MOON

Dear Sue —
Happy Anniversary —
Happy MOST trip!
Love,
Bernice

NICARAGUA

JOSHUA BERMAN & RANDALL WOOD

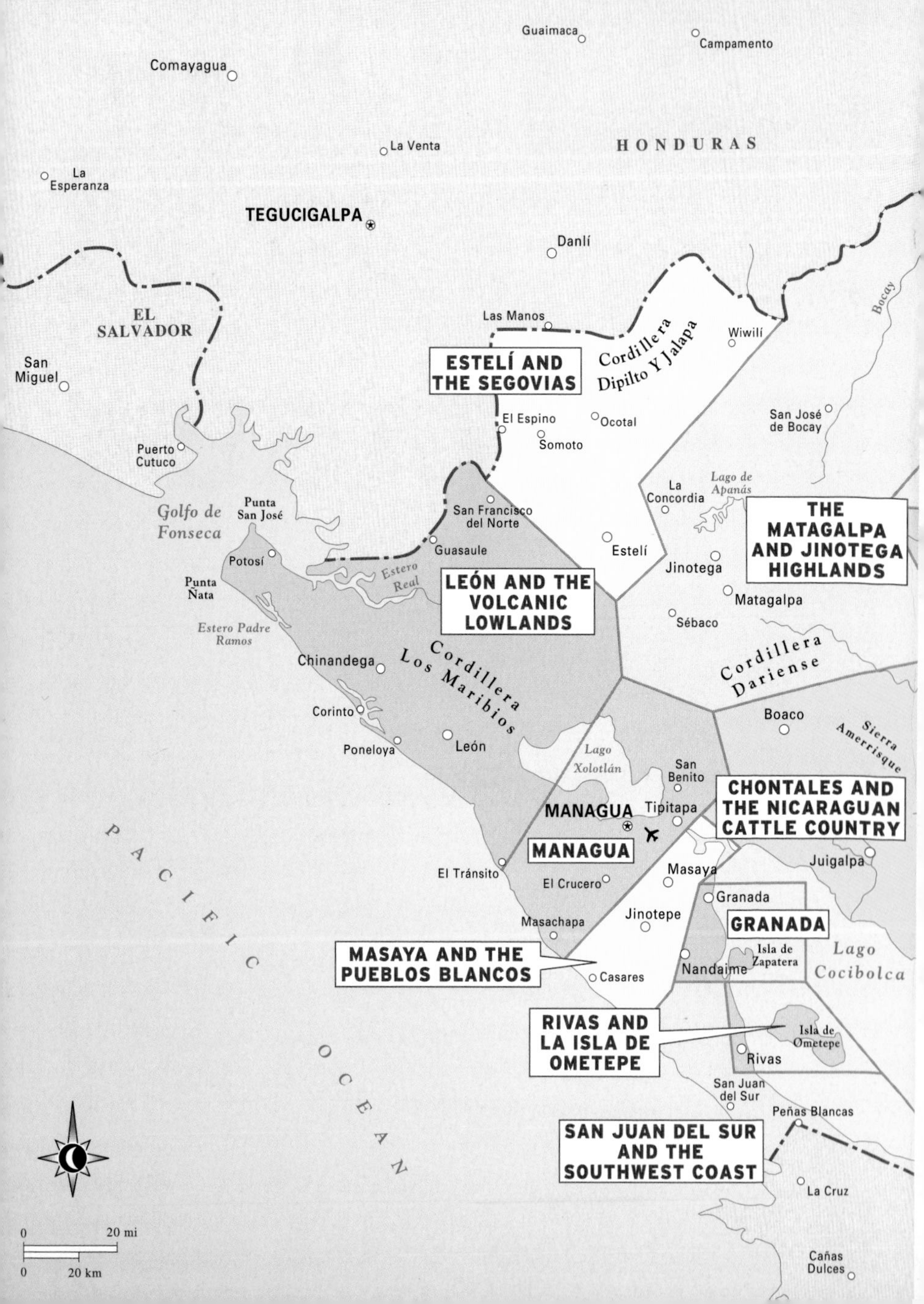

HONDURAS

Guaimaca
Campamento

Comayagua

La Venta

La
Esperanza

TEGUCIGALPA

Danlí

EL
SALVADOR

Las Manos

Cordillera
Dipilto Y Jalapa

Wiwilí

Bocay

San
Miguel

**ESTELÍ AND
THE SEGOVIAS**

El Espino
Ocotal

San José
de Bocay

Puerto
Cutuco

Somoto

Golfo de
Fonseca

Punta
San José

La
Concordia

Lago de
Apanás

**THE
MATAGALPA
AND JINOTEGA
HIGHLANDS**

San Francisco
del Norte

Potosí

Guasaule

Estelí

Jinotega

Punta
Ñata

Estero
Real

**LEÓN AND THE
VOLCANIC
LOWLANDS**

Matagalpa

Estero Padre
Ramos

Sébaco

Chinandega

Cordillera
Los Maribios

Cordillera
Dariense

Corinto

Boaco

Sierra
Amerrisque

Poneloya

León

Lago
Xolotlán

San
Benito

Tipitapa

**CHONTALES AND
THE NICARAGUAN
CATTLE COUNTRY**

MANAGUA

MANAGUA

Masaya

Juigalpa

El Tránsito

El Crucero

Jinotepe

Granada

GRANADA

Masachapa

Isla de
Zapatera

Lago
Cocibolca

**MASAYA AND THE
PUEBLOS BLANCOS**

Casares

Nandaime

**RIVAS AND
LA ISLA DE
OMETEPE**

Isla de
Ometepe

Rivas

San Juan
del Sur

Peñas Blancas

**SAN JUAN DEL SUR
AND THE
SOUTHWEST COAST**

La Cruz

PACIFIC OCEAN

Cañas
Dulces

0   20 mi

0   20 km

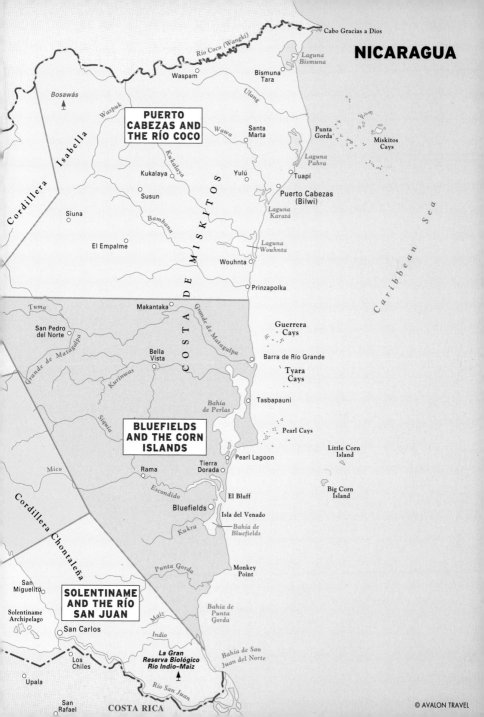

Contents

Discover Nicaragua

Aland of clay-tiled villages and soaring cathedrals, of volcanic heat and Caribbean cool, Nicaragua is the largest and least densely populated country in Central America. Its seven million inhabitants are as varying as their homeland, continuing to reinvent themselves amid unending political, geological, and economic drama.

A decade of economic growth has brought resurfaced roads, refurbished hotels, and a host of new clubs and restaurants. In the southwest today, gated communities and golf courses adjoin sugarcane and cornfields as a part of the terrain. Travelers are less out of place than they were a few years ago — and a growing tourism sector has budded to guide, lodge, feed, and entice them. The change has garnered Nicaragua unprecedented media attention as the country finds itself the subject of scores of articles about tourism, coffee, and foreign investment — and about elections, hurricanes, and the latest corruption scandal in Managua.

Despite travel magazines that hype it as "the next Costa Rica," travel in Nicaragua involves compromises you wouldn't be asked to make in more prosperous countries. Patience is key. Canned tours are nonexistent. Power and water are not guaranteed. Though the travel industry is maturing, the established tourist route or "gringo trail" remains nar-

rowly defined. Getting off the beaten path is as simple as hopping a rainbow-colored bus to a town whose name you can't pronounce.

Volcanoes, lagoons, canyons, rivers, and valleys provide opportunities to go hiking, paddling, and exploring. A vast network of dusty roads can carry curious travelers to country villages throughout the interior. Nicaragua's two coasts are remarkably different: The Atlantic is a remote labyrinth of mangrove swamps and classic Caribbean colors, while the Pacific is a bold stretch of hills, plains, and charming towns, its bays and beaches washed by superb surf.

Nicaragua's revolutionary past – resurrected with the 2006 presidential election of Daniel Ortega – and its transformation into international real estate darling are engrossing examples of living history. But you're better off hearing about it from the Nicaraguans themselves. Their tales of tidal waves, earthquakes, political upheaval, and reconstruction will keep you up till the wee hours – or as long as your

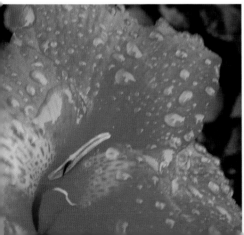

Spanish holds out. If your *español* isn't quite up to the fluid, fast, bawdy Nicaraguan conversation style, then you've discovered another reason to visit the country: Outstanding personalized Spanish language schools offer quality instruction in many settings – from beachfront to crater lakes to colonial cities. Classwork is often integrated with homestays, volunteer work, and trips to waterfalls and coffee farms. Or you can engage in "voluntourism" – the integration of service and assistance into your recreation – in one of the dozens of opportunities listed throughout this book.

Nicaragua offers innumerable chances to challenge yourself, live simply, and witness life at a slower pace. Take time to appreciate what Nicaragua offers – tortillas and red beans cooked over a wood fire, an uncluttered night sky behind a volcano's silhouette, or a friendly exchange with a *campesino* in the town plaza. You'll find that doing so can change your perceptions and teach you something new at every turn.

Planning Your Trip

In general, destinations south of Managua are more developed for travelers, especially Granada and San Juan del Sur, whose exploding number of colonial hotels, upscale surf camps, and convenient shuttle services have altered the tourism landscape considerably. The rest of the country—north and east of Managua, plus the Río San Juan—is a different story. In these places, with some basic Spanish, patience, and persistence, you can pueblo-hop on public buses till the Chontales cattle come home. Basic room and board are found in even small pueblos, as are community homestay and rural tourism programs. Fancier hotels and restaurants are found in most department capitals, usually on or near the central plaza.

Traveling in Nicaragua is easier than it once was. You can get a shuttle from the airport in Managua straight to your hotel in Granada, or choose to rent a car from most international companies, whose offices are right there at baggage claim. You can arrange for a tour guide or your hotel's driver to meet you at the airport as well, then hire them to help you travel between Granada, San Juan del Sur, and León. U.S. dollars and major credit cards are accepted in most hotels in these areas. This is all quite new for Nicaragua—though only in these more popular parts of the country.

► WHERE TO GO

Managua

The most chaotic of Central American capitals, Managua used to be a modern, cosmopolitan center—until it was flattened by an earthquake in 1972, the first of a series of major disasters. Today, amid an ongoing building boom and expansion of the city's middle class, Managua can be a fun stopover if traveling through on business or pleasure. Though you could conceivably pass through Nicaragua without visiting Managua at all, its central location makes it an important transport hub and the place to go for services not available elsewhere. You can see Managua's small cadre of attractions in half a day, but if you're here on a weekend, consider staying to sample the vibrant nightlife.

Granada

The most colorful and comfortable of Nicaragua's cities, Granada has been charming travelers with its red-tiled roofs, grand

Granada's Catedral

IF YOU HAVE . . .

One week: Visit Granada, Ometepe, and San Juan del Sur.
Two weeks: Extend your stay in one of the above, or add León and Chinandega. Add either Estelí/Matagalpa or Bluefields and the Corn Islands.
Three weeks: Add the Solentiname islands and a trip down the Río San Juan. Take the time to hike a volcano or explore the Estero Reál. Or work your way up the Pacific coast, one beach at a time.
Four weeks: Go deep. After visiting the above, get off the beaten track using Matagalpa, Jinotega, or Estelí as a base, or spend a couple days camping in the more remote wildlife reserves of Matagalpa and the Río San Juan.

Granada street

well as Masaya, the Pueblos Blancos, and the Laguna de Apoyo.

Masaya and the Pueblos Blancos
Less than an hour south of the capital, Masaya and the dozens of villages that comprise the Pueblos Blancos are known for their residents' artistry. Start with a trip to Volcán Masaya, where you can peer into Nicaragua's fiery entrails, then visit the shaded stalls of Masaya's craft markets. Spend a lazy afternoon driving through the Pueblos Blancos and have a dip in the Laguna de Apoyo, the country's nicest swimming hole. You could easily devote two full days to this region, either by staying in Masaya or the Laguna, or by traveling here each day from Granada. The Pueblos make a nice diversion for those spending a longer time in Managua, as the hills are markedly cooler.

Rivas and La Isla de Ometepe
An old administrative city with a vibrant colonial history, Rivas may be worth a stop on your way to the beaches of San Juan del Sur or to Nicaragua's crown jewel: La Isla de Ometepe, a few kilometers across Lake Cocibolca. Visible from the entire southern highway, Ometepe's twin volcanic peaks—Concepción is hot and active, Maderas is dormant and forested—offer challenging, unique treks. Or stick to the lakeshore, enjoying island-grown coffee, lagoons, waterfalls, and the call of howler monkeys. The slopes of Maderas are home to an array of rustic, farm-based hostels, surrounded by old-growth hardwoods, petroglyphs, barnyard animals, and memorable views.

San Juan del Sur and the Southwest Coast
Nicaragua's favorite beach town is also the most popular with foreign tourists. In addition to a crescent bay lined with barefoot restaurants and sandy bars, San Juan del Sur

cathedrals, breezy lakeshore, and drowsy lifestyle since the days of the Spanish, who used the city as their first Atlantic port, via Lake Cocibolca and the Río San Juan. Today, Granada is the undisputed hub of tourism throughout the country, and it's got the international cuisine and café culture to prove it. Many visitors opt to stay in Granada throughout their trip, as a tranquil base from which to explore the 365 isletas and the cloud forests of Volcán Mombacho, as

kayaking through Las Isletas de Ometepe

offers a slow-paced, tranquil setting, fresh seafood, and charming guesthouses. Go fishing and sailing, try the canopy tour, or learn surfing and Spanish. From San Juan's bay, the Pacific coastline extends in both directions in series of hidden beaches, hills, and wave-strewn coves. The southwest coast is an important habitat for the Paslama turtle—witnessing the hatching is breathtaking.

León and the Volcanic Lowlands

Lying at the feet of the imposing Maribio volcanoes, León and Chinandega are colonial cities in the arid lowlands of Nicaragua's Pacific northwest. León's importance as a political and economic center over the past four centuries has bequeathed it a rich history. Stop in at the baroque cathedral, the largest in Central America, or wander the indigenous Subtiava neighborhood, with a magnificent church of its own. Most travelers stroll León's streets, walk up (and ride down) Cerro Negro, and then head back south or east. With a week or more, you can work your way farther northwest. In addition to beaches near León, there are a number of remote protected areas throughout the Cosigüina Peninsula.

Estelí and the Segovias

Nicaragua's mountainous north is accessible by comfortable public transportation, its main city, Estelí, only a few hours from Managua. Farther north, the peaks are some of the oldest in Central America, and they boast an unforgettable landscape with hardwood and pine forests, stony river valleys, and fields of tobacco, coffee, and corn. Spend a day at Estanzuela's waterfall and the Tisey wildlife reserve, or head into the hills for a weekend in Miraflor, precious habitat for some of Nicaragua's rarest species of birds and orchids. Press farther northward to the small towns of the Segovias—Somoto and Ocotal—dry as dust but alive with history, legends, and lore.

The Matagalpa and Jinotega Highlands

Nicaragua's rugged interior is coffee country, where the unrushed traveler will find

Estelí flora

the untrodden, as most of Nicaragua's land-mass lies farther afield to the east. A guide in Matagalpa can take you trekking to summits, waterfalls, and forgotten gold mines. Spend a weekend in a rural lodge, tour coffee plantations, or participate in a village guest program for a closer look at *campesino* life.

Chontales and the Nicaraguan Cattle Country

The golden hillsides along the east side of Lake Cocibolca fold upward into the rocky precipices of the Amerrisque mountains, stomping grounds of the Chontal people during pre-Columbian times. Today, the lowlands run thick with cattle ranches that produce most of Nicaragua's cheese and milk. To the north and east, the roads dwindle to rutted tracks and old, rural encampments. It was here that the Chontal people carved their totem-like statues, a few of which are on display in the museum in Juigalpa. Most travelers speed through on buses bound for El Rama and the Atlantic coast, but spending a night in Juigalpa or Boaco, where the wild west vibe hasn't lost its edge, may lead you on to the area's hot springs, petroglyphs, horseback treks, and burly hikes.

rough, undeveloped adventure. Green valleys and steep peaks define the landscape, and the hard-working, sometimes aloof residents define its character. Everyone's got a war story in these mountains, and hearing them adds texture to your travels. Matagalpa has steep streets, famous steaks, and long vistas; Jinotega is the gateway to

outdoor activity in the Cattle Country

path to the beach on Corn Island

Solentiname and the Río San Juan

Life moves slowly along the broad river that drains Lake Cocibolca to the Caribbean. This gorgeous, verdant lowland is Nicaragua's wettest, and its remoteness means you'll spend more time and more money getting around. The Spanish fort at El Castillo has watched over river traffic since the 17th century. Along the southern shore of Cocibolca, you'll find wildlife reserves and cultural curiosities. The Solentiname archipelago isn't easy to get to, but you'll be rewarded with an up-close look at the birthplace of liberation theology and a thriving colony of artists. Explore the wilds of Los Guatuzos, habitat for monkeys, birds, and amphibians, then set sail downstream for San Juan de Nicaragua, home to the bones of English pirates and more ghosts than residents.

Bluefields and the Corn Islands

The isolated Atlantic coast may as well be a country unto itself. Nicaragua's Caribbean is tough, muddy, and quite unlike any Cancún-tainted visions you may harbor. Most tourists fly straight from Managua to Big Corn, but a few hardy souls still make a go for Bluefields to experience Creole culture and crab soup. When you tire of Bluefields's grittiness, board a boat for Pearl Lagoon, the coastal fishing communities, Pearl Cays, or Greenfields reserve. Both Corn Island and Little Corn Island are Caribbean gems as gorgeous below the waterline as above. There are kilometers of coral reef, a handful of hotels, and only one dive shop on each island. Little Corn has no roads so the only sound you hear should be the wind in the trees.

Puerto Cabezas and the Río Coco

The northeast Miskito communities of Puerto Cabezas (Bilwi), Waspám, and the Río Coco are a far removed, embattled region of the country, where resources go more toward fighting the drug trade and recovering from natural disasters than toward developing tourism. Still, there are basic services in Puerto Cabezas, including decent oceanfront accommodations and low-budget tour guides to take you to nearby rivers, beaches, and Miskito communities. Even farther north, Waspám is the commercial center for villages up the Río Coco, mostly indigenous communities where Miskito is still the first language spoken. Puerto is an easy flight from Managua—or a heroic, 24-hour cross-country bus trip.

▶ WHEN TO GO

Generally speaking, the best months—when the land is still green from the rains and the days are sunny and dry—are December, January, and February. June, July, and August are nice as well, with cooler temperatures, fewer North Americans, and more of our European friends. March, April, and May are the hottest, driest months, prone to pervasive dust and smoke caused by agricultural burning; September–November are the wettest months, and also hurricane season, when you can expect periodic tropical depressions to raise the rivers.

Costumes are part of the Palo de Mayo celebration.

Nicaragua's *invierno* (winter, or rainy season) lasts approximately May–October, and *verano* (summer, or dry season) lasts November–April. Rain during these months may mean just a quick shower each afternoon, or it may go on for days. As you travel east toward the Atlantic coast or down the Río San Juan, the rainy season grows longer and wetter until the dry season only lasts the month of April.

Several fiestas are worth planning your trip around: the fiestas in Diriamba around January 19, the Palo de Mayo on the Atlantic coast (throughout May), the Crab Soup Festival on Corn Island (August 27–28), and the Fiesta del Toro Venado in Masaya (last Sunday of October). The first weeks of December, when Nicaraguans celebrate the Immaculate Conception with various *purísima* and *gritería* parades, are particularly lively in Granada and León.

▶ BEFORE YOU GO

Passport and Visa Requirements
Every traveler to Nicaragua must have a passport valid for at least six months following the date of entry. A visa is required only for citizens of the following countries: Afghanistan, Albania, Bosnia-Herzegovina, Colombia, Cuba, Haiti, India, Iran, Iraq, Jordan, Lebanon, Libya, Nepal, Pakistan, People's Republic of China, People's Republic of Korea, Somalia, Sri Lanka, Vietnam, and Yugoslavia. Everyone else is automatically given a tourist pass good for three months.

Vaccinations

Required: A certificate of vaccination against yellow fever is required for all travelers over one year of age and arriving from affected areas.

Recommended: Before traveling to Nicaragua, be sure your tetanus, diphtheria, measles, mumps, rubella, and polio vaccines are up-to-date. Protection against hepatitis A and typhoid fever is also recommended for all travelers.

What to Take

Everything you bring to Nicaragua should be well built and ideally water-resistant, especially if you intend to visit the Atlantic coast or Río San Juan, where you'll inevitably find yourself in a boat. Also be prepared for rain during any part of the wet season. Choose a small, sturdy bag not so large you'll be uncomfortable carrying it for long distances or riding with it on your lap in the bus—and secure its zippers with small padlocks. If you're planning to stay in a midrange or upscale hotel for the duration of your trip, your bag is of less concern, but be sure to take a small daypack or shoulder bag for your daily walkabouts.

CLOTHING

Pick clothes that are light and breathable in the heat, and if your plans include Matagalpa, Jinotega, or Estelí, you may appreciate something a bit warmer, like a flannel shirt. For sun protection, don't forget a shade hat that covers the back of your neck.

No matter what your style, it is very important to look clean. Having a neat personal appearance is important to all Latin Americans, and you'll find being well groomed will open a lot more doors. In the countryside, Nicaraguan men typically don't wear shorts, unless they are at the beach or at home. Jeans travel well, but you will probably find them hot in places like León and Chinandega; khakis are lighter and dry faster.

Roads are rough, even in cities, so good walking shoes will ease your trip considerably; lightweight hiking boots or just sturdy sneakers are sufficient. You'll be hard-pressed to find shoes larger than a men's 10.5 (European 42) for sale in Nicaragua. Take a pair of shower-sandals with you, or buy a pair of rubber *chinelas* anywhere in Nicaragua for about $1.

MISCELLANY

Bring a small first-aid kit, plenty of plastic bags and Ziplocs for protections from both rain and boat travel, and a cheap set of ear plugs for the occasional early-morning rooster.

A lightweight, breathable raincoat and/or small umbrella are a good idea. A small flashlight or headlamp is indispensable for walking at night on uneven streets and for those late-night potty runs in your *hospedaje,* and an alarm clock will facilitate catching early-morning buses. If you wear glasses, bring along a little repair kit. Bring a pocket Spanish dictionary and phrasebook. Photos of home and your family are a great way to connect with your Nica hosts and friends. A simple compass is helpful for finding your way around, as directions in this book typically refer to compass directions (finding the hotel three blocks north of the park is a lot easier if you know which direction north is).

PAPERWORK

Make a photocopy of the pages in your passport that have your photo and information. When you get the passport stamped in the airport, it's a good idea to make a photocopy of that page as well after you get situated in your first hotel, and store the copies somewhere other than with your passport. This will facilitate things greatly if your passport ever gets lost or stolen. Also consider taking a copy of your health/medical evacuation insurance policy.

Explore Nicaragua

▶ THE 21-DAY BEST OF NICARAGUA

Like other countries in the region, Nicaragua has a popular, carved-out tourist route through its principal attractions. Nicaragua's beaten path offers the chance to travel in the company of fellow vagabonds, but always with easy access to offbeat side trips. The Granada–Ometepe–San Juan del Sur circuit can be done in about one week; save another week for tackling the northwestern lowlands and a third week for the Atlantic coast or Río San Juan. Wherever you head, Granada is a good place to ease into things, with colorful surroundings, wonderful cuisine, and more creature comforts than elsewhere in the country.

Day 1

Arrive in the afternoon at Managua's International Airport. Transfer to a hotel in town, catch a performance, enjoy some of the local restaurants, and above all, get accustomed to the heat and relax after your flight.

Days 2-3

Hop a bus to Granada and spend at least two or three days there. Tour the city the first day, visit museums and enjoy the languid waterfront. Your second day, paddle to the nearby *isletas* or go hiking on Volcán Mombacho, whose heights above the city make for a cool day.

Day 4

Using Granada as your base, make a day trip to the city of Masaya and its the active volcano of the same name. Start early at Volcán Masaya National Park, then browse the handicrafts in the Old Market. Return to Granada that evening.

Days 5-7

Pack up and head south. Catch the boat at San Jorge to Ometepe. Spend 2–3 days exploring the island's unique getaways, or arrange a guide to take you to the top of one of the volcanoes for more adventurous travel.

Masaya is famous for its hammocks.

DIVING AND SNORKELING

Despite Nicaragua's gorgeous shorelines, diving is a pastime only beginning to be developed, with only three shops in the whole country: one in San Juan del Sur and one on each of the Corn Islands. Snorkeling is best off the Corn Islands and some of the Pearl Cays. While the Miskito Cays might have good diving as well, they are unfortunately inaccessible. Start on Corn or Little Corn Island and do your part to encourage preservation of these still beautiful but delicate ecosystems. For freshwater diving, inquire at Laguna de Apoyo, which is deeper than you'd guess by looking across the glassy surface of the lake.

Laguna de Apoyo

ATLANTIC SIDE

Corn Island and **Little Corn Island** share a combined 12 kilometers of reef. Each island has a small, personable dive shop to equip divers and take them to the sites. Both islands' reef systems feature a stunning diversity of wildlife, including rays, eels, angels, groupers, sharks, and enormous pools of African pompano. Both shops offer PADI certifications for about $250, plus a range of packages for all skill levels. Although the diving off the Corn Islands is impressive, the most spectacular and undoubtedly world-class site is found nearly 25 difficult kilometers farther out to sea around a sea mount called Blowing Rock.

PACIFIC SIDE

Nicaragua's Pacific side offers diving too, particularly in the south near **San Juan del Sur,** but conditions are predictably unpredictable (visibility can change from 1 to 20 meters from day to day). There are rock reefs here (no coral formations) inhabited by large fish, including colorful wrasses, parrotfish, snappers, and huge surgeonfish. Once abundant, shark populations have thinned severely due to overfishing. The best Pacific diving in Nicaragua is between December and April during periods of clear, cold water upwelling associated with the strong offshore winds. Visibility is significantly poorer during the rainy season (June–November) due to sediment from the rivers, which enrich coastal water and provoke algal blooms.

FRESHWATER LAKES

For freshwater diving, Nicaragua offers the volcanic crater lakes of **Apoyo** (near Masaya) and **Xiloá** (near Managua). The diving in both lakes is part of ongoing biological research of the endemic cichlid fish species, and experienced divers can rent tanks from the folks at the Proyecto Ecológico in Laguna de Apoyo. Apoyo has better visibility, but Xiloá has more colorful fish, and is especially interesting during the peak breeding season in November and December. There are still at least 10 undescribed fish species in the freshwater crater lakes, but hurry, as they are being decimated by introduced tilapia.

Nicaragua is known as the Land of Lakes and Volcanoes.

Days 8-9

Catch the boat back to San Jorge and bus it south through Rivas to the beach at San Juan del Sur. Spend at least one night there, but tag on a few more if the surf's up or the turtles are laying.

Days 10-11

Catch the early express bus to Managua. Transfer directly to León. It's been a long trip, so relax, walk around the hot town, check out a few museums, and save time for ice cream in the park.

Days 12-13

Catch a ride to Matagalpa, then continue east to the village of San Ramón. It will take you the better part of a day to get here, so enjoy the afternoon and that plate of *gallo pinto* waiting for you in the mountains. Spend the next two days hiking to the mines and touring a coffee farm or two.

Days 14-19

Return to Managua and take the afternoon flight to Corn Island. Spend two days on Corn Island and two days on Little Corn, soaking up sun, fresh lobster, island vibes, and perhaps a dive on the reef.

Day 20

Take the morning flight back to Managua to see a few more of the city's sights before last-minute shopping at the Mercado Roberto Huembes.

Day 21

Adios, jodido! Feliz viaje!

► HIKING THE RING OF FIRE

Volcano hopping, anyone? Pack some sturdy boots and hike one or all of the more than a dozen ascents detailed in this book. Nicaragua's Maribio and Dirián mountain ranges contain both dormant and active cones, each one completely unique in scenery, difficulty, vegetation, and length. A few of these hikes have established, well-blazed trails (Mombacho and Masaya Parks are notable), many don't. In undeveloped-for-tourism areas, "hiking" means turning off the pavement, taking a poor dirt road to an even poorer one, and then entering the country's vast network of mule- and footpaths that have connected rural communities for centuries. You'll share the road with horses, cattle, and families walking to and from their fields. You'll discover small adobe chapels, hidden shrines to the Virgin Mary, and cool watering holes, all on your way to or from another crater. Of course, you should always, when possible, hire a local guide, as a way to both support the community and to not get lost, both respectable goals.

Following is a quickie weeklong jaunt up a couple of favorites, but after seeing the long chain of gas-streaming peaks stretching off into the horizon, you'll realize that this is only the beginning.

Day 1
Arrive at Managua International Airport and transfer to Granada.

Day 2
After enjoying the specter of Volcán Mombacho looming over the colonial streets, get a ride to its summit and walk the various ridge trails around its jungled craters; the wonderful loops make a good warm-up for what's to come.

Day 3
Spend the morning at Volcán Masaya's gaping crater, only an hour from Granada and guaranteed to impress. On the way back, enjoy a swim in the Laguna de Apoyo, an unspoiled crater lake, easily accessed by bus from Masaya.

Day 4
Transfer to León and find someone to take you to Cerro Negro, a relatively short but stout and rewarding hike.

Day 5
Rest up on the beach at Las Peñitas and paddle out to Isla Juan Venado.

Day 6
Today's the big day. Hook back up with your guides in León and set out early to tackle

ascending Cerro Negro

Momotombo, a 1,300-meter, eight-hour round-trip on horseback and foot. Celebrate with a fancy dinner in León that night.

Day 7

Back to Managua, back to work, or back to the beach.

▶ THE GREAT GREEN NORTH

Nicaragua north of Managua is offbeat and little-traveled, and gives the creative traveler lots of opportunities. Pueblo-hopping through the Segovia mountains and participating in the Ruta de Café will immerse you in an authentic and sublime world you won't soon forget. Each town has a swimming hole, local hike, or archaeological site that will beckon you farther. Go! Alternate legs include passing through San Juan de Limay and the back roads to León; or from Jinotega, looping through Yalí to Condega. This sample itinerary will give you a taste of what to expect:

Day 1

From Managua, head north to Estelí and spend the day walking the streets of this bustling commercial center, viewing the murals and markets, and enjoying cool weather.

Days 2-3

Take an early-morning bus to the Estanzuela waterfall; stay in a cabin on the Tisey Reserve, where you can arrange hikes, horseback expeditions, and farm tours. Return to Estelí at the end of day three.

Days 4-5

From Estelí, go east and up, into the Miraflor Reserve, where you can experience a rural homestay, photograph orchids, and try to spot elusive wildlife. Even if you don't find any quetzals or ocelots, the locals will regale you with legends and ghost stories. Spend the night, return in the morning, and grab a bus north.

Tisey Reserve

freshly picked coffee beans

Day 6

Stop in for lunch at one of the quiet northern agricultural towns, like Condega, or Palacagüina; press on to Ocotal, and spend the evening roaming the park and city center.

Day 7

Day trips galore await from Ocotal—seek out the ruins, or head northeast to Jalapa if you have the time. Otherwise, check out the humble church and exhibits in the Ocotal *casa de cultura* and hop an express bus back to Estelí.

Day 8

Leave Estelí in the morning and make your way through Sébaco to Matagalpa. Enjoy the city for the day, maybe even take a quick hike up Cerro Apante.

Day 9

Here's your chance to visit a coffee plantation and witness the process that brings us that magical beverage. You can stay in San Ramón, Finca Esperanza Verde, or the relatively upscale accommodations at Selva Negra.

Day 10

Enjoy a beautiful, fun-filled day of monkeys in the trees, hearty country dining, and a guided tour through the farm.

Day 11

Return to Managua, hopefully with a few pounds of freshly roasted coffee in your pack.

the lodge at Selva Negra

HANDICRAFTS AND *ARTESANÍA*

Nicaragua is a nation with a rich diversity of handicrafts as beautiful as they are practical. If you're interested in shopping, the city of Masaya and surrounding pueblos present the nation's best opportunity to admire – and acquire – elaborate pottery, intricately woven hammocks, wood carvings, ceramic miniatures, leatherwork, and embroidered *guayaberas*. Increasingly these treasures are finding their way into Granada tourist markets and boutiques (start with the lobby of your hotel in Granada). For sheer diversity, Managua handicraft shopping is better, but the experience in open markets like Huembes isn't as evocative. Here's a brief guide to some of the items you'll find in Nicaragua:

HAMMOCKS

Nicaraguan hammocks are well made and reasonably priced: around $30-60, depending on size and quantity. Though you can also find good-quality hammocks at the Roberto Huembes market in **Managua,** the heart of Nicaragua's home-crafted hammock industry is **Masaya,** and visiting the many family "factories" is as easy as walking up to the porch and saying *"Buenos días."* Check the weave and the quality of the cord – stiffer cord tends to last longer and tighter weaves tend to be more comfortable.

SOAPSTONE

The soapstone sculptors of **San Juan de Limay** (a small village north of Estelí) produce polished figurines inspired by animals, Rubenesque women, and pre-Columbian designs. Smaller pieces are simple to transport, but at **Masaya,** you can have larger pieces packed and shipped home. You'll see iguanas, parrots, frogs, oxen, wagons, and more, plus ornately carved nativity scenes and chess sets, all carefully rendered in the salmon and ivory hues natural to the Limay soapstone (*marmolina*).

POTTERY

Nicaraguan pottery designs have continued uninterrupted from pre-Columbian times to the present. Today's potters produce all manner of vases, bowls, urns, pots, and other forms in rich earthy hues, some delicately etched, some left crude. You'll find fantastic mobiles and wind chimes of clay birds, bells, or ornamental shapes, like stars and planets. Get gorgeous, export-quality pieces in **Masaya** or **San Juan del Oriente** (Catarina and increasingly the other Pueblos are getting into the act now, too). Or find earthy, rustic pieces not too different from what the Nahuatls must have used up north: **Jinotega**'s black pottery or red clay pieces in **Estelí** and **Matagalpa.**

▶ DOWN THE RÍO SAN JUAN

The watery "Golden Route" through southern Lake Cocibolca and down the Río San Juan is tougher to access than it was when boat service was more frequent, so you'll need a minimum of 7–10 days to get there, get around, and get back. Once you reach San Carlos (by boat, bus, or small plane), public boat transportation is regular and cheap, but limited to a handful of boats per week. As a result, unless you really drop a lot of cash to hire your own personal boat and driver, you may find yourself stranded on one of 36 Solentiname islands for three days, with nothing to do but go fishing or bird- and crocodile-watching in a dugout canoe—we can think of worse. The Río San Juan is unquestionably worth a visit, especially the photogenic fort and river town at El Castillo.

Masaya handicraft market

BASKETWORK

The basketwork you'll find around the country is an extension of the bamboo baskets you see stacked up with produce in countryside markets. Nueva Segovia and the northeast Miskito regions of Nicaragua, in contrast, produce curious baskets and urns from bundles of wrapped pine needles that have been bound into long coils, then wound in concentric coils. Look for them in **Ocotal** and the markets in **Managua.**

PRIMITIVIST PAINTINGS

The first primitivist paintings from the **Solentiname** archipelago came into the world spotlight in the 1960s as an offshoot of Padre Ernesto Cardenal's liberation theology movement on the islands. Instantly recognized the world over as an art form unique to Nicaragua, the vibrant paintings typically portray romanticized scenes of tropical Latin America: markets, oxen, trees laden with fruit, and skies full of toucans and parrots. You'll have a better story to tell if you buy them from the source on the Solentiname islands, but if your schedule doesn't permit, you can do just as well at the Galería Solentiname in **Managua.** Lower-priced pieces are available in Huembes market, but you'll have to look harder to find the better works.

WOODEN FURNITURE

The carpenters and craftspeople of the small towns around **Masaya** turn out gorgeous wooden furniture. Rocking chairs called *abuelitas* ("little grandmothers") or *mecedoras* are sturdy and comfortable, and if you ask, they'll gladly disassemble them and condense their products into well-wrapped airline-suitable packages. You can also find them in **Managua** and **Granada,** though there you are dealing with middlemen and prices are higher.

Note that air and boat schedules require careful timing on this trip, so we've constructed one possible way to coordinate the logistics, which should help get you started in the region. Because schedules can change, be prepared for the worst and bring something to read while you're waiting for the next boat.

Day 1: Tuesday

Fly from Managua to San Carlos in the early morning. If you really want the full-blown adventure, take the slow boat from Granada on Monday, not Tuesday: You'll arrive Tuesday morning. Poke around San Carlos until the afternoon, when the boat leaves for Solentiname.

Days 2-3: Wednesday-Thursday

Enjoy this island artist colony set in a unique area of profound natural splendor. You can hire boats to take you among the islands, enjoy scarlet sunsets, and absorb the intense tranquility of the archipelago. Return to San Carlos Thursday morning to catch the boat to Los Guatuzos. If you'd rather go directly and

The cannons of El Castillo watch over the Río San Juan.

bypass San Carlos, strike a deal with a local Solentiname boat owner.

Days 4-6: Friday-Saturday

Hike and explore the fascinating tropical landscape of the Los Guatuzos Reserve. A two-day stay will give you a taste for the reserve, but real outdoors enthusiasts will probably prefer to stay until the next boat (Tuesday, unless you make other arrangements). Arrival in San Carlos on Saturday means you are just in time to catch a boat downstream. Cast away and start your adventure down the mighty Río San Juan, bound for El Castillo.

Day 7: Sunday

Start your day off in El Castillo early, so you can hear the sky fill with birds. Visit the old Spanish fort or rent a horse for a bush trip.

Day 8 and Beyond

Most travelers return to San Carlos for a flight to Managua at this point, but if the downstream horizon is beckoning, then keep on floating, and happy trails.

MANAGUA

Nicaragua's difficult and nondescript capital rarely charms but will not fail to impress, even if only with its stubborn tenacity. The obstinate survivor of a half dozen catastrophes, Managua is a city in perpetual rebirth; the Managua of the 21st century would be unrecognizable to someone who lived there in the 1980s, the Managua of the '80s would be unrecognizable to someone who lived there in the '60s, and so on. It's dusty and dirty and remarkably devoid of traditional museums and other urban destinations; its sprawling neighborhoods and utter lack of a proper city center make it difficult to navigate, and the traffic can be a hassle. But Managua is home to nearly a third of the population and four of Nicaragua's biggest universities, and as such, is the city that most sets the tone for the political and economic dialogue on the nation's future development. The history of Nicaragua is also writ large here, from earthquake to revolution to economic revival and onward, so the better you understand Managua, the better you will understand the history of Nicaragua itself.

Managua is also, for better or worse, the best place in the country to get your gear repaired, see a doctor or dentist, buy equipment, and run your other errands if you find yourself in a pinch. It's got the nation's best selection of restaurants and clubs, and is bar none the most enjoyable city in which to go out at night, whether it be for a concert, ballet, salsa dancing, or just a drink with some friends at one of the ever more stylish nightlife hotspots. You probably won't plan your trip around a visit to Managua, but if for some

HIGHLIGHTS

◖ **Plaza de la Revolución:** Most of Managua's historical sights are clustered in this four-block area, still the cultural heart of Nicaragua's capital (page 29).

◖ **La Laguna de Tiscapa:** Just one of the area's many volcanic lakes, this is the only one you can zip over while tethered to a steel cable; or just enjoy the view (page 36).

◖ **Las Huellas de Acahualinca:** This glimpse of Managua's mysterious past is haunting for the questions it raises, not the ones it answers (page 36).

◖ **Chocoyero-El Brujo Nature Reserve:** Located just south of Managua, in a gorgeous patch of protected hillsides and ravines, this community-based tourism venture offers some wonderful day hikes (page 52).

LOOK FOR ◖ TO FIND RECOMMENDED SIGHTS, ACTIVITIES, DINING, AND LODGING.

Lago Xolotlán

La Laguna de Tiscapa

Plaza de la Revolución

Las Huellas de Acahualinca

Managua ◖

Chocoyero-El Brujo Nature Reserve ○

La Concepción ○

Granada ○

Jinotepe ○

○ Nadaime

PACIFIC OCEAN

0   20 mi
0   20 km

reason you find yourself there for an evening or a weekend, there are myriad ways to enjoy it. Neither should you feel compelled to avoid it, as Managua has charms of its own you will soon learn to appreciate.

PLANNING YOUR TIME

If you are in Managua to "see the sights," a morning would be more than enough, as the historical attractions are few and found clustered together in a relatively small area. It would be feasible to ride in on a morning bus, have a look around the historical sights, and take an afternoon bus onward. But for everyone except the historical buffs it makes sense to plan to spend an evening in Managua, as that is when it is most fun. Managua's real attraction is the nightlife, which is unparalleled relative to

the smaller towns. Lastly, if you find yourself in Managua for a longer period of time or prefer the wild outdoors to the club scene, do not miss the Pacific Beaches or the Chocoyero–El Brujo Nature Reserve, both highly recommended destinations from which Managua is the most obvious point of departure.

Managua city has no obvious city center but can be broken down into a few zones of interest to the traveler: **Carretera Masaya,** the growing hotspot of restaurants, clubs, and (increasingly) lodging options; **Barrio Martha Quezada,** the neighborhood with all the international bus stations and a long tradition of budget accommodations and petty crime; and **Plaza de la Revolución/Laguna de Tiscapa,** the waterfront and just south of it, where most of the historical sights are found.

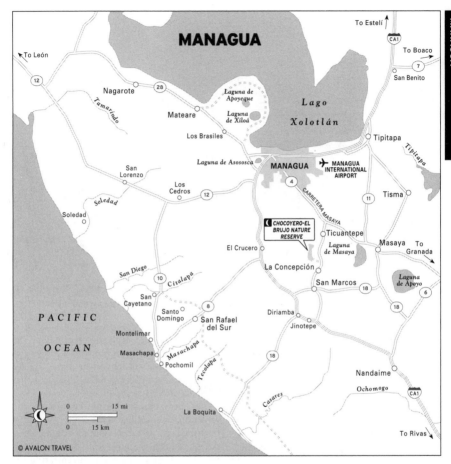

HISTORY

Managua's modern layout is the very embodiment of its history, in a tale that leads inexorably from the water's edge in the direction of Masaya. Mana-huac ("the big water vessel") has been inhabited since 4000 B.C.; you can see the footsteps of some of the earliest inhabitants in the **Museum of the Footprints of Acahualinca** at the city's western edge. The Nahuatls met the Spanish so fiercely there the Spanish retaliated by razing the city in the 15th century; the land remained abandoned another 300 years. By the mid-1800s, when both

León and Granada rivaled for political control of the nation, Managua was again a prosperous fishing village. The Conservatives and Liberals compromised by making Managua the capital, and the fishing vilage began to grow. But in 1931, by which time Managua was a small municipality of 10 square city blocks, an earthquake of 5.6 on the Richter scale leveled Managua and killed more than 1,000 people. For five years, Managuans rebuilt their city, only to see it consumed by flames in the Fire of 1936. Again, they rebuilt.

By the late 1960s, Managua was the most

Old Managua's grandstand was one of the few structures to survive the earthquake of 1972.

© RANDALL WOOD

modern capital in Central America, home to nearly half a million inhabitants, with a modern center and two skyscrapers. But at 27 minutes past midnight on December 23, 1972, an earthquake of 6.3 on the Richter scale laid waste to the five square miles of the city. The quake killed 10,000 people, destroyed 50,000 homes, and reduced the city's entire infrastructure to rubble. Managua was left without water, sewers, or electricity, hospitals lay in ruins, and the roads were choked with debris.

This was a disaster from which Managua has never quite recovered, as little of the initial material aid arrived at its intended destination. President Anastasio Somoza Debayle saw to it that humanitarian assistance channeled through the "emergency committee" under his control ended up in his personal bank accounts. For Nicaraguans who'd lost everything, being forced to purchase donated relief items from the National Guard was the last straw: The revolution would fully erupt only seven years later. Today, the ruins of old Managua have been largely left to rot at the south shore

of Lake Xilotlán, a depressing reminder of the city's glory years. The old cathedral and several other buildings still remain standing, though squatters occupy the derelict buildings that were not cleared away.

But the Sandinista Revolution brought destruction, not healing, to the capital. Managua bore the brunt of the Revolution's final battles. As the Sandinistas advanced, Somoza began bombing his own capital, concentrating his ire on the barrios of Riguera and El Dorado. But Managua remained wrecked throughout Somoza's war against the Sandinistas. And once the Sandinistas took power, fighting the Contras left no money to rebuild Managua according to any sort of plan. It was during this time Managuans shoveled themselves out, and the city began to grow organically, forming the twisting, homogenous neighborhoods of small houses and shanties that make Managua so difficult for foreigners to decipher today.

The end of the Sandinista era brought new investment capital and new opportunities and since 1990 Managua has grown quickly and impressively. But rather than risk rebuilding in the seismic zone, new, upscale establishments stretch down the city's outskirts in the direction of Masaya, where they now form the city's **Zona Rosa.**

SAFETY IN THE CITY

Managua is still less dangerous than other Central American capitals, but the economic slowdown that accompanied Ortega's return to power has led to increased crime. The best way to stay out of trouble is to avoid areas where you'll find it. Rough barrios include Renée Schick, Jorgé Dimitrov, La Fuente, San Judas, Villa Venezuela, Batahola, Las Americas, Bello Amanecer, Vida Nueva, Los Pescadores, Domitila Lugo, Santana, and Hialeah. The formerly popular budget hotel area between the *hospedajes* (hostels) of Barrio Martha Quezada and the Plaza Inter/Hotel Crowne Plaza is increasingly prone to muggings these days, especially at night. Also, watch yourself in crowds, particularly those of the Mercado Oriental, urban buses, and sporting, music, or political events.

The safest and cleanest neighborhoods are Los Robles, Altamira, San Juan, and Bolonia, all of which offer more upscale accommodation and bed-and-breakfasts.

SIGHTS

Managua's significance to tourists is limited at best, but if you appreciate Managua's history, you'll enjoy a walk around some of the crumbling historical sites. Your first challenge is finding your way around. The lack of a city center and the frenetic traffic make Managua a very unwalkable city, and the lack of street names makes it hard to navigate by car: Money you spend zipping back and forth in taxis here is well spent and will keep you from growing frustrated as you explore or just transition from hotel to restaurant to nightclub and back to the hotel.

◖ Plaza de la Revolución

Nothing evokes the absurdity of Nicaraguan politics like the Plaza de la Revolución, and

fortunately a great deal of Managua's more accessible historical landmarks lie around its edges and can be visited in half a morning. And do visit in the morning, when the breeze off the lake is cool, the trees are full of birds, and the streets are less chaotic. As the heart of old Managua, it was known as Plaza de la República. The Sandinistas renamed it and used it symbolically for staging mass rallies against the Republic's old dictator. Renowned Sandinista-hater President Alemán was thus obliged to (symbolically) build an audiovisual fountain in the center of it. Twice a day during the late 1990s the fountain's waters would rise and fall rhythmically in time with a recorded audio soundtrack. So naturally when President Ortega returned to power in 2006 he was thrilled to, symbolically, demolish the fountain and restore the old political landmark, which he again uses for political rallies.

Catedral Santiago de los Caballeros had barely been completed when the earthquake of 1931 struck. It survived that one, but fared more poorly in the earthquake of 1972, which left it still standing, but unusable. **Las Ruinas de la Catedrál Vieja** (as they're known now) have remained a standing testament to the earthquake and are Managua's most captivating tourist sight. Even though it's been closed due to the danger of falling concrete, you can still peer in and appreciate its ravaged, sunlit interior. Across the street, heading toward the lake, the brightly painted **Casa Presidencial** was built in 1999 amid protests over the lavish expenditure, but has been abandoned by the current president in favour of running the country from his own house and Sandinista party headquarters.

The Palacio Nacional de Cultura houses Nicaragua's National Museum but at various times has also housed the Ministry of Housing, the treasury, the comptroller-general, and the National Congress. Sandinista commandos raided the building in 1978 and held the entire Congress hostage, winning international recognition and the liberation of several political prisoners. In addition to the national library,

MANAGUA

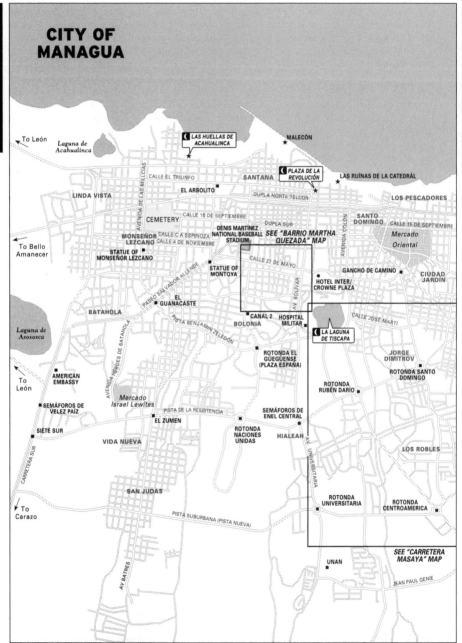

CITY OF
MANAGUA

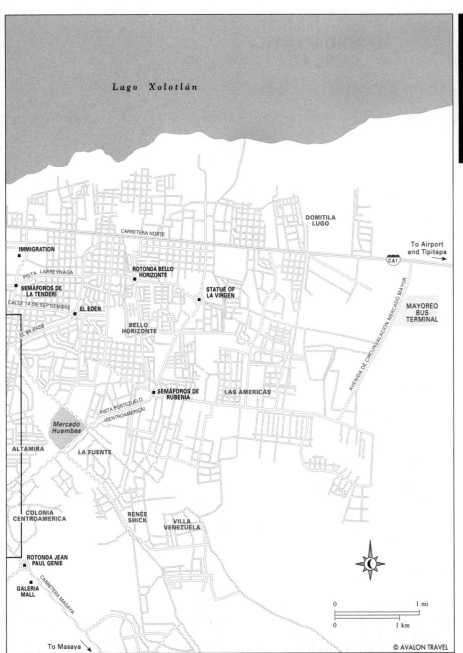

Lago Xolotlán

DOMITILA
LUGO

CARRETERA NORTE

To Airport
and Tipitapa

CA1

IMMIGRATION

PISTA LARREYNAGA

ROTONDA BELLO
HORIZONTE

SEMÁFOROS DE
LA TENDERI

STATUE OF
LA VIRGEN

CALLE 14 DE SEPTIEMBRE

EL EDÉN

MAYOREO
BUS
TERMINAL

AVENIDA DE CIRCUNVALACIÓN MERCADO MAYOR

EL BY-PASS

BELLO
HORIZONTE

SEMÁFOROS DE
RUBENIA

LAS AMÉRICAS

PISTA PORTEZUELO
(CENTROAMÉRICA)

Mercado
Huembes

ALTAMIRA

LA FUENTE

COLONIA
CENTROAMERICA

RENÉE
SHICK

VILLA
VENEZUELA

ROTONDA JEAN
PAUL GENIE

GALERIA
MALL

CARRETERA MASAYA

0   1 mi

0   1 km

To Masaya

© AVALON TRAVEL

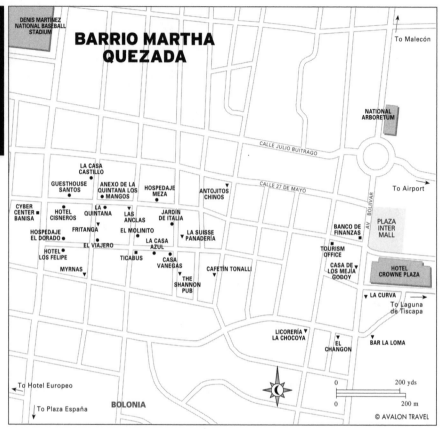

several murals and the Institute of Culture can be found here.

El Centro Cultural de Managua is housed in the first two floors of what was once a much taller Gran Hotel, Managua's principal lodging before 1972. Now a green two-story building with murals on the outside, its first floor offers to the public a café as well as a battery of art exhibits, concerts, puppet shows, and dances. The second floor holds studios of prominent Nicaraguan artists. The hallways are lined with striking black-and-white photographs of old Managua, pre- and post-earthquake and host handicraft fairs the first Saturday of each month. Carved into the southeast corner of

the building is **La Cavanga,** a bar built in the style of 1950s Managua, where you can catch live acoustic music on weekend nights. Sneak up to the roof to see how the upper floors of the old hotel were never replaced, yet another monument to the earthquake. At the building's western end is the old Cinema Gonzalez, reincarnated as a Coca-Cola–sponsored evangelical church.

Set in the small green space of the Parque Central are several monuments of historical significance. An eternal flame guards the **Tomb of Comandante Carlos Fonseca,** father of the Sandinista revolution. Buried across from him is Santos Lopez, a member of

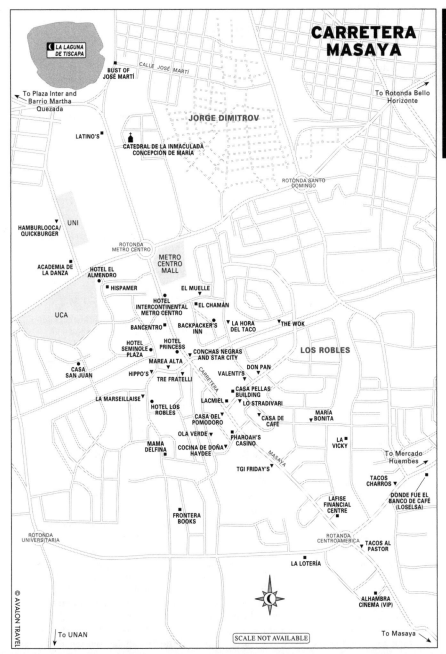

CARRETERA MASAYA

LA LAGUNA DE TISCAPA

BUST OF JOSÉ MARTÍ

CALLE JOSÉ MARTÍ

To Plaza Inter and Barrio Martha Quezada

To Rotonda Bello Horizonte

JORGE DIMITROV

LATINO'S

CATEDRAL DE LA INMACULADA CONCEPCIÓN DE MARÍA

ROTONDA SANTO DOMINGO

HAMBURLOOCA/ QUICKBURGER

UNI

ROTONDA METRO CENTRO

METRO CENTRO MALL

ACADEMIA DE LA DANZA

HOTEL EL ALMENDRO

HISPAMER

EL MUELLE

UCA

HOTEL INTERCONTINENTAL METRO CENTRO

EL CHAMÁN

BANCENTRO

BACKPACKER'S INN

LA HORA DEL TACO

THE WOK

LOS ROBLES

HOTEL SEMINOLE PLAZA

HOTEL PRINCESS

CONCHAS NEGRAS AND STAR CITY

CASA SAN JUAN

MAREA ALTA

DON PAN

HIPPO'S

TRE FRATELLI

VALENTI'S

CARRETERA

CASA PELLAS BUILDING

LA MARSEILLAISE

LACMIEL

LO STRADIVARI

HOTEL LOS ROBLES

CASA DEL POMODORO

CASA DE CAFÉ

MARÍA BONITA

OLA VERDE

MAMA DELFINA

COCINA DE DOÑA HAYDEE

PHAROAH'S CASINO

LA VICKY

MASAYA

To Mercado Huembes

TGI FRIDAY'S

TACOS CHARROS

DONDE FUE EL BANCO DE CAFÉ (LOSELSA)

FRONTERA BOOKS

LAFISE FINANCIAL CENTRE

ROTONDA UNIVERSITARIA

ROTONDA CENTROAMERICA

TACOS AL PASTOR

LA LOTERÍA

ALHAMBRA CINEMA (VIP)

© AVALON TRAVEL

To UNAN

SCALE NOT AVAILABLE

To Masaya

FOLLOWING DIRECTIONS IN MANAGUA

Locating addresses in Managua is unlike any system you've ever seen, but with a few tips, some basic vocabulary, and a couple of examples, you'll master Managua in no time. Street names and house numbers are few and far between, and where they do exist, they are universally ignored. Addresses in Managua begin with a landmark (either existing or historical), which is followed by the number of *cuadras* (blocks) and a direction. Remember this: North is *al lago* (toward the lake); east is *arriba* (up, referring to the sunrise); south is *al sur* (to the south); and west is *abajo* (down, where the sun sets).

Some other key phrases to know are *contiguo a* (next door to), *frente a* (across from), *casa esquinera* (corner house), and *a mano derecha/izquierda* (on the right-/left-hand side). Also note that *varas* are often used to measure distances of less than one block; this is an old colonial measurement just shy of a meter.

Directions throughout this chapter are given in English for consistency's sake, but always

beginning with the landmark exactly as it is referred to in Spanish. By studying the following examples, you should be able to find your way around with few hassles.

De la Plaza España, tres cuadras abajo, tres c. al lago, casa esquinera.
From Plaza España, three blocks west, three north, corner house.

De donde fue el Sandy's, 200 varas arriba, frente al gran hotel.
From where Sandy's used to be, 200 meters to the east, across from the big hotel.

De los Semáforos El Dorado, dos cuadras al sur, una c. arriba, casa lila.
From the El Dorado traffic light, two blocks south, one east, purple house.

Reparto San Juan, de la UNIVAL, 50 varitas al lago, edificio de cinco pisos.
In the San Juan neighborhood, just 50 meters north of the UNIVAL, five-story building.

General Sandino's "crazy little army" in the 1930s, who helped train latter-day Sandinistas in the general's ideology and the art of guerrilla warfare. The historical frieze that circles the **Templo de la Música,** a brightly painted gazebo, highlights the arrival of Columbus, Rafael Herrera fighting pirates, independence from Spain, Andrés Castro fighting William Walker, and more, but it's just as interesting for the antics of the sparrows that inhabit its arches.

The **Plaza de la Cultura República de Guatemala** is a small park dedicated to Guatemalan author Miguel Angel Asturias Rosales, winner of the Nobel Prize in literature in 1967 for his colorful writings about national individuality and Native American traditions. He wrote frequently of the tyranny of dictators, the beauty and hostility of nature, and the struggle against domination by U.S. trusts,

themes with which the Sandinista government felt much empathy.

West of the Parque Central is the former Palacio de Telecomunicaciones (ENITEL). Across the street are two colonial-style homes that also withstood the earthquake—not much else did in this neighborhood, including a *discoteca* (dance club) on the same block that collapsed and killed nearly everyone inside.

Parque Rubén Darío, dominated by a stark, white marble statue, is adjacent to the Parque Central and honors Nicaragua's most-beloved poet. Built in 1933, it was restored in 1998 with the help of the Texaco Corporation (whose logo is displayed a little too prominently on the statue's base). At the water's edge and replete with marble and brass, **El Teatro Rubén Darío** was designed by the same architects that created New York's Metropolitan Opera House. It too survived the earthquake and remains a classy place to take in a performance of dance, theater, or music. The second-floor balcony offers a wonderful view of the lake, and the crowds give you a glimpse of Managua's privileged aristocracy. Check the newspaper for performances, its website www.tnrubendario.gob.ni, or call 505/266-3630 or 505/228-4021 for upcoming events.

Just west of the theater, the decrepit little park in memory of **Samora Moises Machel** honors the leader of the guerrilla movement that brought independence to Mozambique, a nation whose history of attempted socialism, counterrevolution, and democracy parallels Nicaragua's.

The **Plaza de la Fé** (Faith Plaza) was built during Alemán's administration in tribute to Pope John Paul II, who made his second visit to Nicaragua in 1996. Former Managua mayor Herty Lewites, built the acoustic stage **La Concha Acústica** here for mounting live concerts. Managua's northern limit is defined by the blustery shoreline of Lake Xolotlán, which you can admire from the **Malecón,** a public walkway along the water's edge lined with food and drink stands. The brass statue of Simón Bolívar, hero of the Latin American liberation movement greets you as you arrive (even if he is facing the wrong way).

South of Plaza de la Revolución and Avenida Bolívar

Just south of these sights are **Los Escombros,** the grass-lined ruins of old downtown Managua, where no one dares build, and where Managua's poorest squat in the crumbling hulks of what the earthquake didn't pull completely to the ground—not a safe area at any time of day. Pass through instead to the lighthouse-esque and disturbingly apocalyptic **Monumento de la Paz,** designed to oversee a new era of peace. Beneath the concrete are buried the destroyed remains of thousands and thousands of weapons from the Contra war, many of which—including a tank—can be seen protruding through the cement. It is representative of the great strides President Chamorro took during her presidency to ensure

Nicaragua's days of violence and war would be relegated to the past.

The imposing, Hulk-like statue of **El Guerrillero sin Nombre** (The Nameless Guerrilla Soldier) grasps a pick-ax in one hand and an AK-47 in the disproportionately muscular other. This is an important city landmark and a symbol of the revolution's aspirations, inscribed with one of Sandino's most treasured quotations: "Only the laborers and farmers will go to the end." A Liberal government countered with a different statue just across the road, honoring the working class with two cowed and undernourished looking figures, one representing a construction worker and the other a domestic servant, both representative of Nicaragua's growing laborer community in neighboring Costa Rica.

Across from the new *cancillería* (foreign affairs) building, where the old Iglesia de San Antonio used to stand, is the **monument to victims of the earthquake of 1972.** This touching statue, constructed in 1994, was the brainchild of journalist Aldo Palacios. It portrays a man standing amidst the wreckage of his home and is inscribed with the poem, "Requiem a una Ciudad Muerta," by Pedro Rafael Gutierrez.

One of the few Managua streets known by name, **Avenida Bolívar** runs south from the Nameless Guerrilla statue, past several lesser-known historical sites. One block south of the Guerrillero sin Nombre, the southwest corner with a lone wooden telephone pole marks the site of journalist **Pedro Joaquin Chamorro's assassination** as he drove to his office on January 10, 1978. Whether the drive-by was paid for by Tachito or his business partner in the infamous blood-bank business was never determined, but Chamorro's death helped spark the revolution. Look for a concrete monument directly behind the telephone pole. Continuing south, you'll pass some government buildings and basketball courts before coming to the **National Arboretum** (8 A.M.–5 P.M. Mon.–Sat., $0.50) on your left, home to more than 180 species of trees found in Nicaragua. It is practically unvisited except by local school groups but is especially attractive in March, when the fragrant *sacuanjoche* (Nicaragua's national flower) blooms brightly; the scarlet flowers of the *malinche* tree blossom from May through August. The trees are planted atop the remnants of Somoza's Hormiguero (Anthill), a military base belonging to the National Guard and destroyed in 1972 by the earthquake. Popular legend has it that this was the site where, on February 21, 1934, General Sandino was ambushed and assassinated after meeting with President Sacasa at his home on the Tiscapa Crater. Watch for ghosts.

◖ La Laguna de Tiscapa

Continuing south on Avenida Bolívar, pass the Plaza Inter mall on your left, then turn left behind the Crowne Plaza Hotel to find the **Parque Historica,** a breezy spot overlooking a volcanic lagoon and the rest of the city. The twin-towered monument halfway up the road is the **Monumento Roosevelt,** which delineated the southern terminus of the city preearthquake. Twenty meters farther up the hill is the statue of justice, sardonically decapitated ages ago. The statue of Sandino atop the crater lip is one of Managua's most recognizable symbols and is now a public park with impressive views of the old city and lake. The Sandinistas erected it atop the wreckage of Somoza's presidential mansion. A permanent exhibition of old photos of Sandino has been set up in the basement of the ruins. Just up the hill but closed to the public rests Las Masmorras, a prison in which Somoza tortured many political prisoners, including Daniel Ortega.

The Laguna de Tiscapa, once a treasured swimming hole of pristine waters, was defiled in the 1980s when it began receiving surface run-off, including untreated sewage from nearby neighborhoods. A major cleanup began in 2005, in which the drainage channels were diverted, and efforts continue to reoxygenate the water and to make it fit for bathing once again. The mayor's office plans to exploit its potential for tourism, including reviving the floating stage for the presentation of concerts. In the meantime, try out the **canopy tour** (tel.

General Sandino's silhouette still graces the Tiscapa Crater in downtown Managua.

© JOSHUA BERMAN

505/888-2566, 9 A.M.–5:30 P.M. Tues.–Sun., $15 for foreigners, $10 for Nicas) via zip lines that send you rocketing over the crater on three cable-connected platforms. As canopy tours go, Managua's is cheaper than elsewhere with no sacrifice in safety. The broad panoramas around you are some of the best in the capital. When historical figure Comandante Tomás Borge tried the lines, he got stuck halfway across like an old sock, to the delight of crowds that jeered, "Cut the cable!" On the northeast side of Laguna Tiscapa, just two blocks from the Ministerio de Gobernación, is the site of the old U.S. Embassy, leveled during the earthquake.

◖ Las Huellas de Acahualinca

If you visit only one historical site outside of Plaza de la Revolución and the Laguna de Tiscapa, this is the one. Modest but informative, the site is a simple interpretation center built over the fossilized footprints of Managua's earliest known inhabitants who fished Lake Managua 4,000 years before Christ. The prehistoric footprints were found in the last century, four meters below the ground surface. The footprints may represent humans fleeing a volcanic eruption or just heading to the lake to fish, but you'll notice the women's footprints are deeper, indicating they were carrying something heavy, like the children. The museum also has some exhibits on Nahuatl life and the volcanoes of Central America, emphasizing the point that living in the shadow of eminent volcanic destruction is nothing new in town. You are left to draw your own conclusions. The museum (tel. 505/266-5774, open 8 A.M.–5 P.M. Mon.–Sat., $2) is a bit out of the way at the northwest end of the city, so call before going, and find a taxi to take you there and back (about $5 an hour; one hour should be enough). The taxi will inevitably drive you through some of Managua's poorer lakefront neighborhoods, a statement about life in Managua as well.

Elsewhere in Managua

At the center of an immense field of young coconut trees along the Carretera Masaya is the new cathedral, **Catedral de la Inmaculadá Concepción de María,** constructed just two years after the conclusion of the civil war. Commissioned by American Thomas Monahan and designed by Mexican architect Ricardo Legorretta, this dynamic and open cathedral houses the Dutch bells of the old cathedral. Playing on the soaring forms of Spanish colonial architecture and using colors and materials of the Latin culture, the new cathedral is the pulpit of Nicaragua's famous and controversial Cardinal Miguel Obando y Bravo. Mass is celebrated Tuesday–Saturday at noon and 6 P.M. and Sunday at 11 A.M. and 6 P.M.

In the amphitheater of **La Tribuna** (from Hotel Crowne Plaza, a few blocks north to the traffic circle and one block east), 19th-century Presidents Chamorro and Zelaya oversaw grand ceremonies; damage from the 1972 earthquake was never repaired. Hard-core

history fans will appreciate the **monument to Bill Stewart** (one block west and two blocks south of the Semáforo El Dorado), the U.S. journalist for ABC-TV whose death at the hands of the National Guard was captured by his cameraman and destroyed U.S. support for Somoza's faltering regime. A few blocks south in the same neighborhood, the **Iglesia de los Angeles** is a living monument to the revolution, painted on all sides in bright murals that tell the story of Nicaragua. Beautiful on its own, it can be better appreciated with a guide: Contact Solentiname Tours (tel. 505/270-9981, zerger@ibw.com.ni) for an expert who will lead you through the story.

Just west of the petroleum refinery on the road leading west out of town is **La Cuesta del Plomo** (accessible from ruta bus 183), the ravine where Somoza was allegedly fond of making folks "disappear." Families whose loved ones didn't come home after a few days would go to this hillside to search for their bodies. Off in the distance in Lake Managua is La Isla del Amor (Island of Love), the small island where the dictator used to take his lovers to a personal cottage in the days before auto-hotels made the whole thing easier.

Museums and Art Galleries

Nicaragua's museum selection is pretty poor overall, but beside the Huellas de Acahualinca, you can spend a rainy afternoon in **El Museo Nacional de Nicaragua** located in the Palacio de Cultura (tel. 505/222-2905, open 7:30 A.M.–4:30 P.M. Mon.–Fri., 9 A.M.–5 P.M. Sun., $1). It highlights natural history, as well as pre-Columbian ceramics and statues from all over Nicaragua's territories.

Otherwise, it's easy to spend half a day visiting Managua's art galleries, which gather the best of Nicaragua's creative artists. Most galleries showcase a particular artist's work, but you are welcome to browse whether you are just admiring or are interested in making a purchase. The best of these is probably **Galería Solentiname** (Barrio Edgard Munguía Transfer, 600 meters south of the UNAN, tel. 505/277-0939, open 9 A.M.–5 P.M.

Mon.–Sat.) is set in the home of Doña Elena Pineda, a native Solentinameña who has done a great job of promoting the works of painters from the famous archipelago. Related, the **Galería de Los Tres Mundos** (Los Robles, two blocks north of the French restaurant La Marseillaise, open 8 A.M.–5 P.M. Mon.–Fri.) is Ernesto Cardenal's home base and showcases a variety of Solentiname artwork, from paintings to balsa work. More a cultural center than a museum, **Códice** (Colonial Los Robles *segundada etapa,* house #15, tel. 505/267-2635, open 9 A.M.–7 P.M., sometimes later, Mon.–Sat.) displays changing exhibitions of sculpture, paintings, and ceramics, all set around a lovely courtyard. There are often musical performances here in the evenings, and the patio is a peaceful corner in which to enjoy a light lunch and a drink.

ENTERTAINMENT AND EVENTS

Plan your evening with the help of www.2night .com or www.bacanalnica.com, which list special events and parties in the city. Travelers will want to stick to two main areas for enjoying the nightlife: The first is along Carretera Masaya from the new cathedral to the Rotonda Centroamerica (and if you have a car, a bit beyond). Known as Managua's Zona Rosa (hot spot), it's the easiest place to find food, music, and entertainment. Secondary in importance is the region immediately surrounding Hotel Crowne Plaza and Plaza Inter mall, with several decent bars and upscale restaurants, but not as much "buzz."

Discos

Dance is a huge part of Latino culture and Managua's discos are among the best. So even if you're a wallflower, go out and nurse a beer while watching Managuans of all ages dressed to the nines at their exuberant best. Before long you'll be on the dance floor too (conveniently, Managua also has several places to learn salsa and merengue if you are in town for a longer period of time). Venues range from enormous and open to intimate and mysterious.

Thursdays and Fridays are the warm-up for Saturday night, which goes until sunrise.

The line forms early at **XS (Excess);** dance to salsa, merengue, and *reggaetón salseado,* or relax with rum served by the bottle in several different indoor and outdoor settings. **El Chamán** is always popular despite its outdated ambience. Huge among the college crowd and right next door to both Metrocentro and many Carretera Masaya restaurants, this is a good place to finish your evening.

When you've had enough salsa and merengue, go island-style—Managua's Costeño crowd is right at home in **Island Taste** (Km 6 Carretera Norte). Go on a Thursday, when there's enough elbow room to enjoy the Garífuna, *soka,* and reggae vibes—Fridays and Saturdays, the place is typically too full to turn around, much less dance.

Bars and Clubs

Near Hotel Crowne Plaza: The Shannon Pub (from TicaBus, one block east and half-block south) is one of Managua's best, run by "don Miguel," an affable, longtime Irish expat. It features an appealing menu, imported whiskey, a satellite jukebox, dartboard, and lovely pints of Guiness, and it's open daily for breakfast and from 3 P.M.–closing.

Not far away, **El Changon** (two blocks south and 15 meters west of the Crowne Plaza Hotel, open from 7 P.M. Wed.–Sat.) is named for Cuban witchcraft. It has a scruffy, bohemian atmosphere; a soundtrack that includes reggae, rap, and rhumba; and a cozy, open-air dance floor that doubles as a stage for local rock bands. Just around the corner, on the hilly road that goes past the Plaza Inter, both **Bar La Loma** (tucked discreetly behind the Escuela de Manejo La Profesional) and **La Curva** are popular.

Along Carretera Masaya: Your best bet is to take a cab to the Lafise financial center (a large squat green building with a clock tower), and take the side road that parallels the highway for a block or two north and where you will find an area that hosts several (ever-changing) bars, most of which fall out of favor after a year. Two blocks north is **Mangoes Disco.** In the area just south of the monolithic and imposing, all-glass **Casa Pellas building** there is a handful of sidewalk bars that get busy on weekends: the **Iguana Rana, Punto Zero, Tsunami,** and **Marcelo's,** which has a cramped, and thus intimate, dance floor. Opposite Marcelo's is the **Excalibur Sports Bar** with $3 per hour pool tables. For serious pool enthusiasts, **Time-Out** (from the Lafise financial center, half a block east, 3.5 blocks north) has 20 tables for $2.50 per hour, and serves cocktails, beers and snacks. A beer bottle's throw to the south, are two down-at-the-heel disco-bars **Club Manza** and **Arribas** which get noisy around the 15th and 30th of each month, when paychecks are usually cashed. On the outskirts of town, a few hundred meters south of the Galería mall in the Plaza Familiar, **Hipa-Hipa** remains popular in spite of bad service and selective bouncers—if you make the cut (hint: dress well), you'll bump elbows with cell phone–toting Miami Boys and their *fresa* companions (strawberries, as Managua's young glamour girls are affectionately known). Wednesdays ladies drink free. Down the road at the outskirts of Managua, **Moods** in the Galerias Mall is upscale and pricey but gets good reviews; Thursday is ladies night.

Gay Bars
The first openly gay bar in Nicaragua was Locos, now under new management as **Miami** (Estatua de Montoya one block south, one block west) with the same atmosphere as before. **Tabu** (Entrada del Hospital Militar, three blocks north, one west, 10 yards north, tel. 505/851-7495) is newer and cooler, and the dancing lasts until earlier in the morning. The following options are located in slightly sketchier neighborhoods, so use caution: **Le Bistro** (*puente el Eden,* 2.5 blocks north on the right side by the hardware store) and **Galanes** (Ciudad Jardin, main road in front of the Mariscada).

Live Music
Managua's music scene, at once intimate and refined, shows a lot of local talent and energy.

Without a doubt, the single best show in town is **Casa de los Mejía Godoy** (in front of the Hotel Crowne Plaza, tel. 505/270-4928 or 505/278-4913, fmejiago@cablenet.com.ni). Both brothers perform here regularly, Carlos on Thursday and Saturday, with or without his band Los de Palacagüina. Luis Enrique does Latin rhythm nights on Friday, and Sunday features other Nicaraguan or international performers. Both brothers are born showmen and present a theatrical mix of stories, bawdy jokes, and famous songs. The club is expensive by Nica standards, but well worth it by any measure. Buy tickets the afternoon of the performance for $8–15; shows are Wednesday through Sunday only and start at 9 P.M.

The breezy, outdoor terrace of **La Ruta Maya** (150 meters east of the Estatua de Montoya, tel. 505/268-0698, open Thurs.–Sat., $4–6) is a pleasant place to appreciate a wide variety of performers from singer-songwriters to reggae, jazz, and everything in between. Local talent includes names such as Macolla, Llama Viva, Dimensión Costeña, Elsa Basil, and Clara Grun, to name but a few. **Latino's** (600 meters north of the Metrocentro rotunda) gets a similar entourage of troubadors and has an attractive, modern decor and dance floor. This is the place if you want to dance rather than just listen. They have live music from Thursdays to Saturdays, entrance $4. Also look for acoustic performances at the Shannon Pub and Changon.

Brass Monkey on Carretera Masaya (one block south and opposite of the Casa Pellas building—you can't miss the sign) is the town's most popular karaoke bar.

Casinos
Managua sports a growing number of casinos, from government-sponsored **Pharaoh Casino** (Carretera Masaya) which opened the scene in 1999, to **Star City Casino** (across from the Princess Hotel), which is better-appointed and far louder. A younger crowd frequents the **Las Vegas** if they're unable to get into the **Hollywood** strip club adjacent. Other brash additions in the Zona Rosa are **Aladdin's Casino**

and **Palm's Casino** with a decent supply of one-armed bandits.

Movies

Managua now has more than 40 cinema screens in six different complexes, but unfortunately they all show the same 10 films. On the upside the Cinemark and Galería complexes host occasional film festivals in one of their cinemas, offering an alternative to Hollywood dreck, thanks to the support of the cultural attachés of the local embassies. The **Alianza Francesa** (tel. 505/267-8283 or 505/267-8285) features a variety of European films, screened on a large video display on Tuesday nights. Also try the **Cinemateca** (tel. 505/222-3845), located next to the **El Centro Cultural de Managua,** where cinema connoisseurs enjoy film classics.

But if you're looking for something modern, check show times in the newspaper *Revista Cinematográfica* (a weekly bulletin distributed at most gas stations and some hotels and restaurants), or *Patadeperro* a free monthly arts magazine that's hard to find but can usually be picked up at the Casa de Café. Shows change every Thursday and will set you back about $3–5. Tuesdays and Wednesdays are often cutprice. Bring a jacket: Managua's theaters are glacially air-conditioned.

Good cinemas can also be found at **Cinemark** (tel. 505/271-9037 or 505/271-9000) in the Metrocentro Mall, at the **Cinema Plaza Inter** (tel. 505/222-5090 or 505/222-5122) on the third floor of the Plaza Inter mall (remember to take a cab at night; the neighborhoods west of the theater are no longer walkable at night), or at the **Galería** shopping complex located on the Carretera Masaya (tel. 505/276-5065) just southeast of the Rotunda Jean Paul Genie.

Theater and Dance

Managua's finest theater, **El Teatro Nacional Rubén Darío** (at the Malecón, tel. 505/266-3630 or 505/228-4021) hosts top-name international acts. Check the newspaper for performances or call. **La Escuela Nacional de Teatro** (Palacio Nacional de Cultura, tel. 505/222-4449) is primarily a teaching facility that presents performances on weekends by students and small professional troupes from all over Latin America; call for a list of events, as they're not always published. The **Sala De Teatro Justo Rufino Garay** (from the Estatua Montoya three blocks west and 20 meters north, next to Parque Las Palmas, tel. 505/266-3714) is better frequented and offers similar fare on weekends only; a calendar of events is often available at supermarkets and Texaco stations as well as in the arts magazine *Patadeperro* if you're lucky enough to find a copy.

Located across from the UCA, **La Academia de Danza** (tel. 505/277-5557) has frequent performances and concerts. The students deliver professional and talented renditions of traditional, folk, modern jazz, Brazilian, and ballet; call or drop by for a schedule of events, or if you're in town for the long haul, consider taking one of their dance classes to prepare you for the club scene.

Tour Guides

Many of the middle and upper range hotels can organize a guide and/or taxi to take you around the city and see many of the sights and places mentioned in this chapter. A taxi will cost around $20 per half day and a guide a similar amount. If you're lucky you'll get both for the one price. One recommended guide (without taxi) is Raul Gavarrette (tel. 505/876-5702, rgavarrette@hotmail.com), who also runs a Spanish language school in Granada and another in Masaya.

Special Events

Las Fiestas Patronales each August are when Managua celebrates its patron saint Santo Domingo and are the highlight of the calendar year. On the first of the month, the saint (a diminuitive little figure under a glass dome) is brought down from a small church in the hilly neighborhood of Santo Domingo and on the 10th he is returned. On both those dates, and for much of the time in between, Managua

NICARAGUAN FOLK MUSIC AND THE HOUSE OF MEJÍA GODOY

In the wide, vast – and incredibly loud – sea of music flowing through Nicaragua's living rooms, bars, vehicles, and airwaves, music of true Nicaraguan roots is not the easiest to hear. However, once you get to know the distinctive 6/8 rhythms, the sound of the marimba, and the melodies that every single Nicaraguan knows by heart, you'll realize just how much Nicaraguan music is woven into its society.

Only a few musical remnants of Nicaragua's indigenous societies survived the conquistadores; these precious acts of dance, costume, and distinctive melodies are best observed today during the fiestas patronales of Masaya, Diriamba, and the various pueblos dotting the hills between them. These pre-Columbian fragments were further enriched by the different cultures they encountered along the way. Much of this influence was Spanish, and at some point, the African marimba traveled up the Río San Juan, landed in Granada, and found its home among the folkloricos of Carazo and Masaya.

Things are different in the northern hills of Nicaragua, where Carlos Mejía Godoy was born in 1943. The music there, he explains, is composed of campesino versions of the waltz, polka, and mazurka. Born and taught to play the accordion and guitar in Somoto, Carlos Mejía Godoy is neither the "father" nor "inventor" of Nicaraguan folk music, as some would have it. In fact, he is only one in a line of multiple generations of songwriting Nicaraguans. However, his love and passion for Nicaraguan culture, combined with his sheer talent as a musician, songwriter, and performer, have made Carlos Mejía and his long catalog of songs central in any discussion (or jam session) involving Nicaraguan music.

Don Carlos says he wishes he had two lives: one to learn all there is to be learned about Nicaraguan culture and a second to perform and use that knowledge. To most observers (and fans), it would appear he has done an adequate job at squeezing both into the one life he was given. Not only did he join the Sandinista Revolution in 1973 and proceed to compose its soundtrack, but throughout his life, Carlos Mejía has delved deeply into the campo, always in search of the regionally distinct riches of his country's cultural fabric. His songs are vibrant, colorful celebrations of everything Nicaraguan – from its geography, food, and wildlife, to praise for the town gossip and shoe-shine boy.

When asked about the Nicaraguita flower that inspired him to write the most famous song in the country's history ("Nicaragua, Nicaraguita"), Carlos Mejía quoted a passage entitled "La Flor Escogida" (The Chosen Flower) by Profesor Carlos A. Bravo. In that passage, the rare variety of sacuanjoche (Nicaragua's national flower) is described as "roja incendida, un clarinazo, listada de oro" (burning red, a trumpet blast, with golden rays). Carlos Mejía called this "such a beautiful thing," and one is not sure if he was speaking of the flower or the lyrical words describing it – perhaps for him, there is no distinction between the two.

Pick up some of Carlos Mejía's music and learn his lyrics before you leave, but don't stop your discovery there. Carlos's brother Luis Enrique is a world-renowned salsa king, and they can both be found performing at their club in Managua, **La Casa de los Mejía Godoy.**

Other respected Nica folksters include Nandaimeño Camilo Zapata, the granddaddy of them all; also seek out Tino Lopez, Justo Santos, Otto de la Rocha, Norma Elena Madea, and the duo Guardabarranco. Erwin Kruger, is perhaps one of the most celebrated Nicaraguan instrumentalists and composers for guitar. Ask one of the musicians that offer to play at your table in a restaurant like the Munich to play "El Barrio de los Pescadores" or "La Mora Limpia" and you'll get an idea. In addition, every town in Nicaragua has multiple generations of pluckers and crooners, many of whom are a wealth of knowledge and all too willing to sing (or teach) you some songs.

An excellent guide (in Spanish) to Nicaraguan music can be found at www.musicanica.com.

celebrates. Expect parades, horse shows, unlimited quantities of beer and rum, and a lot of fun and colors. INTUR sponsors a series of events during this time, like Las Noches Agostinas, featuring cultural presentations and live music throughout the capital.

Every **July 19th** since 1979, Nicaraguans have celebrated the final victory against Somoza during the Sandinista revolution. July 19th celebrations bring out the Sandinista party faithful, with a rally and presentations in Plaza de la Fé and a show choreographed by President Ortega's wife Rosario Murillo. The truly devout even stay through Ortega's predictable and lengthy speech at the end.

If you are in Managua during the first few weeks of December, be sure to catch the massive **IMPYME** crafts fair on Avenida Bolívar—arts, crafts, and food from all over the country, plus a two-week carnival. **Expica** is a permanent farming-related exhibition site in Barrio Acahualinca (Casa Pellas, two blocks west and one block north, tel. 505/266-9634) and where

in August ranchers descend upon the capital to exhibit and sell breeding stock, and generally show off their latest SUVs, ill-concealed revolvers, and beer-swilling prowess on the bar stool. The Nicaraguan cowboy elite show hundreds of some of the most magnificent and beautifully tended specimens of Brahman cattle in this part of the world, as well as impressive displays of horsemanship in the saddles of purebred Arabian and Peruvian equines.

SHOPPING
Markets

For a gorgeous selection of arts and crafts in a pleasant atmosphere, visit **Mama Delfina** (Enitel Villa Fontana, one block north, tel. 505/267-8288), which collects the work of artisans from all over the country. At the little café on a breezy second-floor balcony, you can mull over your purchases with a tall glass of icy cacao.

Mercado Huembes is full of the exuberance, color, and life that so typifies Nicaragua.

The Rotunda Metrocentro is at the heart of Managua's sprawling commercial center.

Huembes is the most tourist friendly of the markets in Managua. Massive and cacophonous, Huembes offers fruits, vegetables, meat, cheese, flowers, cigars, clothes, shoes, and the best arts and crafts section this side of Masaya. Open every day from around 7:30 A.M. to around 5 P.M., Huembes is also a major bus terminal (see *To Points South* in the *Getting There and Away* section).

The sprawling 30-block labyrinth of Mercado Oriental, on the other hand, is confusing and dangerous: Someone gets robbed here every seven minutes, and travelers should avoid it.

Malls

The five U.S.-style malls built since 1998 (Plaza Inter, Plaza Metrocentro, Galería, Plaza Las Américas, and Plaza Bello Horizonte) have notably dissimilar personalities: At the upper end of the market, Galería hosts the typical bevy of Cartier, LaCoste, and Chanel counters, and a selection of European fashions; at the lower end Plaza Inter has made a go at cheaper-quality imported goods from Asia (the Plaza is wholly owned by Taiwanese investors). The Centro Comercial de Managua is a pleasant open-air strip mall built in the Somoza era, offering a good selection of books, clothing, fabric, and sporting goods, plus two banks, an Internet café, and a post office—not a bad place to get some errands out of the way if malls aren't your cup of tea. Just north of the National Cathedral, is another high-end but smaller shopping complex. DISNISA, located here, has a strong selection of imported wines and liquor.

Bookstores

Hispamer (Reparto Tiscapa, just east of the UCA, tel. 505/278-1210) is the largest bookstore in the city. In the Centro Comercial, several small, but interesting bookstores compete for your attention, including **Librería El Güegüense** (tel. 505/278-7399 or 505/278-5285), one of the better choices for books about Nicaragua and foreign-language dictionaries; and **Librería Rigoberto López Pérez** (tel.

505/277-2240), named for the poet who, for love of his country, assassinated Anastasio Somoza García. The latter features a wide selection and friendly atmosphere. More recently **Frontera Books** (Reparto Los Robles, next to the main office of IBW, tel. 505/270-2345 or 505/270-2382) offers a good selection of English language novels and nonfiction.

SPORTS AND RECREATION
Denis Martínez National Baseball Stadium

Also known as **El Estadio Nacional,** this landmark is a proper metaphor for Managua: partially destroyed and rebuilt after the earthquake to something less than its original grandeur, originally named after Anastasio Somoza García, then renamed by the Sandinistas after that man's assassin, then renamed again, this time after Nicaragua's native son baseball hero. Formerly one of the funkiest operating ballparks on the continent, El Estadio Nacional was condemned and closed in 2008 after geologists found an earthquake fault beneath the already crumbling building.

Golf

It's no surprise that Nicaragua's wave of Miami-raised nouveax riche would get around to reopening the country's old-time exclusive country clubs, notably the 18 holes at **Nejapa Country Club** (tel. 505/266-9652), located between Veracruz and Sabana Grande. The course hosts events, such as the Amigos de la Zona Franca tournament. Shoot 18 holes for about $20. There's also **Club Terraza** in the Villa Fontana area.

ACCOMMODATIONS

If you find yourself complaining too loudly about Managua, try upgrading your accommodations, particularly if you're just spending a weekend here. There are a plethora of budget hotels and hostels, but many are in the not-so-safe Martha Quezada neighborhood. In the more attractive neighborhoods along Carretera Masaya prices rise, but your experience will be much improved. If you can afford to splurge just once, this might be the place to do so, as several of the higher priced independent bed-and-breakfasts, posadas, and guesthouses are well worth the money.

Under $10

The bulk of Managua's cheapest accommodations are found in Managua's former tourist epicenter, **Barrio Martha Quezada** (a.k.a. Gringolandia). The approximately 12 square blocks north and west of the TicaBus terminal are cluttered with budget accommodations and basic services that cater to the backpacker set. Unfortunately, this neighborhood is increasingly dangerous; several muggings at knifepoint have been reported. If you need to be close to the TicaBus station, consider the quirky **Guesthouse Santos,** a backpacker favorite with a massive common space and funky array of rooms with private, postmodern bathrooms (from TicaBus, one block north and 1.5 blocks west, tel. 505/222-3713, $6) or its annex **Tica-Nica** (one and half blocks north of TicaBus, $6). In the same neighborhood, **La Quintana** (tel. 505/254-5487 or 505/254-5492, $5) has fewer rooms but is reportedly safer; the doors shut at 11 P.M. Other recommendable options are the spartan but secure **Hospedaje El Dorado** (tel. 505/222-6012, $6.50 s, $13 d). There are a half dozen other lackluster *hospedajes* in the same category in this neighborhood.

A far better option is the **C** **Managua Backpacker's Inn** (Chaman, 75 meters south, house #55, tel. 505/267-0006, www.managuahostel.com, $7 shared dorm, $15 private room), which is in a safer neighborhood, has better access to the Carretera Masaya nightlife, is generally clean and good value. Reserve and even prepay online if you'd like. Another cheap option is the **Quaker House** (a.k.a. Casa Cuáquera, tel. 505/266-3216, $8), specializing in witness and solidarity groups; it's located in Barrio Las Brisas, *de la entrada al Hospital Lenin Fonseca, 5 c. al lago, 75 varas arriba* (from the Hospital Lenin Fonseca entranceway, five blocks north, 75 meters east)—look for the second to the last house on the left.

You'll find dorm-style accommodations with kitchen, washing machine, telephone, 24-hour security, and limited parking.

$10-25

Not far from the TicaBus station in Barrio Martha Quezada, **C** **Hotel Los Felipe** (1.5 blocks west of TicaBus, tel. 505/222-6501, www.hotellosfelipe.com.ni) is easily the best of the low-priced hotels in this neighborhood—$20 double with fan, a bit more with air-conditioning. Rooms are clean and safe and have cable TV and phone; Internet, parking, pool, a shady patio area under a thatched roof, laundry service, and private baths are also available. **Hotel Cisneros,** just opposite Guesthouse Santos, offers similar comforts but is slightly more expensive: $25 with fan, and $40 with a/c.

Hospedaje Mauricio Babilonia (six blocks south and half a block west of El Zumen, Managua's Civic Center, house #238, tel. 505/260-1258, $25) is located in a quiet and safe area to the south of Managua's administrative centre of El Zumen. It is run by a well-known local artist, Mauricio Mejía, who has his own gallery in the guesthouse which has five comfortable and clean private rooms, all with cable TV, hot water, and private bathroom. Internet is also available.

$25-50

Posadita de Bolonia (three blocks west of Canal 2, then 75 meters south, tel. 505/268-6692, www.posaditadebolonia.com, $40) is a comfortable and quiet place offering cable TV, Internet, hot water, and private showers. Breakfast is included. Other meals can be provided by arrangement. The hotel also offers a full range of tour and guide services. At about the same level of amenities, **Casa San Juan** (Reparto San Juan Calle Esperanza 560, tel. 505/278-3220, sanjuan@cablenet.com.ni, $46) is quiet and close to the universities and offers wireless Internet throughout the hotel, cable TV, and hot-water showers.

Posada de Maria La Gorda (Reparto El Carmen, tel. 505/268-2455 or 505/268-2456,

$35–60) is accustomed to the international set and provides Internet, laundry, and cable TV; check about special group rates.

$50-100

Starting in the Bolonia neighborhood, **《 Hotel Europeo** (75 meters west of Canal 2, tel. 505/268-4930 or 505/268-4933, www .hoteleuropeo.com.ni, $57) is easy to recommend: 35 clean, quiet, and beautifully furnished rooms, plus continental breakfast, a small pool, laundry service, Internet, and cable TV. **Hotel Real Bolonia** (from Plaza España 1.5 blocks north, across from the German Embassy, tel. 505/266-8133, hotelreal@hotel real.com.ni, $75) features 14 rooms adorned with antiques, paintings, and sculpture, all set around a large garden. **La Posada del Angel** (Hospital Militar three blocks west, 20 meters north, across from the Iglesia San Francisco, tel. 505/266-1347 or 505/266-1483, $65) has a long-standing reputation for excellent customer service; rooms have hot water, minibar, laundry service, cable TV, and strongbox.

《 Hotel El Ritzo (from the Lacmiel, three blocks east, 25 meters south, tel. 505/277-5616, hotelritzo@alianza.com.ni, www.hotelritzo .com.ni, $65) is not only tastefully decorated, quiet, and gorgeous, but is the only hotel worth considering within walking distance of the many restaurants and discos of the Carretera Masaya area. A favorite with journalists and close to the UCA and UNI universities is **Hotel El Almendro** (from the Metrocentro rotunda, two blocks west, half block south, tel. 505/270-1260, www.hotelelalmendro .com, $64), which has most of the amenities of a more expensive hotel but at almost half the price. The comfortable and friendly hotel offers wireless Internet, cable TV, private telephone, small pool, and for just $5 extra per night, you can get a studio apartment which includes an equipped kitchen, to cook your own meals and do your own laundry. Around the corner, **Hotel Pyramide** (Reparto San Juan, del Gimnasio Hercules one block south, one east, 2.5 south, tel. 505/278-0687, pyramide@ibw.com.ni, www.lapyramidehotel.com, $60) features hot

water, cable TV, telephone, minibar, wireless Internet, optional airport pickup, and quite possibly the city's only whirlpool tub.

In the Los Robles area just west of Carretera Masaya, **Hotel Los Robles** (in front of Restaurante La Marseillaise, tel. 505/267-3008, www.hotellosrobles.com, $95) is a charming yet professional hotel with a tropical feel, consisting of quiet rooms set around a garden courtyard, pool, restaurant services, wireless Internet, air-conditioning, cable TV in all the rooms, and a business center; their breakfast buffet is splendid.

Situated in a shady, peaceful neighborhood, **Hotel Casa Real** (Rotonda Rubén Darío two blocks west, two blocks south, half a block east, tel. 505/278-3838, www.hcasareal.com, from $65) has a trilingual staff, a small pool, and an excellent menu.

Another good quality bed-and-breakfast in a safe, central neighborhood is **Hotel Brandt** (Reparto San Juan, from the north side of Hercules gym one block east, tel. 505/270-2114, www.brandtshotel.com.ni, $75), with excellent facilities and service.

A convenient place to stay if you have an early flight is the **Best Western Las Mercedes** (tel. 505/263-1011, $85), directly across from the airport. Decompress on the last night before your flight in a decent restaurant or with the mixed bag of travelers and diplomats lounging by the pool.

Over $100

Managua's premium hotels cater to business travelers and offer four- or five-star service. The **Camino Real** (U.S. tel. 800/948-3770, caminoreal@centralamerica.com, $120) is close to the airport, just minutes away on Carretera Norte. At the base of the Tiscapa Crater, the pyramidal **Hotel Crowne Plaza** (located in Plaza Inter, formerly Hotel Intercontinental, tel. 505/228-3530, managua@interconti .com) has been a landmark since the Somoza days. Better situated with respect to restaurants and nightlife is the **Intercontinental Metrocentro** (tel. 505/271-9483, from $160) or **Hotel Princess** (Carretera Masaya, tel.

505/270-5045, $169–219), two blocks south. One block west and one block north of the Princess, and a short stroll from a dozen excellent restaurants, the **Hotel Seminole Plaza** (tel. 505/270-6496, www.seminoleplaza.com, $119) is owned by the Seminole Indian tribe of Florida; the hotel is typically a bit less expensive than the competition.

The **Holiday Inn** (Pista Juan Paul II, tel. 505/270-4515, holidayinn@tmx.com.ni, from $100) is the least conveniently situated of the premium hotels, but its interior is lovely and its service excellent.

Long-Term Accommodations

If you don't mind the grunge, you can surely work out some kind of long-term rate at any of the cheap *hospedajes* for around $150 a month. Otherwise, visiting students tend to gravitate to **Arcoíris** (Barrio Los Robles, two blocks south and one block east of Plaza del Sol, house #97, tel. 505/278-0905, $12), a clean, comfortable, family-run guesthouse in a safe neighborhood. The price includes breakfast, and minimum one-month stay applies. Internet is available, and laundry and other meals can be arranged. **Belinda's House** (Canal 2, two blocks north and 75 meters west, tel. 505/266-3856, $15) is a similar, cozy family-run long-term guesthouse.

For a fully serviced guesthouse, $500 per month is the going rate. **Los Cedros** (Km 13, Carretera Sur, across from the Iglesia Monte Tabor, tel. 505/265-8340) has 30 furnished rooms with bath, terrace, kitchen, pool, and plenty of green space. Next to Las Cazuelas restaurant and across from Guesthouse Santos, **Hotel/Apartamentos Los Cisneros** (tel. 505/222-3535) rents small, fully furnished apartments that include refrigerator, private phone, and parking facilities. Otherwise, dip into your expense account and check in at **Los Robles** (one block west, two blocks south of the Hotel Inter Metrocentro, tel. 505/278-6334), which has 12 safe rooms at $1,300 per month with maid service, cable TV, fridge, kitchen, and air-conditioning. If you're content living outside the city limits, several excellent long-term options line the far reaches of Carretera Masaya. **Hotel Campo Real** (Km 12.5, tel. 505/279-7067, camporeal@ideay.net.ni, www.hotelcampo real.com) has six fully furnished apartments with all the amenities to make you feel at home, from $60 a night, depending on how long you stay.

FOOD

Restaurants change annually in Managua; with the exception of a few perennial classics, most disappear as soon as the Nica jet set moves on to something newer and trendier.

Breakfast

There are numerous bakeries scattered throughout Barrio Martha Quezada, notably **Cafetín Tonalli** (2.5 blocks south of Cine Cabrera), a unique women's cooperative that produces extraordinarily good breads and cakes, and sells juices, cheese, coffee, and more (Swiss training!). Take out or eat in their enclosed outdoor patio. One block west of TicaBus, **Café Myrna** (open 6 A.M.–lunch daily, $3.50 for a full meal) is pleasant and popular and has great pancakes. A block and a half east of the Calle 27 traffic light, look for the colorful storefront of **Frutilandia** (open 7 A.M.–5 P.M. Mon.–Sat.), where you'll find a fresh, delicious menu of fruit smoothies, shakes, and simple meals.

Cafés and Coffee Shops

Managua's premier classy coffee shop is **La Casa de Café** (a landmark in the Los Robles neighborhood, and smaller venues in the Metrocentro mall and the airport) with a selection of pastries, juice drinks, and Nicaraguan coffee all served on a gorgeous, second-story open terrace overlooking the street. **Don Pan** (across from Pizzeria Valentis), also serves sandwiches and baked goods. In Plaza de la Revolución, check out the café at the **Palacio Nacional de Cultura.**

Vegetarian and Healthy Food

One recent upscale sensation is ◖ **Ola Verde** (behind Pharoah's Casino; follow the road to the end and turn right, tel. 505/270-3048, open from 9 A.M. daily, breakfast starts around $4, lunch around $6), offering fresh juices, salads, soups, hummus, and babaghanoush—a pleasant menu of changing vegetarian and chicken dishes. Ola Verde also has a small shop of natural products and is a popular meeting spot for foreigners.

Ananda (half a block east of the Estatua Montoya, tel. 505/228-4140, open 7 A.M.–9 P.M. daily) is Managua's original vegetarian option, with whole foods and fresh fruit juices.

Traditional Nicaraguan

The best traditional food is found grilling at roadside. Barrio Martha Quezada is littered with cheap eateries and street-side grills, notably the *fritanga* one block west and half a block north of TicaBus, open nights from about 6–9 P.M. Or try **La Racachaca** (from the Plaza España, 1.5 km west), a 10-minute taxi ride from Martha Quezada and easily the most famous *fritanga* in Managua; your cab driver will know where it is because he probably eats there himself.

If street food isn't your style, **La Cocina de Doña Haydee** (one block west of Casino Pharoah) serves Nicaraguan traditional specialties in a clean, quiet atmosphere. **El Garabato** (two blocks south of the Hotel Seminole Plaza, tel. 505/278-2944) has made an attractive combination of a wine and cocktail bar combined with a restaurant serving traditional Nicaraguan food, in this more central location. Dishes cost $3–10. You can buy handicrafts here too. Not far away is **Rostipollos** (across from La Lotería, tel. 505/277-1858, about $5 pp), which in addition to chicken has an extensive menu of Nica favorites, a clean establishment, and good service.

Otherwise, if you have a vehicle, head for Carretera Sur. **Mi Pueblo** (Km 9) is worth the trip for lunch or dinner to check out one of the best views in town, bar none. Just a half kilometer farther south out of town is **Asados Milcas,** with large helpings, quick service, reasonable prices, and good charcoal-grilled meats. Here you'll find grilled chicken

for US$2.50, and surprisingly tender *churrasco* steaks for $5. Even father south and newer, **Casa Hacienda** (Carretera Sur Km 15, tel. 505/265-8437), also offers traditional Nicaraguan dishes and grills. Set within a former coffee plantation, this restaurant has superb surroundings (ask to see the 850-year-old ceiba tree for example) where you can get an idea of how the outskirts of Managua looked before all the construction began.

Steak and Burgers

El Puyaso (from El Chamán, 75 meters south, Los Robles, tel. 505/277-2485) is the Managua branch of a Matagalpan favorite, and their steak is top-notch but not expensive. **La Plancha** (from the Semáforos Plaza del Café, 150 meters to the east) is home to some of the best meat in town. Ask for the *parrillada* rack or just go for the grill, *a la plancha*, about $10–12 a plate. Perhaps the best-known steak place in the city, **El Churrasco** is located right on the Rotonda El Güegüense. **Los Ranchos** (Carretera Sur Km 3, tel. 505/266-0526, open noon–3 P.M. and 6–11 P.M. daily) isn't cheap (about $15 per entrée), but they've served a fantastic steak au poivre since the days of Somoza. **Hary's Grill** (next to the Texaco gas station, Las Colinas, Carretera Masaya, tel. 505/276-1067) serves pricey imported Argentinian steak.

Eskimo (next door to the Fábrica Eskimo, tel. 505/266-9701) serves a varied menu of meats, fish, and shellfish, all in the $6–9 range; the *pollo en vino* is a popular choice. If the Nica beef is too tough for you, **Hippo's Bar and Grill** (from the Hotel Seminole Plaza, one block south), **Woody's,** and **Girafe Joe** (tel. 505/270-0471) serve burgers and steaks in an increasingly fun corner of town now called "Zona Hippos."

Spanish

El Mesón Español y Barra La Tasca (Bolonia Mansión Teodolinda 350 meters south, tel. 505/266-8561) serves fantastic paella and shellfish for about $20. **El Bodegon de Don Tomás** (one block north and 200 meters east of La Marseillaise restaurant, tel. 505/278-3287),

MANAGUA

located in a peaceful cul-de-sac in the Los Robles barrio, serves excellent tapas for $4–10, and a main course for $10–15.

Mexican

Tacos Charros (Colonia Centroamérica, tel. 505/278-2337) is the cheapest place to eat tacos, enchiladas, and the like, all for around $3. **María Bonita** (1.5 blocks west of Distribuidora Vicky, tel. 505/270-4326) is another favorite, offering dinner in an open, romantic atmosphere for about $6, and a traditional and European breakfast bar Monday–Saturday 6:45–10 A.M. for $3. Stop in at **Tacos al Pastor** on your way to the Alhambra movie theater. It's a small but charming restaurant that also sells beautiful pottery; dishes run about $3.

Seafood

One of the best seafood places in town, with a choice of outdoor seating and air-conditioning indoors, is **Marea Alta** in Los Robles (from Hotel Seminole Plaza, two blocks south). The restaurant is the former residence of Chema Castillo, where in 1977 the Sandinistas took hostage of diplomats and government officials (Chema himself was killed). The Los Robles branch has become a core around which a dozen other restaurants have sprung up. Next door is **Rock and Grill,** which offers a brash and definitely un-Asiatic mixture of sushi and steak dishes for $8–15, and one set of streetfront tables farther along is **Scampi's,** which specializes in sushi for $10–20 a plate. Just across the road is **Sharky's,** offering an excellent seafood paella for two for $15 and a good selection of other seafood dishes for $7–15. On the opposite corner from Marea Alta and specializing in tapas and seafood is **Piratas.**

El Muelle (one block east of the Hotel Intercontinental Metrocentro, $6–8) also offers excellent seafood cocktails and main courses.

Asian

You'll need a cab to get to **The Wok** (a short hop down the bypass in front of Hotel Princess, tel. 505/278-0932), dishes start at $6. But

Ming Court (adjacent to the Plaza Inter and Hotel Crowne Plaza) is top of the line, and easily the best and most expensive Chinese food in the country; dishes from $8–10. The **Corona de Oro** (two blocks south of the Hotel Crowne Plaza) also provides an excellent variety of Chinese dishes for a similar price. The **Rincón Chino** (1.5 blocks east of Lacmiel) is popular with the expatriate Taiwanese who run the many *maquila* factories dotted around Managua, as is **Xin Tian Di** (two blocks north of the Lafise financial center and 50 meters east, tel. 505/278-1250) where the "Wan Tan" soup will fill you with barely a ripple in your lunch budget.

Sushi Itto (tel. 505/278-4886), a Central American chain of good-quality sushi restaurants, has two branches in Managua, one in the Galería mall, and the other at the Rotunda El Periodista, about two kilometers west of the UCA, with meals starting at $10.

The newest sushi restaurant is the **Bonsai** located in Los Robles (1.5 blocks south of the Monte Olivos funeral parlor, tel. 505/278-8585). Here diners enjoy executive lunches for $5–6 and a veritable sushi feast for $45 that would feed a marauding band of seven samurai.

Italian

◖ **La Casa del Pomodoro** (Carretera Masaya Km 4, a block from Pizzería Valentis, tel. 505/270-9966) is a big favorite, serving large portions of quality food; their $5 calzones will fill you up for two days. **Tre Fratelli** (on Carretera Masaya) sports a modern bar, indoor and outdoor seating, and a high-end menu that includes the Italian classic Fiorentina steak. Expect to pay upwards of $10 per plate for dinner, but the executive lunch goes for about $6, or just enjoy happy hour 6–9 P.M. The best value for your money, **Valenti's Pizza** (Colonial Los Robles, two blocks east of Lacmiel, tel. 505/277-5744) serves inexpensive pizza and beer in a festive atmosphere. Try their fresh pesto and their cannelloni.

Out of town, **La Cueva del Buzo** (Carretera Sur Km 13, tel. 505/265-8336 or 505/868-1241) is probably the best; their formidable whole red snapper is coated in sea salt and baked with olive oil and Mediterranean spices. The Italian owner personally catches the fish he serves. Plates average around $10.

French

La Marseillaise (Calle Principal Los Robles, tel. 505/277-0224) is a city classic since before the war, serving traditional French cuisine and stunning desserts, all in a gorgeous building. Plainer but somehow more pretentious, **Le Cafe de Paris** is one block south and 60 meters to the east of the former where main dishes cost between $20–40, and a bottle of French wine around the same; enjoy the rare opportunity to eavesdrop on high-powered Nicaraguan businesspeople and lawyers cutting deals across the cognac.

INFORMATION AND SERVICES

The daily newspaper will keep you *al tanto* (up-to-date) in terms of events and festivals. INTUR, the government tourism institute (tel. 505/222-3333, www.intur.gob.ni), staffs a kiosk in the airport and an office near the Plaza Inter mall, where they sell maps, distribute local guides and listings, and offer a visitor's desk for tourists, open 8:30 A.M.–2 P.M. Monday–Friday.

Emergency Services

Dial 118 for police, 115 or 120 for the fire department, and 128 for the Red Cross ambulance. There are several hospitals in Managua; the most modern is the private **Hospital Vivian Pellas** (outside of Managua on the highway to Masaya), built in 2004. For less serious ailments and stomach disorders, Hospital Bautista (tel. 505/249-7070, Barrio Largaespada, near the main fire station) is accustomed to dealing with foreigners.

Libraries

A rarity in a nation that reads few books, Managua's public library, **Biblioteca Dr. Roberto Incer Barquero** (behind the bank at Carretera Sur Km 7, tel. 505/265-0500 ext.

COLLEGE TOWN

Nicaragua's next generation of leaders attends more than 30 Managuan universities, the three biggest of which are **La Universidad de Centroamerica** (La UCA, rhymes with "hookah"), **La Universidad Nacional Autónoma de Nicaragua** (La UNAN), and **La Universidad Nicaragüense de Ingeniería** (La UNI). Visiting the courtyards, soda shops, cafés, and bars on campus provides a great opportunity to mingle with up-and-coming revolutionaries and neoliberal capitalists alike. Find out about the latest student strike or tire-burning session in the fight for 6 percent of the national budget, cheaper tuition, and of course, a classless society without corruption, war, or unfair wages. The intersection in front of the UCA and UNI is a regular hotspot during student strife, and a huge social scene otherwise. It is also a transportation hub, with minivans departing the city daily for nearby destinations. With the Sandinistas once again in power, and one of their principal student firebrands, Jasser Martínez, now a Sandinista deputy in the National Assembly, it's probably safe to assume that the students will stay obediently off the streets unless Daniel Ortega's government gets into trouble and needs some agitation to intimidate the opposition.

465, open 8:30 A.M.–4:30 P.M. Mon.–Fri.) was built in 1999 and houses a notable collection of newspapers from the war years. The old National Library is located in the Palacio de Cultura down by the waterfront. INHCA is a remarkable collection of historical and cultural resources housed within the UCA; accessing them requires a library card obtainable from the director by paying a $10 fee.

Banks

Banking hours in Managua are 8 A.M.–4 P.M. Monday–Friday, and 8 A.M.–noon on Saturday. Along Carretera Masaya, you'll find the **Banco** de América Central (BAC), **Bancentro** (in the LAFISE financial center), **Banco de Finanzas (BDF), Banpro, Banco Uno** and the first truly international bank, **HSBC**. For travelers staying in Barrio Martha Quezada, the nearest bank is the BDF near the Hotel Crowne Plaza. Several other nearby banks are clustered around Plaza España, including BAC and Banco Uno, and branches of most can be found in all the main malls. You'll find shorter lines at Multicambios, on the south side of Plaza España.

Europeans will be glad to know that Bancentro will change euros directly to local currency without first changing them to U.S. dollars (and taking another commission). Avoid the *coyotes* (moneychangers) on the streets.

Mail, Fax, and Phone

The Palacio de Comunicaciones, located across the plaza near the ruins of the old cathedral, contains the central office of both **Correos de Nicaragua** and **ENITEL,** with full mail, fax, telex, express courier, and phone services. In the *palacio,* the *oficina de filatelía* sells stamps from previous editions beginning in 1991 (Nicaragua is well known among philatelists for having the most beautiful postage stamps in Central America), plus postcards and greeting cards (open 8 A.M.–5 P.M. Mon.–Fri., 8 A.M.–1 P.M. Sat.). More compact, easier post offices to deal with are found in the Centro Comercial, Altamira, and the airport.

For packages, **DHL** (tel. 505/255-8700) is located in front of the Hotel Intercontinental, and on Carretera Masaya near the Hotel Princess. **Federal Express** (tel. 505/278-4500) has been operating in Nicaragua since 2000. Find it on Carretera Masaya near Subway, and in Ofiplaza El Retiro, Suite 515 (150 meters south of Rotonda Los Periodistas, tel. 505/278-4500). **UPS** (tel. 505/254-4892) is close to Barrio Martha Quezada and can be found two blocks north of Plaza España.

Internet

There's practically a cybercafe on every corner these days; they typically also offer VOIP

(voice over Internet protocol) calling booths. If you're sleeping in Barrio Martha Quezada, **Cyber Center Banisa,** located two blocks south of the stadium, is your best bet, or try the place next door to Shannon Pub. Otherwise, head toward the university area, across from the main UCA gates, where there are a half dozen Internet joints, all with the cheapest rates in the city, usually open till 9 P.M. during the week. Macintosh addicts can get their fix (or get their own Macs fixed) at the **iMac Center** (tel. 505/270-5918, open 8 A.M.–5 P.M. daily), tucked behind the UCA, a few doors down from HISPAMER bookstore.

Supermarkets

The many branches of La Colonial and La Union not only stock their modern aisles with national and imported foodstuffs, they also sell clothing, sandals, books, CDs, cosmetics, and more. The easiest to reach from Barrio Martha Quezada is just up the road at Plaza España (8 A.M.–7 P.M. Mon.–Fri., 8 A.M.–5 P.M. Sat., 9 A.M.–3 P.M. Sun.). If you're in the Carretera Masaya area, you're better off at the La Colonial on the Rotonda Centroamerica. Visit Costco Familiar (located across the street from Valenti's Pizza, open 9 A.M.–10 P.M. Mon.–Sat., 9 A.M.–3 P.M. Sun.) for gourmet goodies, alcohol, and imported bulk items, including dark European beers (and crappy U.S. ones), shiitake mushrooms, chewing tobacco, and specialty olive oils and cheeses. There are several other supermarkets around the city, but most travelers will find what they need at one of the many smaller "mini-supers" and *pulperías* that populate the neighborhoods.

Photography Supplies

Most cybercafes can help you download digital photos and burn a CD, particularly if you carry your own USB card reader and don't require anything fancy. For old-fashioned print film, check the supermarkets. For more complex needs like Ektachrome, slide, or black-and-white film, head over to **Kodak Express Profesional** (behind the CompuMax in the Colonia Centroamérica). **Konica** (across from the McDonald's at Plaza España) will process your film and also sells their own brand of slide film. For expensive black-and-white processing by hand, go to the **Galería Mexico** (Altamira, across from María Bonita, tel. 505/278-1058). The quality of film processing varies wildly, even within the same store.

Laundry and Dry Cleaning

If you're roughing it, you'll have noticed most *hospedajes* have a *lavandero* (cement-ridged washboard). Buy a slug of bar soap ($0.30) at the local *pulpería,* roll up your sleeves, and scrub away like everybody else. Most *hospedajes* have someone who will wash and iron for a reasonable fee as well. Otherwise, try one of the **Dryclean USA** locations. The most convenient branch is located at the Plaza Bolonia right behind Santa Fé Steakhouse, but their prices will make you wish you'd bought the bar soap.

Travel Agents

Many travel agents operate just southeast of the Plaza España and are a short cab ride from Barrio Martha Quezada. **Viajes Atlantida** (one block east and half block north of Plaza España, tel. 505/266-4050 or 505/266-8720) is a renowned agency and the official representative for American Express in Nicaragua. **Turismo Joven** (tel. 505/222-2619, 8:30 A.M.–5:30 P.M. Mon.–Fri., 8:30 A.M.–noon Sat.) is the local representative for STA, the student travel association, and offers students discounted airfare. Close to Barrio Martha Quezada, **Viajes MTOM** (adjacent to Optica Nicaragüense, tel. 505/266-8717) is quite professional.

Classes/Studying Opportunities

You can join classes in Latin dancing any time at **La Academia Nicaragüense de la Danza** (50 meters north of the UCA gates, tel. 505/277-5557). If you think you'll be in Managua long-term, you or your children can learn horseback riding on the beautiful facilities of **Escuela de Equitación Haras de Albanta** (Carretera Vieja a León Km 13, 500 meters north of the Entrada Chiquilistagua, tel. 505/883-8899 or 505/882-0369).

GETTING THERE AND AWAY

For detailed information on traveling between Managua and other countries, see the *Getting There and Away* section of the *Essentials* chapter, and for travel to points around the country, please refer to each regional chapter. Four main bus terminals link Managua to the towns and cities of Nicaragua's farthest corners. In general, buses depart approximately every hour, 5 A.M.–5 P.M.

To Points North and East

Buses to Estelí, Matagalpa, Ocotal, Jinotega, Boaco, Juigalpa, El Rama, and San Carlos operate out of the **Mercado Mayoreo** bus terminal on the eastern edge of town. From the other end of Managua (i.e., Barrio Martha Quezada), you can take the 102 *ruta* bus to get there, but plan up to an additional hour's travel through Managua's heart; a taxi is much quicker and should cost no more than $3 for a solo traveler.

Expresos del Norte services the entire north of Nicaragua with express buses. Their fleet includes a few Scania luxury buses (a rare treat), and they have a posted schedule, ticket window, and office where you can call to check on times (tel. 505/233-4729).

To Points West and Northwest

Buses to León, Chinandega, and Carazo depart from the **Israel Lewites** terminal (named for a Jewish-Nicaraguan martyr of the revolution but sometimes referred to by its post-Sandinista name, El Boer). The terminal is surrounded on all sides by a chaotic fruit market by the same name; watch your belongings and expect a slightly more aggressive crowd of *buseros.*

To Points South

Buses to Carazo, Masaya, Granada, Rivas, Ometepe, the border at Peñas Blancas, and San Juan del Sur depart from **Mercado Roberto Huembes** in south-central Managua. The taxi ride from Barrio Martha Quezada should cost no more than $2 a person. Before you get to Huembes, be sure to specify *parada de los buses* (bus stop) to your driver, as opposed to *el mercado de artesanía* (crafts market), located on the opposite side of the same market. This is a very busy terminal, serving thousands of commuters from points south, and its porters and bus assistants will swarm you as you get out of your taxi.

Fast, express minibuses known as *interlocales* are the best option for Jinotepe, Diriamba, Masaya, and Granada, and depart from a lot across the street from **La UCA.** Service starts around 6 A.M. and runs as late as 9 P.M. You can also get Carazo expresses at **Mercado Israel,** from *el portón rojo* (the big red door).

Finally, **Adelante Express** (tel. 505/850-6070 or 505/850-6064, www.adelante express.com) offers fast, direct service between the Managua airport and San Juan del Sur for people looking to bypass Managua entirely.

GETTING AROUND

Managua is easiest to deal with by taxi, given the lack of landmarks and the lousy public transportation, and the addresses given in this book are written with that in mind (see sidebar *Following Directions in Managua*). Should you set out walking, watch your step. Thousands of uncovered, ankle-breaking manholes abound, sometimes up to three meters deep and popularly disparaged as "gringo traps." Should you fall into one, you will surely be swept into the depths of hell or into the waters of Lake Xolotlán (same thing, really).

Taxis

Not to fear, if you even approach the edge of the street, Managua's 14,000 taxis will circle you like vultures, beeping for your attention. Taxis will take you most places for $1–7, though the ride to and from the airport might cost you as much as $15 if you don't bargain well (see *Money* in the *Essentials* chapter for tips and techniques). Managua taxis have no meters, so settle on a price before getting in the vehicle! Hotel and guesthouse owners can usually arrange a reliable taxi driver if you feel insecure about taking a cab on the street.

Near Managua

◧ CHOCOYERO-EL BRUJO NATURE RESERVE

Less than 28 kilometers away from downtown Managua is a little pocket of wilderness so vibrant with wildlife you'll forget the capital is literally just over the horizon. The Chocoyero–El Brujo nature reserve (tel. 505/278-3772 or 505/279-9774, cnd@cablenet.com.ni) is a 41 square kilometer protected hardwood forest that provides nearly 20 percent of Managua's water supply (20 million gallons of water per day). In the midst of moist hardwood forest and pineapple farms are two 25-meter waterfalls separated by a rocky knife-edge. El Brujo was named The Warlock because to the locals the fact that no river flows out from the waterfall meant it must be enchanted. The other fall, Chocoyero, was named for the incredible number of *chocoyos* (parakeets) that inhabit the adjacent cliff walls.

In fact, this protected area is a naturalist's paradise, with five kinds of *chocoyo* and 113 other bird species (including several owls), plus 49 species of mammals, and 21 species of reptiles and amphibians. Sharp-eyed travelers may even spot small cat species, like *tigrillos* and *gatos de monte,* and you'll likely hear both howler and capuchin monkeys in the treetops. In addition to having well-kept hiking trails, Chocoyero–El Brujo is also one of the few places in Nicaragua that encourages tent camping, making it a great place to spend an evening in the wild. Conditions are simple: a rustic, wooden base camp where guides will meet you and walk you the remaining way to the falls. The two best times to see the *chocoyos* are at around 5:30 A.M. when they leave their nests, and at around 4 P.M., when they flocks return. To catch the morning commute, you'll obviously have to spend the previous night there.

The entrance fee for foreigners is $3.50; guides, available on weekends, charge a nominal fee ($2–5 for a group of 12, usually). You can rent two-person tents on the premises for $11 each, or set up your own. This is a safe, pretty, and easily accessible area in which to camp for a night. If you call ahead and make a reservation, they'll even cook simple, traditional Nica fare for you for about $2.50–$3 per meal. The Reserve is actively promoting low-ropes courses, envirocamps, and more to local schools and church groups.

Unless you have rented a vehicle, you'll need to charter a sturdy taxi from Managua with a group to take you all the way there. Otherwise, take any bus leaving Managua's Huembes terminal bound for La Concepción (called La Concha for short); buses leave Managua every 15 minutes. Get off at Km 21.5, where you'll see a wooden sign for the park entrance, then stretch out for a good, long walk. The dirt road that travels seven kilometers southwest to the reserve will lead you down a series of volcanic ridges and across a broad valley to the falls. It's an easy two-hour walk, passing through fields of pineapples, bananas, and coffee. Halfway down the road, you'll find a small community where you can rent bikes or horses to take you the rest of the way in (horse $1 per hour, guide $1 per hour, bicycle $0.50 per hour). There also may be some buses from Ticuantepe that take you all the way in—ask around.

MONTIBELLI WILDLIFE RESERVE

An award-winning 162-hectare private reserve is set within the biological corridor between Chocoyero–El Brujo and Volcán Masaya National Park. In this setting, you'll find comfortable accommodations with private bathrooms and an ample deck perched on the edge of a valley—great for armchair birding. There are three trails to hike, with views of the Masaya Volcano and surrounding forest. The restaurant features family recipes and Sunday barbecues.

Over 155 bird species have been spotted here, including manakins, motmots, oropendolas, trogons, tanagers, toucans, and hummingbirds. This is one of the most accessible wildlife reserves in the country, making it really easy to escape from the city. To get there, drive south on Carreterra Masaya, taking the turnoff through the town of Ticuantepe, then just after leaving town on the Ticuantepe–La Concha Highway, it's a 2.5-km road to the main lodge, known locally as La Casa Blanca. By bus, find a microbus heading south to La Concha and get off at Km 18.5 where you can take a mototaxi. Better yet, arrange for transport by contacting Claudia Belli in Managua (tel. 505/270-4287, info@montibelli.com, www.montibelli.com).

THE LAGUNAS OF XILOÁ AND APOYEQUE

Less than a half hour from the capital on the highway to León, the Peninsula de Chiltepe protrudes into the southwestern shore of Lake Xolotlán, cradling two ancient volcanic cones drowned in clean rainwater. Part of the Maribios chain, the twin crater lagoons of Xiloá and Apoyeque are a fun day trip if you find yourself in Managua for more than a weekend and anxious for some greenery.

Legend says the **Xiloá** lagoon was formed when an indigenous princess of the same name, spurned by her Spanish lover, went down to the lake's edge to cry. She cried so much that the valley began to fill with tears, and the lagoon formed around her.

Broader and more easily accessed, Xiloá was a popular swimming hole for decades, but former Minister of Tourism director Herty Lewites took the initiative to develop the site more completely, with thatched-roof *ranchónes*, concrete pads, parking areas, and lunch stands. In 1998, Hurricane Mitch submerged the facilities under a meter of water. Rather forgotten, the lagoon will probably be deserted except for yourself and the occasional marine biologist, scuba diving to study the lake's endemic species.

Apoyeque still bears much of its original cone shape—the lagoon is enclosed in steep crater walls that form the highest part of the Chiltepe Peninsula. The Nicaraguan military occasionally uses it for training special forces in the art of rappelling, and a radio tower perches on the southwest lip of the crater. In 2001, Apoyeque was the epicenter of a series of seismic tremors.

Buses leave Managua's Israel Lewites market infrequently and go directly to the water at Xiloá. It's easier to take any León-bound bus from the same market, get off at the top of the road to Xiloá, and walk (30 minutes). Pay $0.25 per person ($1 per vehicle) to enter the park facilities at the water's edge. Getting to Apoyeque is a more challenging hike, requiring good boots and some autonomy (compass, water bottles, etc.). Take the road from Mateare, which you can walk or hitch down until you reach the access road for the radio antenna. That road will lead you to the ridge, from where you'll have to painstakingly and carefully make your way into the crater.

From Xiloá, a well-marked but little-used dirt road circles the entire peninsula (28 km), coming out in Mateare. The rest of the peninsula and the lower slopes of the two volcanic peaks are lush cattle farms, many owned by the Seminole tribe of Florida, which has invested heavily in the area. The view from the northeastern side of the peninsula is particularly beautiful in the late afternoon when the sky fills with colors.

PACIFIC BEACHES

Roughly 65 kilometers due west of the capital are a handful of easy-to-reach beaches, with facilities ranging from low-key, grungy *hospedajes* to all-out, all-inclusive resorts. In fact, the diversity along the coastline couldn't be greater. Pochomíl attracts the casual day-tripper and increasingly, surfers, while Montelimar is a pricey but pleasurable all-inclusive resort. Los Cardones is an ecofriendly offbeat lodge also popular with surfers and families that's a bit harder to get to but worth the effort. But when you hear about all the foreign real estate investment in Nicaragua, much of it is happening right here, so watch for big changes over the

sunset at Pochomíl

next decade unless Ortega scares away the foreigners again.

Pochomíl

Pochomíl was named in the early 20th century by a farmer by the name of Felipe Gutierrez, in reference to all the *"pocho"* (money) he hoped to earn from his ambitious duck and goat farm. These days it's a once-popular beach town left to stagnate and now in the midst of an economic revival, as wealthy investors are building beachfront estates and hotel complexes, including a new Marriott.

Hotel and restaurant rates fluctuate wildly according to the calendar. Semana Santa and Christmas are the most expensive time of year to visit. In the wet season, prices become significantly more flexible, but at any month of the year, traveling with a group gives you significant leverage to bargain for a good deal. Travelers driving their own vehicles will pay a $1 entrance fee at the entrance to town.

One of the longest-established places on the beach, **Hotel Altamar** (tel. 505/269-9204, $11 per room with private bath, $9 per room with shared bath) has 15 basic rooms and a pleasant restaurant overlooking the water. Otherwise, competition among hotel and restaurant owners is particularly fierce—as you get off the bus expect to be assaulted by employees of a dozen restaurants all trying to drag you into their establishments to eat and drink. No one place is any better than another—you can expect beachfront palm thatch huts, fried fish and cold beer no matter where you go.

All the way down the road at the north end of the beach is the luxury **Hotel Villa del Mar** (tel. 505/269-0426, $35 with private bath and a/c). Owned by the Universidad Americana (UAM) and run as part of the university's tourism/business administration curriculum, it has a nice stretch of beach, swimming pool, wading pool, wood-paneled conference room, palm-thatch huts set on a grassy lawn, and a fancy open-air restaurant serving three meals a day. The $7 entrance fee can be applied to meals and beverages served on the premises if you just come for the day. Otherwise try the more humble **Hotel Cabañas del Mar** (tel. 505/269-0433, $18 d or $25 t with private bath and a/c) next door, offering a simple menu and some vegetarian dishes.

Buses leave Managua's Israel bus station for Pochomíl every 30 minutes all day until about 5 P.M. The last bus from Pochomíl back to Managua departs at 5:30 P.M. from the cul-de-sac.

Barceló Montelimar Beach

Somoza's former personal summer palace was converted into a resort in the 1980s and since being purchased by Barceló Resorts is now **Montelimar Beach** (tel. 505/269-6769 or 505/269-6752, U.S. and Canada tel. 800/227-2356, www.barcelomontelimarbeach .com, $72–135 per person), an all-inclusive five-star resort. It offers 88 double guestrooms with queen-size beds and 205 bungalows with king-size beds, private bath, air-conditioning, TV, strongbox, and minibar. The price includes 24 hours of unlimited feasting, drinking, swimming, and playing. Often crowded during weekends with visitors from Managua, it is more peaceful on weekdays when you can swim in the largest pool in Central America by yourself. The Montelimar compound is enormous, with multiple beachside bars, sports, and a spunky coed crew of "animators" to help you have a good time. It also has facilities for groups and conventions, plus airport shuttles, shopping, casino, travel agency, etc. Any bus to Pochomíl will also get you to Montelimar, and there are various tour operators that arrange for transfers from Managua airport or hotels. Ask about deep, off-season discounts.

Los Cardones Surf Lodge

This is a unique, peaceful, highly recommended beach escape with direct access to consistent surf breaks nearly year-round. Set on five acres of organically managed land, **Los Cardones** (tel. 505/618-7314, info @loscardones.com, www.loscardones.com) rents half a dozen simple but elegant bungalows made from wood and thatch; all have solar hot water, soft beds, no electricity, and compost toilets; all are also waterfront. Their inspired and creative menu involves lots of fresh fish, and their commitment to both the local community and the ecosystem is admirable. Rent surf or boogie boards for the waves, collect shells on the beach, or hike to nearby pre-Columbian petroglyphs. Ask about yoga and surf retreats. Rates ($69 plus tax per person) are all-inclusive, for lodging, meals, drinks, and transportation; great deals for a week's stay or other packages. The managers started **Arte Acción,** which promotes social change through art classes in a nearby neighboring village. Many guests often join in and help the class.

They'll send a car to Managua for you; or to get there by bus, take the bus to San Cayetano from Mercado Israel Lewites in Managua (leaves every 45 minutes 4 A.M.–9 P.M.) and get off at "California." Then walk or hitch 15 kilometers toward the ocean and follow the signs. To drive, take the Carreterra Masachapa to Km 49, then drive 15 kilometers on the Playa San Diego Road until you hit the beach.

GRANADA

Arguably Nicaragua's most picturesque town and certainly the one that most captures travelers' hearts, Granada is an easy place to love. Its colonial architecture remains remarkably intact and is now being painstakingly restored by a new generation of homeowners; the street's colorful facades practically glow in the late afternoon sun. It's sultry and tropical here but a fresh breeze blows off the waters of Lake Cocibolca to attenuate it. The views from along the lakeshore's broad, unfettered shoreline—and the silhouette of Volcán Mombacho—make for easy photos and good memories. Granada has always been important politically, and is the home of many of the country's economic and political elite, but increasingly it is now important as the capstone of the country's economic renaissance after decades of stagnation under the Sandinistas. Travelers eschew Managua and flock to Granada because of its easy charm and lethargic tropical lifestyle, making it their base for further exploration. But increasing number of foreigners have latched onto this colonial jewel and decided to stay.

Granada's real estate boom equals or surpasses San Juan del Sur's, hosting growing numbers of retirees, investors, and property managers who have bought and renovated old buildings, opened up shops and restaurants, organized tours, and helped jump-start what was until recently a fledgling tourism industry. The future of Granada will be determined by how this economic boom is managed, as local resentment against the influx of foreigners is or is not tempered by responsible development. But for now, Granada is the talk of the nation,

© JOSHUA BERMAN

GRANADA

HIGHLIGHTS

La Plazuela de los Leones: Witness to centuries of Granada's most exciting events, the Plazuela is Granada's cultural epicenter, bursting with art, music, historical works, and, of course, Internet access (page 62).

Antiguo Convento San Francisco: The towering stone statues displayed in one of the Convento's many courtyards are a stunning glimpse into the nation's pre-Columbian past (page 63).

Iglesia La Merced: Climb the bell tower for the best view in all of Granada (page 66).

Las Isletas: Spend a lazy day swimming, picnicking, and relaxing among the hundreds of gorgeous islands that comprise Las Isletas (page 77).

Volcán Mombacho: More than a gorgeous background for your Granada photographs, Volcán Mombacho has a first-class set of hiking trails, an ecolodge, a canopy tour, and a lot more (page 78).

Canopy Tours on Mombacho: Fifteen platforms, a hanging bridge, and plenty of excitement await you from the treetops on the slopes of Mombacho. Plus, you'll enjoy one of the best views in town – if you can keep your eyes open, that is (page 79).

LOOK FOR (TO FIND RECOMMENDED SIGHTS, ACTIVITIES, DINING, AND LODGING.

and the talk of the rest of the world as well. Beginning in 2006, one major news outlet after another "discovered" Granada, fawning over the blend of cultures, the growing prosperity, and the easy colonial charm, helping to put Nicaragua on the travel itineraries of many a well-off traveler who wouldn't have considered stepping foot in Nicaragua a decade ago.

They're right: Granada is fun. It's a pleasurable city to walk in, more pleasurable to explore by old-fashioned horse carriage. The landscapes, from awesome Volcán Mombacho on one side to the lake on the other, are striking. Nights the sky fills with stars and the neighbors

come out to chitchat from their front stoops; inside even the most nondescript colonial facade is an open, private courtyard designed to capture the evening breeze. Granada's restaurants are varied and high quality, offering something for just about everybody. Granada lacks the five-star luxury hotels of the capital but enjoys instead an enticing gamut of charming guesthouses, bed-and-breakfasts, and colonial lodges. And of course Granada is well-situated as a home base from where you can easily visit the vast majority of Nicaragua's best tourist attractions, from canopy and coffee tours in the Volcán Mombacho cloud forest

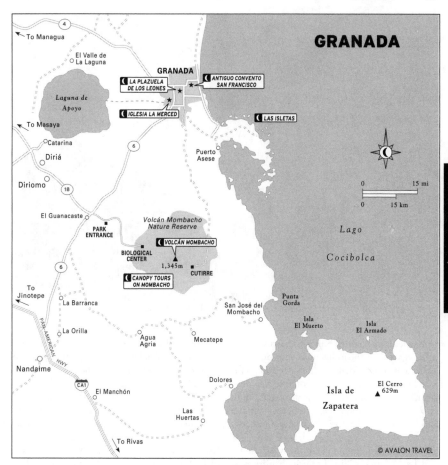

and boat trips through the *isletas* to a cool dip in nearby Laguna de Apoyo (see the *Masaya and the Pueblos Blancos* chapter). It's a place you'll feel happy to come home to.

PLANNING YOUR TIME

A full day and night in Granada is the minimum and allows you to explore the streets, sleep somewhere interesting, and enjoy a good meal or two. But many travelers like it so much they use it as a base over three or four days, day-tripping out to the *isletas* (half day), Volcán Mombacho (full day), the markets in Masaya

(full day), and the Pueblos Blancos (full day) before moving on. While you could conceivably day-trip out to the Laguna de Apoyo as well, the Laguna's hotel options are now sufficient that it's a fun place to stay in its own right. But if you only had 24 hours in Nicaragua, this is the first place you should try to spend them: Don't miss it!

HISTORY

Granada's history is as long as the history of colonial Nicaragua. Founded by Francisco Hernández de Córdoba on the edge of Lake

Iglesia la Merced is one of Granada's many beautiful cathedrals.

Cocibolca, the Spanish built Granada strategically adjacent to the indigenous community of Xalteva, whose residents suddenly found themselves working for their new foreign "visitors." Granada grew quickly as a sort of trade hub; sailing vessels would navigate their way up the Río San Juan and across the lake to Granada. As a result, an affluent Spanish merchant class developed, largely of Veracruz, Cartagena, and La Habana origin. From its beginnings, Granada was a symbol of Spanish opulence, an unsubtle show of mercantile success in the New World. The competing nations accepted the challenge, sacking and burning the city at every available opportunity (the English buccaneers were particularly effective).

After independence from Spain, Granada was the capital of Nicaragua each time the Conservatives took power (León was the capital when the Liberals won). As the Liberal-Conservative feud escalated, it was the Liberals who first called upon the American filibuster William Walker for support. He executed Granada's most ruthless sacking, even by pirate standards. Before he was eventually driven from Granada, he finally burned the whole place to the ground, and buried a symbolic coffin in the central plaza under a wooden sign that read, Aquí Fue Granada (Here Was Granada).

Despite the sackings and reconstruction, Granada remains little changed from its earliest colonial incarnation; if Córdoba were to rise from the grave today and walk the streets of La Gran Sultana as it is sometimes called, he would find it eerily familiar (he would surely blog about it at length). But these days, Granada is changing fast. Less influential than the old families these days is the influx of foreign capital, new ideas, and fast business. A decade ago, Granada was a "sleepy colonial jewel." The hum of the Internet cafés, chic eateries, and trendy hotels would indicate it has woken up.

ORIENTATION AND GETTING AROUND

Granada is an eminently walkable city. Start late in the afternoon after the air has cooled

GRANADA

© JOSHUA BERMAN

WILLIAM WALKER: GREY-EYED MAN OF DESTINY

The year was 1853, and Nicaragua's Liberals and Conservatives were once again at each other's throats in a fierce competition for political power. The León-based Liberals saw a chance to beat the Conservatives of Granada once and for all by hiring foreign mercenaries; so they invited a self-styled North American adventurer, white supremacist, and filibuster from Tennessee named William Walker to join them in battle in Nicaragua. He accepted, and within the year, they realized they'd created a monster.

Walker, the self-proclaimed Grey-Eyed Man of Destiny, arrived from Nashville with a band of 300 thugs and ruffians he'd rounded up in the tough neighborhoods of San Francisco. Walker and his men promptly led the Liberals to a rousing victory, but he had no intentions of going home. Two years later, he usurped power, arranged for elections that he rigged to his advantage, and declared himself President of Nicaragua. His goal was to make Nicaragua a slave state loyal to the American South's nascent confederacy.

The United States, at the brink of civil war, officially recognized Walker as President of Nicaragua. Walker reinstituted slavery and declared English the official language of the country. But Walker did what no Nicaraguan leader has been able to accomplish since: He united the people. In a rare moment of fear-inspired solidarity, the Nicaraguans temporarily forgot their differences, banded together, and with the help of the other Central American nations and some financing from Cornelius Vanderbilt (who'd lost his steamship company to Walker) defeated Walker at the Battle of San Jacinto on September 14, 1856, now a national holiday. Not long afterward, he was captured and executed by a rifle squad in Honduras. The Liberals fell into disgrace, and the Conservatives effectively ruled the nation for the next 30 years.

The scars Walker wrought on the nation run deep. As he and his men fled Granada, they paused long enough to burn the city to the ground and plant a sign that proclaimed Aquí Fue Granada (Here Was Granada). On the highway leading north from Managua to Estelí, a statue commemorates the victory over Walker's troops by a mobilized populace at San Jacinto. And deep inside every Nicaraguan, you'll find a distaste for loud, impudent North Americans with ambitious plans and a confident gait. William Walker's own account, *La Guerra de Nicaragua*, tells his story in no uncertain terms. Just be careful who sees you reading it.

a bit, but before the rich light fades. If you'd rather see Granada at its most peaceful, start just before sunrise to watch the city awake in a splash of yellow and orange, dodge schoolchildren running in their blue and white uniforms, soccer players jogging back from the lake, and skinny dogs darting across the streets.

Granada has several easy landmarks, starting with the central, tree-lined plaza (known alternately as **Parque Central** and **Parque Colón**) and the **cathedral** on its east side. **Calle La Calzada** extends east from the plaza and runs straight to the municipal dock. A number of *hospedajes* and hotels are grouped along this and nearby streets. You can also orient yourself using the long, jagged peak of Volcán Mombacho, rising south of the city.

Walking west from the main plaza, you'll come to the **Xalteva** neighborhood and eventually the cemetery and road to Nandaime. There are many services and a number of attractions along **Calle Atravesada,** one of the city's original streets, which runs north-south between the old 1886 train station (now a museum, which has closed for lack of funds) to the bustling chaos of the municipal market.

Taxis are numerous and cheap, but not much fun. Instead, take a horse-drawn carriage, which you can always find on the western side of the plaza (prices vary, about $10–15 per

Granada by horse cart

hour). Do your part to promote fair treatment of animals by patronizing only those drivers who seem to be treating their horses, telling the others, *"mal tratado"* ("poorly treated").

SIGHTS

In Granada, the whole city—its mellow ambience, colonial architecture, and windblown lakeshore—makes up the experience. As you dart from street to street, soak it all in. You can easily visit the following places in a morning's energetic walk.

Parque Colón (Central Plaza)

If Granada is the center of tourism in Nicaragua, then Granada's central plaza is the heart of it all. The streets that surround and radiate away from Parque Colón are filled with schools, shops, government offices, hotels, and cafés. The colonial yellow building at the southwest corner of the park belongs to the wealthy Pellas family, Nicaragua's version of the Rockefellers. Cross the park to the magnificent cathedral, at whose flank you'll find the

Cruz del Siglo (Century Cross), inaugurated January 1, 1900. Entombed in its cement are coins, pieces of art, and a gilded bottle from the 19th century.

C La Plazuela de los Leones

The pedestrian space guarded by the cannon off the northeast corner of the main plaza is where Henry Morgan set 18 cannons during his sacking of the city, and where, a century later, William Walker was sworn in as President of Nicaragua. On the Plazuela's eastern side, you'll find the **Casa de los Leones,** whose interior has been transformed into an international cultural center. Don Diego de Montiel, governor of Costa Rica, built the Casa de los Leones in 1720. William Walker did not miss the opportunity to burn this place down, leaving nothing standing but the portal bearing the Montiel family crest (still visible). The unique, neoclassical colonnade facade was a product of the subsequent reconstruction. In 1987, the historical monument became the headquarters of the **Casa de los Tres Mundos Foundation** (tel. 505/552-4176, www.c3mundos.org, open 8 A.M.–6 P.M. daily), bearing an art and music school, museum, historical archive, library, concert hall, literary café, bookstore, and exhibition space which hosts resident artists from around the world.

Calle La Calzada

Walk east from the park to the lake along Granada's hippest strip, with its swanky new design of cobblestone, street lamps, and wide sidewalks. Halfway to the lake, stop at the 17th-century **Iglesia de Guadalupe,** first built in 1626 and most recently refurbished in 1945. Continuing along the palm-lined boulevard, you'll reach the *muelle* and *malecón* (dock and quay) on the water's edge. Turn right and pass through "the rooks" (a pair of statues) to enter the **Complejo Turístico,** which is just a short row of restaurants and discos lining the lakeshore, none of which is really as much fun as the places on La Calzada itself. The sidewalks here fill with clamoring hot dog and *chicharrón* vendors. The *complejo* is less a "tourist center"

© JOSHUA BERMAN

for the mothers: sculpture in the Central Plaza

than a broad, unkempt swath of lawn, but its leafy canopy and fresh lake breeze set the tone for languid afternoons along the lakeshore.

❰ Antiguo Convento San Francisco

The grand staircase, stately blue facade, and trio of bells are themselves impressive. But inside the Antiguo Convento San Francisco (one block north and two east of the main cathedral, tel. 505/552-5535, open 8 A.M.–5 P.M. Mon.–Fri., 9 A.M.–4 P.M. weekends, $2), several centuries' worth of art are set around courtyards of tall palm trees. The Convento is most renowned for its collection of 30 alter-ego statues collected a century ago from Zapatera Island. The carved basalt shows human forms with the heads of jaguars, birds, and crocodiles whose spirits were thought to flow through humans' souls—a rare look into the cosmology of Nicaragua's pre-Columbian peoples. There is also a large to-scale replica of the city, and exhibits that represent the lifestyle of the Chorotega and Nahautl peoples.

The towering, sky-blue convent was first built by Franciscan monks in 1529 and lasted 150 years before pirate Henry Morgan burned it to the ground. Since then it has housed William Walker's troops, U.S. Marines, a contingent of engineers surveying a possible canal route in the 1920s, and the National University—a nice place to live and work, given the site's great view of Granada's rooftops, the lake, and Mombacho.

Mi Museo

This is a private collection of hundreds of figurines and ceramics, some thousands of years old. There is no entrance fee, and you can take a 20-minute tour of the exhibits, accompanied by a Spanish speaking guide (also free).

Calle Real Xalteva

La Xalteva (pronounced more or less, with a hard "h") is Granada's second most important street. Walk west from the south edge of the main plaza, past Iglesia la Merced, then a few blocks farther to **Iglesia Xalteva;** at its

GRANADA

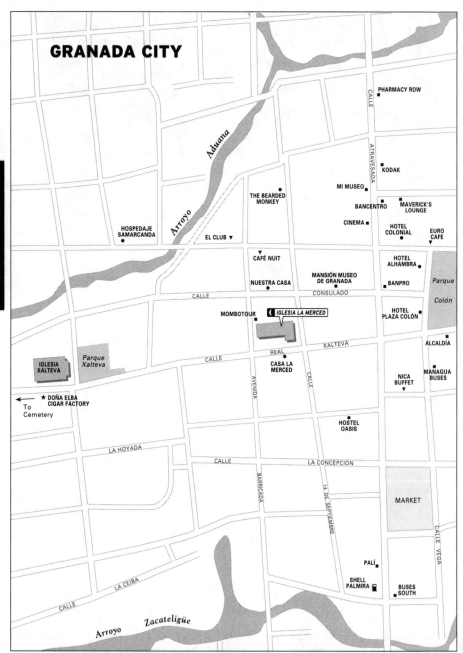

GRANADA CITY

PHARMACY ROW

CALLE

ATRAVESADA

KODAK

MI MUSEO

THE BEARDED MONKEY

BANCENTRO

MAVERICK'S LOUNGE

CINEMA

HOTEL COLONIAL

EURO CAFE

HOSPEDAJE SAMARCANDA

EL CLUB

CAFÉ NUIT

HOTEL ALHAMBRA

NUESTRA CASA

MANSIÓN MUSEO DE GRANADA

BANPRO

Parque Colón

CALLE

CONSULADO

MOMBOTOUR

IGLESIA LA MERCED

HOTEL PLAZA COLÓN

XALTEVA

ALCALDÍA

Iglesia Xalteva

Parque Xalteva

CALLE

REAL

CASA LA MERCED

CALLE

NICA BUFFET

MANAGUA BUSES

AVENIDA

← To Cemetery

★ DOÑA ELBA CIGAR FACTORY

HOSTEL OASIS

LA HOYADA

CALLE

LA CONCEPCIÓN

MARKET

BARRICADA

14. DE SEPTIEMBRE

CALLE VEGA

LA CEIBA

PALÍ

SHELL PALMIRA

BUSES SOUTH

CALLE

Arroyo Zacateligüe

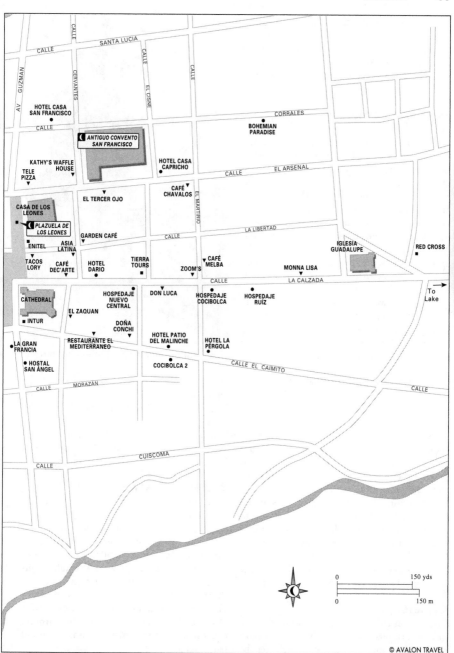

GRANADA

CALLE SANTA LUCIA
CALLE
AV GUZMAN
CALLE CERVANTES
CALLE EL CISNE

HOTEL CASA SAN FRANCISCO
CALLE

CORRALES

BOHEMIAN PARADISE

ANTIGUO CONVENTO SAN FRANCISCO

KATHY'S WAFFLE HOUSE
TELE PIZZA

HOTEL CASA CAPRICHO
CALLE EL ARSENAL

CAFÉ CHAVALOS

EL TERCER OJO

CASA DE LOS LEONES
PLAZUELA DE LOS LEONES

GARDEN CAFÉ
CALLE
LA LIBERTAD

EL MARTIRIO

IGLESIA GUADALUPE
RED CROSS

ENITEL
ASIA LATINA

TACOS LORY
CAFÉ DEC'ARTE
HOTEL DARIO
TIERRA TOURS
ZOOM'S
CAFÉ MELBA
MONNA LISA

CALLE
LA CALZADA

CATHEDRAL
INTUR
EL ZAQUAN

HOSPEDAJE NUEVO CENTRAL
DON LUCA
HOSPEDAJE COCIBOLCA
HOSPEDAJE RUÍZ

To Lake

DOÑA CONCHI
HOTEL PATIO DEL MALINCHE
HOTEL LA PÉRGOLA

LA GRAN FRANCIA
RESTAURANTE EL MEDITERRANEO
COCIBOLCA 2
CALLE EL CAIMITO
CALLE

HOSTAL SAN ÁNGEL
CALLE
MORAZÁN

CUISCOMA

CALLE

0   150 yds
0   150 m

© AVALON TRAVEL

western end, the 10-meter-high arched stone walls known as Los Muros de Xalteva were erected by the Spaniards in the mid-1700s to separate Spanish settlements from those of the locals. There is a relaxing park across the street with interesting stone shapes.

☾ Iglesia La Merced

We recommend ascending the tight spiral stairs of the bell tower of La Merced multiple times during your stay in Granada. It only costs a dollar (which goes to church funds for feeding street children, we are told) and the magical view changes dramatically as the sun moves through the sky. Open 10 A.M.–6 P.M. daily, the tower rises above an ocean of tiled roofs, opening your view to the lake and *isletas,* and Volcán Mombacho over your shoulder. The church was first built in 1534, then sacked and burned by Henry Morgan in 1670, and rebuilt (are you noticing a theme here in Granada?). Climb the tower at sunset, attend a Sunday mass, watch a game of *futbolito* on the concrete plaza in front of the church, then take a few minutes of silence in the great hall or the stairs outside to soak it all in.

view from the bell tower of Iglesia la Merced

Fortaleza de la Pólvora

The old fort and powder storage facility is a great excuse to walk to the terminus of Calle Real Xalteva. The *fortaleza* was built in 1748 to secure Granada's gunpowder supply from marauding pirates. Its medieval architecture speaks of simplicity and strength: five squat towers and one heavily guarded gate with two oak doors. In the 20th century, both the city government and later Somoza's National Guard used La Pólvora as a military garrison, and later, a jail. These days it's a museum of arms or art whose exhibitions rotate regularly. Climb the towers for a breath of wind and a good perspective of the skyline. No entrance fee; watch your head and watch your step.

Cemetery

Located on the southwest corner of the city grid, enormous marble tombs—bigger than the homes of many Nicaraguans—shelter the bones of several centuries of Granada's elite. Note the column-lined Capilla de Animas and the replica of the Magdalena de Paris, both built between 1876 and 1922. The Granada cemetery supposedly houses the bones of five Nicaraguan presidents: happy hunting.

Butterfly Reserve

Continuing two kilometers down the dirt road to the right of the cemetery (by foot or bicycle, the track is too rough for cars at least half the year) will take you to the **Nicaragua Butterfly Reserva** (tel. 505/895-3012, nicaraguabutterfly@yahoo.com, $6); take a bus to Km 50 near the police station, and it's a short walk from there (under a kilometer). Tour the flight house with about 40 species of butterfly, plus all the ones flying around free outside on the lush grounds of an old fruit orchard.

ENTERTAINMENT AND EVENTS

The Casa de los Leones sponsors frequent events, including concerts by local musicians and visiting international artists. One block west of the plaza, Granada's humble movie theater, **El Teatro Karawala,** offers popular (often trashy) American movies; good for rainy evenings. **Cafe Melba** (see *Food*) ups the bar with a better selection of international films.

Bars

Start with a pub crawl down Calle La Calzada, where you'll find crowds enjoying the sidewalk scenes at the **Roadhouse Sports Bar** (open noon–midnight daily), the hugely popular **Zoom Bar** (open from noon daily), and many others: It's hard to go wrong. A decidedly loungier scene is found nearby at **El Tercer Ojo** (Calle El Arsenal across from Convento San Francisco, open 11 A.M.–11 P.M. Tues.–Sun.); swank tapas, wine, cocktails, and more, especially popular during happy hour (4–7 P.M.).

Café Nuit (Calle La Libertad, half block east of Piedra Bocona) is one of the city's prettiest bars, attracting mostly locals and often with live music. On the next corner, the popular **El Club** offers frequent promotional bashes, bikini-clad beer babes, and theme parties.

You'll find a more sedate, but entirely pleasant scene at **El Balcón,** on the second floor of the grand, yellow-painted Gran Francia, just across from the southwest corner of the plaza; sit on the streetside and watch the foot and horse traffic below as you sip your Centenario and enjoy the delicious bar menu. The **Enoteca Wine Bar** (in the Hotel Plaza Colón, open 10 A.M.–11 P.M. daily) has a wide selection of international wines and monthly tastings, often with rum and cigars on hand as well.

Discos

Managua is better for dancers; nonetheless a handful of discos line the lakefront. **Cesar's,** just south of the gate, is one of the most entertaining places to dance; a bit farther into the park, **Pantera** is just as good and hosts the occasional live band. Do not walk to or from the disco strip at night, even in a group, and especially after drinking—the stretch of road between the water's edge and the city center is a notorious hangout for nervous, knife-wielding would-be crooks.

SHOPPING

The municipal market is located one block south of the plaza, but it's geared more for the locals than for tourists. In addition, the excitement overflows, extending up Calle Atravesada, whose sidewalks are often choked with merchants and shoppers. You're better off around the plaza, the artists stands within the park, or the gift shops of the various fancy hotels, but really you should day-trip out to Masaya for the good stuff. Antique lovers will adore **Casa de Antiguedades** (tel. 505/874-2034, haroldsandino@hotmail.com) a block north of the park on Calle Arsenal.

The **Maverick Reading & Smoothie Lounge** (tel. 505/552-4120, mavericks_granada @yahoo.ca, open 9 A.M.–6 P.M. Tues.–Sat., 10 A.M.–noon Sun.) is a great little nook on Calle El Arsenal, behind Hotel Colonial—look for the Canadian flag. Maverick's is a craft shop/café/book exchange run by a friendly Nica-Canadian couple who are a wealth of information about the area. Maverick's has a one-of-a-kind foreign magazine selection, and also sells local publications, maps, patches, snacks, dips, smoothies, and made-to-order meals. They sell and trade books, and are happy to store your bag for $1/day while you explore. Maverick's is also the site of Nicaragua Mia Spanish School.

This is *guayabera* country, and there are several places to buy the elegant Latin shirts, the best (and most expensive) being **Guayabera Nora,** right around the corner from the Bearded Monkey.

Tobacco grown in the hills around Masatepe, often blended with northern Nicaraguan leaves, fills the **Doña Elba Cigar Factory** (located one block west of the Iglesia Xalteva, tel. 505/860-6715, open 7 A.M.–7 P.M. daily). Named after the owner's mother, the

GRANADA

VOLUNTEERING IN GRANADA

As you come to terms with how fortunate you are to be able to go on a tropical vacation to a beautiful – but very poor – country, you may feel the urge to get involved and give something back. If so, there are numerous opportunities in and around Granada. In general, if you are serious about volunteering and making a difference, you should already have basic conversational Spanish skills – and you should consider committing at least two months of your time. Short-term volunteers, though well intentioned, often are more of a hindrance than a help. If you can't commit to two, six, or nine months, there are other ways to help as well, including monetary and material donations, as well becoming active with one of the many U.S.- and Canada-based nonprofit organizations supporting projects in Nicaragua.

Building New Hope (BNH) (U.S. tel. 412/421-1625, www.buildingnewhope.org), based in both Granada and Pittsburgh, Pennsylvania, is a nonprofit organization offering a number of ongoing programs and opportunities to help. Start by purchasing a pound (or six) of Fair Trade–certified organic coffee from their website, then mull over these options while sipping some hot Nica joe: BNH provides career development and skills training workshops to at-risk youth; they also run two neighborhood schools, a community library, and a reading-in-schools program. They operate a veterinary clinic to help control the stray animal population in Granada, which is *always* looking for visiting veterinarians, vet techs, and vet students. BNH is also on the lookout for music teachers for their **Rhythm in the Barrios** project, physical education instructors, and other teachers (intermediate Spanish and one month minimum commitment). During your stay in Granada, be sure to have at least one dinner at **Café Chavalos** (cafechavalos.blogspot.com), a restaurant where former street kids train to become gourmet chefs; low-cost volunteer housing provided to visiting chefs willing to spend a couple of weeks teaching *los chavalos* (the boys). Check their website for more, or contact Donna Tabor in Granada (donna@ buildingnewhope.org); Donna is a former Peace Corps Volunteer who's been living and working in Granada for nearly 15 years.

rolling factory produces some 3,000 cigars daily. Otherwise, try **Sultan Cigars** (tel. 505/803-9569, eddyreyes78@yahoo.es), where Eddy Reyes and family can make you a custom labeled (your name on a cigar label) case in a couple of hours.

SPORTS AND RECREATION

At **El Estadio Roque T. Zavala,** root for local team **Los Tiburones** with the locals—it's great fun and you'll feel less like an outsider. The leagues don't effectively advertise upcoming games, but the locals all know; just ask around.

Sailing

Here's a nice way to experience the breeze and expanses of Lake Cocibolca: sailing lessons and day trips from **Velago Nicaragua Sailing School** (tel. 505/459-4699, elagoGranada @gmx.at, www.velagogranada.com), with a small fleet of Hobie Cats, Jolly Cats, and catamarans to whisk you away. It's located at the Cabana Amarilla (yellow cabin) at the south end of Centro Turistico.

Massage

The Granadan spa scene is just getting started, but fear not **Seeing Hands Massage** (9 A.M.–5:30 P.M. Mon.–Sat.) in the back of Euro Cafe has three blind masseuses who will give you a chair or full body massage (15-minute chair massage under $5). **Swenja Janine** (tel. 505/451-0891) practices reflexology and provides a special Hawaiian healing massage in your hotel room.

Empowerment International (U.S. tel. 303/823-6495 or local tel. 505/678-3341, www.empowermentinternational.org) runs an educational program for impoverished and at-risk youth. Direct work with the families and community is an integral part of their methodology, as are art and photography projects. There are many ways to volunteer for EI both in Nicaragua and from afar. See their website for a list of needs and ways to help. Currently they serve Villa Esperanza and Santa Ana de Malacos, two outlying communities of Granada; as the communities become more self-sufficient, EI hopes to continue to expand it's program.

Hogar Madre Albertina (from Colegio Padre Misieri, two blocks north, tel. 505/552-7661) is an underfunded home for girls where volunteers are sometimes welcome to read to the girls or play games with them. They're also looking for computer and English instructors, for both the girls and the sisters in charge.

Sisters of Madre Teresa de Calcuta in Barrio Sabonetta have a very organized school and residence for girls up to the age of 18. Most have been rescued from precarious conditions in their homes or were at-risk for drug use, prostitution, and other crimes. The school grounds are beautifully manicured and immaculate; the sisters welcome volunteers to teach music (guitar and voice), English, and art; conversational Spanish is a must.

La Harmonía (corner of Calle Atravesada and Carraterra Masaya, billpenny@bill pennyashman.com) is an organization for mentally and physically challenged children and young adults. They accept volunteers with basic Spanish who can teach handicrafts, weaving, haircutting, sign language, or have experience in special education.

La Esperanza Granada (Calle La Calzada, next to Nuevo Central, tel. 505/400-7434, www.la-esperanza-granada.org) works in four small villages on the western outskirts of Granada and accepts volunteers to participate in various education and health-related projects. A two-month minimum commitment and intermediate Spanish is required. There is no fee to volunteer, and inexpensive accommodations are available at their new volunteer house ($2–3 per day), local hostels, or homestays.

ACCOMMODATIONS

The quantity and diversity of good accommodations has exploded in Granada for every budget—from backpacker hostels to midrange rooms to the four-star places in refurbished colonial palaces, usually within a few blocks of Central Plaza. Remember, room prices quoted below are for double occupancy during the high season (Dec.–Apr.); some hotels do not vary their prices throughout the year, others spike rates for holidays, still others offer deep discounts during the rainy season (May–Nov.), which is still a great time to travel.

Under $25

C Hostel Oasis (one block north, one block east of the market, tel. 505/552-8005, www .nicaraguahostel.com, $6 dorm bed, $19–28 rooms) is a quiet retreat from the bustling city, providing a swimming pool, free coffee, a book trade, DVD rental, and lockers. **The Bearded Monkey** (across from the fire station, tel. 505/552-4028, www.thebeardedmonkey .com, $6 dorm, $14–17 rooms) has dorm-style rooms and a friendly, communal atmosphere. Expect cool music on the speakers and an eclectic crowd at the bar, also footlocker and bike rentals, selective book trade, movie nights, and free Internet access. **Hospedaje Samarcanda** (Calle la Libertad, five blocks west of the central plaza, tel. 505/552-8069, www.hospedaje samarcanda.com, $6 dorm, $16–39 rooms) is similar: shared dormitories, rooms with shared or private bath, breakfast, and all-day coffee; lots of traveler services and common space.

Hostal San Angel (a half-block south of

the cathedral, tel. 505/552-6373, $9–14) is a cheery, family-run place: eight rooms with private baths and fans. Around the corner, **Hospedaje Nuevo Central** (Calle La Calzada, 1.5 blocks east of the central plaza, tel. 505/552-7044) has a handful of basic rooms for $10, some with private bath for $12, and offers food, Wi-Fi, coffee, computers, a tour desk, and laundry service. Just down the block, and a few steps up in class, **Hospedaje Cocibolca** (tel. 505/552-7223, www.hospedajecocibolca .com, $14) is reliable and family-run: 24 small rooms with private bathrooms line nice balconies; annex Cocibolca II is similar and around the corner.

Across the park, a couple of blocks west on Calle Consulado, **Nuestra Casa** (tel. 505/552-8115, $18–25) has seven varied rooms in a lively atmosphere, with live music in the restaurant on weekends. Rooms have either fan or air-conditioning, plus private bath, hot water, and TV.

$25-50

☾ Hotel La Pérgola (three blocks east of the park on Calle El Caimito, tel. 505/552-4221, www.lapergola.com.ni, $48) has 11 rooms with private bath, TV, air-conditioning, and access to a gorgeous open balcony (for which the hotel is named), plus tour service, Wi-Fi, and parking. **Hospedaje Cocibolca II** (around the corner from Cocibolca, tel. 505/552-7223, www .hospedajecocibolca.com, $44) is a close second in this price range. Rooms have new tile floors, air-conditioning, private bath, and lovely common space.

$50-100

You'll find no better hotels than Granada's midrange and upscale range, each of which strives to offer an authentic but unique colonial experience with all the amenities. In this price range and above expect hot water, air-conditioning, private bathrooms, cable TV, artsy decor, and the ubiquitous open-air patio with small swimming pool.

This is all certainly true at **☾ Casa San Francisco** (kitty-corner to the Convento San Francisco, tel. 505/552-8235, csfgranada @yahoo.com, www.casasanfrancisco.com, $40–55), a charming colonial cluster of 13 beautifully decorated rooms with breakfast included. Run by a couple of dynamic and well-traveled ex–Peace Corps Volunteer sisters, Casa San Francisco features a small pool and is located in a quiet and central neighborhood. You'll also find a great on-site restaurant and bar.

A few blocks up Calle Corrales from Casa San Francisco, look for **Bohemian Paradise** (tel. 505/552-0286, www.seecentralamerica .com, $60), a small, high-quality retreat in a surprisingly quiet neighborhood, whose handful of über-comfortable rooms around a small garden are excellent (guests rave about the quality of the mattresses and sheets). Most basic services are available (including parking and laundry) except a bar and restaurant, since the owners encourage guests to explore the city; great for small groups, gay friendly.

The Spanish owner of **☾ Hotel Patio del Malinche** (Calle El Caimito, 2.5 blocks east of the central plaza, tel. 505/552-2235, www .patiodelmalinche.com, $75) is attentive to ensuring his guests feel at home. Fifteen rooms surround a huge patio, bar, and pool. **El Club** (three blocks west of the northwest corner of the park, tel. 505/552-4245, www.elclub -nicaragua.com, $55) has a modern look with cozy, windowless rooms and the city's longest—and sometimes loudest—bar.

Better for families in this price range is **Hotel Casa Capricho** (Calle El Arsenal, a block east of Convento San Francisco, tel. 505/552-8422, www.casacapricho.com, $55), with 11 rooms, a kitchen, a dining room, and common areas; it's colorful and pleasant. **Hotel Casa San Martín** (Calle La Calzada, one block east of the plaza, tel. 505/552-6185, www.hcasasanmartin.com, $55) has eight rooms, all with gorgeous hardwood floors.

Finally in this class are two legitimate hotels, not restored colonial houses: **Hotel Alhambra** (northwest corner of the central plaza, tel. 505/552-4486, www.hotelalhambra .com.ni, $60–90) was Granada's first luxury hotel and has the best spot in town, right on the park. Built around a gorgeous, landscaped patio, its 56 newly remodeled rooms (some with pleasing balcony views) have air-conditioning, TV, private bath, hot water, kitchenette, exposed wood beams, and tasteful decorations. The whole place has a classy, mahogany ambience. **Hotel Colonial** (20 meters west of the park's northwest corner, tel. 505/552-7299, www.nicaragua-vacations .com, $90) is newer, with 37 clean, well-appointed rooms surrounding an outdoor patio, pool, and bar.

Over $100

Casa La Merced (Calle Real Xalteva, tel. 505/552-2744, www.casalamerced.com, $90–125) is a stately bed-and-breakfast with eight ample, street-level rooms around an open patio garden. It's right across the street from the church of the same name. But the new king of Calle la Calzada is **Hotel Dario** (tel. 505/552-3400, www.hoteldario.com, $100), whose open walkways, gardens, and rooms make artful use of the available space; some of the 22 rooms enjoy small balconies with spectacular views of Mombacho.

One of Granada's first buildings (and one of few that withstood the fire that consumed the rest of the city in the days of William Walker) has been painstakingly restored as ❰ **La Gran Francia Hotel y Restaurante** (southeast corner of the park, tel. 505/552-6000, www .lagranfrancia.com, $110–150 includes tax and breakfast). A careful blend of neoclassical and colonial elements in hardwoods, wrought iron, and porcelain characterize La Gran Francia's every detail—down to the hand-painted sinks. Twenty-one rooms, some with balconies, are set around a courtyard and pool. The Duke's Suite, named after an 18th-century mystery man, is one of the few accommodations in Granada with a whirlpool tub.

Another class act is ❰ **Hotel Plaza Colón** (tel. 505/552-8489, www.hotelplazacolon.com, $100–130), whose 26 large, elegant rooms feature air-conditioning, hot water, cable TV, and ceiling fan; six rooms have vast wooden porches looking straight across the central plaza to the main cathedral, a beautiful—but sometimes noisy—vista. The other rooms face a quiet street or the sculpted inner courtyards and pool. A restaurant, bar, and wine cellar are on the premises, and parking is available.

Short- and Long-Term Rentals

Many of the homes restored in Granada's real estate boom are occupied only sporadically by their owners, and can be leased on a monthly basis the rest of the year. Granada's several property managers will match you, your family, or group with the home that best meets your needs; expect to pay anywhere from $450–5,000 a month. See **Casa Granada** (tel. 505/552-0407, www.granadarentals.com), **Granada Property Services** (www.gps nicaragua.com), and **Nica Ventures** (tel. 505/875-1978, www.nicacondos.com).

FOOD

Restaurant turnover is unusually rapid in Granada, but you will not go hungry. We've identified establishments with the longest proven track records, and taken a chance with a few newer places. *Buen provecho!*

Breakfast

It's tough to beat the bottomless cup of coffee and massive morning meals at **Kathy's Waffle House** (across from Convento San Francisco, open 7 A.M.–2 P.M. daily, $4), featuring pancakes, biscuits and gravy, eggs and bacon, omelets, and a lot more. Avoid "Managua Sundays" when Nicaragua's upper crust descend from the capital, maids and nannies in tow. **Garden Cafe** and **Cafe Melba** also offer great breakfasts, or try the orange-infused French toast at **Casa San Francisco** (kitty-corner to the Convento San Francisco, from 7 A.M. daily).

Cafés and Vegetarian

Cafe Melba (located on Calle El Martirio near Zoom Bar, tel. 505/552-0261, open 7 A.M.–2 P.M. Tues.–Sun.) is one of the city's only exclusively vegetarian restaurants. Enjoy your meal in the lovely courtyard ambience, or try one of their special cocktails. Wednesdays are movie nights (international, arts-festival quality films); free coffee refills. **Café DecArte** (two blocks east of the park, open after 11 A.M. daily) serves soups, sandwiches, and a variety of specialties like Thai peanut salad, quiche, milk shakes, and fresh pita bread ($4–8). Otherwise, try **The Bearded Monkey** (across from the fire station, tel. 505/552-4028), for bargain veggie chili and a proper, fat burrito.

◖ Garden Cafe (Calle la Libertad, one block east of central plaza, tel. 505/552-8582, thegardencafe.granada@gmail.com, open 7 A.M.–3 P.M. Mon.–Sat., under $4) is a wonderful respite from the heat, with a cool space to enjoy gourmet sandwiches, salads, smoothies, and coffee drinks; the artsy patio is a great place to crank the Wi-Fi. **Euro Cafe** (northwest corner of central plaza, open 7:30 A.M.–9 P.M.

daily) serves homemade gelato, pastries, panini, fresh hummus, fruit juices, and strong coffee drinks; there's free Wi-Fi. There's great coffee and desserts at **El Tercer Ojo** (see the *International and Fine Dining* section). People rave about **Safari Lounge,** just a block west of the main park, for its cappuccino and veggie options.

Traditional Nicaraguan

Besides renowned *vigorón* and *chancho con yuca* (both pork dishes), sold on banana leaves in the plaza, visit Calle La Calzada's various *fritangas* evenings for deep-fried pleasure. **Querubes** serves a popular lunch buffet in the market, and on Calle La Calzada's restaurant row you'll find lots of Nica traditional food; start at the aptly named **Comida Típica** (open noon–11 P.M. daily except Wed.) with rotating daily specials such as *indio viejo* or *baho.* Enjoy chicken and burgers on the north end of Plaza de los Leones at either **Rostipollo** or **Tip-Top,** both Nicaraguan favorites.

The unassuming **◖ Restaurante Las Colinas** (Barrio Las Sabanetas, tel. 505/552-3492, open 10 A.M.–10 P.M. daily, closed Tues. nights), in a nondescript neighborhood south of the main market, has become famous among foreigners looking for the best prepared Cocibolca *guapote* (lake bass) in town—about $10. Any taxi driver will know the way.

"Jimmy Three Fingers" of **Nuestra Casa** (Calle Consulado, 2.5 blocks west of the plaza, tel. 505/552-8115) serves acclaimed barbecue ribs, meatloaf, and a whole lotta soul food (plus occasional live music, if you're lucky).

Pizza

Locals and backpackers rave about the prices at **Telepizza** (Calle El Arsenal, 1.5 blocks east of Bancentro, tel. 505/552-4219, open 10 A.M.–10 P.M. daily), with large pies from $6 and delivery available; the gigantic $3 stuffed calzones may be one of the best deals in town. Also popular is **Monna Lisa** (Calle La Calzada, tel. 505/552-8187). Get real, thin-crust Italian pizza baked in a wood-fired oven at **Don Luca's** (Calle La Calzada, tel. 505/552-7822).

vegetables for sale

International and Fine Dining

Don't miss dinner at **Café Chavalos** (tel. 505/852-0210, www.cafechavalos.blogspot .com, open weekend nights only, reservations recommended). Full dinner (soup, entrée, dessert, and coffee) averages about $10 per person, more with wine or beer; specialties are red snapper baked in a banana leaf, chicken with goat cheese, chile relleno, the best ceviche this side of Lake Cocibolca, and rich lemon desserts. *Los chavalos,* or the guys, are newly trained chefs and servers who have chosen careers in the culinary arts over life on the streets. Their story is as inspiring as the food is delicious. Café Chavalos is supported by the nonprofit organization Building New Hope (see sidebar *Volunteering in Granada*).

For lip-smacking, upscale Nicaraguan dishes and steaks, don't miss **El Zaquan** (open noon–3 P.M. and 6 P.M.–closing daily), located behind the main cathedral—your nose should lead you to the meat-draped open-flame grill and dishes like *churrasco jalapeño* (around $9).

El Tercer Ojo (Calle El Arsenal across from Convento San Francisco, tel. 505/552-6451, open 11 A.M.–11 P.M. Tues.–Sun.) offers everything from Spanish tapas and sushi to gorgonzola pasta, kebabs, and fine wine in a gauzy lounge of candles and soothing music. Find more good vibes around the corner at **Asia Latina** (Calle la Libertad, a block off the central plaza, tel. 505/552-4672, open noon–midnight daily), a bar and restaurant serving Thai and Asian fusion "with a touch of Latino"—amazing dishes with many vegetarian options.

Old-time favorite **Charly's Bar and Restaurant** (located four blocks west of the old hospital mansion on the edge of town, tel. 505/552-2942, open 11 A.M.–3 P.M. and 6–11 P.M. daily except Tues.) is a German-style *rancho* serving schnitzel, sauerkraut, and draft beer in a big, crystal boot—it's a bit far from the city center, but worth the trip, and they'll pay for your taxi if you eat there.

Doña Conchi (Calle Caimito, two blocks east of the cathedral, tel. 505/552-7376, closed Tues.) offers a taste of her native Spain in one of the more intimate atmospheres in Granada—dinner by candlelight under the stars, surrounded by a lush garden patio and live guitar music. Diners enjoy large, fresh dinner salads, seafood, and pitchers of sangria. Ask about the centuries-old bullet holes in the wall. One door west, **El Mediterraneo** (tel. 505/552-6764, closed Mon.) is another elegant Spanish restaurant set in an airy garden patio adorned with colorful artwork; readers love this place. **El Arcángel Restaurant** at La Gran Francia (tel. 505/552-6000, open at 7 A.M. for breakfast, then noon–10 P.M. daily) features an exquisite fusion of Latin American ingredients with international cuisine; fancy entrées like whiskey-glazed steak, pastas, and banana and brown-sugar coated snapper filet run $12–20.

INFORMATION AND TOUR OPERATORS

The local **INTUR** office (across from Iglesia San Francisco, tel. 505/552-6858) is open 8 A.M.–noon and 2–5 P.M. Monday–Friday. They have a good selection of brochures and maps, but so does every restaurant and hotel in town. Granada's homepage **www.granada.com.ni** is prettier than it is helpful.

Walk east on Calle La Calzada from the central plaza and you'll find no shortage of tour companies waiting to whisk you to islands, mountaintops, Masaya markets, and more. We like **Tierra Tours** (Calle La Calzada, two blocks east of park, tel. 505/862-9580, www .tierratour.com) for their clever assortment of half-day, full-day, and overnight trips in the Granada area—about $25 per person, cheaper for groups. In addition to local tours of Granada, Masaya, and Catarina, Tierra offers night tours of Volcán Masaya and overnight cabins and tent platforms at a nearby Butterfly Reserve and coffee farm ($55 pp for full-service camping trip). Ask about shuttle service to other parts of Nicaragua, including León, where they have a sister office.

Mombotours (Calle Atravesada, next to BDF, tel. 505/552-4548, www.mombotours .com) has impressive kayak tours of Las Isletas,

GRANADA

© JOSHUA BERMAN

plenty to do: bulletin board in a Granada hostel

as well as bike tours/rentals and canopy trips at the Cutirre Farm on Mombacho. Homespun, friendly local service at **WOW Tours** (call Jethro tel. 505/646-5628, www.wowtoursnicaragua .com), where a few helpful young guys can arrange all kinds of trips and adventures. They'll accompany you on public buses, or help you rent a vehicle; the office is next to Oasis Hostal on Calle Estrada.

Servitur (tel. 505/838-7820 or 505/552-2955, orvind@hotmail.com) is connected to the Hotel Alhambra, offering travel agent services and a variety of local trips in the Granada area, including a horse-drawn-carriage city tour and fishing trips. Right around the corner, **Amigo Tours** (tel. 505/552-4080, bernal @amigotours.net, www.amigotours.net) is connected to the lobby of the Hotel Colonial. On the more expensive, air-conditioned side of things, Amigo specializes in area tours, national airline bookings, car rentals, and transfers to and from Costa Rica. Same goes for **Nicaragua Adventures** (tel. 505/552-8461, www.nica-adventures.com), located on Calle La Calzada.

SERVICES
Emergency
The biggest hospital, Bernardino Díaz Ochoa, is a few kilometers out of town, on the road toward Managua. On the same highway, a bit closer to town is the Hospital Privado Cocibolca (tel. 505/552-2907 or 505/552-4092). For minor treatments, the section of Calle Atravesada just south of the bridge is occupied by more than a dozen clinics, blood labs, and pharmacies. The National Police station is located on the highway to Nandaime (tel. 505/552-4712) and 75 meters west of the cinema (tel. 505/552-2977 or 505/552-2929).

Groceries
The two major supermarkets are the Palí (on Calle Atravesada just south of the market) and La Colonial, both open till 8 P.M. or so.

COMMUNITY TOURISM NEAR GRANADA

For those seeking a full-immersion cultural experience, the most obvious option is to sign up for a homestay with one of the many Spanish Schools in Granada. This is a good option if you want to stay with a Nicaraguan family and still have access to Granada's many restaurants, Internet cafés, and other distractions. If you'd really like to get out there, then consider arranging a few days (or weeks) with the **Unión de Cooperativas Agropecuarias Tierra y Agua,** also known as the **Earth and Water UCA** (tel. 505/896-9361 or 505/552-0238, turismo@ucatierrayagua .org, www.ucatierrayagua.org). The office in Granada is located 75 yards to the west of the Shell Palmira and is open Mondays, Wednesdays, and Fridays 8:30 A.M.-2 P.M. The UCA is an association of rural farmers on the slopes of Volcán Mombacho and Isla de Zapatera National Park who will be glad to be your hosts. You'll stay in primitive Nicaraguan lodging and eat typical food while getting to know your new neighborhood. Expect to pay about $5 per person per night for lodging in La Granadilla or Zonzapote, and about $3 per meal. Local guides will take you horseback riding, hiking, fishing, and more; cheap transport to and from Granada can be arranged.

Income generated by your visit goes directly to a cooperative collective fund to pay for meals, guides, maintenance, etc., and to distribute to families involved. The UCA also maintains a general fund for tourism, used for training and to make small loans for new tourist-related projects.

Phones and Mail

The main ENITEL building is right off the plaza's northeast corner; the national post office (open 8:30 A.M.–5 P.M. Mon.–Fri.) has moved *four times* since 2005; it was last seen on the east end of Calle Corales.

Internet

Internet cafés throughout the city usually offer service for $1–1.25/hour and Internet phone service for around $0.10/minute. Start at **Alhambra Internet** (across the street from Hotel Colonial, open 8 A.M.–10 P.M. daily); they offer a variety of services and the shop is always air-conditioned. Also pleasant is the **Cafémail** (in the Casa de los Leones, open 7 A.M.–10 P.M. daily), offering a coffee-bar experience with both a row of PCs and Wi-Fi. In fact, most restaurants and hotels have free Wi-Fi in Granada, so you'll have no problem with your laptop.

Banks

Banco de America Central is on the southwest corner of the plaza, and Banpro and Bancentro are on Calle Atravesada, just a few blocks away.

The sanctioned money changers are out in full force along this same section of Atravesada (they're on the street, waving wads of cash) and ATMs in most banks and at the Esso gas station on the edge of town.

Laundry

Mapache Laundry Service (next to Tierra Tours, Calle La Calzada, tel. 505/611-3501, open 7 A.M.é5 P.M. Mon.–Sat.) offers quality service and personal attention as they wash your clothes in their handful of modern machines; delivery and pickup service, $3 per six pounds. There's another laundry place (from the middle of the central park, 1.5 blocks west, tel. 505/552-6532) that also offers pickup and delivery service for about $4/load.

Car Rental

The **Budget** (tel. 505/552-2323, reserve@budget.com.ni, open 8 A.M.–6:30 P.M. daily) office is located in the Shell Guapinol gas station on the road to Managua. Cars rent from about $30–110 a day, and they can make you an offer on a cheap rented cell phone while you're there. There is huge demand for their

© JOSHUA BERMAN

sunrise on Calle La Calzada

28-vehicle fleet, so reservations are necessary, especially in the high season. Hotels also often maintain a list of trusted cars and drivers.

GETTING THERE AND AWAY
By Bus to Other Points in Nicaragua

There are four places to catch a bus out of town. The easiest and most popular way to get to Managua (or Masaya, which is on the way) is to grab a **COGRAN** *expreso* (1.5 blocks south of the central plaza's southwest corner, tel. 505/552-2954); these medium-sized buses leave every 15–20 minutes from 4:30 A.M.–7 or 8 P.M. Monday–Friday (they stop service a few hours earlier on Sunday). Another fleet of minivans leaves from the Parque Sandino on the north side of Granada near the old railroad station, with regular departures from 5 A.M.–7:30 P.M. Both services travel to La UCA in Managua. From there, the same vehicles leave for Granada every 15 minutes, from 5:50 A.M.–8 P.M.

Regular bus service to Rivas, Nandaime, and Jinotepe works out of the **Shell Palmira,** on Granada's south side, just past the Palé supermarket. The first bus to Rivas leaves at 5:45 A.M. and takes 1.5 hours; service continues sporadically until the last one at 3:10 P.M. Nandaime buses leave every 20 minutes. Jinotepe *expresos* take a mere 45 minutes compared to the nearly two-hour *ordinario* trip through the pueblos. Around the corner, behind the Palé, is the bus terminal with service to Masaya (although any Managua-bound *expreso* will let you off in Masaya as well).

By Bus to Costa Rica and Panamá

Avenida Arrellano, on the west end of Granada, is part of the San José– and Panama City–bound routes for Central American bus lines. The three offices are all located on the east side of the street, and reservations should be made at least two days in advance. The **TicaBus** terminal (tel. 505/552-4301) is half a block south of the Old Hospital; be there at 6:15 A.M. for the 7 A.M. bus. **TransNica** (tel. 505/552-6619) is three long blocks south of the Old Hospital, on the corner of Calle Xalteva; three daily southbounders leave at 6:30 A.M., 8 A.M., and 11 A.M.; be there a half-hour before departure.

By Boat

Granada's crusty old ferry departs Granada's municipal dock (tel. 505/552-2966) Monday and Thursday at 2 P.M., arriving in San Carlos around 6 A.M. When weather permits, the boat stops at Altagracia before cutting across to the eastern lakeshore and port calls in Morrito and San Miguelito. The adventure costs about $4 or $8 each way (these are the normal lower/upper deck prices; or pay $50 for the VIP sleeper cabin) and returns from San Carlos at 2 P.M. on Tuesdays and Fridays. The boat can get crowded and uncomfortable, especially around Semana Santa when the lake turns *bravo* (rough) and the weather is hot. Get to the port early and be aggressive to stake your territory. During the rest of the year, the ride is usually languid and uneventful, and you may even be able to get some sleep on the deck.

Near Granada

◖ LAS ISLETAS

This 365-island archipelago formed when Volcán Mombacho erupted some 20,000 years ago, hurling its top half into the nearby lake in giant masses of rock, ash, and lava. Today, the islands are inhabited by a few hundred *campesinos* and an ever-increasing number of wealthy Nicaraguans and foreigners who continue to buy up the *isletas* and build garish vacation homes on them. The natural beauty of the *isletas* is spectacular, and history buffs will enjoy the **Fortín de San Pablo,** a Spanish fort that was largely unsuccessful in preventing pirate attacks on Granada. The islanders themselves are interesting and friendly, maintaining a rural lifestyle unique in Nicaragua: Children paddle dugout canoes or rowboats to school from an early age, and their parents get along by fishing and farming—or by taking camera-toting tourists for a ride in their boats.

To visit Las Isletas, begin at either Cabañas Amarillo or Puerto Asese, both a seven-minute drive south of Granada at the end of the waterfront road (about $1 via taxi). Puerto Asese is more popular, while Cabañas Amarillo (fork left at the Asese sign) provides more shade and wider views—as well as kayak tours. At both docks, you'll find a restaurant, snack bars, and a plethora of boats vying for your business.

Choose a *lanchero* (boatman) and don't expect to haggle over prices, as gasoline is expensive. You'll pay about $10 a person for a half-hour tour, more for longer or farther trips. Beef up your visit by asking to visit an island where a family can serve you lunch—or pull up and "refuel" at one of the mellow island bars before continuing your tour. You can also take a dip in the lake water or have your *lanchero* bring you to the cemetery, old fort, or monkey island.

Note that choosing to tour the islands in a *lancha* is not recommended for those seeking a quiet wilderness experience—the loud motors spew smoke and scare the birds away and keep you far up out of the water. Much more enjoyable is the sound of birdsong over your kayak as you cut silently through the glassy water; sign up for one of several kayak tours in the Mombotour office in Granada (see *Information and Tour Operators* in this chapter). Learn how to sea kayak, then take a tour of the islands and old fort. The introductory class, which includes all equipment, transportation, and tour of the Fortín San Pablo, costs $34 a person and lasts three hours. Special bird-watching kayak excursions run $20–30; Nica guides are available and for the full petroleum-free experience, try the bike-kayak combo tour.

GRANADA

PARQUE NACIONAL ARCHIPIÉLAGO ZAPATERA

About 34 kilometers south of Granada, Zapatera is an extinct volcano surrounded by Isla el Muerto and a dozen or so other islets, all of which comprise 45 square kilometers of land; the whole complex is home for some 500 residents. Zapatera is a natural wonder, rising 629 meters above sea level. Its virgin forest is rife with myriad wildlife such as parrots, toucans, herons, and other waterfowl, plus white-tailed deer, and an alleged population of jaguars no one ever seems to see.

These islands were enormously important to the Nahuatl, who used them primarily as a vast burial ground and sacrifice spot. The sites of La Punta de las Figuras and Zonzapote are particularly rich in artifacts and have a network of caves that have never been researched. Also seek out the petroglyphs carved into the bedrock beaches of Isla el Muerto. An impressive selection of Zapatera's formidable stone idols is on display in the Convento San Francisco, but the islands' remaining archaeological treasures remain relatively unstudied and unprotected and (naturally) continue to disappear.

Officially declared a national park by the Sandinistas in 1983, the Zapatera Archipelago has never been adequately protected or funded. MARENA's thousand-page management plan document is just that—a document—while in reality, only one park ranger visits the islands a couple of times per month. It's no surprise then that inhabitants and visitors litter, loot the archaeological patrimony, hunt, and cut down trees for timber.

Visiting Zapatera

Access the islands from Granada's Puerto Asese, where you can strike a deal with returning Zapatera islanders or hire a tourist boat. The most reliable way is to arrange a trip with **Zapatera Tours** (tel. 505/842-2587, www.zapateratours.com), a small company that specializes in creative lake tours, including overnight camping trips, fishing, waterskiing, you name it. You can also inquire about Zapatera trips with any of the other Granada tour companies

above. With a fast, powerful motor, it's a 20-minute trip from Granada, partly over a stretch of open water that can get choppy.

There are a scattering of places to stay around the island, including a cheap dormitory and homestay options in Zonzapote (see sidebar *Community Tourism*). Or book a room at **Casa Hacienda Hotel Santa María** (tel. 505/884-0606, zapateratour@gmail.com), where the Cordova family's 120-year-old tile-roofed ranch house has been outfitted with comfortably primitive double rooms with mosquito net, fan, and private bathrooms. The cost is $50 per person to use the place for the day, or $120 a night for two people plus meals, transport, and fishing trips. The hotel is on a relaxing sandy beach, looking north toward Isla el Muerte and Mombacho.

◖ VOLCÁN MOMBACHO

Mombacho is unavoidable; it towers over the southern horizon, lurks around every corner, creeps into your panoramic photos. In Granada, you are living in the shadow of a giant. Fortunately, this giant is gentle. Every bit of cool, misty, cloud forest higher than 850 meters above sea level is officially protected as a nature reserve. This equals about 700 hectares of park, rising to a peak elevation of 1,345 meters, and comprising a rich, concentrated island of flora and fauna. Thanks to the Fundación Cocibolca, the reserve is accessible and makes available the best-designed and maintained hiking trails in the nation.

Overgrown with hundreds of orchid and bromeliad species, tree ferns, and old-growth cloud and dwarf forests, Mombacho also boasts three species of monkeys, 168 observed birds (49 of which are migratory), 30 species of reptiles, 60 mammals (including at least one very secretive big cat), and 10 amphibians. The flanks of the volcano, 21 percent of which remains forested, are composed of privately owned coffee plantations and cattle ranches. Maintaining the forest canopy is a crucial objective of Fundación Cocibolca, since this is where more than 90 percent of Mombacho's 1,000 howler monkeys reside (the monkeys

© JOSHUA BERMAN

Mombacho's well-kept trails lead you around the forested rims of several defunct and overgrown craters.

available for $5 (per group, plus tip) for the Sendero el Cráter and $10 for the Sendero la Puma. Note, because of the altitude and the clouds, the visibility from these trails may be much diminished on bad-weather days.

The reserve is closed on Mondays for maintenance, and usually restricts Tuesdays and Wednesdays to organized groups. From Thursday to Sunday, all are welcome. The entrance fee ($7.50 for foreigners, $5 for Nicas and residents, $4 for students and children) includes admission to the reserve, transport to and from the top of the volcano, and insurance. If you've got the time and the strong legs, feel free to hike all the way up the steep road yourself. Allow a couple hours (and lots of water) to reach the top.

Volcán Mombacho Biological Center

Located at the base of one of Mombacho's 14 communications antennas, on a small plateau called Plan de las Flores at 1,150 meters, the research station is also an interpretive center, *hospedaje, cafetín,* ranger station, and conference center, technically completed in 2000 but still expanding. Find drinks and snacks here, including a simple meal for $3.50. As of press time, there are 10 dormitory beds in a loft above the interpretive center. It costs $25 to rent out the whole *albergue* (hostel), which sleeps up to 10 people. The package deal includes dinner, a guided night hike (on which you can search for the famous red-eyed frog and Mombacho salamander), and breakfast; or pitch a tent for $15 and buy meals on the side. To make a reservation, contact the Biological Station at tel. 505/248-8234/35 or 505/552-5858; or contact Fundación Cocibolca in Managua (tel. 505/278-3224 or 505/277-1681, www.mombacho.org). Most tour companies will get you there; start with Mombotours or Tierra Tours.

travel in 100 different troops, and venture into the actual reserve only to forage).

There is a short (half-hour) trail through the coffee farm at the bottom of the volcano, where you wait for your ride up. Once on top, there are two main trails to choose from: **Sendero el Cráter,** which encircles the forest-lined crater, and features a moss-lined tunnel, several lookouts, and a spur trail to the **fumaroles** (holes in the ground venting hot sulfurous air). The fumaroles area is an open, grassy part of the volcano with blazing wildflowers and an incredible view of Granada and the *isletas.* The whole loop, including the spur, is 1.5 kilometers, with a few ups and downs, and takes a casual hour to walk. The **Sendero la Puma** is considerably more challenging—a four-kilometer loop with several difficult climbs that lead to breathtaking viewpoints. It begins at a turnoff from the fumaroles trail, and you should allow a minimum of three hours to complete it (and lots of water). Well-trained, knowledgeable local guides (some with English) are

Canopy Tours on Mombacho

Put yourself on belay at the **Mombacho Canopy Tour** (tel. 505/888-2566 or 505/852-9483,

GRANADA

gloriamaria@cablenet.com.ni, $30 pp), located up the road from the parking lot, just before the road passes through the El Progreso coffee mill. Their 1,500-meter course involves 15 platforms and a 25-meter-long hanging bridge. Many tour operators offer a full-day Mombacho package that involves a visit to the reserve followed by a canopy tour on the way down, or you can arrange it yourself by calling Fundación Cocibolca.

On the opposite (east) face of Volcán Mombacho, cloud-forest coffee farm meets canopy tour at the Cutirre Farm. **Mombotour** (next to BDF, tel. 505/552-4548, www.mombotour .com) offers a range of half-day trips, involving some combination of canopy tour, horseback ride, bird-watching hike, and coffee-farm tour. Trips include transportation to and from Granada and lunch, about $55 per adult (add a kayak tour to make a full day out of it).

The 15-kilometer ride to the Cutirre Farm takes longer than you'd expect. The road turns into a river during the wet season, but the trip is worth it; once you arrive, the views from the lodge are spectacular, looking straight out at Isla de Zapatera, and behind it, the cone of Volcán Concepción. There is also a small but attractive insect museum, with a full butterfly farm in the works. Bird-watchers can take a walk through the plantation with guides experienced in spotting any of the 43 species observed here.

The canopy tour, suspended from 14 of the giant shade trees on the coffee farm, is a professional, safe system of 17 platforms, a hanging bridge, and 13 horizontal zip lines, ending with a 23-meter rappel from a massive ceiba tree. Show up at Mombotour's Granada office to arrange your trip, leaving at either 10 A.M. or 2 P.M. (arrive one hour prior), returning you to Granada about three hours later.

Getting There

Although the majority of Mombacho's visitors arrive as part of a tour package, it is entirely possible to visit the reserve on your own, and it makes a perfect day trip from Managua, Granada, or Masaya. You'll start by taking a bus (or express minivan) headed for Nandaime or Rivas (or, from Granada, to Carazo as well); tell the driver to let you off at the Empalme el Guanacaste. This is a large intersection, and the road up to the parking lot and official reserve entrance is located 1.5 kilometers toward the mountain—look for the signs. The walk to the parking lot is a solid half-hour trek, mostly uphill and in the sun. Water and snacks are available at the parking lot—be sure to drink lots before and during this first leg of your journey. Once you arrive at the parking lot, you'll pay the entrance fee and then board one of the foundation's vehicles to make the half-hour, six-kilometer climb up to the Biological Station. The lumbering troop transports depart at 8:30 A.M., 10 A.M., 1 P.M., and 3 P.M. Thursday–Sunday, and return shortly after each climb up the hill (last bus down is 6 P.M.). In your own four-wheel drive vehicle, you'll be asked to pay $13 in addition to your entrance fee. The park is closed Monday and open on Tuesday by reservation only.

MASAYA AND THE PUEBLOS BLANCOS

Masaya is a city of artisans, metalworkers, leatherworkers, carpenters, painters, and musicians. In fact, no other region of Nicaragua is as blessed with a sense of artistry and creativity as Masaya and the surrounding villages, or Pueblos Blancos. Many of the handicrafts found in markets throughout the country (and throughout Central America) are Masayan: handwoven hammocks, terra cotta pottery, musical instruments, and more. "The City of Flowers," as Rubén Darío christened the town a century ago (he was talking about the girls, not the flora), rarely garners more than a brief afternoon market visit for most travelers. It is a city relatively devoid of monuments, historical buildings, and traditional sights. As a market place however, it is unsurpassed, and wandering through the cool alleys of the crafts markets are a cultural tour through Nicaragua, a vivid expression of this people's vitality, passion, and creativity. If you are eager to come home from your trip with something special, this is the place to find it.

An inextricable part not only of the landscape but of the culture, Volcán Masaya and its adjacent crater lake, are hard to miss. You might even get a whiff of sulphur if the wind is blowing the right direction, because this volcano is still very much active. It's also one of the world's most accessible volcanoes—one of only two on earth where you can drive up to the crater lip and look inside—and Nicaragua's most thoughtfully planned national park. As such it's a rewarding and memorable experience well worth your time, and possibly one of the top three things to do in Nicaragua.

© JOSHUA BERMAN

HIGHLIGHTS

◖ El Mercado Viejo Craft Market: The best handmade pottery, leatherwork, paintings, and more are all handsomely displayed in a professionally run market designed to showcase Nicaragua's finest (page 85).

◖ El Malecón: Take a stroll along the crater's lip, which marks Masaya's western edge, and enjoy the view of the lagoon below (page 85).

◖ Volcán Masaya National Park: Peer into the gates of hell, wherein dwell demon parakeets – then visit the museum of this popular national park (page 90).

◖ Laguna de Apoyo: Get away from it all in what might be the coolest swimming hole in the country, an enticing volcanic crater lake, ringed with forest (page 92).

◖ Catarina Mirador: This crater's lip patio terrace, with one of the best panoramas in Nicaragua, often offers live marimba music to accompany your beverage (page 95).

LOOK FOR ◖ TO FIND RECOMMENDED SIGHTS, ACTIVITIES, DINING, AND LODGING.

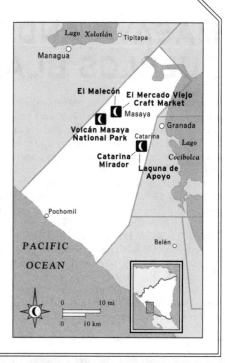

To the south and west of Masaya the charming Pueblos Blancos are a group of artisan villages whose people produce the things you find in the markets. It's easy to spend a day visiting their workshops or just enjoying the casual, friendly atmosphere of each town. In particular, the village of Catarina, perched on the crater lip above Laguna de Apoyo enjoys one of the most spectacular vistas in all of Nicaragua. The Pueblos run into Carazo, another group of small towns, closer to the Pacific, with a pleasant climate and somewhat middle-class feel in a country of economic extremes. Its cooler temperatures favor coffee production, often under the shade of beautiful hardwood trees. The towns of Diriamba and Jinotepe make delightful lunch stopovers on your way through from Managua to Masaya, but both have nice places to stay and Jinotepe's open-air market is worth a visit.

A regional turquoise jewel, the Laguna de Apoyo is probably the most pleasant freshwater swimming hole in the country, imbued with both a sense of tranquility and isolation that make more than just the cool lake water refreshing. It's an easy day trip from Granada, but many choose to stay the night as well, and a growing number of hotels and restaurants make that possible. Unless you are truly water-averse, this delightful place should not be missed.

PLANNING YOUR TIME

Visiting the craft markets, the city, and the *malecón,* and visiting the volcano are probably two separate trips if you're relying on public

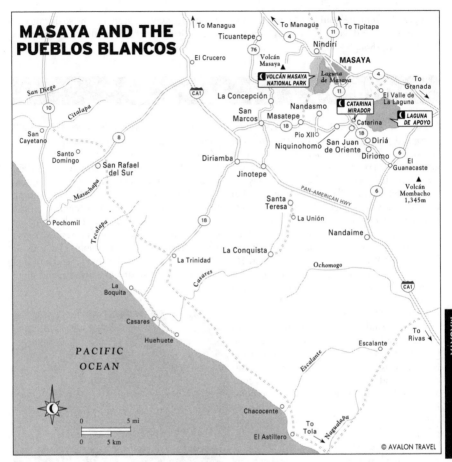

transportation. Naturalists more interested in the volcano can just as easily spend a long day on hiking trails, in the visitors center, and on tours. One way to do both is to spend a night in Masaya in the interim, but most travelers opt instead for Granada, which has a better selection of hotels and restaurants. On the other hand, if you're driving it's feasible to leave town early, spend morning on the volcano, afternoon in the markets, and be back home in time for dinner.

There are lots of side trips that can expand your itinerary if you're traveling slowly. For starters, allow extra time in Masaya city to walk to the cliff-top lookout point near the baseball stadium, where you'll also find the hammock factories. You can spend an hour or two at the Coyotepe fortress, where the views are pleasant and the wind takes the edge off the heat.

A trip through the Pueblos Blancos is a day in itself, even if you are driving. It's fun to start at one end, work your way up to Catarina, have lunch, and then continue. You can visit the Pueblos Blancos by public transportation, as the buses run this route frequently throughout the day, but having the freedom of a vehicle will greatly facilitate your ability to pick and choose as you work your way through the villages. Lastly, though very few travelers stay the night in Masaya, consider doing so during one of the city's colorful festivals, when the town really comes alive.

Masaya City

Masaya (population 90,000) sprawls over a tropical plain nestled against the slopes of the volcano by the same name; at its western edge, paths carved by the Chorotegas trace the steep hillside down to the Laguna de Masaya. Twenty indigenous villages of Darianes used to cluster at the water's edge. Masaya was officially founded as a city in 1819 and has grown ever since. Several centuries of rebellion and uprising—first against the Spaniards in 1529 and later against William Walker's forces in 1856, the U.S. Marines in 1912, and in a number of ferocious battles against the National Guard during the revolution, earned the Masayans a reputation as fierce fighters.

Travelers find Masaya less picturesque than Granada and it's true the streets and building facades in Masaya are less cared for. But the Masayans are a creative people with many traditions found nowhere else in Nicaragua, such as their solemn, mysterious funeral processions. Perhaps Masayan creative energy goes into its delightful arts and crafts instead of the architecture. Your best introduction to these delights is Masaya's Mercado Viejo (Old Market), which is so pleasant and compelling that many visitors choose not to stray beyond its stately stone walls. But it's well worth the money to charter a horse-drawn carriage to carry you to the breezy *malecón,* to see the crater lake 100 meters below.

ORIENTATION AND GETTING AROUND

Masaya sits due south of the Managua–Granada Carretera along the east side of the Laguna de Masaya. The street that runs north along the plaza's east side is the Calle Central, and as you travel it toward the Carretera, it becomes increasingly commercial. One block east of the southeast corner of the park, you'll find the stone walls of the Mercado Viejo (Old Market). Walking six blocks west of the central park takes you to the hammock factories, baseball stadium, and *malecón;* traveling due south leads you to Barrio Monimbó; going five blocks north puts you in the heart of the Barrio San Jerónimo around the church of the same name, situated at the famous *siete esquinas* (seven corners) intersection. The heart of Masaya is easily walkable, but several hundred taxis, buses, horse-drawn carriages, and more

the narrow colorful aisles of Masaya's local market

© JOSHUA BERMAN

MASAYA

LA LAGUNA DE MASAYA

The peaceful waters of the Laguna de Masaya belie the violent origin of the lake. Long before the first Chorotegas settled in 20 small villages around its perimeter, the lake was one of Volcán Masaya's gaping craters, choked off long ago by shifting channels of magma beneath the surface of the earth and abandoned to slowly fill up with rainwater. These days, the most impressive views of Laguna de Masaya are from the 100-meter-high vantage points of the *malecón* in the city of Masaya, or from the restaurants that line Carretera Masaya, just west of the city. It's one of Nicaragua's bigger crater lakes: 8.5 square kilometers set at the foot Volcán Masaya and 73 meters deep in the center. While several trails, some of which were made by the Chorotegas themselves, lead the intrepid hiker down to the water's edge, the lake water receives some of Masaya's municipal sewage, so it's no swimming hole. Dip your heels in nearby Laguna de Apoyo instead.

exotic forms of transport will help you get out to the *malecón* or the highway.

SIGHTS AND ATTRACTIONS

◖ El Mercado Viejo Craft Market

All roads lead to El Mercado Viejo, built in 1891, destroyed by fires in 1966 and 1978, and most recently refurbished in 1997 as a showcase for local handicrafts. Also known as El Mercado Nacionál de Artesanías, or simply the "tourist market," El Mercado Viejo is safe, comfortable, and geared toward foreigners. Here you'll find all manner of delightful leather, brass, iron, carved wood, and textile handicraft, plus paintings, clothing, hammocks, and the best of what Nicaragua's talented craftspeople have to offer. It's the best reason to come to Masaya and even if you don't buy anything, an enjoyable and colorful experience. Right around the corner, **Chincheli** is a shop owned and run by talented local artists and former street kids. Not only do these artists sell high quality paintings, hammocks, and bracelets, they also teach other children, under the tutelage of NGO Los Quinchos.

◖ El Malecón

Cool off after an intense morning in the market on the windswept *malecón,* a beautiful cliffside promenade with long views over the Volcán Masaya crater lake to the north and west. It's easily reached from the city center. Rather than a taxi, this is the best opportunity to charter a horse carriage, which makes a nice ride through some quiet neighborhoods.

Artist Workshops

Nicaragua's most treasured souvenirs, woven hammocks are handmade by scores of Masaya families, and take 2–3 days each. The most obvious place to purchase one is in either of the markets described above. More fun than just buying is to visit one of the many *fábricas de hamacas,* most of which are in people's homes, clustered on the same block near the southwest edge of town, across from the old hospital on the road to the *malecón* and

There are several small guitar workshops in Masaya.

© JOSHUA BERMAN

MASAYA

baseball stadium. There you'll find at least a half-dozen family porch-front businesses; all of these craftspeople will gladly show you how hammocks are woven.

Sergio Zepeda is a third-generation luthier (guitar builder) at **Guitarras Zepeda** (200 meters west of the Unión Fenosa, right behind Hotel Rossyln's, tel. 505/883-0260, guitarraszepeda@yahoo.com). His shop is only a block off the Carretera Masaya. Cheap children's and beater guitars start at $50; professional hardwood instruments with Cocobolo Rosewood back and sides and imported red cedar, mahogany, or spruce tops can go for up to $800. Allow at least two weeks to order, or show up in his shop and see what's available.

Elsewhere in Masaya

Masaya's central plaza is officially called **Parque 17 de Octubre,** named for a battle against Somoza's Guardia in 1977. Plenty of remaining bullet holes are testimony, plus two imposing command towers immediately to the west. The church in the northeast corner is La Parroquia La Asunción. The unremarkable, triangular **Plaza de Monimbó** park on the southern side of Masaya comes to life every afternoon at around 3 P.M. as the throbbing social and commercial heart of the mostly indigenous Monimbó neighborhood. The **Museo y Galería Héroes y Mártires** (inside the Alcaldía, 1.5 blocks north of the park, open 8 A.M.–5 P.M. Mon.–Fri., donation requested) pays tribute to those Masayans who fought Somoza's National Guard during the revolution with a collection of guns and photos of the fallen but the highlight is the unexploded napalm bomb Somoza dropped on the city in '77.

ENTERTAINMENT AND EVENTS

Every Thursday 5–11 P.M., **Jueves de Verbena** consists of dance, theater, art expos, music, and more, all presented in the Old Market on one of several stages. Or rub elbows with the locals at the most popular local bar in town,

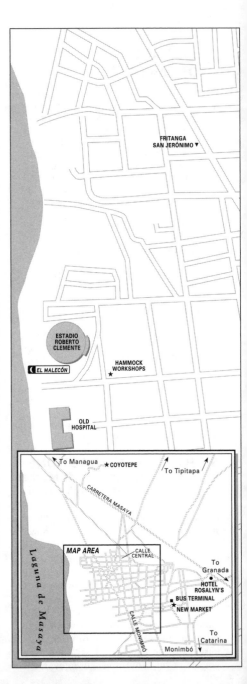

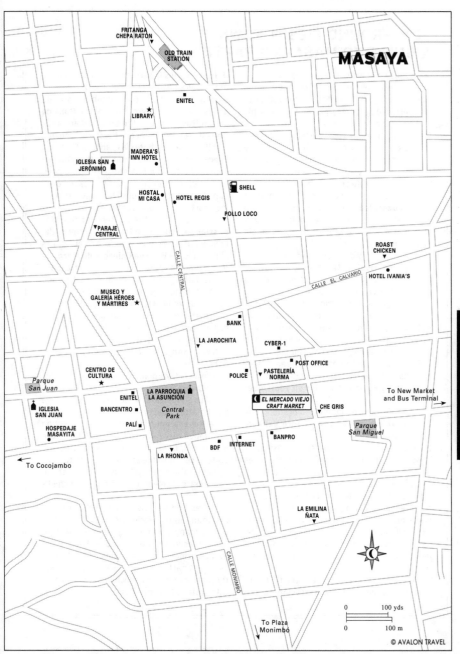

MASAYA

MASAYA

FRITANGA CHEPA RATÓN

OLD TRAIN STATION

ENITEL

★ LIBRARY

MADERA'S INN HOTEL

IGLESIA SAN JERÓNIMO

HOSTAL MI CASA ● HOTEL REGIS

SHELL

POLLO LOCO ▼

▼ PARAJE CENTRAL

CALLE CENTRAL

ROAST CHICKEN ▼

CALLE EL CALVARIO

HOTEL IVANIA'S

MUSEO Y GALERÍA HÉROES Y MÁRTIRES ★

BANK ■

LA JAROCHITA ▼

CYBER-1 ■

POST OFFICE ■

POLICE ■ ▼ PASTELERÍA NORMA

CENTRO DE CULTURA ★

Parque San Juan

ENITEL ■ LA PARROQUIA LA ASUNCIÓN

BANCENTRO ■ *Central Park*

IGLESIA SAN JUAN

PALÍ ■

HOSPEDAJE MASAYITA

EL MERCADO VIEJO CRAFT MARKET

CHE GRIS

To New Market and Bus Terminal →

Parque San Miguel

BANPRO ■

BDF ■ INTERNET ■

▼ LA RHONDA

← To Cocojambo

LA EMILINA ÑATA ▼

CALLE MONIMBÓ

To Plaza Monimbó

0   100 yds
0   100 m

© AVALON TRAVEL

YEAR-ROUND FIESTA TOWN: A GUIDE TO MASAYA'S PARTIES

Masayans celebrate all year long, observing various religious, historical, and indigenous rites with a wild collage of marimba music, traditional costume, poetry, painting, food, drink, and age-old customs. Many of the dances are family traditions, in which certain roles – and their accompanying masks and costumes – are passed from generation to generation. Costumes are a key element of the festivals and are often elaborate and gorgeous.

A few weeks before Easter, the celebration of **San Lázaro** features believers promenading with their ornately costumed dogs, to thank their patron saint for keeping their household animals in good health.

The fiestas only get more interesting.

In the **Festival of the Cross,** celebrated in May, people exchange thousands of palm-thatch crosses in honor of La Señora de la Asunción. The virgin icon is carried to Monimbó in remembrance of the miracle that occurred there during the last eruption of Volcán Masaya's Santiago Crater, in which the virgin saved the city from hot ashes.

September-December are peak fiesta months in Masaya. Things get started with the official **fiestas patronales** on September 20, in honor of Patron Saint Jerónimo. Toward the end of the three-month celebration, look for the extravagant **Fiesta del Toro Venado,** on the last Sunday of October. It's similar to the North American Halloween, but instead of ghosts and goblins, Masayans don disguises that poke fun at their favorite politicians, clergy, and other public figures.

Held on the penultimate Friday of October, the **Fiesta de los Agüisotes** (Fiesta of the Bad Omens) is a nod to Nicaragua's darker side: Folks dress up as scary figures from local legends, such as the *chancha bruja,* the *mocuana,* and the *arre chavalo* (a headless priest from León).

Patron-saint celebrations end the first Sunday of December with the **Procesión de San Jerónimo.** This is perhaps the most stunning of Masaya's fiestas, as the statue of the city's patron saint is paraded through the streets amidst a sea of flowers. Look for the **Baile de las Inditas** (Dance of the Little Indian Girls), **Baile de Negras** (Dance of the Black Women), and the **Baile de Fantasía** (Dance of Fantasy). Every Sunday from September through December features a folk dance of some sort, a competition between rival troops, or even dancers that go from house to house performing short dances to marimba music.

In mid-January, the **Festival of San Sebastian** explodes with life and energy in the indigenous Monimbó barrio. The celebration's highlight is the **Baile de Chinegro de Mozote y Verga,** in which participants engage in a mock battle, hitting each other with big sticks and finally coming together in a peace ritual. The *tunkún* drum (a Maya instrument) beats out the rhythm of the dance, along with a whistle called a *pífano.* At the end of the ritual, everybody screams together:

"¡Viva San Sebastian!" ("Long live San Sebastian!")

"¡Viva el Mayordomo!" ("Long live the Master of the Parade!")

"¡Viva Santa Marta Vencedera!" ("Long live Saint Martha the Conqueror!")

La Novena del Niño Dios is an interesting December ritual in which small children are given pots, pans, whistles, and firecrackers and are sent into the streets at 5 A.M. to noisily call all the other children together for the 6 A.M. mass in celebration of the Christ child's birth.

Pieces and parcels of Masaya's festivals are found in the various *fiestas patronales* of the many surrounding pueblos, each of which present their own peculiar twist to the events. In mid-June, for example, San Juan de Oriente's party involves "warriors" dancing through the streets and whipping each other with stiffened bull penises.

La Rhonda, on the south side of the park, with beer, lots of space, and good appetizers.

If you're here on a weekend during baseball season (Nov.–May), be sure to catch the local team, San Fernando, who plays in **Estadio Roberto Clemente,** named for the Puerto Rico–born Pittsburgh Pirate who died in a plane crash in 1973 delivering aid to Nicaraguan earthquake victims. The tailgating scene atop the *malecón* may be one of the most scenic in the world. Tickets start at $0.50.

ACCOMMODATIONS

Along the highway and outside of town, Masaya's hotels tend to be pay-by-the-hour sex motels; avoid them. In town, lodging is basic but not exciting.

Under $10

◖ **Hotel Regis** (on Calle Central, 3.5 blocks north of the church on the main plaza, tel. 505/522-2300, $5 pp) has a dozen neat, clean rooms (including some for groups and families), with shared bath and fan, and a respectable breakfast for $2. The couple that runs the place is friendly, knowledgeable about things to do in the area, and speaks some English— however, they are strict about running a clean shop, look down on partying, and close their doors at 10 P.M. There are several other options on the same block, including **Hostal Mi Casa** (tel. 505/522-2500, $5 pp or $20 for a simple room with a/c) in a big, open, colorful space which includes the Fruti-Fruti smoothie bar and cafetín.

If you'd rather be closer to the discotecas and baseball stadium, get a bare-bones room in a family's home at **Hospedaje Masayita** (two blocks west of the central park, tel. 505/667-7055, $4 and up).

$10-25

◖ **Madera's Inn Hotel** (two blocks south of the fire station, tel. 505/522-5825, maderasinn @yahoo.com, $15–45). Some rooms have fan and shared bath, and more expensive ones have private bath and air-conditioning. The 12

rooms occupy two floors set around a beautifully furnished common room; you'll also find friendly service, Internet access, parking, tours, and laundry.

$25-50

A reasonable and newly renovated modern hotel, **Hotel Ivania's** (from Calvario church, 3.5 blocks west, tel. 505/522-7632, gerencia @hotelivanias.com, $35 s, 50 d) has 17 clean but plain rooms with air-conditioning, television, hot water, refrigerators, and tiled floors, all surrounding an attractive courtyard.

FOOD

Eateries close to El Mercado Viejo include **Pastelería Norma** (20 meters north of the Old Market), for baked goods, juices, and snacks, and **Che Gris** (on the east side of the Old Market), which offers traditional cooking in an air-conditioned setting. A livelier, more popular option is ◖ **Jarochito's** (tel. 505/522-4831, open 11 A.M.–10 P.M. daily), just north of the central park, for Mexican with a Nicaraguan twist, with plates from $3–8. A bit farther up the calle principal is **Comedor La Criolla** (open 7 A.M.–5 P.M. daily), serving excellent local breakfast and lunch for $2.50–$4. It's a great place to sit and enjoy a fresh juice drink.

Countless small places line both sides of the main street from the central park all the way up to the old train station, and they are great places to find out why Masayans refer to themselves as *"come-yucas"* (yucca eaters). You can sink your teeth into the juicy, greasy, fried, and roasted treasures at one of several locally famous *fritangas:* **Fritanga Alvarez** is across from the entrance to Santa Rosa; **Fritanga San Jerónimo** is a few blocks west of the church with the same name; **La Emilina Ñata en el Barrio Loco,** or Flat-nose Emilina's in the Crazy Neighborhood is open every day from 5 P.M. till its world-famous grilled beef runs out. Still another savory sidewalk barbecue option is **La Chepa Ratona,** next to the old train station.

INFORMATION

The INTUR office is located within the Old Market, open business hours (closed for lunch, tel. 505/522-7615). They might be able to answer specific questions about the area or upcoming events. Then again, they might not.

SERVICES

Hospital Hilario Sanchez Vásquez (on the highway toward Granada, tel. 505/522-2778) is the biggest facility in town. The large, blue police station (tel. 505/522-4222 or 505/522-2521) is half a block north of the Old Market across from Norma's bakery. Besides the multiple ATMs within the Old Market, numerous banks are close by: Bancentro on the west side of the Central Park and a BDF one block north of the Old Market. Several cheap and crowded Internet places line the south side of the central park. Both Correos de Nicaragua and a DHL Worldwide Express are available inside the Old Market compound to facilitate sending gifts and packages, and the ENITEL phone office is a block south of the old train station.

GETTING THERE AND AWAY

Nearly every southbound bus leaving Managua from Roberto Huembes passes Masaya, which is right on the highway, only 27 kilometers from Managua. Faster still are the Masaya- or Granada-bound *expresos* from the UCA leaving regularly 7 A.M.–9:30 P.M., arriving in Masaya's Parque San Miguel; from there, they depart for Managua 6 A.M.–8 P.M. The ride costs under $1. Less recommended is the *expreso* service between Masaya's Plaza de Monimbó and Mercado Oriental in Managua, first leaving Masaya at 3 A.M. and running through 7 P.M. Ordinary bus service leaves and arrives at the main terminal in the parking lot of the Mercado Nuevo.

Near Masaya

◖ VOLCÁN MASAYA NATIONAL PARK

An extraordinary and easy day trip from Managua, Masaya, or Granada, Volcán Masaya National Park (tel. 505/522-5415, open 9 A.M.–4:45 P.M. daily, $4) is Nicaragua's most impressive outdoor attraction and premier tourist site. There are very few volcanoes in the world where you can simply drive up to the crater edge and look into what the Spaniards declared to be the very "mouth of hell": that's exactly what Masaya offers, but there's a lot more. One of the most visibly active volcanoes in the country, Volcán Masaya emits a nearly constant plume of sulfurous gas, smoke, and sometimes ash, visible from as far away as the airport in Managua. From one of its craters, you can sometimes glimpse incandescent rock and magma. A visitors center (where they'll ask you to park your car facing out "just in case") will help you interpret the geology and ecology of the site, as will the park's impressive nature museum. For the more actively inclined, hiking trails cover a portion of the volcano's slopes.

Volcán Masaya was called Popogatepe (mountain that burns) by the Chorotegas, who feared it and interpreted eruptions as displays of anger to be appeased with sacrifices, often human. In the early 1500s, Father Francisco Bobadilla placed a cross at the crater lip in order to exorcise the devil within and protect the villages below. Not long afterward, though, thinking the volcano might contain gold instead of the devil both Friar Blas del Castillo and Gonzalo Fernandez de Oviedo lowered themselves into the crater on ropes to search. They found neither the devil nor gold but probably singed their eyebrows.

The park is actually composed of several geologically linked volcanic craters: Volcán Nindirí, which last erupted in 1670, and Volcán Masaya, which blew its top in 1772. The relatively new Santiago Crater was formed between the other two in 1852, and is inhabited by a

the cross at Volcán Masaya

paintings of the volcano as the Spaniards saw it. Consider one of the several guided tours ($10 pp, sign up at the visitors center), including an exciting night tour beginning at sunset. Of special interest is the walk to the Tzinancanostoc Bat Cave, a lava tube passageway melted out of solid rock.

Though most visitors only snap a few photos from the crater's edge before continuing, the park also contains several hiking trails through a veritable moonscape of lava formations and scrubby vegetation, making it easy to spend at least half a day here; carry lots of water and sunscreen (there is little to no shade); the trails are well worth your time and offer good opportunities to cross paths with some of the park's wildlife, including coyotes, deer, iguanas, and monkeys. The Coyote Trail will lead you east to the shore of the Laguna de Masaya.

Coyotepe

Just south of the volcano on a hill overlooking the highway, the battlements of this fort (open 8:30 A.M.–5 P.M., 365 days a year, $1) overlook the city of Masaya. Take a cab or hike up the road—the view of Masaya, its lagoon and volcano, both great lakes, and the far-reaching surrounding countryside is worth it; that's before you even descend into the dungeons. Built at the turn of the 20th century, this site witnessed a fierce battle between national troops and U.S. Marines in 1912. Somoza rehabilitated it as a particularly cruel prison. Today, Coyotepe is in the hands of the Nicaraguan Boy Scouts, who will accompany you through the pitch-black underground prison facilities in exchange for a small fee (for special attention, or at least a smile, greet your guide with the three-finger Scout salute and their motto in Spanish: *Siempre Listo*—Always Prepared).

Nindirí

Just north of the highway between the entrance to the national park and the city of Masaya, Nindirí was the most important and densely populated of the indigenous settlements in the area—up to 1,500 years before the arrival of the Spanish. In Chorotega, its name means Hill of

remarkable species of parakeet that nests contentedly in the rocky side of the crater walls, oblivious to the toxic gases and the scientists who had thought such a sulphurous environment would be uninhabitable. You might see these *chocoyos del cráter* (crater parakeets) from the parking area along the crater's edge.

As for the sensation of "just in case," the danger is quite real. In April 2000, the Santiago crater burped up a single volcanic boulder that plummeted to earth, crushing an unfortunate Italian tourist's car in the parking lot.

Visiting Volcán Masaya

The exhibits at the **Visitors Interpretation Center** and museum include three-dimensional dioramas of Nicaragua and Central America, models of active volcanoes, and remnants of indigenous sacrifice urns and musical instruments found deep in the volcano's caves; there is also a display of old lithographs and

MASAYA

© RANDALL WOOD

Coyotepe Fortress, near Masaya

the Small Pig, and its principal attraction is the 1,000-artifact collection in the **Museo Tenderí** (named after a local cacique) that celebrates pre-Columbian culture. Also, ask around about the Cailagua site, with petroglyphs overlooking the Laguna de Masaya. During the last week of July, the festival for patron saint Santa Ana employs many of the ancient dance, costume, and music rituals popular to the whole Masaya and Carazo region.

LAGUNA DE APOYO

Nicaragua's cleanest and most enticing swimming hole is Laguna de Apoyo, just outside of Masaya. Actually a lake that formed in the drowned volcanic crater of the long extinct Apoyo Volcano, the lagoon floor reaches 200 meters in depth—the lowest point in all of Central America. Considering how easy it is to reach the lagoon, it is surprisingly untouristed. Despite its continued seismicity—a minor earthquake in 2000 under the crater-rim town of Catarina caused Apoyo's water to slosh back and forth like a teapot and

wrecked a few homes—for the most part the volcano is considered dormant, and a thick green forest has grown up the slopes over the years. These slopes harbor a few hiking trails and are protected from further development by law. The crater hosts a few fish species found nowhere else on earth; scientists at the Proyecto Ecologico are studying them. If you hike through the forests, expect to observe species of toucan, hummingbirds, blue jays, howler and white-face monkeys (which are prone to fling their feces at you if you approach), and rare butterflies. You will find very few places on earth quite like this charming, isolated community.

Accommodations and Food

The number of places to eat or lodge along the western shore of the crater lake is slowly increasing and diversifying, despite local grumbling about illegal development of the waterfront. At any establishment, pay $6–10 to stay for the day and enjoy the docks, pool, inner tubes, hammocks, and other facilities.

The area has no stores or shops to speak of, and few services, so either pack your essentials before coming, or count on one of the local hotels or restaurants.

The Monkey Hut (tel. 505/552-4028, www.thebeardedmonkey.com, $9 dorm beds and hammocks, $15 s, 20 d with shared bath and fan) is a well-liked retreat on a beautiful terraced piece of land at the water's edge, with a fully equipped kitchen and a small selection of rooms. Soft drinks, water, wine, and beer can be purchased at the hut—all other supplies need to be packed in. Make reservations at the Bearded Monkey in Granada. 【 **Crater's Edge** (tel. 505/860-8689, www.craters-edge.com, $11 pp dorm, $22–44 private room) is also geared toward budget travelers, offering terraced patios, waterside bar, and floating dock. A daily shuttle bus leaves Hostel Oasis in Granada at 10 A.M. and returns at 4 P.M. Rooms in the decent dormitory have a fabulous sunrise view. Also offered are three meals a day served at the restaurant, Wi-Fi, and local crafts for sale.

The **Proyecto Ecologico Spanish School and Hostel** (tel. 505/882-3992, www.gaianicaragua.org) is one of the oldest operations in the crater, a not-for-profit research station and Spanish school. Stay for $8 pp shared dorm, $19 d with fan but shared bath, breakfast included. They organize fishing trips, scuba diving expeditions ($60/tank), and the chance to participate in one of several volunteer reforestation brigades each year (see *Spanish Schools* in the *Essentials* chapter for more; all-inclusive Spanish school packages start at $210 per week). There is nowhere better to speak with knowledgeable ecologists who can help interpret this unique region, and the home-cooked meals ($3) are well recommended.

At "Grandma's," **Posada Ecologica La Abuela** (tel. 505/880-0368, www.posadaecologicalaabuela.com, $55 d) find a series of wooden docks, rocker swings for splashing around in the water, and great views. The wooden cabañas are very comfortable and well appointed, with air-conditioning, private bath, nice mattresses; also great facilities for groups.

MASAYA

© JOSHUA BERMAN

Laguna de Apoyo is inviting on a hot day.

Neither hostel nor hotel, **Guest House La Orquidea** (tel. 505/872-1866, www.laorquidea nicaragua.com, $60 per room) is a stylish two-bedroom house, fully equipped for a relaxing stay, from your balcony to the boats and toys. Groups can rent it for just a little over $13 per person, healthy breakfast provided.

On the opposite end of the road, **(San Simian Lakeside Bungalows** (tel. 505/813-6866, www.sansimian.com, $50 includes large breakfast), the sister hotel of Hotel Casa San Francisco in Granada, is a lovely water-side group of five private bungalows, each of which has a slightly different theme built from natural materials like thatch and bamboo. The tasteful, rustic rooms have bamboo beds with comfy mattresses, mosquito nets, fans, and fun outdoor showers and gardens; more features include great on-site meals, bar, and relaxing dock with water toys. Nearby trailheads lead up into the jungle and along the shore.

Norome Resort and Villas (tel. 505/883-9093, www.noromevillas.com; Granada office on the southeast corner of the central park, tel. 505/552-2552), one of Apoyo's originals, is a perhaps overbuilt complex of 66 Caribbean-style villas ($85 d, $200 villa), featuring private bath with bathtubs, air-conditioning, TV/DVD, and kitchenettes. The restaurant and bar perched over the water are stunning, and the food is respectable (meals $4–9). Norome goes for the upscale market with features like massage, whirlpool tub, and a pool. Travelers have given it mixed reviews: Its immensity can make it feel a bit lonely, and the recent power outages have led to some maintenance problems.

Getting There and Away

Laguna de Apoyo is about a 20-minute ride from either Masaya or Granada, and about an hour from the airport in Managua. There are two paved roads that go up and over the crater lip and down to the water's edge; one originates on Carretera Masaya, at a spot called *el*

The Monkey Hut, a backpacker retreat at Laguna de Apoyo

© JOSHUA BERMAN

puentecito; the other branches off the Masaya–Catarina road. They join just before passing through the village of Valle de Laguna, where you'll turn right at the T then make a quick left to begin your descent (pay a $1 entrance fee if driving). The road winds downward until the paved section ends exactly at the gate to former president Alemén's vacation home.

Many visitors split the $15 taxi fee from either Granada or Masaya, though it's hardly necessary to spend that much, with regular backpacker buses leaving Hostel Oasis and the Bearded Monkey in Granada, charging only a couple of bucks each. Public buses headed for *bajo al plan* (i.e., lakefront) cost under $1 and leave the main Masaya market terminal at 10:30 A.M. and 3:10 P.M.; or you can hop one of the hourly buses for Valle de Laguna, then walk (30 minutes downhill) or wait for a stray taxi. Mototaxis run between the *puentecito* and Valle de Laguna. Three public buses can get you back up the hill, leaving at 6 A.M., 11:10 A.M., and 4:40 P.M. (3 P.M. on Sunday is the last bus), or ask at your hotel about booking a spot on the backpacker buses running to Granada—essentially a charter service.

The Pueblos Blancos and Carazo

Escaping the heat of Managua or Granada is as easy as a 40-minute bus ride to the Pueblos Blancos and Carazo, two regions that occupy a breezy 500-meter-high *meseta* south of Managua and are thus far cooler and more relaxing. The Pueblos Blancos, or White Villages, are named for the purity of color of their churches (some of which, inexplicably, are now other colors). They are separated to the north by the Sierras de Managua, to the east by the slopes of Volcán Masaya, to the south by the Laguna de Apoyo and Volcán Mombacho, and to the west by the dry, desolate decline toward the Pacific Ocean. Each town is well known for something particular—bamboo craftwork, wicker chairs, black magic, folk dances, Sandino's birthplace, crater lakes, beaches, or interesting festivals. Visiting the pueblos is an easy day trip best appreciated if you have a car, which permits you to tour furniture workshops, coffee plantations, or outdoor plant nurseries.

In nearby Carazo, the January celebration of San Sebastián is a dramatic and colorful festival not to be missed. Diriamba is home to Nicaragua's national soccer team but baseball is given equal attention; games are exciting and fun. This is also the gateway to several Pacific beaches quieter than their more developed neighbors.

ORIENTATION AND GETTING AROUND

Renting a car or taxi is the best way to visit the Pueblos, but you can get around almost as easily with the *expreso* minivan system. No more than 10 or 12 kilometers separate any two towns, all of which are easily accessible from Masaya, Granada, and Managua. Buses to the Pueblos Blancos leave from Huembes, continue south on the Carretera Masaya, and then turn west into the hills at various points, depending on the route. The Carazo buses—to Jinotepe and Diriamba—travel via Carretera Sur and leave from the Mercado Israel Lewites and from a lot across from the UCA.

◖ CATARINA MIRADOR

This hillside pueblo clings to the verdant lip of the spectacular Laguna de Apoyo crater lake. The Mirador is a blustery cliffside walkway and restaurant complex at the edge of the crater with one of the best panoramic views in Nicaragua—look for the distant red-tiled roofs and cathedral spires of Granada, broad Lake Cocibolca behind, and on a clear day, the twin volcanic peaks of Ometepe. Roaming marimba and guitar players will serenade you for a small fee (negotiate before they begin playing). Locals visit Catarina for its ornamental plant nurseries and the shops of local

© JOSHUA BERMAN

MASAYA

The view from the Catarina Mirador is one of the best in the country.

artisans and basket-makers whose shops begin at roadside. Vehicles pay $1 each to enter the Mirador.

(Hotel Casa Catarina (tel. 505/558-0034 or 505/558-0227, reservaciones@hotelcasacatarina.com, www.casacatarina.com, $65 s, 75 d) is a new, modern, and well-liked three-star hotel. It's the only choice other than the basic but clean **Hotel Jaaris** or **Hospedaje Euro,** both about $10 and one block west (i.e. downhill) from the Catarina church.

Finally, while Catarina is clearly popular with the crowds, some travelers are now also discovering the Diriomito Mirador to be just as fun.

SAN JUAN DE ORIENTE

San Juan potters craft attractive ceramic vases, pots, plates, and more, in both a proud celebration of pre-Columbian styles and modern inspirations. Shop at one of the small cooperatives along the entrance to town, or in the many tiny displays in people's homes as you walk through the narrow streets. Many artisans

are glad to invite you back into their workshops for a tour.

DIRIÁ AND DIRIOMO

Named for the indigenous Dirian people and their leader, Diriangén (the famed rebel cacique and martyr whose spilled blood at the hands of the conquistadores is immortalized in Carlos Mejía Godoy's anthem, "Nicaragua Nicaragüita"), Diriá and Diriomo face each other on both sides of the highway. Both towns are well loved for their unique celebrations throughout the year, mixing elements of pre-Columbian, Catholic, and bizarre regional traditions (like the "dicking" festival in which participants smack each other with dried-out bull penises, sometimes practiced in San Juan de Oriente as well). Diriá, on the east, has a *mirador* smaller and less-frequented than the more famous one at Catarina, as well as additional trails down to the Laguna de Apoyo. Across the highway, Diriomo is renowned for its sorcery: The intrepid traveler looking for a love potion or revenge should seek out one of the pueblo's *brujos* (or at least read the book *Sofía de los Presagios;* see *Suggested Reading* in the *Resources* chapter).

Less famous than Catarina, Diriomo has a crater overlook of its own: **Diriomito Mirador,** which occasionally offers paragliding, or *parapente* (tel. 505/522-2009).

NIQUINOHOMO

"The valley of the warriors," in Nahuatl, produced a famous warrior indeed: Augusto César Sandino, born there at the turn of the 20th century. Sandino's childhood home off the northwest corner of the park has been restored as a library and museum. A 4,000-pound, solid bronze statue of the man, with the famous hat and bandolier of bullets around his waist, stands at attention at the east side of town. Niquinohomo's 320-year-old church is also worth a look.

MASATEPE

Masatepe (Nahuatl for "place of the deer") is a quiet pueblo of about 12,000 that explodes in revelry the first Sunday of every June during its famous **Hípica** (horse parade). Stick around after the festivities for a steaming bowl of Masatepe's culinary claim to fame—*sopa de mondongo* (cow tripe soup), served hot in front of the town's gorgeous, architecturally unique church. The *hípica* is just one part of the *fiestas patronales* in honor of la Santísima Trinidad, the black Christ icon a Chorotegan found in the trunk of a tree during the years of the Spanish colony. Find other meals in the Bar Sarapao or Eskimo shop on the north side of the park.

Outside of the city, both sides of the highway are lined with the workshops of the extraordinarily talented Masatepe carpenters, whose gorgeous, handcrafted hardwood and rattan furniture is prized throughout the country. You'll wish you could fit more of it in your luggage (a set of chairs and a coffee table go for about $100), but console yourself instead with a comfortable, old-fashioned hardwood rocking chair. They'll disassemble and pack it down to airline-acceptable size for you for a small fee.

If driving to Masatepe from the south, save

MASAYA

© JOSHUA BERMAN

Los Pueblos Blancos are named for their white churches.

time for a meal at **Mi Teruño Masatepino** (on the east side of the road, just north of the turnoff for Pio XII and Nandasmo), a delicious open-air restaurant featuring Nicaragua's traditional country cuisine.

SAN MARCOS

San Marcos is sort of the hub of the Pueblos Blancos and hosts Nicaragua's best (and most expensive) university, the **Ave Maria College of the Americas** (three blocks south of the park, www.avemaria.edu.ni), a Catholic, bilingual, four-year liberal arts university with about 400 students and a sister campus in Ann Arbor, Michigan. Before 1998, its modern facilities belonged to the University of Mobile (Alabama). Ave Maria is one of the beneficiaries of Catholic conservative and Domino Pizza founder, Thomas Monaghan. Not much to see here other than the church and town square, though both are lovely. There's one hotel: **Hotel Casablanca** (two blocks east of the church's southeast corner, tel. 505/535-2717, www.hotelcasablanca.com.ni, $40) and several small restaurants; **La Casona** (near the park) is particularly recommended for its food and pleasant owner.

MARIPOSA ECOHOTEL AND SPANISH SCHOOL

Tucked into the forest off the road to the village of San Juan de la Concepción (also known as La Concha, 12 kilometers west of Ticuantepe, under an hour from Managua), this unique hideaway has spurred a stream of rave reviews from our readers. **Mariposa** (tel. 505/418-4638, www.spanishschoolnica.com) is a wonderful example of sustainable tourism, using revenue to fund a range of grassroots environmental and community projects. Guests are invited to help with the projects, from reforestation and chicken raising to literacy, education, and animal rescue. The hotel and rooms have excellent views of Volcán Masaya, use solar and wind power, and there is an organic farm with coffee, bananas, free range eggs and lots of fruit. Meals are typical Nicaraguan breakfast, buffet-style lunch (salads, meat, and vegetarian), and

family-style dinner. The hotel rooms are decorated with local handicrafts, each with their own bathroom and fan. There is also a swimming pool, riding horses, and hiking trails; also a fully stocked library, quality one-on-one Spanish school, and the manager, Paulette Goudge, PhD, offers a three-month course in the "Politics of Development." This is a great place for families. Rooms are only $12 a night, $80 a week, or look into their all-inclusive Spanish school packages for $250 a week.

JINOTEPE AND DIRIAMBA (CARAZO)
Jinotepe

Jinotepe (Xilotepetl, or "field of baby corn") is a sometimes-sleepy, sometimes-bustling villa of 27,000 set around **La Iglesia Parroquial de Santiago** (built in 1860) and a lively park shaded by the canopy of several immense hardwood trees. Thanks to a branch of UNAN, Jinotepe's student population keeps things youthful and lively, and its outdoor market is fun. Don't miss the beautiful two-block-long mural on the nursing school (three blocks west of the park's northwest corner) and the towering statue of Pope John Paul II in front of the church. While you're there, enjoy an icy, chocolatey *cacao con leche* in the kiosk under the shade trees of one of Nicaragua's shadiest parks.

Basecamp International Centers (tel. 866/646-4693, nicaragua@basecampcenters .com) has an inexpensive dorm, private rooms for $28, breakfast, and can arrange volunteer opportunities. BIC is located from ENITEL, two blocks west, half a block south. The **Hotel Casa Mateo** (one block north of the park and two west, tel. 505/532-3284, U.S. tel. 410/878-2252, $35–55) has 40 rooms with TV, private bath, hot water, and fan; also laundry service, a guard for your car, a restaurant, and Wi-Fi. Reservations are required. This is a nonprofit ministry hotel run by Glenn and Lynne Schweitzer, pastors and missionaries from Maryland. They offer special group rates ($15 pp) and also run a health clinic, a home for abused children, and a vocational center.

THE FESTIVAL OF SAINT SEBASTIÁN

Every pueblo's *fiestas patronales* have something that make them unique, but Diriamba's celebration of the Holy Martyr San Sebastián stands above the rest as Nicaragua's most authentic connection to its indigenous roots. Many of the dances, songs, and costumes are true to traditions that predate the arrival of the Spanish by hundreds of years. But this is no nostalgia act – indeed, the integration of pre-Columbian ritual with Catholicism and the telling of modern history is as fascinating as the colors, costumes, and music.

This celebration is actually three fiestas for the price of one, since icons of San Santiago of Jinotepe, San Marcos of San Marcos, and San Sebastián of Diriamba have been observed together since the three of them first traveled from Spain, landing at nearby Casares beach. The icons are still believed to have the special bond they formed during their journey, and they get together to celebrate this three times a year during the fiesta of each of their towns. Santiago and Marcos meet up at the *tope* (end of the road) in Dolores on (or around) January 19, where they are danced around the village to a bombardment of cheers and homemade fireworks. The next day, they reunite with their pal, Sebastián, in Diriamba, where the town has been partying for four days in preparation.

The following day is the peak of activities, the actual **Día del Santo,** marked by special masses and, sometimes, groups of tourists that come to view the long, raucous procession, famous for its theatrical dances and costumes. The following are the most important acts:

The Dance of Toro Huaco is of indigenous ancestry and features peacock feather hats and a multigeneration snake dance, with the youngest children bringing up the rear and an old man with a special tambourine and whistle up front. **El Güegüense,** also called the **Macho Ratón,** is recognizable for its masks and costumes depicting burdened-down donkeys and the faces of Spanish conquistadores. The Güegüense (from the old word *güegüe,* which means something like grumpy old man) is a hard-handed social satire with cleverly vulgar undertones that depicts the indigenous peoples' first impression of the Spanish – it has been called the oldest comedy act on the continent. **El Gigante** is a dance that depicts the biblical story of David and Goliath, and **La Danza de las Inditas** is a group act, recognizable by the white cotton costumes and the sound of the marimba. Most of the dancers are carrying out a family tradition that has been kept for dozens of generations, and each usually has a grandma-led support team on the sidelines to make sure their costumes and performances are kept in order.

A true believer will tell you that Diriamba's fiesta begins not on January 19, but on February 2 of the previous year, when the official *fiesteros* apply for roles in the upcoming celebration; they then begin more than 11 months of preparation, all of which is seen as a display of faith and thanks to their beloved San Sebastián. Those that don't show their devotion by dancing or playing music do so by carrying the icons or fulfilling promises to walk a certain number of blocks on their knees, sometimes until bloody.

Bring plenty of film, and be sure to try the official beverage of the festival: *chicha con genibre,* a ginger-tinted, slightly fermented cornmeal drink. Most of the masks and costumes in the productions are also for sale, as are homemade action figures depicting the various dance characters.

There are dozens of small, decent eateries, but Managua expats actually drive here to enjoy **(** **Pizzería Coliseo** (open 12:30–9 P.M. Tues.–Sun., $5 and up), a legitimate Italian restaurant. Rome *originario* Fausto has been preparing delicious Italian pizzas and pasta for more than 20 years. The place is famous—ask anyone and they'll guide you there.

Diriamba

Diriamba's **Festival of San Sebastian** in the third week of January is an annual religious, theatrical, folklore celebration uninterrupted since colonial days. Featuring both pagan and Catholic elements, it is without rival in western Nicaragua (see sidebar *Year-Round Fiesta Town: A Guide to Masaya's Parties*), comparable perhaps only to Bluefield's Palo de Mayo. Enjoy the **Museo Ecológico de Tropico Seco** (tel. 505/422-2129, open Mon.–Fri.), which provides good background on much of the region's unique dry tropical ecosystem. The MARENA office here ministers some of the local turtle-nesting refuges.

Book early if you plan to stay here the week of the festival: On the boulevard heading out of town, **(** **Jardín and Vivero Tortuga Verde** (tel. 505/534-2948, www.ecolodgecarazo.com, $25–45) has a half dozen clean, comfortable rooms set amidst a beautiful garden filled with statues; truly a pleasant and peaceful guesthouse atmosphere and careful, personal attention by the owner. They can also show you around their converted coffee plantation now rife with lush flowers and vegetation; ask about their beach house in Casares. **Hospedaje Diriangén** (one block east, half block south of the Shell Station, tel. 505/422-2428, $7 pp with private bath and fan), is clean enough and safe. The **Casa Hotel Diriamba** (one block east of the clock tower, tel. 505/523-2523, $11 d) is more central.

Abundance Farm

This is a true rural tourism opportunity, about 30–45 minutes outside Diriamba or Jinotepe.

Abundance Farm (tel. 505/416-5355, www.abundancefarm.com) allows you to get a taste of Nicaraguan *campesino* life, from chopping wood and cooking beans, to harvesting corn, and feeding the chickens; guests also have opportunities to volunteer in a local school and learn Spanish. Your hosts, Alicia and Leonidas, will be happy to show you their local waterfall and tell you the story about the hydroelectric dam. Accommodations (dormitories and rooms) are extremely primitive—and cheap, from $5 a night; fresh, healthy food is only $4 a day for three meals. Abundance Farm is part of the WWOOF program (World Wide Opportunities on Organic Farms) and offers you chicken lovers long-term guest possibilities as well.

Getting There and Away

Sleek, comfortable *interlocal* minibuses leave for both Jinotepe and Carazo from the UCA in Managua until 10 P.M. and much slower *rutas* leave from Terminal Israel Lewites.

From Jinotepe, buses leave from the COOTRAUS terminal—a dirt lot along the Pan-American Highway directly north of the park—at all hours for Managua, Masaya, Nandaime, and Rivas. Microbuses to Managua leave from the unofficial Sapasmapa terminal on the south side of the Instituto Alejandro, 4:45 A.M.–7:30 P.M. ($0.75). Your most comfortable choice is one of the *interlocales* to Diriamba and San Marcos queued up on the street in front of the Super Santiago—only the front one will load passengers, departing when the van is full.

From Diriamba, a fleet of *interlocales* run to and from Jinotepe for about $0.25, 6 A.M.–9 P.M. daily from a spot right next to the clock tower.

Walk east and take your first left to find *microbus expresos* to Managua's Israel Market and the UCA for $1, 5 A.M.–7 P.M. A little farther east at the first *caseta* (booth) on the left, you can ask about all the buses that pass from Jinotepe (Managua: 4:30 A.M.–6 P.M.; Masaya: 5 A.M.–6 P.M.).

CARAZO BEACHES

Humble, rundown **La Boquita** and **Casares** still attract local families rather than the real estate-hawking jet set. That's their attraction. On a big swell, the surf is up at both places, and you'll likely be the only gringo in the lineup. On shore, visiting the volcanic rock outcrops will keep you entertained. Note that this area—particularly La Boquita—is worth avoiding during Semana Santa and New Year's Day when they are overrun by a drunken mob scene.

Rent some shade under one of the ranchos, where you can order drinks, food, and wandering musicians. There is one nice hotel on the beach, **Hotel Palmas del Mar** (tel. 505/552-8715, pglo@tmx.com.ni, $40) and a few undifferentiated *hospedajes* with cheap, basic rooms for under $15.

Just down the coast, the beach at Casares is uncomfortably short on shade—but it's also short on crowds, has a decent hotel, and features a long, wide beach great for watching the fishing boats coming in and out. On the drive between La Boquita and Casares, seek out **El Pozo del Padre,** a self-contained rocky bathtub that's loads of fun at high tide.

La Boquita and Casares are 35 kilometers due west of Diriamba. Public transportation leaves from the main market on the highway east of the clock tower. Express microbuses leave every 20 minutes for the 40-minute, $0.75 ride to La Boquita 6:20 A.M.–6 P.M. Regular buses take 90 minutes and leave between 6:40 A.M. and 6:30 P.M.—they like to turn off their engines and coast the last part. From the beach at La Boquita the first bus leaves at 5 A.M., the last one at 6 P.M.

Centro Ecoturístico La Máquina

This is one of the "private wild reserves" protected by MARENA and managed by the landowners; it remains almost completely unvisited by tourists. Visit a waterfall, overlook, and picnic facilities, and enjoy a shallow bathing area; short hiking trails lead through the forest. Take a bus or drive from Diriamba toward La Boquita; La Máquina is located halfway (15 minutes) around Km 58 (look for the sign on the right).

MASAYA

RIVAS AND LA ISLA DE OMETEPE

South of Managua, the land crumples suddenly into high cloudy ridges and the wind-blown peak of Las Nubes (934 meters) and then falls off slowly until it spills into south-western Nicaragua's verdant plains. Here Lake Cocibolca presses the land into a narrow belt that barely separates the lake from the Pacific Ocean. In fact, geological evidence suggests at one point, it didn't separate them at all, and Lake Cocibolca once flowed across this slim margin of land to the west, emptying into the Pacific near the fishing community of Brito rather than down the Río San Juan into the Atlantic Ocean, as it does today.

The isthmus of Rivas is rich with history. Although known as the land of Nicarao, the area was first inhabited by the Kiribisis tribe, whom the more powerful Chorotegas pushed aside. The Nicaraos came afterward, and by the time the Spanish "discovered" the region, had been resident there for at least seven generations. Rivas, a languorous colonial town of traders and farmers, watched hundreds of thousands of passengers sailing between New York and California pass through in horse-drawn carts between San Jorge and San Juan del Sur; this was the only dry land crossing of the entire gold rush journey. At about the same time, one of filibuster William Walker's first military defeats took place here. These days, Rivas draws less attention than the coastal communities of San Juan del Sur and the island of Ometepe, but retains a colonial charm appreciated by many.

But it's hard to compete with Ometepe for attention. The magnificent twin-peaked

HIGHLIGHTS

Iglesia Parroquial de San Pedro: This old church in Rivas has changed very little since the days thousands of gold rush passengers rode by it in horse-drawn carriages (page 105).

Punta Jesús María: This gives you a unique sand-spit beach experience where you can mingle with the locals and drink a cold one in Concepción's shadow (page 119).

Reserva Charco Verde: The beaches, short trails, abundant vegetation, and friendly accommodations make this a pleasant retreat (page 120).

Volcán Maderas: On the sleeping volcano's slopes you'll find the inspiring farm Finca Magdalena, pre-Columbian petroglyphs, and forests full of wildlife (page 125).

Río Istián: Paddling a kayak through these still waters early in the morning or during sunset is breathtaking (page 127).

Cascada San Ramón: A rewarding hike and a frigid mountain waterfall you'll never forget (page 127).

LOOK FOR (TO FIND RECOMMENDED SIGHTS, ACTIVITIES, DINING, AND LODGING.

Isla de Ometepe rises like a crown from the center of Lake Cocibolca. An intensely volcanic island steeped in tradition and mystery, Ometepe is the ancestral home of the Nahuatl people and an increasingly enjoyable destination for travelers, with multiple sandy beaches, secluded swimming holes, a network of trails, and of course two breathtaking volcanoes: one hot, one cold (the former remains quite active). It's worth visiting Nicaragua to see this island alone.

Travel in southwestern Nicaragua is pleasant because it does not suffer the same intense, grinding poverty prevalent in the drier lands of the north and west. It rains more in the south, and the rivers flow nearly year-round. The volcanic soils on Lake Cocibolca's western shore are rich and productive. Cattle graze lazily in immense, lucrative ranches and sugarcane fields drape the valleys south of the foot of Mombacho, one of Nicaragua's most picturesque peaks.

PLANNING YOUR TIME

Ometepe should not be missed on all but the shortest trips to Nicaragua, as the scenery, water sports, hiking possibilities, and overall ambience are among Nicaragua's finest. Ometepe offers in a nutshell a little bit of everything Nicaragua has to offer, from history to swimming holes and waterfalls, and from volcanic trekking to horseback riding, all in an environment travelers routinely rave about as relaxing and delightful. You could feasibly travel to and

RIVAS

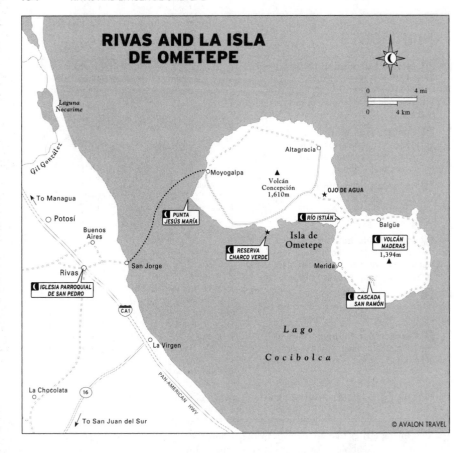

RIVAS AND LA ISLA DE OMETEPE

Laguna Nocarime

Gil González

To Managua

Potosí

Buenos Aires

Rivas
IGLESIA PARROQUIAL DE SAN PEDRO

San Jorge

CA1

La Virgen

La Chocolata   16

PAN-AMERICAN HWY

To San Juan del Sur

Moyogalpa

PUNTA JESÚS MARÍA

Volcán Concepción 1,610m

Altagracia

OJO DE AGUA

RÍO ISTIÁN

Isla de Ometepe

RESERVA CHARCO VERDE

Merida

Balgüe

VOLCÁN MADERAS 1,394m

CASCADA SAN RAMÓN

L a g o

C o c i b o l c a

0   4 mi

0   4 km

© AVALON TRAVEL

from the island in a single day, but it would be folly, as you would barely scratch the surface and miss out on the fun activities, all of which require a more languid pace. Rather, allow at least two days and a night (and an extra day and night if you'd like to hike a volcano, which is a full day activity in itself).

You will probably visit Rivas on the way to and from San Juan del Sur; half a day is acceptable to walk around the historical sites, appreciate the cathedral, and perhaps take in a museum, and this is an appropriate way to

stay connected to Nicaragua, as San Juan del Sur by contrast is increasingly gringo. Travelers with a more leisurely schedule can easily spend another half day enjoying the lakeshore in San Jorge before continuing to Ometepe.

Note though that travel in this region requires careful coordination of transport, as you can easily lose up to a half day waiting for boats and buses. Sunday on Ometepe is particularly difficult unless you have rented a car, which can be expensive but might save you a valuable travel day.

Rivas

Southern Nicaragua's most important town center, Rivas is a commercial center whose small population (under 50,000) help it retain an old-world charm. Few travelers travel specifically to Rivas as a destination proper, but it remains an important companion town for San Juan del Sur, providing a better selection of medical, banking, and shopping services. Rivas is also the site of a Costa Rican consulate, in case you have immigration issues. Don't discount it as inconsequential however; it's one of Nicaragua's more pleasant cities, charismatic and enjoyable in its own right, and not lacking in historical sites worth visiting.

Rivas is often hot because of its low altitude, but a cool lake breeze from Lake Cocibolca makes it bearable. Rivas is known as Ciudad de los Mangos due to the abundance of the trees in and around the city; swarms of chatty *chocoyos* (parakeets) feast on the fruit, their calls filling the skies around sunset. Rivas was known as Valle de la Ermita de San Sebastián until 1717, when a delegation of pious villagers traveled to Guatemala, the capital of the republic at that time, to request their little town be declared a villa with the name of La Pura y Limpia Concepción de Nuestra Señora la Virgen María. Capitán General del Reino Francisco Rodríguez de Rivas granted the request, and to thank him, the villagers modified the name to La Villa de la Pura y Limpia Concepción de Rivas de Nicaragua. Thankfully for travelers and mapmakers, over time the name contracted to something shorter.

SIGHTS AND ATTRACTIONS
◖ Iglesia Parroquial de San Pedro

Rivas's obvious centerpiece is a well-loved historical monument repainted in 2007. Built in the 18th century, the Church of San Pedro has witnessed the California gold rush, William Walker, the Sandinista revolution, and the 21st-century real estate boom. As you take in the details of the church's pleasing colonial

design, remember that every single gold rush–bound passenger that traversed Nicaragua in the days of Cornelius Vanderbilt's steamship line passed under its shadow. It is today, as always, a peaceful place to seek refuge; mass is held evenings around 6 P.M.

Other Churches and Museums

Four blocks west of the park at the town's center, the **Iglesia de San Francisco** was built in 1778 and was the first convent of the Franciscan friars. A beautiful statue commemorates the devotion of the friars to both God and their work. When they began construction of the nearby Bancentro, an underground tunnel was discovered that linked the Iglesia de San Francisco with the plaza (the open area adjacent to the central park's north side); the tunnel passes beneath the library (one door east of Bancentro). Researchers speculate it was probably dug at the same time as the church, meaning it was in place and probably used during the Battle of Rivas, when the plaza was the site of a military barracks.

Rivas is also the birthplace of several presidents of the republic, including Máximo Jérez (Liberal, governed from June 8, 1818 to August 12, 1881), Adén Cárdenas (Conservative, governed from March 1, 1883 to March 1, 1887), and most recently, Violeta Barrios de Chamorro (Coalition, governed from April 25, 1990 to January 10, 1997). Chamorro's childhood home is located across the street from the Iglesia Parroquial de San Pedro's south side. Several direct descendants of William Walker also continue to reside in Rivas.

Rivas has its own history museum: the **Museo de Historia y Antropología de Rivas** (open 8 A.M.–noon and 2–5 P.M. Mon.–Fri., only in the morning Sat., foreign travelers $1), set on the western side of town in a 200-year-old house that was once part of a cacao and indigo plantation. Once known as the Casa Hacienda Santa Úrsula, on June 29, 1855, William Walker and his men were defeated

RIVAS

To Managua

To San Jorge and Ometepe

ESSO

SHELL

HOSPEDAJE PRIMAVERA

HOSPEDAJE COCO

SUPERMERCADO PANAMERICANA

TEXACO

HOSPEDAJE LIDIA

INTERNET

MONUMENT TO EMMANUEL MONGALO Y RUBIO ★

FARMACIA RIVAS

PAN-AMERICAN HWY

BASEBALL STADIUM

RESTAURANT AND BAR EL PRINCIPE

CAT

To San Juan del Sur, Peñas Blancas, and Costa Rica

HOSPEDAJE HILMOR

IGLESIA PARROQUIAL DE SAN PEDRO

RESTAURANTE/ HOSPEDAJE EL ESPAÑOL

PASTRIES

PIZZA HOT

ESKIMO

BAR & RESTAURANTE LA CARRETA

EX-PRESIDENT CHAMORRO'S BIRTHPLACE

Central Park

CHOP SUEY

TITO'S BAR

LABORATORIA-CLINICA MARIA INMACULADA

BANKS

COMSIS

EL MERCADITO (EXPRESS BUSES)

PALI

HOTEL NICAROL

BDF

BANCENTRO

POST OFFICE

SODA RAVUELA

POLICE

SUPER POLLO

HOSPEDAJE Y BILLARES LOS LAURELES

BUS TERMINAL

MUSEO DE HISTORIA ★

To Costa Rican Consulate

FARMACIA LA MERCED

IGLESIA DE SAN FRANCISCO

RESTAURANTE EL MESSON

To Cemetery and La Chocolata

200 yds
200 m
0
0

© AVALON TRAVEL

Rivas's cathedral, the Iglesia Parroquial de San Pedro, witnessed the Gold Rush.

here in a heroic battle Nicaraguans are still proud of. The Battle of Rivas, as it became known, was one of the first manifestations of Nicaragua's growing sense of independence in the late 19th century; in fact, los Rivenses claim that "nationalism began in Rivas." The museum has a healthy collection of pre-Columbian pottery, as well as domestic utensils from the 18th and 19th centuries including kerosene lamps, silverware, and hand tools. The building itself evokes the lifestyle of the old farming community; more exciting are several old maps of the region. Some books are for sale.

The **Monument to Emmanuel Mongalo y Rubio** marks the final resting place of a young Rivas teacher who lived here in the mid-1800s. Mongalo y Rubio gained his fame during the Battle of Rivas by setting fire to the Mesón (the museum building) where Walker and his men had sought refuge; as they abandoned the blazing building, they were captured or shot.

Another museum piece in its own right, the **Biblioteca Pública de Rivas** next to Bancentro is one of the oldest still-standing buildings in Nicaragua, dating back to at least the early 17th century. Among its various incarnations it was a secondary school founded in 1872 by Máximo Jérez and El Colegio de la Inmaculada Concepción. Still easily visible in the building is a stray bullet hole incurred during the Battle of Rivas.

At the southeast end of town not far from the road to La Chocolata, the Rivas **cemetery** is set on a little hill with a nice view of town and the surrounding hillsides. It's worth visiting in the late afternoon, as Rivas sunsets are often blazing washes of red and orange, thanks to the humidity from Lake Cocibolca.

ENTERTAINMENT AND EVENTS

The **Restaurante y Disco El Principe** (next to the baseball stadium on the highway to the border) is the most popular and laid-back nightspot. The ambience at **Bar y Restaurante La**

© RANDALL WOOD

Carreta (one block north of the Iglesia San Pedro) is Wild West meets Latin America; it offers traditional fare dishes and appetizers and is open late on weekends. At **Tito's Bar** (one block north of Bancentro, tel. 505/532-2150), the atmosphere is casual and friendly, and the beer is ice cold. Tito's has a small dance floor and a couple of pool tables. But the billiards are better at **Billares Los Laureles,** where games cost about $1 each.

No one enjoys baseball as much as Rivenses; at last count, there were 138 officially registered baseball teams and more than 3,900 registered players in the municipality, with stadiums or makeshift diamonds in every village in the department! Attending a Sunday afternoon game in Rivas's main stadium on the highway is a great way to experience the city and the energy of its people; tickets are $1, and in lieu of chili dogs, there are plenty of *vigorón* (fried pork and yucca) and enchiladas in the grandstand.

ACCOMMODATIONS

Few travelers find a reason to spend the night in Rivas, and the Ometepe-bound tend to prefer the lakeside places in San Jorge. But if you're visiting from San Juan del Sur, there's no reason not to spend the night.

Under $10

For budget travelers, **⟨** **Hospedaje Lidia** (half a block west of the Texaco station, tel. 505/563-3477, $5.50 a night pp for shared bath or $6.50 for private) is the most popular and has a dozen clean rooms, including large rooms for up to five people. At the northeast and southeast corners of the church are two alternatives: **Hospedaje Hilmor** (tel. 505/830-8157) with beds for $6 per person or doubles for $10 with a shared bath, TV, and fan; $15 for private bath. **Restaurante-Hospedaje El Español** (tel. 505/563-0006, $10 pp) is a pleasant corner place with a friendly and atmospheric bar and smoking room in the front *sala*. In the back are four simple rooms; each pair of rooms shares a bath. Along the highway outside of town

you'll find a handful of unremarkable and inexpensive places to stay.

$25-50

Hotel Cacique Nicarao (a block west of the park, tel. 505/563-3234, $55 d plus tax) is efficient and modern with cable TV, air-conditioning, Wi-Fi, a guarded parking lot, and attentive staff. You can also rent Alamo cars here.

FOOD

Buy fresh pastries and juice at **Repostería Don Marcos,** a block east of the park, an easy breakfast en route between San Juan del Sur and the boat to Ometepe. Possibly the lowest-price lunch in town is **Soda Rayuela** (open 7 A.M.–10 P.M. daily), serving $1 sandwiches and burgers and $4 dishes. Across the street from the Iglesia San Pedro is **Pizza Hot** (closed Mon.); the outdoor tables are a nice place to watch the crowds go by. There's an **Eskimo**

Rivas market

next door for dessert. Another decent option is **Hooter's Pizza,** around the corner from the Texaco, and although there won't be any busty blondes serving your pie, there is karaoke until late at night on Wednesdays.

Eat fried, baked, broiled, breaded, and roasted chicken in **Pollo Dorado** (closest to the center of town) or **Super Pollo,** near the market. On the southwest corner of the park is **Chop Suey** ($5–7 a plate), a Chinese place not far off the mark, though all the dishes have been subtly adapted to suit the Nicaraguan palate.

For lunch, visit **El Messon** (south side of Iglesia de San Francisco), a classic Nicaraguan buffet also serving *caballo bayo,* a traditional dish heated over coal in a specially designed pot with ears and a face (you can get your own pot in Huembes Market in Managua). Also, during the evening, a number of typical *fritangas* set up shop in the plaza, notably **La Gitana** (the gypsy), who shows up in her pickup truck around 11 P.M. and serves the meanest *gallo pinto* in town.

The best upscale restaurant is in the **Hotel Cacique Nicarao,** which—besides its traditional menu of well-prepared foods—is one of the only places outside Managua where you can get buffalo wings with hot sauce. Most of the bars listed in the *Entertainment and Events* section have reasonable food as well.

Along the Highway

Near the southern limits of the city are a number of slightly better quality restaurants that cater to truckers, travelers, and businesspeople heading through on their way to and from the border with Costa Rica. Highly recommended is **La Estancia** on the east side of the highway, with a rustic ambience; well-prepared chicken or beef dishes go for $6, and fresh shrimp dishes are $10 and up. Almost directly across the highway is **El Mariscazo,** a word that is difficult to translate directly, but means something like "A huge slap in the face with seafood." It's a good option for fish, shrimp, and lobster, all of which run in the $10–15 range, and none of which you'll be smacked with.

SERVICES

There are several well-stocked pharmacies in town if you're looking for suntan lotion, aloe, painkillers, or medication. The biggest and best is right across from the park on the side of the plaza, **Farmacia María Inmaculada** (open 7:30 A.M.–7:30 P.M. daily), which has on staff both a well-respected doctor (consultation 2–4 P.M. Mon.–Fri.) and professional massage therapists. Another well-stocked pharmacy is the **Farmacia Rivas** (two blocks east of the park at the intersection of the boulevard, tel. 505/563-4292).

The **post office** (a block south of the police station) has fax service and is open 7:30 A.M.–4:30 P.M. Monday–Friday and 7:30 A.M.–noon Saturday.

Of the many Internet cafés in town, two of the most popular ones are one block south of the park.

There are several banks in town including BDF, Bancentro, Banpro, and BAC, all of which operate essentially on a schedule of 8:30 A.M.–4:30 P.M. Monday–Friday, 8:30 A.M.–noon Saturday. Because BAC owns Credomatic, you can take advances against your credit cards there.

The Costa Rican Consulate in Rivas offers help with immigration issues for Costa Rica–bound travelers. It's located about one kilometer west of town and is open 7 A.M.–5 P.M. Monday–Friday and 7 A.M.–noon Saturday.

GETTING THERE AND AWAY

Buses leave Managua's Roberto Huembes terminal for Rivas every 30 minutes. Several express buses depart in the early morning before 8 A.M. Express buses to San Juan del Sur and the border at Peñas Blancas will let you off on the highway at Rivas. They leave Huembes at 5 A.M., 8 A.M., 9:30 A.M., and 3:30 P.M.

Regular buses leave from the market on the northwest side of Rivas: every hour for Jinotepe and Granada, every 25 minutes for Nandaime, Masaya, and Managua. The last bus for Managua leaves from the Texaco station on the highway at 6 P.M. Four daily buses go to Belén and six for Las Salinas (9 A.M.,

11 A.M., 12:40 P.M., 2:30 P.M., 4 P.M., and 4:30 P.M.). A better way to reach Carazo and the Pueblos Blancos (such as Catarina) is to take one of the express minibuses, which leave from El Mercadito on the other end of town about once every hour.

To and From Costa Rica

Bus service to Peñas Blancas and the border begins at 5 A.M. and continues every 30–45 minutes. The last bus leaves Rivas at 5:30 P.M. (the ride takes less than an hour and costs less than a dollar). You can also share a *colectivo*. On the highway in the Supermercado Panamericana (next to the Texaco station), you can buy tickets for the TicaBus, which passes by Rivas each morning bound for Costa Rica between 7 and 8 A.M., and between 3 and 4 P.M. every afternoon bound for Managua. Buy your tickets the day before ($10–12 to San José, Costa Rica).

Taxis to San Jorge and San Juan del Sur

To San Jorge and the ferry to Ometepe, a taxi should cost you no more than $1 per person, whether you take it from the highway traffic circle or from Rivas proper. Ignore any taxi driver that tries to charge $2 or more. Taxis from Rivas to San Juan del Sur cost around $8 per person, or $1 if it's a *colectivo*, which only run during daylight hours.

Near Rivas

NANDAIME AND DOMITILA WILDLIFE RESERVE

Just south of where the highways from Granada and Carazo join to continue on to Rivas and the border, you'll pass by the mid-size city of Nandaime, located on the Pan-American Highway in the shadow of Volcán Mombacho. This is a humble, unassuming pueblo with the most basic of traveler's amenities, a small-town tranquility, and a passion for music. Nandaime's most famous son is Camilo Zapata, a key founder of the Nicaraguan folk style, who composed the song, "El Nandaimeño." Nandaime is also home to three *chichera* groups, ragtag bands composed of a bass drum, a snare, cymbals, a sousaphone, and loud, clashing brass. Known as "orchestras," they participate frequently in parades and bullrings, and their music is happy, loud, and scrappy.

Just south of Nandaime, the private wildlife reserve of Domitila ($45 pp in the dorm, $65 private room; $5 pp for day-trippers, tel. 505/881-1786, www.domitila.org) sits on 230 hectares of tropical dry forest and lakeshore. They have tree nurseries, hiking trails, and oodles of wildlife. Domitila is ecofriendly and uses composting toilets and its own wastewater treatment facility. You'll find comfortable, private cabins, complete restaurant service, and facilities for groups of up to 25 researchers, scientists, or travelers. The $45 per person rate includes three meals per day; gourmet lunch is $10. Call ahead to arrange one of their popular wildlife tours ($20 pp) for bird-watching, butterfly tours, or horseback riding. They also arrange luxury trips to the island of Zapatera, where hot meals are prepared and served to you on-site. The entrance is located five kilometers south of Nandaime (Km 72) on the road to Rivas; turn off the highway onto a dusty dirt road, which will lead you 10 kilometers past the Lagunas de Mecatepe to Domitila.

SAN JORGE

A traditional village with a strong Catholic spirit, San Jorge is primarily a port town and farming community that produces plantains. Nearby Popoyuapa, true to its Nahuatl-sounding name, cultivates cacao, the tree whose seed is used to produce cocoa and eventually chocolate, and which was

RIVAS

once used by the Nicarao people as a form of currency.

The tiny lakeside port of San Jorge is your access point to La Isla de Ometepe and as such, most travelers breeze straight through it on the way to catch a boat. If you have an hour to kill before your ferry departs, there's no reason to spend it dockside sitting on your luggage. Some travelers even find San Jorge a pleasant place to spend a night, and the locals are turning out increasingly acceptable hotel accommodations (mostly targeting the backpacker set) hoping that's exactly what you'll do.

Be advised that at certain unpredictable times of the year, a southern wind brings plagues of *chayules,* small white gnats that swarm the lakeside in San Jorge and eastern shores of Ometepe. They neither bite nor sting, but are relentless and always seem to wind up in your mouth.

Sights

Halfway down the long road to town, you'll pass under **La Cruz de España,** a graceful concrete arch that suspends a stone cross directly over San Jorge's main drag. This main street runs through town down to the water's edge and the docks. The monument commemorates—and is ostensibly built over the very place where—on October 12, 1523, Spanish conquistador Gil González Dávila and indigenous cacique Nicarao-Calli first met and exchanged words.

Across the street from the base of the arch is a mural commemorating the same event, with the words attributed to Nicarao, *Saben los Españoles del diluvio, quien movía las estrellas el sol y la luna. Dónde estaba el alma. Cómo Jesús siendo hombre es Dios y su madre virgen pariendo y para qué tan pocos hombres querían tanto oro.* (The Spanish know about the flood, who moved the stars, the sun, and

© RANDALL WOOD

The *rancho* at Domitila is frequented by scientists and tourists alike.

© JOSHUA BERMAN

In San Jorge, all signs point to the great lake.

the moon. Where the soul was found. How Jesus, a man, is God and his virgin mother giving birth, and why so few men wanted so much gold.) Many believe that the Spanish went on to refer to Nicaragua as The Land of Nicarao, which over time evolved into the modern word Nicaragua.

The squat **Iglesia de las Mercedes** is one of Central America's earliest churches. Built around the year 1575, it was renovated and repainted a bright yellow in 2001. Most tourists keep their bathing suits packed until they get to Ometepe, but San Jorge's kilometer-long **beach** is hugely popular among Nicaraguans, who flock there during Semana Santa to enjoy the lake and the awesome view of twin-peaked Ometepe on the horizon.

San Jorge celebrates its *fiestas patronales* in honor of their eponymous saint every year April 19–23 (the date changes to accommodate Semana Santa when necessary), at which time you can expect the beach to be packed.

San Jorge usually has a parade or two during the celebrations, and there are performances of traditional dances, including **Las Yeguitas** (The Dance of the Little Mares) and **Los Enmascarados** (The Dance of the Masked Ones).

Accommodations and Food

If you missed the last boat to La Isla and don't feel like backtracking to Rivas, book one of the rooms at **(Hotel Las Hamacas** (tel. 505/563-1709, $18 double with private bath and fan, $25 with a/c, includes breakfast), no more than 100 meters west of the dock. Also consider **Hotel Restaurant Azteca** (from the dock, go two blocks past the castle, make a right, and go two more blocks, tel. 505/879-9512, $20 d with a/c and TV). There is a nice restaurant plus a pool and pleasant common areas.

You won't go hungry in San Jorge's numerous food-and-drink joints lining the beachfront, but neither will you be surprised by the menu: chicken, beef, fish, fries, burgers, and sandwiches.

Getting There

Many tour operators in Granada now run shuttles straight to the dock for about $15. Take any southbound bus from Managua's Huembes Terminal to Rivas and get off at the traffic circle on the highway at Rivas. From there to the dock at San Jorge is four kilometers, accessible by Rivas buses once an hour ($0.25); they pass the traffic circle approximately 20 minutes after the hour. Unless you happen to be there right at that moment, however (or are traveling on an extraordinarily tight budget), take a taxi to San Jorge for $1 per person—ignore anyone who tries charging more. There is one Managua–San Jorge express, departing Huembes at 9 A.M., arriving in San Jorge at 10:50 A.M. The same bus departs San Jorge evenings at 5 P.M., arriving in Managua at 10:50 P.M.

La Isla de Ometepe

The island of Ometepe is Nicaragüense to the core yet remains remarkably insulated from the rest of the country (and the world) by the choppy waters of Lake Cocibolca. Ometepe's 38,000 proud residents live a mostly agrarian lifestyle, harvesting plantains, rice, tobacco, sorghum, sugarcane, corn, and coffee. Not even the violence of the 1970s and 1980s reached the island from mainland Nicaragua, which the locals call "over there." Story has it that in 1957, as Volcán Concepción rumbled and threatened to erupt, the government ordered the islanders to evacuate Ometepe; they soundly refused, claiming they preferred to die on their island than live anywhere else. They may get their chance: since early 2005

Ometepe's beach on the sweet sea

RIVAS

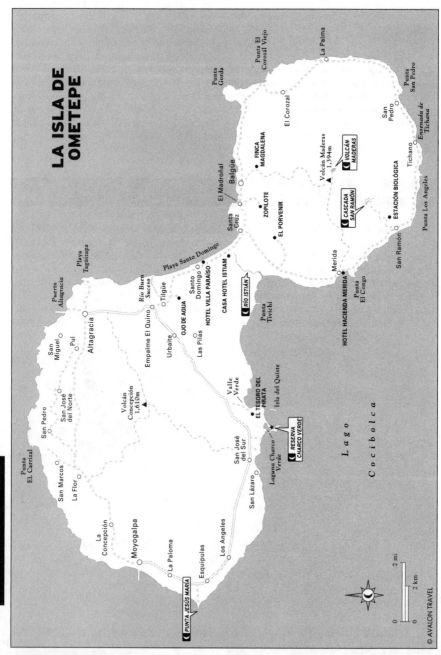

LA ISLA DE OMETEPE

La Palma

Punta El Corozal Viejo

Punta Gorda

El Corozal

Punta El Corozal

Punta San Pedro

San Pedro

Ensenada de Tichana

El Madroñal

Balgüe

FINCA MAGDALENA

Volcán Maderas 1,394m

▲ **◄ VOLCÁN MADERAS**

Santa Cruz

ZOPILOTE

EL PORVENIR

◄ CASCADA SAN RAMÓN

ESTACIÓN BIOLÓGICA

Tichano

Punta Los Angeles

San Ramón

Mérida

Playa Taguízapa

Puerto Altagracia

Río Buen Suceso

Playa Santo Domingo

Tilgüe

Santo Domingo

OJO DE AGUA

HOTEL VILLA PARAÍSO

CASA HOTEL ISTIÁN

◄ RÍO ISTIÁN

Punta Tivichí

HOTEL HACIENDA MÉRIDA

Punta El Congo

San Miguel

Pul

Altagracia

Empalme El Quino

Urbaite

Las Pilas

Volcán Concepción 1,610m ▲

Valle Verde

Isla del Quiste

EL TESORO DEL PIRATA

San José del Sur

San José del Norte

San Pedro

San Marcos

La Flor

La Concepción

Moyogalpa

La Paloma

Esquipulas

Los Angeles

San Lázaro

Laguna Charco Verde

◄ RESERVA CHARCO VERDE

Punta El Carrizal

Punta Jesús María

◄ PUNTA JESÚS MARÍA

L a g o   C o c i b o l c a

N

0   2 mi

0   2 km

© AVALON TRAVEL

A LOVE STORY – THE LEGEND OF OMETEPE AND ZAPATERA

It is said that long ago, neither Lake Cocibolca nor the islands existed. In their place was a broad green valley called Caopol, inhabited by animals that lived in thick forest. Not a single human lived in the forested valley, but the Chorotega, Chontales, Nagrandan, and Niquirano tribes all inhabited the edges of the valley, where they fought battles between tribes.

In the Niquirano tribe there was a lovely Indian maiden by the name of Ometepetl, who caught the eye of the young Nagrandan warrior named Nagrando. He fell deeply in love with her, and she with him. Their love remained a secret because the Niquiranos and Nagrandans were sworn enemies. The day Ometepetl's father learned of the illicit romance he grew furious and swore he would chase Nagrando to his death, rather than see his daughter marry a Nagrandan. Ometepetl and Nagrando fled to the valley where they hid in the forest to escape the fury of Ometepetl's father. There they decided the only way they'd ever be able to have peace would be to die together. Ometepetl and Nagrando slit their wrists with a sharp blade and died in each others' arms.

Ometeptl, as death overcame her, leaned backwards, and her breasts swelled. The sadness that overwhelmed the valley caused the sky to darken and an intense rain to fall. The valley began to flood, and her breasts became the twin peaks of Concepción and Maderas. Nagrando grew into an island as well, the volcanic island of Zapatera, located halfway between the lands of the Nagrandan people and his love Ometepetl. Ometepetl's father and the men who accompanied him in the search to kill Nagrando all perished in the flood. They became the Isletas de Granada and the Solentiname archipelago.

Ometepe's Volcán Concepción has increasingly rumbled, fumed, and ejected tons of volcanic ash, smoke, and debris, in spectacular, frightening eruptions.

Ometepe is awash in myths and legends, some of which date back to the days of the Nahuatl. Long before the Spanish arrived, the islanders considered Ometepe sacred ground, inhabited by gods of great power; even today an uncommon sense of mystery and magic permeates the place.

Ometepe's allure attracts Nicaraguans from other regions of the country in addition to foreigners, and a visit here is a sensory experience unlike any other. At night, the slopes of the volcanoes echo with the deep roar of howler monkeys, and by day the air is filled with the sharp cry of the thousands of parakeets and *hurracas* (bright blue jays that scold you from the treetops). Retaining much of its original forest, Ometepe represents what Nicaragua may have been like in 1522 when Gil González Dávila first set eyes on it: broadleaf trees, clean lake water, and fresh air, all under the towering presence of Concepción and Maderas, two immense volcanoes that together make up the bulk of the island.

Nicaragua's pre-Columbian history may have begun on and around Ometepe. According to legend, the Nahuatl people in what's now Mexico, under pressure from the more powerful Aztecs, followed the Central American isthmus southward in search of a new home, guided by a vision of two volcanoes in the middle of a broad lake. When they saw Ometepe (Nahuatl for "two hills"), they knew their exodus had come to an end. Today, Ometepe is a mosaic of small farms on rich soil that produce plantains, avocados, grazing grass, milk, coffee, and honey. Its two principal towns, Moyogalpa and Altagracia, are formerly sleepy commercial centers, port towns, and transportation hubs enjoying an upswing in tourism and accommodation.

The twin Cenozoic volcanic peaks of Volcán Concepción and Volcán Maderas dominate every aspect of being on the island. The island of Ometepe has been called the edge of the tropics, and the dividing line between tropical and dry falls right between the two volcanoes. Southernmost Maderas is an extinct volcano whose crater is filled with a shallow lagoon and whose slopes are carpeted with more tropical and humid species, including actual cloud forest at the top. Concepción is an active volcano whose slopes are covered with tropical dry forest species like *guacimo* and *guanacaste*. Beginning December 8, 1880, Volcán Concepción erupted with such force that lava and smoke flowed out of the crater for nearly a year. It was this eruption that created some of its more distinctive features visible today, like the Lava de Urbaite, Peña Bruja (a broad cliff visible from Altagracia), and Peña de San Marcos. Concepción erupted again in 1883, launching large rocks from the crater, and again in 1889 and 1902, ruining crops in Rivas. However, Concepción remains quite active even now, and has erupted sporadically since 2005.

MOYOGALPA

Moyogalpa is Ometepe's principal port town and major commercial center. This is your first stop on the island (unless arriving on the boat from Granada, which lands in Altagracia). The small port's name, to the chagrin of local tourism promoters, is Nahuatl for "place of the mosquitoes" despite the reality, which isn't so buggy. While many tourists pass straight through Moyogalpa, the town makes a fine base for island explorations should you decide to stay.

Sights and Entertainment

A good place to start your exploring is the **Fundación Entre Volcanes,** located across the street from the Moyogalpa ENITEL office. This small NGO is involved in several community projects across the island and may be able to help you find ways to volunteer your time while on the island. They also have some representative handicrafts of the region on display.

At the top of the hill, Moyogalpa's **Catholic church** is charming, with a bell tower just high enough over the tree line to afford you a great view of the town, coastline, and lake. In the park in front of the church are two statues: a Native American with a spear and a boy urinating—the islanders definitely maintain a sense of humor.

La Sala Arqueológica (or El Museo), located toward the top of main street, has a small but interesting collection of pre-Columbian artifacts found on the island over the years. Owner and amateur historian Herman García and his wife Ligia are very knowledgeable about island history and lore, and can point you to local artisan communities. The store in front of the museum sells contemporary works.

On the main street, the **Ranchon El Chele** is a popular place to drink and relax. **Disco Johnny Bar,** just north of the dock, and **Disco Cocibolca,** near El Indio Viejo a few blocks east of the dock, also vie for the dancing crowd on the weekends.

The town of Moyogalpa celebrates its patron saint, Santa Ana, June 23–26. The **Baile de las Inditas** is performed in much the same way as the indigenous dance it replaced, with traditional costumes and the resonant sound of the marimba.

Shopping

In addition to more than 200 museum pieces that represent the indigenous peoples of Ometepe, **La Sala Arqueológica** (one block west of the park) sells examples of local handicrafts, including something called the hickory fruit–style. Many of the museum pieces were found by Ligia González de García, on her own farm outside of town.

Hikes and Beaches

Besides the challenging trek to the top of Volcán Concepción (see sidebar *Hiking Ometepe's Volcanoes*), many other trails run along the slopes of the volcano without actually climbing to the crater's edge. Take plenty of water, a healthy curiosity, and enough Spanish pleasantries to talk your way from farm to farm. The people of Ometepe are friendly and

VOLUNTEERING ON OMETEPE

There are numerous opportunities on the "Oasis of Peace" to get involved in community projects: From long-standing solidarity partnerships to sustainable agriculture work and research projects, Ometepe awaits voluntourists.

Learn more about the **Bainbridge-Ometepe Sisters Island Association** (www.bosia.org), and start helping by buying a bag of organic, fair trade coffee on their website; beans are grown at Finca Magdalena and profits are sent back to Nicaragua in the form of development projects around the town of Balgüe.

There are several projects on the island that lend a hand to youth at risk from around Nicaragua; a high level of Spanish is recommended, as this can be frustrating, difficult work (and equally rewarding, of course). One is the residential center of **¡Sí a la Vida!** (Yes to Life!, www.asalv.org), an organization that welcomes international volunteers who can expect to work with the kids in sports, arts, handicrafts, and tutoring, as well as specialized services like health care, construction, and agriculture. Volunteers accompany Nicaraguan staff on field trips to the streets and markets of Managua. To volunteer, contact Bob and Millie Royce (U.S. tel. 206/842-8517, bomiki@bainbridge.net). There's also the **Quincho Barrilete** chapter in the town of San José del Sur, which sometimes accepts volunteers.

In the community of San Lázaro, just to the east of Punta Jesús María, is the **Nuestros Pequeños Hermanos** (NPH, www.nphamigos.org) orphanage, run by Our Little Brothers and Sisters, who provide "a Christian family environment based on unconditional acceptance and love, sharing, working and responsibility." Adopt a godchild, come for a visit, or visit their website to apply to their volunteer program.

In the community of Santa Cruz, you'll find the **Fundación Entre Volcánes** (tel. 505/569-4118), which runs projects all over Volcán Maderas. Contact Raúl Mayorga or Martín Juarez for details — Raúl works in Moyogalpa (two blocks south and one block east of the Shell station, tel. 505/882-5562) and Martín is based out of the town of Los Angeles (Ometepe, not California).

The Ometepe Biological Field Station in San Ramón collaborates with the Washington, D.C.-based **Smithsonian Institution Migratory Bird Center** in their Bridging the Americas educational program for schoolchildren of both Nicaragua and the United States. To volunteer, send a brigade, support financially, or to donate educational equipment, like field guides and binoculars, contact Mary Deinlein at the National Zoo (U.S. tel. 202/673-4908), or Alvaro Molina in Nicaragua (tel. 505/453-0875, merida@ibw.com.ni, www.lasuerte.org). Alvaro can also get you involved with local schools in the town of Merida — feel free to bring supplies down for local teachers.

To learn everything there is to know about organic agriculture, permaculture, and horticulture, spend a week (or four) at **Finca Bona Fide** (about 300 meters past Finca Magdalena, tel. 505/616-4566, www.projectbonafide.com). Chris and Michael run a beautiful farm, have 18-day organic agriculture workshops (free for locals), have a nutritional kitchen in Balgüe, where they feed 70 kids breakfast every morning, and offer farm work internships and volunteer opportunities. Enjoy rustic lodging and three meals a day for $5-8 depending on how long you stay. The view from the communal tree shower hidden in the bushes is alone worth the work. Similar agricultural work arrangements can be made at **La Finca Ecologica El Zopilote** (tel. 505/419-0246, www.ometepezopilote.com), where volunteers are expected to stay for at least a week and receive a 20 percent discount on lodging, but have to cook for themselves.

RIVAS

welcoming enough to let you traipse through their land in search of adventure, but remember that how you behave while "trespassing" will determine how travelers who follow you will be received.

From Moyogalpa to the north, travel along the beach to the community known as Barrio de los Pescadores. Augusto Rodríguez will take you out on fishing and boat tours—talk to him about a trip around the south side of Ometepe to the tiny Isla de Quiste, where you can camp. In the same town, Carlos Loco (Crazy Charlie) is a local painter who has done some impressive paintings of Ometepe. From Barrio de los Pescadores, follow the path closest to the beach, which will lead you through hardwood forest, farms, and clusters of bamboo huts. Three kilometers past the little lagoon of Charco Pelota, you'll find the farm of César Mora; ask for permission to cut through, then follow the path up to the main road and cross it; walk back down the road toward Moyogalpa. An interesting side trip is the farm of Oscar Mora, which you'll reach via a small path on your left as you

HOMESTAYS AND COMMUNITY TOURISM ON LA ISLA DE OMETEPE

Community-based tourism, in which native residents organize to provide accommodations and services to visitors, is one of the most sustainable forms of tourism. Fortunately, the island of Ometepe boasts several such arrangements, in addition to the long-standing **Finca Magdalena,** a coffee cooperative and guesthouse on the slopes of Volcán Maderas. By supporting these organizations you can ensure that more of your tourism dollars stay in the community, benefit the local population, and supports tourism projects with noble goals.

Comunidad Indígina Urbaite-Las Pilas (tel. 505/569-4180, redometepe@guegue.com .ni, ask for Ulises Hernández) organized itself in 1931, democratically electing a board that makes major decisions in the community. Tourists enjoy the flora and fauna of the island, live with local farmers and fishermen, and go on guided walking or fishing tours. More private lodging arrangements are also available for $4 per person. To get to this community, take the bus from Moyogalpa to Urbaite and walk 15 minutes to Las Pilas.

In Moyogalpa **Escuela Hotel Teosintal** (tel. 505/569-4105, tecuilhotelesc@intelnett .com or tecuilturismo@intelnett.com, contact Migdalia Tórrez, $10 pp) has been operating since 2005 and can connect you with a network of agricultural cooperatives, many of which specialize in the production of sesame seeds for export. The focus of the tourism school is to provide an additional source of income for the local producers and improve customer service and tourism services on the island. The theory is reinforced by the students' interaction with foreign hotel guests. The hotel can arrange tours around the island or up to the volcanoes. Escuela Hotel is located just north of the ENITEL office in Moyogalpa.

Moyogalpa is also home to **Pueblo Hotel** (tel. 505/617-1405, pueblo_hotel@yahoo.com, www.islaometepe.org, contact Danelia López Ponce), a network of 25 women from various communities on Ometepe who produce organic fertilizer, conduct workshops on issues associated with domestic violence, and host tourists in their homes. The goals of the program are to increase intercultural exchange (or *intercambio*), promote local culture, and share ecological knowledge and experience. The cost of a stay in one of the houses is $12 per person, which includes three meals per day and a complete immersion personal experience. Aside from traditional tourism activities offered elsewhere on the island, the Pueblo Hotel members can teach you traditional fishing techniques, take you to one of the local botanical gardens, and explain the incredible medicinal value of the Ometepe flora.

(Contributed by Roman Yavich, Fulbright scholar and Nicaragua tourism expert; Roman resides in San Juan del Sur, where he works with Comunidad Connect, a local nonprofit organization.)

head back to town. From his farm, the view of the island is unforgettable, and his farm has other paths you can explore, just ask his family for permission.

Accommodations

For budget travelers, **(El Indio Viejo** (three blocks east of the dock, one south, tel. 505/569-4262) is popular, offering 17 dorm beds for $3 each, $10–14 for a private room for up to four people with clean beds, private bath, and fan. This is where backpackers turn for the familiar funkiness extended from Granada's popular Hospedaje Central; take a hammock or camp outside for less than $2. The bar/*comedor* has a hip world music soundtrack, satellite TV, movie lounge, washing machine and book exchange. Volcano hiking arrangements ($10–15 per group) can be made with Will. Artists are welcome to add to the organic murals and may even receive free lodging; El Indio has the only espresso machine in Moyogalpa.

Hotel Restaurant La Bahía (located across from the Shell Station, tel. 505/823-5743, $4 pp) offers second-story rooms with tons of light and air, and a view of Concepción from the back porch. **Hotelito Ali** (a few blocks up from the dock, tel. 505/456-3270) has 11 rooms set around a garden patio and a decent restaurant that serves three meals. Rates are $5 per person with shared bath, $6 private bath, and $25–35 for nicer rooms with air-conditioning.

Easily recommendable is **(Hotel Ometepetl** (a few blocks up from the dock, tel. 505/569-4276, $12–25 private bath, a/c) whose staff is friendly and can help you with the logistics of preparing your trip (guides, cars, etc.). They have a gift shop on-site and accept credit cards. The rooms at **Hotel Casa Familiar** (half a block south of main street, tel. 505/459-4240) are similar and the establishment is clean and comfortable. Otherwise, there are plenty of other hotels along Moyogalpa's main drag; just get off the boat and walk uphill.

Food

All the aforementioned accommodations serve food, the nicest of which is found at the restaurant at Ometepetl, with meals for about $5. **La Casa Familiar** serves traditional Nicaraguan meals. **El Indio Viejo** offers spaghetti, burritos, and other favorites, but more importantly serves a large breakfast—important if you're off to hike a volcano. Doña Esperanza Jimenez, a half-block east of the park, serves huge, inexpensive meals as well, but not breakfast.

(Los Ranchitos (four blocks up the hill from the dock, then half a block south, tel. 505/569-4112, open 7 A.M.–9 P.M. daily) is a favorite among locals and Peace Corps volunteers; its huge menu features surprisingly good pizza (large pie for only $6). Not far behind is **Yogi's Cafe and Sports Bar** (half a block west of El Indio Viejo, tel. 505/403-6951), dishing out burgers, reggae music, and movies on a big projector screen.

Services

The ENITEL office is located 1.5 blocks east of the main street and is closed on Sundays. The Moyogalpa hospital (tel. 505/569-4247) is three blocks east of the park along the highway out of town. For Internet, go to the **Arcia Cyber Café,** which is air-conditioned and open 8 A.M.–9 P.M. daily, or continue up the main street and use one of the computers at the museum. The nearest cash machine is in Rivas and the only place that accepts travelers checks is Hotel Ometepetl (minus 10 percent).

NEAR MOYOGALPA
San Marcos

Just northeast of Moyogalpa along the "back way around the island" is the small community of San Marcos, home to a women's group that makes and sells ceramic pieces, including authentic replicas of pre-Columbian art. Ask around in town for the *taller de artesanía*.

(Punta Jesús María

The long, sandy peninsula of Punta Jesús María is lovely for swimming and relaxing. The restaurant will give you a beer to take with you on your walk up the kilometer-long sandbar with waves lapping at both sides. This

RIVAS

© RANDALL WOOD

The beach at Charco Verde is one of Nicaragua's most beautiful.

is a good place to watch the sun set or enjoy a meal after a swim in the lake. Owner Joaquín Salazar may let you set up your tent on the beach and spend the night with the crickets. The entrance is a long driveway just north of the town of Esquipulas that takes 15 minutes to walk. Take the bus and ask to get off at the **Punta de la Paloma**, as the locals call it. Ask somebody why (hint: it has nothing to do with doves).

(Reserva Charco Verde

At Charco Verde you can swim in the lake accompanied only by the call of the monkeys in the treetops and the whir of colorful birds. This is still a relatively wild area, with enough tall trees remaining to harbor some very exciting wildlife. The entire area has been cordoned off to prevent development, leaving this cove an oasis of peace to be shared by you and the monkeys (who, incidentally, do their own part by throwing excrement at intruders from the trees).

The three local hotels are each owned by

a different Riveras sibling. Each rents horses and offers boat trips along the shoreline, fishing trips, and outings to Isla de Quiste. The family owns a cattle farm just up the beach you can also visit. **Hospedaje Charco Verde** (tel. 505/887-9302) is next to the reserve with easy trail access; cabanas cost $20–30 with fan or $35–55 with air-conditioning. Reservations are recommended during the high season.

Up the beach toward Moyogalpa, Rubén Riveras runs a family-style guesthouse on the beach called **Hotel Finca Venecia** (tel. 505/872-7668, $35–45 for cabins, $5 pp for rooms with private bath). The hammock pavilion is quiet and, during the high season, not a bad place to spend the night (for $2) when all the beds are taken. The restaurant serves well-prepared pasta, chicken, fish, and beef dishes. From his place, it's an easy walk along the shore into the reserve of Charco Verde and to Playa Balcón. The entrance along the beach is free, but your voluntary contribution helps maintain the reserve—$1–2 if you enter through the Hospedaje Charco Verde.

THE LEGEND OF CHICO LARGO

Over the years, this famous legend has taken two forms. In the first version, an old man by the name of Chico Largo lives in the wetlands of Charco Verde. There he appears to people at night and offers to make a deal with them: wealth and prosperity during the entirety of their lives, in exchange for their souls, which upon death, he converts into cattle. Many of the cows on the island, then, are the souls of Ometepe's previous generation, which opted for a life of decadence instead of hard work.

In the second version, the cacique Nicarao is buried with his throne made of solid gold along the edge of the Charco Verde. In this version, Chico Largo is a descendant of Nicarao and roams the area guarding and protecting Nicarao's tomb. Chico Largo, since he is already guarding the tomb, has now taken it upon himself to guard the forest, animals, and fish as well, and is the primary protector of Ometepe's wildlife.

Right next door is **La Posada de Chico Largo** (tel. 505/886-4069 or 505/830-7608, chicolargo@yahoo.com, $4 dorm beds, $5 pp for room with private bath), the most economic of the three. Despite their nickname, "Los Diablos" are accomodating hosts and their restaurant is good. Ask about La Mirador del Diablo trail.

Isla de Quiste
Really just an islet, Quiste means cyst in Spanish, probably in reference to its small size. It's overgrown and vacant, and a scant 100 meters long—a perfect place to pitch a tent and camp. Many Moyogalpa hotels will help you make arrangements with someone with a small boat. Otherwise, in Charco Verde, Rubén Riveras will drop you off on the island in his motorboat and pick you up again later (or the next day) for about $15, depending on the number of travelers. But you can just as easily strike a deal with any of the locals in the small communities to the north of Moyogalpa, like Barrio de los Pescadores.

Valle Verde and El Tesoro del Pirata
The pirate's treasure is, in this case, an isolated retreat on a wide, black-sand beach rather off the beaten track. Reach the cove by hiking through the Charco Verde Reserve or by getting off the bus at the entrance just beyond the community of San José del Sur, then walking 15 minutes or so from the highway, following the signs. **El Tesoro** (tel. 505/832-2429) is located just far enough off the beaten track to encourage the local wildlife to whoop it up for you. The view is excellent, as is the swimming and boating, and several readers claim they serve the best tasting fish on the island. Pay $25 for a cabana with air-conditioning and private bath, and $2 per person to camp with a $6 tent rental. Group discounts are available.

ALTAGRACIA
The second largest community on Ometepe and an important island port, Altagracia is more picturesque than Moyogalpa, but definitely plays second fiddle with regard to attractions and services. In 2000, *National Geographic* filmed a documentary about vampire bats here—and while there are indeed many vampire bats, they are a threat only to the local chickens, which the bats like to suck dry by hanging from the chickens' nerveless feet.

Sights and Entertainment
Altagracia's *fiestas patronales,* in celebration of San Diego, are held November 12–18. In addition to the traditional festivities, the **Baile de las Ramas** (Dance of the Branches) is a major component of the celebration. The dancers tear off smaller branches of the *guanacaste* tree, and hold them to their heads while dancing to imitate the worker *zompopo* (leaf-cutter) ants carrying leaves off to the ant hills.

RIVAS

El Museo Ometepe (open 9 A.M.–5 P.M. daily, $1) has a few exhibits of the flora, fauna, and archaeology of Ometepe, including statues and ceramic pieces unearthed around the island. The church courtyard makes for a peaceful retreat with a few interesting pre-Columbian stone idols for added irony. You might get yelled at by a group of bright green parakeets that make their home in the roof of the dilapidated old church (next to the freshly painted new church). Across the street in the central park, you'll find the *artesanía cooperative,* comprised of eight local artisans who take turns working in the shop. Some of the pieces are original and exhibit the pride that the islanders have for their home.

Accommodations

Altagracia's accommodations are all located within a block of each other, so feel free to walk around and compare before settling in. **Hotel Central** (two blocks south of the park, tel. 505/552-8770) is a traveler favorite, with a nicely furnished reading room, small garden, and friendly staff. Expect to pay $5 per person for a private bath and fan, slightly less for a shared bath, and $7 per person for a private cabin out back.

Hotel Castillo (tel. 505/552-8744, $4 pp shared bath, $6 private bath) is similar and sports one of the nicer bars in town. Across from the park, **Posada Cabrera** (tel. 505/820-4499, anamariacabrera@yahoo.com, $4 pp) has a pleasant feel, nice staff, and a green backyard. The rooms, however, are extra small, and not as private (the walls don't go all the way up to the ceiling). Doña Ana Maria's father runs El Ojo de Agua, for which she can provide additional information.

Try a homestay with a local family, courtesy of **La Peñita** (tel. 505/855-1380, $3.50 pp). The friendly owner has bikes to rent and will take you on a guided tour of the island. To get there, take the bus from Altagracia to El Quino (at the fork for the isthmus) and walk 300 meters north. This is about as close as you can stay to El Ojo de Agua.

Services

The Camara de Turismo in the park has decent information about the island. The ENITEL phone office and the post office are found diagonally across from the park on the same corner as the Museo Ometepe. The Casa Cural, located on the south side of the park, has six computers and Internet service Monday–Friday. There's also one computer at Tienda Fashion, a block south of the park. You'll have no privacy there, as the computer is located in the middle of the store, but it's open late and on weekends. Check out the crafts while you're waiting.

The small Centro de Salud (on the southeast corner of the park, tel. 505/552-6089) can treat patients 24 hours a day, but for serious injuries go to the hospital at Moyogalpa (get the owner of your hotel to take you in a vehicle).

NEAR ALTAGRACIA

From the park, walk east down a sandy road about 30 minutes to the bay of Playa Tagüizapa, a fine sandy beach for swimming. You can pick up supplies in town for a picnic and make a lazy day of it. Located three kilometers north of the town of Altagracia, the port has boat service between Granada and San Carlos (Río San Juan). The road that leads to the port is shady and makes a nice, short walk—allow about 45 minutes each way. On the way, you'll pass Playa Paso Real, an out-of-the-way bathing beach you'll likely have all to yourself. If you're heading to the port to catch the boat to Granada or San Carlos, it's worthwhile to speak with the owner of Hotel Central. They offer pickup truck service to the port, so you don't have to carry all your luggage that far. Be aware that when the water is too rough, the boat may not show up at Altagracia, preferring to hug the eastern shore of the lake.

PLAYA SANTO DOMINGO

Playa Santo Domingo is the narrow wedge of land that connects the volcanoes of Concepción and Maderas, the product of rich volcanic soil that washed down from the slopes of Concepción and Maderas over millennia, gradually connecting the two islands. The several-kilometer-long stretch of black sand on the northern part of the Istián Isthmus has Ometepe's most upscale accommodations. The swimming can be nice, but with the near-constant onshore breeze, the water is usually choppy.

Accommodations and Food

Rent a charming stone cabin at **▌ Villa Paraíso** (tel. 505/563-4675, ometepe@hotel villaparaiso.com, www.hotelvillaparaiso.com). Rates are $20 double for rooms with private bath and air-conditioning; $55 for suites with air-conditioning, fridge, satellite TV, and hot water; $18 for small, simple rooms upstairs. The breezy waterfront restaurant is fabulous but occasionally prone to *chayules* (gnats). Call early for reservations as the place fills up quickly, especially on weekends and holidays. Next door, **Hotel Finca Santo Domingo** (tel.

505/552-8761, $15–30) is less exciting, and rooms are simple and uninspired though some are air-conditioned.

Two kilometers farther down the beach toward Maderas **Casa Hotel Istiam** (tel. 505/868-8682) provides excellent value, and its beach is clean and pleasant with a wonderful view of Volcán Maderas. The service is friendly and the restaurant good. Make reservations in Moyogalpa at Hotel Ometepetl. Rooms cost $8 per person with private bath, $5 per person with shared bath; there is one for $20 double with air-conditioning and private bath. Camping is possible.

El Ojo de Agua

Located near the town of Tilgue, on the northern part of the isthmus, El Ojo de Agua consists of crystal clear spring-fed waters captured in two simple pools—one large, one small and more private. Swing in Tarzan-style on a rope

RIVAS

the Santo Domingo beach on Isla de Ometepe

HIKING OMETEPE'S VOLCANOES

The volcanoes that form La Isla de Ometepe are irresistible temptations for many an intrepid backpacker, some of whom climb one – or both – mountains while visiting the island. The two peaks are nearly the same height, but radically different in personality. Don't underestimate them – both volcanoes have led to injury and even death, plus frantic, multiple-day rescue searches. You are required to hire a guide before setting out.

Ascending **Volcán Concepción** (1,610 meters) is the more arduous climb, particularly the last third of the way, which is treeless and rocky. It may also be off-limits when you arrive, as recent volcanic eruptions (there have been several eruptions since 2005) have convinced the authorities to restrict access to the upper half. Should the trek be permitted, you will be buffeted by a cold wind all the way up the slope until the moment you reach the crater lip, where a blast of hot sulfurous air rushes out of the bowels of the earth to strike your face. It's that mixing of hot and cold air that

forms the almost permanent cloud cover at the top of the volcano, but on the off chance the clouds thin, the view from the peak is unforgettable.

There are several guides in Moyogalpa and Altagracia, and almost all the hotels have their own guides as well. Berman Gómez at the Hotel Ometepetl is highly recommended (he was trained in Costa Rica in guide services and travels with first-aid supplies and a radio). You can hire a guide for $10-20 per group of five people. Most travelers hike Concepción by way of the towns La Concha or La Flor, and there is an eastern approach from Altagracia that takes you through an impressive amount of monkey-inhabited forest before hitting the exposed section. Allow a full day for the hike, five hours up and four hours down. Take plenty of water, sun protection, and good shoes and socks to protect your feet.

Volcán Maderas (1,394 meters) is more accessible and thus more frequently hiked. It is, however, still difficult, and has led to at

Volcán Concepción suddenly came back to life in 2005 in a puff of ash.

© RANDALL WOOD

least two deaths. Now a national park whose boundaries begin at the 400-meter mark all the way around the volcano, the most commonly used trail to the top starts at Finca Magdalena, leads to the crater lip, then down into the crater to a mist-swept lake straight out of Tolkien. This final descent down to the crater lake requires a rope and should not be attempted without proper safety equipment – make sure your guide packs one. The trail, unfortunately, has seen better days. Lack of appropriate maintenance has made a mud pit out of much of the upper stretch. Allow four hours to go up and two or three to come back down, and count on spending an hour at the crater lake (58 minutes of which you'll spend deciding whether or not to jump in the cold, mushy-bottom *laguna*). If you're not staying at the Finca Magdalena you must pay a trail fee to enter and pass through the coffee plantations. You'll pass a petroglyph or two on the way up.

The other ascent leaves from Merida, and, after a rigorously steep three-hour start, includes more time in the upper reaches which one tourist called "the enchanted, magical" part of the hike. Hotel Hacienda Merida offers this excursion, including transport back from Magdalena if you choose to descend the other side.

into the revitalizing waters, then climb out to drip-dry in the sun with an ice-cold beer in hand. The little bar there also serves food. The botanical garden surrounding the pools is the frosting on the cake. If you are feeling under the weather, buy some medicinal herbs or tea from the garden. Your $1 entrance fee helps with maintenance.

◖ VOLCÁN MADERAS

Maderas is now officially a national park, which will hopefully encourage preservation of the thick forests. Maderas is a pleasant volcano to climb, since you hike in the shade, and is less demanding than its truly active twin, but a guide is now obligatory since a pair of hikers got lost and eventually perished on the mountain. But even if you're not a peak-bagger, there's lots to do here, starting with a visit to the fields of old petroglyphs, a relic of the island's Nahuatl past. In addition, a host of unique places to stay (many based on working farms) are fun and interesting.

As you approach the southern half of La Isla de Ometepe, you'll cross the isthmus and come to a fork in the road near the settlement of Santa Cruz. Turning left takes you to a pair of backpacker-oriented accommodations, both extremely rustic.

A 10-minute walk up the trail from the village of El Madroñal leads to **La Finca Ecologica El Zopilote** (tel. 505/419-0246, www.ometepezopilote.com, $3–10 pp for raised platforms), a hillside cluster of thatch huts and platforms run by a few peace-loving Italians and their pack of hound dogs. Meals are not provided, rather fix your own in the open-air communal kitchen; the compound has compost toilets, an artisan's workshop, and a clay oven for bread and pizza. Check out the organic products in the gift shop, from coffee to liqueur, and enjoy the permaculture plantation throughout the grounds. Tents for camping are also available. Volunteers willing to work on the farm for at least a week get a 20 percent discount and all the fruit they can eat.

Just uphill from the town of Balgüe is the famed **Finca Magdalena** (tel. 505/880-2041, www.fincamagdalena.com, $2 dorm, $8 private d, $15 half a cottage, $40 family-size cottage), a coffee cooperative established in the 1980s on land confiscated from the Maltodano family that now employs 27 families. Magdalena and its barnlike second-story accommodation has been a must-see stop on the Central America backpacker trail since the 1990s. Everyone showers in the same bracing cold water piped

NAHUATLS AND THE PETROGLYPHS OF OMETEPE

In the days of the Nahuatls, Volcán Maderas was called Coatlán, "the place where the sun lives," and Concepción was known as Choncotecíguatepe, "the brother of the moon," or Mestliltepe, "the peak that menstruates." In the lush forests of the lower slopes of the two volcanoes, the Nahuatls performed complicated rituals in honor of many different gods: Catligüe, the goddess of fertility; Ecatl, the god of air; Migtanteot, the god of death; Tlaloc, the god of soil; and Xochipillo, the goddess of happiness. The Nahuatl gods were all-powerful and vindictive, and spent their days in the land where the sun rises doing what all-powerful gods do best – feeding on human blood.

The concept of a soul was an important part of the Nahuatl belief system, as were the concepts of an afterlife and some form of reincarnation. Their calendar consisted of 18 months of 20 days each, for a total of a 360-day calendar year. They believed in a cycle of catastrophic events that recurred every 52 years, and according to that cycle the Nahuatls would store grains and water, in case this were the year.

Scattered around the island of Ometepe, but principally on the north and northeastern slopes of Volcán Maderas, are the statues and petroglyphs, carved around the year A.D. 300, that paid homage to the Nahuatl gods. Spirals are a consistent theme, representing perhaps calendars or the Nahuatl concept of time and space. It has been suggested the spirals may also represent the islands themselves, or that the twin-spiral shape of Ometepe gave the island even more significance to the islanders, as it fit in with their ideas about the cosmos. More mundane images can also be identified in the carved rocks: monkeys, humans hunting deer, and a couple in coitus, suggesting Nahuatl wishes for prosperity and fertility, or just a bit of monkey business.

directly from a spring up the slope. Horseback rides and coffee tours are also offered, and the petroglyphs are on their property. Also contact them about volunteer and work opportunities. Camping is available.

Their new satellite Internet connection ($3/hr) may or may not be a precursor to linking a good part of Ometepe via wireless ethernet—but don't get so caught up checking your email that you forget to watch the moon set over the silhouette of Concepción while meals are cooked over a woodstove ($1–4). You can purchase fresh roasted coffee and fresh honey—a good way to help support the farm.

To get to the Finca Magdalena, take the bus to Balgüe and follow signs along the 20-minute walk up the road to the farm (arrive before dark). Five daily buses depart the dock in Moyogalpa, the last at 3:30 P.M.

Así Es Mi Tierra (tel. 505/421-3132, $6 pp includes breakfast) in the town of Balgüe proper has seven clean rooms, and taxi services;

it's a good spot to go when you tire of farm life. Just a bit north of the hostel, Jairo and his mellow friends have a fresh fruit and vegetable store and are adding a vegetarian restaurant, serving Indian and Thai meals. At **Isabella's Cafe** (located at the entrance to the elementary school) both vegetarians and meat lovers find fresh meals filled with love for $1–3.

Off the road to San Ramón, up a left-hand entrance and steep driveway you'll find **Albergue Ecológico El Porvenir** (tel. 505/855-1426, $4 pp shared bath), a wonderful hillside retreat with modern buildings, incredible views, and a full menu of food and activities. See the owners of Hotel Central in Altagracia or Hotel Villa Paraíso on Playa Santo Domingo for more information about transport and booking.

Merida

Some 250 families get by on Volcán Maderas's southwestern shore, mostly by fishing and growing basic grains and *plátanos,* but the tourism potential is phenomenal and the area is increasingly being developed. Representatives from the following accommodations will pick you up in Moyogalpa, just call ahead.

Formerly a private coffee hacienda prior to the revolution, **⟨ Hotel Hacienda Merida** (tel. 505/868-8973, haciendamerida@gmail .com, www.lasuerte.org, $6 dorm, $15 d with private bath, $3 pp campsite) is now a quiet, lakeside compound with a friendly atmosphere and scarlet sunsets. Second-floor rooms have balconies with views of the volcanoes and the lake. Myriad activities run the gamut from biking, hiking, fishing, paddling, horseback riding, and windsurfing to card playing and chess; don't miss the great food including all-you-can-eat buffets ($5 pp)—listen for the dinner bell. They pride themselves on fresh, healthy food, baking whole wheat bread and harvesting most ingredients from their own irrigated garden. Internet, Wi-Fi, and Skype calls all are available. The Nicaraguan owner, Alvaro Molina, speaks perfect English and is a walking guidebook for Ometepe and beyond—he has also collected a great resource library for travelers and naturalists, and is an activist on many local and national issues, especially concerning the environment.

More of an upscale guesthouse, **La Omaja** (300 meters past Merida, tel. 505/885-1124, laomaja@hotmail.com, www.laomaja.com, $45 d with private bath) offers well-appointed cabins with two or four beds and hot water; the owners can help arrange all sorts of excursions on Maderas or elsewhere. Enjoy special deals during the off-season. Three meals are available in their restaurant.

⟨ Río Istián

The paddle trip in a kayak or canoe from Merida to Río Istián is not to be missed, especially early in the morning or during sunset. If the wind is up, it can be a difficult trip (allow 1–2 hours of hard paddling to get there), but as you enter the still waters of the marshy isthmus choked with all sorts of trees and birds under the reflection of two volcanic peaks, you will

agree it was worth it. Bring plenty of water. The shorter paddle to Isla el Congo, just offshore, is nice as well, but beware the monkeys!

A rigorous and none-too-obvious trail leads up to Maderas's crater lagoon and down the other side from Merida; hire a guide and get an early morning start. The Hotel Hacienda Merida offers this excursion, including transport back from Magdalena.

⟨ Cascada San Ramón

Four kilometers up the road from Merida, in the tiny village of San Ramón is a biological station frequented by student groups and researchers from all over the world and, of late, tourists as well. The **Estación Biológica de Ometepe** (tel. 505/883-1107, www.lasuerte .org) is home to Fundación Ometepe. Their main lodge has a huge kitchen, as the staff here are accustomed to accommodating large groups. Researchers use the station's kayaks and small boats to explore the Río Istián. Rooms go for $10 per person for shared bath,

© JOSHUA BERMAN

RIVAS

The hike to the San Ramón waterfall is worth it.

$13 per person for private double rooms, and a $50 suite with TV, massive bed, and whirlpool tub.

The most popular attraction by far is the stunning 56-meter waterfall, Cascada San Ramón, on the south slope of Maderas, visible at the end of a two- to three-hour hike up from the lake (a $3 fee is charged at the gate below). The signs say it is a three-kilometer trail, but it's likely more than that. You can drive your four-wheel drive vehicle part way up to the water tank for an extra few dollars; from there, it's less than an hour walk to the falls. Those kilometers are straight up hill, mind you, so don't overestimate your hiking prowess.

The East Coast of Maderas
The lonely east coast of Maderas is one of the most isolated spots in Nicaragua, connected tentatively by a poor excuse of a road with no bus service. The locals are not used to receiving guests. It's potentially feasible to circumnavigate the entire volcano on foot or on one of Hotel Hacienda Merida's mountain bikes (about 12 or 6 hours, respectively). The coast of Tichana hides lots of unexplored areas, including, reportedly, caves full of paintings as well as some petroglyphs near Corozal.

Getting to San Ramón and Merida
Three daily buses leave Moyogalpa for Merida at 8:30 A.M., 2:40 P.M., and 4:30 P.M.; from Altagracia buses depart at 7 A.M., 10:30 A.M., and 2 P.M. (these buses continue to San Ramón, returning the following day starting at 5:30 A.M.). From Merida to Moyogalpa, buses leave at 4 A.M., 8:30 A.M., and 3:30 P.M. The trip now takes only an hour on the newly paved road.

GETTING THERE AND AWAY
By Boat from San Jorge
Lake Cocibolca can get rough when the wind is high. At those times, choosing a larger vessel

the ferry to Ometepe

RIVAS

OMETEPE FERRIES FROM SAN JORGE

San Jorge-Moyogalpa		Moyogalpa-San Jorge	
7:45 A.M.	Ferry	5:30 A.M.	Boat
9 A.M.	Boat	6 A.M.	Ferry
9:30 A.M.	Boat	6:30 A.M.	Boat
10:30 A.M.	Ferry	7 A.M.	Boat
11:30 A.M.	Boat	8 A.M.	Boat
12:30 P.M.	Boat	9 A.M.	Ferry
1:40 P.M.	Boat	11 A.M.	Boat
2:30 P.M.	Ferry	11:30 A.M.	Boat
3:30 P.M.	Boat	12:30 P.M.	Ferry
5 P.M.	Boat	1 P.M.	Boat
5:30 P.M.	Ferry	3 P.M.	Boat
		4 P.M.	Ferry

These times are subject to change. For the most up-to-date schedule, or to be sure that your boat is running, call Ometepe Tours (tel. 505/563-4779). The smaller, older (more adventurous) boats cost $1.50; the lower deck of the ferry is $2; and the upper decks of the ferry are $3 and well worth it for the view. Don't worry – when you pull into port, the men climbing the rails and jumping aboard are not pirates, they are taxi drivers in San Jorge or bag porters in Moyogalpa.

may make all the difference between a leisurely ride and a tumultuous vomit-marathon. Avoid the rough seas by traveling early morning and late evening. If you are prone to motion sickness, try to get a seat toward the center of the ship, where the pendulum motion will be less noticeable, and when the nausea comes on, fix your sight on the horizon. There are a handful of old boats that ply the waters between San Jorge and the port at Moyogalpa, all of which you may share with boxes, bananas, cattle, and crowds of islanders on their way home from doing errands in Rivas and Managua. We prefer the *Ferry Ometepe*, a big steel boat with radar and life jackets and from whose roof you can travel in the fresh air (note, however, that even this, the safest of the fleet, briefly sank dockside in 2006 while unloading a banana truck; best not to think about it). A one-way trip costs $2–3.

Be aware that the various vessels you can hire are independently owned and, unfortunately, few give honest information about the others, so if you're told, "The next boat doesn't leave for four hours," keep asking. **Volcano Lake Tours** (office near the port, tel. 505/827-7714) will give you reliable information about the schedule.

RIVAS

By Boat to the Río San Juan

The **Empresa Portuario de Nicaragua (EPN)** ferry leaves Granada on Mondays and Thursdays at 3 P.M., arriving in Altagracia between 5 P.M. and 7 P.M. The ship then continues onward to San Miguelito on the southeastern lakeshore, arriving in San Carlos around dawn. You can usually stay on the boat until the Río San Juan boats begin operating at 6 or 7 A.M. (instead of having to get a room). An upper-deck ticket costs a couple dollars more and earns you more room to hang a hammock.

On the return trip, the ferry leaves San Carlos on Tuesdays and Fridays at 2 P.M., passes Altagracia at 11 P.M., and arrives in Granada at sunrise. The price for a one-way passage between Granada and Ometepe is $3, but when seas are high, the ship will skip Ometepe altogether, preferring to hold tight to the lee shore of the lake.

GETTING AROUND LA ISLA DE OMETEPE
By Bus

Fully 90 percent of the buses leave the Moyogalpa dock, travel straight up the hill along the main street, stop at the park, then head east out of town; the other 10 percent turn left, passing through La Flor and San Marcos on their way to Altagracia. In general, there's a bus to meet every boat. For the most up-to-date schedule, ask around the dock, or look for a posting in the tour offices or El Indio Viejo in Moyogalpa.

From Altagracia, buses depart for Moyogalpa and for the small towns of Maderas (San Ramón, Merida, Balgüe, and Santo Domingo). If you board a bus in Moyogalpa that's heading to Maderas, remember you'll pass through Altagracia first, where you'll spend 30 minutes waiting for more passengers before continuing to Maderas. From Moyogalpa to Altagracia, it's approximately one hour, and from Altagracia to Balgüe it's another hour. The island is bigger than you think.

Be very aware that buses are few and far between on Sundays, which remain a tough day to get around the island in anything but a

rented car or by availing yourself of the services of your hotel.

Rental Cars and Taxis

Either arrange a transfer with your hotel beforehand or chip in with friends and hire one of the many taxis that will mob you when you get off the ferry. A taxi from Moyogalpa to the beach resort of Santo Domingo is around $15, though you have more leverage if you're traveling in a group. Likewise, you can rent vehicles, but they're not cheap. Check out Hotel Ometepetl's "fleet," usually a late-model Toyota or Suzuki Samurai; rental is about $35 per 12 hours. The *Ferry Ometepe* is the only vessel that will permit you to drive your personal vehicle onboard, though space is extremely limited. If you're interested in taking your vehicle across, call 505/459-4284 at least 72 hours in advance, and then again the day before your trip (more than one reservation has gotten lost). The price for transport of your vehicle is $28, plus your passenger fare.

Island Tour Operators

CITOMETEPE, the island's tourism commission, offers overview information at www.visitaometepe.com. As for tour operators, your first encounter will be at the ferry dock in San Jorge: **Ometepe Tours** (tel. 505/569-4242, maquipi1@hotmail.com) arranges package tours of the island, including guides, vehicles, and hotel reservations. By the time your boat crosses the waters of Cocibolca, the arrangements will be made, and one of four Ometepe Tours vehicles will pick you up at the dock. It doesn't get much easier than that. The Nicaraguan family company is friendly and honest and provides the only day trip of Ometepe, leaving San Jorge at 9:30 A.M., then driving a relaxing five-hour loop around Concepción with well-planned visits to the sites, after which they'll have you back in San Jorge by 5 P.M., so you can hurry back to your hotel in San Juan del Sur or Granada.

In Moyogalpa, Horacio Galán of **Volcano Lake Tours** (tel. 505/827-7714, volcanolake tours@gmail.com) has 13 years of experience as a guide on the island and is incorporating bird-watching into the standard fare offerings of the island. **Ometepe Expeditions** (tel. 505/664-6910, ometepexpeditions@hotmail .com) is home to locally famous guide Berman Gómez (tel. 505/647-5179), who recently led a team from the BBC on a tour around the island and both summits. All of these operations are reputable and offer fairly creative trips. Most hotels will gladly help to arrange tours as well, getting you up both volcanoes or on a number of hikes or horseback rides.

SAN JUAN DEL SUR AND THE SOUTHWEST COAST

Once a quiet fishing village in a forgotten corner of the country, San Juan del Sur is now Nicaragua's primary Pacific coast destination—for both national and foreign tourists. Many of the pueblo's 18,000 residents still make a go at fishing, but most are putting their money on the steady stream of big-spending foreign visitors. Everyone and their mother, it seems, is developing a new shuttle service, bar, surf camp, or *hospedaje,* and in 2002, San Juan del Sur celebrated its 150th anniversary by declaring itself "Nicaragua's Tourist City."

San Juan's principal resource is its perfect protected harbor and crescent beach, open to the setting sun and protected by La Cara del Indio (The Indian's Face), a rock formation in the cliffs at the north end of the bay. Surf's up, and so is foreign investment—and in San Juan del Sur, business and pleasure mix easily, usually over heaping plates of pasta, butter, and fresh snapper. In addition to curious tourists and the surf crowd, you'll meet property pimps, land sharks, and a frenzied flock of checkbook-toting prospectors madly scouring the coastline for a piece of the pie. It's easy to draw parallels to the California gold rush of the mid-19th century—the last time gringos flocked to this port, in transit to either boom or bust—but San Juan's new influx is unique. This time, many North Americans and Europeans have decided to stay and build.

Whether San Juan del Sur is the next Cancún remains to be seen and will depend largely both on Nicaraguan management of this unprecedented development opportunity

© JOSHUA BERMAN

HIGHLIGHTS

(Sunset: Feel the earth turn downward, man, while sitting on San Juan del Sur's public beach; surfboard optional (page 134).

(Da Flyin Frog Canopy Tour: This 17-platform canopy tour offers a lively forest and views of the ocean (page 134).

(La Flor Wildlife Refuge: Even if you miss the spectacular nighttime turtle-nesting events, a simple walk along this protected beach and up the forested river is remarkable (page 148).

(Playa Gigante: Somewhere around here, a wave is arching around the point with no one around to ride it (page 152).

LOOK FOR **(** TO FIND RECOMMENDED SIGHTS, ACTIVITIES, DINING, AND LODGING.

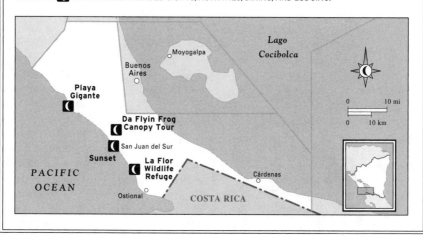

and the ability of investors to prove they are contributing locally and being responsible members of the community. Locally, opinion over the matter is largely divided, with the younger San Juaneños more receptive and the older generation less of the new paradigm. Investment has also meant a rise in crime, drug use, and deforestation, and a rise in prices prevalent through Nicaragua is locally blamed on the foreigners.

But it's hard not to appreciate San Juan del Sur's exciting new personality. Travelers flock there for a reason, and the panoply of interesting accommodations, chic restaurants, and bars with great vibes ensure travelers will continue to feel comfortable in, and continue enjoying,

this up-and-coming beach resort. And if you look under the town's glossy new veneer, you will undoubtedly notice San Juan del Sur remains a quiet fishing village in a forgotten corner of the country.

PLANNING YOUR TIME

San Juan del Sur proper is a relatively small town; you could walk every street in town in a morning. But most visitors spend at least two days and a night here, and if you start exploring the surrounding beaches and coves, beach lovers can stretch it into a full week, as can surfers (best swell is May–December). At a minimum, count on one full day wandering around town, one trip north to Playa Madera and another

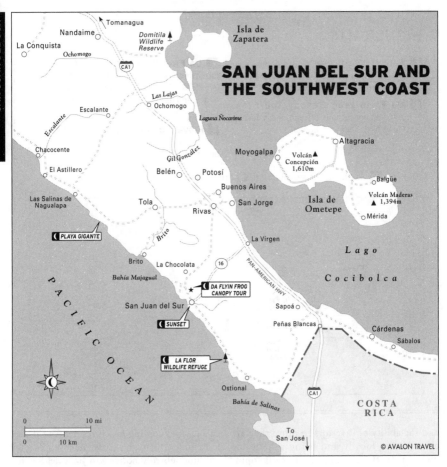

SAN JUAN DEL SUR AND THE SOUTHWEST COAST

(Map labels:) Tomanagua, Nandaime, Domitila Wildlife Reserve, Isla de Zapatera, La Conquista, Ochomogo, CA1, Las Lajas, Ochomogo, Escalante, Escalante, Laguna Nocarime, Moyogalpa, Volcán Concepción 1,610m, Altagracia, Chacocente, Gil González, Belén, Potosí, Balgüe, El Astillero, Buenos Aires, Volcán Maderas 1,394m, Las Salinas de Nagualapa, Tola, San Jorge, Isla de Ometepe, Mérida, Rivas, PLAYA GIGANTE, Brito, La Virgen, Lago Cocibolca, Brito, La Chocolata, 16, PAN-AMERICAN HWY, Bahía Majagual, DA FLYIN FROG CANOPY TOUR, San Juan del Sur, Sapoá, SUNSET, Peñas Blancas, Cárdenas, Sábalos, PACIFIC OCEAN, LA FLOR WILDLIFE REFUGE, Ostional, CA1, COSTA RICA, Bahía de Salinas, To San José, 0 10 mi, 0 10 km, © AVALON TRAVEL

---

trip south to Playa el Coco or La Flor Wildlife Reserve; plan an extra half-day for a canopy tour, sportfishing, or sailing excursion.

SIGHTS AND SPORTS
Sunset

The main show in town is the crimson day's end over the languid harbor waves; San Juan sunsets can go on for hours if conditions are right; make sure you're on the beach with a Toña in hand, watching the silhouetted fishing boats and protective face of El Indio.

Da Flyin Frog Canopy Tour

The newest canopy tour in the country and arguably the best, Da Flyin Frog (tel. 505/611-6214, tiguacal@ibw.com.ni, $25 pp, closed Sun.) is a 17-platform, two-kilometer ride through the trees with great views of the ocean. It's located just outside town on the mayor's cattle ranch on the Chocolata road.

Organized Sports

The renovated basketball court, next to the Casa de Cultura on the main beach drag, now also features **volleyball** and **soccer.** League games on weeknights attract many spectators cheering on their favorite local teams (for information on sponsoring a team, see sidebar *Volunteering in San Juan del Sur*). During the rest of the day, the Sports Park is open for (often competitive) pickup games. Otherwise, expect soccer games to be played at low tide on either end of the bay.

Hikes from Town

Hiking opportunities are rapidly diminishing in the context of property boundary–sensitive developers, so tred lightly and ask for permission. Some of the closer beaches, north and south of town, make for good day hikes as well, as does rock hopping the northern curve of the bay and around the point—mind the tides and bring lots of drinking water.

The **cross** is easily reached via the driveway past the Pacific Marlin neighborhood or the ladder that winds its way from about 500 meters around the rocks on the northern point of the bay. The steep walk takes about 30 minutes each way and leads to one of the best overlooks of the bay. For a panorama from the **antennas,** take a bus toward Rivas and ask the driver to let you off at Bocas de las Montañas. From there, head through the trees and pastures to the breezy and beautiful *mirador* (lookout)— an hour each way.

Some 1,700-year-old **petroglyphs** are accessible via a 90-minute countryside walk beginning east of the Texaco station. Consider asking for a local guide. Take a left (north), pass the school, and walk through a gate after about 500 meters; find the farmhouse and ask permission to cut through. Follow the water pipes and the river until you find the stone with the carvings. Continue upstream to reach the waterfalls, impressive only during the rainy season—wear good shoes and long

© JOSHUA BERMAN

catch of the day, near the park in San Juan del Sur

pants to avoid being stung by the nettlelike *pica-pica* plant.

Sailing and Surfing

Charter the *Pelican Eyes* yacht for an all-day jaunt (tel. 505/568-2110, www.piedrasyolas .com, $70) including lunch on a deserted beach and an open bar. The Pacific beaches are well appreciated by surfers and body boarders alike, and surf mags now proudly hawk Nicaragua the same way they do Baja California and

Pipeline. Surfers tend to make base camp in San Juan del Sur and then drive out to the better breaks, though you can camp on many—but not all—beaches. Learn more online at www.nicaraguasurfreport.com. Many of the best breaks are only accessible by boat, so pull a group together to pitch in for diesel.

Local shredders Byron and Kervin López can be found in their shop, **Arena Caliente** (tel. 505/636-1769, www.arenacaliente.com), next to the market. They rent boards for

SURFING IN NICARAGUA

Year-round offshore breezes generated by the vast, blustery surface of Lake Cocibolca collide with incoming Pacific swells to create ideal surf conditions. Surfers have been prowling the southwest coast of Nicaragua for more than a decade, and a multiplying supply of beachside surf camps has finally risen to meet the demand. San Juan del Sur is the undisputed center of the scene, but there are respected surf camps all the way to Jiquilillo, spanning the entire Pacific coast. Despite the rising popularity of Nicaraguan surf, most waves still sport plenty of gaps in the lineup for a skilled rider like yourself.

$10/day and, for an extra $20, teach you to use them. They also offer a ride to the beach for $5 per person, round-trip and offer inclusive weeklong surf packages. Around the corner heading towards the beach is **San Juan Surf & Sport** (tel. 505/479-3868), which also rents all manner of sports equipment. **Dale Dagger Tours** (tel. 505/568-2492, www.nicasurf.com, www.daledaggertours.com) has been scouting breaks for more than a decade, ever since he shipwrecked here in the early 1990s. He can book weeklong packages based either in upscale hotels or in one of his lodges on an isolated beach up the coast (see *Playa Gigante* under *Tola and Pacific Beaches*). Horseback rides, canopy tours, golf, fishing, and walking tours of San Juan del Sur—and just about anything else you can think of—can also be arranged.

Joey of **Action Tours** (tel. 505/843-8157, www.actiontoursurfnica.com) runs private surfing, fishing, and chilling charters on his authentic *panga*. The $180 full-day trip includes lunch. **El Rana** runs trips to the popular beaches north of town leaving from in front of Hotel Estrella at 11 A.M. But you can just as easily strike a deal with any local fisherman

for a water taxi out to the other beaches: This makes sure the locals get a cut.

If you get worked by the overhead swell, ask around for Mosco or Cambute to get your board fixed. For now there are no shops that sell new boards in San Juan del Sur, but a used one is easy to find. For more information, see the *Tola and Pacific Beaches* section in this chapter.

Diving

The Pacific lacks the visibility of the Caribbean, but fish are plentiful and there's a sunken Russian shrimp boat offshore. San Juan has two dive shops willing to take you underwater ($75 for two tanks, $275 for open-water certification): **Pacific Divers** (just west of the Texaco station, tel. 505/867-8194, www.abucear.com) and **Scuba Shack** (on the beach road just north of Eskimo, tel. 505/568-2502, www.scubashack-nicaragua.com). The latter also rents surfboards and runs half- and full-day surf charters. Upon request they will take you diving in the Laguna de Apoyo, a crater lake in an ancient extinct volcano near Masaya, and can make arrangements for diving the Corn Islands in the Caribbean.

Mind and Body

Nica Yoga (www.nicayoga.com) is a new venture offering all-inclusive yoga retreats or custom packages that include yoga and surfing (retreats start at $700). Alternatively, track down "Yoga Larry" of **Bodhin Adventures** (tel. 505/680-6015, www.bodhin.com) for low-key classes held on the beach when the tide is low. **Luna Bella Spa** (one block south of the east side of the church, tel. 505/803-8196, www.lunabella.org) offers three different types of massage, energy work, reflexology, aromatherapy, beauty treatments, and yoga classes; an hour-long massage is $40. Call for appointments.

SHOPPING

During weekends, holidays, and cruise ship arrivals, street vendors—usually Masayan—work the beachfront. **El Papagayo Artesanía** (open

9 A.M.–7 P.M.) is French-owned with goods from around the world. Most everyday items, including fresh vegetables and those dollar flip-flops you've been looking for, can be purchased in or around the **Municipal Market** (center of town, open 7 A.M.–7 P.M.). Purchase surf gear, from threads to wax, at **Nica Surf Shop** (near the center of town, open 8:30 A.M.–6 P.M. Tues.–Sun.).

ENTERTAINMENT AND EVENTS

San Juan del Sur's mellow, year-round party scene picks up around Christmas, New Year's Eve, and Semana Santa when the town is flooded with visitors. Managuan club owners set up beach discos during the high season. The rest of the year, the town's only disco, **Otangani Beach,** is open Thursday–Sunday (Saturday night is the best). San Juan del Sur's Bermuda triangle of bars, **Iguana, Marie's Bar,** and **Tsunami,** cater to locals and foreigners alike, and differ only in their choice of music.

Carin (one block east of Eskimo on the beach) and **El Lago Azul** have karaoke on Fridays and Saturdays, respectively.

San Juan del Sur's *fiestas patronales* take place June 16–24, with bull riding, pole climbing, greased pig catching, and Coca-Cola chugging contests; if these aren't enough of a cultural experience, stick around for the events of July 17: the **Procesión de la Virgen del Carmen** is a celebration of the Patron Saint of Fishermen. Locals parade the icon through town and to the docks where waiting boats take her (and as many locals as possible) for a lap around the bay. **September 2** is the commemoration of the tidal wave of 1992, a 62-foot monster that swept across main street, destroying many structures (and farther up the coast, entire villages, like El Tránsito).

ACCOMMODATIONS

San Juan's lodging runs the gamut from grungy to chic. Nearly all the cheapest *hospedajes* are near the center of town, are Nicaraguan owned, and are usually extensions of someone's home.

The beachfront road has a few nicer hotels and most of San Juan's restaurants and bars. It is safe to assume that nicer hotels have backup generators and water tanks, but you should still ask unless you like candlelight bucket showers. During the high season, around New Year's and Easter, hotel prices double or even triple the rates listed below.

Under $25

◀ La Casa Feliz (one block east of the market, tel. 505/689-7906, www.lacasafeliz.com, $7 pp dorm) caters to surfers, offering a bunk, a key to the front door, kitchen, and bamboo showers. Surfboard rental and lessons on call; after the session enjoy their lush courtyard. Surfers also like **Arena Caliente** (tel. 505/636-1769, www.arenacaliente.com); call for package rates.

Elizabeth's (east end of market street, tel. 505/568-2270) has 19 rooms that run $7 double for shared bath, $20 for a refurbished room with private bath. Elizabeth is well liked and the ambience is relaxed.

One street over is **Hotel Beach Fun** (tel. 505/568-2441, $6 shared bath), a 20-year-old *hospedaje* in a 90-year-old building. The 16 rooms are small, but the open courtyard is nice and so are the owners.

Hotel Estrella (located where the market road meets the beach, tel. 505/568-2210, hotel estrella1929@hotmail.com) was the first hotel in San Juan del Sur, constructed in 1929. Less glamorous than its glory years, Estrella is still the only place in town where you get an oceanfront balcony for $5 a person. Drawbacks include bats and having to walk downstairs to use the 1929 bathroom.

Casa Oro (tel. 505/568-2415, www.casael oro.com) is a dorm-style youth hostel in a big, old, wooden building just west of the central park; rates are $5–7 bunk/hammock, $18 double with private bath. Also on offer are $30 guided tours to La Flor and surf beach shuttles for $5 round-trip.

You'll find a warm welcome, a kitchen, and parking at **Rebecca's Inn** (25 yards west of the park, tel. 505/675-1048, martha_urcuyo

CRUISE SHIPS: *LOS CRUCEROS* COMETH

In 1998, the Holland America Line added San Juan del Sur as a port of call on several of their cruises. The announcement sparked hope in the people of San Juan del Sur, who began preparing their sleepy town to receive the thousands of cruise ship passengers scheduled to disembark.

After several years of regular biweekly stops however, whether or not *los cruceros* have benefited San Juan del Sur depends entirely on whom you ask. The well-to-do Careli Tour company, which enjoys a monopoly on the buses and guides who whisk passengers straight from the dock in San Juan to day trips in Granada or Masaya, isn't complaining. These passengers never set foot in San Juan proper, and the few hundred who decide to remain in town do not spend money in restaurants or hotels. A few bars have made a good business

catering to thirsty crewmembers, but passengers themselves don't do much onshore imbibing or eating. The *ciclo*-taxis and their drivers that cart passengers to and from the dock are imported from Rivas and few of the crafts vendors that display along the tree-lined beachfront strip are Nicaraguan. In fact, the majority of San Juaneños have not gained a dime from the arrival of the cruise ships and would only notice their absence by the lack of tinted-window bus convoys rumbling past their doors every two weeks.

Concerned cruise passengers should attempt to leave some dollars behind for someone other than their ship-sponsored tour operators, whether in San Juan del Sur or in other Nicaraguan cities they visit – and if you like what you see, come back and spend a night or two.

@yahoo.es, $16–20), run by Martha, who grew up in this house and can tell you about the local lore in English. **Hotel Costa Azul** (from the park, one block west, one block north, tel. 505/568-4294, $10 shared bath, $20 private bath and TV) is *tranquilo* and clean but you'll share your common space with customers of the in-house Internet café. An extra $10 is charged for running your room's air-conditioning.

The small but clean **Posada Puesta del Sol** (one block west of the municipal park, tel. 505/568-2532, lalacard98@yahoo.com, $10–15 with breakfast) has five rooms and a friendly, welcoming feel. A $2 rate reduction is given to students studying Spanish in town.

$25-50

[**Royal Chateau Hotel** (one block east of the market, tel. 505/568-2551) is Nica-owned, and their friendliness, the security of the compound, private parking, a big wooden porch, and a filling breakfast make the Royal Chateau an easy pick for the midrange hotels. Rooms run $35 double with fan, private bath, and TV, and $10 more for air-conditioning.

Hotel Colonial (half a block from the park, tel. 505/568-2227, $54) has 12 cramped rooms with private bath, TV, air-conditioning, and continental breakfast. Right around the corner, **Hotel Gran Océano** (tel. 505/568-2219, hgoceano@ibw.com.ni, $46) is similar. **Hotel El Pacifico** (tel. 505/568-2557, pacifico@ibw.com.ni, $46) is located across the river in Barrio El Talanguera, well removed from the hustle and bustle of the city. Get there via the Chocolata road turnoff before the bridge at the entrance to town. Rooms are basic and comfortable, with wood floors, air-conditioning, private bath, parking, pool, restaurant, and bar.

$50-100

Most of the places in this category include breakfast in the room rate. **Frederica's B&B** (waterfront, tel. 505/568-2489, rapido1@ibw.com.ni) has a pair of lovely, fully equipped doubles for $55, or $60 with air-conditioning. [**Hotel Villa Isabella** (tel. 505/568-2568, www.sanjuandelsur.org.ni/isabella) charges $75 for large rooms with private bath, air-conditioning, TV, Wi-Fi, heated pool, and $95–150 for full condos. This pristine, 13-room bed-and-breakfast is two minutes from the beach, and offers a small pool, business services, full accessibility, and a huge selection of free DVDs. Their breakfast is no meager continental affair: homemade waffles, cinnamon rolls, banana pancakes, eggs your way, fresh fruit, and great coffee. Discounts are available throughout the year.

Hotel Casa Blanca (tel. 505/568-2135, casablanca@ibw.com.ni, $70 plus tax) is also a good choice, with small pool, parking, laundry, breakfast, kitchen, and 24-hour security.

(La Posada Azul (half a block east of BDF bank, tel. 505/568-2524, www.laposada azul.com, $80–120) has lovely rooms, breakfast included, Wi-Fi, and pool. Tasteful decor and classy wood-grained ambience echo the remodeled building's 90-year history.

Just south of town, in the Las Delicias neighborhood is **Las Cascadas B&B** (tel. 505/689-8008, www.lascascadasbandb.com, $65–95 d). All rooms have air-conditioning, satellite TV, and hot water. Massage, pool, and a menagerie of animals from Captain Jim, the three-foot-tall parrot, capuchin monkeys, iguanas, toucans, and a couple of friendly pooches.

Farther south and closer to the Remanso surf break is the relaxing **Gaby Mar** (tel. 568-2358, jorsan@ibw.com.ni, $70), with one of the nicest pools in the area, air-conditioning, and hot water. Or, come for lunch and enjoy the pool.

Over $100

Featured in nine out of ten gushing travel articles about Nicaragua in the last few years, **(Pelican Eyes Piedras y Olas** (tel. 505/568-2510, www.piedrasyolas.com, $120–250) has fully equipped homes with kitchenettes and

Sunsets from Pelican Eyes Piedras y Olas are a main attraction.

outdoor decks; this was one of the first resorts to raise the luxury bar in San Juan del Sur and Nicaragua. This compound of straw-bale and adobe construction built into the hillside on the east end of town features two bars, a world-class restaurant, and three infinity pools overlooking the ocean. The 50 rooms and large villas are built against a 10-acre nature reserve (open to exploration). Their **Bistro La Canoa** is one of the best places in town to enjoy a sunset.

Long-Term Accommodations

Weekly or monthly rentals are increasingly easy to arrange. For the low budget set, most Spanish schools in town have packages combining lessons and a homestay, which can be arranged (whether or not you are attending class) for around $10 per day including three meals. Read about Comunidad Connect's services in the sidebar *Volunteering in San Juan del Sur* and check the *Spanish Schools in Nicaragua* section in the *Essentials* chapter for more.

For something fancy, fear not: The property flippers are all hoping to rent you their recently refurbished digs, and the streets are flush with For Rent signs. See **Vacation Rentals Nicaragua** (www.vacationrentalsnicaragua.com) or stop by **Aurora Beachfront Realty** (tel. 505/568-2498, U.S. tel. 323/908-6730). A fully furnished two-bedroom place goes for $800/week and a big house is double that.

FOOD AND BARS
Cheap and Local

Eat three *corriente* meals a day at one of the counters inside the municipal market—under $3 a meal. Evenings, try the *fritanga* across from Elizabeth's *hospedaje,* or walk to the southwest corner of the park for **Asados Vilma,** a.k.a. "The Chicken Lady," with grilled meat dishes, mountains of *gallo pinto,* and delicious juices or *frescos* from $3.

Nearly every *hospedaje,* hotel, and beach restaurant makes a variety of breakfasts, usually for $2–3. Locally owned *sodas* offer a variety of deliciously fried food for about $4. **Soda Margarita** (just west of the Pelican Eyes

entrance, open 7 A.M.–10 P.M. daily) is one of the best. We prefer **Comedor Las Pampas** (located across from the baseball field heading south from town, tel. 505/442-0314, open 7:30 A.M.–9 P.M. daily) for its authentic open-fire cooking and tender *guardatinaja.*

Rinconcito Mexicano (at the upper entrance to the Sports Park, open noon–9 P.M. daily) serves commendable *chilaquiles* ($4) and other authentic Mexican specialities, plus real flour tortillas.

Cafés and Bar Food

The **Panadería** (two blocks north of Hotel Villa Isabella and the park, open early, closed Sun.) serves delicious cinnamon rolls, and **El Gato Negro** (open 7 A.M.–3 P.M. daily) serves wonderful espresso and breakfasts in an excellent bookstore setting.

A mellow bar with great food including a monster Philly cheesesteak, **Big Wave Dave's** is open early for breakfast, then serves bar food, drinks, and darts all day long, meals from $4. Half a block away, **Iguana** has the best burgers, curly fries, and fish tacos in town.

The best food on the go is at **Captain Jim's** sandwich shop, right by the Texaco, where you can order the Daniel Ortega sub, fresh salad, and a fresh smoothie for pocket change.

Seafood

A long row of virtually identical thatched-roof *rancho* restaurants runs along the central part of the beach, serving fresh fish dishes from $5 and shrimp and lobster dishes from $10–14 until 10 P.M. Of note is the seafood soup at **Rocamar,** located at the north end of the beach road, and **Jocelyn's,** near the BDF bank, with delicious fish dishes and a comfy atmosphere. **El Timon** even serves octopus, and is the most expensive of the *ranchos.*

At the south end of the bay or at **ExpoMar** (just east of BDF bank) you can buy grouper, swordfish, or red snapper fresh from the boat (they will filet it for you), particularly on Wednesday and Saturday when the boats return from sea.

VOLUNTEERING IN SAN JUAN DEL SUR

If you'd like to spend some time working with the community, the environment, and the children of San Juan del Sur, there are numerous options.

Comunidad Connect (tel. 505/408-3376, www.comunidadconnect.org) is a local nonprofit with a bilingual, multicultural staff, dedicated to supporting sustainable economic and community development in the area; they run the Sports Park by the beach, started a recycling program in cooperation with the mayor's office, work with real estate agencies and developers to facilitate private sector donations to community projects, and invite voluntourists like yourself to help with their projects. CC can arrange an all-inclusive vacation with a local family homestay, volunteer project, Spanish lessons, and a range of tourism activities. Contact director and long-time San Juan del Sur resident Jon Thompson (jon @comunidadconnect.org) to find out how to get involved in local projects – physically or financially.

The local book-lending project has been a smashing success in a country largely devoid of lending libraries. The **San Juan del Sur Biblioteca Movil** (www.sjdsbiblioteca.com) is a part of the town library, located across the street from the park, and, besides offering books and reading space to San Juaneños, brings books to young and old in outlying communities. The project was founded by Jane Mirandette (janem101@aol.com), the proprietress of Hotel Villa Isabella and is supported by a U.S.-based nonprofit organization, the Hester J. Hodgdon Libraries for All Program (www.librariesforall .org). Besides helping monetarily, tourists can volunteer at the library by teaching English, organizing books, and reading to youngsters. Volunteers can also join the library staff on a visit to one of 27 rural schools to which the Biblioteca Movil brings books for children to bor-

© JOSHUA BERMAN

Donate your time, money, and books to San Juan del Sur's lending library.

row. There is a formal volunteer program for librarians, library school students, and others held twice a year. Book donations are always welcome. Bring them with you or send Spanish-language books to a storage space at: 1716 Del Norte Blvd., Loveland, CO 80538 (visiting Coloradans who bring a suitcase of books from Loveland get a free night in Jane's hotel).

There are several other opportunities to **teach English** in San Juan del Sur. At the Newton Montegri preschool, near the entrance to Pelican Eyes, track down the director Mercedes Rivera Navarro to work with four- and five-year-olds. A range of opportunities working with children and adults is available at the town library, across the street from park. Contact Heidy Herrera Obando (tel. 505/568-2338 or 505/696-8969, heidyho23@yahoo .com) to find out about short- and long-term commitments. The library can provide teaching materials for other projects. At the *instituto* (high school), you can teach English on Saturdays. Contact Director Rosa Elena Bello by calling 505/568-2402 or 505/858-0326. Finally, those wishing to arrange a longer-term experience in a rural setting, possibly staying with a family in the *campo*, can contact Mara Jacobsohn (tel. 505/853-2767).

Fundación A. Jean Brugger (tel. 505/568-2110, fundacion@piedrasyolas.com, www.piedrasyolas.com) was created by the Pelican Eyes folks in 2000 to support the education and training of the promising young people of San Juan del Sur. The Foundation provides scholarships, uniforms, school supplies, and job training for dedicated area students. It also supports antilitter campaigns and a newly built art gallery, which hosts daily workshops for young and not-so-young artists. In addition, the Foundation maintains a 10-acre nature reserve, runs baseball camps for area youths, and hosts a monthly luncheon for senior citizens. Pelican Eyes Piedras y Olas Hotel underwrites all administrative costs for the Foundation, so 100 percent of your donation goes toward the good causes. Monetary donations are always needed and materials, such as school supplies, are appreciated as well.

San Juan del Sur has no fewer than five sister cities around the world: two in Germany, one in Spain, one in Norway, and one in Massachusetts. The **Newton-San Juan del Sur Sister City Project** (david.gullettte @simmons.edu, www.newtonsanjuan.org) sends brigades down twice a year (medical, dental, optical, construction, English instruction, etc.) and also directly supports the library project. They also have an appropriate technologies workshop in which volunteers can help build and install improved stoves, latrines, and water filters. To make a tax-deductible contribution, send a check to Treasurer Fiora Houghteling, 15 Bullough Park, Newton, MA 02460. The local contact in San Juan is Rosa Elena Bello at the Servicios Medicos Comunales (rosaebel@ibw.com.ni).

Also, check the listing for **Esperanza del Futuro** in the *Tola* section of this chapter.

Bambu Beach Club (located at the north end of San Juan del Sur's main beach, tel. 505/568-2101, www.thebambubeachclub.com) is a Mediterranean-influenced restaurant serving seafood *bocas*, sandwiches, and entrées. It's also a full bar, relaxed beach hangout, seaside cinema, and acoustic concert space.

Italian

◖ **Pizzería San Juan** (just west of the playground at the municipal park, tel. 505/568-2295 for delivery, open from 5 P.M. daily) is also authentic, with great pasta and real Italian pizza by the slice or $7 a pie.

Fine Dining

Bar y Restaurante La Cascada (in Pelican Eyes Piedras y Olas Hotel, tel. 505/568-2511, $11–20) offers tables set above the village with a prime view of the ocean and sunset. The chef is world class, serving delights like parmesan-crusted baked mahi over herb spaetzle.

Breakfast and lunch start at $7; or just sample from the exotic tropical drink menu.

◖ **El Colibri** (one block south of the east side of the church, tel. 505/568-2861, $6–12) offers a reasonably priced assortment of delicious Mediterranean specialties from paella to polenta to chicken breast stuffed with walnuts, raisins, and basil in a red wine sauce. Reservations for large parties during the high season are recommended. **El Pozo** (half a block south of the market, tel. 505/806-5708, open from 6 P.M. Thurs.–Mon., $8–12) is a modern bistro featuring contemporary American dishes.

El Jardín (tel. 505/880-4765, open 5–9:30 P.M. Wed.–Sun., $6–8) is located outside of town on the Chocolata road heading north, but is well worth the drive. They complement Asian fusion cuisine with an assortment of margaritas and fancy tequilas; leave room for the cheesecake.

INFORMATION AND SERVICES

From home, start your exploration online at **www.sanjuandelsur.org.ni.** Many of the businesses listed in this chapter can be found on this local network of websites and they post updated rates. The new **Municipal Tourism Commission** at the northwest corner of the park can provide information on activities, and free maps and flyers around town advertize local goings-on.

Health Services

The few pharmacies in town have limited supplies; for medical needs, the Centro de Salud provides free consultations 8 A.M.–7 P.M. Monday–Saturday, 8 A.M.–noon Sunday. However, for any serious medical concerns, plan a trip to Rivas, as the Centro is typically understaffed and crowded.

Banks and ATMs

Nearly all of the nicer hotels (and restaurants) accept major credit cards, but the three banks in town all have ATMs. BDF, located half a block from the Casa de Cultura; Banco

ProCredit, one block west of the market; and Bancentro, next to Big Wave Dave's, all offer similar services but do not change travelers checks. The ATM at Casa Blanca gives out U.S. dollars along with *córdobas,* as does the ProCredit ATM.

Internet

San Juan's handful of Internet cafés are more expensive than other places in Nicaragua but are plentiful and easy to find. There's one at Hotel Costa Azul and another up the block at Leo's, both good. The completely solar- and wind-powered **Nica Geeks** (open 8 A.M.–6 P.M. daily) has more expensive but faster service, located on the street coming into town from the Texaco station.

Laundry

Most of the nicer hotels provide laundry service, as will the inexpensive hotels if you strike a deal. If you'd rather go to an independent *lavandería* (laundromat) with modern machines, you'll find **Gaby's** (tel. 505/837-7493) uphill from the market, charging $5 per load (wash, dry, fold).

GETTING THERE AND AWAY

The trip from Managua is about 2–2.5 hours in your own vehicle or express bus but nearly 4 hours in an *ordinario.*

To San Juan del Sur

Going to San Juan del Sur, catch express buses from Roberto Huembes terminal ($3–5 pp) about every hour around the middle of the day; the best and last one leaves at 4 P.M. Slow, crowded, *ordinario* service to Rivas from Huembes Market in Managua operates 5 A.M.–5 P.M. From Rivas you can take a *colectivo* ($1.50 pp) or taxi ($7) the rest of the way. *Colectivos* don't run after dark and taxi prices double because not even the most skilled drivers can see the potholes at night.

Beware! The handlers at the Huembes bus terminal can be unusually aggressive. They will grab your bags out of the taxi, push you onto a slow Rivas bus, lie by claiming it's an express,

San Juan del Sur in all its natural glory

and then demand a tip. Read the windshield of the bus and ask the other passengers to verify.

Managua Airport Direct Shuttles

This convenience is a brand new service in San Juan: **Adelante Express** (tel. 505/850-6070, www.adelanteexpress.com) charges about $40 one-way, cheaper per person for groups. There are new shuttle services to Granada and León popping up all the time; check Tierra Tours (see *Information and Tour Operators* in the *Granada* chapter).

To Managua

Express buses leave from the corner in front of the market at 5 A.M. (this is the nicer *lujo* bus), 6 A.M., and 7 A.M. *Ordinarios* to Rivas and Managua leave every hour 5 A.M.–5 P.M. You can also catch a *colectivo* taxi to Rivas from 4 A.M. to about 3 or 4 P.M. and then catch any northbound bus toward Managua.

Going to and from Costa Rica

From the Costa Rican border at Peñas Blancas, buses for Rivas leave every half hour. Get off at **Empalme la Vírgen** and flag a bus, taxi, or ride going between Rivas and San Juan del Sur. The beach is 18 kilometers due west of La Vírgen; taxis from the border to San Juan charge $11–20.

To the border at Peñas Blancas, get a ride to La Vírgen in a bus or taxi, then catch a lift south; the first Rivas–Peñas Blancas bus passes at 7:30 A.M. Or book a ticket with TicaBus (tel. 505/877-1407) in Rivas.

GETTING AROUND

You won't need a taxi to get around town (you'll only see them trolling for passengers to Rivas): from one end of town to the other it's just a 15-minute stroll. Instead walk or rent a bike from Elizabeth's.

To travel up and down the coast, you'll

¿PURA VIDA? NICARAGUA'S ROCKY RELATIONSHIP WITH COSTA RICA

Costa Rica is a wealthier, more politically stable country than Nicaragua. In his 1985 travelogue, *So Far From God,* Patrick Marnham called Costa Rica "the most European of the countries of the isthmus." To keep it that way, the Costa Rican economy is wholly dependent on low-cost Nicaraguan laborers for harvesting their sugarcane and coffee and filling the ranks of the construction workforce in urban centers. In an effort to control immigration, Costa Rican officials conduct regular roundups of illegal aliens, returning as many as 150 to Nicaragua daily. As you travel south into Costa Rica, you can expect patrolmen to stop and search your bus several times for illegals. Some estimates put the number of Nicaraguans living in Costa Rica at more than a million, but with the constant flux and large percentage of illegals, no one knows for sure. The real number might be half that. But many Ticos are sure of one thing: Nicaraguans are "lazy, no-good, poor, and dirty." Oh yeah, they're *"Indios,"* to boot.

The tense relationship between these incongruous Central American neighbors loosely parallels the relationship between the United States and Mexico: namely, a massive flood of poor immigrants crosses the border into a more prosperous and stable nation and is subsequently accused of driving down wages, taking all the jobs, and straining social services without paying taxes. As the immigrants are darker skinned and easy to distinguish, they're easy to blame.

Nicaraguans, for their part, generally mistrust Ticos and don't appreciate their arrogance. "The truth is," wrote none other than Carlos Fonseca, founder of the FSLN, from exile in San José in 1960, that Costa Rica "doesn't even seem to be located next to Nicaragua – it is so totally different.... And even though this country is different from Nicaragua, and I am longing for a different Nicaragua, Costa Rica doesn't appeal to me, and I wouldn't want the Nicaragua of the future to be anything like Costa Rica."

Cultural tensions predate these new immigration issues; in fact, only 50 years ago, Ticos used to emigrate to Nicaragua to work on cattle farms. A hundred years before that, after helping to defeat William Walker's army in Rivas, Tico soldiers occupied southern Nicaragua, withdrawing only after being granted the Guanacaste Peninsula in an 1858 treaty. During the 1980s, U.S.-backed Contra forces illegally based operations in Costa Rica, prompting an irritated Costa Rican President Oscar Arías Sanchez to help negotiate an end to Nicaragua's conflict.

Costa Rica continues to press for a resolution to Nicaraguan immigration issues. Too much blustery rhetoric from Managua regarding other issues, like the sovereignty of the Río San Juan, may tempt the Ticos to crack down even more on illegal immigrants, something Managua would very much like to avoid. Even today, Nicaraguan immigrants have reported irregular and inhumane incarceration by Tico authorities, often for weeks at a time without formal charges (and sometimes without daylight, toilets, or sufficient food).

Rhetoric aside, the two neighbors desperately need each other. Costa Rica's most recent census puts the total number of legal and illegal Nicaraguan immigrants at around at between a quarter and half a million, all of whom make the Tico service economy, from agriculture to construction, function. In turn, the remittances those workers send home keep Nicaraguan families afloat. Perhaps pragmatism will win out over politics in the end.

need a sturdy and preferably four-wheel drive car or a decent mountain bike and some stamina. Taxi drivers lounge around the market and can take you up and down the coast, but if you are going surfing to Madera or to Majagual for the day, you're better off catching a ride with one of the surf shops, or with the "gringo shuttles" from Casa Oro. Casa Oro also runs turtle tours, and water taxis operate from in front of Hotel Estrella. Casa Blanca, on the central park of the beach, rents cars.

Arrange a car and driver in advance by contacting Ricardo Morales (2.5 blocks south of Hotel Villa Isabella, tel. 505/882-8368 or 505/568-2618, richardsjds@hotmail.com), a San Juan native with a few "4-Ronners" and a great deal of local contacts and knowledge; he'll pick you up at the airport or in Granada if you like.

BEACHES TO THE SOUTH

Between San Juan del Sur and Ostional on the Costa Rican border are a number of excellent beaches (see *By Bus along the Ostional Road* for bus access to all of the following). You'll first pass through Barrio Las Delicias, which includes San Juan del Sur's stadium and cemetery, followed by a fork in the road known as "El Container." Turn right here to get to **Playa Remanso,** about a kilometer down a path infamous for robberies: Don't go alone. For $10, which goes towards food and drinks, you can park at a small hotel. Take the creek road to the right of the entrance to get to the slow surf break on one of the most scenic beaches near town. At low tide, look for bat caves, tidepools, blowholes, and various wildlife.

Walking 30 minutes south around the rocks brings you to **Playa Tamarindo,** followed by **Playa Hermosa** just under an hour later (it's a

© JOSHUA BERMAN

Playa Yanqui, just south of San Juan del Sur

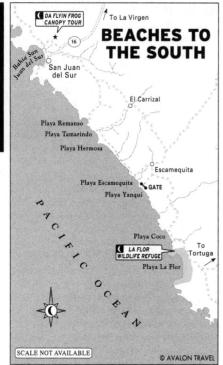

BEACHES TO THE SOUTH

DA FLYIN FROG CANOPY TOUR
To La Virgen
16
San Juan del Sur
Bahía San Juan del Sur
El Carrizal
Playa Remanso
Playa Tamarindo
Playa Hermosa
Escamequita
Playa Escamequita ← GATE
Playa Yanquí
PACIFIC OCEAN
Playa Coco
LA FLOR WILDLIFE REFUGE
To Tortuga
Playa La Flor
SCALE NOT AVAILABLE
© AVALON TRAVEL

20-minute walk from the bus stop at El Carizal, farther down the road toward Ostional). Ask in the surf shops in town about safety precautions and public access to these beaches.

A 20-minute drive south of town is **Playa Yanqui.** This powerful and fast wave that rolls into a giant beach was almost destroyed by one of the new developments when the owner decided to build a "viewpoint" going out into the sea. An effort by local surfers and activists prevented the construction and for now, this break remains one of the best in the area. Look for a sign at a fork on the main road before you get to the Yankee Beach development; go right and then left at another sign, then over a hill for a photo-worthy view of what awaits. Park at the small house on a hill at the south end of the beach for $3 to prevent theft. At low tide you can park right on the beach.

Playa El Coco

Eighteen kilometers south of San Juan, this jewel of a beach is great for swimming, fishing, and access to the turtles at La Flor; this is where you'll find **Parque Marítimo El Coco** (tel. 505/892-0124, www.playaelcoco.com.ni), an extensive compound on a wide beach with a popular restaurant called **Puesta del Sol** (open 8 A.M.–6 P.M. daily, closed Tues.) with meals from $7. Accommodations range from furnished apartments to fully equipped bungalows and houses; prices start at $80 and go to hundreds of dollars per night—weekend packages are very reasonable with a group of people. Houses have air-conditioning, satellite TV, hot water, and kitchen, and sleep up to eight people. You should come prepared with supplies; there is an on-site minimarket, plus bike rental, Internet, and a new conference facility.

La Flor Wildlife Refuge

One of the two Pacific turtle nesting beaches in Nicaragua, the park at La Flor is comanaged by the government and **Fundación Cocibolca** (tel. 505/248-8234), an NGO that has organized the local stakeholders in the management of the park. Foreigners pay $10 per person to enter, another $25 for a group for camping (bring your own gear). Try to catch one of the nighttime *arribadas,* or mass nesting events.

Ostional

This picturesque bay and community at the extreme southwestern tip of Nicaragua is still more of a fishing town than a tourist destination, but curious visitors can seek out the rural tourism cooperative, **Community Tours** (tel. 505/846-2272, communitytours@yahoo .es), for tours of the area and nearby bays—along with simple accommodations. All trips are about four hours and have a local guide, whether by boat or horseback. A portion of the profits goes toward 30 university scholarships for promising youths of the community.

By Bus along the Ostional Road

Buses from Rivas to Ostional pass through the San Juan del Sur market at 1 P.M., 4 P.M.,

TURTLES

The Olive Ridley (or Paslama) sea turtle *(Lepidochelys olivacea)* is an endangered species well known for its massive synchronous nesting emergences. These seasonal occurrences, called *arribadas,* occur several times during each lunar cycle in the July-February nesting season and, at their peak (Aug.-Oct.), result in as many as 20,000 females nesting and laying eggs on a single beach.

In Nicaragua, the two beaches that receive the most turtles are **Playa Chacocente** and **Playa La Flor,** both on the southwestern Pacific coast. Playa La Flor, located about 15 kilometers north of the Costa Rican border and 18 kilometers southeast of San Juan del Sur, is a 1.6-kilometer-long beach that has been protected as part of a wildlife preserve. However, some 4,000 people in nine nearby communities have long derived some form of income from the turtle-egg harvest. During the nesting season, government officials work with local community leaders to allow for a semi-controlled harvest of 10-20 percent of the total eggs deposited on the beach. Despite this management strategy, hatchings have been less successful every year. Fly larvae, beetles, coyotes, opossums, raccoons, skunks, coatimundi, feral dogs, pigs, and humans all prey on Olive Ridley sea turtles in one form or another. High tides and beach erosion sweep away other eggs, and once they emerge from their shells, they are pounced on by crabs, frigate birds, caracara, vultures, and coyotes before they can reach the sea. Once in the water, they must still battle a host of predatory fish.

In general, females lay two clutches of eggs per season and remain near shore for approximately one month. The mean clutch size of the females differs from beach to beach but averages about 100 eggs; incubation takes 45-55 days, depending on the temperature, humidity, and organic content of the sand.

The *arribadas* and hatching events both occur during the night and witnessing these phenomena is an unforgettable experience. Tourism can protect the turtles, as it provides an incentive to continue protection efforts, but it can just as easily be disastrous (since the first edition of this book was published, the rangers have been permitting people to "swim with the turtles," an injurious practice). It is too easy to harass, injure, or frighten the turtles if you're not careful. Don't count on park rangers to tell you what's acceptable; use your common sense to respect this inspiring natural process and *please* pay close attention to the following rules during your expedition to the beaches of La Flor or Chacocente:

TURTLE-VIEWING ETIQUETTE

1. Do not take use your camera's flash when taking pictures of turtles coming out of the sea, digging a nest, or going back to the ocean – the light can scare them back into the ocean without laying their eggs. The only time that you can take a picture of them is when they are laying eggs; the flash will not disturb them as much, as they enter a semitrance state.

2. Keep your flashlight use as minimal as possible; use a red filter over the lens or color it with a temporary red marker. If the moon is out, use its light instead.

3. Do not dig out any nests that are being laid or are hatching.

4. Do not eat sea turtle eggs, whether on the beach or in a restaurant. Despite their undeserved reputation as an aphrodisiac, the raw eggs may carry harmful organisms and their consumption supports a black market that incentivizes poaching.

5. Do not touch, attempt to lift, turn, or ride turtles.

6. Do not interfere with any research being performed on the beach (i.e., freeing hatchlings from nest boxes).

7. If camping, place your tents beyond the vegetation line so as not to disturb the nesting turtles.

(Thanks to Shaya Honarvar, PhD, Department of Bioscience & Biotechnology, Drexel University)

and 5 P.M. and onwards (two hours) to Ostional. They depart the center of Ostional at 5 A.M., 7:30 A.M., and 4 P.M., but confirm with the driver and anyone else you can find waiting around.

BEACHES TO THE NORTH

By land, access these beaches via the road to Chocolata, just east of the Texaco station. Much of this road served as the old railroad grade for a railroad never built. Seven kilometers along this road, turn left at Chocolata to a fork in the road: left goes to Marsella and Madera, right to Majagual.

Playa Marsella

This pleasant, breezy beach is one of the closest to San Juan del Sur and you can drive right up to the sand, making it a popular day trip for Frisbee throwers and sunset watchers. On the weekends a small restaurant on the beach serves up *ceviche,* fried fish, and cold beer.

Playa Madera

One of the most consistent, easy-to-access surf breaks from San Juan, Madera is enjoyed for its medium-speed hollow wave that breaks both right and left, best on incoming tides. There's parking right on the beach, and the place turns into a popular hangout around sunset.

A simple wooden bunkhouse with a kitchen offers cheap lodging for $5 per person and cheap meals ($2 breakfast, $5 lunch), and rents boards by the hour.

A short walk north is **Hideout Surf Camp** (ddwysdwy@hyahoo.com, $10 pp dorm, $20 private room) followed by, another five minutes north along the beach, **Matilda's** (tel. 505/456-3461 or 505/818-3374, camping _matilda's@hotmail.com, $4.50 for a "permatent," $8 dorm, $30 d private room with bath) right on the beach, perfect for swimming. **Buena Vista Surf Club** leans towards luxury (tel. 505/863-4180 or 505/863-3312, www. buenavistasurfclub.com), located in the hills above Madera, from where you can watch

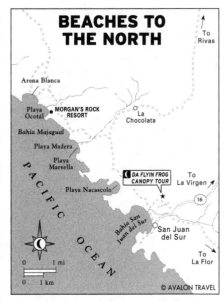

BEACHES TO THE NORTH

To Rivas

Arena Blanca

Playa Ocotál · MORGAN'S ROCK RESORT

La Chocolata

Bahía Majagual

Playa Madera

Playa Marsella

DA FLYIN FROG CANOPY TOUR

To La Virgen

16

Playa Nacascolo

Bahía San Juan del Sur

San Juan del Sur

PACIFIC OCEAN

To La Flor

0   1 mi
0   1 km

© AVALON TRAVEL

the waves while doing yoga on an incredible wooden deck.

To get to and from Madera, stop by any of the surf shops in San Juan. Rides cost $5 round-trip. More options are available in Bahí Majagual.

Bahía Majagual

Twelve rough kilometers from San Juan del Sur, this is one of the most beautiful beaches on the coast, popular with surfers. Formerly a peaceful backpacker retreat, it is now home to a 15-foot-tall cement tower. For the moment, the beach remains accessible, but hurry.

Majagual is perfect for day trips. You can also take a water taxi from San Juan del Sur, the boat leaves from in front of Hotel Estrella at 11 A.M. and comes back at 5 P.M.; round-trip is $7 per person. Another choice is the "gringo shuttle" from Casa Oro. These usually leave around 11 A.M. By bus from Rivas, head toward the Chocolata road—19 kilometers west of Rivas—and walk 5 kilometers west. A private taxi costs around $20.

© JOSHUA BERMAN

Playa Ocotál, as seen from the exclusive Morgan's Rock Hacienda & Eco Lodge

Morgan's Rock Hacienda & Eco Lodge

Continuing north along the coast, Playa Ocotál is the home of a much-hyped ecolodge at the vanguard of Nicaragua's upscale tourism market. **(Morgan's Rock Hacienda & Eco Lodge** (tel. 506/296-9442, www.morgans rock.com) is an exclusive resort surrounded by a 1,000-hectare reforestation project and an 800-hectare private nature reserve; its 15 elegant, hardwood cabins are built into a bluff above the crashing surf on the beach below. As few trees as possible were felled during construction, so you'll have to walk a 110-meter-long suspension bridge through a lush canopy to reach your cabin, which is the most luxurious and beautiful treehouse your childhood fantasies ever dreamed up. The structures—as well as the main lodge, which features a

gorgeous infinity pool—were designed with all local materials and feature ingenious architecture and attention to detail. Check out the photo tour on the website if you don't believe us.

You're on vacation here, so no phones or Internet, but there's plenty to do: sunrise kayak tours of the estuary, tree-planting excursions, and tours of their shrimp farm and sugar mill, where they brew their own Morgan's Rum. More than 70 workers are employed to grow and produce much of the restaurant's vegetables, dairy products, herbs, and other needs. A cool $250 per person per night gets you a cabin, three meals, all you can drink of local, nonalcoholic beverages, and two tours a day. Prices vary by season, so call or email to reserve your room. The facilities and services are for guests only, so sorry, no day trippers.

Tola and Pacific Beaches

Ten kilometers west of Rivas is the agricultural community of Tola, gateway to the steadily improving shore road and a string of lonely, beautiful beaches that make up thirty kilometers of Pacific shoreline. Until very recently, you would have been the only foreigner on any of these beaches, but the word is out and land prices are rising. Still, there are few tourist facilities and only a few isolated lot developments. A nine-hole golf course at Playa Iguana may be open by the time you read this, as well as other projects, but until then, the beaches west of Tola are still an adventure.

TOLA

Tola is famous in Nicaragua as the subject of a common expression: *"Te dejó esperando como la novia de Tola"* ("He left you waiting like the bride of Tola"), which recalls the real-life soap opera of a young woman named Hillary, who, on the day of her wedding, was left at the altar at Belén while the groom, Salvador Cruz, married his former lover, Juanita.

There are a few decent eateries in Tola, the most popular of which are **El Naranjito** and **Lumby's.** Operating since September 2001, **Esperanza del Futuro** (tel. 505/563-0482), a community-development program run by Doña Loida (an influential Sandinista leader, elected Mayor in 2004), aims to provide better education to people in rural areas. They have a library, classrooms, sewing co-op, and gardens, and give classes in guitar, agriculture, herbal medicine, and computers. Many travelers have stayed and worked with Doña Loida, from a week to six months. They'll help arrange cheap room and board. Esperanza del Futuro is located on the road that leads from the park to the baseball field/basketball court, about 100 meters past the baseball field.

◖ PLAYA GIGANTE

North up the coast from San Juan del Sur, and an hour outside Rivas, Gigante is the first beach you come to after Tola and is named after the Punta Pie de Gigante (The Giant's Foot), a local rock formation. The community of Gigante consists of a beautiful crescent beach, a few dozen poor homes occupied by about 500 locals, and a growing number of surf camps. Avoid this beach during Semana Santa, when it gets crowded with locals who camp out on the beach, get phenomenally drunk, and run cockfights. For local information and guide services, ask at Hotel Blue Sol or El Mirador for Zacarias, a well-recommended guide who can help you arrange trips, and find food and lodging and some waves. He also has a *palapa* (shack) on the beach where you can hang your hammock.

Accommodations

Giant's Foot Surf Lodge (tel. 505/606-9071, www.giantsfoot.com) rents out two adjacent beachfront lodges with air-conditioning, fan, and private bathroom; full capacity is 12 guests. Amenities include table tennis, a fire pit, hammocks, DVDs, books, and board games. Weeklong packages cost about $1,000, everything included except your airfare; discounts are available in the off-season. **Hotel Brio** (tel. 505/552-8422, www.hotelbrio.com, $20–30 with fan and private bath) is 300 meters back from the beach, with ocean views, Wi-Fi, and a restaurant serving three meals a day. They also have two 25-foot *pangas* for surfing and fishing tours. **Hotel Blue Sol** ($5 with fan and shared bathroom) is a great place to feel the local Nica vibe and eat the best tacos in town.

At Dale Dagger's **Hidden Bay Surf Lodge** (www.nicasurf.com), about $1,000 a week lets you explore some of the best and least-known breaks in Nicaragua, returning to the luxury of air-conditioning, wireless Internet, and running hot water. Dale encourages his guests to eat at local restaurants so as to directly support and authentically interact with the local community.

Momo's Camp (tel. 505/695-6639, www.surfcamp-nicaragua.com), run by Vincent

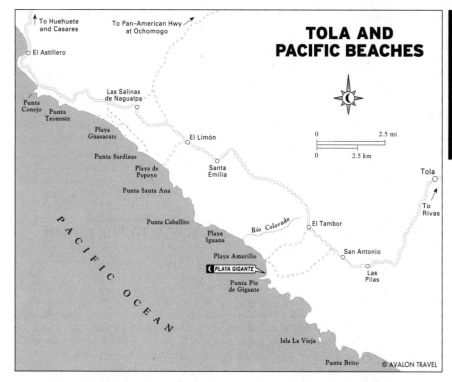

TOLA AND PACIFIC BEACHES

and Theresa, has all-inclusive packages with two daily boat trips to the best waves between Popoyo to the north and Manzanillo to the south.

Food

La Gaviota is famous for its *plato típico de Gigante* featuring seasonal seafood ($4–11). **El Mirador** prepares popular breaded fish nuggets *(deditos de pescado)*. Buy fresh seafood in the mornings from three local *acopios* (storage houses) and buy everything else from **Pulpería Mena.**

Getting There and Away

Take the Las Salinas bus from Tola or Rivas and get off at either of the two entrances to the beach (the second one is a bit easier to follow). If you are not traveling by car, you'll need to walk or bike about seven kilometers to the beach on a hilly dirt road. Look for Rivas–Tola–Gigante buses, leaving around 8 A.M. and returning late in the afternoon. Travelers pay $1 for a round-trip ticket.

LAS SALINAS DE NAGUALAPA

Las Salinas is a poor fishing community whose lovely beach is popular among surfers. **La Tica** is a simple and pleasant restaurant and *hospedaje* where the owners are friendly and helpful; rooms cost a couple dollars per person. Nearby hot springs are worth exploring if you get sick of the beach (ask at La Tica for directions) but are also used by local families to wash clothing, so they're not exactly pristine.

The Surf Sanctuary (tel. 505/894-6260, www.thesurfsanctuary.com) is a surf camp with restaurant, bar, TV, Internet, movies, and the works. For $50 per day, guests enjoy a private house with four beds, bath, hot water, air-conditioning, private porches, and pool; weeklong all-inclusive packages cost about $1,500 per person. But **Two Brothers Surf Resort** (tel. 505/877-7501, www.twobrothers surf.com) offers more luxury, comfort, and security. Villas range $80–150 a night. The big one fits up to six people; the resort features a pool, lounge, hand-carved Indonesian temple doors and archways, locally crafted Granada floor tiles, fully equipped kitchens, air-conditioning, ceiling fans, and indoor and outdoor showers.

GUASACATE AND POPOYO

Guasacate, a huge stretch of gorgeous shoreline that remains, for the moment, little visited and mostly undeveloped, is now the site of some upscale home construction, so transformation has begun. The entrance to Guasacate is 5–8 kilometers down the first left-hand road after crossing a bridge in Las Salinas, paved the whole way. What this means for the renowned Popoyo surf break remains to be seen. **Popoyo Surf Lodge** (tel. 321/735-0322, www.surf nicaragua.com) has a variety of basic rooms as well as fancy lodging with private bathrooms, air-conditioning, and tile floors. The restaurant serves three square meals and lots of fresh fish; reservations and packages available online at www.wavehunters.com.

"Mama" Gloria Mendoza's **Casa/Bar Mendoza** (a.k.a. the "Tiltin' Hilton") also offers basic lodging, including hammocks for $2, camping $3 per person, and a few small, cleanish rooms; three meals a day are available for $2–4. **Surfing Martinez,** in a smaller building across the street, has $2 hammocks and dark, sandy, tiled rooms, all with shared bath, for $5 per person.

Also in the neighborhood, about 300 meters from the beach, is **Surfari Charters** (tel. 505/874-7173, www.surfaricharters.com), which specializes in all-inclusive surf and fishing trips, so check their website for more information (or just to see some really amazing surf pics).

At least one bus a day leaves Roberto Huembes in Managua bound for El Astillero via Ochomogo (not Tola). From San Juan del Sur or Costa Rica, you'll be driving through Rivas and Tola, following the signs to Rancho Santana, then continuing past this development's gates until you reach Las Salinas. Buses depart Rivas about every hour. A taxi to Guasacate from El Astillero costs $7, from Rivas $30. The road to the beach will take you past several austere salt flats, from which the nearby town of Las Salinas gets its name.

EL ASTILLERO AND BEACHES TO THE NORTH

Most of the little deserted beaches in the 10-kilometer strip between Las Salinas and El Astillero don't even have names. El Astillero itself is a fishing village full of small boats and is, in fact, the first safe boat anchorage north of Gigante. North of El Astillero, the road turns inland away from the coast. Accessing the beach anywhere along this area requires a boat and a lot of dedication. Ask around in El Astillero. There are plenty of underemployed sailors and fishermen that would be glad to strike a deal with you if you're interested in exploring the coastline.

Refugio de Vida Silvestre Río Escalante-Chacocente

One of the only Nicaraguan Pacific beaches where the Paslama turtle lays its eggs, Escalante-Chacocente Wildlife Refuge (tel. 505/532-3293, www.chacocente.info) is a protected wildlife area whose beach provides habitat for numerous other species as well, including white-tailed deer, reptiles, and many interesting types of flora. There's lots to do, including guided wildlife tours, sportfishing, scuba diving, and projects with various local communities. Getting to Chacocente isn't easy which, for the sake of the turtles, is just as well. One early morning bus leaves Diriamba daily for Chacocente, spends the night, and returns to Diriamba before dawn the next day. Campers can bring their own tent or stay in the visitors center's wooden bungalows for only a couple of dollars. To get there, the turnoff from the Pan-American Highway is just south of the Río Ochomogo bridge, or take a taxi from Rivas (about $20 for the 90-minute ride).

Peñas Blancas and the Costa Rica Border

Peñas Blancas is the official border crossing into Costa Rica. Since 1999, this post has undergone massive construction and renovation, making it a nicer—and better organized—post than even Costa Rica's (although the Ticos have a cafeteria on their side, something still lacking on the Nica side of the border). A major effort is underway, with financing from the United States, to make this border crossing a bottleneck and entrapment point for drug traffickers headed north. Many of the buildings you see in the compound are inspection points for the hundreds of tractor-trailers that cross the border every day. Needless to say, this is one place you don't want to be caught smuggling furs. Sniffing dogs are common.

Border hassles can last anywhere from 1–10 hours! The longest waits happen at times when the hundreds of thousands of Nicaraguans living across the border are traveling to and from their country—this happens a week before and after Christmas, Easter, and any Nicaraguan election. The best time of day to cross is during the afternoon. Usually you can squeeze through in under an hour.

HOURS AND FEES

The border is open 6 A.M.–10 P.M. on all days, except Sunday when it closes at 8 P.M. There is a small fee for exiting ($2–4) and entering ($7–9) Nicaragua. Everyone traveling to the border on an international bus service like TicaBus or TransNica will pay $1 to the town government of Cárdenas before reaching the border, "just because."

Inside the Customs and Immigration building, find a branch of Bancentro, which can help you change money if necessary. Its schedule is generally tied to that of the border post itself.

PAPERWORK

Just a passport and some cash is all that's required of North American and European travelers, but don't forget to get stamped on both sides of the border to avoid subsequent headaches! To enter Costa Rica, Nicaraguan citizens must have a Costa Rican visa from the consulate either in Rivas or Managua. Upon entering Nicaragua, most North American and European travelers are granted a 90-day visa, with the exception of Canadian and Japanese citizens, who for some reason are only given 30 days.

By law, folks entering Costa Rica must have a ticket to leave the country. They usually don't check, as long as you're dressed like you have money. If they do, you lose your place in line and go to the table outside, where Transport Dendu will sell you an open-ended ticket from San Jose to Managua for $7.

ENTERING NICARAGUA WITH YOUR VEHICLE

If you are driving your own vehicle, the process to enter Nicaragua from Costa Rica is lengthy but usually not too difficult (rental vehicles cannot cross the border). You'll present your title *(Título de la Propiedad),* as well as your driver's license and passport. Get proper stamps from Hacienda (Timbres de Hacienda), and a property certificate from Hacienda. Also make sure you have a current tag and Tico insurance; all of this can be taken care of in the town of Liberia, just to the south. You will be given a temporary

(30-day) permit to drive in Nicaragua that will cost $10—should you lose the permit, you will be fined $100. Travelers driving their own vehicles north from the border will be forced to pass through a dubious "sterilization process" on the Nica side, in which the exterior of the vehicle is sprayed with a mystery liquid to kill porcine and bovine diseases; it costs $1 and takes five minutes unless the line is long. Roll up the windows.

GETTING THERE AND AWAY

International bus services like TicaBus, TransNica, and NicaBus are popular ways to get across the border easily and comfortably, the best service being the new TransNica Plus, since you travel with 30 instead of 55 passengers. In many cases, the bus has a "helper" who collects your passports and money and waits in line for you. The disadvantage is that the bus won't pull away from the border post until every single traveler has had their papers processed, which can be time-consuming in some cases (waits up to four hours are not unheard of). More confident travelers like to take a Nicaraguan bus to the border, walk across to Costa Rica, and take a Costa Rican bus to San José, which is often faster. Express buses from Managua to Peñas Blancas depart Mercado Huembes at 5 A.M., 8 A.M., 9:30 A.M., and 3:30 P.M. Buses and microbuses leave the market in Rivas every 30–45 minutes. On the Costa Rican side, the last bus leaves the border bound for San José at 10 P.M. (about a six-hour ride).

CONTINUING INTO COSTA RICA

After crossing the border, you've got two choices: Buy a ticket to San José from the TransNica booth across from customs ($7 pp); the ride takes 6–8 hours, with departures daily at 5:15 A.M., 7:30 A.M., 9:30 A.M. direct, 10:45 A.M., noon, 1:30 P.M. direct, 3:30 P.M., and 6 P.M. Or, get a Liberia–Pulmitan bus to Liberia ($1.50 pp, two hours, last bus at 5:30 P.M.). From Liberia, 14 daily buses go to San José ($4, 3–5 hours); buses leave every 20 minutes to the Nicoya Peninsula and its beaches. Liberia, the capital of Guanacaste, is also a good base for Santa Rosa National Park (where William Walker and company were resoundingly defeated) and Rincón de la Vieja National Park, with impressive volcanoes. In fact, Guanacaste used to belong to Nicaragua and some say it still feels connected, or at least socially and physically independent of Costa Rica proper. Many locals still have family in Nicaragua, and this is the only department with its own flag. You can overnight in **Hotel Liberia** (tel. 506/666-0161, www .hotelliberia.com, $5 pp with shared bath, $9 pp with private bath and really nice room) and thereafter continue easily to Nicoya (but not Monteverde, which is a challenge). For the rest, we highly recommend Christopher P. Baker's *Moon Costa Rica*.

LEÓN AND THE VOLCANIC LOWLANDS

North and west of Managua are broad plains of corn, beans, sorghum, and sugarcane. The fecund soils that make this the most agriculturally productive region in Nicaragua are a gift from the Maribio volcanoes, an uncommonly exposed chain of peaks, rises, and cones stretching from Lake Xolotán to the Gulf of Fonseca. On any given day, one or more may be seen disgorging gas and white ash—and sometimes more.

Fire gives way to water—the beaches beyond León and Chinandega are some of the longest, most isolated in Nicaragua. They exist among coastal islands, estuaries, and virgin mangrove stands rich in marine life and waterfowl like herons and kingfishers. Large tracts of this region remain difficult to access, meaning for the moment, the birds retain the upper hand.

You can't help but feel itinerant here. Blame it on the heat—this is the driest, most scorching corner of the country. Volcanism seeps from the land in boiling mud pits, geothermal vents, and the occasional tremble. The ruins of León's first incarnation are a testament to impermanence. Leóneses and Chinandeganos know that life can be short and even violent, and should thus be enjoyed. Indeed, this region suffered tremendously during Hurricane Mitch in 1998, when more than two meters of rain fell in three days. Nowhere in Nicaragua was the destruction as intense, and the still-visible landslide at Las Casitas is a silent reminder of the worst of it.

León is the principal city of the northwest, a colonial town with the architecture and languid lifestyle of centuries past. This bastion of liberal thought in Central America has narrow

LEÓN

HIGHLIGHTS

🌙 **Museums:** Begin your art immersion at **La Casa de Cultura** and then continue around the corner to the fabulous **Centro de Arte Fundación Ortiz-Gurdián** (page 163).

🌙 **Volcano Boarding on Cerro Negro:** Whether you go sitting down on a toboggan or standing up on a modified snowboard, hurling yourself down a 40-degree pitch of tiny black pebbles on an active volcano is a scream (page 169).

🌙 **Las Ruinas de León Viejo:** As old as Nicaragua's colonial history, this legitimate archaeological dig exposes the bones of Spain's earliest settlement (page 175).

🌙 **Poneloya and Las Peñitas Beaches:** Relaxing and peaceful accommodations at the ocean's edge all offer easy access to the impressive Isla Juan Venado (page 177).

🌙 **Padre Ramos Wetlands Reserve:** If you're into isolated beaches and protected bird-filled estuaries, the bouncy trip north is worth it (page 189).

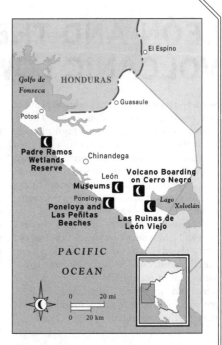

LOOK FOR 🌙 TO FIND RECOMMENDED SIGHTS, ACTIVITIES, DINING, AND LODGING.

streets lined with cathedrals, universities, and cafés. For five hundred years, León's political history has consisted of long stretches of peace, punctuated by the staccato call of uprising, resistance, and war.

In contrast, Chinandega, Nicaragua's most northwestern city, is the agribusiness capital of the country. A provincial capital quickly becoming not only the heartbeat of the sugarcane but also the shrimp industry, Chinandega is at once the gateway to Honduras, the Padre Ramos Reserve, and the almost totally isolated Cosigüina peninsula. It's also the region most likely to cause you to redefine what "hot" feels like.

PLANNING YOUR TIME

León city is one of few Nicaraguan destinations with more attractions than you can see in a single day. Plan on two to explore the city; another if you plan to hike a volcano, and another if you head to the shore. Las Peñitas, Padre Ramos, Isla Juan Venado, and other points from León require more effort to get to but are excellent destinations for those traveling on a slightly slower schedule. It's worth slowing down in fact, so you can paddle boats through the estuaries and observe the wildlife (like nesting turtles on Juan Venado).

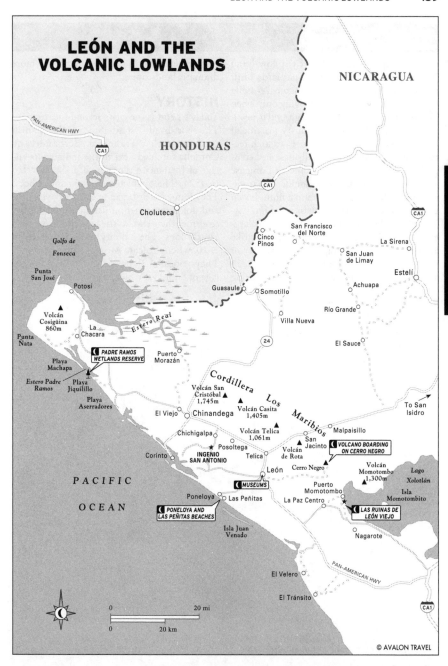

© AVALON TRAVEL

LEÓN

City of León

The principal metropolis of the low-lying Nicaraguan northwest, the Spaniards built the first city of León—now abandoned—along the shore of Lake Xolotlán, moving only when Volcán Momotombo shook the ground beneath their feet. Modern León, a dusty provincial capital with latent aspirations, is an architectural delight where traditionally designed colonial homes, stately churches, and an immense cathedral stand shoulder to shoulder in a tropical torpor that keeps city life to a hum. It's an easily walked city, with a plethora of interesting cafés and restaurants, Latin America's largest cathedral, and an ambience quite unlike anywhere else in Nicaragua, plus a variety of lodging and accommodations that make León a pleasant place to rest a day or two, venturing out farther afield to take in some of the more dramatic landscapes.

HISTORY

Today's León is the city's second incarnation. The short-lived first attempt was the Spanish settlement that Francisco Hernández de Córdoba founded next to the indigenous village of Imabite on the shore of Lake Xolotlán in 1524. The Spanish were lousy neighbors. They immediately began to enslave the Imabite and doled out cruel punishments: Many natives met their ends at the jaws of the Spanish attack dogs. The old city was abandoned in 1610 when Volcán Momotombo erupted. They relocated alongside the indigenous village of Subtiava, which over the centuries was

one of León's numerous colonial cathedrals

© JOSHUA BERMAN

LEÓN

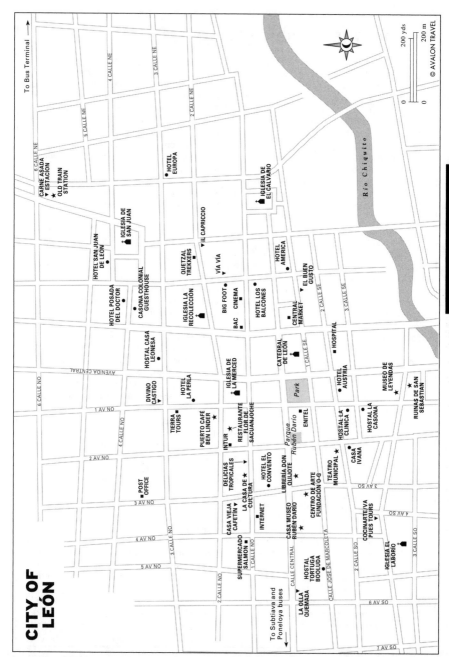

CITY OF LEÓN

To Bus Terminal →

CARNE ASADA ESTACION ▼
OLD TRAIN STATION

HOTEL EUROPA •

IGLESIA DE EL CALVARIO ✝

6 CALLE NE
5 CALLE NE
4 CALLE NE
3 CALLE NE
2 CALLE NE

Río Chiquito

IGLESIA DE SAN JUAN ✝

HOTEL SAN JUAN DE LEÓN ✝

IL CAPRICCIO ▼

QUETZAL TREKKERS ★

VIA VIA ▼

HOTEL AMERICA ■

HOTEL POSADA DEL DOCTOR •

CASONA COLONIAL GUESTHOUSE ■

IGLESIA LA RECOLECCION ✝

BIG FOOT •

BAC ■ CINEMA

HOTEL LOS BALCONES •

EL BUEN GUSTO ▼

CENTRAL MARKET ■

2 CALLE SE
3 CALLE SE

HOSTAL CASA LEONESA ■

AVENIDA CENTRAL

DIVINO CASTIGO ■

HOTEL LA PERLA ★

IGLESIA DE LA MERCED ✝

CATEDRAL DE LEÓN ✝

1 CALLE SE

HOSPITAL ■

6 CALLE NO
1 AV NO

TIERRA TOURS ■

PUERTO CAFÉ BEN LINDER ★

INTUR ■

RESTAURANTE FLOR DE SACUANJOCHE ★

Park

HOTEL AUSTRIA •

MUSEO DE LEYENDAS ★

4 CALLE NO
2 AV NO

POST OFFICE ■

DELICIAS TROPICALES ▼

LA CASA DE CULTURA ■

HOTEL EL CONVENTO •

LIBRERIA DON QUIJOTE ★

Parque Rubén Darío

ENITEL ■

HOSTAL LA CLINICA •

HOSTAL LA CASONA •

RUINAS DE SAN SEBASTIÁN ★

3 AV NO

CASA VIEJA CAFETIN ▼

INTERNET ■

CENTRO DE ARTE FUNDACIÓN O-G ★

CASA MUSEO RUBÉN DARÍO ★

TEATRO MUNICIPAL ★

CASA IVANA •

3 AV SO

4 CALLE NO
3 CALLE NO
4 AV NO

SUPERMERCADO SALMON ■

1 CALLE NO

COCINARTE/VA PUES TOURS ▼

4 AV SO

5 AV NO

To Subtiava and Poneloya buses

LA OLLA QUEMADA ▼

HOSTAL TORTUGA BOLUDA •

CALLE CENTRAL

CALLE JOSE DE MARCOLETA

2 CALLE SO

IGLESIA EL LABORIO ✝

3 CALLE SO

6 AV SO

7 AV SO

2 CALLE NO

N (compass)

200 yds
200 m

0
0

© AVALON TRAVEL

HIKING THE MARIBIO VOLCANOES

Nicaragua has been called "a violent expanse of volcanic strength," and there is nowhere better to feel that force than on the hot, baked slopes of its mountains of fire. Start early and bring a minimum of three liters of water per person. None of these hikes should be attempted without a local guide.

Momotombo, 1,300 meters
(8 hours round-trip)
The quintessential cone-shaped volcano, Momotombo rises up from the shores of Lago Xolotlán in a particularly menacing posture — and history has proven that the menace is real. Momotombo is climbable, but it's not easy, especially when you hit the loose volcanic gravel that comprises the upper half of the cone. Your triumphant reward will be one of the best views possible of Lago Xolotlán without use of an airplane. From the Ruinas de León Viejo, head out of town to the main highway and turn right (north) along the highway. Follow that to the geothermal plant, where you'll have to convince the guard to let you through to hike. They're sensitive about people traipsing across their installation, so honor whatever promises you make.

Telica, 1,061 meters
(5-7 hours round-trip)
Despite its tendency to spew ash over its namesake town, Volcán Telica makes for a good climb. Take a bus from León to Telica, then follow the road to the community of La Quimera and keep going until the road disappears beneath your feet and becomes the volcano. Alternatively, access the volcano from Santa Clara, the town adjacent to the Hervideros de San Jacinto.

Cerro Negro, 675 meters
(2 hours round-trip)
This is the most frequently active volcano in the chain (its last eruption was August 1999). The lowest and youngest of the Maribios, Cerro Negro rises like a black-sand pimple from the landscape, completely free of vegetation and scorching hot when there is no cloud cover. A road takes you from León to the base; from there, follow the makeshift "trail," part of which will have you scrambling over awkward rocks and fighting surprisingly strong wind. The trail loops around the steaming crater, which the brave may enter at their own risk — if the gaseous wind blows across your path, move fast to get out of it. You can also descend into the second crater accessible from the summit, again at your own risk. Getting out of this one is much harder and much hotter, so make sure you are in good shape. Going down is easy — just run, skip, and hop down the back side or zoom down on a board (see *Volcano Boarding on Cerro Negro* in the *Sports and Recreation* section of this chapter). There are a number of approaches; the most common heads due east from León, near the town of Lechecuago. Leave early in the morning to beat the heat and avoid the afternoon thunderstorms. The metals in Cerro Negro attract lightning better than the taller volcanoes nearby, so don't test it.

La Casita, 1,405 meters
(8 hours round-trip)
Access can be very difficult because of property issues. Near the top of the climb, the guides will lead you into the saddle between La Casita and San Cristóbal and then to the peak of La Casita itself. There are some radio towers here, and the terminus of an access road damaged during the landslide. Though it's also possible to hike to the top along the slide itself, it's a treeless, sun-baked hike, not to mention possibly disrespectful to the thousands who remain buried beneath it. Although not as tall, La Casita offers a better view of Managua and the lake than San Cristóbal does.

San Cristóbal, 1,745 meters
(8 hours round-trip)
This is the granddaddy of volcano hikes in the Pacific region; it's long but the grade is moderate and even easy compared to some of the hikes listed previously. You'll need a guide to help you wend your way through the myriad fields, farms, and fences that obstruct the path upward (and which change every planting

season). Find your guide in Chichigalpa. Enrique Reyes and his brothers are experienced at leading trips up San Cristóbal, and can be found in the Barrio Pellisco Occidental, across from the Escuela Hector García. If they're not around, finding a guide in Chichigalpa is easy. Horses cost $2 a day, and you should pay the guides at least $8 per group.

Cosigüina, 860 meters
(6 hours round-trip to edge of crater, 11 hours round-trip to crater lake)
Literally, a walk in the woods and then you're at the vegetation-carpeted crater lip with crazy views. Start walking from Potosí, or rent horses ($2 per day). Head back along the road toward the community of La Chacara, where the slope of Cosigüina is most amenable for climbing. From the edge of the crater, you can see across the Gulf of Fonseca into El Salvador. There are competing claims about whether one can descend to the crater lake without the use of ropes. If you intend to descend the approximately 300 meters down to the crater lake, you should take 30 meters of good rope with you (you can purchase it in El Viejo or Chinandega) and consider a guide from La Chacara. Luís Mejía Castro in El Viejo (from the Cine Imperial, two blocks west, tel. 505/886-5477) knows the Reserva Natural and its volcano intimately. Be careful: Careless hikers have died on this volcano.

subsumed by the growing commercial center of León.

León has been the capital of Nicaragua during Liberal governments several times before 1852. It has also, since colonial times, been both a university town and a hotbed of leftist thought. The Sandinistas found ready supporters here in the 1960s and '70s, and Somoza retaliated ferociously, even torching the central market at one time.

In September 1978, Sandinista forces attacked key locations in León, including National Guard installations at the famous XXI building. In response, Somoza bombed the populations of both León and Chinandega, and tortured or executed anyone suspected of sympathizing with the Sandinistas. Sandinista troops took León on June 4 after two days of vicious battle whose bullet holes remain to the present, as does a sympathy for the Sandinista party other areas of the country no longer share.

ORIENTATION AND GETTING AROUND
León is laid out in the traditional colonial grid system with the central park and cathedral at the center. The main bus station and market are located nearly a kilometer northeast of the park, and Barrio Subtiava is 12 blocks due west. Within the city, taxis charge $0.50 during the day and $1 at night. Small city buses and converted pickup trucks also crisscross León and charge about $0.15; ask about your destination before getting on.

SIGHTS
◖ Museums
León's museums are exceedingly eclectic, covering the political, natural, and all things cultural. Start at **La Casa de Cultura** (tel. 505/311-2116, open 8 A.M.–noon and 2–7:30 P.M. Mon.–Fri., until 6 P.M. Sat. and Sun.), housed in an old colonial home; enjoy a collection of artwork that includes a disparaging painting of Ronald Reagan and Henry Kissinger. Entrance is free.

La Casa de Rubén Darío (tel. 505/311-2388, open 8 A.M.–noon and 2–5 P.M. Tues.–Sat., 8 A.M.–noon Sun.) is a glimpse into León in the 19th century. Nicaragua's favorite son lived here with his aunt and uncle until the age of 14. Fellow poet Alfonso Cortéz later inhabited the same house as he battled insanity (the room he

LEÓN

A WALKING TOUR OF CHURCHES AND RUINS

La Catedral de León is the largest cathedral in Central America and the modern city's focal point. One (probably apocryphal) story claims the architect accidentally switched two sets of plans while on the ship from Spain, and the larger of the two cathedrals, originally intended for Lima, Peru, was built in Nicaragua. The cathedral was constructed in 1747 at the request of Archbishop Isidoro Bullón y Figueroa and inaugurated in 1860 as a basilica by Pope Pius XI. It's an imposing and majestic baroque structure whose grandeur is magnified by the open space of the park in front of it. You can observe elements of late Gothic and neoclassic architecture, primarily from inside. Check out the paintings of the stations of the cross and the 12 apostles. The **Tomb of Rubén Darío** is a notable element of the cathedral – look for the golden statue of a lion. The cathedral holds the mortal remains of the musician José de la Cruz Mena and several religious figures. Look for the famous *Cristo de Pedrarias*, a painting that once hung in the cathedral of León Viejo. The particularly beautiful **Patio de los Príncipes** is a small courtyard of Andalusian design, with a fountain in the center and colorful beds of flowers. Ask in the INTUR office about **rooftop tours.** The conglomerate of white towers and domes that form the roof of the Catedral de León is fascinating in its own right – and the view of the city and nearby volcanoes is unsurpassed.

© JOSHUA BERMAN

from the roof of León's cathedral

NORTH AND EAST FROM THE CENTRAL PARK

Iglesia de la Merced, 1.5 blocks north of the main cathedral, is the church considered most representative of León in the 1700s. It was originally built in 1762 by the Mercedarian monks, the first order of monks to arrive in Nicaragua during the years of the conquest. It is essentially baroque in style but has neoclassical elements in the front and colonial on the south. It faces a small but lovely park popular amongst León's skateboarders. Particularly attractive is the church's side bell tower.

Passing the Iglesia de la Merced and walking two blocks east along 2 Calle NE, you'll find the yellow **Iglesia de la Recolección** on the north side. This church has the most perfect baroque style of the León churches and a massive, functional bell tower. It was built in 1786 by Bishop Juan Félix de Villegas and is the only church in León constructed using carved stone.

From the Iglesia de la Recolección, continue one more block and turn north. Walk two blocks until you reach the picturesque **Iglesia de San Juan.** The old train station is a block farther north from the east side of the church. Built 1625–1650 and rebuilt in the 1700s, the Iglesia de San Juan's architecture is a modern interpretation of neoclassicism. This neighborhood of León will give you a good feel for what León was like in the 1700s:

church, park, small houses of adobe using traditional *taquezal* construction techniques, and the nearby market.

Walking four blocks south down the same road, you'll find the **Iglesia del Calvario** on your left side. It is set at the top of broad steps on a small hill overlooking one of León's narrow streets. Renovated in the late 1990s, Calvario was built 200 years previous in a generally baroque style, but with neoclassical ornamentation in the front that reflects the increasing French influence in Spain in the 18th century. Inside are two famous statues known as *El Buen y el Mal Ladrón* (The Good and the Bad Thief).

SOUTH AND WEST FROM THE CENTRAL PARK

La Iglesia y Convento de San Francisco, three blocks west of the park on the north side, and across the street from the Casa Museo Rubén Darío, contains two of the most beautiful altars of colonial Nicaragua. The church was built in 1639 by Fray Pedro de Zuñiga and rebuilt and modified several times afterwards, notably in the mid-1980s to restore the damage done to it during the revolution. Its small, tree-lined courtyard is

a pleasant place to escape from the hot sun and relax.

Turning and walking a block south, you come to the unassuming **Iglesia de San Juan de Dios,** built in 1620 as a chapel for León's first hospital (now gone). Its simplicity and colonial style reflect the wishes of Felipe II when he designed it in 1573.

Two blocks farther south and one short block to the west is the **Iglesia del Laborío,** a graceful, rural-feeling church in the old mixed neighborhood of El Laborío. This church, one of León's earliest, formed the nucleus of the working-class neighborhood that provided labor to León's wealthy class in the 17th century. The street from Laborío east to the Ruinas de la Ermita de San Sebastián is known as **Calle la Españolita** and was one of the first streets built in León.

The **Ruinas de la Ermita de San Sebastián** consist of the shattered remnants of the outer walls, and inexplicably, the intact bell tower. The Ermita was built in 1742 on a site long used by the indigenous people for worship of their own gods. It suffered major damage in 1979 during Somoza's bombardment of León. El Museo de Tradiciones y Leyendas is across the street.

inhabited still has the iron bars he bent during one attempted escape). Darío's bed and the rest of the furnishings of the museum are typical of middle-class León in the late 19th century, as is the building itself, built from adobe with a clay-tile and cane roof. On display are original copies of his most famous works translated into several languages and copies of a magazine he published in Paris. The silver crucifix given him by Mexican poet Amado Nervos, correspondence from when Darío was the consul to Argentina and ambassador to Spain, and period coins and currency are also displayed; donations of $1–2 are accepted for the upkeep of the building.

A block west of the Parque Casa de Rubén Darío occupying two facing buildings, the **Centro de Arte Fundación Ortiz-Gurdián**

(open 10:30 A.M.–6 P.M. Tues.–Sat. and 9 A.M.–5 P.M. Sun., $0.75 admission, free on Sun.) has reputedly the best collection of Latin American artwork in Nicaragua, with an emphasis on colonial America.

El Museo de Tradiciones y Leyendas (Barrio Laborío, open 8 A.M.–noon and 2–5 P.M. Mon.–Sat., 8 A.M.–noon Sun., $1) celebrates Nicaragua's favorite folktales: the golden crab, La Carreta Nagua, the pig-witch, and La Mocuana. The building itself is the former XXI jail and base of the 12th Company of Somoza's National Guard. Built in 1921, **XXI** meted out 60 years of brutal torture. The mango tree that now shades this museum was planted by a prisoner and watered from the same well that was used for electric shock and water-boarding sessions.

LEÓN

RUBÉN DARÍO (1867-1916)

Poet, journalist, diplomat, and favorite son of Nicaragua, Rubén Darío has become the icon for all that's artistic or cultural in Nicaragua. Born Felíx Rubén Garcia Sarmiento in 1867 in the quiet agricultural town of San Pedro de Metapa (now Ciudad Darío), Darío hardly knew his parents. He was raised instead by an aunt and uncle, Colonel Félix Ramírez Madregil and Bernarda Sarmiento, in the colonial city of León. Darío was a fast learner who was able to read at the age of three. He studied in the Jesuit school Iglesia de la Recolección in León and began composing poetry at the age of 11. In 1882, he was sent to El Salvador by friends who wanted to dissuade him from marrying Rosario Murillo. There he met, befriended, and was inspired by the renowned poet Francisco Gavidia. In 1884, he returned to Nicaragua to work in the National Library of Managua.

Darío departed for Chile in 1886, where he worked as a journalist for the newspaper *La Nación*. His epic poem about the glories of Chile won first prize in a contest sponsored by a Chilean millionaire. His breakthrough came with the publication of *Azul* in 1888, in which Darío introduced a profound change in the aesthetic conception of Spanish-American literature. The stories in *Azul* revealed Darío's encounter with Prussian literature and exotic themes of a fantastic world: fauns, gnomes, fairies, nymphs, swans, azure lakes, and grand parks and castles. He was influenced by many, but his style was unique, playing off elements of the naturalism and symbolism movements of the era.

In 1893, he was named ambassador of Colombia to Argentina. He moved to Buenos Aires, a cosmopolitan city that suited him well. His friends there were the educated and elite, and he continued to publish his writings while the Latin American modernist literature movement began to organize under his influence.

In 1898, Darío resumed writing for *La Nación* in Europe. In 1910, he published what is largely considered to be his finest work: "Poema de Otoño." He was director and founder of the international publication, *Magazine*, while in France. In 1905, Darío published one of his best, and last, works: "Cantos de Vida y Desesperación," in which he introspectively reembraces his Latin roots and examines themes of the passage of time, the suffering of a youth gone by, the pain of the loss of physical pleasure, the tiredness of life, man and his inevitable destiny, and the North American advance into Latin America during that period.

Shortly thereafter, in 1908, he became ambassador of Nicaragua to Spain. He remained in Europe until 1916, when, with his health failing, he returned to Nicaragua where he received a hero's welcome. Darío passed away in León on February 16. One of his most quoted phrases is: *"Si la patria es pequeña, uno grande la sueña"* ("If one's nation is small, one makes it large through dreams").

Murals

León's many colorful and noteworthy murals are mostly products of the 1980s. Across from the north side of the cathedral is a long, horizontal piece telling the history of a proud and turbulent nation. Starting on the left with the arrival of the Nahuatl, the mural traces the planned interoceanic canal, the exploits of William Walker, Sandino's battle with U.S. Marines, the revolution of 1979, and a utopian ending image of a fertile, peaceful Nicaragua; flanking a doorway across the street, Sandino steps on Uncle Sam's and Somoza's heads. One block to the west the CIA, in the form of a thick serpent, coils through the Sandinistas' agrarian reform, literacy campaign, and construction efforts, to strike at a Nicaraguan hand at the ballot box. The trend seems to be reviving in the 21st century; to wit, the intricate anticorruption mural on the basketball court.

Other Sights

The shady and pleasant **Parque Rubén Darío**, a block west of the central park, pays tribute to four famous Nicaraguan writers, all sons of León: Azarías H. Pallais (1884–1954), Salomon de la Selva (1893–1959), Alfonzo Cortéz (1893–1969), and of course, the beloved Rubén Darío (1867–1916).

León's **Old Train Station**, built in 1884, was Nicaragua's first and most majestic. It has been rebuilt since being gutted by fire in 1956, now housing a boisterous market.

The creepy yet captivating **El Fortín de Acosasco** sits on a low, grassy hill just south of the city. Conservative president Sacasa built it in 1889 to keep an eye on the Liberals that would overthrow him four years later. Abandoned until Anastasio Somoza took interest and rehabilitated it, El Fortín has since served as both a military base and jail, and is presently abandoned once again. From the Subtiava church, it's an easy 45-minute walk or $6 by taxi (don't walk alone): Go one block east and head due south up the hill along the shady dirt road. The panorama of the city and volcanoes is worth the walk.

On September 21, 1956, the poet-student Rigoberto López Pérez, disguised as a waiter, gained access to the ballroom of León's **Old Social Club** where he fatally shot Anastasio Somoza García. The National Guard killed López immediately, making him a much-revered martyr to the cause of the revolution. In the mural at the **Park of Heroes and Martyrs**, a block north of the cathedral, this event is vividly depicted in the black-and-white tiled floor and pistol.

Sights in Barrio Subtiava

The indigenous neighborhood of Subtiava (Maribio for "land of the big men") retains a trace of both its cultural identity and political autonomy. Besides the thrill of walking the streets of a village predating Columbus, note several interesting ruins here. Just about any of the microbuses that circulate through León will take you to Subtiava if you're not up for the 12-block walk.

La Catedral de Subtiava, beautiful in its aged simplicity, is second only to the Catedral de León in size and is the keystone of the community. Construction began in 1698 and finished 12 years later, but the indigenous inhabitants of Subtiava kept worshiping their own gods despite Spanish proselytism. In an effort to get the locals into the church, the Spanish mounted a carved wooden image of the sun representing the local god on the church ceiling of the church, a compromise that left everyone satisfied, even if, during a church service the Spanish and locals were simultaneously worshiping different gods. The beautifully crafted sun remains, as do the immense wooden columns that evoke the kind of forest that surrounded León three hundred years ago. Next to the cathedral is the Casa Cural, which predates the cathedral of Subtiava by 160 years but was rebuilt in 1743.

Across the street from the cathedral on the north side is the **Museo Adiact** (open 8 A.M.–noon and 2–5 P.M. Mon.–Fri., 8 A.M.–noon Sat., $1–2 donation), a run-down but captivating museum that houses many of the area's archaeological treasures. Sadly, some of the better idols and statues were stolen in the late 1980s and sold to foreign museums.

Five blocks east of the cathedral's southern side is a small park dedicated to the last cacique of Subtiava, Adiact, and his daughter, Xochilt Acalt. From the cathedral of Subtiava, three blocks south and two blocks west is **El Tamarindón,** an enormous tamarind tree from whose branches the Spanish hung the last cacique—now a small park.

There are two sets of ruins in Subtiava, **Las Ruinas de Veracruz** (one block west of the cathedral, set in high weeds) and **Las Ruinas de Santiago** (one block north of the cathedral on the other side of Calle Central, look for a small sign). The church at Veracruz was Subtiava's first, built sometime around 1560 and abandoned in the late 1700s due to its small size. The eruption of Volcán Cosigüina in 1835 caused its subsequent collapse. The church at Santiago, constructed in the early

LEÓN

THE LEGEND OF ADIACT AND THE TAMARIND TREE

Several competing versions of this tale have been passed down over three centuries of Nicaraguan history. When Subtiava was still a rebellious Native American village and the Spanish were trying to subdue its inhabitants, victory appeared in the form of a young woman named Xochilt Acalt (Flower of the Sugarcane). Her father was Adiact, the cacique of the Subtiava people and a ferocious warrior renowned for his victories in battle with the Spanish. But legend goes Xochilt fell in love with a young Spanish soldier. Some say the Spanish took advantage of the love affair to capture and hang Adiact; others say that when he learned of the illicit relationship, he hung himself in shame. Xochilt Acalt disappeared from town, and legend has it she too committed suicide (though some say she banished herself to Poneloya, where another tribe took her in). Either way, everyone agrees that the 300-year-old tamarind tree that still stands proudly in the center of Subtiava is where Adiact was hanged. To modern Subtiavans, the tree still represents the rebelliousness of the indigenous people and is a source of much community pride.

1600s, is significant because its small square bell tower remains intact.

ENTERTAINMENT AND EVENTS
Bars and Discos

It's no surprise that a university town like León would have thriving nightlife. **Las Ruinas** (Calle Central, one block west of the park, tel. 505/311-4767) is a cavernous disco popular among the younger crowd. **Dilectus** (south of the city center on the highway, tel. 505/311-5439) is the fanciest and most expensive disco in town, with a fun crowd and

well-mixed music; it's also an upscale and attractive restaurant with occasional live music and karaoke. Thursday is mariachi night and Friday is teen night; entrance fee is $2, but budget in a taxi ride home at the end of the night. Across from Parque La Merced, the **Don Señor** complex—disco, restaurant, downstairs dive, and upstairs patio lounge with a view of the nightlife—attracts the college crowd and foreigners. The disco is open from 8:30 P.M. Tuesday–Saturday. The restaurant and the bars are open for lunch and dinner, and close late on Saturdays. The latest of the late-night options is **Salon Estrella** (one block south of La Iglesia de la Recolección) which lasts until 3 A.M. on the weekends.

Several bars and cafés host a weekly live music night. Friday nights at **Vía Vía's** can be good; for current listings, check in at Restaurante Flor de Sacuanjoche and CocinArte. **Divino Castigo** (a block north of Iglesia de la Merced) is good on Tuesdays. **La Olla Quemada** (a block west of Ruben Darío's House Museum on Central Street) features a nice atmosphere and celebrated female vocalist Carola, who entertains about one Wednesday a month. **Tequetzal** (half a block west of the central park) hosts live music on Thursday nights.

Don't miss León's answer to London's double-decker bus tours: **El Bus Pelón** (The Bald Bus) runs 30-minute rides around the city, weekends only, from about 5–10 P.M., sometimes featuring live *chichero* music. Line up at the southwest corner of the central park with your own booze. The locals love it.

Cinemas, Theater, and Special Events

León's **cinema** is in the Plaza Siglo Nuevo (from the cathedral, one block north, one block east, tel. 505/311-7080). Look for the *cartelera* (schedule) at shops around the city for show times or call; tickets cost $3. **El Teatro Municipal José de la Cruz Mena** (one block south of the southwest corner of the central park, tel. 505/311-1788) is the cultural heart of the city, open to the public for half-hour

© TOMÁS STARGARDTER

Local artisans craft sawdust paintings during Semana Santa in León.

theater tours during the day with all kinds of events at night. Some big-name performers prefer León over Managua.

The INTUR office will know about events planned during your stay. June 1 is the celebration of Somoza's defeat in León and August 14 is **La Gritería Chiquita,** when devout Catholics celebrate being spared from Cerro Negro's frequent eruptions. The first week of December is huge, with loud, firework-festooned celebrations of the Immaculate Conception. León celebrates its *fiestas patronales* on September 24 and the weeks surrounding it.

León's **Semana Santa** celebrations are acclaimed throughout Nicaragua as the nation's most lively. In addition to tons of food and drink, local artisans craft religious scenes in beds of colored sawdust worked painstakingly by hand.

SHOPPING
The market immediately behind the cathedral focuses more on the locals than on foreigners. **Librería Don Quijote** (two blocks west of the park, open 8 A.M.–7 P.M. Mon.–Sat.) is an interesting new and used book shop that sells many old Sandinista titles.

SPORTS AND RECREATION
Baseball
León ballers have earned more baseball championships than any other city in Nicaragua. Catch a game during the season (January–May). Ask any taxi driver when the next game is and if he'll take you to the stadium on the edge of town.

◖ Volcano Boarding on Cerro Negro
Scooting down the black sands of Cerro Negro (which has, in places, a 40-degree slope) on a board has evolved quickly to become León's most exciting outdoor adrenaline rush (wear sturdy shoes). **Big Foot** hostel runs daily trips for $19. The tour includes equipment (from jumpsuit and goggles to gloves and pads), guide, transportation, a board ("fast" or "extra fast"), and a celebratory drink at the bar upon return. The ride out in the back of the Big Footed Toyota is half the fun. Alternatively, **Va Pues Tours** has a standing tricked-out snowboard model for $20. Either way, plan on a 45-minute ascent and a 45-second descent.

At the entrance to Cerro Negro you will find a small information center, a *ranchón,* some bathrooms, and a friendly and informative

© JOSHUA BERMAN

volcano surfing on Cerro Negro

local tourism cooperative called **Las Pilas-El Hoyo.** The $3.50 entrance fee goes to support conservation efforts and pays a portion of the members' salaries. Cooperative guides can take you on other hikes in the area, including the two taller volcanoes—El Hoyo and El Pilas—a nearby swimming hole, and a larger reservoir (see sidebar *Hiking the Maribio Volcanoes*).

ACCOMMODATIONS
Under $10

The cheapest alternatives surround the bus terminal but are universally dismal and in a potentially dangerous neighborhood. Safer, more comfortable, and closer to the town center, ◖ **Tortuga Booluda** (1.5 blocks west from the San Juan de Dios church, tel. 505/311-4653, www.tortugaBooluda.com) offers book exchange, coffee, Wi-Fi, breezy courtyard, and shared, convivial common areas. The place feels homey. Prices range $5 per person dorm,

$10 per person room with shared bath, $15 with private bath, $30 second-story room with air-conditioning and private bath.

Casa Ivana (across from the Teatro Municipal's south side, tel. 505/311-4423, $8 d) has seven clean, quiet, safe rooms with private baths along a long garden in a family house. Around the corner, two more small, low-key hostel-type accommodations face each other, two blocks south of the central park: **La Clinica** (tel. 505/311-2031, $4 with fan, $25 with a/c) and **La Casona** (tel. 505/311-5282, $3 dorm, $10 d with private bath).

Vía Vía (75 meters south of the Servicio Agrícola Gurdián, tel. 505/311-6142, www.viaviacafe.com, $4 dorm, $12–20 d) is popular and has one of the most pleasant multicultural bar scenes around, plus tours, salsa dancing and Spanish classes, and a book exchange. Across the street **Big Foot Adventure Hostel** ($3–5 dorm, $10 d) caters to the same

Hotel El Convento offers upscale digs, set in the city's center.

© JOSHUA BERMAN

LEÓN

backpacker crowd, with a foot-shaped pool, multiple common areas, and a café. Lockboxes and a 24-hour laundry service ($4–6) are available. This is the biggest hostel in León, so expect a lively social scene, but the rooms are quiet.

$10-25

◖ Casona Colonial Guesthouse (half a block west of the Parque San Juan, tel. 505/311-3178, $20) has rooms with private bath, hot water, and a fan and is quite possibly the best bargain in León, complete with high ceilings, flower-filled courtyard, and beautiful wooden furniture. Breakfast is available for $2, or try the cafetín next door. **Hotel America** (one block east of the market, tel. 505/311-5533, hotel americaleon@gmail.com, $20) has rooms with private bath and fan in a large and high-ceilinged old hotel whose black-and-white tiled floors date back to the days of Somoza. Breakfast available or get fresh pastries from the bakery across the street.

$25-50

In a converted colonial home, the **Hostal Casa Leonesa** (from the cathedral, three blocks north and half a block east, tel. 505/311-0551, lacasaleonesa@gmail.com, www.casaleonesa .com, $45) has nine gorgeous rooms around a small pool and garden, each with air-conditioning, TV, hot water, and Wi-Fi. The beautiful common space makes you feel like León royalty.

Hotel San Juan de León (on the north side of the Plaza Iglesia San Juan, tel. 505/311-0547, hsanjuan@ibw.com.ni, www.sanjuandeleon .com.ni, $35 with fan and private bath, $40 with a/c) has 20 smallish rooms on two floors surrounding a tasteful courtyard and kitchen for guests' use. All rooms have TV, and breakfast is included. Around the corner, **◖ Hotel Posada del Doctor** (one block west of Parque San Juan, tel. 505/311-4343, www.posadadel doctor.com, $40–50), with 11 lovely, fully equipped rooms around a very bright and pleasant garden.

The imposing 30-room compound of **Hotel Europa** (from the Iglesia San Juan one block south and one east, tel. 505/311-6040, heuropa @ibw.com.ni, $25–35) has been around since the 1960s, when it catered to the train passenger crowd. Recently remodeled and kept clean, it offers a restaurant, lounge areas, Wi-Fi, guarded parking for your vehicle, and its own water and electricity supply.

$50-100

Expect old colonial stateliness in the 20 wood-adorned rooms at **◖ Hotel Los Balcones** (three blocks east of the cathedral, tel. 505/311-0250, www.hotelbalcones.com, $55). Upstairs rooms enjoy a small balcony, in addition to standard amenities: TV, air-conditioning, hot water, Wi-Fi. In the center of León, **Hotel Austria** (from the cathedral, one block south and half a block west, tel. 505/311-1206 or 505/311-7178, haustria@ibw.com.ni, www .hotelaustria.com.ni, $57–79) is a very practical hotel, with spotless, modern rooms with air-conditioning, TV, phones, and hot water;

also continental breakfast and guarded parking for your vehicle. There is an on-site restaurant and comfortable space for relaxing or group meetings.

❰ Hotel El Convento (next door to the San Francisco Church, tel. 505/311-7053, www.hotelelconvento.com.ni, $95) offers comfortable, bathtub-equipped rooms and luxurious grandeur within its walls, several of which were rebuilt from stones used in the convent's original 1639 construction. From the beautiful centerpiece garden and fountain to the long, cool corridors adorned with art and antiques, El Convento impresses. In addition, the hotel offers business and conference services, a ballroom, a restaurant, and local tours for guests.

Over $100

The rooms at the four-star, colonial-style **Hotel La Perla** (1.5 blocks north of Iglesia de la Merced, tel. 505/311-3125, www.laperlaleon.com, $105) juxtapose classic wooden furniture with plasma-screen TVs and Wi-Fi. The luxury suite, with mirrored dressers, king bed, and minibar is possibly the nicest room in the city. The upper balcony has a superb view of León's tiled roofs and churches and the restaurant and bar are dazzling; consider taking your drink to the pool just as the sun's last rays hit the patio.

Long-Term Accommodations

A college town, León caters easily to those looking to stay on longer. In general, expect to pay about $200 per month for a simple, furnished room or apartment. Quetzal Trekkers (see *Information and Tour Operators*) offers cheap housing for its volunteers, but you can also make arrangements with the family-minded Tortuga Booluda (see *Under $10* this section) or failing that, in Delicias Tropicales (see *International* in the *Food* section).

FOOD

León is slowly shedding its reputation for uninspired restaurants. Though Leónese eateries cater to the student crowd—i.e., *típica* (traditional), burgers, and pizza—new restaurants are gradually diversifying the menu.

Comida Típica

Enjoy a substantial traditional breakfast in the picturesque Hotel Colonial for about $2.50, and have lunch for under $2 at **Comedor Lucía** (across from Vía Vía). The best finger-lickin' *fritanga* in town is **El Buen Gusto** (a couple blocks east of the cathedral's south side); mix and match from their sidewalk smorgasbord and hubcap grill between 10 A.M. and 10 P.M.; it's closed Sundays. The carne asada at the **Estación** offers strong competition for León's best *fritanga* crown; several large grills serve mountains of *gallo pinto,* plantains, and fried cheese to an appreciative crowd.

❰ Restaurante Taquezal (half a block west of the central park's southern end) has a pleasant atmosphere and a varied menu and receives positive reviews from readers; typical dishes cost $5–9. Try the Nicaccino: cappuccino with a shot of Nicaraguan rum.

Restaurante Flor de Sacuanjoche (Barrio Zaragoza, 75 meters west of UNAN) serves a varied menu of beef, seafood, and vegetarian specialties, including salads, "soysage," and veggie burgers. Meals run $4–6, and it's open 10 A.M.–midnight daily.

Cafés

Right in front of the cathedral, **El Sesteo** (open 8 A.M.–9:30 P.M. daily) is a trendy, high-priced, open-air corner spot and the international crowd's favorite place to sip cappuccino or enjoy their famous *churrasco* (steak, about $9). **❰ Puerto Café Benjamin Linder** (Barrio Zaragoza, two blocks north of ENITEL, tel. 505/311-0548, open 7 A.M.–3 P.M.) is a restaurant, coffee shop, bar, Internet café, and massage parlor, whose profits help support local children with disabilities. The shop is a tribute to the only U.S. citizen killed in the Contra war. A beautiful indoor mural depicts his life in Nicaragua; enjoy it while ordering from their creative, veggie-friendly food and coffee menu (also lots of sandwiches, snacks and bar food, with special $2 lunches). The vegetarian restaurant and coffee shop at **CocinArte** (across from the north side of La Iglesia el Laborío, tel. 505/854-6928) has large chess boards and

A GUIDE TO LEÓN'S STREET FOOD

León's street food is particularly enticing for reasons no one seems to know. Is it that the delicious, salty, and greasy fare replenishes something after a long day of sweating in the sun? Or is it the friendly, tropical atmosphere and convivial social scene? More than one traveler has reported picking up a couple of extra pounds after an extended stay in León. Don't sweat it, just enjoy!

Aside from the many taco stands a few blocks west of Parque Rubén Darío, which give you the choice of beef, chicken, or cheese (all good), and the numerous bread ladies with simple, sweet, and triangle options, look for these delicious treats on the streets.

SAVORY

Buñuelos: deep fried ground yucca mixed with salty cheese, served with sugar or honey and lemon sauce.

Manuelitas: deep fried soft flour tortilla with sugar, cinnamon, and cheese on the inside.

Güirilas: thick tortillas made of young corn and grilled on top of a plantain leaf, best enjoyed with cheese.

Maduro con queso: whole-fried plantain with a piece of cuajada cheese served in a plantain leaf.

Nacatamales: a plantain leaf-wrapped cultural experience of pork, potatoes, rice, pepper, onion, and corn, usually eaten on Friday nights or on Sunday mornings (safer bet). They're delicious, but as a Sunday breakfast, a bit heavy.

Tamales de elote: young corn cooked in the corn leaf. The "relleno" version comes with sweet cheese on the inside.

Enchiladitas rojas de León: just like a regular enchilada but with paprika, served with cabbage and spicy pepper salad.

Jocote con sal: this fruit is in itself a piece of Nicaraguan culture dipped in salt. It has the texture of a young apple and a slightly bitter but enjoyable taste. *Jocote* is also used in *almibar,* a traditional marmalade made during Semana Santa.

Cosas de horno: a type of corn bread baked with a sweet milled corn and lots of sugar.

SWEET

Bollo de coco: cooked coconut with sugar.

Cajetas de leche: cooked milk with sugar, somewhat like molasses.

Dulce de papaya: cooked papaya with sugar.

Raspados: shaved ice served with thick fruit syrup and/or condensed milk.

(Contributed by Roman Yavich, Fulbright scholar and Nicaragua tourism expert; Roman resides in San Juan del Sur, where he works with Comunidad Connect, a local nonprofit organization.)

a comfortable reading and lounging space, plus creative and low-priced vegetarian favorites.

Among the new favorites in town is **Il Capriccio** (tel. 505/311-6339, open 9 A.M.–12:30 P.M. and 2–7 P.M. Mon.–Sat.), located across from Quetzal Trekkers, with some of the best Italian desserts and Nicaraguan coffee in town, plus a menu of sandwiches, salads, and pasta. To escape the León heat and enter a tropical, fruit-filled retreat, head just east of the Casa de Cultura to **Delicias Tropicales** (tel. 505/311-2818, open 7 A.M.–6 P.M. Mon.–Sat.). They use all-natural ingredients for their refreshing smoothies and juices and prepare filling sandwiches to order.

International

Enjoy pizza and authentic Lebanese dishes at **Restaurante Italian Pizza** (half a block north of the cathedral, tel. 505/311-0857 delivery, open 9 A.M.–9 P.M. daily). The pizza at **Hollywood Pizza** (located in the movie theater complex, tel. 505/311-0636, open 11:30 A.M.–9:30 P.M. Mon.–Fri., later on weekends) is less exciting but the air-conditioning provides a good respite. They also deliver. The **Mediterraneo** (half a block north of the Iglesia Guadelupe, open at 4 P.M. Tues.–Fri., at 11 A.M. weekends) is perhaps the best option for Italian dishes and pizza. Enjoy the pleasant green patio, nice art, and good service.

LEÓN

The only reasonable Mexican option is **Guadalajara** (across from Puerto Café Benjamin Linder, tel. 505/311-6748). This loud, simple, and very pink restaurant offers home delivery as well. Meat lovers should try the *mula terca* (stubborn mule), a combination of pork, beef, bacon, ham, cheese, and other meats.

For dark-lit, slightly mysterious ambience, slink into either the **Casa Vieja Cafetín** (one block north of Hotel El Convento entrance) or **Allante Bar Café** (across from the Teatro Municipal), both with standard surf, turf, and bar-food menus; both are open Monday–Saturday for dinner. León's fanciest, most expensive restaurants are found in the top hotels in town.

INFORMATION AND TOUR OPERATORS

The official **INTUR** office (from the central park, one block west and 1.5 north, tel. 505/311-3682) has brochures, postcards, and updated bus schedules; a more centrally located **Information Office** (a few meters north of the Cathedral, tel. 505/311-3992) also offers mounds of brochures, plus a gang of eager UNAN students waiting to help you with local information and maps. Both offices operate Monday–Saturday during normal business hours, including a two-hour lunch break. Also check in the Casa de Cultura for local tour services or simply visit **www.leononline.net** for local events.

Several tour operators provide transport and guides to all the nearby sites, including León Viejo, San Jacinto Hot Springs, Isla Juan Venado, and volcano expeditions. **Julio Tours Nicaragua** (from the cathedral half a block north, julio tours2000@yahoo.es) offers relaxed, homespun service, enthusiastically recommended by several readers. **Va Pues Tours** (tel. 505/315-4999, www.vapues.com) are based in their adjoining vegetarian restaurant and art center, CocinArte, across from the north side of Iglesia Laboría. They offer reasonably priced trips to all of these places and then some—ask about their overnight turtle-viewing trips with a local biologist, the romantic trip out to Las Isletas in Granada, many

volcano trips, and a rum factory tour as well. The newer **Tierra Tours** (tel. 505/311-0599, tierra tour@dds.nl) offers similar services at "competitive prices," in addition to shuttle service to Granada and San Juan del Sur and countrywide all inclusive trips.

Quetzal Trekkers (tel. 505/311-6695, 1.5 blocks east of Iglesia de la Recolección, leon @quetzaltrekkers.com, www.quetzaltrekkers .com) is a highly recommended, nonprofit volunteer-run organization that specializes in volcano hikes, including overnight options; profits go directly to **Las Tias,** a León nonprofit that provides support to local street kids and orphans. They are almost always looking for short-term volunteers. If you are lucky enough to be in town during the full moon you will want to summit Volcán Telica at night with a well-experienced Quetzal Trekker guide.

SERVICES
Banks

Bancentro is only a block north of the cathedral, and most of the other banks are within a block east and north of there. A cluster of ATMs sits one block east of the cathedral, in the BAC, at La Union Supermarket, and in Plaza Siglo Nuevo (movie theater complex).

Medical Services

The hospital is in the center of León, one block south of the cathedral, though you're probably better off in one of the two private clinics with emergency rooms. On the block west of Café Puerto Benjamin Linder, Policlinica la Fraternidad (tel. 505/311-1403) and Policlinica Occidental (tel. 505/311-2722) face each other from opposite sides of the street. Even there, on weekends and after normal business hours, they may not have a doctor on-site.

Internet

Internet cafés are too reliable to even list; odds are you're standing within a block of one as you read this. But the better ones have backup generators to deal with power failures; it's worth asking if you are doing anything you can't afford to lose. Of note, **CompuService** (across from Policlinica la Fraternidad, open 8 A.M.–9:30 P.M. Mon.–Sat., 9 A.M.–6 P.M. Sun.) is well air-conditioned with all kinds of fast services, including docks for laptops and cold beer from the restaurant next door. Also excellent, spacious, and well cooled is **Club en Conexion** (from the cathedral, three blocks north, half a block east, open 7:30 A.M.–9:30 P.M. Mon.–Fri., till 7 P.M. Sat.).

Mail, Phones, and Other Services
The Correos (two blocks west and 1.5 north of Puerto Café Benjamin Linder, open 8 A.M.–5 P.M. Mon.–Fri., 8 A.M.–noon Sat.) deals with faxes as well as mail. Agencia de Viajes Premier (across from the Rubén Darío park, tel. 505/311-5535) is León's only authorized UPS agent. International calls are extra cheap in León and can be made from most any Internet café.

Of the several huge supermarkets, the most central is **La Union** (a block east of the cathedral, open 7:30 A.M.–8 P.M. Mon.–Sat., 8 A.M.–6 P.M. Sun.).

Travel Agents and Tickets
Viajes Mundiales (from the cathedral, three blocks north, half a block east, tel. 505/311-6263 or 505/311-5920, viajesmu@ibw .com.ni, open 8 A.M.–noon and 2–6 P.M. Mon.–Fri., until 1 P.M. Sat.) is a full international agency and official representative of major airlines. Two blocks west is an authorized **TransNica** agency (tel. 505/311-5219) with bus service to Costa Rica, Honduras, and El Salvador. **Agencia de Viajes Premier** (by the Iglesia San Juan, tel. 505/311-5535) is the authorized agent for La Costeña airline tickets, to plan your flight to the Atlantic coast or Río San Juan.

GETTING THERE AND AWAY
The main bus station (La Terminal) is in the northeast corner of town, where you'll find transportation to all points except Poneloya and Las Peñitas (buses to these beaches depart from their own terminal in Mercadito Subtiava). Big, yellow buses and small, white *interlocales* depart regularly for Managua, Chinandega, and points along the Telica–San Isidro highway. There are also daily expresses to Estelí and Matagalpa (5 A.M. and 8:40 A.M.). Buses for Managua's UCA terminal run from 4 A.M. till about 7 P.M.

Near León

SOUTH OF LEÓN
◖ Las Ruinas de León Viejo
The sleepy ruins of Spain's first settlement in Nicaragua are an easy and worthwhile day trip from León. They are located just adjacent to Puerto Momotombo; turn off the highway at La Paz Centro. Francisco Hernández de Córdoba founded the first León in 1524 and Pedrarias Dávila governed it. After two years, for reasons unknown, Dávila had Hernández de Córdoba decapitated in the town square. In 1610, Volcán Momotombo erupted, burying the site under ash. But León may have already been abandoned following a series of premonitory earthquakes that convinced the settlers to look elsewhere for a place to call home.

(Momotombo has erupted several times since then, most recently in 1905.)

Dr. Carlos Tünnerman and a team from the National University (UNAN) first uncovered the ruins of old León in 1966, but in 2000, archaeologists found the remains of both Córdoba and Dávila and placed them in an on-site mausoleum. León Viejo is now a World Heritage Site. The Nicaraguan Culture Institution has completed fascinating excavations and has trained many local guides to take you around, most of whom are friendly, enthusiastic, and speak passable English. Entrance is $2, plus a small fee to take photographs or video.

The site is open seven days a week, with tour

the ruins of León Viejo

guides 8 A.M.–5 P.M. Catch a bus from León to catch either an 8 A.M. or 11 A.M. connection in La Paz Centro; last return bus from the ruins is 3 P.M. Call 505/222-2905, ext. 112, for the Palacio Nacional de la Cultura in Managua or visit any of León's tour agencies.

Volcán Momotombo and Momotombito Island

Volcán Momotombo is the most challenging Pacific volcano to climb (see sidebar *Hiking the Maribio Volcanoes*), and it is one of Nicaragua's more active volcanic peaks. While the small town of El Cardón, on the other side of Volcán Momotombo is closer, the town itself is difficult to get to from the highway.

Momotombo's little sibling, the island of Momotombito was once a pre-Columbian religious sanctuary, when the islet was called **Cocobolo.** Today, it is an uninhabited natural reserve of tropical dry forest. It's not easy to get to, but persistence will pay off in the town of Puerto Momotombo, where for the right price, many fishermen would be eager to transport

you the 25 kilometers along the north shore of Lake Managua to the island. Bring water and supplies to last two days in order to camp on the island, and don't pay your boatman until he returns to take you off the island. The island reportedly contains petroglyphs and the faintest remnants of the previous civilization who would be horrified to see what has become of their precious lake.

Nagarote

About halfway between Managua and León, the historic village of Nagarote (Chorotega for "the road of the Nagarands") is representative of Nicaragua's small agricultural and cattle villages. Its claim to fame is an enormous old *genícero* tree said to date to the time of Columbus, whose broad branches shade the small market. The tree and a statue of Diriangén are two blocks north and one block west from the central park. The Casa de Cultura is located one block south of the tree. Nagarote is nationally renowned for its *quesillos,* a snack of mozzarella-like string cheese, sour cream, and onions wrapped in a hot tortilla. Enjoy them at any of the roadside restaurants that cater to the León–Managua travelers, many of whom plan their trips around a stop in Nagarote for some cheesy goodness.

NORTH OF LEÓN
Los Hervideros de San Jacinto

On the southeast flank of 1,060-meter Volcán Telíca, Los Hervideros de San Jacinto are a warren of boiling mud pits and thermal vents which have formed a veritable martian landscape not far from León. The vents testify to the region's geothermal electric potential, an opportunity that has not gone unnoticed by potential foreign investors—some Israeli— that continue to explore the idea of producing energy from the vast reserves that are forming the vents. To get there, take a bus bound for Estelí, San Isidro, or Malpaisillo and get off at the town of San Jacinto (approximately 25 kilometers from León). The entrance is marked by an enormous arch and a posse of women and children selling "artifacts" from the hot springs. The young boys will offer to guide you around for $0.20, a good deal considering the danger of falling into a scalding mud bath. Community-based tourism projects and trail improvements are in the works, as is a new hotel.

El Sauce and Achuapa

In the foothills of the Segovia Mountains, to the north and east of León, El Sauce (rhymes with WOW-say) was once the eastern terminus of the railroad that received Nicaraguan coffee bound for the port at Corinto. In the 1800s, caravans of mules lumbered into town, laden with thousands of pounds of coffee beans. El Sauce has since faded into a sleepy cowboy village whose pride and joy is a breathtaking colonial church built in 1750 in tribute to the patron saint, the Cristo Negro de Esquipulas (the Black Christ). El Sauce celebrates its *fiestas patronales* on January 18 and causes a massive pilgrimage from all over Nicaragua to view the Black Christ icon. El Sauce is off the

beaten track but makes a good first stop on forays toward Achuapa, San Juan de Limay, and Estelí. There are a couple of places to eat, and several *hospedajes:* try **Hotel El Viajero** (tel. 505/319-2325, $3 shared bath, $5 private bath and TV).

WEST OF LEÓN
C Poneloya and Las Peñitas Beaches

Only a 20-minute drive from León, Poneloya is the most popular beach in the area and has been a playground of the Leónese elite for generations. Nearby, less-visited Las Peñitas beach has recently become a popular destination for foreign travelers bound for Isla Juan Venado Wildlife Reserve. Both beach towns are tight-knit communities of a few thousand souls, with the family names displayed proudly on the houses; during Semana Santa, hotels at both beaches swell to capacity and double their rates.

The road from León splits when it reaches the coast, the right fork placing you in Poneloya where you'll find two hotels. **Hotel Lacayo** (tel. 505/886-7369, $5 pp shared bath), with its sagging cots and your own dilapidated balcony overlooking the ocean, is a massive, breezy beachfront barn on stilts that continues to defy gravity after 70 years of hosting beachgoers. Don't mind the bats; they eat mosquitoes. Across the street, **Hotel La Posada** (tel. 505/317-378, León tel. 505/311-4612, $20–25) has 19 concrete rooms with private bath, fan, and air-conditioning. It's simple but essentially clean. The best restaurant in Poneloya is **El Pariente Salinas** located in the middle of town. For a more refreshing option, walk all the way to the north end of the beach where you will find a group of restaurants frequented by locals. The last one, **El Chepe,** is said to be the best but all allow you to pick the fish you want whole-fried. The *estero* here is safer than the ocean, a fact not overlooked by lots of children who come to enjoy splashing around.

Traveling several kilometers south along the coast will bring you to a series of accommodations that make up Las Peñitas, presented here in the order you'll find them. **Casa Surf** (tel. 505/407-5549 or 505/317-0275) is located right on the sand behind a row of houses that line the street. Tents to sleep on the beach cost $1.50. They also serve refreshments and hope to serve real meals soon. **Playa Roca** (tel. 505/858-3656, www.playaroca.com, $6 dorm, $15–20) has seven cozy rooms, offers similar services as its competition, but stays open later at night (till midnight on weekdays and 2 A.M. on weekends). The view of the rocks and the waves is one of the best on the beach. **Hotel Suyapa Beach** (tel. 505/317-0219, frobertoreyes@yahoo.com, $21–45) is a modern, well-kept hotel/restaurant with 23 rooms around a small pool. The food and service is here is reportedly the best on the beach. Continuing south, Nicaraguan-owned **Mi Casita** (tel. 505/852-9766, $15) offers seven brightly painted rooms, two of which have private balconies, with soft beds, fan, and the sound of the surf.

French-owned **Hotelito El Oasis** (tel. 505/839-5344, www.oasislaspenitas.com, $6 dorm, $15 d) has reasonable rates, spacious rooms, and slow service. But what's the rush? Rooms have fans and private baths. Enjoy the small *rancho* and hammock area with a great second-story view of the beach. Like most other places on the beach, they rent surfboards and can arrange tours of Isla Juan Venado, horseback trips ($10), and Spanish lessons ($4/hour). Around the corner and past the local bars of Los Cocos and El Calamar, you'll find the Canadian-owned **La Samaki.net** (tel. 505/640-2058, $20), with pool, Wi-Fi ($3/hour), and nice paintings. They serve different vegetarian options, including Indian curry, and will soon be the first place in Nicaragua with kite surfing instruction and rentals. Just a bit farther is **(La Barca de Oro** (tel. 505/317-0275, tortuga@ibw.com.ni, $6 dorm, $22 d); rooms come with fan, mosquito net, and private bath and there is a honeymoon suite with air-conditioning for $30. La Barca looks directly out to the northern tip of Isla Juan Venado, only 100 meters away across a protected lagoon. They can help you arrange all kinds of local (and inland) excursions. You can also rent kayaks or hire locals to give a massage or pedicure at this popular backpacker getaway.

Buses for Poneloya leave every half hour from the Subtiava Mercadito, from early in the morning until 6 P.M. They stop first in Poneloya, idling for 10 minutes, then continue to Las Peñitas; the trip to the end of the road at Barca de Oro can take up to an hour. You'll save a lot of time and pay a bit more (about $7, not bad if you have three or four people) with a taxi from León. The last bus back to León leaves Barca de Oro at 6:40 P.M.

Surfing and Water Sports

The waves along this stretch of Nicaragua's Pacific shoreline are less forgiving than the beaches down south; they break faster and and with more force, and the currents are stronger. Poneloya in particular has a vicious undertow that makes it dangerous for casual swimmers: Take more caution than you would elsewhere. At Las Peñitas you can rent boards and stay the night; farther north along the coast, you will have to have your own transportation and more than likely, local guidance.

Isla Juan Venado Wildlife Reserve

The 21-kilometer strip of tropical dry forest, mangroves, and inland estuary south of Las Peñitas provides habitat for hundreds of species of migratory birds, as well as crocodiles and other wetland creatures, and is also an important nesting beach for sea turtles. The park is named for a man who, in colonial times, made his living hunting deer on the island and selling the meat in the market of Subtiava.

Many León-based tour operators run trips to Isla Juan Venado, but you can just as easily strike a deal with one of the many boatmen in Las Peñitas to explore the endless, tree-lined channels. Arrange your trip at least one day in advance, especially if you plan on a sunrise excursion, when you'll see the most wildlife (late afternoons are good, too). Take sun protection and lots of water. You'll need to purchase tickets at the ranger station/youth club ($2 pp includes life vest), a two-story house 100 meters down the beach from Barca de Oro. The youth

© RANDALL WOOD

volcanic rock formations on the beach at El Tránsito

club helps with reforestation of the mangrove forests, turtle monitoring, and other types of ecological research in cooperation with the organization FUNDAR. Like many protected areas in Nicaragua, Isla Juan Venado is comanaged by the local community and an NGO, in this case LIDER. This is one of the most successful examples of the COMAP (co-management) program in Nicaragua, and the ranger station can be a good source of information on this topic, as well as other issues concerning the flora and fauna of the reserve. They can also arrange boat trips to the island for $50 per group of up to 14 or $20–30 for a smaller boat with one of the community members. Also available are nighttime turtle-viewing trips (seasonal) for $10 and mandatory guided camping also for $10. Some of the hazards in the reserve include caimans, bees, snakes, and crab and turtle egg hunters frustrated by poverty, so bringing a local guide is a really good idea.

You can also access the reserve from the rustic community of Salinas Grandes on the south side of the island, where you can rent kayaks and stay in beachfront *ranchos* at **Rigo's Guest House** (tel. 505/311-3306 or 505/868-1569, rsampson@ibw.com.ni). Make arrangements at least one week in advance to make sure that Rigo is ready.

El Velero and El Tránsito Beach Communities

South from León, the gorgeous two-kilometer stretch of white-sand beach known as **El Velero** (The Sailboat) has tremendous tourist potential but instead is simply occupied by summer homes for wealthy Leóneses. Buses for Puerto Sandino and El Velero leave from the station at León. The limited options for travelers are not cheap and have fallen into total disrepair, an ignoble end to one of Herty Lewites's more ambitious tourism projects in the 1980s. It's better to visit for the day.

A quiet fishing community 60 kilometers from Managua along the old highway to León, **El Tránsito** was devastated by the tidal wave of December 1992. The Spanish helped them recover and built what is now the new town on the hills above the old one, which was at the shoreline. The swimming here can be a bit tricky, as there's a strong undertow that will pull you north along the cove, but walk south along the shoreline to see the rock formations and popular swimming holes behind them. These rocks run parallel to the shoreline and buttress the full blow of waves. Splash around in one of them at high tide, when the waves strike the rocks and rush up and over in an exhilarating saltwater shower. Ten minutes' walk north along the shoreline takes you to the wreckage of El Balneario, an old abandoned vacation spot. Enjoy cheap, cold beer and fresh fish on the south end of the village. Buses leave Managua every afternoon from Israel Lewites at 11:15 A.M., 12:40 P.M., and 2 P.M. Buses leave El Tránsito every day at 5 A.M., 6 A.M., and 7 A.M.

LEÓN

Chinandega

Chinandega, a provincial capital grown out of the agriculture business is the last major town before the Güasaule border with Honduras, and the gateway to Nicaragua's distant corner of the Gulf of Fonseca. It's a town you'll get to know well if you are stocking up for a visit to the desolate coastline or the unvisited crater wall of Volcán Cosigüina. It's also the undisputedly hottest corner of the nation.

The same threatening volcanoes that loom over the city of Chinandega and its surrounding plains are also responsible for the high fertility of the soil. This attracted the Nahuatl, who called their new home Chinamilt ("close to cane"). Chinandega suffers the same poverty as the rest of the nation, but also boasts a prosperous community of old and new money, based primarily in sugar, bananas, peanuts, sesame, soy, and shrimp. Cotton used to be the number-one cash crop in the 1960s, but the deforestation and agro-chemicals essential to its production caused monumental environmental damage, like poisoned aquifers and toxic soil, still affecting life to this day. The agricultural activity of the region and proximity to the northern borders and Port of Corinto make Chinandega Nicaragua's most important agribusiness center.

Did we mention that it's hot in Chinandega? It's so hot in Chinandega, expect to break a sweat in the shower. This is what it feels like to be a rotisserie chicken. You can easily see Chinandega's colonial churches and central market in a couple of hours before stopping to catch your breath. Keep your wits about you, as the areas south of center can be a bit dangerous due to the presence of *pandillas,* or street gangs.

ORIENTATION AND GETTING AROUND

Chinandega's two hubs of activity are the area surrounding the Mercado Bisne (from the English word "business"), and the town center, or simply, *el centro.* The Mercadito is located two blocks north of the central park,

and the Central Market a few blocks east of the park, along the Calle Central. La Rotonda los Encuentros and the Texaco StarMart are both important reference points you'll pass on your way into town. Everything is walkable, but drink lots of water. Taxis are plentiful and cost $0.40 within city limits; *ruta* buses are $0.10.

ENTERTAINMENT AND RECREATION

For a classy dancing experience, the **Dilectus Disco** (located just east of town on the road to León) is one of the nation's finest. If you prefer a looser, younger crowd and still want air-conditioning, try **Montserat** on the highway to Guasaule. **La Terraza** (on the road to El Corinto) is very pleasant, with dancing on the weekend, decent food, and a clean swimming pool! There is also a great air-conditioned bar at the Hotel El Chinandegano.

If you really enjoy sweating, join in a pickup basketball game at the courts by the park. If watching **baseball** is more your style, catch Team Chinandega in season (the stadium is located west across the river, on the road to El Viejo). You'll find a clean public swimming pool at the Instituto San Luis (on the east end of town, open Fri.–Sun., $1.50 for the whole day), complete with high dive, cheap beer, and a hot dog and burger stand. There are also plenty of waves to surf up and down the entire coast and zero surfers. This means the waves are yours alone, but so are the equipment, logistics, and responsibility.

Several places in town can arrange a trip up to the giant San Cristóbal volcano (a.k.a. El Viejo), but only Don Alvaro from **Casa Grande** (tel. 505/341-0325) can take you to his family's 130-year-old farm where you can stay the night in the hacienda or camp outside before your climb. One- or two-day trips are available for $20–25, depending on group size.

For a different kind of fun stop by the office of **Fundación COEN** (tel. 505/341-2906,

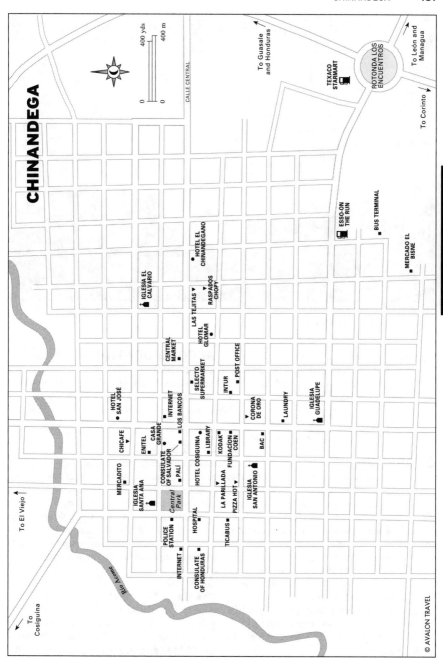

CHINANDEGA

To El Viejo

To Cosiguina

Río Acome

© AVALON TRAVEL

CALLE CENTRAL

To Guasale and Honduras

To León and Managua

To Corinto

ROTONDA LOS ENCUENTROS

TEXACO STARMART

ESSO ON THE RUN

BUS TERMINAL

MERCADO EL BISNE

LEÓN

IGLESIA EL CALVARIO

HOTEL EL CHINANDEGANO

LAS TÉJITAS

RASPADOS CHOPY

HOTEL GLOMAR

CENTRAL MARKET

SELECTO SUPERMARKET

POST OFFICE

INTUR

CORONA DE ORO

LAUNDRY

IGLESIA GUADELUPE

HOTEL SAN JOSÉ

INTERNET

LOS BANCOS

CHICAFE

ENTEL

CASA GRANDE

MERCADITO

IGLESIA SANTA ANA

Central Park

CONSULATE OF SALVADOR

PALI

HOTEL COSIGUINA

LIBRARY

KODAK

FUNDACION COEN

BAC

LA PARILLADA

PIZZA HOT

IGLESIA SAN ANTONIO

POLICE STATION

HOSPITAL

TICABUS

INTERNET

CONSULATE OF HONDURAS

0   400 yds
0   400 m

LEÓN

© JOSHUA BERMAN

The San Cristóbal Volcano lords over the scorching streets of Chinandega, occasionally powdering them with a layer of white-gray ash.

www.fundacioncoen.org), just south of the Kodak store, where informal volunteer arrangements can be made to work with children with disabilities or with chemotherapy patients. For more information on volunteering contact Vittoria Penalba in Managua (tel. 505/266-5401 ext. 115, vpenalba@fundacioncoen.org).

SHOPPING

Buy crafts and homemade wine at **Chicafe,** where your purchase will support the efforts of several local women's craft cooperatives. The three markets (Bisne, Central, and the Mercadito) are dark and deep and are all surrounded by several square blocks of additional retail action—whip out some moist *córdobas* and go nuts. The **Kodak** store (two blocks east and one south of the central park) has an impressive stock of photo and computer supplies (and extreme air-conditioning). Chinandega has two fully stocked **supermarkets:** El Palí in front of the park, and El Selecto, 3.5 blocks farther east.

ACCOMMODATIONS
Under $10
At less than $5 a night, **Hotel Chinandega** is the best dump in town: centrally located, 15 rooms, relatively clean, and only slightly depressing and dingy.

$10-25
Hotel Glomar (a block south and a block east of the Selecto, tel. 505/341-2562) has passable doubles for $18–21; the place is clean enough, a few rooms with air-conditioning. Similar accommodations are in the **Casa Grande** (tel. 505/341-0325, $10–15); there's free laundry service, and the friendly owner, Don Alvaro, can help organize volcano expeditions.

$25-50
The Hotel San José (tel. 505/341-2723, movalles@starband.com, $35) has rooms with private bath, TV, air-conditioning, breakfast, and hot water in a converted home. **C Hotel El Chinandegano** (tel. 505/341-4800,

hotelchdgano@turbonett.com.ni, $30) offers air-conditioning, private bath, breakfast, phone, and Wi-Fi; in addition guests enjoy professional hotel service, laundry, parking, and lovely, bird-filled common spaces.

The plushest digs in the city center are at **Hotel Cosigüina** (located half a block south of *la esquina de los bancos,* corner of the banks, tel. 505/341-2129, www.hotelcosiguina.com, $45 plus tax) with air-conditioning, hot water, and private bath. They also rent cars and serve food and drinks in the Fumaroles Restaurant.

FOOD

You won't go hungry in Chinandega, with choices ranging from every type of street food imaginable staring at you from thousands of coolers, stands, and baskets all over town, to the *comida corriente* in any of the markets (meals for less than $2) to a host of expensive restaurants. Located on the Calle Central, seven blocks east of the park, **Las Tejitas** (open evenings) may be the best *fritanga* in Nicaragua; so say the stream of regular clients. Sit outside on the sidewalk and enjoy a heaping plate of juicy roasted chicken, *gallo pinto, tajadas* (fried plantain chips), and any number of deep-fried delicacies, all for under $3, drink included. Another good *fritanga* is **La Parrillada** (about 100 meters south of Palí, tel. 505/341-3745, open all day long) with free delivery and buffet, grill, fry, and rotisserie options.

The relaxed, tasteful **Chicafe** (half a block west of the Almacen Quinonez, open 8 A.M.–6 P.M. Mon.–Sat.) sells coffee, fruit smoothies, and local *artesanía* to help fund Chinantlan, a local NGO that supports small farmers and distributes international donations to local education and health centers. If you can find **Raspados y Soda "Chopy"** (located around the corner from El Chinandegano) the sugar buzz from the traditional shaved ice might snap you out of the heat coma. Otherwise, experience very Nicaraguanized Chinese food at **Corona de Oro** (a block and a half east of Iglesia San Antonio), with large portions (about $5) and good service.

Many fancier restaurants abound along the highways in and out of town, and gringo fare is plentiful, including a Jerry's Subs and Pizza in the StarMart and all kinds of junk food and sandwiches at On the Run. **Sport Burger** (tel. 505/341-3264) or **Pizza Hot** (505/341-8730) will deliver great and greasy food right to your hotel.

INFORMATION AND SERVICES

INTUR (block and a half south of Selecto, tel. 505/341-1935, chinandega@intur.gob.ni) maintains an office full of brochures and has a staff who are surprisingly helpful as long as you sign in. The police occupy the entire block along the west side of the central park, and the hospital is right across the street to the south. Money changers work the streets near the central market, and most of Chinandega's banks are clustered on *la esquina de los bancos,* two blocks east of the park.

The post office is three blocks east of the park and 1.5 north. Also, the TicaBus agent will send FedEx packages via their Managua office. The ENITEL phone office is one block east of the park—look for the giant red and white tower. ATMs can be found at Banco America Central (BAC), as well as at StarMart and On the Run. Get your laundry done just north of the Iglesia Guadelupe.

Chinandega's abundant cybercafes are in constant flux, though you'll want to seek out the ones with air-conditioning, such as the one located one block north of the corner with all the banks.

International Consulates

The Consulate of El Salvador (tel. 505/341-2049, open 8 A.M.–2 P.M. Mon.–Fri.) is two blocks north of *la esquina de los bancos.* When applying for a visa, leave your passport before 11 A.M. The Honduras Consulate (tel. 505/341-0949, open 8:30 A.M.–4:30 P.M. Mon.–Fri.) is across from ENITEL. The Costa Rica Consulate (tel. 505/341-1584, open 8:30 A.M.–5 P.M. Mon.–Fri., until noon Sat.) is located half a block north from Banpro.

LEÓN

GETTING THERE AND AWAY

The main bus station is at Bisne Market, just past Rotonda los Encuentros. From La Rotonda, highways run north to Somotillo and the border with Honduras at Guasaule (this is easily the most deteriorated stretch of the entire Nicaraguan highway system, a real bone-crusher), east to León and Managua, south to Corinto, and west into Chinandega. A second bus station located at the Mercadito (just north of the central park) provides service to El Viejo, Jiquilillo, Potosí, Cosigüina, and Puerto Morazán.

Car rentals starting at $35 a day are available at the Avis office in the Hotel Cosigüina

and Budget in Hostal Las Mañanitas. Local buses ($1), expresses ($1.85), and microbuses ($2.20) run regularly between Chinandega and Managua's Israel (Boer) Market, beginning at 4:30 A.M. and ending around 8 P.M. Service to and from León is even more frequent and hitching in any direction from La Rotonda is a cinch.

Even though there is a TicaBus agency in town, those traveling north into Honduras or El Salvador will have to go to Managua to catch the bus, which no longer stops in Chinandega. Be advised: Any foreigner who enters El Salvador must have a visa. Get yours at the Salvadoran Consulate.

Near Chinandega

EL VIEJO

Only a few kilometers west of Chinandega, El Viejo is a cheerful town of some 35,000 El Viejanos, as they like to be called. Less service-oriented than its big neighbor, El Viejo can still launch you on your next adventure. El Viejo is much older than Chinandega. Originally an indigenous community called Texoatega, for the fierce cacique who once ruled it, the town was renamed for the old Spaniard who arrived in 1562 carrying a sacred image of the Virgin Mary. According to legend, when the Spaniard tried to sail back to Spain, the Virgin created a hurricane so that she would be returned to her new home in Nicaragua. The old man complied, and the image soon became the most important Virgin Mary in the country. Her fame has lasted through the centuries, and in 1996 the Pope himself recognized her when he came to declare El Viejo's church a Basilica Minor. The church is impressive and worth your time to visit.

Buses arrive half a block north of the basilica, across the street from the market where you'll find the cheapest eats. Buses called *interlocales* back to Chinandega leave from behind the basilica and run until about 11 P.M.

Entertainment and Accommodations

Nightlife in El Viejo is exciting and sometimes downright rowdy. Local volunteers say it's all "beer and bark" though, and everyone makes up and shakes hands the next day. Just south of the basilica is **Texoatega,** a nightclub whose fame spreads as far as León. It is clean and has good food and service, with a huge variety of music (check out mariachi night on Thursdays). **Los Coquitos,** on the same block, presents boxing matches and super cheap pitchers of beer. **La Piscina,** two blocks north of the basilica and half a block east, serves great meals and appetizers, and opens the dance floor Thursday–Saturday. Their *piscina* (swimming pool) is reportedly drained and cleaned once a week and costs $0.75 to use all day. An outdoor movie theater, one block south of ENITEL and behind the hardware store, shows a daily double feature for under $0.50. The first flick is for the whole family and the second is . . . um . . . for adult, single men only.

El Viejo's *fiestas patronales* fall the week of December 6, with firework-spitting bulls every night, culminating in the **Lava la Plata,** when even the president often

VOLCÁN CASITAS AND HURRICANE MITCH

On October 30, 1998, the quiet municipality of Posoltega (whose Nahuatl name, Posolitecatl, means "neighbor of the boiling place") was catapulted into a horrendous sort of fame as the site of one of the worst naturally caused disasters in Nicaragua's history. After Hurricane Mitch dropped two meters of rain in just three days, the southwest flank of Volcán Casitas transformed into a gigantic wave of mud and rock more than three meters high and nearly 1.5 kilometers wide. The communities of El Porvenir and Rolando Rodríguez were instantly consumed by the very soil on which they were built. Some 2,500 people immediately lost their lives, and those who were not buried lived through the horror of losing nearly everything and everyone in their lives. Immediate relief efforts were held up by the political shenanigans of President Alemán, who stalled help to the Sandinista leadership of Posoltega.

A survivor told one Witness for Peace volunteer, "You should have seen how the children, the little ones, fought to survive.

People were pulling themselves up out of the mud naked, completely covered in mud. They looked like monsters in a horror movie. All you could see were their eyes. Children didn't even recognize their own parents. For days we could hear the ones who were still half-buried crying for help."

A decade later, the slide is still clearly visible from the León-Chinandega highway. International efforts helped construct several new communities for survivors, despite reports of disappearing relief funds reminiscent of Somoza's postearthquake "emergency committee." The new suburban communities, however, provided no means of production for a people accustomed to living off the land. Many were psychologically devastated and eventually made their way illegally to search for work in Costa Rica.

The entire slide area has been declared a national monument, and a memorial plaque personally delivered by U.S. President Bill Clinton can be visited in the Peace Park on the highway, near the turnoff for Posoltega.

shows up to help "wash the church silver." Until recently, the only places to stay were in "hotels of love." Now, **Casa de Huesped La Estancia,** two blocks north of the basilica, has six simple rooms with shared bath for $3.75 a night.

Marina Puesta del Sol Resort (www.marinapuestadelsol.com) is Nicaragua's only luxury marina, painstakingly conceived and elaborated by Nicaragua-born and California-raised Marc Membreño and father, two frustrated hydrogeologic engineers who decided to pursue another passion instead of energy. The marina employed over 200 local community members when constructed and the owners continue to invest in the community. It's a bit out of the way for the casual traveler, but for the coastal sailor it's the only marina worth docking at, and careful environmental management means it will stay that way.

CHICHIGALPA

Set in the middle of hundreds of square kilometers of sugarcane, Chichigalpa's **Ingenio San Antonio** is Nicaragua's largest and most powerful sugar refinery, and more importantly, the Compañía Licorera, Nicaragua's alcohol monopoly and source of all the Toña, Victoria, Flor de Caña, and Ron Plata you've been drinking. The two companies belong to the wealthy Pellas family, who founded the sugar refinery in 1890 and have produced sugar and liquor ever since (except 1988–1992 when the Sandinista government briefly expropriated it—the Chamorro government subsequently returned it).

As alcohol is a mainstay of Nicaraguan culture and legend, the refineries and distilleries have been important parts of Nicaraguan life for more than a century. If you're interested in seeing how the cane is crushed, processed, and distilled, arrange for a tour of the Flor de Caña distillery by calling the plant in advance (tel. 505/343-2344, try asking for Simón Pedro Pereira) and requesting a guided tour. At the moment, there is no charge for the tour, but neither are there free samples.

CORINTO

The barrier island and economically important port town of Corinto lies 20 kilometers southwest of Chinandega. Because of its shipping activity and beaches (one of which cradles a giant shipwreck reminiscent of *Planet of the Apes*), Corinto is fairly well developed for tourists with a small range of simple hotels and seaside restaurants. Corinto's 20,000 inhabitants live on 49 square kilometers of island, connected to the rest of Nicaragua by two small bridges.

The Spanish first made use of the harbor in the 1500s, but didn't completely conquer the region until 1633, when an armada of 26 ships, 500 Spaniards, 227 horses, and 2,000 slaves arrived, swiftly defeating Texoatega's troops and taking many of them as additional slaves. The original port, placed at El Realejo (which still exists as a faint shadow of its former self), was transferred closer to the ocean at Corinto in 1858 after mangroves and sediment had choked the waterways.

Even when Corinto's first dock was built in 1875—then nothing more than a wooden pier jutting into the harbor—Corinto was a vital link in Nicaragua's transport and shipping facilities. Nicaragua's railroads transported coffee from El Sauce to Corinto, from where ships took it to the United States and elsewhere. A railroad constructed during Zelaya's presidency further expanded the port and its strategic significance.

In 1912, nearly 3,000 U.S. Marines landed in Corinto in response to Benjamin Zeledón's revolution, beginning what would be a 20-year occupation of Nicaragua. In October 1983, CIA operatives stole into the harbor under cover of night, where they mined the harbor and blew up several oil tanks on the docks. The economic and psychological damage strained an already suffering Sandinista government,

but the "covert" operation, when publicized later, earned the Reagan administration international condemnation and enraged U.S. citizens who, before Corinto, remained unaware of the until-then unpublicized American intervention.

From 2000–2001, the Alemán administration revitalized the port and dredged the harbor with project financing from the World Bank in order to increase export production. Today, Corinto remains what it has been since the days the Spanish landed with their horses and slaves: a vibrant coastal community with all the headaches and spice of a port town.

Sights and Entertainment

Besides soaking up the sun and rum at Playa Paso Caballo, the curious traveler will want to take a look at the beached oil tanker, a short walk up the coast. The ship washed up here sometime in the 1980s after it caught fire (nothing to do with the war) and its owners decided to salvage what they could and let the rest drift to shore and burn. Both the beach and the tanker are located on the northern tip of the island, and all buses from Chinandega pass by here before continuing to the center of town. Be careful, as the rip currents are notoriously strong. Paso Caballo fills up on Sundays and holidays, during which times you should keep a good eye on your stuff—in fact, keep an eye on your stuff year-round. Several *ranchos* on the beach provide shade, food, and alcohol.

In town, what was once the **Old Railroad Terminal and Customs House** is now a museum in tribute to the old train, well worth a visit. Two discos, **Ali Baba** and **Centauro,** are on the road between town and the northern beaches.

Festivals

If you are in the neighborhood around the weekend that falls closest to May 3, don't miss the **Féria Gastronómica del Mar** (Seafood Festival), where you can try more than 100 different Corinteña recipes with fresh fish, shrimp, and other local delicacies. The festival takes place in the central park, 10 A.M.–3 P.M. Saturday and Sunday.

Accommodations, Food, and Services

The family-run **Hospedaje Vargas** (about a block west of the Texaco station where buses arrive, $6 s shared bath, $8 s private bath) is simple and has fans in all 10 of its rooms. **Hospedaje Luvy** (1.5 blocks west of the central park, tel. 505/342-2637, $8 s, $11 d with fan, shared bath) is similar. All 10 rooms in the **Hotel Central** ($30 s, $40 d, with a/c, private bath, cable TV) enjoy a view of the industrial container loaders of Corinto's docks.

As always, your best bargain is the *comida corriente* in the town market. Otherwise, numerous *cafetíns* dot the town and a row of restaurants flank the town beach. **Restaurante Costa Azul** and **El Peruano** have typical dishes and seafood starting at $5. They are both very pleasant, breezy, open-air *ranchos* with views of the harbor and islands. Also consider **New Orleans** (one block east of the minisupermarket), with free crab soup for serious drinkers. It's run by a recently returned Nica who has brought a little culture back from his old home in the French Quarter.

The best restaurant in town got nudged out of the main plaza and can now be found toward Playa Paso Caballo on the main road to Chinandega, near the bridge (from which you can jump into the water)—it's called **El Español** and the owner makes a mean sangria. **Corinto Online** (half a block north of the park) will connect you to Internet for $2.50 per hour. Getting to and from Corinto is a snap from Chinandega's Bisne Market, or by hitching from the Rotonda.

PUERTO MORAZÁN

Accessed by bus from Chinandega, Puerto Morazán is the gateway to the magnificent and sinuous Estero Real, whose mangrove estuary provides habitat for countless marine species and birds. Morazán was built at water level, so it's no surprise that during Hurricane Mitch it flooded so severely only the church steeple appeared over the surface of the water. Shortly after Mitch, the community rebuilt itself on its original site, disregarding the humanitarian assistance community's plan to relocate the community to higher ground.

Morazán has not always been so poor. During World War II, Morazán's port, railway terminus, and customs office saw the movement of tons of cargo bound for European and North American destinations. When the war ended, so did Morazán's brief period of prosperity, and when Volcán Chonco erupted, damaging the railroad tracks, the final nail was put in Morazán's coffin.

The estuary itself is gorgeous, even if its "protected" status has been largely ignored by MARENA officials and the shrimp industry. Take a bus from El Viejo and pay someone to take you out into the estuary to bird-watch: The local boat owners are better equipped to do so than you'd expect. You won't be disappointed by the extraordinary variety of wildlife, nor by the amazing view of Volcán Cosigüina.

COSIGÜINA PENINSULA AND BEACHES

Nicaragua's northwest corner is a magnificent volcanic knuckle jutting out into the Golfo de Fonseca. The scenery is stunning, the beaches isolated, and the people strongly rooted in their indigenous past. All buses to the area leave from Chinandega's Mercadito and make stops in El Viejo before continuing on. Many of the following spots only have bus service once a day, which means you'll be making an overnight trip if you don't have your own wheels. Bring a hammock, flashlight, food, and plenty of water. El Viejo's nuns know the area well—find them for additional information on any of the following.

Reserva Natural Volcán Cosigüina

Not only does this nationally protected reserve provide incredible views from the volcano's rim, but the dense vegetation inside the crater is the haunt of the only scarlet macaw population this side of the Segovia Mountains. Hiking or horseback riding to the rim is not to be missed (see sidebar *Hiking the Maribio Volcanoes*). Your journey begins in the poverty-stricken town of Potosí, former trading port with El Salvador until the Contras blew it up (the El Salvador–Nicaragua ferry was nearly reconstructed in Potosí recently, but plans shifted the project to Corinto). Of note is the three-day festival around May 19 on Meanguera, an El Salvadoran island that allows for unchecked passport access during the fiesta. You can reach Potosí at the end of a miserable 3.5-hour bus ride down "the crappiest road ever." Six buses leave daily and cost $1.50 each way. Fifteen kilometers past Potosí in the community of **El Rosario,** the park's official ranger station, run by a nonprofit organization called LIDER, sits below the volcano and is the best place to begin your exploring. LIDER links anxious tourists with the community tourism organization called Centro Ecoturístico de Aguas Termales, which offers two-day, one-night all-inclusive visits to the reserve during which you will take a horse ride up to the crater rim, take boat rides past mangrove forests, go on hikes, and cook (yourself) in the hot springs—all for $60 which goes to support the community and the comanaged conservation efforts. Contact Irving Caballeros at the LIDER office in El Viejo (tel. 505/625-4607, turismocosiguina @yahoo.com).

The Cliffs at Punta Ñata

One bus a day leaves Chinandega at 12:10 P.M. for the 3.5-hour ride to the town of Punta Ñata. It is worth the time and hassle! Five-hundred-meter cliffs preside over the Pacific Ocean and the Farallones Islands (formed by Cosigüina's last eruption). Find a guide in Punta to show you the hike and how to climb down the cliffs.

Los Aserradores Beach

Playa Los Aserradores is quiet and desolate, and the waves are either pleasant or devastating depending on the swell. You can stay at **Hotel**

Chancletas (tel. 505/868-5036 or 505/879-0014, www.hotelchancletas.com) for $10 per person in a dorm or $30–75 for a luxury room with or without air-conditioning. Activities include surfing, fishing, hiking, horseback riding, or relaxing in a hammock. Chancletas sits in front of one of the best waves around and has a full bar and restaurant for when the tides aren't perfect. Owner Shay O'Brien is a great source of information and can point the way to the nearby breaks. Catch one of the two daily buses at the Mercadito in Chinandega. The last one leaves at 1 P.M.

Nearby **Bahía Santa Maria** is good for beginner surfers. The bus leaves Chinandega at 12:30 P.M. and returns the next day at 5 A.M. Another option is **Playa Mechapa,** one of the longest, shallowest stretches of pure beach in Nicaragua. Buses leave Chinandega at 1:40 P.M. and return at 4 P.M. Buses to Punta San José, on the tippy tip of the peninsula, depart at 9:30 A.M. and 1:10 P.M., returning for Chinandega at 2:30 P.M. and 5 P.M.

Jiquilillo Beach

Less than a one-hour bus ride out of El Viejo, Playa Jiquilillo makes for a beautiful day trip all year—except during Semana Santa, when the place is a madhouse. Relatively deserted and undeveloped, this is a beach like no other. Long gone is the town that once stood here, demolished by the 1992 tsunami.

For accommodations, Jiquilillo has one of the region's most creative hostels, **Rancho Esperanza** (tel. 505/879-1795, www.rancho .esperanza.bvg3.com). Comfortable and clean dorm accommodations for $5 and bamboo cabins for $7 per person. This idyllic backpacker getaway combines low-impact natural living with projects that actively benefit the village. Volunteer with the kids club, or just lounge in a hammock on the beach. The hostel offers great local food (three meals a day for $6), has an impressive book exchange, and will organize excursions to nearby Padre Ramos estuary and Volcán Cosigüina. Six buses make the daily round-trip from Chinandega to Jiquilillo, starting at 6 A.M.

Padre Ramos Wetlands Reserve

Relax in the gentle waters of this protected estuary, laze in a hammock under the shade of a *palapa,* or be lulled to sleep on a deserted starlit beach. Padre Ramos is a little-visited part of Nicaragua that will reward you with an expanse of serene coastline and an overflowing supply of hospitality, wilderness, community, and culture.

The bus to Jiquilillo continues up the coast, past Hospedaje Los Zorros, and arrives at the end of the road in the community of Padre Ramos. A simple fishing village of some 150 dispersed families, Padre Ramos is the gateway to the neighboring protected wetlands, and consequently the site of several grassroots tourism projects. The estuary is a decidedly mellower place to swim than the ocean and is home to all the wildlife—especially birds—you could hope to see. Check out the visitors center when you arrive to ask about fishing and boat trips into the wetlands. In Padre Ramos, you'll want to pay a visit to **Comedor Comé Pues** (the Eat Now! Restaurant, formerly known as Doña Elli y las Chavalas). It's located on the right as you turn into the community, and offers enormous fish dishes for under $4 a plate.

Alternatively, dine at **Don Roque's** traditional *rancho* on the water's edge. You can get a quick boat ride to the community of Venecia across the estuary, where you'll find long stretches of utterly deserted beach. The entire area is a breeding ground for sea turtles, the eggs of which are laid and hatch between November and January.

Ask around for **Eddy Maradeaga** (tel. 505/874-5724) for mangrove tours by boat, hiking, or horseback riding. Eddy is one of the most engaged community members and is very knowledgeable about the local ecosystem and conservation efforts. He is working with a group of local students to develop a community-based tourism program for Padre Ramos. If you want to spend a few days in this incredibly peaceful rural community, stay at **La Tortuga Booluda** ($3 pp), a family-run hostel behind the school, just 50 meters from the beach and 100 from the estuary; the place was started with the help of its sister hostel in León with the same name. Simply tell the bus driver to let you off in front of Doña Reyna's house, and she and her seven granddaughters will make you feel like you are part of the family. Expect your couple of days stay here to turn into weeks.

KAYAKING AND CANOEING IN NICARAGUA

So much water, so few boats. Some of the country's most incredible paddle-accessible attractions are serviced by few and small fleets of open, nonmotorized free craft. That's because the demand to glide through Granada's maze of *isletas,* Ometepe's Río Istián, or the mangrove estuary at Padre Ramos is still surprisingly low, considering the extraordinary outdoor opportunities offered by these, and other, places in Nicaragua. In many cases, you'll have to be creative to find ways to float the endless lakes, rivers, estuaries, archipelagos, and coastlines of Nicaragua that gave the country its name. Any water-bordering community will likely have small boats the owners use for fishing or transport. Ask for a *canoa,*

panga, or *botecita,* and see what shows up. Dugout canoes are common throughout the country, and you can ask to rent one along the Río San Juan and other areas.

For the glory-seeking paddler, Nicaragua is the place to make the cover of an extreme sports rag: the 700-kilometer stretch of the Río Coco from Wiwilí to the Caribbean at Cabo Gracias a Dios has (as far as we know) only been navigated end to end by pirates, guerilla soldiers, and indigenous boaters. There may be some hairy portages around some of the legendary waterfalls, and rumor has it that no one has ever even published a photograph of the falls between Raiti and San Carlos.

One of the best ways to explore Estero Padre Ramos is by sea kayak, paddling amongst the birds, sea turtles, and mangroves that inhabit this rich environment. The best tours are operated by **Ibis Exchange** (tel. 505/621-2778, U.S. tel. 415/663-8192, ibis.exchange@yahoo .com, www.pointreyesoutdoors.com). Ibis's professional guides provide delicious meals, kayak gear, and camping equipment for day tours and overnight adventures. Trips cost $35–95 per person. All ages and skill levels are welcome. Ibis Exchange offers eight-day package tours that include León, Estero Padre Ramos, and Juan Venado Nature Reserve.

HONDURAN BORDER AT EL GUASAULE

Located about 1.5 hours north of Chinandega on the Pan-American Highway, El Guasaule is the principal Pacific-side border crossing with Honduras. It is six kilometers beyond the town of Somotillo, where you'll find a large number of trucker and traveler services. At the actual border, there is a Bancentro branch and some basic food services. Reach the migration office at Guasaule by calling 505/346-2208.

Hours and Fees

El Guasaule is open 24 hours, and there is always heavy truck traffic and road repair problems on the Nicaraguan side. It costs $2 to leave Nicaragua and $7 to enter the country. Just a passport and some cash is all that's required of North American and European travelers, with the notable exception of El Salvador—United States citizens must purchase a visa for $30 (available at the consulate in Chinandega or during your trip, bring cash), even if you are only passing through the tiny country on your way to Guatemala.

Crossing the Border with Your Vehicle

If you are driving your own vehicle, the process to enter Nicaragua is lengthy, but usually not difficult. You must present the vehicle's title, as well as your own driver's license and passport. You will be given a temporary (30-day) permit to drive in Nicaragua, which will cost you $10—should you lose the permit, you will be fined $100.

Getting There and Away

There are numerous and regular buses traveling between the Bisne Terminal and El Guasaule, and the main international bus lines (TicaBus, etc.) heading to Honduras and El Salvador pass through Chinandega on their way to the border.

ESTELÍ AND THE SEGOVIAS

As you travel north and up out of the sultry Pacific lowlands, your introduction to Nicaragua's hilly interior begins with the Sébaco Valley, green with rice, carrot, and onion fields. From there, the Pan-American Highway struggles upward to the pleasant city of Estelí, "Diamond of the Segovias," then continues through mountains and valleys dotted with rural villages whose inhabitants are proud to call themselves *norteños*. Most folks here get along by subsistence farming and ranching, while cash crops like tobacco and coffee also define the land; a few communities boast talented artisans in pottery, leather, and stone. Underneath the north's gentle exterior of pine trees and tended fields are minor ruins of ancient cities, deep pools and cascades, and rugged communities of farmers and cowboys.

The north of Nicaragua is poorer than the rest, and suffers acutely from drought, poor soils, and deforestation: Nowhere else is the six-month dry season so intense. The challenging living conditions however make for a hardy and hardworking people, quick with a smile or a story. The curious and unrushed traveler will not regret breaking away from the highway and going deep into this northern countryside.

PLANNING YOUR TIME

If you've only got a day and a night, spend them in the city of Estelí to sample fine cigars and admire the town's inspiring collection of murals. With a second day, the bird-watcher, hiker, and historian should focus on nearby attractions like the Estanzuela waterfall, the lodge and trails at Tisey, or the orchid-rich

© JOSHUA BERMAN

HIGHLIGHTS

◖ **Custom Cowboy Boots:** They're custom-made from high quality leather, so don't leave Estelí without a pair for long rides into the wild or just dancing, northern-style (page 200).

◖ **El Salto Estanzuela and the Tisey Reserve:** Visit Estelí's premier swimming hole and ecolodge, where you can hike, ride horses, or just jump in for a swim (page 206).

◖ **Miraflor Nature Reserve:** This is the best place in Nicaragua to get back to nature and spot the elusive quetzal or other exotic wildlife (page 207).

◖ **San Juan de Limay:** Rumble over the mountain pass and down into the valley to seek out one of the famous soapstone workshops (page 213).

◖ **Iglesia de Nuestra Señora de la Asunción:** Ocotal's church has seen it all, and even withstood the world's first air-raid bombing in the 1930s (page 216).

◖ **Grand Canyon of Somoto:** The nicest swimming hole north of Estelí is also a great example of responsible community-run tourism (page 221).

LOOK FOR ◖ TO FIND RECOMMENDED SIGHTS, ACTIVITIES, DINING, AND LODGING.

broadleaf forest reserve of Miraflor. With a little more leisurely pace however, you can easily spend another day exploring Miraflor. Or spend it getting a feel for the *campesino* lifestyle by spending a lazy afternoon in any of the small northern towns off the Pan-American—like Condega, La Trinidad, or Pueblo Nuevo—or find yourself in the highland border towns of Ocotal or Somoto. If you're really curious, go deeper still, by traveling long loops eastward to Jalapa and Quilalí, or to Cusmapa, the highest town in Nicaragua.

HISTORY

Upon the Spanish arrival to this part of the isthmus, the Nahuatl cacique Mixcoatl, or Snake of the Clouds, ruled the countryside. The Spanish conquistador Francisco Hernández de Córdoba personally founded the city of Segovia on the banks of the Río Coco where it met the Jícaro, and the first settlers began exploring for veins of gold in the nearby hillsides. Both the ferocity of the natives' attacks on the Spanish and the proximity of better sources of gold led the Spanish to abandon this early settlement and move farther north

ESTELÍ AND THE SEGOVIAS

HONDURAS

0 | 10 mi
0 | 10 km

Teotecacinte

Jalapa

Santa María

Las Manos

Cerro Mogotón 2,107m

Cordillera Dipilto y Jalapa

Murra

Santa Clara

Ciudad Sandino

San Fernando

Susucayan

Macuelizo

Ocotal

Ciudad Antigua

IGLESIA DE NUESTRA SEÑORA DE LA ASUNCIÓN

Totogalpa

Quilalí

GRAND CANYON OF SOMOTO

Telpaneca

San Juan del Río Coco

Palacagüina

PAN-AMERICAN HIGHWAY

Somoto

Yalagüina

Río Coco

CA1

El Espino

Ducualí Grande

Pueblo Nuevo

Las Sabanas

Condega

San Sebastián de Yalí

CA1

MIRAFLOR NATURE RESERVE

Cinco Pinos

San José de Cusmapa

La Concordia

San Rafael del Norte

San Francisco del Norte

SAN JUAN DE LIMAY

La Sirena

Río Estelí

CUSTOM COWBOY BOOTS

Jinotega

Somotillo

Achuapa

EL SALTO ESTANZUELA AND THE TISEY RESERVE

Estelí

Santa Cruz

To Matagalpa

Villa Nueva

Río Grande

La Trinidad

San Isidro

San Nicolas

El Sauce

Sébaco

CA1

To Chinandega

To Léon

To Managua

© AVALON TRAVEL

ESTELÍ

along the Río Coco. The Xicaque, Miskito, and Zambo tribes attacked the new settlement with growing ferocity, however, strengthened and emboldened by shiny new firearms from the British. What the natives started, English pirate Henry Morgan finished in 1654, when he sailed all the way up the Río Coco, guns blazing, and reduced the city to rubble. The Spanish packed up shop and moved west to the present village of Ciudad Antigua, which became the capital of the Segovia region. There was no respite here either, though, and while some settlers bravely duked it out with the natives, others looked for a quieter lifestyle farther south in the broad valley of Estelí. Not until the early 19th century did the little village of Ocotal begin to assume any importance, when the Catholics transferred valuable religious artifacts to the new church of Nuestra Señora de la Asunción. The faithful followed the relics westward, and Ocotal began to grow.

Until 20 years ago, violence and hardship continued to plague the region. In the early 1930s, General Sandino and his men were firmly entrenched in the mountains north of Ocotal, and the American government, intent on capturing him, sent in the Marines. The gringos remained based in Ocotal while they scoured the countryside around Cerro Guambuco and built the country's first airstrip in Somoto, from which they launched strikes on the city of Ocotal, the first city in the history of the world to experience an air raid. During the 1980s, much of the conflict between Sandinistas and Contras took place in the same area, fiercely punishing outpost towns like Jalapa.

These days, military conflict has been relegated to distant memory, and the new danger is ecological: The notorious pine bark beetle swelled to crisis populations in the late 1990s, chewing through the thick stands of Ocote pine trees more quickly and efficiently than axe-wielding campesinos had been able to do.

City of Estelí

Spread across a flat valley 800 meters above sea level, Estelí is an unassuming city whose 110,000 merchants, ranchers, artists, and cigar rollers are prouder than most. In Nahuatl, Estelí means something like "river of blood," an apt moniker for an area so saturated with Sandinista rebels in the days that led up to the 1979 revolution that Somoza carpet-bombed the city (ask locals where to find *"la bomba,"* a relic from the air strikes). But these days, most Estelíanos live a bucolic life of farming and commerce.

ORIENTATION AND GETTING AROUND

Buses to Estelí will deposit you in one of the two bus terminals on the east side of the highway, and express buses bound farther north will drop you off at the nearby Shell Esquipulas. In either case, proceed in the same way: Take a cab to the central park ($0.50) to start your exploration. Estelí is quite possibly the only city in the country to take the trouble to name avenues (north-south) and streets (east-west). Still, the Nicaraguan penchant for giving directions in terms of landmarks and number of blocks completely overrides the best of intentions.

The two avenues that border the park, and one additional avenue on either side, make up the bulk of the commercial district. Avenida Central, on the west side of the park, hosts the greatest number of businesses and restaurants. Estelí is a long city; you can cut short the walking by hopping a cab for the fixed price of $0.30–$0.60 anywhere in the city (except La Casita restaurant on the south side of town). *Urbano* buses run a big loop around the city, including up and down the main avenues.

You're essentially safe in Estelí, but exercise more care here than elsewhere, in the barrios

© RANDALL WOOD

Estelí is an unassuming city of about 100,000.

east of the highway and west of the river be especially cautious. Keep an eye out for harmless but annoying Jimmy Loco, a one-armed, purple-faced elderly man with a penchant for harassing blondes.

SIGHTS AND RECREATION
El Parque Central

Estelí's central **park** is a hub of mellow activity and a magnet for local characters. Buy an ice cream cone, kick back on a bench, and watch it all swirl by. The **Iglesia de San Francisco** was built in layers starting in 1823. It began as nothing more than a humble adobe chapel with a straw roof. Rebuilt in 1889 to a grander scale and given a roof of clay tiles with a baroque facade, the church was later redesigned as a modern building, with stately columns, a neoclassic facade, and twin bell towers topped with crosses.

La Galería de Héroes y Mártires

Located half a block south of the church, La Galería (tel. 505/713-3753, emayorga70 @yahoo.com, open 9 A.M.–4 P.M. Mon.–Sat., donations accepted) is only one of the projects of the Association of Mothers of Heroes and Martyrs of Estelí, a support group of 300 women who lost children during the battle against Somoza's National Guard. After your visit, sign up for a class in piñata and pastry making. The gallery itself is a single room in what was once one of Somoza's jails, filled with memorabilia from the days of the revolution—photos of Estelí as an urban battleground, quotes from Sandino and Che Guevara, weaponry and shell casings, and portraits of young men and women killed in action, sometimes accompanied by uniforms and other personal effects.

Connected to the Galería, you'll find the less powerful, but still interesting **Museo de Historia y Arqueología** (open 9 A.M.–noon Mon.–Fri., closed Wed.), with a small display of petroglyphs, artifacts, and revolutionary photos.

Still in the same building, on the south side, the **Casa de Cultura** offers a series of music,

ESTELÍ

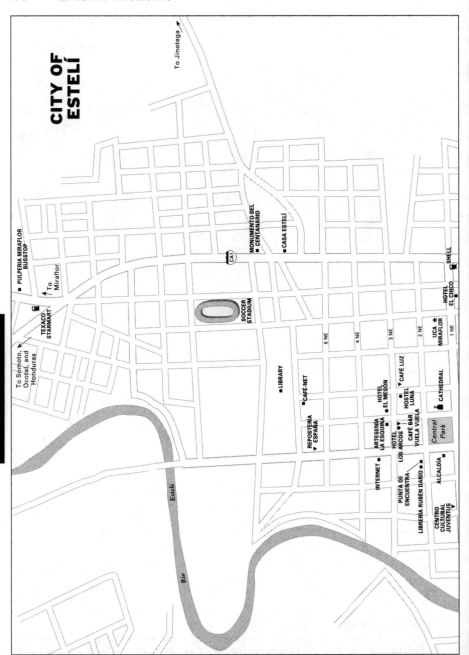

CITY OF ESTELÍ

To Jinotega

To Somoto, Ocotal, and Honduras

PULPERÍA MIRAFLOR BUSSTOP

To Miraflor

TEXACO STARMART

MONUMENTO DEL CENTANARIO

CASA ESTELÍ

CAT

SOCCER STADIUM

SHELL

HOTEL EL CHICO

LIBRARY

CAFÉ-NET

REPOSTERÍA ESPAÑA

HOTEL EL MESÓN

CAFÉ LUZ

HOSTEL LUNA

UCA MIRAFLOR

5 NE

4 NE

3 NE

2 NE

1 NE

INTERNET

ARTESENÍA LA ESQUINA

HOTEL LOS ARCOS

CAFÉ BAR VUELA VUELA

CATHEDRAL

Central Park

PUNTA DE ENCUENTRA

LIBRERÍA RUBÉN DARÍO

ALCALDÍA

CENTRO CULTURAL JUVENTUS

Río

Estelí

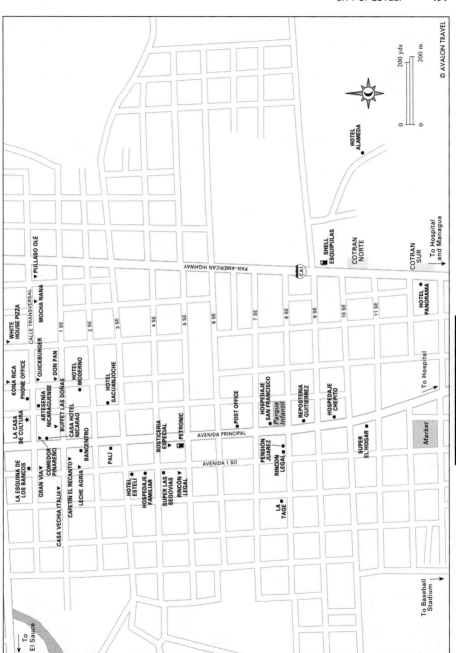

ESTELÍ

© AVALON TRAVEL

THE CHILDREN'S MURAL WORKSHOP

In 1987, in response to a request for help from community leaders in the struggling Barrio Batahola in Managua, three former art students began teaching mural workshops to children. The program was a success and two years later, the three muralists passed their roles on to other youth in Managua and moved to Estelí to continue their program. The idea was to empower the people while at the same time reclaiming Nicaraguan culture and promoting the participation of children in society. They found that painting murals was an empowering achievement for the participants, and the creation of the murals was invariably tied to further community activities and social work (and lots of pretty pictures to look at).

Today, the mural project is known as the **Fundación de Apoyo al Arte Creador Infantíl** (FUNARTE), a nonprofit, nongovernmental organization run by a group of young adults who grew up through the original mural workshops. They offer weekly painting workshops to hundreds of Estelíano children for free and give special workshops for imprisoned teenagers and children with disabilities. The murals depict their history, culture, and the daily reality in which they live.

There are well over 100 murals in Estelí, the majority of which were painted by participants of FUNARTE's workshops. The murals are best viewed and photographed in the late afternoon sun, as many of the best are on west-facing walls. The paintings are everywhere, but take special note of those on the Alcaldía (mayor's office), Casa de Cultura, and in and around the Parque Infantíl (nine blocks south of the main plaza). Also, be sure to get a good look at the long, horizontal mural on the wall of the army base along the Pan-American Highway, just south of the main bus station.

To visit FUNARTE's headquarters (tel. 505/713-6100), walk four blocks south from the southwest corner of the plaza, then two west to reach the main workshop, itself covered in powerful paintings; continue another block west, turn right past the mural depicting the book *The Little Prince*, and make your next left to arrive at the offices and classroom.

art, and dance classes to the public; the Casa also often has a display of local artists in its spacious lobby. The entire block used to belong to a prominent Estelíano family before it was confiscated by the Sandinistas.

Yoga

If you want to study a traditional form of hatha yoga from a guru-trained Nicaraguan yogini, be at **Licuados Ananda's** (one block south of the central park, next to the Casa de Cultura) 10 minutes before 6 A.M. with a towel or mat. Or ask Doña Edith in the Hospedaje Familiar about classes in yoga and eastern medicine.

Estelí Cigar Factories

In the past Estelí cigar factories were often closed to the casual visitor, unless you sought permission from distant owners. Today, many offer tours and discount cases of *puros*.

Following are our favorites but there are other options as well; the local INTUR office or the information desk at Casa Estelí can provide a comprehensive list of factories offering tours.

The **Estelí Cigar Factory** (tel. 505/713-5688) produces more than 60 brands of cigars, almost entirely for export to the United States and Europe; their most popular are Cinco Vegas, Cupido, and Badge of Honor. Don Kiki, the owner and master roller of Cuban and eastern European descent (a "Jewbano," he says), is a portly, amiable craftsman, who may even give you a tour of his establishment if you call ahead to make an appointment. Hop a bus northbound and get off near El Rancho de Pancho.

Empresa Nica Cigars (around the corner from the COTRAN Sur, tel. 505/713-2230) will also allow curious visitors to come inside and take pictures of their rollers. You'll smell the tobacco from blocks away. They are famous

Puros, or cigars, grown and rolled in Estelí are acclaimed around the world.

© JAMES SAVAGE

for the *padron,* a cigar manufactured using organic tobacco which has received international awards and acclaim.

Tabacalero Santiago (tel. 505/713-2230) is a newer company, which gained fame with endorsements from Arnold Schwarzenegger, Bruce Willis, and Charlie Sheen—and a contract to provide cigars to the Playboy mansion. The owner's family won its first cigar factory in a poker game in Cuba shortly after World War II. Now with a factory in Panamá as well as Estelí, don Francisco provides Churchills, Figurados, Magnums, El Presidentes, and other brands to a global market.

ENTERTAINMENT AND EVENTS

Estelí's *fiestas patronales* take place around October 12 and most years include a famous *hípica* (horse parade).

Bars and Discos

The **Rincón Legal** (one block west of Parque Infantíl) is the brainchild of Frankie Legall and is a bar-shrine to the FSLN and Cuban Communist Party; Carlos Mejía Godoy plays here when in town, and this is the home turf of many artists—and a place for wandering lefties to toast the light arms and photos of Carlos Fonseca on the wall. **La Etage** (one block west of Rincón Legal) is a bit more politically diverse, with a relaxed environment and comfy seats. **El Punto de Encuentro** (40 meters west of the northwest corner of the central park) features rocking chairs, sofas, and recliners in which to enjoy cheap eats and drinks. For a popular expat hangout, head for the garden out back.

For dancing, **Studio 54** is Estelí's biggest. Thursday is ladies' night; says one local resident: "Lots of pretty young women, lots of ugly old men." Also very popular, **Rancho Bar El Semáforo** (on the south side of Estelí on the Pan-American Highway) is especially lively on Saturday; the outdoor dance floor attracts a mixed croad. Just before Semáforo is **El Chaman** with a thatched roof and a jungle motif, and sometimes live music.

SMOKIN' NICARAGUA

There is history in that cigar you're smoking – stories hidden among the tightly packed folds of tobacco and along the delicate veins of its wrapper leaf. As you light the *puro* in your hand and watch it turn into ash and smoke, take a sip of rum and ponder the unique legacy of the Estelí cigar industry.

It all began with the 1959 Cuban revolution, when capitalist Cuban cigar lords found their businesses liquidated into the new socialism. These artisans of the finest cigars in the world quickly gathered illicit caches of the precious tobacco seeds their families had been cultivating for centuries and fled to Miami. From there, it was only a couple of years before they discovered Nicaragua. One grower told *Cigar Aficionado* magazine that Cuba and Nicaragua "have the most fertile dirt in the world for tobacco. It's almost like God said, 'I'm going to pick these two countries and I'm going to use them for tobacco.'"

And so the core of the old Cuban cigar aristocracy moved to Estelí and, with their precious seeds from the homeland, began turning out world-renowned cigars once again. They endured another popular revolution in 1979, the ensuing civil war and land redistribution, and then survived the cigar boom and bust of the 1990s, followed by the waters of Hurricane Mitch that tore through their fields in 1998. But the business is sunk deep into the rich soil, and the handful of familial cigar dynasties that first came to Nicaragua 30 years ago are still here, and still rolling world-class cigars.

Most of the tobacco fields and giant wooden drying barns are found across the Estelí valley as it runs north away from the city, as well as in many upper reaches all the way to Jalapa. In Estelí there are about 10 serious cigar producers, a few of which will let travelers in their doors for an informal tour and perhaps a taste test. Most businesses are *zona franca* (free-trade zone), however, which prohibits them from selling their product within Nicaragua. Don Orlando Padrón, head of Cubanica Cigars, keeps the doors to his Estelí factory shut for another reason: to protect the trade secrets that produce one of the most internationally acclaimed cigars in the world, El Padrón, which is also organic.

Some of the other heavy hitters are Latin Tobacco, Estelí Cigar, Tabacalera Perdomo (formerly Nick's Cigars), Plasencia, and

SHOPPING

Provided you're not interested in fruits and vegetables (in which case you want the *mercado*), the entire length of Avenida Principal is lined with boutiques whose shop girls might whistle and catcall to entice you into their stores.

Artesanía

Two shops—**Artesanía La Esquina** (one block north of the cathedral, tel. 505/713-2229) and **Artesanía Nicaragüense** (one block south of the cathedral, tel. 505/713-4456)—each have a huge selection of Nicaraguan arts and crafts from all over the country. In general, prices are cheaper in the Managua and Masaya markets, but for locally produced items, like soapstone carvings and Ducualí pottery, these are good places to shop. Plans are in the works for a government-sponsored crafts market in the Hospital Viejo building on Avenida Principal.

Custom Cowboy Boots

Estelí is the place to buy handmade **leather goods** like belts, saddles, and cowboy boots: Find them all along the southern half of Avenida 1 S.O. A pair of quality cowhide boots (or deerskin or snakeskin, the latter of which might get confiscated at your home customs office) go for about $45 and take a week to make when custom fit to your foot. Order a pair on your way north and pick 'em up on the way back to Managua. **Guitarras y Requintas el Arte** (located adjacent to INISER, tel. 505/713-7555) sells handmade guitars, mandolins, and *guitarrónes* (the bass guitar used by

tobacco harvest near Estelí

Nicaraguan American Tobacco (NATSA). Don Francisco's Tabacalero Santiago is the newest company, one that grows and rolls organic tobacco. The factories are scattered across Estelí, and unless you've got pretty good Spanish, bring a translator. Although the main tourist office will tell you all the factories in Estelí offer tours, hospitality varies widely. Don Francisco's production manager can arrange a tour if arranged a day in advance, and Don Kiki, of Estelí Cigars, sometimes gives casual tours, maybe even a cup of Cuban coffee and a smoke.

Cigar making is a proud family tradition here and elsewhere in the world, and there's no denying the craftsmanship of a fine cigar. But as the blunt you're smoking burns lower, and the heat of the cherry seeps into the leaf between your fingers, consider the yang side. Organic tobacco is grown in Nicaragua, but barely; most production employs massive quantities of chemicals, which invariably find their way into the earth, the water, or the lungs, hands, and feet of the workers. Tobacco handlers often absorb the toxic elements of the leaf, and although at least several of Estelí's factories have impressive, airy environments for their workers, conditions for the rollers are often no better than the worst sweatshops. And the history burns on.

---

mariachis) out of a tiny barber shop for around $90–120; the floor is littered with wood shavings and hair clippings.

Bookstores

Tiny **Librería Leonel Rugama** (on Ave. Principal, across from the Kodak) is run by the famous poet-martyr's parents. Rugama's dramatic death at the hands of Somoza's National Guard is legendary: Cornered in a building in Managua, the young soldier single-handedly held off a contingent of guardsmen while Carlos Fonseca escaped through the sewers. Ordered to his knees by the Guardia, he was commanded, *"Rindase, Sandinista!"* ("Surrender, Sandinista!"). Rugama retorted, famously, *"Que se rinda tu madre!"* ("Let your mother surrender!") before he was shot.

Otherwise, **Mocha Nana** has a small English language bookstore, where no one has to surrender at all.

ACCOMMODATIONS
Under $10

Estelí's least expensive lodging is on the south side of town by the Parque Infantíl. **Hospedaje Chepito** (one block south of the park, tel. 505/713-6388, $4) is a favorite with the backpacker set, with passable rooms and shared cold-water bath. A better choice is **Hospedaje Sacuanjoche** (2.5 blocks south of ENITEL, tel. 505/713-2862), a family-run and peaceful lodging. A bit closer to the action, **Hospedaje Familiar** (half a block north of Super Las Segovias next to the Tip-Top distributor, tel. 505/713-3666, $10–13) is

ESTELÍ

© RANDALL WOOD

Travel in style with a custom pair of kickers.

run by Edith Valenzuela Lopez, a tried-and-true Sandinista with more than 33 years of hosting *internacionalistas;* rooms have private bath and TV.

$10-25

Hostel Luna (one block east and one block north of the cathedral, tel. 505/441-8466, www.cafeluzyluna.com) is run by British expat Jane Boyd, offering dorm beds for $7 and private rooms for $15. Breakfast is served at **Cafe Luz** across the street where you can hang in the garden hammocks. Jane is a valuable source of knowledge on activities in the area and can help arrange anything from a trip to Miraflor, a cigar factory tour, or a walking mural tour with a local guide. A few doors north of Hospedaje Familiar, **Hotel Estelí** (tel. 505/713-2902, $10–15) has 13 rooms on two stories with private bath, TV, and parking; there are several nice, furnished doubles and matrimonials. The eight rooms at **Hotel El Mesón** (one block north of the cathedral, tel. 505/713-2655, $23–27) have private bath

and fan (a few with a/c); this place is quiet and clean, and the hot water makes January mornings a lot more bearable. They have parking, a bar and restaurant, a garden, a travel agency, car rental, and will change travelers checks. Not far away, **Hotel Moderno** (one block east of the park and two south, tel. 505/713-2378, $30) consists of 11 rooms—all with private bath, hot water, TV, and fan—surrounding a shaded courtyard, conference room, bar, and restaurant.

$25-50

The gorgeous **Hotel Los Arcos/Café Vuela Vuela** (one block north of the cathedral, $35–75) is run by a Spanish development organization in a charming colonial edifice. All profits go toward development activities like their schools, continuing education programs, and street children. If you're more interested in a relaxing evening than a night in town, **Hotel Cualitlán** (from COTRAN Sur, two blocks south, four east, and one north, tel. 505/713-2446, $50) is a walled-in guesthouse compound unlike any other in Estelí. It has a verdant sitting area with a tree-canopy roof, soothing music, and a creative menu geared to the international traveler. Choose one of several delightfully appointed cabañas—something like Swiss chalets—set around the lush tropical courtyard, all with hot water and cable TV. They have two rooms that can house up to six for $20 per person, all with breakfast included.

Long-Term Accommodations

All of the Spanish schools (see *Spanish Language Schools in Nicaragua* in the *Essentials* chapter) have networks of families accustomed to housing foreigners for a weekly or monthly rate. Doña Edith at the **Hospedaje Familiar** offers extended room-and-board deals, starting at $150 a month. **Centro Cultural Juventus** (tel. 505/713-3756) can offer housing for visiting students or those in language school. For house and apartment rentals, call **Bienes Raices Gomez** (tel. 505/713-3835).

FOOD

The Esteliano diet is hardy and satisfying, but simple. Local venues tend to mostly serve steaks, fried chicken, and bowls of soup big enough to drown in. The nicest restaurants are found in the town's upscale hotels and on the blocks around the park. Many of the places where locals eat are in the *Entertainment and Events* section.

For the money and finger-lickin' goodness, the many *fritangas* and pizza trucks in the park are hard to beat. Also easy on the wallet is **Don Pollo's** fried chicken, one block north and half a block east of the catheral. Easy to recommend is **Comedor Pinareño** (one block south of the park, $2–7), with its Cuban menu and selection of fine cigars. **Cafe Luz,** one block east and one block north of the church, serves a variety of international and *comida típica* fare that is particularly appealing to the *gallo pinto*–weary traveler. **La Gran Vía** (just south of the *la esquina de los bancos,* closed Sun.) serves Chinese meals from $4.50. **Leche Agria** (2.5 blocks south of *la esquina de los bancos*) serves

---

NATURAL MEDICINE IN ESTELÍ

Knowledge of folk medicine and the use of natural plants and herbs in curing all types of ailments is common throughout all of Nicaragua, especially in rural areas where natural meds are cheaper and more available than modern drugs. However, nowhere in the country is the use of natural medicine as well institutionalized as it is in Estelí.

There are several organizations devoted solely to the production, marketing, and selling of natural medicines. The two most prominent are CECALLI and ISNAYA. The former maintains a nursery and nature museum at its gardens south of Estelí, right next door to the La Casita café. They sell their herbs, teas, and other natural products in a store on the Avenida Principal, 1.5 blocks north of the plaza.

Managed by the Centro Nacional de la Medicina Popular Tradicional, ISNAYA maintains a beautiful farm called El Cortijo, located near La Sirena, eight kilometers north of Estelí on the Pan-American Highway. They also run several stores and a lab and packaging plant in the city of Estelí. Check with ISNAYA's offices (from the park, three blocks south, 1.5 to the west, tel. 505/713-4841) if you are interested in living and working on the farm for an extended period.

---

excellent *quesillos* (cheese and tortilla snack), juices, and cheeses. **Comedor Popular La Soya** (on Ave. Principal, 2.5 blocks south of the park), true to its name, serves soy-based meals and soy milk drinks.

For a bit of a splurge, try **El Pullazo Olé** (open 5–10 P.M. daily, $4–9) and join the fierce Nicaraguan competition for the best beef in the nation; they also serve fantastic sausages and desserts. For Italian, try **Casa Vechia,** one block south and one block west of *la esquina de los bancos.*

ESTELÍ

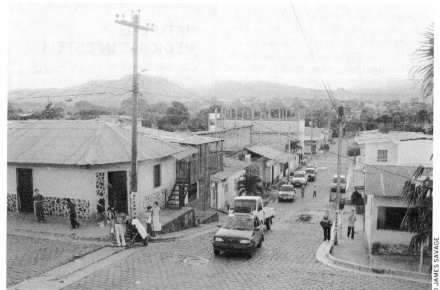

getting around the quiet northern city of Estelí

© JAMES SAVAGE

Bakeries and Coffee Shops

There is an excellent Spanish bakery, **Repostería España,** 3.5 blocks north of the central park, and a German one, **Repostería Alemán,** behind the cathedral. **(Mocha Nana** (five blocks east of Casa de Cultura, tel. 505/713-3164, mochanana@hotmail.com, 9 A.M.–7 P.M. Mon.–Sat.) is a perfect afternoon respite from the sun; in addition to fine cappuccinos, mochas, coffee, and espresso they have a small English language bookstore and trade library.

Licuados Ananda has health foods, yogurt, natural juices, and fruit smoothies in a patio surrounding a pool. Try the vegetarian *nacatamales,* veggie burgers, and sandwiches. They also have educational opportunities on many facets of eastern and natural medicine.

The menu is simple, healthy, and homegrown at **(La Casita** (across from La Barranca, south entrance, tel. 505/713-4917, casita@sdn nic.org.ni). open). Yogurt, home-baked breads, fresh cheeses, vegetables, granola, juices, and coffee drinks are all served in a pleasant garden atmosphere along the shore of a babbling brook. It's on the Pan-American Highway a few kilometers south of the city, and is open 1–7 P.M. Monday, 7 A.M.–7 P.M. Tuesday–Saturday, and 9 A.M.–7 P.M. Sunday—closed first Monday of every month. Take an *urbano* bus to the new hospital, then walk south around the bend in the road; or hail a taxi for about $1.50—it's well worth the trip. In addition to featuring wonderful food and mellow music, La Casita sells local crafts and plants, including herbs, ornamentals, and much much more.

Juventus Centro Cultural (two blocks west of the central park's southwest corner, tel. 505/713-3756, open 9 A.M.–6 P.M. Mon.–Sat.) is situated on top of the hill that drops down to the river, making for great panoramas of the river and mountains to the west as you enjoy *licuados,* granola, open-face swiss and brie sandwiches, and hot drinks.

INFORMATION

Casa Estelí (tel. 505/713-4432 or 505/713-2584, casaesteli@nortedenicaragua.com, www.norte

denicaragua.com) is a highly informative tourist office with maps, translators, Internet access, and an on-site café as well.

INTUR's tiny, tucked-away office in the back of the Hospital Viejo (tel. 505/713-6799, open 7 A.M.–2 P.M. Mon.–Fri.) was useless to the tourist at last check, but stop in and see if they're offering any services. The public **library** (tel. 505/713-7021, open 8 A.M.–noon and 2–5 P.M. Mon.–Fri.) is in a huge, brand new building built with foreign donations four blocks north and one east of the central park.

SERVICES
Emergencies
El Hospital Regional de Estelí (tel. 505/713-6300) was donated by the Spanish in the mid-1990s and is located just south of the city. Avenida Principal has many private clinics—offering both western and eastern medicine. La Policía Nacional (tel. 505/713-2615) is located on the main highway, toward the northern exit.

Banks and Exchange
There are three respectable banks at *la esquina de los bancos* (the corner of banks), one block west and one south of the park; Bancentro is 2.5 blocks south on Avenida Principal. All have ATMs, as does the Texaco station on the northern border of the city. The travel agency in Hotel Mesón changes travelers checks, as do most of the banks. The street money changers will find you on the main avenue. It's okay to use their services.

Mail and Phones
The post office is open 7 A.M.–8 P.M. The Farmacia Corea (one block north of the main market, tel. 505/713-2609) offers mail and package service, as well as money transfers. ENITEL (one block south of the church and half a block east, tel. 505/713-2222) is open 8 A.M.–8 P.M. Monday–Friday and 8 A.M.–5 P.M. Saturday.

Travel Services and Car Rental
Agencia de Viajes Tisey (in Hotel El Mesón, tel. 505/713-3099, fax 505/713-4029, barlan @ibw.com.ni) is a modern and professional agency that deals with airlines, international reservations, and Budget rental cars.

Casa Estelí has a Budget rental car office. A four-wheel drive truck costs about $80/day; it's open 365 days a year, and is located, from the *monumento centenario,* 20 *metros* to the south on the Pan-American Highway. The Dollar car rental agency is located with the Toyota dealer; it rents a Yaris for $25 per day and a four-wheel drive Hilux for $60 per day.

Internet
The most convenient cybercafe is **Soluciones Computarizadas** (off the northwest corner of the park), but there are several others north of there, such as **PCnet** (1.5 blocks north of the park). There are several Internet cafés any direction within two blocks of the park, most are open 8 A.M.–9 P.M. Monday–Saturday, 8 A.M.–6 P.M. Sunday.

GETTING THERE AND AWAY
Express and ordinary buses for Estelí leave from Managua's Mayoreo terminal. Seven *expresos* per day pass Esteí bound for Managua, making stops along the highway. If you're arriving from Honduras, buses leave frequently daily from Somoto and Ocotal, the last one leaving at 5 P.M.

From Estelí, *ordinario* buses leave the COTRAN Norte at regular intervals for Ocotal, Somoto, and points north 4 A.M.–5 P.M.; they leave COTRAN Sur for Managua, Matagalpa, León, and Yalí. Ocotal *expresos* stop of at the Shell Esquipulas approximately every hour on the half hour.

From COTRAN Sur there are dozens of daily buses to both Managua and Mataglapa, leaving from the wee hours until 6 P.M.; three express buses to León depart before 7 A.M., plus a few daily microbuses to León (they leave when they fill up, and competition is fierce).

ESTELÍ

Near Estelí

◀ EL SALTO ESTANZUELA AND THE TISEY RESERVE

El Salto Estanzuela is the region's most famous swimming hole, a gorgeous 15-meter, rainy season–only cascade that plunges into a cold, shady pool, all smothered in colorful native flora and fauna. It's just southwest of the city. Swim behind the falls for a refreshingly cool perspective on Nicaragua. You can hike to the waterfall from the highway. The road to Estanzuela leaves the Pan-American just south of the new hospital and is sandwiched between two *pulperías* (markets) where you can stock up for the journey. This is the terminus of the *urbano* bus routes which start at the central park, or take a taxi from the city center for about $0.50. The five-kilometer walk should take 60–90 minutes each way. It's an easy hike, but with lots of ups-and-downs. Otherwise, hop a bus for the 20-minute ride (buses leave COTRAN Sur at 6:30 A.M. and 1:30 P.M.). Before you reach the hamlet of Estanzuela, for which the waterfall is named, look for a gated road on your right; the waterfall is at the bottom of a hill after the first two dilapidated wooden homes of the village. Villagers charge 30 cords ($1.50) to hike down to the falls. Head downward for about 10 minutes until the track veers steeply down to the left. If you take one of the side trails to the left now it will lead you to the top of the falls. Before the road turns to the right again, take the path in front of you straight down to the falls, there is a large sign for the Ministerio del Ambiente. You should now be able to hear the falls.

Reserva El-Tisey

Down the same road as the waterfall, Reserva El-Tisey, a 9,344-hectare reserve comanaged by the Nature Conservancy and supported by U.S. Agency for International Development (USAID), makes available a rustic ecolodge, fields of organic vegetables, a network of hiking trails, and trips on horseback, not to mention some of the best panoramic views in the nation, hands-down. From the top of Tisey on a clear day, you can make out the Pacific coastal plain and the entire chain of volcanic peaks from Cosigüina to Lake Managua and Momotombo, the Estelí valley, and north to the mountains of the Segovias on the horizon. The reserve has an office in Estelí (tel. 505/713-3918) and an office in Managua (tel. 505/249-6039).

Start by settling in at **Eco-Posada Tisey** (tel. 505/713-6213 or 505/836-6021), which charges $3 per person for communal living, $10 for a double bed and some privacy, and $1.50 per meal. They will find you guides, rent horses, or show you around the organic farm that stocks most of Managua's supermarkets with fresh veggies. There's more to see there than you'll likely have time for, so plan a few days at least. One trail climbs to a lookout (1,300 meters) where you'll enjoy the phenomenal view and the falls. The folks at the Posada can show you some of the reserve's

mountain scenery in Reserva El-Tisey

© JAMES SAVAGE

other highlights, like the septuagenarian sculptor who picked up hammer and chisel to absorb some of his nervous energy when he quit drinking, or the bat cave, local hangout for more than 10,000 winged friends (hint: bring a hat). Closer to the lodge, taste fresh cheeses and vegetables, or spend a night in the farming community of La Garnacha. To get there, catch a bus to El Jalacate.

La Ganarcha is the heart of the El-Tisey reserve; the only way to get here is to hike or hire a truck from Eco-Posada Tisey. The biological station is the headquarters for the reserve where you can get maps, talk with the rangers, and arrange for guides. There are five-person cabins here with fantastic views of the surrounding forest and hills for $10/night, or dormitory lodging for $3–5 per night. Food can be arranged with a local family for under $5 a day. There are many marked trails that leave from either the biological station, or the guest quarters—one heads due west from the station and winds through rocky hillsides and pine forest to several highpoints with views of the volcanoes to the west. Winds stir the trees and the smell of pine needles is everywhere.

LA TRINIDAD

Just as the Pan-American Highway begins its curvy climb north into Nicaragua's mountains, a midsize pueblo straddles the road and monitors your entrance into the north country. It would be easy to stay on the bus as you pass through La Trinidad toward Estelí, only 22 kilometers farther north, but it would be just as easy to get off at the Texaco station and wander up to the park, where few tourists have ever set foot. La Trinidad, named for the three hills that surround it, is a festive village of bread bakers, bus drivers, musicians, and cowboys. Its unhurried and friendly populace can often be found hanging out in the well-tended central plaza—kept green even in the height of the dry season. The Catholic church, although decidedly ugly by Latin American standards, may be worth a visit during mass to hear the dueling mariachi choirs. La Trini's rip-roaring *fiestas patronales*, celebrating La Virgen de

Candelaria and Jésus de Caridad, occur during the last week of January and roll raucously into the first week of February, with a famous *hípica* (show-horse parade) that attracts riders from all over Central America.

Take a walk up to the old **Spanish cross** or west up the river valley road to the **Rosario shrine**—allow about an hour each way. The hill to the east of the highway is the legendary Mocuana, with its caves of witches, gold, snakes, and a tunnel to Sébaco, if you believe everything you hear.

Hotel y Restaurante Tzolkin (tel. 505/437-6067, winstonmairena@yahoo.com, $15–20) is located just off the southwest corner of the park, if you'd like to spend the night in a friendly pueblo or get a nice meal for under $4. Another good spot for food is **Don Juan's Las Sopas,** on the southern outskirts of town; this is a popular stopover for Pan-American commuters and truck drivers, with an open-air patio and a fantastic menu of soups—including *huevos de toro* (bull balls), ox tail, and chicken soup. To fit in with your fellow lunchers, squeeze in plenty of lime, and down a shot of Extra Lite rum after every couple of spoonfuls (tell the bus driver to let you off here, or take a taxi from the town's center).

◖ MIRAFLOR NATURE RESERVE

More than a trip into Estelí's misty mountains, a visit to Miraflor is a trip backward in time. Perhaps this is what Costa Rica's Monteverde was like 40 years ago before it was populated with four-star resorts and laced with splinter-free wooden walkways. Miraflor is unabashedly rustic, natural, and unpretentious. Declared a protected natural reserve in 1990, this rudimentary tourist infrastructure was developed by locals, with their own sweat and labor and in the absence of any external help.

Miraflor as an entity is totally unique even if, as an entity, it's a little vague. There's no town, per se, or even a real center. Rather, the 5,000 Mirafloreños live dispersed throughout the 206 square kilometers of the reserve in a geographically dispersed but socially united community.

ESTELÍ

© ERIKA BRICEÑO

Miraflor offers both cultural and natural attractions, including wildflowers galore.

The Miraflor Reserve is privately owned, cooperatively managed in many parts, and almost entirely self-funded by associations of small-scale producers. Most notable among these is the UCA Miraflor (or in full, the Union de Cooperativas Agropecuarias Héroes y Mártires de Miraflor)—not to be confused with the University of Central America—an association of 14 small farmer cooperatives and 120 families living within the protected area. UCA Miraflor is primarily an agricultural credit and loan institution, but it has also tackled issues and begun programs, such as community health and education, organic agriculture and diversification of crops, cooperative coffee production, gender and youth groups, and conflict resolution. Tourism, Miraflor's greatest potential, was just an afterthought,

Sights and Attractions

Miraflor has something for everyone—nature lovers, hikers, social justice workers, organic farmers, artists, horse lovers, orchid fanatics, birders, and entymologists—each of whom will find their own personal heaven here. You can certainly visit parts of Miraflor in a day

trip from Estelí, but read on and consider experiencing the unique accommodations.

It should be noted that every attraction in Miraflor is privately owned, often by poor *campesinos.* Your financial support is the driving force that will lead to the continued preservation of these magnificent forests, because, "hey, this would be a great place to chop down the trees and plant some beans."

Fauna: The distinct bird species number 236, belonging to 46 different families which inhabit or fly through these mountains—that's nearly 40 percent of all bird species in the country, including four species of the elusive quetzal *(Pharomachrus mocinno),* toucans, the *ranchero (Procnias tricaruntulata),* with its three dangling chins, and the Nicaraguan national bird, the *guardabarranco.* Miraflor is also one of your best chances to spot coyotes, sloths, deer, howler monkeys, or one of six different feline species, not to mention raccoons, skunks, armadillos, and exotic rodents.

Orchids: Miraflor is one of the richest and most unexplored orchid-viewing regions anywhere. Among the more than 300 identified species is an enormous colony of *Cattleya*

To Somoto

To San Sebastián de Yalí

Cerro Yeluca
1,426m

Cerro Las Nubes
1,321m

CA1

MIRAFLOR
NATURE RESERVE

La Naranja

Cebollal   FINCA
LINDOS
OJOS

Laguna
Miraflor

El Zarzal

POSADA LA
SOÑADA

La Mesa Moropotente   LA RAMPLA

La Concordia

To
Jinotega

MIRAFLOR
VISITOR CENTER

CA1

Las Palmas

**MIRAFLOR
NATURE RESERVE**

PAN–AMERICAN HWY

Río Estelí

0   12 mi

0   12 km

Estelí

© AVALON TRAVEL

ESTELÍ

skinniri (the national flower of Costa Rica), not to mention scads of bromeliads and a museum of other orchids from throughout the reserve.

Hikes and Adventure: Short hikes are possible through any of the hundreds of pockets of forest, but ask your guide to take you on one of the more adventurous trips. Although difficult to access, the 60-meter waterfall at **La Chorrera** is one of the wildest spots in the reserve. **The Caves of Apaguis** were dug in pre-Columbian times by gem seekers and have been occupied ever since by *duendes* (dwarves), as any local will inform you. The mature cloud forest of **Bosque Los Volcancitos** is Miraflor's highest point at 1,484 meters and is

known habitat for howler monkeys and quetzals. If the monkeys don't snatch away your binoculars, expect fantastic views from El Tayacán, Cerro Yeluca, Cerro El Aguila, La Coyotera, and Ocote Calzado. Furthermore, the forests are replete with mysteries, such as the *casa antigua,* a 1,200-year-old foundation in the Tayacán area, surrounded by dozens of other unearthed *montículos* (mounds). Archaeologists haven't even begun to investigate the rest of them.

Progressive Agriculture: If you enjoy inspired agriculture and alternative farming practices, the *campesinos* at Miraflor will gladly show you their cutting-edge lifestyle, including

SWAMP THINGS: LEGENDS OF THE MIRAFLOR LAGOON

La Laguna de Miraflor is, compared to other *lagunas* (lakes) in the country, a mere puddle, whose marshy banks are crowded with vegetation and birdsong. Its fame lies not in its grandeur, but in its myth. There are at least five legends surrounding the lagoon, stories passed down over the years that have smothered the 10-hectare body of water in a shroud of mystery as thick as the white clouds sweeping over its surface.

The most famous of these legends is the **Ramo de Flores:** Every Thursday of Semana Santa (Holy Week), a cluster of beautiful flowers rises to the surface of the lagoon and circulates around and around. The flowers, say some, are bringing a message to the people that they should unite. The name Miraflor (flower view) comes from this legend, and variations tell of a tiny dancing prince in the middle of the flowers and dwarfs bearing the flowers to give to local girls.

Also well known is the story of the **Ciudad Perdida** (The Lost City). Only the oldest of Mirafloreños know of the hidden entrance, but everyone knows of the vast fields of exotic fruit-bearing trees at the bottom of the lagoon (which, by the way, has been measured at 27 meters deep, plus three meters of sediment). One can eat all they want when in the city, but if they try bringing the fruit back to the surface world, they will not be allowed to pass.

Every now and then, the water of the lagoon turns jet black; evidence, say some, of the giant **black serpent** that lives in the water and occasionally stirs up the sediment on the bottom. The snake may or may not have something to do with the lagoon's vengeful nature, punishing anyone who speaks disrespectfully of it or disbelieves its power. One unfortunate young man did so "recently" while swimming in the middle – he had barely spoken his blasphemy when a whirlpool formed, sucked him under, and then spit him back up, whereupon he apologized profusely and pledged his eternal respect for the enchanted waters.

Just across the road, the **Laguna de Lodo,** or Lagoon of Mud, has its share of legends as well. The mud pond is half the size of its counterpart and lies above the subterranean river that feeds the main lagoon. One day, a local *leñador* (lumberjack) was working near the Laguna de Lodo and dropped his axe into the mud, which promptly swallowed it up. He cried and cried and cried, until his axe finally rose to the surface . . . with a head and blade of shining gold.

---

organic compost, natural pest management, watershed protection, live fences, crop diversification, soil management, reforestation, worm farming, and environmental education. In addition, Miraflor's small-scale, fair trade, organic coffee cooperatives and cupping lab (in Cebollál) are among the nation's finest.

What to Bring

At 1,400 meters above sea level, Miraflor is remote, cloud-covered, and sometimes downright chilly. Be prepared for inclement weather (buy a sweatshirt at one of Estelí's millions of used-clothing stores) and bring your own bottled water if you're concerned. A flashlight or candles will be helpful on that midnight walk to the latrine.

Accommodations and Food

Accommodations are all well kept, but primitive; some do not have electricity. Start with a call or visit to the UCA Miraflor office in Estelí (from the cathedral three blocks east, half a block north, tel. 505/713-2971, miraflor@ibw.com.ni, www.miraflor.org, open 8 A.M.–12:30 P.M. and 2–5 P.M. Mon.–Fri.). They will present your options and help arrange lodging, taking care to distribute guests fairly among the various families who have agreed to host guests. Expect to pay $13–17 per person per night, with all meals included. The UCA Miraflor–affiliated lodging is distributed between four main communities, and they'll ask you to pick a zone: either the cloud forest with the communty of La Rampa, the middle zone (best for birders as it has more species diversity) with the communities of Sontule and El Cebollál, or the low, dry zone with the communities of Coyolito and La Pita.

Campesino Homes: This option features a network of families trained in the subtle art of entertaining picky travelers; their homes, while clean and well-maintained, are usually quite rustic. But they're getting better all the time, and some families are reinvesting quite a bit of money in their guest quarters.

Cabins: Although there are numerous guesthouse cabins throughout the reserve (the UCA Miraflor will tell you all about them), the following are the most well-known and professionally run operations to date. Doña Corina Picado's **Posada La Soñada Inn** (contact Doris, tel. 505/713-2161 or 505/713-6333, Corina _picado@yahoo.com) offers several cabins of cut pine, each furnished with bunk beds or a collective room, candles, and an overarching sense of peace and quiet, best experienced with a hot cup of homegrown manzanilla tea, sitting on the porch and watching the clouds roll through the forest in her backyard. Doña Corina is an experienced and well-traveled cook.

Doña Maribel Gonzales's **Las Perlas de Miraflor** ($12 pp includes three meals) offers lovely accommodations with very reasonably priced tours and horseback rides.

Just down the road, hidden in its own clump of cloud forest and coffee, is the **Finca Lindos Ojos** (tel. 505/713-4041, kahrin@ibw.com .ni, $25 pp per weekend, $10 day trips), run by a German couple in Estelí and boasting two queen-size beds for couples. The farm produces organic coffee and vegetables and has a solar panel and generator for the water pump and lights. Lindos Ojos is affiliated with the UCA Miraflor, but handles its own business. Ask about package trips that include meals, guided hikes, and organic agriculture demonstrations.

Getting There and Away

Until the road from Estelí is finally paved, expect bumps, dust, and mud on the slow ride into the hills. There are four buses a day from Estelí: two leave for La Pita from Pulpería Miraflor by the Texaco Starmart at the north end of town (6 A.M. and 1 P.M.). The buses to Sontule and La Perla leave from COTRAN Norte at 2 P.M. and 3:40 P.M. The UCA Miraflor office may also be able to arrange transport.

Returning to Estelí, buses depart La Pita at 8:10 A.M. and 3 P.M., from Sontule at 8 A.M., and from La Perla at 7:30 A.M. The bus from Yalí passes by La Rampla at 7 A.M., 11 A.M., and 4 P.M. Hitching in this remote area of the Estelí countryside is very difficult, as there are not many rides.

CONDEGA

The 9,000 inhabitants of the "Tierra de los Alfareros" (Land of the Potters) eke out a living raising cattle, corn, and beans as did the Nahuatl centuries before. Truckloads of pre-Columbian pottery have been dug out of area cornfields, and the tradition lives on today with a women's pottery cooperative in Ducualí Grande.

Before the revolution, only three *terretenientes* (landowners) owned all the land from Condega to Yalí. Condegans roundly supported the Sandinistas, which led to lots of harassment from Somoza's National Guard (Commandante Omar Cabezas once hid out for months with his troops in the mountains outside Condega, reportedly in a cave near El Naranjo). In 1979, the Sandinista government confiscated those properties and redistributed them to the locals.

Contra soldiers found easy pickings in the unprotected farms of the Canta Gallo Mountains east of Condega, where several major skirmishes took place during the 1980s. Most locals can tell you some of the horror stories. In 1998, Hurricane Mitch destroyed more than 200 homes and two of the three local industries (a cigar box factory and a tannery).

Condega's sister city in the United States is Bend, Oregon; to get involved or join a

ESTELÍ

delegation, contact Timoteo Jeffries, coordinator of the **Bend-Condega Friendship Project** (tjeffries77@yahoo.com).

Sights

"In Condega, we don't have an airport, but we've got a plane," locals will tell you, referring to the famous wreckage on a hillside at the edge of town. Toward the end of his grip on power, Somoza took to strafing the northern regions with his air force. When, on April 7, 1979, the Sandinistas downed one of his planes, it was considered a major victory and huge morale booster. Follow the dirt road behind the cemetery, then 100 meters to the top of the hill, where you can take in the view and pieces of plane.

Founded in 1977, the **Casa de Cultura** occupies the former command post of the National Guard. One of its elements, a public library, enjoyed widespread community support during the Sandinista years, when each family donated a book to the room. Now there are guitar and sewing classes, and a **musical instrument workshop** where you can order a custom-made guitar, *guitarrón,* or violin. Among other attractions, the **Julio Cesár Salgado museum** (open 9 A.M.–5 P.M. Mon.–Fri., reading room open 1–5 P.M. Mon.–Fri.), named after the town's first archaeologist, has a collection of pre-Columbian ceramic work that local farmers have unearthed. Take in some baseball weekends at the ballfield just north of town, or catch the *fiestas patronales* on May 15, traditionally the first day of the rainy season—a double cause to celebrate in this rain-starved region.

A couple of blocks north of the town square and half a block toward the river (east) is a **cigar factory,** where you can ask to see the process and buy really fresh *puros* at a great price.

The **Taller de Cerámica Ducualí Grande** is an artisan's workshop founded in the 1980s with the help of a Spanish volunteer; the 13 workers continue to create charming ceramics using the simplest of wheels and firing the pieces in a woodstove. Pottery costs about $1–7.

To get there, take a bus north about two kilometers and get off where a large concrete sign points west to the workshop. Follow that road one kilometer across the bridge and through the community of Ducualí Grande. Turn left when you see the small church, and look for the white sign on the right side.

Venecia Coffee Farms

Venecia only dates back to the 1980s, when the Sandinistas created it to house the local coffee workers for the cooperative. As a standout Sandinista position, it was attacked by the Contras relentlessly, who burned it mostly to the ground in the mid-1980s. The city has plans to establish an ecotourism park called Canto Gallo, with trails between San Jerónimo and Venecia, including huts, family hosts, and opportunities to work on the coffee *fincas.* Until then, you're on your own: From Condega take the early-morning bus (5 A.M.) east to the coffee cooperative of Venecia (45 minutes). There are several small trails starting in Venecia that wind down and around the hillside through pine trees and coffee fields. The view is fantastic and the air is cool compared to Condega. There are neither lodging facilities nor restaurants in Venecia (but ask about staying with a family), so travel prepared to take the last bus from Venecia back to Condega at 5 P.M.

Accommodations and Services

A mainstay in the village for decades, the **Pensión Baldovinos** (south side of the park, tel. 505/715-2222, $3) has simple rooms with shared bath and decent meals. Expect one of the three mothers who run the kitchen to scold you with "breakfast is the most important meal of the day!" if you try to leave without eating. Next door, **Hospedaje Framar** (tel. 505/715-2393, $3) is newer and clean, offering seven rooms with shared bath; doors close at 10 P.M. The owner scrupulously weeds out the shady elements (or young couples sporting no luggage), so be presentable. The newest of Condega's lodging facilities, owned by a Belgian-Nicaraguan couple, **Rincón Criollo**

La Gualca (tel. 505/715-2431) has cheap rooms with shared bath, or $13 double with private bath.

Getting There

Any bus that travels between Ocotal, Somoto, or Jalapa and Managua or Estelí can drop you off on the highway in front of Condega, a two-block walk from the center of town. Or take the Yalí/La Rica buses from Estelí (5 A.M.–4:10 P.M.). Make sure to ask if the bus goes through Condega, as there are two routes to Yalí. Express buses will let you off on the highway by the cemetery; *ordinarios* will let you off in front of the park. From Condega, walk out to the Instituto on the highway to try to catch north- or south-bound *expresos,* or wait for slow buses at the park.

PALACAGÜINA AND COFFEE COOPERATIVE

The town of Palacagüina is best known as the pastoral setting for Carlos Mejía Godoy's revolutionary religious anthem, "Cristo de Palacagüina," in which Jesus is born *"en el cerro de la iguana, montaña dentro de la Segovia."* In the song, the Christ child's *campesino* parents, Jose and María, are dismayed when, instead of becoming a carpenter like his father, he wants to be a guerrilla fighter.

One of Nicaragua's largest fair trade coffee cooperatives, **PRODECOOP** is comprised of 2,000 coffee-growing families; they export as many as 30,000 *quintales* (100-pound bags) a year. PRODECOOP can house and feed up to six guests in brand-new accommodations atop the cupping lab overlooking the drying beds, which bustle with activity during the harvest. There is also a swimming pool and a 360-degree view of the surrounding hills. For reservations, contact their office in Estelí (75 meters west of *la esquina de los bancos,* tel. 505/713-3268, www.prodecoop.com). The coffee compound is between Palacagüina and the northern exit to the highway.

Most *ordinario* buses (not *expresos*) traveling between Estelí and Somoto or Ocotal pass through Palacagüina. If you take an *expreso,* the walk from the highway into town will be long and dusty.

PUEBLO NUEVO

First inhabited in 1652, Pueblo Nuevo is one of the few northern towns that was not affected much by the Contra war. There are about 3,000 folks in town and another 19,000 living off the land in the surrounding countryside. Pueblo Nuevo honors San Rafael Arcángel during the week leading up to October 24.

Doña Selina will rent you a room in her house, feed you, and should be able to help you find a local guide to go hiking in the surrounding hills or to view some of the organic agriculture by the river. One nice hike is to the community of Pencal, across the river and about 1.5 hours each way. You can also stay in the farmhouse/*hospedaje* Finca La Virgen. While in Pueblo Nuevo, take a look at the infrequently visited **Museo Arqueologico** (next to the phone office, tel. 505/719-2512, open 8 A.M.–noon and 2–5 P.M. Mon.–Fri.) in the Casa de Cultura, exhibiting pottery, old farm implements, and archaeological pieces found in the area.

Twelve kilometers west of town on the road to Limay, you'll find **El Bosque,** an archaeological dig site where the bones of several mastodons, glyptodons (predecessors to modern armadillos), and early ancestors of the horse species have been uncovered. At 18,000–32,000 years old, the bones are considered one of the oldest archaeological sites in the Americas. Closer to the surface, remnants of Paleolithic weapons were discovered on an upper stratum of soil.

Buses leave Estelí twice a day at 11:45 A.M. and 3:10 P.M., leaving Pueblo Nuevo at 6:30 A.M. and 8:30 A.M.; ask in the park about transportation that continues farther west into the country.

◖ SAN JUAN DE LIMAY

Since 1972, Limay's claim to fame has been its *marmolina* (soapstone) sculptors, trained by a priest named Eduardo Mejía so they could improve their living conditions. Padre Mejía helped the new artists mine the soapstone from nearby Mt. Tipiscayán (Ulúa-Matagalpa for "mountain of the toucan"), develop their talent, and market their beautifully polished long-necked birds, kissing swans, iguanas, and Rubenesque women. After the revolution, minister of culture Ernesto Cardenal, helped the sculptors organize a short-lived cooperative. A core of local carvers still lives and works in Limay, and you can watch them work and purchase some pieces with little effort. In town, just ask for the *artesanos de piedra*.

Nearby Río Los Quesos meanders outside the city limit. Ask a local kid to show you the Poza La Bruja swimming hole, ringed with pre-Columbian petroglyphs. Find a place to bed down for the night at **Pensión Guerrero** (a pink corner building located one block north of the Catholic church, $2.50 s). Limay is part of a sister-city program with Baltimore, Maryland.

San Juan de Limay is a 40-kilometer bus ride from Estelí that traverses a 1,000-meter mountain pass through coffee fields. Buses follow

soapstone sculpture of San Juan de Limay

© JOSHUA BERMAN

two routes to Limay (via la Shell and via El Pino) and leave Estelí's COTRAN Norte at 8:45 A.M., 9:15 A.M., 12:15 P.M., and 2 P.M.

Ocotal

Built on a thick bed of red sand and surrounded on all sides by mountains draped with green Ocote pines, Ocotal is the last major settlement before the Honduran border at Las Manos and the unbroken wilderness that stretches eastward to the Caribbean. Since 2000, it has seen a lot of development: Formerly sandy streets are now paved, there's a big supermarket instead of a handful of little markets, and the feeling is one of progress. For most travelers, Ocotal may be nothing more than a place to sleep before hitting the border—but for many coffee growers and subsistence farmers, Ocotal is still "the big city" for supplies and business. And in many ways, Ocotal marvelously represents the kind of quiet, steady growth that goes unnoticed until you've been away for awhile and then takes you by surprise. Steadily, Ocotal is reinventing itself as a great place to do business. Here you are indeed getting close to the frontier

however, and you only have to head a mile out of town in any direction before you are back to the rutted dirt roads, soporific cow towns, and sweeping valleys that make Nicaragua at once so charming and so challenging.

ORIENTATION AND GETTING AROUND

Buses will deposit you at the COTRAN bus station, about eight blocks south and three blocks west of the main plaza. Two main *entradas* (entrances) to the city, one from the south, and another from the highway to the west, lead straight into the town center. If you enter from the west, pause at the top of the monument to San Francisco to appreciate the layout of the city before continuing into town. Most of the commercial activity occurs between the park, the market, and around the Shell station on the highway. Ocotal is walkable but has numerous taxis anyway.

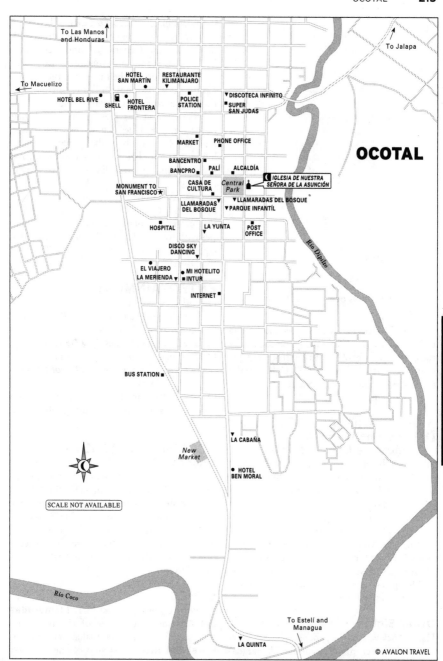

ESTELÍ

Saint Francis looks over the northern city of Ocotal.

If you'd like a friendly, bilingual local **guide** to accompany you to any attraction (especially the Grand Canyon of Somoto), call Sarahi Sofia Gutierrez Gomez (tel. 505/732-1089, sofia gomez1984@yahoo.com), world-renowned tourist guide, translator, and Nicaraguan traveler.

SIGHTS AND ATTRACTIONS
◖ Iglesia de Nuestra Señora de la Asunción

Start with this three-naved church in the center of town. Construction began in 1804, and the northern bell tower (the left one) wasn't completed until the 21st century! Two centuries of inhabitants have taken the liberty of scratching their names into its soft adobe walls, including U.S. Marines in the 1930s. The church looks out over Ocotal's **central plaza,** one of Nicaragua's most gorgeous. Shady and green, it fills up in the evenings with sparrows and gossiping *campesinos.*

Other Sights

Half a block west of the park's southwest corner (across the street from Restaurante Llamaradas del Bosque), the **Casa de Cultura** boasts an impressive collection of photos of gringo military defeat and General Sandino's resistance. Yes, "boast" is the right word there. Ironically, the Marines lodged their troops in the Casa de Cultura as well as most buildings surrounding the park during their stay in Ocotal.

Take a dip at Las Tres Señoritas and their two swimming holes (known as Las Pozas la Ladosa y Salterín) by walking west (or grabbing a taxi) on El Nuevo Almanecer road, and then crossing the river. Explore on your own, find a guide in town, or ask locals for more specific directions, but be careful—the rivers here are said to be *encantada* (enchanted). To the south of Ocotal, stout Cerro Picudo bristles with trails and allegedly contains a hidden lagoon on top, not to mention the "Caves of the Dwarf."

ENTERTAINMENT

Ocotal's two discos compete for crowds Friday–Sunday. **Discoteca Infinito** (four blocks north of the cathedral) currently has the advantage over **Disco Sky Dancing** (three blocks south and one block west of the central park). Ocotal celebrates its *fiestas patronales* August 14–15, when you can expect to find Ocotaleños blowing their hard-earned cash on horse shows, live music, gaming tables, and the like.

ACCOMMODATIONS
Under $10

Ocotal has nearly a dozen cheap and spartan *hospedajes.* Backpackers will do fine in secluded ◖ **El Viajero** (five blocks north and one block east from the bus station, tel. 505/732-2954, $4 s, $10 d, $15 t), offering TV and private bath. It's quiet, clean, and the service is exceptionally friendly in an area not really accustomed to tourists.

$10-25

A favorite among travelers is **Llamaradas del Bosque** (south side of the park, tel. 505/732-2643, $18), a good value for the money. **Hotel Bel Rive** (west side of the highway across from the Shell, tel. 505/732-2146 or 505/732-3249, $15) has doubles with private bath, phone, TV, fan, and parking. This is a big step up in quality.

Ocotal's finest is **Hotel Frontera** (just east of the Shell station, tel. 505/732-2668, $25 s, $45 d) offers private bath, phone, and TV, plus a slick poolside bar, conference room, parking, Internet, restaurant, and pleasant airy porches overlooking the city and mountains. More expensive rooms are by the pool, cheaper rooms in the back.

FOOD

The menu in these parts is chicken, steak, and fish, and we usually recommend avoiding the fish this high in the mountains. **Llamaradas del Bosque** (on the south side of the park, open 6:30 A.M.–8 P.M. daily) is a favorite, serving three meals buffet-style for around $2. **La Merienda** (one block east and one south of Hotel El Viajero) serves it up in a would-be disco atmosphere. At **La Yunta** (one block east and one south of Hospedaje El Viajero), you'll find higher quality and higher prices: If you've got the time, it's worth the money.

INFORMATION AND SERVICES

The Ocotal INTUR office (from the central park, three blocks south, one block west, one block south, tel. 505/732-3429, open 7:30 A.M.–4:30 P.M. Mon.–Fri., 8:30 A.M.–12:30 P.M. Sat.) is better than most regional branches. They train waiters and hoteliers, and organize cultural exchanges with other parts of Nicaragua. Bancentro and other banks are located one block west and one north of the park. The post office (open 8 A.M.–noon and 2–5 P.M. Mon.–Sat.) is one block south of the cathedral and one east. ENITEL (open 7 A.M.–5 P.M.) is two blocks north of the park. Find a cybercafe across from the police station, or a half-block west of the northwest corner of the park. In either you'll pay about $0.75 per hour for dog-slow connections.

GETTING THERE

At least 11 express buses leave Managua's Mayoreo terminal for Ocotal, stopping along the highway in Estelí to pick up additional passengers. Sixteen buses ply the route between Somoto and Ocotal daily, 5:45 A.M.–6:30 P.M. If you miss the *expreso* buses, there are countless additional, painfully slow ordinary buses from Mayoreo.

NEAR OCOTAL
Mozonte

An easy 60-minute walk from Ocotal, Mozonte, of largely indigenous descent, is notable for its workshops of potters who produce ceramics from a particularly fine clay. You can spend the better part of a morning (start walking early to avoid the heat) in Mozonte admiring the craftsmanship of these potters. Both the **Centro de Artesanías** and the **Centro de Artesanía Ojos de Mujer** exhibit a variety of ceramic pieces for sale.

Ciudad Antigua

Ciudad Antigua was the second Spanish attempt to settle Nueva Segovia (the remnants of the first settlement, built in 1543 at the bequest of then-governor Rodrigo de Contreras, are called Ciudad Vieja, and can still be seen near Quilalí at the junction of the Jícaro and Coco Rivers). The wooden church doors still bear the scorch marks of one attempted sacking of the city by pirates. You can pore over some well-loved religious pieces and a few historic documents and other colonial structures that survived the onslaughts of the 19th century at the **Museo Religioso de Ciudad Antigua** (next to the Iglesia Señor de los Milagros, open 8 A.M.–4 P.M. Mon.–Fri.). Two buses a day depart from Ocotal at 7 A.M. and noon.

Macuelizo

If sitting in a completely undeveloped, natural hot spring appeals to you, grab a *camión* at the Shell station and settle in for the 90-minute ride for a day trip to **Macuelizo Termales.** Find a guide in town.

ESTELÍ

San Fernando and Pico Mogotón

San Fernando is a notably picturesque village of thick adobe-walled homes set around the town park and **Templo Parroquial.** Its 7,000 inhabitants live on more than 200 individual coffee farms and produce an estimated 25,000 *quintales* of coffee annually. More famous than its coffee, however, are its inhabitants, who since the colonial days have been a little lighter-skinned and a little more Spanish-looking. Many have blue or light brown eyes. How do they do it? Well, just don't ask about those last name combinations: Herrera-Herrera, Urbina-Urbina, and Ortez-Ortez, though many attribute the blue eyes to the town's occupation by the U.S. Marines 1927–1931. Life revolves around coffee in San Fernando, and many homes double as coffee-processing mills *(beneficios).*

You can stage a hike to Pico Mogotón, Nicaragua's highest point (2,106 meters) from San Fernando, but even from there, Mogotón is 20 kilometers away. A better hike is to the **Salto San José,** where water rushing off the Dipilto mountain range cascades into a small pool. Take a bus to the community of Santa Clara and get off across from the ball field, turn left (north), and walk the 6–8 kilometers to the river. To be sure of the trail, hire a local kid for some food and a couple *córdobas* to take you. They all know the way and might even jump in for a swim with you.

CROSSING THE BORDER AT LAS MANOS

The Honduran border is 24 kilometers north of Ocotal, and is open 24 hours. You will be charged $2 to leave Nicaragua and $7 to enter (or $4 exit, $9 entry after normal business hours or on weekends). There are several small eating booths, two places to change money, and not much else. Fill out the immigration form at the little grey building and walk 100 meters farther down the road to the immigration building to pay and get your exit stamp. Honduran buses to Danlí stop running after 4:30 P.M., so get there early unless your hitchin' thumb feels lucky. To get to the border from Ocotal, buses leave 5 A.M.–4 P.M. ($0.50), or take a cab (around $4–6, depending on how hard you bargain).

JALAPA

Tucked back in one of Nicaragua's farthest populated corners, Jalapa enjoys a cool, moist microclimate suitable for the production of tobacco and vegetables which its drought-stricken neighbors could only hope for. Only four kilometers from the border with Honduras, Jalapa is also separated from the rest of Nicaragua by 60 kilometers of rutted, disintegrating, nearly impassible road. Surrounded on three sides by Honduras and only surpassed in its remoteness by nearby border outpost Teotecacinte, Jalapa struggles to remain integrated with the rest of Nicaragua.

Throughout the 1980s, that isolation made Jalapa prime stalking ground for Contra incursions from three nearby bases in Honduran territory—Pino-I, Ariel, and Yamales. The city of Jalapa was flooded with refugees from farming communities farther afield in response to Contra attacks like that of November 16, 1982, when a Contra unit kidnapped 60 *campesinos* at Río Arriba.

Jalapa is a peaceful and laid-back place these days, most concerned with good tobacco harvests and the repair of the road that connects it to Ocotal. The whole town comes to life every year at the end of September for the **Festival de Maíz** (Corn Festival).

Look for local *artesanía* of baskets made of coiled and lashed pine needles. **Grupo Pinar del Norte** has lots of fine examples of this unique craft.

QUILALÍ

Starting in the 1930s when Sandino dug into the area of El Chipote and held off the U.S. Marines, Quilalí has been bloodied by decades of battle. You won't find a family in town that didn't lose a loved one to the struggle between Sandinistas and Contras in the 1980s; in fact, the town remains steadfastly Contra to this day and is home to both El Chacál (José Angel Talavera) and El Chacalín (Alex Talavera), the leaders of the Resistance Party (made up of ex-Contras). Upon entering town, you'll notice Quilalí is surprisingly well developed, courtesy of international aid money destined to support the Sandinista government's opponents. Rumor has it Quilalí's main street was used as an airstrip during the 1980s. Many of the Contras here were trained for battle in the United States or in bases whose locations were unknown even to participants. Their mementos from the U.S. military are treasured today: Look for U.S. Army tin cups, knives, and mosquito nets—not to mention stashes of large weaponry that weren't turned in to Doña Violeta's postwar government. The area is also well known for its marijuana production. A recommended read if you travel this area is *White Man's Burden* by William Easterly, who uses the town of Quilalí

as a case study for the effectiveness of development assistance.

The road to Colina La Gloría offers beautiful views of surrounding mountains and passes at least two swimming holes, one each in the Río Jícaro and Río Coco. **Hospedaje Tere** (on the main street) costs $4 a night and is the cleanest place in town. Several informal, family establishments, including **Comedor Jackson and Sholla,** serve typical food for about $3 a plate. Quilalí has a very good hospital supported by Médicos sin Fronteras, and standard services like ENITEL and Correos.

Four buses a day leave Ocotal via Santa Clara. The first one is at 5 A.M. From Estelí, five buses depart (5:45 A.M.–1:40 P.M.) for a five-hour bone-cruncher through San Juan del Río Coco and onward to Wiwilí.

Somoto

Located on the south side of the Pan-American Highway as it veers westward toward the Honduran border at El Espino, Somoto is an average-size city of 15,000 and capital of the department of Madriz. Tucked into the Cordillera de Somoto at 700 meters above sea level (the highest point of this range is Cerro Tépec-Xomotl at 1,730 meters), Somoto enjoys a fresh climate most of the year. Originally named Tépec-Xomotl, or Valley of the Turkeys, Somoto is known today more for its donkeys, *rosquillas* (baked corn cookies), and blowout carnival each November. A tributary of the Río Coco traverses the city.

U.S. Marines built an airstrip here, three blocks south of the park, to try out a military technique they'd just invented: the air strike. They used the base in Somoto to bomb Ocotal in the 1930s in a failed attempt to root out General Sandino.

The Ciudad de Burros has not much more to offer than a quiet evening in its quaint and friendly park, and a friendly, curious populace.

© RANDALL WOOD

Somoto is known as "The City of Burros."

ESTELÍ

ROSQUILLAS SOMOTEÑAS

Baked corn *rosquillas* are Somoto's most famous export.

Although *rosquillas* are baked in adobe wood-burning ovens all over Nicaragua, Somoto is particularly renowned throughout the country for the quality of this baked treat. The *rosquilla* is a crunchy ring of salted corn-dough baked with cheese. When they're not baked the traditional way, you'll find them as flat, molasses-topped *ojaldras* or thick nugget-pockets called *pupusas*. Serve 'em up with a cup of steaming hot, black coffee, still fragrant with smoke from the wood fire, and enjoy: The two tastes naturally complement each other. The two main producers in town are **La Rosquilla Somoteña Betty Espinoza** and **Rosquilla Garcia,** both two blocks west of the COTRAN on either side of the street. *Somoteñas* are the most famous regional variety of *rosquillas* – if you're traveling anywhere else in the country, they make a cheap, simple gift, greatly appreciated by any Nicaraguan.

SIGHTS AND EVENTS

La Parroquia Santiago de Somoto is one of Nicaragua's oldest churches. Construction began in 1661, some 86 years before León's great cathedral. If you're around Somoto on the eighth of any month, consider joining the religious masses on their pilgrimage to the tiny community of **Cacaulí,** all hoping for a glimpse of the Virgin Mary. Ever since she appeared to a young farmer named Francisco in the late 1980s, thousands of people have arrived to try

to repeat the miracle. They each carry a clear bottle of holy water, which they hold up to the sun at exactly 4 P.M. The Virgin—not parasites—should appear in the water. Whenever the eighth falls on a Sunday, the believers turn out in larger numbers.

Somoto's *fiestas patronales* fall on July 15–25, but the town is more famous for the **carnival of November 11** (or the second Saturday of the month), when it celebrates the creation of the department of Madriz in 1936. All of

Nicaragua's best party bands make the trip north, each setting up on one of seven stages—plus mariachis, dance parties, and the standard bull and cockfighting. As for nightlife, try the **Hotel Bambú,** on the highway just east of the bus terminal.

(GRAND CANYON OF SOMOTO

"Discovered" in 2006, Somoto's best swimming hole instantly became a national sensation when it was covered in an article in the national paper *La Prensa.* Float through clear green pools of water gazing up the steep canyon walls hanging with lush vegetation. There are cliff bats, rare birds, and a calm and peaceful feel to the air. The deep pools are separated by shallow bits which make it impossible to take a boat on the river. Instead, spend all day splashing from pool to pool. Bring a picnic and plastic bags to keep things dry.

This is possible as a day trip from Estelí, though it's nearly three hours each way to get there and the last express bus back to Estelí leaves at 3:30 P.M. See the *Ocotal* section for information and guides to hire a local pro to take you. If you're on your own, catch a bus to Somoto, then another to El Espino (every 45 minutes or so). Tell the driver to let you off at *entrada para Cañon de Somoto* (25 minutes from Somoto). Walk down the path about one kilometer to the river. Cross over the river to follow the path on your left along the river about 200 meters, until you get to a man sitting under a tree. He will charge you 10 *córdobas* and give you a ticket. He points you to walk another 500 meters. Cross the river again and come upon a small house with rowboats. A man will charge you 15 *córdobas* per person to row you another 500 meters where you can rent inner tubes for 40 *córdobas* a piece. A lovely example of spontaneous community tourism.

ACCOMMODATIONS AND FOOD

The **Hotel Panamericano** (on the north side of the park, tel. 505/722-2355, $6–15)

has hot water and additional amenities in a variety of rooms; there are a few interesting animals in captivity here. The nicest accommodation in Somoto is no doubt the (**Hotel Colonial** (half a block south of the church, tel. 505/722-2040, $25) for private bath, cable TV, and parking, breakfast included.

Comedor Soya (on the plaza) serves a soy with a smile; all kinds of surprising meals available inexpensively. For excellent *frescos* and fries, check out **Café Santiaguito** (1.5 blocks south of the church). Other options can be found in the market area, as long as you like things fried.

The Almendro (across from the Colonial, open 10 A.M.–9 P.M. daily) was mentioned in a Mejía Godoy song *("el almendro de donde la Tere")* and has nicer meals from $5.

INFORMATION, SERVICES, AND TRANSPORTATION

There is a bank across the street from the Alcaldía. The post office is across from the Hotel Colonial, and ENITEL is behind the church (open until 5 P.M.). A modern health clinic, Profamilia, is two blocks south of COTRAN and open 24 hours a day. Buses to Somoto from Estelí run every hour 5:30 A.M.–5:20 P.M. There are also regular express buses from Mayoreo in Managua.

EL ESPINO BORDER CROSSING

The least used border crossing in Nicaragua, El Espino is open 24 hours. To get there from Somoto, take one of the regular buses ($0.50) that head toward El Espino, or chip in for a cab (about $4). It's a 40-minute ride from Somoto. At the crossing, you first receive and fill out an immigration form at the booth next to the steel railroad crossing–style gate, then proceed 100 meters up to the little building on the right where you'll pay $2 to exit ($4 after hours) or $7 to enter ($9 after hours). Continuing bus service into Honduras is just over the hill and runs until 4:30 P.M.

THE MATAGALPA AND JINOTEGA HIGHLANDS

As you turn eastward from the Pan-American Highway and begin the gradual climb upwards, the particular character of the Matagalpan and Jinotegan highlands will attract your attention immediately. This rugged, determined region of blue-green hillsides, sometimes thickly forested mountains, and small, farming villages of adobe homes and clay-tile roofs is unlike anywhere else in Nicaragua. As highlands go, Nicaragua's center is not that high, rising to barely 2,000 meters above sea level, but after visiting the torrid plains around Granada and Managua, the relatively cool air and the smell of pines will be a welcome surprise. The temperatures favor vegetable production, though many quiet valleys are still thick with corn and red beans. They also favor the production of coffee and east of Matagalpa, the rumpled landscape of hardwoods and coffee plants dominates. Coffee's preference for shade has encouraged the preservation of some of this region's forests, and the mornings resonate with birdcall and the bellow of the howler monkeys.

Matagalpa is the more elegant and historical of the region's two big cities, with a gargantuan cathedral and several big, shady parks. A city draped over the curves of more than one hill, your legs will quickly notice the changes in altitude as you explore. Jinotega is farther north into the mountains, higher, and smaller. Emphasizing its sense of isolation are the green walls of the valley in which it nestles; even the cathedral in the town's center is dwarfed by the immensity of nature in its lush plaza. Jinotega remains somewhat of a cowboy town, the uncouth little brother of more cultured

HIGHLIGHTS

🌙 **Parque Darío:** End your self-guided walking tour of Matagalpa City here, in this shady plaza where you can watch the world go by and listen to the deafening calls of the birds in the treetops (page 233).

🌙 **La Catedral de San Pedro de Matagalpa:** One of the north's finest structures, this gorgeous cathedral can be spotted from anywhere in town (page 233).

🌙 **Grupo Venancia:** Rub shoulders with Matagalpa's enlightened citizens and visitors while you enjoy stimulating theater and great music (page 234).

🌙 **Finca Esperanza Verde:** Call ahead to reserve space at this award-winning ecotourism effort in the hills above San Ramón, with hiking trails through area coffee farms and deep, fertile valleys (page 244).

🌙 **Hotel de Montaña Selva Negra:** A hotel quite unlike any other, Selva Negra has enough farm tours, mountain hikes, good food, and quiet, peaceful relaxation to rest any weary soul (page 248).

🌙 **San Rafael del Norte:** Visit this cool and historical village in the hills outside Jinotega for a unique taste of the north country; poke through the Sandino Museum and hike to several waterfalls (page 259).

LOOK FOR 🌙 TO FIND RECOMMENDED SIGHTS, ACTIVITIES, DINING, AND LODGING.

Matagalpa. Jinotega feels like the end of the road, the gateway to the thousands of remote kilometers that separate the Atlantic coast from the rest of Nicaragua.

Both Jinotega and Matagalpa suffered mightily during the revolution and ensuing Contra war. But today's *norteños* work their farms without the fear of war, bending their backs instead in the struggle against rural poverty, drought, and the whims of the world coffee market. Residents of Matagalpa and Jinotega are accustomed to adversity and live bright, intense lives anyway. Spending time among them will give you a perspective you won't find in the more frequently visited corners of Nicaragua.

PLANNING YOUR TIME

Two or three nights is sufficient for seeing Matagalpa and Jinotega, but allow an extra day or two if you plan to explore any of the surrounding countryside. Those looking for

MATAGALPA

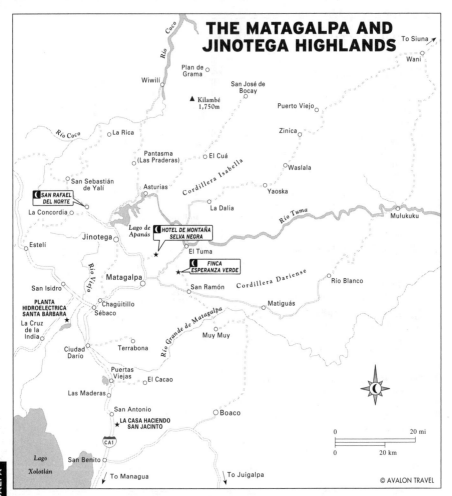

THE MATAGALPA AND JINOTEGA HIGHLANDS

© AVALON TRAVEL

a peaceful mountain retreat often spend 2–3 nights at either Hotel Selva Negra, Finca Esperanza Verde, or with a homestay program run by a coffee cooperative. Combining such a trip with a night or two in the city can easily consume five or six days—more if you visit the more remote communities.

HISTORY

Periods of tremendous violence and warfare have racked the mountainous north for well over a century. In the early 1930s, Augusto César Sandino fought U.S. Marines and the National Guard here; 40 years later, young revolutionary Sandinistas faced Somoza's National Guard in several bloody battles, particularly between San José de Bocay, Matiguás, and Bilampi. Far more devastating than either of those conflicts, however, were the 1980s, when Matagalpa and Jinotega (along with the RAAN, or North Atlantic Autonomous Region) experienced the worst of the war

© JAMES SAVAGE

coffee pickers near Matagalpa

between the Sandinista military and Contra troops. Travelers along the region's few roads were frequently ambushed and soldiers from both sides raided villages as a matter of course. Farmers learned to tend their crops with rifles slung over their shoulders.

Peace swept the region at the start of the 1990s and the past decade has transformed Matagalpa and Jinotega into an agricultural powerhouse. Gone are the thousands of cold, wet, and hungry guerrilla soldiers that muddily marched through these hills. Some of the same rugged trails are now popular with a few foreign travelers intent on visiting coffee cooperatives, climbing mountains, and swimming in waterfalls.

MATAGALPA

The Road to Matagalpa

The road from Managua climbs from the verdant plains of sugarcane and rice up through a series of plateaus with long horizons and broad panoramas before reaching the long mountain valleys that characterize the north. Most travelers take an express bus straight through most of the landscape and beeline for the mountains, but Matagalpa's dry lowlands hide a few interesting places of their own.

ROADSIDE ATTRACTIONS
La Casa-Hacienda San Jacinto

A must-see on the high school curriculum of all Nicaraguan history students, the Casa-Hacienda San Jacinto, located about 35 kilometers north of Managua along the Pan-American Highway, merits its own roadside statue. The monument guards the turnoff to the battlefield of San Jacinto and depicts a defiant Andrés Castro standing atop a pile of rocks. This is the site where, in 1856, the Liberals—supported by William Walker and his band of filibusters—and Conservatives battled fiercely. Conservative Andrés Castro, out of ammunition, picked up a rock and hurled it at the enemy, killing a Yankee with a blow to the head. Today, Castro represents the fighting spirit of Nicaraguan nationalism that refuses to bow to foreign authorities.

Three kilometers east of the highway (a flat, 20-minute walk), the museum at the restored San Jacinto ranch house is run-down and little visited except by occasional hordes of high school students. But for $1 admission, you can explore the period relics and admire the displays. If no one's manning the ticket window, just shout until the caretaker rides her bike down from the main building. Bring water: There are no facilities at the site itself, and just one mediocre restaurant at the highway turnoff.

La Laguna de Moyoá and Las Playitas

After conquering the first big ascent on the highway from Managua (known as Cuesta del Coyól), you'll be greeted by the Laguna Moyoá (Nahuatl for "place of the small mosquitoes") on the west side of the highway and the swampy Laguna Tecomapa to the east (unless it is a dry year, when both disappear). Geologists believe they are the remnants of the ancient Lake of Sébaco, a giant reservoir that formed the heavy clay soils of today's Sébaco Valley. A tectonic shift ages ago sent the Río Grande de Matagalpa flowing eastward toward the Atlantic instead of into Lake Xolotlán through Moyoá, and the lake gradually disappeared. It experienced a brief revival during Hurricane Mitch, when Lake Moyoá rose to the edge of the highway and Tecomapa became a legitimate lake through which wading cattle grazed.

Moyoá was once home to the Chontaleña people, and it is possible that they had a fixed settlement on the island in the lake. Some clay pottery has been uncovered from the A.D.

500–1500 period, which would indicate they at least frequented the site, probably to fish and hunt.

The locals do a good business catching fish out of Moyoá—mostly *mojarra* and *guapote*—both very good for eating, and both of which you'll see held up on strings along the side of the road. To visit the lake, stop in at Comedor Treminio and ask for Anita Vega or Humberto Treminio, the owners of the land that borders the lake. You can eat your meals at their establishment, and strike a deal with them for the right to camp out on their land. Try the shady grove down at the end of the road that leads to the lake. Birds you might see at Moyoá include *playeritos, piches, zambullidores,* and several types of heron.

CIUDAD DARÍO

Named after the prized poet of Castilian literature, Ciudad Darío was known by the indigenous name of Metapa in 1867 when Rubén Darío was born. Today, a handsome brass statue of the author stands at the southern approach to the city.

Darío's primary attraction is the unassuming **Casa Natal Rubén Darío** (along the main street in front of the ENITEL building, 8 A.M.–12:30 P.M. and 2–5 P.M. Mon.–Fri.). Darío was born here and then moved to the city of León shortly afterward to live with relatives. The eastern part of the house has been converted into a small amphitheater for the presentation of cultural shows.

For a plate of *pinto,* hit the **Comedor Clementina** (from the mayor's office, two blocks north and half a block west) for a hearty beef soup or her famous chicken and *ayote* (a type of squash). There are plenty of fresh fruit juices to sip while you wait for your meal and try to talk with her pet parrot, who speaks Italian (so she claims!). A half a block east from Clementina's is a big *fritanga* that opens up around 6 P.M., $1–2 a plate.

Restaurante El Coctél (from the Pulpería Masaya, go west one block and north a half-block) likes to serve crowds coming out of the museum, and specializes in *carne a la plancha; a* bit pricier than the other options in town—you can pay more than $7.50 for some things—but it's one of the few restaurants with a real ceiling overhead. The favorite restaurant among the NGO and businessperson crowd is **Doña Conchi's** (a block north of the Shell station toward the north end of town), a relatively upscale place with a full menu ranging $2–8 per dish.

Express buses between Managua and points north save an hour off the trip by not entering Ciudad Darío. So, if you're headed there by bus (from Managua's Mayoreo terminal), make sure to take an *ordinario*. Any local bus leaving Matagalpa or Estelí headed to Managua will go by way of Darío.

Near Ciudad Darío

Anyone between the ages of 7 and 15 will know exactly how to help you find the following historical and geological destinations in the Darío neighborhood of Santa Clara, located about one kilometer east from the town's park (not far from the Carlos Santí baseball stadium).

To get to the **petroglyphs,** start at Darío's mayor's office in the park and head east toward the stadium at the top of a hill (0.5 km). On the other side of the stadium is a school for deaf children. Beyond that, the paved road will turn to dirt as you enter Barrio España. There is a *pulpería* (market) on the corner where you can get directions to the petroglyphs, less than a 30-minute walk.

La Posa de Las Yeguas (The Mare's Pool) is a deep spot in the creek where, supposedly, women who weren't faithful to their husbands were turned into mares and went to live. Several rocks there bear petroglyphs and more modern graffiti. It is said the friars of old would go to meditate at **La Cueva del Fraile** (The Friar's Cave), not far from La Posa de Las Yeguas.

SÉBACO

The name Sébaco comes from the Nahuatl name Cihuacoatl (the "snake-woman"). In 1527, the Spanish founded the city they called Santiago de Cihuacoatl on the banks of the Río Viejo alongside the indigenous settlement of Cihuacoatl, capital of the Chontales people.

THE LEGEND OF CIHUACOATL

At the edge of the Río Viejo, there was once a powerful community ruled by a mighty cacique. His wife was considered the most beautiful woman in the country, but she made regular suspicious trips down to the river with great quantities of carefully prepared foods: beverages of seeds and berries, and birds prepared with spices and grains. One day, one of the cacique's men decided to follow the woman down to the river to see what she did. There, he watched as the woman sat calmly on a rock at the river's edge and struck the palm of her hand against the water's surface several times with a sharp smacking sound. From out of the ripples on the water's surface emerged a giant snake, which rose halfway out of the water and placed its head on the woman's beautiful smooth thighs. She fed the snake, its head resting on her lap, and afterwards the two made love at the water's edge. Then the serpent slithered back into the river, down to its underwater cave, and the woman gathered her things to leave.

The cacique's servant ran quickly back to tell the story, trembling as he related the infidelity to the cacique. When the woman returned home, her husband, in a jealous rage, killed the woman with a single stroke of his knife. The snake, upon realizing his lover had been slain, agitated the river with its tail, causing it to rise up violently and destroy the entire community. The goddess Cihuacoatl (Snake Woman) has been worshipped ever since by the Nahuatl people in the area.

But when a major flood put the town under water in 1833, Sébaco was moved to the hill east of town, where the remnants of Sébaco Viejo can still be found: The **Templo Viejo** houses a simple collection of archaeological artifacts, including pieces of pottery and ceramics, some small statues, and a wooden carving of the deity Cihuacoatl. When they moved, the residents of Sébaco packed up their buildings piece by piece and transported the materials to the new location, where they reconstructed the buildings to approximately their original form. Since then, the houses slowly crept down the hill and back to the water's edge, waiting for history to repeat itself. And that's exactly what happened. In 1998, Sébaco was hit so hard by Hurricane Mitch it became one of the primary obstacles separating Managua from the north. The large bridge at the south end of town resisted the floods of the Río Grande de Matagalpa, but the river overflowed its banks just south of the bridge and sliced a new channel through the road hundreds of meters wide. The combined torrent swelled into a deadly wall of water that ripped through Ciudad Darío.

No matter where you travel in the north of Nicaragua, at some point you'll pass through Sébaco. Located right where the highway splits to take travelers to either Estelí and the Segovias (fork left) or Matagalpa, Jinotega, and the northeast (fork right), Sébaco, a.k.a. La Ciudad de Cebollas (City of Onions), is known throughout the region for its lively roadside commerce. If you're traveling at night, Sébaco is a sudden blast of streetlights, traffic, and bustle after two hours of darkness since Managua.

While travelers are more typically interested in the Texaco station's restrooms, most Nicas pick up fresh produce—carrots, beets, and of course, onions—through the window of their bus or vehicle. Sébaco's aggressive road vendors will scale the side of your bus and display their goods through your window (hope you don't mind a faceful of carrot tops). If you have a long bus ride ahead of you, this is a good place to pick up bags of fruit juice, snacks, or veggies which make good gifts for your Nicaraguan hosts.

Accommodations and Food

Although there are a few cheap, seedy places to crash in town, you'd be much wiser to continue to Matagalpa or Estelí, each no more than an hour away. The dozens of decent roadside restaurants offer similar menus of chicken,

tacos, beef, and sandwiches. **◖ El Sesteo** is the best sit-down spot, with uniformed waiters, an air-conditioned *sala,* and the nod of the expat community, which has been enjoying lunches there since it opened. On the east side of the intersection across from the triangle, the cheaper **Sorbetería Mac-et** serves sandwiches, hot dogs, light lunches, fruit juices, and ice cream.

If you need to get out and stretch your legs, or have urgent errands, Sébaco also has several banks, a telephone office, and a private health clinic.

Chagüitillo

About two kilometers north of Sébaco along the highway to Matagalpa, Chagüitillo is a small community with access to several dozen pre-Columbian petroglyphs scratched into the stone walls of a canyon just outside the village. The site **Apamico** is named in Nahuatl for "place of the monkeys." Relics depicting monkeys, shamans carrying human heads, and hunting scenes line the banks of the Aranca Burba stream. The locals can easily help you find the two streambeds and show you the petroglyphs; both sites are an easy walk from the center of town. Particularly good guides are Orlando Dávila and Melvin Rizo, who speaks some English. Dávila lives in front of the school whose tall green wall is painted with representations of the petroglyphs; Rizo lives a block or two closer to the highway.

In town, find the *pulpería* run by Bernabe Rayo (located on a side street off the main road through town). Chagüitillo is the source of a water project for the city of Matagalpa, and engineers digging the trenches for the pipelines have unearthed many additional artifacts. Some are scattered amongst the many houses of the community, but Rayo has done an admirable job of collecting some of them and trying to form a small community museum out of the pieces. You can support him by purchasing something from his store. He's got an interesting collection of old ceramic pots, cups, and small statues, plus some larger pieces he's reconstructed from the shards.

El Atajo de Guayacán

About 25 kilometers before arriving in Matagalpa, El Atajo de Guayacán (the Guayacán Shortcut) is a dirt road leading north along the west side of a pretty mountain valley to the city of Jinotega. Drivers headed from Sébaco to Jinotega can bypass the city of Matagalpa completely and save an hour's drive. Hikers (use the Matagalpa, Sébaco, and Jinotega INETER quad maps) can use it to penetrate some fantastic mountain valleys. Your first hike should be Cerro Los Chiles, a peak that forms a half-basin along the side of El Atajo de Guayacán.

Matagalpa City

The department of Matagalpa is the most mountainous in Nicaragua, and its capital city remains true to form. As you walk up and down the steep streets, you'll realize the city is draped like a blanket over the rolling valley floor beneath it. Nicknamed La Perla del Septentrión (The Pearl of the North), Matagalpa's true precious stone is a ripe, red coffee bean, the production and harvest of which is essential to the region's— and the nation's—economy. Matagalpa enjoys clean, mountain air, but water is another story. Radically depleted by deforestation and human contamination, clean water is in dreadfully short supply here. During the driest times, city officials cope with the problem by implementing draconian rationing schemes. The surrounding mountains have been mostly scraped clean of trees, but during the wet season, they turn emerald green and remain so throughout the Christmas season, when the coffee harvest turns the city of Matagalpa into a lively center of coffee pickers, prospectors, packers, and processors.

Nahuatl influence is more prominent in Matagalpa than elsewhere, particularly in regional vocabulary, which retains much pre-Columbian vocabulary. The Nahuatl word *chüisle,* for example, is used instead of the Castilian *quebrada* for stream. The city's central office for the region's indigenous community settles land disputes and other issues. Modern-day Nicaraguan politicians prize Matagalpa because its high population can often swing the vote, but tourists will prize Matagalpa as a welcome respite from the heat of the lowlands, plus a chance to sip the best coffee in the world while plotting their forays deeper into the mountains. Ignore the inflated population sign as you enter the valley—the latest figures put Matagalpa's urban population at just over 100,000.

HISTORY

Matagalpa has been settled for as long as anyone can remember. The beautiful valley where the city of Matagalpa now sits was already a cluster of Nahuatl communities—including Solingalpa and Molagüina, which still exist

© JOSHUA BERMAN

Matagalpa's steep streets

MATAGALPA

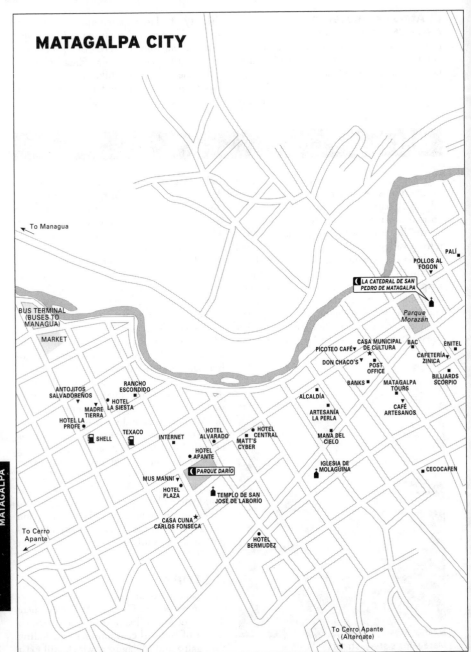

MATAGALPA CITY

To Managua

BUS TERMINAL
(BUSES TO
MANAGUA)

MARKET

PALÍ

POLLOS AL
FOGON

LA CATEDRAL DE SAN
PEDRO DE MATAGALPA

Parque
Morazán

CASA MUNICIPAL
DE CULTURA

PICOTEO CAFÉ

DON CHACO'S

POST
OFFICE

BAC

ENITEL

CAFETERÍA
ZINICA

BILLIARDS
SCORPIO

BANKS

MATAGALPA
TOURS

CAFÉ
ARTESANOS

ANTOJITOS
SALVADOREÑOS

RANCHO
ESCONDIDO

HOTEL
LA SIESTA

MADRE
TIERRA

HOTEL LA
PROFE

SHELL

TEXACO

INTERNET

HOTEL
ALVARADO

HOTEL
APANTE

MATT'S
CYBER

HOTEL
CENTRAL

ALCALDÍA

ARTESANÍA
LA PERLA

MANA DEL
CIELO

CECOCAFEN

MUS MANNI

PARQUE DARÍO

HOTEL
PLAZA

TEMPLO DE SAN
JOSE DE LABORÍO

IGLESIA DE
MOLAGUINA

CASA CUNA
CARLOS FONSECA

HOTEL
BERMUDEZ

To Cerro
Apante

To Cerro Apante
(Alternate)

MATAGALPA

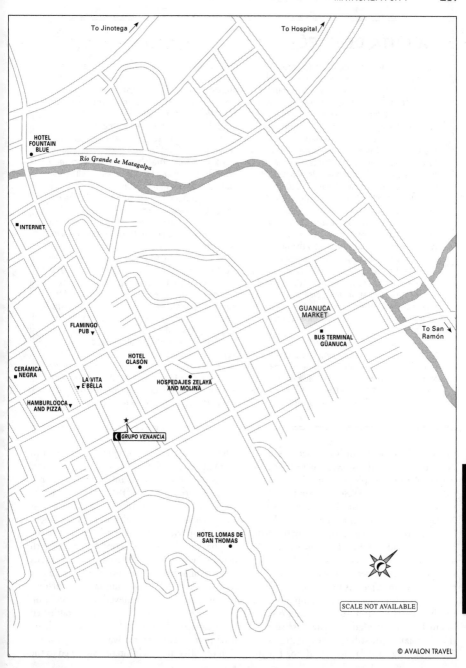

To Jinotega

To Hospital

HOTEL
FOUNTAIN
BLUE

Río Grande de Matagalpa

INTERNET

GUANUCA
MARKET

FLAMINGO
PUB

BUS TERMINAL
GÜANUCA

To San
Ramón

HOTEL
GLASÓN

CERÁMICA
NEGRA

LA VITA
E BELLA

HOSPEDAJES ZELAYA
AND MOLINA

HAMBURLOOCA
AND PIZZA

GRUPO VENANCIA

HOTEL LOMAS DE
SAN THOMAS

SCALE NOT AVAILABLE

© AVALON TRAVEL

MATAGALPA

LA RUTA DE CAFÉ

Today, both international coffee merchants and *café-turistas* can travel a circuit of coffee cooperatives scattered through the mountains of Jinotega, Matagalpa, and the Segovias. As a participant in this Ruta de Café not only will you sample coffee in special cupping labs, you'll also visit coffee-growing families and their farms, which are often magical cloud forests shrouded in cool mists; you can stay for a couple of hours or a couple of days, living with the families, eating meals with them, picking coffee, and learning about all stages of the process. As a *café-turista,* you'll experience the communities of real people who have been behind every sip of coffee you've ever taken. What's more, you will learn why the quality of a coffee is inextricably tied to the quality of life of those that produce it, as well as the quality of the environment in which they live. Finally, you will learn what organic, bird friendly, and fair trade-certified coffees are (visit www .transfairusa.org and www.globalexchange .org for details).

To experience the most activity, be sure to arrange your visit during the peak of the harvest, usually mid-December–February. Make your arrangements in advance. Start your tour at **CECOCAFEN** (Center of Northern Coffee Cooperatives, tel. 505/772-6353,

turismo@cecocafen.com), whose main office in Matagalpa city is located two blocks east of Banco Uno. They can arrange anything from an afternoon coffee cupping at their Sol Café *beneficio* (coffee-processing mill) to a day trip, visiting some of their farmers, to a multi-night excursion, staying in *campesino* homes and touring their farms (or even putting some work in during the harvest). Trips include transportation and food, and hikes (with pickups) can be arranged between towns. Prices fully depend on the trip. Or consider a stay at **Finca Esperanza Verde** (www.fincaesperanza verde.org), an acclaimed accommodation and working organic coffee farm, located outside San Ramón.

In Jinotega, **SOPPEXCA** (Society of Small Coffee Producers, Exporters, and Buyers, tel./fax 505/782-2617, soppexcc@tmx.com .ni) is eager to serve as your tour guide of the region, arranging any number of hikes, trips, and homestays among its growers in the surrounding hills. Their office and cupping lab is located in Jinotega, one block west of the Ferretería Blandón.

There are also several welcoming coffee cooperatives in the hills north of Estelí with similar tours available, notably **PRODECOOP** in Palacagüina and **Venecia** near Condega.

today—when the Spanish first set eyes on it. Nahuatl traditional histories don't include any stories of their people having arrived in this valley—as if they have always been here. Long before it was called the Pearl of the North, Matagalpa was known as the City of Ten in Nahuatl, in reference to the 10 small settlements that made up the valley. The name is also attributed to the powerful cacique Atahualpa, who governed the area during the time of colonization (Solingalpa was his wife).

The Spanish established a camp alongside the Nahuatls around 1680. Some powerful Spanish families made up the first settlers; their last names are still common in the region: Alvarado, Castañeda, Reyes, Rizo, Escoto.

They set up extensive cattle ranches and planted fields before coffee was even a dream. In 1838, the area was named Departamento del Septentrión, and in 1862, Matagalpa was elevated to the status of city. Even with that status, the city of Matagalpa was of far less economic importance to the nation than Sébaco.

That changed in the second half of the 19th century when Matagalpa became the focus of a sizeable immigration of Germans. They had not arrived in Nicaragua to plant coffee, as is commonly believed, but to develop the gold mines in the east. Once established in Nicaragua, however, they quickly realized how perfect the climate was for the cultivation of coffee and their interest switched to the crop that would define Nicaragua's economy for more than 100 years. Matagalpa had developed a new reason for being, and coffee has been the focus of Matagalpa ever since.

Today, several problems constrain Matagalpa from the prosperity it enjoyed in the 19th century. Most critical is the lack of potable water—even the Chagüitillo water project may provide water for no more than 10 years—but developing rural roads and dealing with the growing solid waste problem will both be necessary before Matagalpa returns to its status as a pearl.

SIGHTS
◖ Parque Darío

Grab a bench in Parque Darío and buy a crushed ice *raspado* to enjoy while people-watching. There are probably more trees jammed into the park's tiny confines than any other in Nicaragua, and come sunset the branches fill with thousands of birds. A permanent fixture in the park is a vendor with rows and rows of handmade ceramic piggy banks for sale, none of which costs more than $1.

Churches and Museums

El Templo de San José de Laborío sits at the edge of the Parque Darío at the south end of town. It's probably as old as the colonial presence in Matagalpa, but no one is quite sure exactly when it was built. It was rebuilt in 1917 on top of its old foundation, but underneath that foundation are the ruins of another that date to at least 1751, and possibly a bit earlier. In 1881, an indigenous uprising used the church as its garrison.

Matagalpa was the birthplace of the founder of the FSLN, Carlos Fonseca. The house he was born in has been converted into a museum. Known as **La Casa Cuna Carlos Fonseca** (one block east of Parque Darío's south side, tel. 505/772-3665, open 8 A.M.–noon and 2–5 P.M. Mon.–Fri., small donation), the tiny corner building has the original brick floors, mud walls, and tile roof, and has an interesting assortment of documents, photos, and memorabilia, including Carlos's typewriter and his gear from military training in Korea.

The history of **La Iglesia de Molagüina,** found in the center of the city, has been forgotten. It was probably constructed between 1751 and 1873, though those dates have been questioned by historians. Simple and monastic, it is a well-used and well-loved church: Molagüina is home to a Catholic order of nuns and the College of San José.

Museo de Café (located on the main street two blocks east of the mayor's office, across from Teatro Perla, open 8 A.M.–5 P.M. Mon.–Fri., closed for lunch, open Sat. mornings) displays some interesting murals and photographs from Matagalpa's history, plus a small collection of indigenous artifacts. Entrance is free and local coffee is available for sale.

◖ La Catedral de San Pedro de Matagalpa

At the northeastern end of town, La Catedral de San Pedro de Matagalpa was a disproportionately large cathedral—the third largest in the nation—when it was built in 1874, reflecting the opulence of Matagalpa at the time. The cathedral is built in the baroque style, with heavy bell towers set at both sides and an airy, spacious interior. It's the most prominent building in town and is easily visible from the hillsides north of town on the road to Jinotega. The cathedral's interior is crisp and cool, tastefully adorned with bas- and medium-relief sculpture, carved wood, and paintings. Mass is held nightly at 6 P.M.

Cemeteries

There are two adjacent cemeteries on the hillside east of the city, about a 30-minute walk from town. One is for locals and one for foreigners, a rare arrangement in Nicaragua. Both contain headstones hand carved from dark rock, something seen only in Matagalpa. Buried in the cemetery higher up on the hill in the local section is one of the most famous casualties of the 1980s war: Benjamin Linder. An American, Linder was an avid juggler and unicyclist, and his headstone reflects those passions, along with some doves, the symbol of the peace he never lived to see.

MATAGALPA

MATAGALPA, WATER, AND THE LEGEND OF THE SERPENT

Matagalpa is a water-stressed city. In some neighborhoods, the water pressure is only turned on once a day; in others, Matagalpinos are forced to walk to distribution points to fill up containers from tanker trucks. You may see these trucks along the city streets in the early mornings, when everyone comes out with buckets and pans to get what water they can.

At the same time, there's more water in Matagalpa than some people know what to do with. Time and time again, shallow excavations in the city for routine projects have turned up a moist layer of earth just several meters below the surface. When a well-loved priest died in the 1990s, his tomb was dug underneath the floor of the cathedral. Before they had finished digging, the hole had begun to flood. Studies have determined the water under the city of Matagalpa isn't exploitable in quantities great enough to supply the city, and so other alternatives are being developed.

Much of Matagalpa's limited water supply comes from the forested hillsides that surround the city, hillsides that are rapidly being stripped of their timber. Matagalpinos speak of an old legend: The hill known as Apante, just southeast of the city, was said to be an enormous upwelling of water trapped within a pocket of soil and rock. Within the water lived a great snake. One day the snake began to shake, and the hillside began to crumble, threatening to unleash a massive landslide upon the residents of the city. In despair, they turned to the Virgin Mary for protection. Mary fought the snake and subdued it by planting its tail underneath the foundation of the church of Molagüina in the center of the city.

But the snake grows stronger each day . . . when it finally has enough strength to break free, it will shake its tail again, causing the hills to crumble and collapse upon the city. If the deforestation of the hillsides surrounding Matagalpa continue, this prophecy may very well come true.

ENTERTAINMENT AND EVENTS

Matagalpans celebrate their *fiestas patronales* on September 24, and the anniversary of their becoming a city on February 14. Every September there is a rowdy country fair that brings in crowds from the north and east, and cattle traders from all over the country. This is the best time of year to catch Matagalpa's traditional music of polkas, mazurkas, and *jamaquelos,* performed by the roving street bands that play at restaurants. **Noches Matagalpinas** are held the last weekend of every month in Parque Darío; the weekend typically involves a street stage with live music and stands set up by the local restaurants.

In 2001, a new dance academy started up, under the able direction of Marcos Valle, who studied modern dance in Spain. The **Academía de la Danza de Matagalpa** puts on dance presentations several times a year. If there's going to be a show, they advertise it at the Casa Municipal de Cultura, next to the fire station.

Local radio stations include Radio Norteña, FM 94.1; Radio Stereo Apante, FM 94.9; and Radio Yes, FM 90.1. The latter has several programs for a rural audience, including impersonations, jokes, and news commentary. Their morning news program is worth a listen in the early hours of the day while you're taking a cold-water mountain shower. A women's cooperative runs the show at FM 101.7.

◖ Grupo Venancia

Grupo Venancia (tel. 505/772-3562, Thurs.–Sat.) is a low-key, convivial open-air bar surrounding a stage and sometimes dance floor. They host music, dance, theater, artsy international films, and both local and global activism. The place is renowned for its free shows every Saturday night. Grupo Venancia is also a nonprofit women's group that can probably be called ground zero of Nicaragua's feminist movement. It was founded in 1990 and in addition to the gathering space, runs urban and rural workshops on women's rights and domestic violence. Ask about their published materials, ways to volunteer, and try to catch their Saturday morning radio show, "La Hora Lila," on Radio Yes (FM 90.1) at 8:30 A.M.

Nightlife

There's no doubt that the Matagalpinos like to shake their boots as much as other Nicaraguans, though they prefer *ranchera,* merengue, and *reggetón* over salsa. Matagalpa's various *discotecas* may be open Thursday–Sunday, in general, but the only consistently happening night—with guaranteed crowded and electric dance floors—is Saturday. For dancing, **Las Tequilas,** just past the Hora del Taco restaurant on the left if heading out of town toward Managua ($2 or less taxi ride from downtown), is popular, as is **El Rancho Escondido,** which also offers *corriente* meals for less than $2. The newer **Hot Dance** is popular among a younger crowd. More mature revelers and couples enjoy the hassle-free dance floor at **Rincón Paraíso.** For a friendly testosterone-filled cantina atmosphere, order a few liters at **El Rincón Nica,** sometimes with live music on Fridays, located near Rancho Escondido. Open all week for mediocre lunch and dinner, **La Casona** comes alive as Matagalpa's premiere Friday night fiesta, with live music in a crowded, open-air back patio.

The bohemian hang of choice is **Cafe Artesanos** (a half-block up from BAC next to Matagalpa Tours), one *norteño's* unique cathedral to coffee. Noel Montoya offes a close look—and taste—of Nica beans at their best, and is happy to introduce you to the art of roasting and brewing. Mix the black liquor with Flor de Caña. Open for breakfast, dinner, and into the night, the place features local artists' paintings and murals on the walls of an old colonial building.

Madre Tierra (one block south and 2.5 blocks west from Parque Darío) is run by a pair of Italians serving good, simple foods; they host occasional live music and foreign films, with funky cushions, couches, and high benches to perch on. You'll recognize it by the massive red painting of an ancient earth mother.

SHOPPING

The north's famous black pottery—darkened by a particular firing technique—is unique in Nicaragua, where pottery is typically a natural reddish-orange color. Find it for sale throughout the city. Multiple shops bearing the name **Cerámica Negra** are spread throughout the city, offering similar selections. Even La Vita e Bella restaurant offers an excellent variety of ceramics and jewelry.

You'll find a great selection of local crafts at **Centro Girasol** (a bright yellow corner building right across the first bridge as you enter Matagalpa from Managua, tel. 505/772-6030). They've also got local jams, honey, coffee, and yogurt.

El Castillo del Cacao (The Castle of Chocolate, tel. 505/772-2002, www.elcastillo delcacao.com) is the Willie Wonka Chocolate Factory of Nicaragua, located 500 meters north of Las Marias Esso station (about a five-minute cab ride from the city center). Here you can tour the factory, visit a chocolate museum, and learn about the production of organic chocolate in Nicaragua. Nicaraguan cacao is known as a *landrace,* or a traditional variety almost identical to pre-Columbian cacao. It has a rich, complex, nuttier flavor than the heavily cultivated and hybridized strains grown elsewhere in the world. To get the best tour of the factory go in the afternoons.

HIKING AND TOURS

Start by picking up a map at the **Centro Girasol** (a bright yellow corner building right across the first bridge as you enter Matagalpa from Managua or two blocks south and one west from the COTRAN Sur, tel. 505/772-6030). The *Treasures of Matagalpa* map costs less than $2, benefits local children with disabilities, and outlines a number of walks, offering guide service as well.

Matagalpa Tours (a half-block east of BAC, tel. 505/772-0108 or 505/647-4680, www.nicaraguatravels.net) is a guide service, travel agent, and backcountry outfitter, run by a Dutch expat and his Nicaragua wife, who manages their on-site Spanish language school. Let them arrange a variety of packages, shuttle service from Granada, homestays, Bosawás treks, coffee plantation tours, and community tourism. Anywhere from $15 per day to $60 per day depending on the extent. Arien has explored, hiked, and camped throughout the Matagalpan countryside and has even drawn a number of trail maps. The Bosawás tours are major wilderness excursions that need to be arranged long in advance. Granada shuttles cost $25per person.

Hiking Cerro Apante

Immediately recognizable by the cluster of antennas on its peak, Cerro Apante (1,442 meters) towers above Matagalpa. Officially, it is a natural reserve, though most of its steep flanks are privately owned, covered by thick vegetation and a handful of small farms. Apante is a well-preserved piece of tropical humid forest that contains decent stands of oak and pine, as well as several hundred types of wildflowers. It is protecting an important source of water for the city (*apante* is Nahuatl for "running water"). It is crisscrossed with many small trails that lead to its streams and lagoons, all of which are easily accessed by foot from the city.

The two routes to the top both begin by standing at the northwest corner of Parque Darío (in front of Hotel Alvarado). Walking south on the *calle principal* (main street) will take you up to the Apante neighborhood on the edge of town (also serviced by the Chispa–Apante Rapibuses). Continue up the road, keeping the summit to your left and continually asking if you're on the right track to *el cerro*. From the same corner in town, travel due east up a road that climbs steeply, eventually deteriorating into a rutted road. The road

switches back a few times, ending at a hacienda atop a saddle in the Apante ridgeline. From there, find a footpath to the top. The actual summit is off limits, and is guarded by a caretaker and his dog, but the nearby ridge enjoys a breathtaking view of its own. You can link the two hikes into a three-hour loop; bring lots of water for the trail.

ACCOMMODATIONS
Under $10

Hotelito Reposado (located two blocks east of the northeast corner of Parque Morazán) offers simple rooms from $7 shared bath to $10 private bath. However, you're better off choosing from the many options along the *calle principal* and, in particular, the few places around the Parque Darío.

Hotel Plaza (on the south side of Parque Darío, tel. 505/772-2380) has been a stalwart in the Matagalpa lodging scene for decades. The 18 rooms range from $2.50 cubby holes with shared bath to $10 doubles with private bath, TV, and fan. On the west side of Parque Darío, **Hotel Apante** (tel. 505/772-6890) charges $7.50 per person for shared bath, fan, and TV in its bright, clean rooms. **Hotel La Siesta** (one block south and 2.5 blocks west of Parque Darío, $7 pp shared bath) is a family-run place with a quiet coffee balcony; the seven rooms range from singles to quadruples.

One of the best, safest budget options is **[Hotel Alvarado** (across from the Parque Darío's northwest corner, tel. 505/772-2830 or 505/772-2252, $8 pp), run by a friendly Christian doctor couple who run a pharmacy downstairs. Ask for one of the top-floor rooms which boast private bathrooms, a breeze, and views of the city and mountains from the small balconies. If their eight rooms are full, ask about their other location across town.

$10–25

[Hotel Fountain Blue, a.k.a. Fuente Azul (third entrance to Matagalpa just west of the bridge, or from Salomón López 1.5 blocks west, tel. 505 /772-2733), has a dozen practical rooms—$21 double with private bath, hot water, TV, and fan or $10 pp for smaller rooms with shared bath. This place is quiet and comfortable, with a pay phone, Internet, free coffee, continental breakfast, and guarded parking.

The choice of many visiting Nicas, **Hotel La Profe** (across from Shell El Progreso gas station, tel. 505/772-2506) offers rooms for $10–15; ask for the quiet rooms in the back. North along the *calle principal*, **Hotel Central** (across from the Supermarket Matagalpa, tel. 505/772-3140) has doubles from $11, or pay $19 for private bath and fan. The rooms are secure and clean, but a bit musty in the rainy season.

$25-50

Hotel Lomas de San Thomas (350 meters east of Escuela Guanuca, tel. 505/772-4189, www.hotellomassnthomas.com, $35–75) lords over the city, a mustard-colored, three-story establishment on a breezy hill just east of town. The 25 rooms have private bath, hot water, TV, and telephone, many with an excellent balcony. There is also a bar and restaurant on-site. It gears itself for business conventions and the NGO crew, offering secretarial services, conference rooms, fax, Internet, and a tennis court. To get there, leave the highway at the third entrance to Matagalpa and pass straight through town following the signs. At the eastern edge of Matagalpa, turn left and climb the hill on a cobblestone road to the hotel.

FOOD
Comida Típica and Cafés

As always, there's tasty street food in both parks, and as always, it's *vigorón* or *chancho con yucca* (both dishes served on banana leaves). However, during the lunch hour, several *fritangas* at Parque Morazán serve a more robust menu.

Sniff around just east of Bancentro, and you will surely catch a whiff of warm, fresh breads and pastries wafting out from the **Panadería Belén** (open 8 A.M.–6 P.M. Mon.–Sat.). **C Repostería Gutierrez** (one block east

and half a block south of the southeast corner of Parque Morazán, open 7 A.M.–8 P.M. daily) is a favorite among locals, with savory cheap Nica dishes. On the corner of Parque Darío, **Mus Manni** (open 6 A.M.–8 P.M. daily) also has great bread and pastries.

One of the friendliest and most famous *comedores* is **C Don Chaco's** (1.5 blocks east of the Alcaldía, open 7:30 A.M.–9 P.M. Sun.–Thurs., 7:30 A.M.–5 P.M. Fri.), where in addition to heaping plates of *comida típica* (with great veggie options), you'll find a delicious *batido* (smoothie) menu of fruits, vegetables, and even soy milk. If you prefer buffet, lunchline style, with a smorgasbord of Nica food lined up in front of you, the ragingly popular **Mana del Cielo** (located 2.5 blocks south of the banks) will satisfy; it's owned by a retired baseball player who played in Nica's pro leagues for a number of years.

To taste the sweet goodness of Matagalpa's best *güiríla* (a sweet-corn pancake wrapped

BLACK GOLD: THE STORY OF NICARAGUAN COFFEE

In 1852, Germans Ludwig Elster and his wife Katherina Braun were passing through Nicaragua on their way to the California gold rush. They never made it to California, but they did find gold. Rather, Katherina did.

While crossing Nicaragua, Ludwig met many disheartened travelers returning home from failure in California. He and Katherina decided to cut their journey short and look for gold in the mines of San Ramón, Matagalpa. While Ludwig worked the taxed gold deposits of Matagalpa, Katherina Braun established a home garden and planted some of the coffee beans they'd picked up in Managua. Her discovery – that Matagalpa's climate and soils were just right for the cultivation of the bitter but full-bodied arabica coffee bean – dwarfed the importance of San Ramón's gold mines and changed the course of Nicaragua's history.

Coffee fever gripped Matagalpa in the 1880s, and the Nicaraguan government, eager to capitalize on the crop that neighbor-states Costa Rica and Guatemala had already been growing for 40 years, threw its weight behind the Germans. Laws were passed encouraging young Germans to immigrate to Nicaragua. One such law gave them free land to work; many of these family farms are still operating today.

At first, coffee was shipped in bean (parchment) form through the port of Corinto, around Cape Horn to European importers in Bremen and Hamburg. By 1912, though, the Nicaraguan German community had established their own processing plants where they milled and processed the coffee beans. They used a new "wet" method that stripped the beans of their pulp over grated steel cylinders. Today, more than 40 wet coffee mills, plus thousands of micromills on individual farms process coffee throughout the nation.

FROM MATAGALPA TO MOCHACCINO: HOW NICARAGUAN COFFEE IS PROCESSED

One of the truly unique aspects of Nicaraguan coffee, besides its exceptional quality, is how much of the process is performed on the farm, before the product is shipped elsewhere. This is a significant difference from the routine adopted by Costa Rican coffee growers, most of whom send off their harvest immediately after picking.

Also, an increasing number of small-scale Nicaraguan coffee farmers are learning to recognize and judge the quality of their product and eliminate the middlemen, or *coyotes*, who have traditionally taken the lion's share of coffee profits. One tool that allows them to do

© JOSHUA BERMAN

Coffee harvest begins in December.

this is the cupping lab – a specially equipped kitchen where Nicaraguan cooperative members are trained to grind, brew, and rate their own coffee using internationally recognized criteria. One of the key figures in the cupping lab project was Paul Katzeff, CEO and roastmaster of California-based Thanksgiving Coffee Company (there are wonderful stories about exchanges with Nicaraguan coffee farmers and a whole lot more at www.thanksgivingcoffee.com).

But before you cup it, you must grow, harvest, and process it. Following are the steps involved:

1. Coffee berries are picked during the harvest months December–February. The fleshy berries are red and yellow and called *café en uva* (meaning grape or cherry coffee).
2. The berries are de-pulped, i.e., the fleshy covering is removed. This is done the same day they're picked to prevent fermenting, which would affect the flavor. This is either done dry or while they're suspended in water ("wet processing").
3. The coffee beans at this stage still have a mucilaginous coating on them. The beans are allowed to sit for 24 hours to allow the coating to ferment, facilitating the removal of the mucilage.
4. After 24 hours, the beans are soaked in water and stirred with wooden paddles. The mucilaginous coating dissolves. During this stage, the good beans sink to the bottom of the vessel, and the bad beans float to the surface, where they're removed.
5. The beans are now called *café en pergamino* (parchment coffee). Small growers sell their beans to the coffee cooperatives at this point. They still have a hard shell around them.
6. The beans are laid out in the sun on broad concrete slabs to dry and raked continuously to prevent burning.
7. When the beans reach 12 percent humidity, they are stored for around one month in a cool, semi-dark building. During this time, the coffee beans' flavor is enhanced.
8. When ready for shipping, the beans are milled to remove the hard shell. What is left after milling is the familiar coffee bean, in two halves. At this stage, the coffee is considered *café oro* (gold or green coffee).
9. The beans are sorted. All broken, burned, or blackened beans are removed by hand.
10. The beans are packed in 150-pound burlap sacks and sent to the port of Corinto for shipments to the western United States and Asia, or Puerto Cortéz, Honduras for shipments to the eastern United States and Europe.
11. The green coffee beans are roasted, ground, bagged, and brewed into the beverage so many people can't do without. A few cooperatives and companies in Nicaragua roast and package their coffee for distribution in country – you can find these at co-op headquarters or any local supermarket.

GOOD BEANS: WHAT MAKES GOURMET COFFEE

As much as 80 percent of Nicaraguan cooperative-produced coffee can be considered "quality coffee" because it fills the following internationally recognized requirements:

- They are arabica beans (not robusta) grown at an altitude of 900 meters or higher.

- Consisting of big beans, the lots are aromatic, well sorted, and free from broken or burned beans and small stones.

- Beans are given one month to sit during processing and are not de-hulled until just before shipping.

- Beans are transported in sealed containers.

- Beans are adequately stored by the purchaser.

- Upon toasting, the beans are sealed immediately in special one-pound vacuum-packed bags that prevent the introduction of light, air, and moisture, but permit carbon dioxide to escape.

- The consumer can buy the coffee in whole-bean form, not ground.

MATAGALPA

around a hunk of salty *cuajada* cheese, about $0.35), you'll have to brave the chaos of the crowds that cluster around the smoky stands across the street from Palí. For *pupusas* and fruit drinks, seek out the cute **Antojitos Salvadoreños** (1.5 blocks south of El Rancho Escondido, open 11 A.M.–9:30 P.M. Tues.–Sun.), where three deliciously greasy, stuffed pancakes cost $1.50. For ridiculously delicious roasted chicken, look for the flames in the window of **Pollos el Fogón** (on the corner across from the cathedral's northwest corner, delivery tel. 505/772-6004, open 10 A.M.–10 P.M. daily, $3 a plate).

Everybody loves Don Tano's **Picoteo Café** (located just east of the post office, open 7:30 A.M.–10 P.M. daily), serving chicken, burgers, pizza, and lots of beer. The walls are covered with platitudes painted on wooden plaques; most dishes run around $2.

Pique's (not far from the Parque Morazán) is a stylish Mexican joint, with dishes in the $2.75–4 range. Their *chalupas* and mole are especially good, and the atmosphere is relaxing.

La Casona (on the main drag, across from the mayor's office) offers a lunch buffet and a variety of bar-type foods for $3–4. It's open 9 A.M.–11 P.M. daily, later on weekends when it turns into a popular bar. Look for the big 7-Up sign outside. **Cafetería Zinica:** in the words of the proprietress herself, "We don't have a menu. We just serve hamburgers—the best damn hamburgers in the country." Actually, they do have a menu and serve several other things, including fresh fruit juices. Super-clean, the place is named after the Matagalpa town where Carlos Fonseca, founder of the FSLN, was killed by Somoza's National Guard.

☾ Café Artesanos (a half-block up from BAC next to Matagalpa Tours, open 8 A.M.–noon and 3 P.M.–midnight daily) is one of the most relaxing hangouts in the city for a bite, a cup of coffee, and if you're lucky, live music. It's open for breakfast and dinner and is especially soothing in the morning. Also try **Madre Tierra** (one block south and 2.5 blocks

west from Parque Darío) for dinner. Both cost about $2–4.

Finer Dining

One of the cornerstones of Matagalpa's dining scene, **☾ La Vita e Bella** (tel. 505/772-5476, vitabell@ibw.com.ni, 12:30 P.M.–10:30 P.M. Tues.–Sun.) is tucked into an alley in the Colonia Lainez, serving Italian and vegetarian dishes, and desserts that will make you glad you found the place. This is possibly the best restaurant in the city for non-chicken and non-beef dishes; entrées are under $4, large pizza $6, and there's an excellent wine selection.

There are three notable restaurants on the highway to Managua, all on the right-hand side, a few kilometers south of the first entrance to Matagalpa. **La Hora del Taco** (open 11 A.M.–11 P.M. daily) offers the same finger-licking Mexican menu as its Managua counterpart, with an added outdoor balcony looking out into the Valle Las Tejas; margaritas are less than $2, and the $4 fajita plate is to die for.

Around the next bend in the highway, **El Pullazo** (open for lunch and dinner) just might serve you the best piece of beef tenderloin you'll taste in Nicaragua, but they won't tell you their secret recipe. They have a few other beef dishes too, but no one orders them. Your *"pullazo"* of meat (a vulgar play on the word for injection) is accompanied by a sweet *güiríla* pancake and hunk of *cuajada* cheese. Wash it down with a beer and you're only $4 in the hole.

Popular with locals for special occasions, **Parradea** (open 7 A.M.–11 P.M. daily, $5–15), 75 meters north from the Shell at the Virgin, offers seafood, steaks, and even such delicacies as bull testicle soup, as well as *comida típica* breakfasts.

There's also the **Sacuanjoche Restaurant and Bar** at the Hotel Lomas de San Thomas, offering standard fare like steaks, fajitas, shrimp dishes, and salads (entrées $4–9), a ceramic shop, and taxi service ($1 to or from the town center).

SERVICES
Emergencies
All emergency services are covered in Matagalpa—fire (tel. 505/772-3167), police (tel. 505/772-3870), and hospital (tel. 505/772-2081). The hospital is located at the north end of town on the highway to San Ramón. But you'll get better medical treatment at the Clínica Maya Flores.

Banks
There are a half-dozen banks in Matagalpa—BAC, Banpro, Banexpo, Banco Caley Dagnall, Bancentro, and Banco Mercantíl—and a fistful of money changers that hang out around the southeast corner of Parque Morazán. The banks are mostly clustered in a three-block strip, starting at the southeast corner of Parque Morazán. Nearly all have ATMs.

Internet
The fastest most advanced cybercafe in town is **Matt's Cyber** (located two blocks north of Parque Darío, 8 A.M.–10 P.M.). **CyberCafe Downtown** (a half-block west of the southwest corner of the Parque Darío, open 8:30 A.M.–8 P.M. Mon.–Sat., 10 A.M.–7 P.M. Sun.) is popular and fast. Walking north on the *calle principal,* about halfway to Parque Morazán, you'll find **NetCom** just past La Casona; it provides decent service, and is open 8 A.M.–9 P.M. daily, closing a bit earlier on Saturday and Sunday (8 P.M. and 7 P.M. respectively). One of the fastest servers in town is at **Cybercafe Matagalpa** (a half-block north, one block west from the Palí supermarket, across the street from Mi Favorita store, open 9 A.M.–9 P.M. daily, to 7 P.M. Sun., about $2 an hour), with cheap membership deals available.

Mail and Phones
Correos de Nicaragua Matagalpa (tel. 505/772-4317, open 8 A.M.–12:30 P.M. and 2–5:30 P.M. Mon.–Fri., 8 A.M.–1 P.M. Sat.) is located one block west of Parque Morazán, tucked into a side street that runs south from the main drag. Fax, phone, and mailbox services are available.

There are a number of card-based public phones and BellSouth posts all over town, especially along the main *calle principal,* and the main ENITEL building (open 7 A.M.–9 P.M.) is located to the east of Parque Morazán (look for the big antenna jutting out from the city skyline). Cheap, web-based international call service is available at all three Internet places above.

Laundry
A block and a half east of the Cancha Brigadista is a washer and dryer for rent. It's open 8:30 A.M.–5 P.M. Monday–Saturday and charges $4 a load, including wash, dry, and fold.

Haircuts
The male hairdressers at Max Salon (across from the cinema) are proud, flamboyant, and terribly excited to give you a makeover; let them pamper you with a new 'do, pedicure, and manicure, as they chat away and laugh; expect U.S. or European quality ($8 for a cut and dry, more for coloring and highlights). For a simpler, more old-fashioned cut, try the old-school barber shop next to Mana del Cielo, where a cut and straight-edge shave costs under $4.

Car Rental
Prices are standard. Budget (tel. 505/772-3041 or 505/266-6226, reserve@budget.com.ni) has a small lot at the La Virgen Shell Station, just as you enter town from the south. Dollar (tel. 505/772-4100 or 505/772-4640, $40/day) has an office in the Toyota dealership.

GETTING THERE AND AWAY
From Managua
Express buses from Managua leave the Mayoreo bus terminal every hour 5:30 A.M.–5:30 P.M. The ride takes two hours and costs about $2.50. If heading north from Granada or Masaya, you can bypass Managua by grabbing one of two direct buses from the Masaya

bus terminal, leaving at 5 A.M. and 6 A.M. and taking less than three hours (these are full-size buses and run every day except Thursday and Sunday).

From Other Cities

From León, there are two daily expresses, leaving at 4:30 A.M. and 2:45 P.M.; this ride takes less than three hours and costs about $2.50 per person. Matagalpa-bound buses leave every half hour, starting about 5 A.M. from both Estelí (last bus leaves at 5:45 P.M.) and Jinotega (last bus leaves at 7 P.M.). There is one direct bus from Chinandega to Matagalpa, leaving at 5 A.M.

From Matagalpa

Matagalpa has two bus terminals—which one you head to depends on your destination. At the south end of town, the **COTRAN Sur** (tel. 505/772-4659 or 505/603-0909) services Managua, Estelí, León, Masaya, and Jinotega. There's a public bathroom there ($0.10) and several small eateries.

Express buses to Managua depart every hour 5:15 A.M.–5:15 P.M. Nonexpress Managua-bound buses leave every half hour 3:30 A.M.–6 P.M. Direct buses to Masaya leave at 2 P.M. (daily except Thursday and Sunday).

To León via San Isidro and Telíca, there are two daily expresses, leaving at 6 A.M. and 3 P.M. There are also *interlocales* minivans that leave whenever they fill up; or take any bus bound for Estelí, get off at the Empalme León, and catch a bus to León (departing just about every 20–30 minutes).

There is a constant flow of buses to Estelí and Jinotega, leaving every half hour 5 A.M.–5:40 P.M. (Estelí) and till 6 P.M. (Jinotega). One daily direct bus to Chinandega leaves Matagalpa at 2 P.M.

At the north end of town, the **COTRAN de Guanuca** services the interior of Matagalpa, including El Tuma–La Dália, San Ramón, Río Blanco, Muy Muy, and Bocana de Paíwas.The ride to San Ramón takes about 45 minutes. Road conditions in these areas are bad in the dry season, horrible in the rainy season when bus service sometimes slackens. Buses to points east depart approximately every 15 minutes to an hour until around 4:30 P.M.

GETTING AROUND

Matagalpa is a perfectly good city for walking, except for all those hills, where you'll sweat out all that *fritanga* grease; the taxi fare within town is $0.35. City buses ply three different routes back and forth across town, and cost about $0.10. Particularly useful is the bus route called El Chispa.

Near Matagalpa

Segmented by dozens of rivers—some of which are impassible in the wet season—and bereft of roads throughout much of the area, the lands east of Matagalpa made good training grounds for the guerrillas that followed Fonseca into battle against Somoza's troops in the 1970s. Thirty years later, the *campesino* population has grown but the wild and rugged landscape is as impenetrable as ever. The sparsely populated and mostly undeveloped hillsides that stretch from Matagalpa to the Honduran border vary from dense tropical jungle to pine forest to shallow, bushy hillsides.

EAST OF MATAGALPA

Heading into the geographic heart of the nation, the traveler encounters broad hillsides of shiny coffee bushes beneath shady canopies, plots of corn and beans, and small communities of tile-roofed adobe houses sitting among the rugged mountains that are the eastern reaches of the Cordillera Dariense. The *campesinos* in the folds of these mountains live much the way they have for centuries, even as governments, revolutions, and natural disasters have swirled violently around them.

The major communities of the east, Río

Blanco, Matiguás, and Muy Muy, serve as commercial and transportation centers for the region, and they offer rudimentary accommodations for the traveler. But don't expect any luxury rides here: The roads east of Matagalpa are some of the most neglected in the country, notably the stretch between Siuna and Mulukuku, which is practically impassable during the wettest months of the year. That said, you will be traveling through some of the most beautiful—and least visited—parts of an already undertouristed nation. Except for some fledgling ventures in San Ramón, traditional tourist facilities are nonexistent in the entire region. That shouldn't stop the more adventurous traveler from seeking out some of the following destinations.

THE SAN RAMÓN-MULUKUKU ROAD
San Ramón

Only 12 kilometers from Matagalpa, the village of San Ramón is nestled in a lovely valley at the base of several steep hills. Founded in the late 1800s, San Ramón got its start around the La Leonesa and La Reina gold mines, and today is a peaceful, friendly hamlet, about five blocks square and surrounded on all sides by green farms and forests penetrated by a number of roads and trails. San Ramón has two parks, a health clinic, a gas station, and a number of nonprofit and coffee-related administrative offices. Because of sister-city relationships with Catalan (Spain), Henniker (New Hampshire), and Durham (North Carolina), small groups of wandering foreigners are not uncommon and San Ramón adeptly hosts both foreign groups and individuals in one of several guesthouse and homestay programs.

Use San Ramón as a more rural alternative to Matagalpa (travel to and from the city is a cinch), or sample one of the short local excursions, such as the walk to the La Pita coffee cooperative. On the way, you'll pass the 100-year-old ruins of the Leonesa mine, overtaken by moss, ferns, and giant ceiba trees. **Cesar Davila** (tel. 505/772-9734 work or 505/478-3519 cell) has a privately owned

San Ramón's central plaza is cool and lush.

© JOSHUA BERMAN

MATAGALPA

nature preserve that he has reforested practically right in San Ramón. Cesar, an ex-soldier, is full of stories of the war, and has knowledge about forestry, birds, and herbs. He has built a trail across his lands for a half-hour hike to the point of the cross above San Ramón with beautiful views of surrounding hills.

El Suena de la Campagna (fundacionla campana@gmail.com)—located just down from the gas station, across the creek at the bridge and on the left—is not only a hostel but a Spanish NGO that supports work with children with disabilities in San Ramón as well as a Casa de Cultura. The hostel has 11 rooms from dormitory accommodations for $10 per person to $25 for a private matrimonial. The restaurant has excellent *comida típica,* laundry service, library, Internet, 24-hour reception, and trails on the property. Stay as a guest or get involved in some of the projects.

Find the office of Finca Esperanza Verde (an ecoresort outside town) by walking east from the Shell station past the police station, and through a small gate at the dead end. This is the place to inquire about the **Club de Guías** (trained young guides, $10/day, some with English) and the local **Casa de Huespedes** or guesthouse system (tel. 505/772-5003, U.S. tel. 919/489-1656, www.durham-sanramon.org, fincaesperanza@gmail.com), which offers a secure room, private bath, and three meals for $15 a day.

There are no true restaurants in San Ramón, but plenty of more casual eateries, including tasty *comedores* along the sidewalk across the highway from the Shell station. **Doña Nelys Arauz** serves heaping plates of originally styled Nica food for under $2.

Buses to and from San Ramón are frequent, leaving the Guanuca terminal every hour or more 6 A.M.–7 P.M., in addition to the many other eastbound buses that pass through San Ramón on their way elsewhere. A cab from Matagalpa costs about $3 per person, if you're interested in day- or night-tripping into the city of Matagalpa.

Finca Esperanza Verde

Although its office and many of the community programs it supports are in the village of San Ramón, Finca Esperanza Verde (FEV, tel. 505/772-5003, www.fincaesperanzaverde.org, reservations required) is very much its own destination. A cool, green getaway 18 km east of San Ramón and 1,180 meters above sea level, travelers will find a range of peaceful accommodations, as well as beautiful sunsets, delicious food, and a menu of educational and recreational activities. FEV was conceived by an ex-Peace Corps couple from North Carolina and is closely associated with the Durham, NC–San Ramón Sister City Project; in 2004 FEV won first place in a *Smithsonian Magazine* sustainable tourism contest, and more recently the 2007 Virgin Holidays Responsible Tourism Award for best small hotel. Their coffee is certified as the 10th best coffee in Nicaragua.

The open-air lodge and cabañas have wide, west-facing vistas, surrounded by shade-grown, organic coffee plantations and second-generation cloud forest, through which winds an impressive and varied trail system; hike it on your own or, to see more of the 150 species of birds, howler monkeys, numerous orchids, and medicinal plants, hire one of the farm's guides ($5 per hour, per group, well worth it if you speak Spanish, or want to help them learn English).

Don't miss the day trip to Wabule Falls ($110 for the whole group), which includes a truck for the day, guided hike, picnic lunch, and rope assisted descent into the canyon. FEV's property features several waterfalls, a butterfly house and breeding project (tours $6 pp), and a delicious spring-fed, potable water supply. From November through February, pick, process, and sort the coffee beans, then follow the coffee to Matagalpa where it is sun dried, sorted, graded, cupped, and exported. The farm's all-Nicaraguan staff enjoy teaching visitors about coffee and are proud that their care of the farm makes it a home to hundreds of species of birds, butterflies, mammals, trees, and orchids. Other possible activities include a cooking demonstration and class, and a folk music concert. Or just relax on the hammock terrace watching the jungle and the sunset.

The lodge and cabins, built of handmade brick and other local materials, can accommodate up to 26 people and are equipped with solar electricity, flush toilets, sinks, and warm sun showers. There is a range of accommodations—bunks cost $14 per person, and a private cabin for two with a view, $50, all with private toilet (the bigger your group, the better the deal). Meals ($5–6) include fresh juices, fruits, vegetables, and eggs from neighboring farms, and of course, homegrown organic coffee. A gorgeous camping area features tentsites and a roofed picnic table in the middle of a coffee and banana grove ($6 pp, bring your own gear). You can book a variety of package tours, and get a detailed breakdown of pricing at their website.

If you have a vehicle with moderate clearance (and 4WD for the rainy season), FEV is a 40-minute drive from San Ramón. Follow the road to Yucúl, then turn left and follow the signs to the *finca*. By bus, take the Pancasan/El Jobo bus from the COTRAN Guanuca terminal in Matagalpa, and get off in Yucúl past San Ramón; then follow the signs to FEV, a beautiful 3.5-kilometer uphill walk that should take under an hour. Don't forget a long sleeve shirt and a rain jacket.

Río Blanco and Cerro Musún

Cerro Musún, one of Nicaragua's youngest and least visited parks, encompasses the 1,460 meter peak of the same name and is still the haunt of some of Central America's more elusive mammals, like the puma. In 2004, however, Musín ("water mountain" in Nahuatl) lived up to its name when heavy rains caused several of its lower slopes to collapse, destroying several hillside communities in a massive mudslide.

The town of Río Blanco is your jumping-off point for hikes in this tremendous reserve area. Rest up at **Hotel Bosawas** or **Hotel Nicarao** (both $15 s, a/c, TV) before tackling hikes up

to the seven waterfalls or the peak itself. Your hikes start at the FUNDENIC guide station (about one km out of town), where you can hire a guide to lead you through the reserve (about $6/day).

While you're in town, check out the statues in the Catholic church, artifacts from the pre-Columbian civilizations that occupied these lands. They left behind some petroglyphs at the river's edge (visible only during the dry season). Start searching near the red hanging bridge on the exit to Barrio Martin Centeno.

Two express buses leave for Río Blanco from Managua's Mayoreo terminal around noon; additional service is available from the COTRAN Guanuca in Matagalpa.

Bocana de Paíwas

Bocana de Paíwas has a *hospedaje* and several restaurants, including the well-liked **Restaurante Mirador,** located on a long peninsula overlooking the Río Grande de Matagalpa. This is also the site of some pre-Columbian petroglyphs, tucked into the rocks alongside the Río Grande de Matagalpa.

Mulukuku

Founded primarily to support a Sandinista military base in the 1980s, Mulukuku quickly became a refugee center for those fleeing battles farther north; today's descendants of that time live in a humble but vivacious village on the edge of the mighty Río Tuma.

Mulukuku is well known for one of its expat residents, Doña Dorotea, a nurse born in 1930, who's lived and worked in the community for decades. Because of her work with Sandinista charities, she became a target for former president Alemán's political mischief and blind personal vengeance—he even ordered her deported after falsely accusing her of performing abortions. Over a period of several weeks in 2001, Dorotea's fellow townspeople rallied behind her as Alemán continued threatening to throw her out of Nicaragua and she pleaded that she had nowhere else to go.

Though she was never deported, she spent several frustrating years hassling with her residency permit and is finally back in Mulukuku and continuing her work; Alemán was never asked to explain.

THE EL TUMA– LA DÁLIA ROAD

This paved, patched-together road, usually in a sore state of disrepair, heads due east from the north end of Matagalpa, then curves north, crosses the Río Tuma, and continues to the town of La Dália. From there, it stumbles along as the northern route to Wani and Siuna, first passing through Waslala, which used to be the most populated pueblo east of Matagalpa.

A few kilometers east of the turnoff to San Ramón, look on the left for the **Madre Tierra Panadería** (Mother Earth Bakery, Km 37.5 Carreterra La Dalia, next to CESESMA and La Praga coffee farm, open 8 A.M.–5 P.M. Mon.–Fri.). In the shaded bamboo hut, you'll find mouthwatering home-baked wheat bread, plus yogurt, coffee, and an array of local medicinal herbs and remedies. Under construction at press time, an adjoining bamboo structure plans to house **Tonantzin,** a natural healing, massage, acupuncture, and reflexology center. The **Center for Health and Environmental Educational Services, CESESMA** (tel. 505/772-5842, cesesma@ibw.com.ni), is a nonprofit that provides educational opportunities (theater, dance, crafts, gardening, etc.) for youths in the rural coffee sectors. They accept qualified, long-term (a year or more) volunteers.

Santa Emilia and Salto El Cebollál

The farming community of Santa Emilia is marked by a left turn at about Km 145; a bit farther, you'll find a 15-meter waterfall spilling impressively into a wide hole flanked by thick vegetation and a dark, alluring rock overhang. The falls are known alternately as Salto de Santa Emilia and Salto el Cebollál. Before jumping in, consider that the stream flows through at least one upstream community and may be contaminated. Still, the spray from the falls is refreshing and the site is gorgeous in a romantic, popping-the-question kind of way (if she can hear you over the water's roar, that is). Access is just beyond the Puente Yasica, a bridge at about Km 149; look for a small house and parking area on the right, where a soft-drink sign reads Balneario El Salto de Santa Emilia. You'll be asked to pay a $1 parking fee unless you're just jumping off the Tuma–Dália bus. From there, walk down the steep trail, following the sound of the falls—and don't forget the ring.

Piedra Luna

About 10 kilometers (15 minutes) southwest of the mountain town of La Dália is a top-notch swimming hole called Piedra Luna by the locals. This makes a great day trip from Matagalpa and will give you a chance to appreciate some of the remaining monster trees in the area. Ask your bus driver to let you off at Piedra Luna and descend the steep hillside down to the river's edge. The swimming hole was formed by the waters of the Río Tuma as they swirled around a several-ton rock sitting midstream. The swimming hole is easily seven meters deep, and local kids come from all over to dive off the rock into the pool. How did the rock get there? Ask the locals, who will relate the fantastic legend of the spirits that carried it there from someplace far away. To get there, take any bus from the north terminal at Matagalpa bound for Waslala or El Tuma–La Dália and ask to be let off at Piedra Luna (approximately a one-hour trip from Matagalpa and a 30-minute walk down to the river).

Peñas Blancas

Located on the road that leads between El Tuma–La Dália and El Cuá, the cliffs of Peñas Blancas (1,445 meters) are several hundred meters high and carved out of the top of a massive hillside. This is unquestionably one of the most stunning natural sights in northern Nicaragua. At the top of the cliff is a copious waterfall, gorgeous and little known, even by

El Salto de Santa Emilia

Nicaraguans who live outside of the immediate area. The cliffs and waterfall are easily visible from the highway, next to property owned by Alan Ball. He's currently developing hikes and tours to the waterfall, but you can be proactive and get there yourself by asking around.

Getting there requires some effort, more so if you're using public transportation. Take the El Cuá–Bocay bus from Matagalpa (leaves Guanuca station at 7 A.M.), and about an hour after La Dália get off at the entrance to the reserve and Centro de Entendimiento con la Naturaleza. From there, ask for the best route to the falls. The hike is only possible in the dry season, and there is no well-established trail to the falls. The walk is worth it, as you'll pass through a series of humid forest ecosystems of orchids and mossy trees. Near the falls, the wind is full of spray. The hike up and down can be done in two hours but expect to get extremely muddy and wet. A Matagalpa-bound bus will pass the entrance to the reserve at 2 P.M. Peñas Blancas is run by a *cooperativa* and costs about $5 to go up with a guide. There are screened-in cabins for hikers that want to stay the night.

THE MATAGALPA-JINOTEGA HIGHWAY

The sinuous mountain road between Matagalpa and Jinotega is considered one of the most scenic roads in all of Nicaragua. The road was first opened around 1920 by the English immigrant and coffee farmer Charles Potter for use by mules and wagons taking coffee from his farm to Matagalpa. No small feat of engineering, the road had to negotiate over 100 curves, the worst of which was the Disparate de Potter (still legendary). A stubborn old man, Potter built his road in spite of the naysayers, and it's

The lodge at Selva Negra is one of Nicaragua's most established tourist destinations.

said he used the road to carry a piano—strung atop two mules—all the way to his farm.

The long valley panoramas are often breathtaking: Momotombo and the Maribio Volcanoes are visible when the sky is clear. You'll pass neatly arranged coffee plantations shaded by windrows of cedar and pine, banana trees, and canopies of precious hardwoods. There is also an endless succession of vegetable and flower fields, and roadside stands that sell farm-fresh goods. Should you take the express bus, you'll miss the opportunity to stop and take photographs, buy fresh vegetables, and hike into the coffee plantations. But if you drive, you may need to concentrate on the road so much that you'll miss the scenery. The best alternative is to take it easy: Hop on and off passing buses and offered rides over the course of an afternoon, enjoying the following sights until you get to Jinotega.

Mirador de La Chispa (Km 133)

Just three kilometers outside of the city of Matagalpa, La Chispa is an impressive overlook on the right side of the highway, with a view of the city.

◖ Hotel de Montaña Selva Negra (Km 140)

The entrance to Selva Negra is marked by an old military tank on the side of the road, a relic from the revolution and painted over with the rainbows of Doña Violeta's UNO coalition in the early 1990s. The Black Forest Montain Resort has been an anchor in Nicaragua's tourism scene since well before there ever *was* a tourism scene. It remains popular for people looking to hike, dine, monkey-watch, or even tie the knot. Hotel de Montaña Selva Negra (tel. 505/772-3883/5713, reservaciones@selva negra.com, www.selvanegra.com) is located at

Km 140 on the highway between Matagalpa and Jinotega. It is, at its heart, a coffee farm by the name of La Hammonia, owned and run by Eddy Kühl and Mausi Hayn, third- and fourth-generation German immigrants and members of the founding families of the country's coffee industry. The farm—considered one of the most diversified in Central America, and winner of the 2007 Sustainability Award from the Specialty Coffee Association of America—is based on the German tradition of chalets set around a peaceful pond with access to short hiking trails up the adjoining 120-hectare hillside and along its ridge. Rooms run from $8 for a spot in the youth hostel to $35 for a double overlooking the lake, or $60 for a private bungalow. There are larger bungalows for groups and families. The restaurant serves hearty, home-cooked meals using organic ingredients produced entirely on the farm; you'll dine on a gorgeous outdoor patio overlooking the water. Needless to say, the coffee is superb and fresh (and sold at Whole Foods Market in the United States).

© JAMES SAVAGE

the Cloudforest Chapel at Selva Negra

The *finca* is a birder's paradise with some 200 species of birds that have been identified. You can see a list of identified bird species on their website, and try to spot them with one of the professionally trained bird guides. Tours of the coffee farm, flower plantations, the cattle, and livestock start at 9 A.M. and 3 P.M.—in Spanish, English and German when Mausi is available. Almost everything on the farm is recycled even down to using the plastic bottles as pest control. The tour is an amazing education in permaculture and innovative organic methods. Or you can easily rent a horse for the day and ride the many roads that crisscross the plantation on your own. In 2000, the Kühls built a gorgeous, orchid-adorned stone chapel for the wedding of their daughter, and they now rent out the facilities—chapel, horse-drawn carriage, and fresh-cut flowers—for guests who come to get hitched.

Expect to have a chat with the owners while you're there—Eddy is a wealth of knowledge, a prolific writer, and a well-loved amateur anthropologist; many of the family's ideas have come from the suggestions and talent of the guests who visit them. Especially charming is the original *finca* house built by Otto Bosch in 1893. To get to Selva Negra, take any bus from Matagalpa heading to Jinotega. They'll let you off at the entrance to the hotel.

Also, you can arrange tours and buy their coffee from their daughter's U.S. coffeehouse in Atlanta, Georgia: Java Beano (www.java beano.com).

Disparate de Potter (Km 143)

This was the worst, rockiest curve of all the obstacles that Charles Potter faced when building the road between Matagalpa and his farm La Fundadora. There was no way around the rock that made up that part of the mountain, so he stubbornly blasted his way straight through it. The hill's two pieces remain exactly as he left them, with the single addition of a lookout platform on the needle of rock left standing on the outside of the curve. At the side of the road is a well-liked restaurant serving traditional Nicaraguan food. It's open 8:30 A.M.–8 P.M. daily, and serves meals in the $4–6 range, as well as snacks and beverages to accompany the amazing vista from the dining room. Climbing the stairs to the platform is well worth the small fee ($0.30 pp). Ask about the country house for rent at the Finca Peor es Nada, a fully furnished ranch with private bedrooms for up to three couples, $200 per weekend (tel. 505/772-2553, speak with Delia Pérez)

Santa Lastenia (Km 148)

At 1,555 meters above sea level, Santa Lastenia is the highest point along the road, after which one drops rather precipitously into the valley of Jinotega.

Vegetable Stands (Km 152)

Jinotega and Matagalpa are the two most copious producers of vegetables in Nicaragua, and a set of small farm stands along the road are evidence of the rich harvests of this area. Whether you want to eat them or just photograph them, the stacks of fresh cabbage, carrots, broccoli, radishes, beets, lettuce, squash, and greens are a culinary feast for the eyes. The stands are typically run by the family's older children, who might just sweet-talk you into making a purchase.

Jinotega City

When walking the cobbled streets of Jinotega, you can't help but feel you're at the edge of the world, with all kinds of unknowns in the hills to the north and east. Medieval mapmakers would have emblazoned the valley of Jinotega with "Beyond Here Lie Dragons," referring to the hundreds of kilometers of wild, lush mountain country that beckon to the east. East of the city the pavement stops, the roads turn rutted and bumpy, bus service is less frequent, and the accommodations dwindle— at least the kind where they leave a mint on your pillow and fold the edge of the toilet paper into a little triangle. But the immense department of Jinotega is comprised of hundreds of small communities and thousands of farmers who make their livelihood in the hills around them—including many who have barely ever traveled beyond this land in their lives. Jinotega is replete with fragrant valleys of orange groves, white corn, plantains, sweet vegetables, and a whole lot of cattle. But in between the small farms, Jinotega is open space—virgin forest, small freshwater lagoons, stately mountain ranges, and some of the loveliest rivers in Nicaragua, including the mighty Río Coco (which forms the northern border of the Jinotega department) and the Río Bocay, one of the Coco's most important tributaries.

Jinotega, or La Ciudad de las Brumas (The City of Mists), is the watering hole and commercial center for the department of the same name. Farmers from the north and east inevitably find their way here to do their business and trading, and Jinotega City has built itself into a clean, prosperous community around the business needs of those farmers. It's a working town whose streets are lined with cobblers, tailors, barbers, blacksmiths, watch repairmen, and merchants that deal in housewares, veterinary supplies, saddles, cowboy hats, firearms, auto parts, and an endless stock of farming tools. It's a town very much in tune with the rugged and self-sufficient life of the Nicaraguan *campesino,* and you will learn much just by wandering its streets among such hardy characters. Jinotega, your gateway to the wide-open expanses of the east, is at once charming and thrilling. As late as the mid-1960s, it wasn't uncommon to find wild monkeys in the old-growth park canopy of *lechito* trees.

Travelers enjoy Jinotega because its high elevation (a full kilometer above sea level) gives it a pleasant climate, especially nice in the

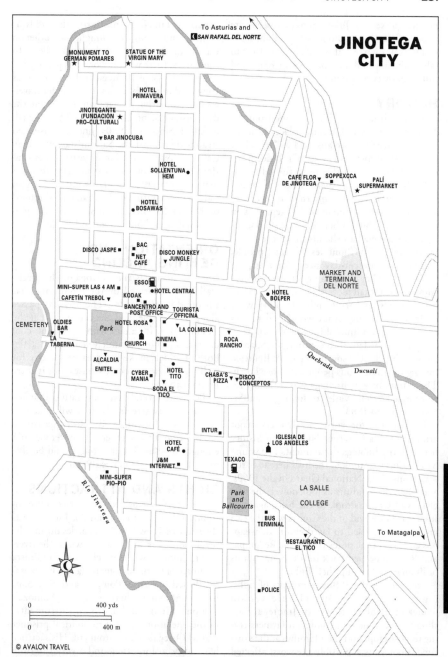

JINOTEGA CITY

To Asturias and
◄ SAN RAFAEL DEL NORTE

MONUMENT TO
GERMAN POMARES ★

STATUE OF THE
VIRGIN MARY ★

HOTEL
PRIMAVERA ●

JINOTEGANTE
(FUNDACIÓN ★
PRO-CULTURAL)

▼ BAR JINOCUBA

HOTEL
SOLLENTUNA
HEM ●

CAFÉ FLOR
DE JINOTEGA ▼

SOPPEXCCA ■

PALÍ
SUPERMARKET ★

HOTEL
BOSAWAS ●

DISCO JASPE ■

BAC ■
NET
CAFÉ ■

DISCO MONKEY
▼ JUNGLE

MARKET AND
TERMINAL
DEL NORTE

MINI-SUPER LAS 4 AM ■

CAFETÍN TREBOL ▼

ESSO ⛽
● HOTEL CENTRAL

KODAK ■

BANCENTRO AND
POST OFFICE ■

TOURISTA
OFFICINA ■

HOTEL
● BOLPER

CEMETERY

OLDIES
BAR ▼

LA ▼
TABERNA

Park

HOTEL ROSA ●

CHURCH

CINEMA ■

▼ LA COLMENA

ROCA
▼ RANCHO

Quebrada

Ducualí

ALCALDIA ■

ENITEL ■

CYBER
MANIA ■

HOTEL
● TITO

SODA EL ▼
TICO

CHABA'S ▼
PIZZA

▼ DISCO
CONCEPTOS

INTUR ■

HOTEL
CAFÉ ●

J&M
INTERNET ■

TEXACO
⛽

IGLESIA DE
✝ LOS ANGELES

MINI-SUPER
PIO-PIO ■

Río Jinotega

Park
and
Ballcourts

LA SALLE

COLLEGE

● BUS
TERMINAL

▼ RESTAURANTE
EL TICO

To Matagalpa ▼

● POLICE

0   400 yds

0   400 m

© AVALON TRAVEL

picturesque setting. Jinoteganos themselves are at once friendly and aloof—they might leave you to your own, but if you make the effort to talk to them, you'll find them warm, open, and full of country hospitality.

HISTORY

The name Jinotega is said to come from the Nahuatl name Xilotl-Tecatl ("place of the ji-ñocuabo trees"; also translated as "the place of the eternal men and women"). Indeed, the natives who lived in this peaceful valley enjoyed healthy and prosperous existences and were known to live to more than 100 years of age. Today's department of Jinotega was in those days the border between two diverse indigenous peoples: to the north, in the Bocay region, lived the Chontales (Kiribie) people, and near the present-day city of Jinotega, the Chorotega. They were an agricultural people who lived off small plots of corn, beans, cacao, roots, tubers, and fruit orchards. They wove their own clothing from wood and cotton fiber, as well as animal skins tinted with plant extracts. In the late 18th century, the Spanish chose to inhabit the southern part of Jinotega, forcing the indigenous peoples to move north. The community of Jinotega was officially recategorized as The Valley of Jinotega in 1851, and as a city in 1883.

For better or for worse, nearly every major armed uprising in recent Nicaraguan history began in the Jinotega department. The young Sandinistas first took to the hills here to battle squadrons of the National Guard in the 1960s, and when the Sandinistas took power, the first groups of Contras took to the hills, again in Jinotega. At the end of the Contra war, the two groups that refused to lay down their weapons and accept the peace treaty (the Recompas and Recontras) fled back into the mountains of Jinotega to keep up their fight.

For most of the 1990s, remnants of fighting groups, like FUAC, plagued certain wilder areas of northeastern Jinotega, hassling the peace-loving Jinotegan farmers trying to raise crops and their families at the same time. Jinotega was possibly the worst affected

department in Nicaragua during the 1980s, as Contras and Sandinistas fought each other on the mountain roads and the deep valleys. In those days, there was only one bus per day between the city of Jinotega and Managua (as compared to one every hour now), and travelers intent on driving their own vehicles ran the daily risk of being ambushed, robbed, raped, or killed. Since the 1980s, Jinotega has voted steadfastly against the Sandinistas, who they claim are responsible for 10 years of devastation. The survivors of the generation that was marched off to the mountains as machine-gun fodder are resentful and frustrated now, robbed of their adolescence, and desperately trying to make a decent, honest living off the land.

ORIENTATION AND GETTING AROUND

Jinotega occupies the bottom of the steep-walled bowl formed by the mountains that surround it on all sides. The highway passes along its east side, and the cemetery is at the western edge. It's a city with a pleasant, cool climate and not too much vehicular traffic, both of which make it a pleasurable city for walking. There are no city buses, nor is there need for them.

There are several taxi cooperatives that circulate the city streets and that will take you across town for $0.35. But Jinotega isn't a big place, and the temperature never gets hot enough to be unpleasant. You should be able to walk anywhere you need to go.

SIGHTS AND ATTRACTIONS

There are few traditional tourist sights in Jinotega, but lots to see and do. Jinotega was the scene of a few ferocious battles during the revolution years, and it was down by the riverside in Jinotega where much-loved Sandinista commander German Pomares (a.k.a. El Danto) was killed in battle. Pomares and his troops had fought many battles against Somoza's National Guard and had been instrumental in the operation that led to political prisoner Daniel Ortega's release from jail. His sacrifice has not been forgotten, and a very carefully maintained red-and-black memorial marks the spot where he was killed.

Don Pilo is a second-generation medicine man who lives in an unknown location in the mountains west of Jinotega city. Twice weekly, he climbs down out of the mountains with his bags of herbs and potions and sets up camp at the cemetery to sell them. He's a well-loved town character who some put off as a charlatan, and others consider a true magician and physician. Regardless, both rich and poor wait for him Tuesdays and Fridays to see if he can cure their ills, from intestinal parasites and coughs to bad marriages, naughty children, and spurned lovers. And you don't need a prescription, just a strong stomach. The cures are all natural and brewed out of the stronger medicinal plants of the region, plus bark, moss, and sometimes even soil.

The town cemetery is an interesting place to wander. The graves started at the entrance to the cemetery and have worked their way south over time. The victims of the war in the 1980s are located at the south end of the plot. Some of the older gravestones are particularly ornate and well crafted in stone.

Festivals and Celebrations

Jinotega's *fiestas patronales* begin on May 1 and continue through May 15. You can expect to see folks from all over the north of Nicaragua showing up for the occasion. The *fiestas patronales* of San Juan de Jinotega are June 24. In addition (perhaps just to round out the year with parties), the Aniversario de la Creación del Departamento de Jinotega is celebrated on October 15.

ENTERTAINMENT AND NIGHTLIFE

The best bar in town, and a common expat hangout, is **La Taberna** (on the right just before the cemetery gate, open daily except Mon.) serving food, booze, and a list of unique cocktails. This place takes the cowboy motif to an extreme with a woven bamboo roof and barstools with saddles. However, the carefully partitioned and cozy feel lends a romantic

air. Also a friendly bar, **Roca Rancho** (a couple blocks east of the park across from the Beneficio Ducalí, tel. 505/782-3730, open noon–midnight daily) is a unique space where the Victoria flows smoothly and you sit in a kingly, high-backed bar stool.

There are two small discos in town. Start with the tried-and-true **Conceptos,** not far from the center of town, formerly a house but was converted into a dance hall with a house-party feel. Newer and more modern **Monkeys Jungle** is a half-block north of the downtown Esso in an old theater. For a surprising scene ("reminiscent of Los Angeles in 1982," wrote one reader), the **Oldies Bar** features music from the 1970s and '80s; food is served, and the lighting and bright white decor combined with occasional dry ice create a serious *Saturday Night Fever* set (open 2:30 P.M.–1 A.M., closed Tues.).

SPORTS AND RECREATION

Basketball is the game of choice in Jinotega, and there are pickup games most evenings on the *cancha* (town court). Jinotega has an active youth league and both women's and men's teams; the players are better than you'd expect, if you're thinking about getting in a game.

Hikes from Town

The western wall of the Jinotega valley makes a popular climb for a Saturday morning. Start at the cemetery and work your way upward to Peña de la Cruz, where the cross is planted. Depending on how ambitious you are, the hike is 30–90 minutes, and you'll be rewarded with an impressive view of the city and the verdant valley of Jinotega. The cross isn't the original—locals say its predecessor was bigger and "better"—but the modern cross is illuminated, thanks to an electric cable that climbs the same steep hillside you just did. Look for the shining beacon of Christianity at night from the city. During misty nights, it's particularly eerie, emitting a diffuse white glow through the mists.

The eastern wall of the valley is steeper and longer, and there are no trails. That doesn't stop many locals from making their way to the top for a look around. Plan on two hours for this one. The easiest way to do it is the steep, windy dirt road that climbs abruptly out of the city and snakes its way to the top of the ridge. By road, it's around an hour on foot, but it's still not an easy walk, as the road is exceptionally steep. Watch your step on loose gravel.

ACCOMMODATIONS

Keep in mind that Jinotega's chief clientele are the small-scale farmers of the east who come in for weekends at a time to see a dentist, sell some corn, and have their boots fixed. They don't require many luxuries and don't want to waste too many *córdobas* while they're in town, as evidenced by all the under-$2 *hospedajes* that spot the neighborhood around the market. The following are some more "upscale" options. As you choose your lodging, remember to ask about hot water, which you will appreciate here more than in other parts of the country—Jinotega is chilly.

Under $10

Hotel Rosa (tel. 505/782-2472) is the oldest gig in town, and a hundred years ago, when it first opened its doors, it was the only gig in town. Its 19th-century feel remains in massive wooden beams, simple rustic rooms, and a laid-back atmosphere. Somewhat dark and dingy, the 30 rooms cost $2–3 per person.

El Hotelito (just east of the park, next to Sopas Coyote's Bar, tel. 505/782-2079) has 10 rooms with tiled floors, comfy-looking beds, and shared baths for about $4 per person. It closes its doors at 10 P.M.; knock to be let in after-hours.

Toward the north end of town, but still in a quiet residential area, **Hotel Primavera** (tel. 505/782-2400) is run by a family that expects you to behave; 28 small rooms set around a courtyard are nothing special, but they're clean, simple, and cheap—$3.50 per person. There are rooms with private bath for a relatively steep $10. Inside the family's living room, there's a pay phone available. The doors close at

10 P.M. and don't open until morning—make sure you're on the right side of the door and mind the sign No Women of Bad or Dubious Conduct.

$10-25

Hotel Central (only a block from the park, tel. 505/782-2063, $14) is indeed central and features a massive lobby leading back to 23 well-lit rooms not much larger than their beds. There are nice rooms upstairs with cable TV, private bath, and hot water; meals are available at the dining room for around $2 each. Both the hotel and restaurant are closed Sundays.
Hotel Fuente (located on the south side of the El Carmen Shell station, tel. 505/782-2966) has 13 clean but loudly-furnished rooms with old art deco furniture, private baths, hot water, and TV for $12 single or double. The owner tries very hard (there's even a suggestion box in the hallway!).

Hotel Sollentuna Hem is owned by a Swedish-Nica woman (the name is Swedish for home of the green valley). In business since 1988, the hotel has 17 different rooms (Scandinavian clean, with a unique, mismatched style) with private baths and hot water for $8–25. Meals are available for $2 breakfast, $3 lunch and dinner, and she can accommodate vegetarians. Complete laundry service is also available, as are tours of her farm on the outskirts of town.

$25-50

Jinotega's classiest accommodations, the ◖ **Hotel Café** (one block west, a half-block north of the Texaco station, tel. 505/782-2710, www.cafehoteljinotega.com, $60) stands heads and shoulders above the rest with its 16 tidy, comfortable, and tastefully decorated rooms, taking up two stories and surrounding a lush garden and spiral staircase. The rooms feature private baths, hot water, cable TV, telephones, desks, and air-conditioning; minisuites for a few bucks more, continental breakfast included. You'll find valet parking and laundry service. Hotel Café accommodates groups and has a conference room, business center, and some great views of the surrounding city and countryside, as well as Jinotega's nicest restaurant and bar. Hotel staff can assist in planning your visit and tours of the area.

FOOD

Meals are simple but hearty in this neck of the woods. After dark, the streets fill with *fritangas,* and families open their front doors to create cheap eateries in their living rooms and front parlors. You can eat your way to greasy happiness for under $2 with no effort at all. Start at the southeast corner of the park and troll the two main streets through a sea of enchiladas, *papas rellenas* (stuffed and fried potatoes), and *gallo pinto* (the national dish of rice and beans).

Soda El Tico, a local lunch favorite, is just east of the park and has a clean and inexpensive lunch buffet and simple menu. Meals go for around $3–7. **Cafetería Trebol** is a popular, charming option with a simple menu of burgers, chicken, and sandwiches; located on the north side of the park, this is a great place to enjoy a hot chocolate or *café con leche* with a plate of French toast. It's open for breakfast at 8:30 A.M., 11 A.M. on Sunday.

Look for **Chaba's Pizza** (2.5 blocks east of the park, next door to Dance Magic, tel. 505/782-2692, open 11 A.M.–10:30 P.M. Tues.–Sun.), serving a variety of thin-crust pies for $7–11, delivery service anywhere in town. You'll find excellent, reasonably priced meals and a friendly open-air atmosphere at **Roca Rancho** (tel. 505/782-3730, open noon–midnight daily); local volunteers rave about the jalapeño steak here.

Restaurante La Colmena (The Beehive) is one of the nicest restaurants in town with a menu of beef, chicken, and fish ($5–9), good service, and a pleasant atmosphere. But a close rival is the **Restaurante Borbón** at the Hotel Café, with sandwiches and meals $6–12, and a full wine and foreign drink list at the bar; the chicken cordon bleu is spectacular.

As you enter town from Matagalpa look for the corner building on your left before you get to the Texaco. About 15 minutes on the highway before Jinotega is **La Perrera,** a bar and restaurant owned by an American-trained chef.

For baked goods hit **Repostería Silvia** next to the BAC, and be sure not to miss ◖ **Cafe Flor de Jinotega,** located next to the Soppexcca coffee exchange, a small-scale coffee producers' cooperative. Here you can have a cappuccino as good as in Nicaragua, check out educational displays on coffee, and coffee economics, and check out packages as they're sold in the U.S. Hit it before or after you get on the bus for the hinterlands at COTRAN Norte.

INFORMATION AND SERVICES

There are two bilingual websites about the city: **www.jinotega.com** and **www.jinotegalife .com.** Also check out the **Alianza Turística,** one block east and one block south of the church.

Not only does Luis Lautaro Ruiz (tel. 505/ 782-4460, lautaror@ibw.com.ni) seemingly know all there is to know about his native Jinotega and the surrounding mountains, he speaks some English and is a professional writer, film producer, musician, and clown. He is a flexible freelance tour guide and will charge comparable prices to guides in Managua ($15–20 a day). He also claims his house, located a half-block north of the Escuela Mistral, is a museum.

Banks

There's a bank on practically every corner in Jinotega. All the major players are present— Banpro, Bancentro, BAC, and more. Bank hours are standard; check your firearm at the door, please. The most reliable ATM is found at BAC, 1.5 blocks north of the central park.

Internet

Rates are standard at about $0.75 per hour. **Cybermania,** across from Soda El Tico is the largest in town with the fastest connection.

J&M Internet Café (three blocks south of the park) has five machines, and a scanner and CD burner are also available. **NetCafe** (across the street from Restaurante/Disco Jun Shan, open 8 A.M.–10 P.M. daily) has speedy service.

Phone and Mail

The ENITEL office is located just north of the park along the main street. It's open 7 A.M.–5 P.M. daily. The post office (open 8 A.M.–4 P.M.) is a bit hard to find: It's tucked into a business complex behind Bancentro. As you're facing the front door of the bank, look for a sidewalk that leads behind the building to the offices that are part of the same complex. A fax machine is available.

GETTING THERE AND AWAY

Buses at the Terminal del Sur head south to Matagalpa and Managua, including several express buses that make one stop along the highway at Matagalpa without entering the city itself, then continue straight on to Managua. Express buses to Managua ($4) leave every hour, and more express buses are being put into service every day, so ask ahead of time to find out what your options are. These buses may or may not make a brief stop along the highway at Matagalpa before continuing straight on to Managua (3–4 hours).

To Points South

The bus terminal (actually, just a parking lot) is located across from La Salle (a Catholic high school). Several eateries line the road behind the station, where you can relax and wait for the bus to leave, as the terminal doesn't have any facilities for passengers. Buses to Matagalpa leave every half hour 5 A.M.–6 P.M. (the trip takes one hour). Buses leave for Estelí from the COTRAN Norte on a long, roundabout overland route that may require making a connection in La Concordia or San Rafeal del Norte. It is much easier to get to Estelí by simply taking any Managua bus to Sébaco, and transfer to a northbound bus heading to Estelí, Ocotal, Somoto, or Jalapa.

To Points North and East

Buses at the Terminal del Norte go to points inland in Jinotega and beyond, including El Cuá, San José de Bocay, San Rafael del Norte, and Wiwilí. This is where the adventures start, and the rugged conditions at the terminal should prepare you mentally for what awaits you inland: mud, livestock, and a lot of friendly people moving sacks of produce, selling grains and cheap merchandise, and laughing. There are five express buses for Estelí at 5:15 A.M., 7 A.M., 9 A.M., 1 P.M., and 3:30 P.M. There are 10 regular buses for San Rafeal del Norte, starting at 6 A.M. with the last bus at 6 P.M. Regular buses for Wiwilí leave starting at 4 A.M. then 6:30 A.M., 8:45 A.M., 11 A.M., and 1:15 P.M. (seven hours). Regular service to El Cuá–Bocay at 4 A.M., 5 A.M., 6:30 A.M., 10 A.M., and noon (four hours). There is regular service to Pantasma about once per hour (4.5 hours) until 4:40 P.M. Pantasma buses go past Asturias and the dam at Lago Apanás.

The northern terminal also has regular bus service to San Sebastián de Yalí and La Rica, via San Rafael del Norte and La Concordia, from where you can get back-road bus service to Estelí—a fun way to make a loop through some really beautiful country.

NORTH AND EAST OF JINOTEGA
El Valle de Tomatoya

Located just north of the city of Jinotega on the road to San Rafael del Norte, this is the home of a women's cooperative that produces the region's famous black pottery. The production of black pottery is a little more intricate than other types of ceramic arts, and these women have produced some very beautiful pieces of art, including faithful replicas of some pre-Columbian designs. **Grupo de Mujeres de Las Cureñas** has some fine pieces for sale.

Along the highway is **El Centro Recreativo de Tomatoya,** a bathing area created by damming up the San Gabriel stream. Your host, Blanca Dalla Torre, regularly empties out the pool and lets it refill with fresh water. Drinks and snacks are available, as well as a complete selection of beer.

Lago de Apanás and the Mancotal Dam

Lake Apanás is the largest artificially constructed body of water in Nicaragua. Luís Somoza Debayle's administration created it in 1964 by damming the Río El Tuma, flooding the broad valley just north of Jinotega, which until that time was pasture, small farms, and an airstrip that serviced the north of Nicaragua. Today, Lake Apanás is a long, irregularly shaped lake. It feeds the twin turbines at the Planta Hidroelectrica Centroamérica, which produces 15 percent of the nation's hydropower (downstream along the Río Viejo, the same water passes through the turbines at Santa Bárbara and Lago La Virgen, which produce an additional 15 percent). Apanás is not a typical reservoir; unlike many hydropower plants that are located at the dam itself, the Planta Centroamérica is located at the upstream end of the lake, so keeping the lake full is essential. The water passes underneath the highway through massive steel pipes where it drops and passes through the turbines. The hydropower project actually forces the water to change watersheds: Water from the Río El Tuma watershed is discharged into the tributaries of the Río Viejo, where it flows south to Lake Xolotlán (Managua) instead of the Atlantic coast.

Hurricane Mitch nearly sent the whole works downstream in 1998, when waters overtopping the "morning glory" spillway (the concrete structure that looks like a flying saucer on its head in the middle of the lake), flowed through the secondary spillway under the bridge, and down a long stair-step energy dissipater. The volume of water rushing through the channel quickly eroded it away along with all of its concrete, nearly destroying the dam itself and nearly causing a wall of water that would have raged for hundreds of kilometers downstream. The loss of the lake would have been economically catastrophic, affecting irrigation, fishing, and hydropower production, not to mention the loss of life and property downstream on the Río El Tuma. The government has been negotiating since 1999 to find a way to repair the spillway and return the dam's safety structures to normal, while the IMF and World Bank have been trying to privatize the whole system.

To get to the dam, take any bus headed toward Pantasma and get off at Asturias (60–90 minutes from Jinotega). The highway crosses the dam, so you'll know when you've arrived. The lake itself is picturesque, but equally impressive are the remains of the damaged spillway. On the lake side of the road are the remains of an old military base built in the 1980s to prevent Contra troops from destroying the dam. (The Planta Centroamérica was a highly sought Contra target in the 1980s and was similarly tightly guarded to prevent its destruction. Some land mines still litter the hills around the hydropower plant.)

You can fish here, for giant tilapia and guapote, or take a dip. There are several grassy areas at the lake's edge where you can jump in the surprisingly cold water of Apanás. From the dam, walk along the highway in either direction and choose your place. The lake is safe— there are no underwater structures or water intakes to be afraid of, and the water is quite deep and refreshing. Obviously, stay away from the spillover drain.

Lago Asturias and the El Dorado Dam

The El Dorado dam was completed in 1984 and filled in 1985 as a supplement to the Mancotal Dam. Water is captured in Asturias and pumped up to Apanás, where it flows through the turbines for energy production. Anglers in the know realize that Asturias is home to some monster freshwater fish. To get there from the Mancotal Dam, walk back toward the city of Jinotega about one kilometer to the first major intersection. That road descends quickly past a few coffee farms and small farming communities to the El Dorado Dam.

BEN LINDER

As the only reported incident in which a United States citizen was killed by Contra soldiers, Benjamin Linder's death had enormous repercussions, stemming primarily from the fact that he was shot with weaponry purchased by his own government, and by soldiers carrying out a hotly contested policy of violence supported by the same government. Linder's death was elevated to the status of martyrdom by those that shared his values. He was one individual in a huge wave of international supporters of the Sandinista revolution, leftists from Europe and North America who saw a chance to take part in the real-world political laboratory of Nicaragua. Some came to make a stand against the policies of the Reagan administration; some to physically help as development workers, teachers, and coffee pickers; and some came simply to experience the new world order at ground level.

Oregon native Ben Linder graduated from the University of Washington in 1983 with a degree in mechanical engineering, and because he believed in the ideals of the revolution, came to Nicaragua like thousands of other *internacionalistas* to help the revolution reach the poor. He moved to Nicaragua shortly after graduation, where he shared a small apartment in the capital and worked for the electric company. In his free time he would delight the Nicaraguan children by dressing up in a clown suit and rubber nose and pedalling around on a unicycle.

In mid-1985 Linder moved to Jinotega to help install a minihydroelectric plant in the town of El Cuá. This was an area overrun with raiding Contra, and the danger in the region was real. But rather than avoid the danger, his engineer's passion for solving problems led him farther into the bush, to San José de Bocay, to repeat the success he'd had at El Cuá. Bocay was even farther out of Sandinista control than El Cuá, and the Contra were everywhere. On April 28, 1987, Linder and a crew of Nicaraguans went into the field to build a small concrete weir that would measure the flow in a stream Linder thought would be a good site for a hydroelectric plant. His crew crossed paths with a squadron of Contra that had been stalking Sandinista supporters. He, and several others with him, were assassinated at point blank range by a bullet to the temple.

The political repercussions were enormous and the Sandinistas, the Contras, and the U.S. government all angrily accused each other. Though the Contras claimed that Linder had been dressed in combat uniform, was carrying a weapon, and that Linder's team had fired the first shots, the evidence did not support it. That an American had been killed in Nicaragua, with a bullet also paid for by the American people, resonated deeply.

Linder was buried in a small, neat grave in the Matagalpa cemetery. Today, his legend and inspiration live on; if you wander through the peaceful community of San José de Bocay, you'll notice the town has been electrified, courtesy of the Benjamin Linder Mini-Hydroelectric Power Plant, constructed after his death. The Benjamin Linder School is down the road, and one of Bocay's more newly settled neighborhoods was christened Barrio Benjamin Linder.

In the early 1990s, when the Sandinistas handed power over to Doña Violeta's administration and it became obvious the great socialist revolution of the 1980s was not to be, most of the international crowd packed up and returned home, but what Ben Linder set out to do – bring progress and hope to the people whose lives are the most difficult – is an ideal that did not die with the revolution.

Today, the Asociación de Trabajadores de Desarrollo Rural Benjamin Linder (The Benjamin Linder Association of Development Workers) continues to do what Linder was doing the day he was killed: build small-scale hydroelectric plants to promote rural development. The association is located 25 meters south of the Hotel Bermúdez in Matagalpa (tel. 505/612-2030) and is managed by Linder's coworker Rebecca Leaf. To learn more about Ben, visit the Quaker House in Managua, the Ben Linder Café in León, or read the book, *The Death of Ben Linder: The Story of a North American in Sandinista Nicaragua* by Joan Kruckewitt (Seven Stories Press, 2001).

El Dorado also experienced severe damage during Hurricane Mitch. As you look at the lake, imagine that the same massive deluge that destroyed Mancotal's spillway also flowed through that placid little lake and out the other side—then appreciate how fortunate it is to have withstood the hurricane.

There's a little grassy hill on the upstream side of the dam where you can pitch a tent and do some fishing. If you'd like to try to hitch a ride with all your catch, occasional vehicles transit this road—mostly old IFAs and pickup trucks—bound for the communities east of El Dorado.

◖ San Rafael del Norte

This remote, cloud-shrouded town has a cool climate and is surrounded by green hills year-round.

To know San Rafael is to know history. A visit to the **General Augusto César Sandino Museum** (right off the park) gives you a sample of the small town's pride at having served as the proving grounds for the general's legendary battles with the U.S. Marines in the 1930s. Sandino's wife was a San Rafaelina, and Nicaraguan folk musician Carlos Mejía Godoy wrote moving lyrics about love and war in Sandino's hills there.

There are some precious swimming holes around San Rafael, the easiest of which to access are in the two creeks that meet at **Los Encuentros** restaurant, a 10-minute walk on the road to Yalí. You can also hike into the gorge that runs on the north edge of town; descend from the Hospedaje Rolinmar, and then start upstream to where cold water rushes out of a narrow canyon.

La Iglesia de San Rafael del Norte is more impressive than you'd expect for such an out-of-the-way town; some call it the most beautiful church in all of Nicaragua. Pastel-colored windows admit a calming light in which to view the many bright murals, reliefs, and shrines. Many locals distinguish between Sandino the man and Sandinismo as practiced by Daniel Ortega. Look closely at the inside left wall of the church, where a painting of the devil implies that Daniel has betrayed the ideals of Sandino.

The church was a project of Italian priest Odorico d'Andrea who gave much more than that to this town. From his arrival in 1953 to his death in 1996, Father Odorico achieved virtual sainthood among the people of San Rafael and surrounding communities. His image, a smiling man in plain brown robes, can be seen in nearly every home, business, and vehicle in the town. Among his achievements are a health clinic, library, several neighborhoods for the poor, and the renovation of the church. Odorico's soul has multiplied posthumously; many believe he performed miracles and that his body has not decomposed. You can check for yourself at its resting place, called the **Tepeac,** on the hill overlooking the town. Ascending the stairs, you'll pass the 12 stations of the cross until you reach the shrine on top where the tomb lies—as well as gorgeous views. An impressive stand of old trees shades the hilltop. Virgin pine forests carpet the countryside.

There are great eats at **Doña Chepita's,** and there are two places to stay: ◖ **Hotel Casito San Payo** (2.5 blocks north of the park) is a cute family-run place that doubles as a local watering hole. A room will run you $10 and you can get meals here as well. **Comedor y Hospedaje Aura** (on main street east of church) is a typical Nicaraguan *hospedaje* catering more to the traveling *campesino* than foreign traveler.

Near San Rafael del Norte is the ecotourism project **Finca el Jaguar** (tel. 505/279-9219, www.jaguarreserve.org), a 105-hectare stretch of land, of which 60 percent is cloud forest. The *finca* was established to monitor over-wintering survival of migratory birds, and now offers a variety of lodging options. They require reservations at least 10 days in advance—a unique way to get under the forest canopy.

Buses pass through San Rafael del Norte regularly on the route between Jinotega and San Sebastián de Yalí/La Rica. There is also one express bus to Managua that leaves at 4:30 A.M.,

boat traffic on the Río Bocay

passes through Jinotega at 5:30 A.M., and continues south through Matagalpa to Managua. The same bus leaves Managua at 3 P.M. and retraces the route to San Rafael del Norte, arriving sometime after 7 P.M.

El Cuá and San José de Bocay

El Cuá is best known for Benjamin Linder, the only known American casualty of the Contra war. El Cuá and San José de Bocay are illuminated by minihydroelectric power plants he helped design and implement. Both towns were completely enveloped in conflict during the 1980s, overrun first by Contras and then by the FSLN.

El Cuá has three *hospedajes,* a gas station, and several places to eat. There's one *hospedaje* in Bocay, a few small eateries, and a gas station.

Ayapal

Ayapal is a small community on the banks of the Río Bocay. From here, you can hire boats to take you downstream to several Miskito communities (not cheap).

Wiwilí

The upstream capital of the Río Coco region lies snug near the Honduran border and a long, bumpy, five-hour slog north of Jinotega. Wiwilí is a mestizo town, meaning it's of Spanish, not indigenous origin. Waspám, 550 kilometers downstream, is the other anchor at river's end, and is mostly indigenous.

Wiwilí is split by the Río Coco which runs through the middle of town. Several hundred inhabitants of Wiwilí lost their lives to the river during Hurricane Mitch, and political fallout outlasted the storm. Post-Mitch, the two sides of the community went their own separate ways to find international aid, and subsequently decided to become independent. While they retained the same name, Wiwilí on the north side of the river is now part of the department of Madriz, while Wiwilí on the south bank remains part of Jinotega. Both are important port towns with access to the deep waters of the Río Coco.

Local coffee cooperative members can lead individuals or groups on community-led tours to nearby Kilambé National Park and other surrounding treasures. This is some truly wild country and we've only heard of a couple of souls who have attempted the epic six-day trip downstream to Waspám, braving crocodiles, bandits, and drug smugglers; there are reportedly guides that will take you on rafts, camping along the river, and hanging out with wandering, dugout canoe–paddling fishermen, known as *nomados,* by locals.

There are a few decent *comedores* and two accommodations in Wiwilí: **Hotel Central** charges $3 for a bed with shared bath, or $19 double with private bath. **El Hotelito**

has standard singles with shared bath for less than $4.

Wamblán

Wamblán saw some ferocious battles during the 1980s. The last part of the drive to Wamblán is notable for a stunning descent into the city along a mountain ridge. If your trip happens to coincide with the end of the day, the long mountain shadows falling into the ridges will ensure you never forget the moment you entered Wamblán. Those pleasant memories will hopefully outlast your memory of the town's one unpleasant *hospedaje.*

MATAGALPA

CHONTALES AND THE NICARAGUAN CATTLE COUNTRY

East of windy Lake Cocibolca lie hundreds of thousands of hectares of rolling hillside in a broad ecological transition zone where undulated, scrubby pastureland gradually unfolds into the pine savannas and wetlands of the Caribbean coast. Less populated than the Pacific region, Chontales and Boaco's residents are easily outnumbered by their cattle, and in reality it's the cattle that make this area famous, because the broad cattle ranches here produce more than 60 percent of Nicaragua's dairy products, including dozens of varieties of cheese and millions of gallons of milk.

Some of the cattle ranches belong to small families involved in subsistence farming, as both areas bore the brunt of resettlement and land distribution schemes during the Sandinista years, but Chontales in particular is home to some spectacular cattle ranches, and although it's less apparent than in urban centers like Granada, a number of Nicaragua's most wealthy families. Looking out the bus window though, you'll see not enormous farm houses but rather broad, unkempt fields dotted with bovines and the occasional country village.

Boaco's history is long and troubled, but its present is a story of struggle. Aficionados of Nicaraguan literature might enjoy walking the streets of the city that inspired a number of Nicaragua's literary giants, and Boaco makes a reasonable base for some hard-core treks or drives into the wilderness that separates it from Matagalpa, all of which is firmly off the beaten path. But in spite of a few architectural gems and some engaging views, it's less well-to-do and less enticing than its upscale

HIGHLIGHTS

◖ **San José de los Remates and Esquipulas:** These backwoods cowboy towns offer a great opportunity to hike, ride horses, see petroglyphs, and cool your heels in a waterfall (page 271).

◖ **Santa Lucía:** The most charming and picturesque of Boaco's mountain villages, Santa Lucía is rich with gorgeous mountains, river valleys, and opportunities to hike (page 273).

◖ **Museo Arqueológico Gregorio Aguilar Barea:** This warehouse of statuary is filled with treasures the Chontales carved long before Columbus (page 275).

◖ **Juigalpa *Fiestas Patronales:*** Juigalpa throws a cowboy party unsurpassed in the nation. Join Juigalpans for rodeo, mechanical bull-riding contests, and down-on-the-farm good times (page 277).

◖ **Punta Mayales Nature Reserve:** This isolated peninsula jutting into Lake Cocibolca is a fine example of rural tourism (page 279).

LOOK FOR ◖ TO FIND RECOMMENDED SIGHTS, ACTIVITIES, DINING, AND LODGING.

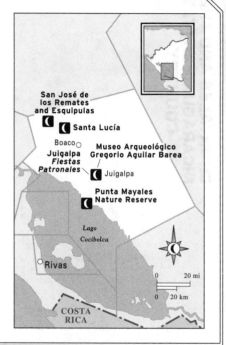

brother Juigalpa, which dwarfs it in every sense. Juigalpa is a much bigger and much more important urban center. Here you rub shoulders with legitimate cowboys sporting their cleanest boots on their twice-a-month trip to the city to pick up supplies, strike a few deals, and do their errands.

Juigalpa's patron saint celebrations are among the best in Nicaragua and draw a crowd from as far away as Managua to enjoy the elaborate bull-riding competitions, horsemanship contests, and traditional dances, all under the magnificent backdrop of the Amerrisque mountain range, which makes Juigalpa both picturesque and enticing. These mountains remain little explored, and the continual discovery of ancient Chontal statues and sculpture imply the grandeur of the mysteries this area still retains.

Many travelers treat this whole region as an uninteresting and unavoidable expanse to be traveled through as quickly as possible en route to the sandy beaches of Nicaragua's Atlantic coast, but the flavor of Chontales and Boaco play no small part in the flavor of Nicaragua as a whole, from the cowboys, to the wide open sky, to the pre-Columbian relics and the small-town lifestyle. Travelers who tire of the Granada hype and the overwhelming presence of other foreign travelers will be amply rewarded for gearing their trip to Nicaragua around these less visited, authentic Nicaraguan experiences.

PLANNING YOUR TIME

Neither Boaco nor Chontales is a region you visit to see what sort of tourist attractions have been developed for your entertainment; rather,

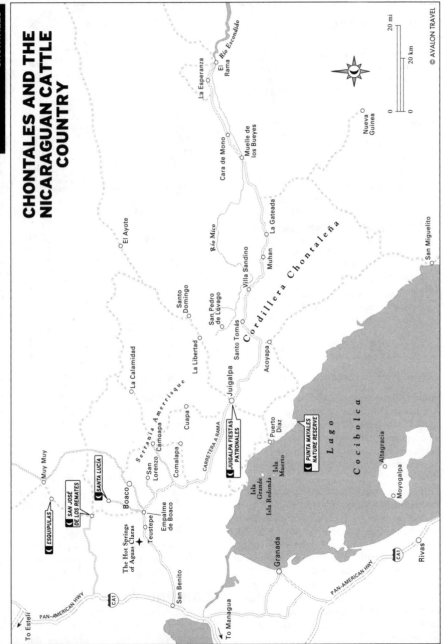

CHONTALES AND THE NICARAGUAN CATTLE COUNTRY

© AVALON TRAVEL

© RANDALL WOOD

Boaco has lots of open skyline.

you go to see what Nicaragua looked like before tourists noticed Nicaragua. As such, how much time you'll need depends dramatically on your inclination for adventure, ability to forgo some creature comforts, and navigate traditional culture, for in many of these small towns you will be the only foreigner on the streets. You could easily spend a day in one of many quiet agrarian towns. Boaco, Camoapa, and Cuapa all have a bucolic rural lifestyle, and offer basic accommodation and small sites of historical, cultural, or geologic interest. Add an additional day if the bouldering and hiking opportunities at Cuisaltepe or Cuapa whet your appetite, and another day on horseback in San José de los Remates (you can even continue on the high road to Matagalpa). Juigalpa is the most interesting and engaging city of Nicaragua's cattle country; its *fiestas patronales* in mid-August draw a crowd from all over the country. If you are planning an overland trip to the Atlantic coast, Juigalpa makes a logical and enjoyable way station that permits you to break the long drive in two, get out and stretch

your legs, and enjoy the landscape before continuing the next day.

HISTORY

The lands now known as Boaco and Chontales were first settled by the Chontal people (not their own name for themselves—the word is Nahuatl for the "mountain people," implying "savages" or "foreigners"). Less is known about them than the Nahuatl, but we know the Chontals were responsible for much of the statuary and stone monuments unearthed over the past decades in the Amerrisque mountain range north of the highway.

The first Spanish settlements of El Corregimiento de Chontales suffered often at the hands of aggressive Miskitos and Zambos, whose frequent attacks devastated 7 out of 12 Spanish settlements. The British not only encouraged but also armed them to do so. In 1749, Camoapa, Boaco (today Boaco Viejo), and Juigalpa were attacked; the towns were nearly destroyed and the churches burned to the ground. Boaco's then-governor, Alonso

Fernández de Heredia, returned the aggression, leading an excursion that returned with more than a hundred Miskito prisoners. The settlers reestablished their communities eight kilometers to the south. Nothing remains of Boaco Viejo today. From 1750 to 1760, these same indigenous groups attacked Juigalpa, Camoapa, Lóvago, Lovigüisca, Yasica, Guabale, Santa Rosa, and nine other communities. In 1762, Boaco was reestablished by Father Cáceres, who was killed shortly thereafter by yet another Miskito attack. In 1782, the church in Juigalpa was—you guessed it—burned to the ground.

As the threat of attack diminished, the lands east of Lake Cocibolca were developed into extensive cattle ranches. Coffee was introduced around the Boaco area, but before long its production had been pushed up into the better lands in northern Boaco and southern Matagalpa. Cattle quickly became the economic mainstay, followed by the extraction of gold from the mines at La Libertad and Santo Domingo.

The social and economic reorganization of the Sandinista years earned the unbridled antipathy of the people of Chontales and Boaco, who were generally frontier-minded people uninterested in government regulation. As their lands were confiscated and reorganized, they naturally had more sympathy for the Contra forces, whom they clandestinely supported throughout much of the 1980s. Much of the violence of the 1980s occurred in the towns that border both sides of the highway and inland. Since the 1990s, both departments have voted against the Sandinista party with overwhelming margins.

Boaco

Nestled snugly in a 379-meter-high notch in the Amerrisque mountains, Boaco is a departmental capital set back in the hillsides like a common country villa, an agriculture center whose soil struggles to support both cattle and corn, and a commercial center beset with poverty. Modern Boaco (the city's name is a combination of Aztec and Sumu words that mean "land of the sorcerers") is the third city to bear the name: In the 18th and 19th century, two previous Boacos were built and destroyed in the same place. In 1749, an expedition of Zumos, Miskitos, and Zambos armed with English rifles sacked the original Boaco, killed the priest, took several females hostage, and burned the town to the ground. The settlers started over along the edge of the Río Malacatoya in what's now the town of Boaquito, and in 1763, due to a brutal outbreak of cholera and the difficulties the land presented for agriculture, moved to the present site of Boaco. By the 19th century, Boaco was a cow town, though residents raised several crops (such as *cabuya,* for making rope)

to sell in the markets of Masaya, a four-day mule-drawn wagon trip.

The modern city of Boaco began on a hilltop and crept down the hillside into a valley, earning the nickname "The City of Two Floors." During the Contra war, Boaco was spared from direct battles, but in the hillsides that surrounded the city, Contras and Sandinistas fought skirmishes in Muy Muy, San José de los Remates, and San Francisco. The violence dislodged countless *campesinos,* all of whom eventually found their way to the city of Boaco seeking refuge. Many decided to stay, and Boaco has swelled over the past 20 years, faster than it can provide for its new inhabitants, most of whom occupy neighborhoods of small concrete homes around the outskirts of the city.

Boaco was an inspiration to several notable Nicaraguan authors and scholars, four of whom—Diego Sequeira, Antonio Barquero, Hernan Robleto, and Julian N. Guerrero—won the Nicaraguan Rubén Darío prize for

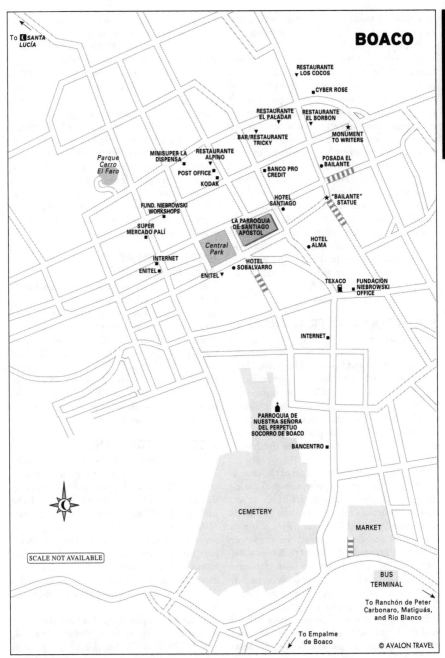

BOACO

To ◆ SANTA LUCÍA

RESTAURANTE LOS COCOS

CYBER ROSE

RESTAURANTE EL PALADAR

RESTAURANTE EL BORBON

MONUMENT TO WRITERS

BAR/RESTAURANTE TRICKY

MINISUPER LA DISPENSA

RESTAURANTE ALPINO

POSADA EL BAILANTE

Parque Cerro El Faro

POST OFFICE

BANCO PRO CREDIT

KODAK

HOTEL SANTIAGO

"BAILANTE" STATUE

FUND. NIEBROWSKI WORKSHOPS

LA PARROQUIA DE SANTIAGO APÓSTOL

SUPER MERCADO PALÍ

Central Park

HOTEL ALMA

INTERNET

ENITEL

ENITEL

HOTEL SOBALVARRO

TEXACO

FUNDACIÓN NIEBROWSKI OFFICE

INTERNET

PARROQUIA DE NUESTRA SEÑORA DEL PERPETUO SOCORRO DE BOACO

BANCENTRO

CEMETERY

MARKET

SCALE NOT AVAILABLE

BUS TERMINAL

To Ranchón de Peter Carbonaro, Matiguás, and Río Blanco

To Empalme de Boaco

© AVALON TRAVEL

literature. A monument in their honor, just east and north of the park, overlooks the city from a sort of balcony.

Boaco's best mayor was a man of the cloth, Father Niebrowski of Poland, who arrived in 1916. While preaching to an underserved community, Niebrowski took it upon himself to better their lot in life and used his determination and practical know-how to bring Boaco into the modern world. Niebrowski built a cinema, a brick factory whose bricks he used to rebuild the church, and a small hydropower plant on the Río Fonseca, which provided electric light to the city for the first time. Niebrowski also established the first hospital, the first community music band, and countless other things that contributed to Boaco's social welfare. To this day, the Niebrowski Foundation is active in the city and provides for small programs in the Boaco area, while the church, factory, and hydropower plant have all faded into memory.

SIGHTS AND ATTRACTIONS

Boaco's patron saint is Santiago Apóstol, and the *fiestas patronales* in his honor are particularly interesting and historic. The festival lasts the entire month of July, during which time the saint's statue is paraded daily from one neighborhood to the next. The crux of the ceremony is July 23–25 when the procession is accompanied by dancers whose performance tells an elaborate tale of the expulsion of the Moors from Spain.

A statue located one block east of the church represents a dancer, complete with snake stick in one hand and brass knuckles in the other. Boaco's churches neatly serve the residents of Boaco's two levels without their having to traipse up and down the hill. In the lower half, the **Parroquia de Nuestra Señora del Perpetuo Socorro de Boaco** is an elaborate nontraditional church whose architecture is nearly Greek orthodox. A statue of the Virgin Mary keeps watch over the earth from its starched white rooftop. Inside, statues of Jesus and the Virgin Mary line up side by side with the carved stone statuary of Boaco's Chontal

and Sumu ancestors, an intriguing compromise between the religions of new and old.

The freshly painted **Parroquia de Santiago Apóstol,** located at the top of the hill, has been a Boaco landmark since the mid-1800s. Mass is held every day, plus several on the weekends, when the ringing of the church bells fills the town square and scatters the pigeons.

Boaco's highest point is **Cerro El Faro,** the lighthouse without a sea. A concrete pedestal and tower, the Faro offers a good view of the city and the valley of the Río Mayales. Technically, the tower is open all week, but the caretaker closes it when he pleases. Underneath is the town convention center and a popular gymnasium. Evenings, the Faro is one of Boaco's more popular places to steal a few kisses.

ENTERTAINMENT AND NIGHTLIFE

Boaco's sole disco is **El Ranchón de Peter Carbonaro,** a kilometer or two out of town along the highway to Muy Muy. Its relaxing atmosphere is perfect for a drink and some traditional Latin music: salsa, *cumbia,* and merengue are popular—and the occasional Mexican *ranchera* cowboy song. By 10 P.M., the dance floor is packed, especially when there's live music. Take a taxi for $1. There are many bars in town offering cheap beer and a relaxed atmosphere until about 11 P.M.

ACCOMMODATIONS

Because of Boaco's constant water problems, ask about reserves and be prepared to grin and bear it with a manual (i.e., bucket) shower if need be. At the south edge of the park, █ **Hotel Sobalvarro** (tel. 505/542-2515, $10–25) has been lodging travelers and passersthrough since before the revolution and still retains the faded charm of yesteryear. It has a few rooms with air-conditioning in a once grandiose building of wooden rooms set around a courtyard with a balcony overlooking the lower half of town.

Near the stoplight, just where the steep road turns nearly vertical, **Hotel Alma** (tel. 505/542-2620, $8–20) has clean, newly painted

© RANDALL WOOD

Parroquia de Santiago Apóstol

rooms with either private or shared bathroom, plus a good view. **Posada El Bailante** (tel. 505/542-2380, $20–25) is another easy recommendation. It's down the block from the dancer's statue, and offers cable TV in all rooms and Wi-Fi. At **Hotel Santiago** (tel. 505/542-4915, hotelsantiago@aol.com, $11–26) English-speaking Carlos David offers eight rooms in an old building with a homey atmosphere. Ask about visiting his nearby cheese and coffee farms and horseback riding.

Note: Many of the hotels and *pensiónes* near the bus terminal and along the main road of Boaco's lower level do a brisk trade in prostitution and romantic getaways for young couples and should be avoided.

FOOD

Pastries and snacks are for sale in the park; wash 'em down with a shake from Hotel Sobalvarro—where you can also grab a sandwich or burger, all served on the best front porch in the city. Several restaurants on the top floor of Boaco serve traditional Nicaraguan dishes, burgers, sandwiches and similar, of which, the least expensive is **Restaurante Maraíta,** also a popular drinking hole. A little pricier than the others but still reasonable, **Restaurante Alpino** (the name is a result of the owner's former business selling Christmas trees in Tipitapa) hits the spot with great beef *churrasco* ($8.50) and seafood. Locals and foreign NGO workers like **Restaurante Borbon,** which is known for its *pollo al vino* and pork chops, among other classics, for around $3–5 a dish, plus huge glasses of *fresco* (juice) served on a breezy balcony overlooking the hills. **Restaurante Los Cocos** (a block farther north on the same street) is cheaper but equally tasty and has a nice back patio lined with trees and plants.

SERVICES

There are two banks in Boaco, one on each of the floors. In the lower part, Banpro is located on the main street. In the upper part, ProCredit is a block north of the back side of the church. Western Union is near the market, and open 8 A.M.–4:30 P.M. Monday–Saturday.

Boaco market

One of the better Internet joints is Cyber Rose (near the writer's monument), which has six computers and a nice smoke-break balcony. The post office is 1.5 blocks north of the church on the left side. There's a pay phone out front (open 8 A.M.–5 P.M. Mon.–Fri., until noon Sat.). ENITEL is located across from the cathedral's northeast corner (open 8 A.M.–9 P.M. Mon.–Fri.).

GETTING THERE AND AWAY

Buses to Boaco leave every 30 minutes or so from the Mayoreo terminal in Managua. From Boaco, the most comfortable way to travel to Managua is by microbus. Two leave each day from the terminal, at 6:30 A.M. and 12:30 P.M. ($2). Regular buses leave every 30 minutes for Managua until 5:40 P.M.

Five buses leave each day for Santa Lucía, 10:30 A.M.–5 P.M. (one hour). Buses bound for Río Blanco (three hours) and Muy Muy leave 5:50 A.M.–5 P.M. For the traveler masochists, the 12-hour Boaco–Siuna kidney-bruiser will take you over some of the worst dirt roads in the nation.

NEAR BOACO
The Hot Springs of Aguas Claras

The *aguas termales* at **Aguas Claras Hot Springs and Hotel** (tel. 505/856-7306, www .termalesaguasclaras.com) are rumored by locals to be heated by an underground volcano, which probably isn't too far from the truth. In 2000, an entrepreneur channeled the geo-thermally-heated waters into pipes and a series of conrete pools protected by palm-thatch roofs. The hotel and resort complex has six pools available to the public and another two reserved for hotel guests. All pools are clean and professionally maintained. The water isn't boiling hot, but it's extraordinarily warm, and is therefore more enjoyable at night. While you lounge in the pool, you can order from an extensive menu of traditional Nicaraguan food and drink. Under the *ranchos* are several hammocks, and in the lobby is a pair of better-than-average billiards tables.

The hotel features 17 private rooms with air-conditioning for $35. The larger rooms for up to five people go for $60. Just coming in for the day costs about $1; credit cards are accepted for hotel and restaurant expenses, but not the entrance fee.

During Semana Santa and weekends in the dry season, the hotel can fill quickly, so make reservations. The *aguas termales* are located seven kilometers west of Empalme de Boaco and are slightly difficult to navigate to without private transportation.

The Baseball Field at Empalme de Boaco

Years ago, a North American traveler named Jake Scheideman fell ill during an ambitious bicycle tour of Central America and was taken in by a family at Empalme de Boaco. Over several days, they nursed him—a complete stranger—back to health. In 1998, after Hurricane Mitch, Scheideman returned to Nicaragua after many years of having been away, wanting to do something for the community that had taken care of him when he was ill. He asked what they would like, and they chose a ballpark.

The ballpark, constructed in Empalme de Boaco (the intersection of the road to Boaco) took more than two years to complete but is now the best of its kind east of Lake Cocibolca; games are Saturday and Sunday afternoons in season. The construction team then started a community housing program that has built 65 homes, a high school, and a community center, and they're still going. Contact Jake and friends to participate, donate, or learn more through the website of his bike shop in Northern California: www.sthelenacyclery.com.

La Cebadilla

Around the turn of the 20th century, a farmer from the mountain town of Cebadilla was surprised to see the Virgin Mary appear before him amongst the rocks where he was tending his cattle. The site has been treasured by the locals ever since.

La Cebadilla is no easier to get to than it ever was, and if you're interested in a hike through an out-of-the-way corner of Nicaragua, try walking up the mountain to La Cebadilla. At one time a small chapel was erected in honor of the Virgin, and there was a small well where it was said the water was blessed. Today, the chapel has mostly fallen to bits.

The hike starts 1.6 kilometers east of Empalme de Boaco, where on the south side of the highway there's a dirt road leading south to the community of Asedades and a steel sign with a picture of the Virgin Mary and the words La Cebadilla. The road leads south one kilometer to Asedades, a poor community of adobe houses, flower gardens, and rocky fields. It's imperative that you find a guide in Asedades to take you up the mountain to La Cebadilla. There are many small footpaths that lead up the hill, but they intertwine and none is more obvious than the others. The walk up the hill will take you between three and four hours—take water and food and make sure you have something to share with your guide. The walk back to Asedades can take 2–3 hours. Your guide will recommend that you stay at the top of the hill through midday and do your walking in the cool of the afternoon.

At La Cebadilla, you may or may not have visions of the Virgin Mary, but you will certainly have a fantastic view of the valley below and the hills of Boaco to the east, sometimes all the way to the big lake.

◖ San José de los Remates and Esquipulas

These picturesque cowboy towns can be the backdrop to your guided horse tours and hikes to local waterfalls. Catch a ride to **Cerro Cumaica Natural Reserve** from either town. The weather here is usually a perfect 20°C (70°F) with a slight breeze almost year-round. Consider visiting both of these towns on the back road to Matagalpa. The bus trip is bumpy but the views are grand. One of the main attractions is the "original black Jesus." In fact, thousands of national and international pilgrims descend each year on Esquipulas during the *fiestas patronales* (January 14–15) to catch a glimpse of **El Señor de Esquipulas,** housed in one of the best kept churches in Nicaragua. Locals believe that only due to the power of their patron saint was the town spared from all the wars that over the centuries had engulfed the surrounding hills.

Four buses leave Teustepe daily and a direct bus from Managua's Mayoreo terminal leaves daily at 12:30 P.M. ($2).

In San José de los Remates, **Jorge Isaac** (tel. 505/542-2359) will help you find accommodations in the 10-room town hostel (hot water) or with a local family. Also look for Doña Rosinda (from ENITEL, half a block east), who is involved in the San José tourism committee and can help you get horses, guides, or maps. The view from Cruz del Milenio is worth the walk: On a clear evening, you can see the lights of Granada and Cerro Negro in León.

Nearby Esquipulas, straddling the border between the Boaco and Matagalpa departments is similar, but has its own charm, waterfall, and friendly tourism committee representative: Doña Berena (tel. 505/426-8238 or 505/772-9262). She can arrange visits to Salto de Limon in the nearby Cumaica Nature Reserve, petroglyph walks, and all-inclusive

HIKES IN THE CAMOAPA AREA

Cuisaltepe's imposing rock face

HIKING MOMBACHO

In the early 1900s, Nicaraguans from Granada transferred their homes and possessions to Camoapa to try growing coffee on the area's hillsides. They chose the slopes of one mountain in particular because of its rich soils and named the peak Mombacho, in memory of their Granada homeland. Camoapa's Mombacho is a forested mountain with a rocky protuberance jutting out of the top. It is lined with several coffee plantations and a handful of radio towers and makes a pleasant day hike from Camoapa. Long ago, Mombacho was the site of a moonshine distillery, the products of which were sold under the name Mombachito.

Hiking the hill is significantly easier than hiking the Cuisaltepe and offers a beautiful view of Camoapa's open ranges. From Camoapa, the road to Mombacho can be accessed by the Salida de Sangre de Cristo (Sangre de Cristo is the name of a church found along the first part of that road). From ENITEL in the center of Camoapa, walk six blocks west, crossing over a small bridge and arriving at the public school. Turn right at the school and head north until you see the Iglesia de Sangre de Cristo. Continue on that road until you reach Mombacho. The hike from town takes 3-4 hours. There's a dirt road that leads up Mombacho from Camoapa to the radio towers. In Nahuatl, *mombacho* means "steep," so be prepared.

HIKING PEÑA LA JARQUÍNA

At the entrance to Camoapa on the southeast side of the highway (to your right as you head toward Camoapa) is a broad, rocky cliff face at whose base is a hardwood forest. This is Peña la Jarquína, named after a prominent local family. It's an easy 90-minute hike from the entrance to Camoapa, around the back side of the hill to the top. Skilled climbers might find it makes a suitable technical ascent; the rock is solid and has plenty of cracks – and is almost assuredly unclimbed.

HIKING CUISALTEPE

Unless you breezed by it on the midnight bus to El Rama, Cuisaltepe inevitably caught your eye: a massive, rocky promontory that juts out of the hillside between San Lorenzo and the entrance to Camoapa. Approaching it from the west, its silhouette resembles the tip of an upturned thumb, pointing in the direction of the highway. In Nahuatl, Cuisaltepe means "place of the grinding stone"; it was a good source of the volcanic rock the indigenous peoples used for making long, round stone implements with which to grind corn into dough. Cuisaltepe was the home of the last cacique of the region, Taisigüe.

Hiking Cuisaltepe is no casual endeavor. More than 300 meters high, much of the south side of the rock is a series of vertical crevasses and overhangs and much of the rest of it is prohibitively steep. However, there is one summit approach – from the north side of the rock – which you can reach from Camoapa. Hike with caution. The climb takes around six

hours round-trip, but adjust that estimate according to your own hiking ability. You should have good shoes, as much of the route is loose, slippery gravel.

Your point of entrance is the road to Camoapa. Any bus traveling between Managua or Boaco and the east will take you there, leaving you at Empalme de Camoapa (also called San Francisco) along the highway. A better option is to take a direct bus to Camoapa, 10 of which leave per day from Managua (five on Sundays). From the highway, the road that leads to Camoapa climbs 25 kilometers. Get off the bus before you reach Camoapa at Km 99, where a small turnoff to the west leads to the community of Barrio Cebollín with a little red bus stop at the entrance. Access to the summit is neither obvious nor easy, and involves climbing partway up, crossing the small forest in a notch in the hillside, then climbing the ridge to the summit. You can find guides in Barrio Cebollín in the first house on the left after you pass the school (the house nearest the utility pole). Euclídes and brothers know the mountain well and climb it periodically.

tourism packages with rural, cultural, and historic elements in and near Esquipulas. Ask about Cerro El Padre (a giant granite rock on top of a large hill) and the *miradores* (viewing points) that some of the locals are putting up in their backyards.

For food, try **El Quelite** or **El Campero,** both on main street. **El Hotelito** (near the park, tel. 505/772-9132, $11) has seven cozy rooms.

◖ Santa Lucía

The town of Santa Lucía was created in 1904 by decree of President José Santos Zelaya in an effort to concentrate the dispersed and poorly administered farming communities of the hillsides north of Boaco. Its well planned and organized beginning boded well for Santa Lucía which, a century later, remains a picturesque

and enchanting mountain village in a valley ringed with green mountains.

Santa Lucía itself doesn't have hotel rooms or fancy restaurants but travelers sometimes come for the scenery around Cerro Santo Domingo, the long rocky precipice of Peña La Brada, and **Las Máscaras** petroglyphs in the valley of the Río Fonseca. For hikes in the Santa Lucía area, Osmin is the right gentleman to accompany you. He can be found in the ENITEL office, where he works—he's a fun tour guide.

Nearby **Salto de los Americas** is a seven-meter waterfall with a deep pool, located a short walk up the river off the road to Boaco. There are several families of monkeys that live in the area. **Peña La Brada** is a cliff edge outside town, with an amazing panoramic view of Boaco and beyond.

There are no official accommodations in Santa Lucía, but the **Comedor Santa Lucía** will put you up and feed you in a pinch. More good food can be found in the *comedor* in the park, which specializes in grilled meat. A direct bus leaves from Managua for Santa Lucía at 10:30 A.M. ($1.50), bypassing Boaco entirely. The same bus leaves Santa Lucía for Managua early in the morning.

Camoapa

A cow town of 13,000 set in the mountains east of Boaco, Camoapa got its name from a Nahuatl phrase that can be translated as either "place of the parrots, place of the dark rocks," or "place of the yams." (How's that for precision?) Once an indigenous community ruled by the cacique Taisiwa, it was later absorbed by the Spanish settlers and incorporated under the name San Francisco de Camoapán.

Today, besides the abundant commerce in dairy products, Camoapa is best known to Nicaraguans for its production of woven straw hats. In the 1960s, a school for promoting the art of weaving was formed, and the art passed through several generations; there are still several hundred weavers in Camoapa. The hats they are known best for are created from intricately and tightly woven strips of fibrous white *pita* and are sold all over Nicaragua's craft markets.

Camoapa's economy is largely dependent on three dairy cooperatives, the workers of which like to have a good time on the weekends when they return from their farms and ranches outside of town to party and relax. Camoapa's *fiestas patronales* begin on October 2 in honor of San Francisco de Asís, with bull riding, cattle contests, and the like. Camoapans boast that they have the toughest bulls and best horses around. Other weekends, the disco at **Atenas** is the place to be, unless you're a true cowboy, in which case the party is at **La Asociación** (Asogacam) out by the ballfield: beer, mariachi music, and the occasional brawl—just like the old days.

Stay at ◖ **Hotel Las Estrellas** (seven blocks east of the church's north side, tel. 505/849-2240, $10–13), a former auto-hotel

turned honest, which offeres the best value rooms in this price range. Smaller but closer to town along the main road, **Hotel Taisiwa** has 11 rooms for $5 with private bath. In addition to **Atenas** solid meals are found at **Camfel** (one block west of the church's north side), a clean place run by seven women; and **Bosquecito** (just down the road that leads to Comalapa), a restaurant filled with potted plants and flowers.

SERVICES

You'll locate the ENITEL phone office by its imposing tower planted on the premises. The post office is on the south side of the church. The Miscelanea Urbina (one block north of the park's northeast corner) is a good place to pick up snacks or supplies, especially if you're gearing up to hike Cuisaltepe.

A doctor is always on call at Camoapa's **Centro de Salud;** or the **Clínica San Francisco de Asís** (a half-block east and a half-block north from the Colegio San Francisco).

GETTING THERE AND AWAY

Buses from Managua to Camoapa depart Mayoreo Monday–Saturday, starting at 4:30 A.M. and running through 4:10 P.M. There's a reduced schedule on Sundays, but still adequate transportation. Buses to Managua depart from the shady side of the church (whichever side that is as the day progresses), Monday–Saturday beginning at 6:25 A.M. and running through 5 P.M. The reduced Sunday schedule begins at 5:25 A.M., leaving roughly every two hours until 5 P.M. There is a minibus that shuttles between the Empalme del Camoapa (San Francisco) and Camoapa, but it's irregular. A ride between the two points will cost you $0.50.

Comalapa

In 1752, Friar Morel de Santa Cruz visited Comalapa and described it as follows: "This is a town of Indians located in a land that's stony, mountainous, and fenced in by hills. Its church is of straw, reduced and indecent, lacking a vestry, but possessing an altar . . . 100 families and 484 persons both Indian and Ladino." Comalapa is largely the same 250 years later, though the church is now a quaint stone structure. Access to Comalapa is through Camoapa, 20 kilometers down the road. There is one bus per day, leaving Camoapa at 6:30 A.M. The same bus leaves Comalapa at 4 P.M. At other times of the day, hitch a ride with pickups traveling between the communities, or try hiking a piece of the road.

Juigalpa

The last big settlement on the road southeast to El Rama, Juigalpa is a prosperous city of cattle ranchers and farmers with famous *fiestas patronales.* Juigalpa bears the traces of its indigenous roots in elaborate statuary and other archaeological pieces still being discovered in the mountains east of town. Juigalpa in Aztec means "great city" or "spawning grounds of the black snails." Its first inhabitants were likely the Chontal, displaced from the Rivas area by the stronger Nicaraos. They resisted the Spanish occupation fiercely in the 16th century, rising up no fewer than 14 times to attack the installations of the colonial government.

Upon Nicaragua's independence, the land that comprised Chontales and Boaco was controlled by Granada. In 1858, the Department of Chontales was formed. Juigalpa and the now desolate Acoyapa were the departmental heads at different times. In the 18th and 19th centuries, travelers bound for the gold mines of Santo Domingo and La Libertad crossed Lake Cocibolca, landed in Puerto Díaz, and spent a night in Juigalpa before proceeding.

SIGHTS AND ATTRACTIONS
◖ Museo Arqueológico Gregorio Aguilar Barea
Juigalpa's most interesting attraction is the Museo Arqueológico Gregorio Aguilar Barea, an airplane hangar–like building housing a collection of more than a hundred examples of pre-Columbian statuary uncovered in the folds of the Amerrisque mountain range. Ranging from one meter to seven meters tall, the pieces are reminiscent of totem poles, elaborately carved in high- and low-relief, with representations of zoomorphic figures and humans (the latter often clutching knives or axes in their hands, or presenting their arms folded across their chests). The statues, thought to be 1,000 years old, were the work of the Chontal people, driven to the east side of Lake Cocibolca by the more powerful Nicaraos some 1,500 years ago.

Unlike the Nahuatl and Nicarao, relatively little is known about the Chontal culture and its statues, more of which are continually being discovered in the Amerrisque range. The museum was built in 1952 by the well-loved former mayor of Juigalpa, Gregorio Aguilar Barea. It also exhibits Nicaraguan coins from across two centuries, gold figurines, original paintings by the museum's namesake, and several historical paintings and photographs. The museum is open 8 A.M.–noon and 2–4 P.M. Monday–Friday, and only in the morning on Saturday; closed Sunday. The entrance fee is less than a dollar. The building has an open front, so even if the gate to the museum is locked, all the statues can be seen from the street.

Parque Palo Solo
The view from the park at the north end of town, **Parque Palo Solo,** is elevated above the surrounding streets, giving the impression of looking over the bulwark of a fortress. The fortress feeling isn't entirely accidental: Juigalpa was built at the top of the hill to offer it some means of defense from the Miskito and Zambo peoples who once raided it from those same mountains 200 years ago. The park was built by Mayor Aguilar Barea in the 1960s and named after the one tall tree that dominated its center. The tree has since been replaced by a fountain adorned with images of the mainstays

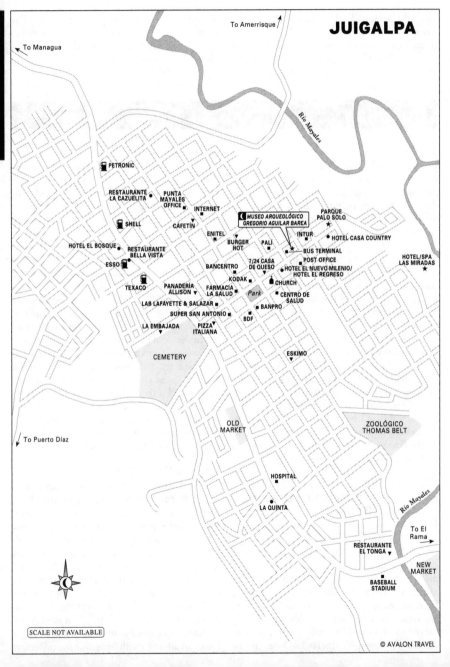

JUIGALPA

To Amerrisque

To Managua

Río Mayales

PETRONIC

RESTAURANTE LA CAZUELITA

PUNTA MAYALES OFFICE

INTERNET

MUSEO ARQUEOLÓGICO GREGORIO AGUILAR BAREA

PARQUE PALO SOLO

SHELL

CAFETÍN

ENITEL

INTUR

HOTEL CASA COUNTRY

HOTEL EL BOSQUE

RESTAURANTE BELLA VISTA

BURGER HOT

PALÍ

BUS TERMINAL

HOTEL/SPA LAS MIRADAS

ESSO

BANCENTRO

7/24 CASA DE QUESO

POST OFFICE

HOTEL EL NUEVO MILENIO/ HOTEL EL REGRESO

TEXACO

KODAK

PANADERÍA ALLISON

FARMACIA LA SALUD

Park

CHURCH

CENTRO DE SALUD

LAB LAFAYETTE & SALAZAR

SUPER SAN ANTONIO

BANPRO

BDF

LA EMBAJADA

PIZZA ITALIANA

CEMETERY

ESKIMO

To Puerto Díaz

OLD MARKET

ZOOLÓGICO THOMAS BELT

HOSPITAL

LA QUINTA

Río Mayales

To El Rama

RESTAURANTE EL TONGA

NEW MARKET

BASEBALL STADIUM

SCALE NOT AVAILABLE

© AVALON TRAVEL

of the Chontales economy: corn and cattle. A restaurant at the edge of the park serves fancy lunches and dinners.

Juigalpa's other park, in the center of town, is an orderly and clean place, whose statue of a boy shining shoes is unique in Nicaragua. Made by a former mayor who spent his early years earning money as a shoe-shine boy, the statue bears the inscription: "Hard work dignifies a man."

◖ Juigalpa *Fiestas Patronales*

Juigalpa's *fiestas patronales,* August 11–18, attract visitors from the entire nation and even Honduras and Costa Rica. Much of the festivities take place on the north side of town in the Plaza de Toros, but you'll find parties all over. Expect bull riding, rodeos, and horseback games. In one of these, called the *carrera de cinta,* mounted riders gallop underneath a wire from which is suspended a small ring. If a rider successfully puts a pencil through the ring at full gallop, he can present it—and a kiss— to the woman of his choice among the contestants vying to be queen of the festival. The woman who receives the most rings is crowned the queen.

During the rest of the year, you can test your merit as a cowboy for $1.50 on Nicaragua's only mechanical bull at **La Quinta,** but no kissing.

NIGHTLIFE AND ENTERTAINMENT

The best disco in town is **La Quinta** (out on the highway, entrance $1 most nights, $1.75 Sat.). On weekend nights—and particularly Saturdays—the dance floor tends to collect the young people of the city. Second best is **Caracoles Negras** (a half-block south of the Petronic station along the highway, formerly Hotters), which picks up the slack on Sunday night and appeals to the cowboy crowd more so than La Quinta. Toward the center of town, **Casa Bravo Club** is an upscale pool hall behind tinted glass and in the comfort of an air-conditioned hall. The party never has to stop at **7/24** right near the park. It's never closed, has loud music, a giant projector screen, and

serves a variety of local cheeses for snacking. The baseball field is located by the river at the south end of town in Barrio Paimuca; games are on Sundays.

ACCOMMODATIONS

Many of Juigalpa's cheapest *hospedajes* are intended to be occupied one hour at a time. Two otherwise obvious places to the west of the park, Hospedaje Angelita and Hospedaje Central, fall into that category and should be avoided.

Stay to the east (rear) side of the church instead. **Hotel El Regreso** (the one-story establishment, tel. 505/512-2068, $4.50 pp with shared bath) has 18 clean rooms, and a friendly owner. The room closest to the street is a bit noisy. Immediately next door, **Hotel El Nuevo Milenio** (tel. 505/512-0646, $10 with shared bath, $11 private) has 22 not-so-clean rooms, but also a pleasant balcony overlooking the street. For a bit more, ◖ **Hotel Casa Country** (located a block from the Parque Palo Solo at the north end of town, tel. 505/512-2546, $15–20) has five luxury rooms on the second story of a gorgeous colonial-style house, all with private bath and TV.

La Quinta (tel. 505/512-2574, $18–28) farther east along the highway, almost directly across from the hospital, has 38 rooms, some with air-conditioning. The fanciest place in town, with the best view bar none, is ◖ **Las Miradas Hotel & Spa** (tel. 505/512-4525, hotel lasmiradas@yahoo.com, $50). Just follow the series of signs from town, each telling you that it's just a few blocks away, to the most stunning view in the city, luxury accommodations, a full hair salon, massage studio, private barbecue lounge, small gym, and a glass-wall sauna with that same five-star view. Las Miradas only has five rooms, so make reservations. The pool is coming soon. Ask Doña Edelmira about the *guardabarrancos* that nest in the hotel wall.

FOOD

Juigalpa has a variety of food—often at reasonable prices—naturally, with massive quantities of beef and dairy on the menu. Case in

CHONTALES

fresh honey for sale on the Juigalpa roadside

© RANDALL WOOD

point: **La Embajada** (difficult to find, but everyone knows it, just ask around). The only thing on the menu at this hole in the wall is meat, ordered by the pound (about $4.50). The "Meat Lady" has a secret marinade recipe she learned from her grandmother and is currently passing down to her granddaughter. It's served with salty *cuajada* cheese and tortillas. Native Chontaleño Daniel Ortega has been known to make an appearance here, and it is also frequented by the bigwigs of Chontales.

◖ **La Cazuelita** (three blocks east and two north from the Esso) sells a remarkable barbecue-chicken sandwich (less than $3 with fries). This newly remodeled, air-conditioned restaurant is popular with Peace Corps volunteers and well-off Juigalpans for its excellent Nicaraguan food, all of which you can sample via a *surtido* ($11, serves 2–3).

Right across from the cathedral is **7/24 Casa de Queso,** offering cheeseburgers, Nica-Chinese cuisine, and a good assortment of cheese. There are a few more places in and near the park, and for good, fresh bread and pastries, stop by **Panadería Allison** (open 5 A.M.–7 P.M. daily). They have a refrigerator full of cold milk to wash it all down.

On the highway in front of the Esso station, **Restaurante Tacho** has great chicken and steak at moderate prices ($3–5) in a pleasant atmosphere. Roving bands of mariachis frequent the place, which has a mostly male crowd. Across the street, and next door to the Esso, is **Bella Vista,** serving up a large choice of meat ($5–7) with a dance floor open till 2 A.M. on the weekends. For more upscale dining, try **Restaurante La Tonga,** with plates from $5 and up, and, of course, Juigalpa's favorite, **La Quinta,** with a juicy *churrasco.*

SERVICES

For Internet, check behind the Texaco station or just walk around town.

There is an ATM located off of the central park outside the Banpro. The post office is located down the street from the church, and ENITEL (open 8 A.M.–noon and 1:30–5:30 P.M. Mon.–Sat.) is four blocks north of the park. The INTUR tourist office, located a block east of the museum, can provide you with brochures and recommendations on where to stay and what to do.

One of the better pharmacies in town is Farmacia La Salud (at the northwest corner of the park, tel. 505/512-0932). Hospital La Asunción (on the southeast side of town along the highway) doesn't have very good facilities. A better option for travelers is the Lab Lafayette & Salazar (two blocks west of the park, tel. 505/512-2292), a private clinic and doctor's office. There is a Centro de Salud across the street from the church, which is open 8 A.M.–9 P.M. Monday–Friday and 8 A.M.–1 P.M. Saturday–Sunday.

The old movie theater is now a Pali grocery store, but Supermercado San Antonio has a better selection and is locally owned.

GETTING THERE AND AWAY

Microbuses to Managua depart from the north or east side of the church at 6 A.M. and 1:40 P.M. (2.5 hours). The larger buses depart Juigalpa from the cramped bus terminal in the market, which at the time of publication was being rebuilt. Ask around to be sure from where your bus departs. Buses leave hourly for El Rama, 4:30 A.M.–1:30 P.M. and every half hour to Managua, 4 A.M.–5 P.M. You'll also find daily service to Nueva Guinea until 3:20 P.M., to Boaco (via Camoapa and Comalapa), and other local destinations.

NEAR JUIGALPA
◖ Punta Mayales Nature Reserve

Located an hour from Juigalpa, Punta Mayales is home to 250 species of birds including owls and hawks; mammals like porcupines, anteaters, sloths, and monkeys; and an incredible assortment of flora with a backdrop of Lake Cocibolca and the Isla de Ometepe and Zapatera volcanoes. There are three cabins of various sizes and tents for camping. There are five trails, ranging 1–3 kilometers, and each offering a unique view of the peninsula.

Stop in the Juigalpa office (near ENITEL, tel. 505/512-2322, arbagar@yahoo.com) to arrange a day trip or an overnight stay. Camping

is $12 with breakfast; cabins cost $80 a night, which includes three meals, guided walks, and an aquatic tour down the Mayales River and out into the lake. If you'd just like to visit for the day, entrance is $2, a land tour is $6 with the option to take horses, and the river tour is $5. Snake shows and caiman-watching trips are easily arranged.

Balneario el Salto

Juigalpa's favorite swimming hole is located an easy two kilometers out of town on the highway to Managua. Look for the big blue sign on the northeast side of the highway; the falls are located a scant 100 meters from the highway. El Salto is formed by a concrete dam that causes water to pool up in a natural reservoir. In the dry season, there's no waterfall at all, though the swimming hole remains quite deep. In the rainy season, the water from the Río Mayales tumbles first over the concrete dam and then through a gorge of enormous boulders carved into fantastic shapes by the flowing water. The near shore gets littered with the remains of old picnics after major holidays (like Semana Santa, when the place is packed), but the far shore is tree lined and grassy. Consider swimming across to the far side and watching the local kids turn somersaults off the wooden-plank diving boards. There is supposedly a $1 fee to get in, but the locals have skirted the fee for so long by entering downstream and walking up the streambed that, with the exception of Semana Santa, no one seems to try to charge any more.

Puerto Díaz

It's a short and uncomfortable ride from Juigalpa down to the village of Puerto Díaz, a sleepy lakeside town of fishing families that pretty much live off what they catch. Puerto Díaz doesn't have any facilities for travelers but is worth a day trip on a lazy Saturday to see how the "far" side of the lake (i.e., the world across the lake from Granada) lives. Buses leave from Juigalpa three times a day at 5 A.M., 2 P.M., and 5 P.M. From the bus terminal, they cross the highway at the Esso station before working their way slowly down to the shoreline.

Balneario el Salto

Cuapa and the Monolith of Cuapa

Tiny, isolated Cuapa, once just another anonymous farming town in the foothills of the Amerrisque mountain range, gained an awful sort of notoriety during the 1980s, when it came to represent the worst of what the Contra war had become. In 1985, Contras attacked and took control of Cuapa, holding it for several hours. They captured the Sandinista mayor Hollman Martínez but later released him when the townspeople pled for his life. Twelve other Sandinista activists, sent from the capital to work in Cuapa, weren't so fortunate: The Contras marched them out of town and executed them at the roadside. When the Sandinista military got wind that Contras occupied the town, they dispatched a truckload of 40 soldiers to defend the town. Contras ambushed the vehicle along the road to Cuapa, killing nearly all of them. A small roadside monument bearing the Sandinista flag commemorates both the civil servants and the soldiers killed during the war.

On a lighter note, Cuapa is famous among devout Catholics. In late 1980 and early 1981, the Virgin Mary appeared several times—bathed in radiant light and dressed in pure white—to local farmer Bernardo Martínez. She told Martínez she had a message for the world and for Nicaragua: "Don't preach the kingdom of God unless you are building it on earth. The world is threatened by great danger." She later asked for prayers for unbelievers and for peace on earth. Devout Catholics were overjoyed at the appearance of the Virgin, but even that moment became rapidly politicized in the toxic climate of the 1980s. Some claimed her message was a coded recrimination of the Sandinista government, and the Sandinistas responded by clamping down on all press coverage of miracles not previously accepted by the Vatican. An elaborate and well-maintained statue and sign greet you at the entrance to Cuapa with Bienvenido a la Tierra de María (Welcome to Mary's Land). Believers from all over eastern Nicaragua flock to Cuapa on May 8, the anniversary of the day the Virgin first appeared.

Whether you've come to see the shrine to Mary or to climb the impressive, needlelike

HIKES NEAR JUIGALPA

EL MONOLITO DE CUAPA

The Cuapa Monolith is a 75-meter-high chunk of granite that projects like a giant needle out of a field, as though it dropped from the sky and pierced the ground; it's first visible on the bus ride to Cuapa.

Climbing El Monolito isn't easy, but it isn't impossible either. It's a hike, not a technical rock climb. The locals in Cuapa know all the trails that lead there, and any young *campesino* will be glad to show you the way to the top to see the cross. From the town of Cuapa, it's a 2.5-hour hike to the top, including several extremely steep sections. Hike with good shoes; locals recommend not climbing it on particularly windy days. Ask around for Nicolas, an English-speaking resident of Cuapa (originally from Bluefields), who can be a guide. He runs a tire repair shop next to Parque Zapera.

SERRANÍA AMERRISQUE

A powerful backdrop to Juigalpa, the Amerrisque mountain range forms a rocky backbone to the history of the city. Most of the archaeological pieces in the Juigalpa museum were unearthed in the Amerrisques, and countless other sites have yet to be explored. Although the area is undeveloped for tourists, the rocky peaks make a tempting hike and the locals claim the east side of the range contains several caves.

Your starting point is the road called the Camino de la Vaticana, built by Rome and Holland in the late 1990s. It will lead you nine kilometers east toward the range and the tiny farming community of Piedra Grande. From there, you can strike into the hills to explore. You can try hitching a ride out there to trim down the flat, boring part of the hike, but it won't be easy, as traffic along the road is sparse at best. There are few communities along its length. Consider hiring a pickup truck in town; a group of five travelers offering $15–20 might be able to convince someone to drive them out there. Try to swing a deal for the ride back while you're at it.

Daniel Molina can serve as a guide (tel. 505/512-2940). He is a young man who speaks English and can help you arrange a trip out to the mountains, where he'll help you find a local guide to show you the trails.

---

monolith outside of town, Cuapa isn't a bad place to spend the night. One option for the climb is to arrive in the evening, spend the night at Cuapa, and set off to climb the monolith the following morning. You can find accommodations and meals at **Restaurante Hospedaje La Maravilla,** with rooms in the $1.50–3.50 range. The hotel fills up the week of June 19–27, when Cuapa celebrates its patron saint, San José.

Six buses leave Juigalpa for Cuapa every day, starting at 6 A.M. and the last departing at 6 P.M. Buses from Cuapa to Juigalpa leave from the town center every day, 6 A.M.–4:30 P.M.

Thermal Vents at Agua Caliente

While eastern Nicaragua lacks the volcanoes of the Pacific horizon, it too was formed volcanically and the hot springs are evidence that under the surface, even quiet old Chontales is bubbling and tectonically active. When they're hot they're hot, but when they're not, a trip out to the hot springs at Agua Caliente yields nothing more than a trickle of water seeping out of the side of the creek bed. When they're active, however, expect torrents of bubbles gushing out of the creek bed in water too hot to touch.

To get there, take the Camino de la Vaticana as though you were going to the Amerrisque mountains, but take the first major left-hand turn instead; Aguas Calientes is 4.8 kilometers down the road. You'll know you've reached the site when you get to a relatively new school building followed immediately by a streambed. The hot springs are located about 100 meters upstream from where the road crosses the stream.

© RANDALL WOOD

dusty road in the Amerrisque mountain range

La Libertad and Santo Domingo

These two pueblos have been the site of small-scale gold mining for well over a hundred years. British mining engineer Thomas Belt was surveying in the Santo Domingo area when he wrote his famous book, *A Naturalist in Nicaragua,* in 1874. The mines were run by a Canadian organization that ceased activities around 2000. The curious may be interested in poking around either town, both of which, though run-down and slightly decrepit, still very distinctly bear the traces of a small boom-town atmosphere. La Libertad is the birthplace of president Daniel Ortega as well as Nicaragua's outspoken and politicized Catholic archbishop Miguel Obando y Bravo.

The Road to Rama

During the 1980s, the highway from San Benito (Managua) to Rama, known as the Rama Highway, was a hotly contested military prize. At stake was control of the port at Rama, through which Managua received much of its oil and supplies from the Baltic states and the Soviet Union. The Contras finally succeeded in capturing the highway in 1987 with a massive offensive of 2,500 troops, who laid waste to government buildings in La Gateada, Santo Tomás, and San Pedro de Lóvago and demolished five bridges, all but the crown jewel—the bridge at Muelle de los Bueyes which, standing 150 meters high over the Río Mico, remains the highest and most irreplaceable bridge in Nicaragua. The highway, a pothole-ridden disaster by the end of the war, was completely resurfaced during 2002–2005.

Between Villa Sandino and La Campana are hundreds of pre-Columbian petroglyphs in situ, around which the **Parque Arqueológico**

"**Piedras Pintadas**" (tel. 505/850-2121, $3 entrance fee) was developed in 2008 with help from Finland. From Villa Sandino it's 20 minutes by bus but you can easily walk it. Stay in Villa Sandino at **Hotel Santa Clara** (tel. 505/516-0055, maisalar@hotmail.com) where you'll find rooms for $20 with air-conditioning and hot water, $15 with fan; or the more economical **Hospedaje Chavarria** across from the Medical Center.

EL RAMA

At the eastern terminus of the highway from Managua, El Rama straddles the frontier between Atlantic and Pacific more perceptibly than any other Nicaraguan town. A longtime riverine port and trader town, El Rama is a melting pot, where mestizo cattle traders meet Caribbean steamer captains, and dark-skinned Creoles mix with "Spaniards" from the Pacific.

The name Rama is a tribute to the Rama people who once inhabited the shores of the Siquia, Rama, Escondido, and Mico Rivers. The inhabitants of today's El Rama, however, are the progeny of immigrants from Chontales, Boaco, and Granada, all of whom swarmed here in the late 18th century to take advantage of the boom in the wood, rubber, and banana trade. Before 1880, the original port of El Rama was located on the southwest shore of the Río Siquia but was relocated to the present location due to the unbearable mud, floods, and swamps that plagued the original location.

While Nicaraguans from all over the country resented the stringent rationing of food and basic goods during the war years of the 1980s, no one was more indignant than the people of El Rama, whose international port was where the millions of metric tons of military hardware were brought onshore from Eastern-bloc freighters to be shipped up the Rama Highway to military bases around the nation. In the 1980s, while locals were forming lines to receive a half-bar of soap and one pound of rice, they watched steel-armored convoys of tanks, fighter planes, and trucks full of rifles, grenades, and antipersonnel land mines pass

through their town bound for the battle lines. Short of the trenches of the front line, nowhere was the military buildup—and the irony of the shortage of basic goods—more obvious.

El Rama, though wholly dependent on the river, is also at the mercy of it. El Rama has been under water several times, including during Hurricane Joan, when for three days the only thing seen above the surface of the boiling, muddy waters of the swollen Río Escondido was the church steeple. Deforestation upstream means the river floods more and more frequently these days, and with less advance warning. An electronic system of flood warning devices installed along the river in 2000 will hopefully give residents a chance to evacuate.

The folks at El Rama are interested in developing a tourism infrastructure; they just don't know how to do it yet. Any adventuring you do in the region will require ingenuity and patience. Divided by rivers and swamps, the lands around El Rama are teeming with places to explore and look for wildlife. **Los Humedales de Mahogany** is a wetlands reserve important for the reproduction of local species. It's a 4–5 hour trip by boat downstream in the direction of Bluefields along the Mahogany River near the entrance to the Caño Negro (Black Creek). **Cerro Silva** was declared protected in 1997; it's located 2.5 hours along the Río Rama in the direction of San Jerónimo. Once you disembark from your boat, it's a 2.5-hour hike from the river's edge to the park; find a guide in San Jerónimo to lead you there.

The falls of **Salto Mataka** are found along the Río Siquia, 2.5 hours from La Esperanza (the town with the big bridge, just west of El Rama). Also located near La Esperanza is **El Recreo,** a popular swimming hole three kilometers north of town.

The typical traveler spends no more than 15 minutes in Rama between the time he or she gets off the bus and onto a boat to Bluefields. But should you find yourself stuck here (let's face it, few travelers will brave the nine-hour bus ride just to go to Rama), you may find El Rama to be worth a second look, and even useful as the base for an expedition or two.

Accommodations

Not recommended are the two sketchy places down by the port, Hotel Amy and Hotel Manantial, where for $7 you get nasty bathroom facilities, questionable security, and probably prostitutes and their company for your neighbors. The locals direct foreign travelers to **Hotel Johana** (tel. 505/517-0066, $2 pp), which is simple and safe and has more than 30 rooms in a large wooden building. A bit cleaner and far quieter is **Hospedaje García,** with singles for $2.75, double beds for $5, and fancier rooms on the second floor with air-conditioning and a view of the river for $10.50.

Eco Hotel El Vivero (Km 290.5 on the highway from Managua, tel. 505/517-0340, $25) is a quiet, peaceful place within a private reserve, located two short kilometers from the city of El Rama. The wooden cabins and decent meals have been recommended by several readers.

Food and Services

Without a doubt, the best place in town for a meal is **Restaurante El Expreso,** whose name has no relation to the speed of the service; enjoy lots of seafood, soups, chicken, and steak. Across from the market, **Antojitos Mexicanos** is popular with the locals for Mexican dishes and beer. The **Eskimo** sells sandwiches in addition to ice cream. A good *fritanga* sets up shop evenings near the market (approximately across from Antojitos Mexicanos).

The **ENITEL** and **post office** are located across the street from each other. ENITEL is open 7 A.M.–9 P.M. Monday–Saturday. For late-night phone calls, try the Pepsi booth on the street that leads to the municipal pier (i.e., the pier with boats for Bluefields). There's a phone there that the owner will let you use. **Farmacia El Carmen** (open 8 A.M.–1 P.M. and 2–6:30 P.M. Mon.–Sat.) is well stocked with medicines, sanitary supplies, and more.

Getting There and Away

El Rama is approximately six hours from Juigalpa. Two bus companies leave from Managua for El Rama—from the Mayoreo terminal (tel. 505/248-3005) daily at 3 P.M. and from Mercado Ivan Montenego (tel. 505/280-4561) daily at 9 P.M. Call ahead for seats on these buses. Express buses don't linger in Juigalpa or stop along the road, shaving two hours off the trip. All boat transportation to Bluefields is found at the municipal wharf: *Pangas* cast off from the dock as they fill up, 6 A.M.–4 P.M. (1.5-hour trip to Bluefields, approximately $10 pp). There's a bigger ship that carries freight and passengers, but it is much slower than the nimble *pangas.* It leaves every Tuesday and Saturday at 11 A.M. (five hours, approximately $5 pp).

Nueva Guinea

This region is nearly as off the beaten path as you can get in Nicaragua. Technically, the town of Nueva Guinea is part of the RAAS (Southern Atlantic Autonomous Region), but it is more easily accessed from the Rama Highway and Juigalpa than Bluefields and the Río Escondido. A full 293 kilometers southeast of Managua, Nueva Guinea lies in the tropical, humid, rolling lowlands that stretch toward the Caribbean. It's one of the rainiest corners of Nicaragua, receiving an average of 8,000 millimeters (yes, that's eight meters) of rainfall each year, but that varies from town to town, based on the forest cover of the area. In terms of population, it is the second largest municipality in Nicaragua, with a de facto population of 120,000 people, many of whom technically live in the municipality of Bluefields but whose transport and public services are provided via Nueva Guinea.

In the 1960s, Nueva Guinea was a rich, dense, tropical rainforest with a wide variety of animal life, but since then, due to poor public policy, misguided development projects, and inadequate agricultural practices, much of the territory has been transformed into barren, useless pasture. Forested areas include the land that borders the Reserva Indio-Maíz and the Reserva Natural Punta Gorda. Even that land is in the process of being slowly and illegally colonized and exploited, and poor farmers in desperate need of land overwhelm the capacity of the Nicaraguan government to prevent their homesteading.

Nueva Guinea was founded as part of U.S. President John F. Kennedy's Alliance for Progress, a program meant to defuse demands for land reform across Latin America in the wake of the Cuban revolution and the postcolonial struggles in the rest of the world. Original settlers were given one *manzana* of land (about one hectare) in the urban center, and 60 in the countryside. The same program was applied to help victims of natural disasters—victims of both the Managua earthquake of 1972 and the eruption of Cerro Negro near León in 1973 were shipped out to Nueva Guinea. In the 1980s, the area was a hot spot of Contra activity under the command of Edén Pastora's group, ARDE, based across the Costa Rica border.

These days, farmers in the area of Nueva Guinea live in some 140 neighborhoods and produce an uninspiring variety of the same thing everyone else does—corn, beans, and rice—plus ginger. Nueva Guinea is a wild place, with horses parked outside of bars and people walking their pigs or herding cattle down main street. The town of Nueva Guinea has few facilities, but the curious traveler may appreciate visiting a place so out of the way.

SIGHTS AND ATTRACTIONS

For the extreme wilderness adventurer, Nueva Guinea is also your base for exploration of two of Nicaragua's most pristine nature reserves—**Punta Gorda** and **Indio-Maíz.** Retrace the steps of colonial Spanish captains, Calero and Machuca, who sought the best route to the Caribbean coast through the communities of Puerto Prinicipe, Atlanta, and others, concluding in the coastal community of Punta Gorda. Arrange for a guide at the mayor's office. Less demanding is the one-hour hike to the falls at **Salto Esperanza:** Take the bus to the community of Esperanza and ask around.

At **Finca La Esperanzita,** you can glimpse an organic agriculture project where small farmers are growing cacao, vanilla, pepper, and several species of tropical hardwoods. They'll gladly provide you with a tour of the facilities, including a coffee-, cacao-, and cinnamon-processing plant run by World Relief one block south and one block east of the hospital.

ACCOMMODATIONS AND FOOD

There are three options in Nueva Guinea: **Hotel Nueva Guinea** (on the main drag, tel. 505/575-0090, $10–25) has a variety of rooms, some with air-conditioning, cable TV, and bath. Newer, quiet **Hotel Miraflores** (300 meters south of URACCAN, tel. 505/575-0039, $10) has good mattresses. Backpackers tend to settle for **Las 24 Horas Hospedaje** (municipal market 1.5 blocks north, across from the police station, $2.50 pp).

Llamas del Bosque (next to the Esso station) serves the best meal in town for about $5. Sit poolside at **Ranchón Kristofer** (three blocks north of the park) or join the crowd on the dance floor. **Comedoría Dalili** (across from the mayor's office) is the least expensive *comedor* in town; less than $1 for a meal.

GETTING THERE AND AWAY

Buses leave for Nueva Guinea from Managua's Mayoreo terminal approximately every hour (eight-hour trip).

SOLENTINAME AND THE RÍO SAN JUAN

The Spanish, intent on piercing the Central American isthmus, focused intently on the Río San Juan, which nearly reaches the Pacific shore. In 1524, Hernán Cortés wrote King Carlos I of Spain, "He who possesses the Río San Juan could be considered the owner of the World." The strategic and economic importance of this region has not diminished since.

The Río San Juan carries the waters of Lake Cocibolca to the Caribbean through a lush landscape of Nicaragua's most extensive nature reserves—and significant stretches of riverside ranchland.

San Carlos is an edgy port town you'll inevitably pass through on the way to adventure, thick with itinerants, rowdies, farmers, fishers, swindlers, and the works. Catch a boat there to the Solentiname Archipelago, quiet islets as pertinent to the revolution years as to Nicaragua's prehistoric past, and a center of production for some of Nicargua's most gorgeous paintings. Or, take a wooden boat down the river towards the Atlantic, a sun-baked ride back through time. El Castillo, one of Spain's most permanent colonial legacies, remains little changed from the 17th century and the days of marauding pirates. From there downstream fishing village follows pasture follows rapids until you reach San Juan de Nicaragua, the little town where it all began and where it all ends, remote and untamed. It's not easy to get here, and thornier still to get around, so bring some patience and determination to this isolated corner of Nicaragua, which is well worth getting to know, and the dramatic landscapes and lacustrine lifestyle are unforgettable.

HIGHLIGHTS

◖ **La Isla Elvis Chavarría:** One of the Solentiname archipelago's jewels, "La Elvis" features a museum, a hiking trail, an arboretum, and a wonderful host community of farmers, fishers, and artists (page 300).

◖ **Los Guatuzos Wildlife Refuge and Centro Ecológico:** This is one of the best places in the south to get down and dirty with nature; start by identifying a few of the 389 species of tropical birds (page 302).

◖ **Sábalos Lodge:** Bamboo, thatch, lazy afternoons, and the burbling river – this lodge is close to the jungle and far away from everything (page 305).

◖ **El Castillo:** The mighty embattlements of this historic mud-river fortress have watched over the river since the days pirates prowled the Spanish mainland (page 306).

◖ **San Juan de Nicaragua:** Remote and thick with history, San Juan de Nicaragua is an adventure in itself; the local blue lagoon swimming hole is dramatic and an easy dugout-canoe ride away (page 309).

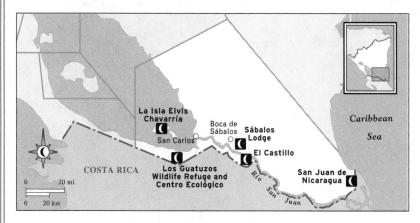

LOOK FOR ◖ TO FIND RECOMMENDED SIGHTS, ACTIVITIES, DINING, AND LODGING.

PLANNING YOUR TIME

Here you've got to have either time or money. Public transportation is slow and the schedules capricious, but it's cheap. You can see and do more if you hire a boat and driver or make arrangements with a tour company, but it will affect your budget by an order of magnitude (organizing a group of like-minded travelers to share costs is one way to offset the price). You'll also experience about 25 percent higher costs for most goods due to transport to this more-isolated region (35 percent more on

Solentiname). It's wise to allow a full week for exploration of this region: Make your plane reservation from Managua to San Carlos early, as seats fill up fast.

On public transportation, you could make it to Solentiname and back in two days if the stars align, but it will more likely be three or four depending on boat schedules. It's only a day more to see El Castillo, and you should make sure to include it on your tour. Once you leave San Carlos and begin exploring downstream, you need more buffer time as you are more at the

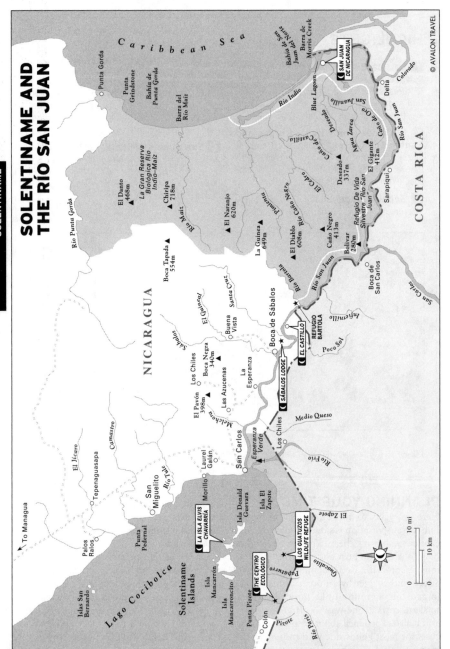

SOLENTINAME AND THE RÍO SAN JUAN

© AVALON TRAVEL

whims of passing boats. The same goes for any potential travel to Los Guatuzos, which will require at least another day of travel time just for boat connections back and forth. A final travel tip: The Río San Juan is a border area where any petty bureaucrat or intimidating sergeant can demand to see your papers, so play it safe and have them in order and on your person.

HISTORY
Colonial Times to Independence
The mouth of the Río San Juan, choked with labyrinthine estuaries, had eluded explorers for years, including Christopher Columbus, who failed to find it in 1502. The Spanish founded Granada in 1524 (the same year Cortés was writing the king and setting off to explore southern Lake Cocibolca). Not until 1539 did Spanish explorers finally reach the Atlantic by sailing downstream from Granada. This made Granada Spain's first quasi-Atlantic port in Central America. To consolidate their hold on the river the Spaniards began persecuting the indigenous people living along the river and the Solentiname Islands.

In 1567, the first Spanish trade expedition set sail from Granada: three ships laden with agricultural products for Panamá. They made it as far as the Caribbean, where English pirates plundered the vessels and fed the surviving sailors to the sharks. Tension and conflict between European nations over the next 300 years led to a virtual state of war between Spain's colonial holdings in Nicaragua and English, Dutch, and French pirates whose respective governments encouraged them to give the Spanish hell. Until the Spanish improved their fortifications along the Río San Juan, the pirates were disastrously successful at sacking and burning Granada, which suffered repeatedly. By 1724, however, fortresses guarded the river at San Carlos, Pocosol, El Castillo, Bartola, El Diamante, Machuca, Río San Carlos, Río San Francisco, Sarapiqui, Concepción Island, and San Juan del Norte—and the pirates' pillaging came to an end.

Throughout the 19th century, the Río San Juan grew in importance for commerce and for its value as a shortcut through the isthmus for foreigners traveling between New York and California (the most famous of whom was Mark Twain). Cornelius Vanderbilt built up a steamship business that forever changed the region and made San Juan del Norte a major destination. But when the steamship business came to a halt, the river slipped back into bucolic obscurity for a century.

During the Contra War
As a sensitive border area during the 1980s, the Río San Juan was a southern front for Contra forces, particularly for the Alianza Revolucionaria Democrática (ARDE), under the leadership of Edén Pastora, a.k.a. Comandante Cero, who fought on the southern front years after the CIA stopped supporting him. Troops from both sides planted fields of antipersonnel mines, and entire communities evacuated the war zone, fleeing south to Costa Rica or west to other points in Nicaragua. The population of the region dropped to fewer than 40,000, then nearly doubled in the 1990s as people returned with new families, stressing already environmentally sensitive land.

Today
In spite of relentless "El Río San Juan is ours!" chest thumping up in Managua, the Nicaraguan government has all but abandoned the river, whose lower reaches have long been neglected. Tens of thousands of Nicaraguans emigrate to Costa Rica, legally or otherwise, in search of work and better living conditions. And for those Nicaraguans living along the river, the news, radio, and television stations come from Costa Rica, as do occasionally the schools and health services. Many towns—especially San Juan del Norte—use the Costa Rican *colón* in lieu of the *córdoba*. But increased government attention should ensue as wealthy Managua legislators purchase land along the river for their own use and development. Costa Ricans bristle at being denied the opportunity to promote tourism along the San Juan if Nicaraguans aren't going to do it. Keep your eyes peeled for Costa Rican–run excursions on the river.

SOLENTINAME

CANAL DREAMS PAST AND PRESENT

After realizing the coveted natural water passage across America was nonexistent, geographers discovered that the lowest point along the entire north-south American divide – from Alaska to Tierra del Fuego – is found in Nicaragua. The fact that it is possible to go no higher than 40 meters above sea level in crossing from the Pacific to the Atlantic Ocean has maintained a fierce interest in the building of an interocean canal there since the early 1500s.

U.S. Army engineer Colonel Orville Childs carried out the first systematic study of the canal route in 1852, at the invitation of U.S. millionaire Cornelius Vanderbilt, who, three years earlier, had set up a transisthmus transit route across Nicaragua to carry gold prospectors between California and New York.

The original Childs proposal, designed to move sailing ships from ocean to ocean, was followed by another half-dozen U.S. Army and Navy surveys over the next 100 years, with the greatest interest occurring at the turn of the century. At this time, Panamá and Nicaragua were vying for the construction of a U.S.-controlled Pacific–Atlantic canal. After intense lobbying by promoters of both projects, the U.S. Congress finally opted to buy out the

bankrupt French company that had already started building the Panama Canal.

The 1914 Bryan-Chamorro treaty, signed by the U.S. and Nicaragua in the year the Panama Canal opened, gave the United States exclusive rights – in perpetuity – to build a canal through Nicaragua. Two further U.S. Army studies for a Nicaraguan canal were commissioned by Congress during the 20th century, one in 1929-1931 for a deep-draft canal similar to that in Panamá, and another in 1939-1940 to build a shallow-draft barge canal. However, despite wartime fears of damage being caused to the Panama Canal, the U.S. Congress never saw sufficient economic merit in either variant to approve construction funds.

The Bryan-Chamorro treaty was abrogated in 1970, at around the same time as containerized cargo traffic began to grow exponentially in international maritime trade. These facts, together with the signing of the Carter-Torrijos treaty in 1979, which would hand over the Panama Canal to Panamá at the end of 1999, spurred renewed interest in the Nicaraguan canal.

During the Sandinista period, a proposal was made by a Japanese consortium to construct a canal that would accommodate ships four

San Carlos

Surrounded on three sides by a watery horizon, San Carlos's sky is often pierced by bright rainbows; unlike drier parts of the country, afternoon showers can occur throughout the year here. But this is no nirvana—San Carlos is a raucous and spirited hamlet of mostly transients. San Carleños are lively people. Some manage to beat the poverty by finding work in the thirty-odd NGO offices in San Carlos as *tecnicos*, secretaries, and support staff. Many of today's San Carleños were born elsewhere in the country and ended up here on their way to

somewhere else. They are field hands on their way to Costa Rican harvests, remotely posted border soldiers, and lake and river merchants trading with Chontales cattlemen.

Nearly everyone traveling in the Río San Juan region is obliged to pass through San Carlos. San Carlos is the departmental and economic capital of the region with all the services generally not available deeper in the countryside. Make use of your time here to get updated boat schedules and supplies for your trip.

times the size of the largest that can squeeze through the locks at Panamá. The Sandinistas were busy fighting the Contra war, with their economy in tatters, and the proposal never prospered.

In the 1990s, two "dry canal" projects surfaced (CINN and SIT-Global), with proposals to build high-speed, transisthmus railways connecting ports on both oceans, which would transport containers on specialized railcars between ships berthed at either terminal of the railway. The routes are being proposed as a potential alternative to the Panama Canal and the U.S. transcontinental rail system, both of which are becoming increasingly congested for the east-west container trade between Asia and the East Coast of the United States. The construction cost has been estimated at $1-2 billion.

In 1999, Nicaragua's National Assembly approved a 30-year concession to a private company named EcoCanal for the construction of an inland waterway to permit the navigation of shallow-draft barge traffic along the Río San Juan from Lake Cocibolca to the Caribbean. Although not an interocean project as such, the $50-million waterway could be converted to one with the excavation of the 18-kilometer stretch of land between the Pacific Ocean and Lake Cocibolca – at an additional cost of some $300-400 million.

Politicians from the two leading parties, the Liberals and Sandinistas, have also revived variants of the 1980s Japanese proposal for building a huge, post-Panama canal, with a price tag in excess of $20 billion.

Until now, recent proposals have been paralyzed by a lack of venture capital to finance full feasibility studies, necessary to convert them into bankable projects for construction. Until such studies are completed, doubts will persist over their economic and environmental viability. Nonetheless, despite potential backing from U.S. investors, the Nicaraguan government has been unwilling to lend its wholehearted support to the project, and instead continues to talk of an interocean rail and pipeline project, possibly financed by Venezuela. This, together with President Ortega's rhetoric about "U.S. imperialism," has made EcoCanal investors nervous and unwilling to commit.

(Contributed by Tim Coone, a journalist by training, who has lived and worked in Nicaragua since the Revolution years.)

ORIENTATION AND GETTING AROUND

If you are landing at the "airport," grab one of the rickety four-wheel drive taxis to take you the couple of kilometers into town—the five-minute ride costs $0.50. The bus station is more or less in the town center, across from the gas station and docks. Coming by boat dumps you right in the middle of the action. The main center of San Carlos is only about a dozen city blocks, all south of the central park on the flank of a hill looking south over the water. The waterfront can be a little confusing, especially if you find yourself in one of the narrow market aisles, but all in all, there's not much actual "town" in which to get lost. Main Street would be the one running along the waterfront. The city sprawls northward along the muddy highway to the hospital and airport.

SIGHTS AND ENTERTAINMENT

The old **Spanish fort,** renovated in 2005, enjoys a nice view overlooking the town and lake. Its cultural center and library were founded with Cuban support—to wit, countless volumes of communist propaganda—and has since been supported by the Netherlands. At the *mirador,* you'll find old cannons, a romantic sunset setting, and one of the nicest restaurants in town.

Solentiname islanders arrive in San Carlos to do some trading.

For nightlife, locals make their way to **La Champa,** a bar so popular, its name has become a verb among locals (as in, "Let's go *champear!*"). **El Bocano** is newer and located just north of the water tower. Bars line most streets throughout town, with the rowdiest ones down by the waterfront; try the **Granadino** or the **Kaoma** for a mellower vibe. The annual **sportfishing competition** in September is a big deal for Nicaraguan anglers and attracts crowds from across the nation for prizes like outboard motors and more. Enjoy the *fiestas patronales* on November 4. Most radio stations in the area are Costa Rican and feature Spanglish reggae and *soka*. Radio San Carlos is at 94.9 FM; Radio Trópico Humedo is at 590 AM.

ACCOMMODATIONS

San Carlos's half-dozen sleazy *hospedajes* on the main drag charge as little as $3 per person, but you get what you pay for. If you're short on cash, or just into slumming, try **Hospedaje Peña** (a block back from the water, tel. 505/583-0298, $2.50 pp), whose 10 rooms and streetside balcony enjoy a view of the Solentiname Islands. **Hotel San Carlos** (tel. 505/583-0265, $3 s, 5 d, $8 with private bath) offers about the same quality accommodation, i.e. not much. **Hotel Costa Sur** (on the road past the bus station, tel. 505/583-0224) costs $4 single, 10 double with shared bath, a few dollars more for private bath; rooms are a little musty, but clean and far quieter than the others.

Hotel Carelys (a half-block south of the park, tel. 505/583-0389, $11) is also known as Aquiles or Doña Coco. Its 10 rooms are the cleanest and most pleasant in the city and include private bath, fan, and complimentary soap, drinking water, and old magazines in Spanish. Another popular choice is the **Cabinas Leyko** (two blocks west of the church, tel. 505/583-0354). Its 22 rooms start at $11 for a double, but they have some higher-end alternatives with air-conditioning and cable TV for $50.

SOLENTINAME

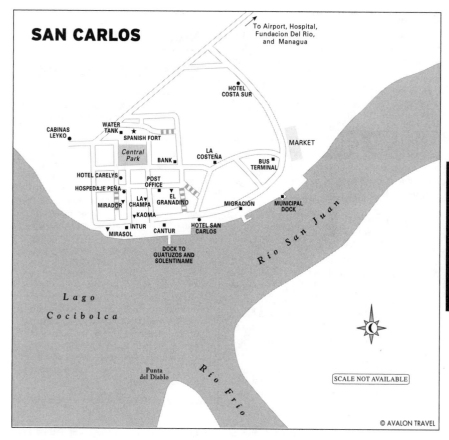

FOOD

The dockside *comedores* or market stalls are the best deal. Otherwise, **El Granadino** serves chicken plates from $4, fish from $5. Its food is the best in town though slow to get to your table. Down the block, popular ◖ **Kaoma** has a similar menu but better service with prices starting at $7; it's open late on weekends. **The Mirador,** aptly named for the landmark on which it sits, has good food and pleasant lake views from the outside seating area. Try the jalapeño steak and imagine shooting cannonballs at pirates. Just below the cannons in the same area is the less impressive **Mirasol,** with similar fare.

INFORMATION AND SERVICES
Tourism Offices

INTUR (near the dock for Los Guatuzos and Solentiname, tel. 505/583-0301) may be able to help you arrange for special transport and can provide a brochure or two about the region. Directly in front of the same dock is the office for CANTUR, which when staffed can provide information on public boat schedules, contacts for private services, and a list of tours offered on Solentiname. The kiosk selling tickets near the entrance to the municipal dock can provide the balance of the updated boat schedules.

Emergency

The police station (tel. 505/583-0350) is located three kilometers from the center of San Carlos on the road to Managua. The fire station can be reached by calling 505/583-2149. Hospital Luis Felipe Moncada (tel. 505/583-0238 or 505/583-0244) is north of town on the highway; or try the Centro de Salud (tel. 505/583-0361). San Carlos's medical services may be okay for minor problems, but for any real emergencies, you're better off chartering a boat south to the hospital in Los Chiles, Costa Rica (one hour or less by boat) or trying to get a flight back to Managua.

Communication

There are cheap Internet cafés all over town; start near the park. You can make phone calls from most Internet places, and both Nicaraguan cell phone companies offer service around San Carlos. Only ENITEL is available in other municipalities of the region.

The San Carlos post office (located a block south of the park, tel. 505/583-0276, tel./fax 505/583-0000, open 8 A.M.–5 P.M. Mon.–Fri., 8 A.M.–1 P.M. Sat., closed for lunch) receives and sends mail via the daily La Costeña flight. But Carlos Reyes (near Hospedaje Peña, fax 505/583-0090) can also receive a fax for you.

Banks

There is no ATM in town, or anywhere else in the Río San Juan. Furthermore, only a handful of businesses in the region take credit cards, so bring enough cash to last for the whole trip. Banco de Finanzas (one block east of the park, tel. 505/583-0144, open 8:30 A.M.–4 P.M. Mon.–Fri., until noon Sat.) will exchange dollars, but will not deal with travelers checks, Costa Rican *colónes,* or credit-card cash advances. There are plenty of *coyote* money changers down by the Migración office, trading *córdobas,* dollars, and *colónes.* Otherwise, head for the Western Union just southwest of the church.

GETTING THERE AND AWAY

You have three choices to get to San Carlos: a horrid nine-hour bus ride from Managua

---

NICARAGUA'S FAMOUS FRESHWATER SHARK

How the *Carcharhinus leucas* became the only shark in the world able to pass between saltwater and freshwater is a fascinating story. After thousands of years of hunting in the brackish outflow of the Río San Juan, Nicaragua's freshwater sharks made their way up the river and formed a healthy population in Lago de Nicaragua. The tale continues with the arrival of humans and their role as both victims and hunters of Nicaragua's bull shark, told in full in Edward Marriott's 2001 book, *Savage Shore.* Indigenous tribes on Ometepe worshipped the shark, sometimes feeding their dead to it. This fear and reverence only faded when the Asian market for shark-fin soup helped to create an industry around harvesting the famous fish, culminating in the late 1960s, when Somoza's processing plant in Granada butchered up to 20,000 sharks a year. Today, the only freshwater shark in the world is seldom seen, although it is still inadvisable to swim in the waters near San Juan del Norte.

---

down the east side of the lake, a slow boat across the lake from Granada or Ometepe, or a quick flight from Managua. Even the locals prefer the third option, making reservations essential.

By Land

While a highway project connecting Managua and San Carlos is in the works, for now the second half of the journey remains a back-breaker, as the bus batters its way at walking speed for hours through gullies, rutted tracks, and mud pits. When the road hasn't been closed entirely, buses leave Managua's Mayoreo market, starting at 5 A.M. with the last night bus leaving at 6:30 P.M. The first of the seven buses to Managua is at 6:30 A.M., the last at 10 P.M.

© JOSHUA BERMAN

The ferry to San Carlos leaves Granada twice a week for the long ride south.

The 300-kilometer trip costs under $10. In San Carlos, buses for all destinations leave from the terminal near the municipal dock. If driving on your own, be sure to have a spare tire and jack, plus water and provisions, as you will need all of them.

By Boat from Granada

The old ferry departs Granada's municipal dock Monday and Thursday at 2 P.M., making stops at Ometepe at 6 P.M. and San Miguelito just before arriving in San Carlos around 5 A.M. the next morning. Be there before 12:30 P.M. to get your ticket—$7 for padded first-class seats with too much air-conditioning, or $3 down below on the hard, wooden benches. Expect both sections to be overcrowded. The same boat leaves San Carlos bound for Granada on Tuesdays and Fridays at 2 P.M.; be there at least an hour in advance to get your ticket. This boat passes Ometepe around 1 or 2 A.M.

The boat gets crowded at times, especially around Semana Santa, when the hot easterly winds chop the lake into steep swells, and the voyage degenerates into a 16-hour puke-fest. Get there early and be aggressive to stake your territory topside. At other times of the year, the ride is long but generally pleasant, and sailing west is always easier than sailing east.

Down the Río San Juan

All boat tickets are sold at the Venta de Boletos Transporte Acuático (tel. 505/583-0200 or 505/892-0174, open 7 A.M.–3 P.M. Mon.–Sat.) on the main drag toward the gas station. Inside the little shack you'll find up-to-date schedules and advance ticket sales for its fleet of *lanchas*. Four slow, three-hour boat trips to El Castillo depart daily, costing $3. Fast boats leave at 10 A.M. and 4 P.M. and for $5 are more than worth it. The same fast boats come back at 5:30 and 11 A.M. from El Castillo. The last boat back is at 2 P.M. All boats for El Castillo also stop in Sabalos.

Boats to San Juan del Norte are less frequent. Only two boats make the trip, one fast and one slow. They leave on Tuesdays and Fridays and come back on Thursdays and Sundays. The

SAN JUAN'S STEAMERS: CORNELIUS VANDERBILT'S NICARAGUAN VENTURE

Entrepreneurs and fortune-hunters heading to California in the famed '49 gold rush found it easier to traverse Central America than to brave the long, perilous overland trek across the United States. American businessman Cornelius Vanderbilt formed the first company that provided passage between New York and San Francisco via Nicaragua. The 45-day trip from New York to California cost $145. Vanderbilt made the first successful voyage himself in 1851. Upon reaching the Nicaraguan shore at Greytown in great, square-rigged clipper ships, passengers boarded side-wheeled *vapores* (riverboats), including the 120-ton iron-hulled *Director* and the smaller *Bulwer*, which worked different stretches of the river (to get around unnavigable rapids, passengers disembarked and transferred to the next upstream ship). The second leg sailed past San Carlos, then traversed the lake to the town of Virgen; there, passengers boarded horse carriages and traveled overland to San Juan del Sur where another clipper ship took them to California.

The route was an immediate success, and by 1853, Vanderbilt's company could scarcely provide enough ships to meet the demand. Vanderbilt's company remained uncontested and by 1854, had transported more than 23,000 passengers between New York and California. Business was booming along the route, which now included a short railway to avoid the rapids at El Castillo. San Juan del Norte became a rip-roaring port town with 127 foreign consulates and embassies, and a stream of adventuring gringos, foreign investors, and New Orleans whores, prompting U.S. envoy E. G. Squier to remark on the town's "general drunkenness and indiscriminate licentiousness."

The most famous of Vanderbilt's passengers was also one his biggest critics: After Mark Twain made the voyage in 1867, he took Cornelius to task in "An Open Letter to Commodore Vanderbilt." In it, he complained about the wretched quality of the steamship line. More of Twain's comments on Nicaragua are found in a posthumously assembled collection called *Travels with Mr. Brown.*

The boom lasted another half century, fueled after the end of the gold rush by the prospect of an interoceanic canal. The dream all but died when the bid went to Panamá in 1902, and communities up and down the Río San Juan began to wither. Outside San Juan del Norte, the remains of an old iron steamdredge stand in the shallows of the river where it foundered, testament to the boldest of dreams and the still-unwritten future of transoceanic shipping in Nicaragua.

slow boat leaves San Carlos at 6 A.M. and San Juan del Norte at 5 A.M. The fast boat ($25, 6 hours) leaves an hour after the slow boat ($13, 12 hours).

Arrange private boat trips at the Venta, INTUR, or directly with a *panguero* (private boat owner). Armando Ortiz's Viajes Turísticos (near the Western Union, tel. 505/583-0039) is one option. Rising gas prices make chartered trips expensive (we're talking hundreds of dollars). As the demand for transportation continues to grow and shift, so do boat schedules. Always check departure times at the docks well in advance, and be sure to get a second (and third) opinion.

By Air

There are two daily 50-minute flights from Managua on weekdays, one at 9 A.M. and one at 1 P.M. Only the morning plane leaves on Saturdays and just the afternoon plane makes the flight on Sundays. The return flight departs San Carlos immediately after landing and unloading. The round-trip costs $120. Contact La Costeña in Managua (tel. 505/263-2142). In San Carlos, the La Costeña office is run by Doña María Amelia Gross out of her home (one block west of the BDF bank, tel. 505/583-0271). Always reserve your spot as far in advance as you can, as flights fill up fast and reservations are free to make. In a case of desperation you can get on the waiting list and show up for a stand-by attempt, which works more often than you would think for a 12-person plane.

RÍO FRÍO BORDER CROSSING

Boating south into Costa Rica begins with a visit to the shabby, blue-and-white Migración office on Main Street in San Carlos, recognizable by the long queue that forms before 7 A.M. The office is open 8:30 A.M.–6 P.M. daily. You'll wait in both lines: The first where a very self-important official will curiously scrutinize your passport; the second where you'll pay $2 to be showered with seals, stamps, and signatures. Boats leave from the dock just past the passport window at 10 A.M., 12 P.M., and 3 P.M. The hour-long chug up the Rio Frío to Los Chiles, Costa Rica costs $10 each way.

Once in Los Chiles, there are two more lines: one to search your bags, another to stamp your passport (Costa Rica Migración is located 200 meters up the road from the dock—be sure to stop and get stamped). If you're entering Nicaragua from Costa Rica, you'll need to buy a Cruz Roja (Red Cross) stamp for about $1, either across the street from Migración, or four blocks away in the Nicaraguan consulate (a half-block north of the church, open 8:30 A.M.–noon and 2–4:30 P.M. Mon.–Fri.). Boats leave regularly for San Carlos through about 3 P.M. Daily direct buses depart for the six-hour trip to San José. (Note: Be aware that a second town by the name of Los Chiles is about two hours northeast of San Carlos, in Nicaragua. Be sure to distinguish between the two when asking for directions.)

The Solentiname Islands

The 36 volcanically formed islands in southern Lake Cocibolca have a long history of habitation and signs of its original residents are abundant, in the form of petroglyphs, cave paintings, and artifacts. The name Solentiname comes from Celentinametl, Nahuatl for "place of many guests."

The islands are of volcanic origin with rocky, hard-to-farm soils. More effort is going into avocados these days. Somoza's logging companies deforested most of the archipelago, and Boaco cattlemen cut the rest to make pasture. In the last three decades, however, much of the forest has been allowed to regenerate, and the rebirth has attracted artists and biologists from all over the world. Fishing, of course, remains a mainstay of the islanders' diet.

Today, 129 families (about 750 people) share the archipelago with an amazing diversity of vegetation, birds, and other wildlife. Solentiname's most unique and well-known attraction is the creativity of its inhabitants, a talent Padre Ernesto Cardenal discovered in 1966 when he gave brushes and paint to some of the local *jícaro* carvers. Cardenal, recently returned from a Trappist monastery in Kentucky in the late 1960s, formed a Christian community in Solentiname and stayed on Isla Mancarrón to work and write for the next 10 years (he is locally referred to as "El Poeta"). Under his guidance, the simple church at Solentiname became the heart of Nicaragua's liberation theology movement, which represents Christ as the revolutionary savior of the poor. It inspired Carlos Mejía Godoy to write "La Misa Campesina" in 1972. Masses were communal, participatory events, and Cardenal's book, *The Gospels of Solentiname,* is a written record of the phenomenon, with transcriptions of a series of *campesino*-led services throughout the 1970s.

On October 13, 1977, a group of anti-Somoza Solentiname islanders staged a daring

© JOSHUA BERMAN

There are 36 islands in the Solentiname Archipelago.

and successful assault on the National Guard post in San Carlos. Somoza retaliated by torching the islands. In 1979, Ernesto Cardenal, now the Sandinista Minister of Culture, formed the Asociación Para el Desarollo de Solentiname (Solentiname Development Association, or APDS). Under APDS, much of what had been destroyed was rebuilt, and the arts continued to flourish and receive much attention from the rest of the world. Today, there are no fewer than 50 families who continue to produce balsa-wood carvings and bright "primitivist" paintings of the landscape and community.

ORIENTATION AND GETTING AROUND

Essentially, only the four largest of the nearly three dozen islands are inhabited: Isla Mancarrón, Isla Elvis Chavarría (a.k.a. Isla San Fernando), Isla Donald Guevara (a.k.a. Isla la Venada), and Isla Mancarroncito. Only the first two have services for tourists. If you are on a budget, getting around the islands will be your biggest challenge, especially considering that

the *colectivo* water taxis only run twice a week, ensuring a minimum stay of three days. To get around, you can either catch a free or discounted ride in someone's *panga,* or you can rent a dugout canoe or rowboat and do some paddling.

MANCARRÓN

The biggest (20 square kilometers) and tallest (at 257-meter Cerro las Cuevas) island, Mancarrón is populated by 34 families—about 200 people. The "town" of Mancarrón, built up in the 1980s, is simply a cluster of houses, a health center, school, and *pulpería,* five minutes up the muddy path from the dock. **Casa Taller de la Cooperativa** has a large collection of works by artists from different islands. The cooperative shares the profits from the individual sales. Much of the rest of the island is off-limits and has supposedly been purchased by cattle ranchers from Boaco, though conspiracy and corruption theories abound.

Ernesto Cardenal's project began in the 1960s in the church, which he reconstructed and designed. It is unlike any house of worship you've ever seen, featuring children's paintings

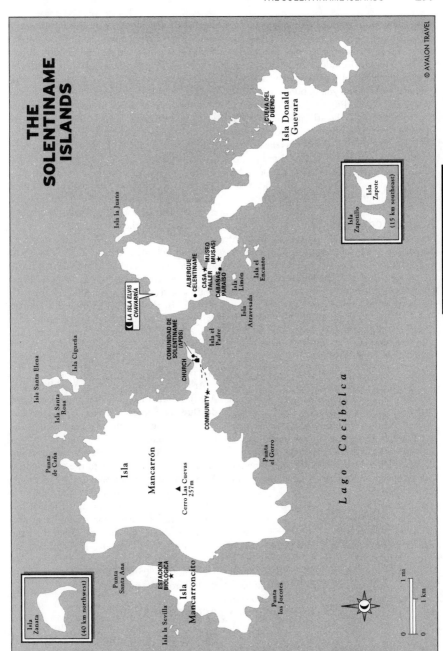

THE
SOLENTINAME
ISLANDS

© AVALON TRAVEL

Isla
Zapotillo

Isla
Zapote

(15 km southeast)

CUEVA DEL
DUENDE

Isla Donald
Guevara

Isla la Juana

LA ISLA ELVIS
CHAVARRÍA

ALBERGUE
CELENTINAME

CASA
TALLER

MUSEO
(MUSAS)

CABAÑAS
PARAÍSO

Isla
Limón

Isla el
Encanto

Isla
Atravesada

COMUNIDAD DE
SOLENTINAME
(APDS)

Isla el
Padre

CHURCH

COMMUNITY

Isla Santa Elena

Isla Santa
Rosa

Isla Cigueña

Punta
de Caña

Isla
Mancarrón

Cerro Las Cuevas
257m

Punta
el Gorro

Lago Cocibolca

Isla
Zanata

(40 km northwest)

Punta Santa Ana

ESTACIÓN
BIOLÓGICA

Isla
Mancarroncito

Isla la Sevilla

Punta
los Jocotes

1 mi

1 km

0

0

on the whitewashed adobe walls, a unique crucifix sculpted by Cardenal, and an altar decorated in pre-Columbian style. The nearby
APDS compound includes a library, a museum,
an art gallery, a display of indigenous artifacts,
and an eclectic collection of books in a variety
of languages, including the complete works of
Ernesto Cardenal, who still maintains a residence in the APDS compound. There are other
works on liberation theology, plus the original
primitivism painting by local resident Eduardo
Arana that helped start the whole project. Ask
if they can show you the 1970s BBC video documentary about the Solentiname Islands.

Accommodations

Several families offer **homestay accommodations** with three meals for around $10
and up. Just ask around. In the community
center you will find **El Buen Amigo** (tel.
505/869-6619, $6 pp). One of the rooms has a
private bath and meals run $2–3. Right next
door is **Villa Esperanza** (tel. 505/583-9020,
$25 pp including three meals). On the hill,
Hotel Mancarrón (tel. 505/583-9015, $50) is
a fenced-in miniresort with 15 basic rooms, a
bar, a restaurant, and a contentious and bitter
recent history. As the locals battle for its ownership, it may or may not be open when you
visit. Ask here about the Lights and Computers
project run by a Vermont NGO and its volunteers, who teach English, computer classes,
and are working to bring reliable electricity to
the island. Students are usually college-bound
kids from the community and volunteers are
more than welcome.

◖ LA ISLA ELVIS CHAVARRÍA

"La Elvis" owes its name to a young martyr
who participated in the 1977 raid on San
Carlos and was subsequently captured and
killed by the National Guard. The island has a
health center, a school (Escuela Mateo Wooten,
named after the Peace Corps volunteer who
promoted its construction in the mid-1990s),
a museum, and a hiking trail.

El Museo Archipiélago de Solentiname
(MUSAS) (at the top of the steep path out of
town, open 7 A.M.–noon and 2–5 P.M. Mon.–
Sat., $2) was built in September 2000 to pre-
serve and display the natural and cultural
heritage of the Solentiname Islands and its
people. The flowers along the path on your
way up were planted to attract butterflies
and hummingbirds. Inside, local artists have
painted scenes of the islands' early history. Also
find interesting maps of the area, archaeological information, and a display of traditional
fishing techniques and the balsa-wood carving process. Behind the museum are a natural
medicine garden, arboretum of 42 tree species,
a model organic avocado and balsa-wood plantation, and a weather station.

The Fundación MUSAS (made up of six
community leaders, the Italian NGO ACRA,
and several other organizations) also organizes
environmental education workshops in the island's school and supports a number of research
projects in the area. The museum is open
daily, but if you find it closed, ask around for
Socorro, the local curator, caretaker, and key
master. For more information, contact ACRA
in the Managua office (tel. 505/249-6176,
musasni@yahoo.com).

At the peak of the dry season (March and
April), be sure to ask whether or not **La Cueva
del Duende** is accessible. The Dwarf Cave, underwater for most of the year but feared by the
locals year-round, is an important archaeological site that the islands' past inhabitants believed to be the entrance to the underworld.
They painted faces to represent their ancestors,
whom they believed to reside there, and left
other markings as well, including a female fertility figure. The cave is located on the nearby
Isla Donald Guevara, but you can arrange the
tour with CANTUR here. Tours around the
islands can also be arranged with Esmeralda
Sequiera (tel. 505/455-9095), who lives down
the hill from the museum.

Accommodations

Doña María Guevara has been running the
◖ **Albergue Celentiname** (tel. 505/893-1977)
since 1984 on a beautiful point at the western

edge of the island. She and many of her family members are painters, participating in Cardenal's project since its earliest days. All of the electricity in the hotel is solar generated. The eight cabañas have capacity for up to 25 people, all with private bath. There is a picturesque porch, a bar, and a *comedor*. The flower-framed views are priceless, but prices for the rooms start at $15 per person and meals are $5. Kayaks and fishing gear are available for rent. Try to make reservations in advance if possible. They can help arrange for transportation when it's available, but expect round-trip transportation from the island to run upwards of $120.

Several hundred meters east, with his own dock on the southern shore of the island, **Don Julio** rents three rooms in his rustic and comfortable, lakefront homestead for $6 per person. Don Julio's brother, Chepe, runs transport to and from San Carlos and can arrange any custom trip you desire. Their sister Doña Maria Magdalena Pineda has her own hotel another couple minutes east along the shore. The **Cabañas Paraíso** (tel. 505/278-3992, gsolentiname@amnet.com.ni, $35 d with three meals and private bath) also has a *comedor*, rents kayaks, and offers tours around the island and beyond.

DONALD GUEVARA, MANCARRONCITO, ZAPOTE, AND ZAPOTILLO ISLANDS

Also known as Isla la Venada, or "La Donald," Isla Donald Guevara's namesake was martyred alongside his *compañero* Elvis Chavarría. La Venada is home to Rudolfo Arellano, one of the original artists from the islands. His family has a total of seven artists now who exhibit their work at the gallery/family house on the south side of the island.

Mancarroncito is the most well preserved, wild, and least inhabited of the main islands. Its steep, thickly vegetated hills rise to a 100-meter peak. The newly opened **Estación Biológica** is run by a local NGO, Fundación del Río, and offers lodging for up to 12 people at $21 per person including three meals and guide services around the reserve. Make reservations

in advance by contacting Fundación del Río in San Carlos (tel. 505/583-0035, fdrio @turbonett.com.ni).

Zapote and Zapotillo are the two closest islands to the mainland and are both owned by APDS, which has essentially decided to leave them alone. Zapote is a key nesting area for a variety of birds and turns into a whitewashed, foul-smelling squawk-fest in March and April, when some 10,000 breeding pairs build nests there. Observe the reproductive mayhem from your boat only, as landing there disturbs the birds. Smaller Zapotillo has less bird activity and a more sordid history, involving a fruit farm, an orphanage for boys, and a pedophile Evangelist priest who was eventually chased into Costa Rica, barely escaping with his life.

ISLAS EL PADRE AND LA ATRAVESADA

Located just off the western tip of La Elvis, El Padre island became a howler monkey sanctuary when a single breeding pair introduced in the 1980s subsequently reproduced into a family of some 50 members. Isla la Atravesada, just off La Elvis and to the east of Isla el Padre, is owned by a North American but inhabited by Solentiname's densest crocodile populations.

TOUR PACKAGES

The same foundation that runs the museum on Isla Elvis Chavarría has also arranged a fully-guided, four-day exploration of the entire Solentiname archipelago and the Río Papaturro in Los Guatuzos, including all its natural, archaeological, and cultural attractions. Prices vary with group size and the number of islands you choose to visit. Stop by the CANTUR kiosk near the west dock in San Carlos for updated information on custom packages. Many of the bigger, Managua-based tour companies listed in the *Essentials* chapter also have packages to Solentiname. Local transport companies in San Carlos might strike a better deal; try **Transporte San Miguelito** (tel. 505/828-6136, anyeljba@yahoo.es). However, professional tour operators tend to have better-informed guides.

SOLENTINAME

GETTING THERE AND AWAY

From San Carlos, boats depart on Tuesday and Friday at 1 P.M. for the two-hour trip to the archipelago (about $2.50 pp). The return trip leaves Solentiname on the same days at 4 A.M., arriving in San Carlos in time to catch the boat to Managua. Should you want to leave the islands at any other time, be prepared to fork over upwards of $70–100 for a private boat, more if you are traveling in a group. CANTUR can also arrange transportation to Los Guatuzos or San Carlos.

Near San Carlos

◖ LOS GUATUZOS WILDLIFE REFUGE AND CENTRO ECOLÓGICO

The 438-square-kilometer strip between Nicaragua's southern border and Lake Cocibolca is a protected wetlands and wildlife reserve replete with myriad species of animals and inhabited by some 1,700 fishermen and subsistence farmers in 11 small communities. The locals are descendants of the Zapote and Guatuzo (or Maleku) peoples as well as the mestizos who arrived in the late 19th century to cultivate rubber. These same *huleros* reverted to the slave trade when the world rubber market crashed, selling Guatuzos for 50 pesos a head to the gold mines of Chontales. Today, only a handful of full-blooded Maleku exist, mostly over the border in Costa Rica.

In the 1930s, settlers introduced cacao to the region, which, because of the crop's need for shade, preserved much of the area's original forest canopy. When plummeting cacao prices and a deadly fungus wiped out the industry in the 1970s, hardwood logging ensued. Only military conflict in the 1980s stopped the logging, but it also drove nearly the entire population of Los Guatuzos into Costa Rica. When families returned in the early 1990s, the area's ecosystem was still largely intact, and the new government quickly acted to protect it from destruction.

Today, residents count on the richness of their natural surroundings to attract visitors and scientists. No fewer than 389 species of birds have been observed here, and between February and April, flocks of migratory species fly through in spectacular concentrations.

Los Guatuzos contains dense populations of crocodiles; caimans; feral pigs; jaguars; and howler, white-faced, and spider monkeys. This is also home to a rare, ancient species of fish called the gaspar *(Actractoseus tropicus)*, a living, armored relic of the Jurassic age that uses its snout and fangs to eat other fish, crabs, and even small turtles.

The research center and guest facilities are located 40 kilometers from San Carlos, up the Río Papaturro, which drains the slopes of

© DANIELLE VAUGHN

All three of Nicaragua's primate species have been sighted throughout the Los Guatuzos Wildlife Refuge.

© ROMAN YAVICH

keel-billed toucan

Costa Rica's northern volcanoes. The narrow river's fauna-rich jungle gradually swallows you as you approach the community of Papaturro. Research station, nature center, and isolated backpacker's hideaway, the **Centro Ecológico** has two eight-bed dorms at $11 a night, plus campgrounds (tents and sleeping pads for rent). Arrange your meals in advance in the nearby village for about $4.

Activities include photo/bird-watching safaris, fishing trips, kayaking the intimidating, still river, nighttime wildlife viewing, boat trips in the wetlands and lake, and tours of local villages (most tours cost $11 pp). A multiplatform suspension canopy bridge allows for incredible bird and wildlife viewing in the upper reaches of the rain forest. There is also an orchid display of over 100 species including the tiniest one in the world, a butterfly farm, a turtle nursery for export to the pet industry, and a caiman nursery for scientific research, export, and tourist adrenaline production. The center also has a conference room, workshop facilities, and support for anyone coming to do field research (GPS equipment, bird nets/traps, and field assistants). They will gladly work out deals for researchers and students. Your host and guide, Armando, offers rubber boots for the mud, and an incredible wealth of knowledge from over 13 years of working in the jungle. Ask him about the time he manhandled a fer-de-lance (one of the most poisonous snakes in the world) to the fear and amazement of four backpackers. Bring quick-drying clothes and

adequate protection from the sun, rain, and especially bugs.

For more information or reservations contact FUNDAR in Managua (tel. 505/270-5434, centro.ecologico@fundar.org.ni, www.fundar.org.ni) or Armando Gómez (tel. 505/674-3559 or 505/677-8082). In San Carlos, FUNDAR works out of the Amigos de la Tierra office (inside the Red Cross building, tel. 505/583-0139); they can help arrange transport to Los Guatuzos or down the river to El Castillo.

Getting There and Away

From the west dock near the CANTUR kiosk in San Carlos, *colectivos* leave for Papaturro at 7 A.M. Monday, Tuesday, and Thursday; the four-hour trip costs $3.50 a person and stops at the small island of Chichicaste where fried fish and soup are available for about $1. The same boat returns to San Carlos the day after arriving, leaving Papaturro at 7 A.M. Or you can rent a private *panga*—which costs $120, but can take up to 10 people to Los Guatuzos in only 1.5 hours.

ESPERANZA VERDE

Also a part of the Guatuzos Reserve, this 5,000-hectare protected area 15 minutes from San Carlos is accessible by *colectivo* heading up the Río Frío toward Los Chiles. Daily departures are at 10 A.M., 12 P.M., and 3 P.M. The return boat leaves at around the same time from Los Chiles. The reserve is part of an effort to reforest and protect the overgrazed watershed of the Río Frío and the Río San Juan. From the dock of Esperanza Verde and the military post walk 500 meters downstream to the **Centro de Interpretación Ambiental Konrad Lorenz,** and a row of six guest rooms with 20 beds ($10 pp or $30 pp with transportation and food); inquire about special rates for NGOs, students, and Nicas. The barren area immediately surrounding the guest facilities is uninteresting, but a 40-minute walk up the road brings you straight into the heart of the rainforest—monkeys, 200 species of birds, giant spiders, mosquitoes, pumas, you name it—and you can spend all day hiking and soaking in the jungle vibe. There are a total of three hiking trails and numerous aquatic trips. Contact Leonel Ubau with FUNDEVERDE in Hotel Cabinas Leyko in San Carlos (tel. 505/583-0127, fundeverde @yahoo.es).

NORTH OF SAN CARLOS

Dozens of small, waterfront fishing villages define the coastline of Cocibolca north of San Carlos, each one at the end of an unimproved spur road from the San Carlos–Managua highway. Given the terrible condition of the road, they're more isolated than you'd expect, but by rented boat you can visit several in a day. The locals don't get many visitors, so you will likely be the only traveler in town.

San Miguelito

A peaceful, lakeside community, San Miguelito has an interesting Casa de Cultura, women's bakery, and access to the island of El Boquete. You can also venture up various rivers, into local wetlands, or over yonder to Solentiname. There are accommodations in the hardwood, Italian-run **Hotel Cocibolca** (tel. 505/552-8803)—16 rooms for $6 with shared bath. Don't miss the great sunset views of Ometepe island's silhouette. They also have tours to a nearby island and wildlife reserve. One daily direct bus leaves Managua's Mayoreo at 7 A.M.; in San Carlos, ask at the bus station. You can also take the slow boat from Granada and get off in San Miguelito before it reaches San Carlos.

Down the Río San Juan

The 190-odd-kilometer journey to the sea takes you down the broad, lethargic San Juan River through forests and isolated cattle farms. You'll have the opportunity to stop in several villages, isolated clusters of stilted homes, or in one of several river resorts and research stations. There are a few minor *raudales* (rapids) where the channel suddenly narrows, including the infamous **Raudal el Diablo** in front of El Castillo. Enormous, silver *sábalos reales* (tarpon) are often seen rising just upstream from these fast waters. Downstream of El Castillo, things become decidedly wilder, especially on the Nicaraguan side, where the enormous Gran Reserva Río Indio-Maíz spills over the left bank. Finally, you'll reach San Juan del Norte, with all its ghosts, and a long sandbar, beyond which lies the Caribbean. (Note: In the following section, the terms "river right" and "river left" refer to a boater traveling downstream).

BOCA DE SÁBALOS

A two-hour *lancha* ride brings you to this town long overshadowed by El Castillo and the famous fort just six kilometers farther

downstream. Boca de Sábalos is a working town of about 1,200 souls, located at the mouth of one of Río San Juan's nearly 1,000 tributaries. Boca de Sábalos has more bars, *hospedajes,* and places to eat than its neighbor, and is the de facto seat of the El Castillo municipality (it was transferred here from El Castillo temporarily during the war, and then never moved back).

Attractions

Don Julio Murio (across from the big bar on the walkway leading north from the dock, tel. 505/414-3620) speaks English, organizes tours on Río Sábalos, and rents canoes and kayaks for $5 per hour without a guide and $10 per hour with a guide. He can also arrange an all-inclusive adventure kayaking to San Juan del Norte ($250 pp) or take you on one of the 10 tours designed by the Sábalos tourism collective.

El Quebracho Wildlife Reserve, located in the part of the biosphere reserve allocated for ecotourism development, has two trails (one of which is self-guided) through a wildlife-rich setting. The reserve can accommodate up to 25 people for $20 per person including three meals, and guides can be hired for $10 per day (discounts for groups larger than 10). Count on spending the night, as its isolation makes day trips challenging. Make arrangements at the office of Fundación del Río (a block south of the *alcaldía* in Sábalos, tel. 505/583-0035), which owns and operates the reserve or the main office near the hospital in San Carlos.

Hire a vehicle to take you to the shady, pleasant 2,000-hectare **African palm plantation**, about a half hour outside of town, one of only two such operations in Nicaragua. Before being purchased by the Chamorro family, it employed hundreds of locals.

You can also hike down the Río San Juan to the 100-year-old **steamship wreck**—a rusted hulk half-buried in sand. To go tarpon fishing, get a permit from the town MARENA office (hook only, no spears), and then hire a guide and boat to take you to just above the Toro Rapids, less than five minutes down the Río San Juan.

For nightlife make your way to the dock/central area and look for Punto Lodge, open daily 2 P.M.–midnight. Or find the several other bars in town simply by following the blaring music.

Accommodations

Walking up from the dock, you'll first come to beautiful hardwood **[** **Hospedaje Katiana** (tel. 505/583-0178, $4 s with shared bath, $7 s with private bath) on your right, with 14 rooms. Next door is **Hospedaje Clarissa** ($4 pp, mosquito net, fan, shared bath), with 11 rooms; it's also one of the most popular eateries in town. Across the street, the **Hotel Central** ($3 s with fan) is inexpensive but basic and not quite as nice.

[**Hotel Sábalos** (tel. 505/659-0252, $12 pp) is located across the way at the confluence of the Río Sábalo and the Río San Juan. The view from the deck might be the best in the entire Río San Juan area. Also enjoy hot water, private bathrooms, classy accommodations, and a *panga* that can take you on tours around the area. Arrange a ride across the river to the

hotel at their family's store next to Hospedaje Katiana on main street.

[SÁBALOS LODGE

A one-time amphibian farm, growing everything from poison dart frogs to snakes for export to the United States, Sábalos Lodge (tel. 505/583-0046 or 505/278-1405, www .sabaloslodge.com, $25–60) now focuses on tourism, with 10 riverside bamboo and wood cabins with thatched roofs, hammock lounge, gym, and a dining area. The meals and the service are world-class yet only cost $5 for breakfast and $10 for lunch and dinner. Hiking trails and inner tube floats are available, plus three *pangas* for pickups from San Carlos and tours to the sunken ship, nighttime caiman-watching, the Rio San Juan reserve, and farther afield. To get to the lodge from Sábalos take a boat bound for El Castillo and get off after five minutes, or walk from town for 15 minutes on the only dirt road that follows the river (difficult during the rainy season; cross several barbed-wire gates en route).

The lodge is associated with San Juan Rio Relief (sanjuanriorelief@cox.net, www.san juanriorelief.org), a privately funded nonprofit organization that helps bring much-needed medical supplies to the area and pays to staff several rural health centers.

MONTECRISTO RIVER RESORT

Six kilometers downstream from Sábalos, on river right (only 20 minutes before El Castillo), Montecristo (tel. 505/649-9012, www.monte cristoriver.com, $35) is a tourism complex offering sportfishing, hiking trails, horseback riding, and tours of local shrimp and fish farms. Backpackers can stay for $15 per person including breakfast; private rooms available, or pay $50 for an all-inclusive package with three meals, riding, and other activities.

Getting There and Away

Six boats make the trip to El Castillo from San Carlos and back every day (reduced service on

Sunday), stopping at Boca de Sábalos and the lodges upon request.

EL CASTILLO

The fortress of El Castillo de la Inmaculada Concepción de María was strategically placed with a long view downriver, right in front of the shark- and crocodile-infested Raudal el Diablo (still one of the biggest challenges for upstream vessels). Now dark, moss-covered ruins, the Fortress of the Immaculate Conception has more successfully attracted tourists than repelled English pirates, and if you're in the area, this is the one place you should not miss.

The nearby town (pop. 1,500) has neither roads nor cars—reason enough to visit. Its residents work on farms in the surrounding hills, fish the river, commute to the sawmill in Sábalos, the palm oil factory up the Río San Juan, or one of the new resorts up and down the river. In between harvests, a lot of folks cross illegally into Costa Rica—an easy 45-minute walk. The town celebrates its *fiestas patronales* on March 19.

History

Ruy Díaz, on the first Spanish exploration of the river in 1525, built the first fortification in 1602, on a section of the river he called "The House of the Devil." In 1673, Spain commissioned the building of a new fort, which, when completed two years later, was the largest fortress of its kind in Central America, with 32 cannons and 11,000 weapons. Granada, at long last, felt safe.

But in 1762 Spain and Britain began the Seven Years War, prompting the governor of Jamaica to order an invasion of Nicaragua. An expedition of 2,000 soldiers took all the fortifications until they reached El Castillo, where a massive battle commenced on July 29. Rafaela Herrera, the 19-year-old daughter of the fort's fallen commander, Jose Herrera, seized command of her father's troops and succeeded in driving the British off, who retreated to San Juan del Norte on August 3.

Eighteen years later, 22-year-old Horatio Nelson entered the Río San Juan with a force

El Castillo

of 3,500 men. He captured the fortification at Bartola on April 9, and then, two days later, El Castillo via a surprise, landside assault. Nine months later sans reinforcement, the soon-to-be Lord Admiral Horatio Nelson and his handful of surviving soldiers—all rotting from sickness—pulled out and went home.

Visiting the Fort

Celebrating 500 years in the Americas, the government of Spain restored the fortress at great cost, building both a historical museum and lending library, plus the nearby school and Hotel Albergue. The museum (open 8 A.M.–noon and 1–5 P.M., $2) is pertinent and interesting, showing the history of the fortress and a collection of arms and other items dating as far back as the 1500s, including a pile of cannon balls and early rum bottles. A nearby *mariposario* (butterfly farm) was also built by the Spanish, although much more recently.

Fishing, Hikes, and River Tours

AMEC can help with boat rental ($10 per hour for two people) and fishing (rods and lures for $5 per day, $10 to replace a lost lure), or charter fishing (from $140 per day). These prices keep rising as El Castillo becomes more popular, so be sure to check at the *caseta* near the dock.

The AMEC *caseta* can also help you arrange full- or half-day river/tributary tours and hikes, jungle tours (popular, $75–90 for up to six people), canoe trips ($10 pp for two people), horseback tours ($15 pp), or a nighttime caiman-watching tour ($45 for a group

© JOSHUA BERMAN

Río San Juan as seen from El Castillo

of four). Unfortunately smaller groups pay the same minimum price.

Accommodations

Most *hospedajes* are downstream from the dock. The ones closest cost $4 a night but don't offer much. On a side street there's **Nena Lodge and Tours** (tel. 505/821-2135, www.nenalodge.com, $5), with 10 rooms and a streetside balcony, and **Hotel Richarson** (tel. 505/644-0782, $15). The most comfortable of the budget options is (**Casa de Huesped y Restaurante El Chinandegano** (tel. 505/583-0191, $4 pp shared bath, $2 extra private bath).

The Spanish built the two-story, wooden (**Hotel Albergue El Castillo** (tel. 505/892-0195) in 1992 when they refurbished the fort. Its comfortable double balcony overlooks the town, the river, and rapids beyond. It sleeps up to 35 people, with shared bath, and the $15 per person price includes an excellent breakfast and bottomless cup of coffee (legitimate coffee, not instant—a rarity in these parts) in the roomy, elegant bar and restaurant. **Hotel Victoria** (tel. 505/583-0188, $20 pp

includes breakfast) is newer and cleaner than some of the cheaper hotels, and has hot water. Many of the rooms have bunk beds, however, and most have shared baths. Victoria is at the very end of the road leading downstream from the dock.

Travelers on a larger budget will want to treat themselves to **Posada del Rio** (on the left side of the walkway down from the dock, tel. 505/616-3528, $60 s, 70 d includes breakfast). In Granada, Hotel Colonial is owned by the same family, and the luxury is similar. The rooms are well decorated and all have private balconies overlooking the water, private state-of-the-art bathrooms, hot water, and air-conditioning. Laundry service available.

Food

There's delicious and frighteningly large river shrimp at **El Cofalito** and steaming bowls of soup at **Soda Conchita,** served on a nice second-story deck. **El Chinandegano** is the best value ($1.50 for basic meals), but there is lots of similar fare down by the dock. **Border's Coffee** (open 7 A.M.–10 P.M. daily), located across the

SOLENTINAME

THE RIVER THAT DIVIDES

If the Nicaraguan government is sure of one thing, the river and its various communities is theirs – and theirs alone . . . to completely ignore. Nicaraguan sovereignty of the Río San Juan has soured relations with Costa Rica, which were already strained by the thousands of illegal Nica immigrants continually slipping over the border. You'll see the bumper stickers in Managua and elsewhere – El Río San Juan es 100% Nica – the most visible sign of increasing jingoistic patriotism that has swelled along with border tensions.

In July of 1998, the Costa Rican government began patrolling the river in armed boats, ostensibly to better police a border Nicaragua has made no effort to control. But the international boundary is the southern bank of the river, not the midpoint, and Nicaragua loudly and immediately challenged the Ticos. Costa Rica responded by blockading the Atlantic coastline from the mouth of the Río San Juan south to Barra del Colorado, forcing the fishermen that would have otherwise purchased gasoline for their boats in Costa Rica to travel 30 kilometers north to Greytown. They explained later that the blockade was an endeavor to investigate a supposed black market in tax-free gasoline and was not retaliation for the dispute over the river. The locals disagree.

Since the 1858 Treaty of Jerez-Cañas, Costa Ricans have had the right to use the river for commercial transport but not police it; this has been the starting point for all subsequent negotiation. But Nicaraguans along the Río San Juan distrust armed Ticos on the river. Costa Rica suggested a compromise of joint patrols, which Nicaragua promptly rejected. The situation remains unresolved.

Cooler heads will be needed on both banks to find a solution. The river's watersheds span both sides of the border, and joint ecological management will be essential to stem rapid deforestation and sedimentation currently choking parts of the channel. The river already runs far lower than it did when the Spanish and Cornelius Vanderbilt navigated its broad waters.

© ROMAN YAVICH

traveling down the Río San Juan

dock from El Cofalito, has an espresso machine, tasty pastries and desserts, fresh juices and milk shakes, all in a great ambience.

Information and Services

The tourist *caseta* in front of the dock is actually a group operation known as the Asociación Municipal Ecoturismo El Castillo (AMEC) and headed up by a guy named Cofal. AMEC is constantly working on an updated list of local guides, boat services, and has compiled a series of hikes and other things to do while in town; contact them via the phone at the Albergue (tel. 505/892-0195). The most reliable phone

in town is the satellite phone at the Albergue, but you can also ask to borrow someone's cell phone and pay them a dollar or two.

Getting There and Away

Lanchas colectivas (to El Castillo $3.50, three hours or $1.50, five hours) depart San Carlos daily at 8 A.M., 10 A.M. (fast boat), noon, 2:30 P.M., 3:30 P.M., and 4:15 P.M. (fast boat). The last fast boat makes part of the journey after dark, which is more dangerous. Returning, boats leave for San Carlos 5 A.M.–2 P.M., with two fast boats at 5:30 A.M. and 11 A.M.

To go downstream, call Don Marcial (tel.

505/406-9559) or stop in the Albergue. Boats for San Juan del Norte pass through on Tuesday and Friday around 9 A.M. On the way back on Thursday and Sunday they pass El Castillo in the early afternoon. It costs $11 to get to San Juan del Norte from El Castillo and $17 on the fast boat, which is more than worth it for the six hours it saves you.

REFUGIO DE VIDA SILVESTRE RÍO SAN JUAN

This two-kilometer-wide belt that follows the north side of the river is part of the Río Indio-Maíz Biosphere Reserve, a 3,618-square-kilometer virgin rainforest, inaccessible to all but the most persistent scientists armed with a permit from the MARENA office in Managua. The first access point to the Refugio is just six kilometers downstream of El Castillo (or about three hours by boat from San Carlos). The western border of the reserve is made up by the Río Bartola at its confluence with the Río San Juan. Arrange a hike through the local MARENA post, with AMEC in El Castillo, or at the self-described ecolodge and research station, **Refugio Bartola** (tel. 505/880-8754, www.refugiobartola.com, $50 pp with breakfast and private bath). The compound and natural history museum is surrounded by rainforest and fueled by solar energy but is difficult to contact: You may need to wait until you're in El Castillo. Farther down the river you can access the Refugio de Vida Silvestre Río San Juan through any of the army posts including Boca San Carlos, Sarapiqui, and Delta. Do not expect much more than a place to pitch your tent and friendly, if camouflaged, company.

◖ SAN JUAN DE NICARAGUA

Also known as San Juan del Norte, San Juan is 100 winding kilometers beyond El Castillo. This hot, historic village in Nicaragua's extreme southeast corner is inhabited by about 900 residents. Sir Charles Grey, governor of Jamaica, first seized the land for the English in 1848 and built the rowdy port of Greytown, which lasted about 150 years. When the British

pulled out, it melted into a forgotten backwater, and these days nothing but a historic cemetery of segregated plots and both British and American headstones remains.

Present-day San Juan lies hidden in the brackish swamps at the confluence of Río Indio with the Río San Juan. San Juan del Norte suffered during the Contra war in the 1980s, during which time Hurricane Joan also flattened it. In the 1990s, Comandante Cero returned to torch it, "just because."

This is about as isolated as you can get, and returning home means creeping back up the river, because the obvious next step, an openwater boat trip to Bluefields, is nonexistent owing to danger and expense (around $500).

Sights and Tours

The most popular attraction in town is the **colonial cemetery,** a short boat ride away across the mouth of the river. At the time of publication the dock at the cemetery was in bad shape, which made landings a bit difficult. Just beyond is the Caribbean, often rough and not suitable for swimming. Rather, the locals prefer to *costanear* (walk the coast), which occasionally yields treasure (and cocaine—be careful). Don Enrique (of Hotelito Evo) offers several **tours** around the area including visits to the largest coconut farm in Central America, sportfishing, and visits to the indigenous Rama Kay community. His son Raul is an INTUR-certified guide, which gives him access to the Río Indio-Maíz reserve. A two-day trip for four people, including hiking to hot springs, sleeping in hammocks, food, transportation, and a visit to an indigenous village costs $250. Contact Don Enrique or Raul at their Hotelito Evo (tel. 505/273-3719 or 505/859-0275).

Accommodations and Food

◖ **Hotelito Evo** (located on the fourth walkway parallel to the river, tel. 505/273-3719, $6 s, $11 d) has seven clean rooms, one with a private bath. The all-wood **Hospedaje Anderson** (third walkway, tel. 505/414-1368, $5 s, 6 d) is basic but adequate. Otherwise

SAN JUAN DEL WHAT?

Sometimes knowing a place's name is all you need to understand its history. San Juan del Sur is an elegant example. The story begins in the 16th century. Spanish explorer Diego de Machuca first reached the mouth of the winding river the Spanish called *el desaguadero* (the outlet or the drain) on June 24, 1538, feast day of Saint John the Baptist. They added "del Norte" to denote the North Sea (the Atlantic), as it was known at the time (the Pacific was the South Sea).

Rodrigo de Contreras, Nicaragua's first Spanish governor, renamed it San Juan de la Cruz in 1541, upon establishing the area's first military garrison. And so it ostensibly remained for the next 300 years, except that owing to the proliferation of Spanish San Juans around the Caribbean, traders began calling it San Juan de Nicaragua. In 1796, the Spanish declared San Juan de Nicaragua a Free Port, which the British, slowly expanding their Atlantic Coast protectorate, must have found amusing: Soon it would be theirs alone.

In 1821 Central America declared its independence from the Spanish crown, and in the ensuing power vacuum, the British took possession of the Atlantic coast with the assistance of their well-armed allies, the local Miskito Indians. At first the British helped the Miskitos take control in 1841 in return for the right to explore. In gratitude, the Miskito King Mosco renamed the town in honor of the Jamaican Governor, Sir Charles Edward Grey, who became the de facto governor of the British protectorate.

Greytown, as it was now called, grew to be the eastern terminus of one of the most popular interoceanic trading routes, and the English sent in the army to occupy the settlement in 1848, now far too important for indigenous control. Cornelius Vanderbilt's steamships made Greytown into a booming port town that received thousands of interoceanic visitors each year. During this period, Greytown was destroyed twice, once by the American Navy and once by flooding in the Río San Juan. But before it could fully recover the steamship line closed down, gold rush traffic trickled off, and the world forgot about the little town at the end of the world.

San Juan del Norte has essentially remained in that condition ever since, but its name continues to change. In his coup de grace in the eternal war of words with Costa Rica over ownership of the river, former president Arnoldo Alemán did not hesitate to rename the town again in 2002. What he chose, given the nationalistic jingoism of the period, should surprise no one: San Juan de Nicaragua.

(Contributed by Roman Yavich, Fulbright scholar and Nicaragua tourism expert; Roman resides in San Juan del Sur, where he works with Comunidad Connect, a local nonprofit organization.)

---

try the thatched-roof cabins in **Cabinas El Escondite** (tel. 505/414-9761, $10 pp with private bath) owned by a Caribbean-Cajun Rastafarian. To find Rasta's *cabinas* ask around near the military post at the north end of town, or walk down the third walkway until it ends and turn left.

Hedley Acton Thomas Barss, a.k.a. Chalí, is the end of earth's most popular bar. For dancing some *soka*, at almost any time in the day or night, it's **Disco-Bar de Pulú Fantasía,** located at the very southern end of the first walkway. For food, try **Doña Marta,** across the street from Chalí, **Soda El Tucán,** near the center of town, or **El Ranchón,** at the southern end of town.

Getting There and Away

The easiest way to get to San Juan del Norte is to fork over some major dollars to a tour company. The most realistic way is a long boat ride downriver from San Carlos. The most adventurous way is a canoe or kayak multiday trip involving camping in the jungle. Not your flavor? The slow motorboat leaves San Carlos Tuesday and Friday at 6 A.M. (buy tickets the day before), takes at least 11 hours, and costs $13 each way. The same vessels leave San Juan del Norte Thursday and Sunday at 5 A.M. On the same days there is a fast boat that leaves an hour after the slow boat, costs double, and takes half the time.

The proposed airstrip is still just that—proposed. Nevertheless, with big money (and the country's most important families) investing in the area, regular flights to Managua can't be too far away.

The Blue Lagoon

Located across the river from the town of San Juan del Norte, the Blue Lagoon or La Laguna Azul is a small pool of clean, blue, and perfectly pleasant water surrounded by coconut palms and lush vegetation, in the center of which floats a giant structure. Doña Angela's children

(their house is next to the Ranchón) can take you over for about $5 in a dugout canoe; for another $5 continue on to the beachfront.

The Río Indio Lodge

Since 2002, the $1.2-million, five-star Río Indio Lodge "ecotourism and sportfishing resort" (tel. 506/296-3338 in Costa Rica, U.S. tel. 866/593-3176, www.rioindiolodge.com), fully Costa-Rican owned and operated, has run fancy sportfishing trips on this Nicaraguan river. This place is geared to the luxury adventure traveler, not the backpacker: A night in one of the 34 rooms will run you about $200 per person. Activities include guided fishing trips, bird-watching, kayaking, hiking, and visits to nearby Laguna Silico.

SOLENTINAME

BLUEFIELDS AND THE CORN ISLANDS

At the end of a broad eastward ecological transition zone from the Amerrisque mountains, through descending hills and pine savanna, to mangroves and estuaries, the Atlantic coast is a land unto itself. Culturally, it is influenced more by the English than the Spanish and ethnically more by indigenous and African blood than by mestizos. Nicaragua's Atlantic coast is sometimes explained as a Caribbean island that through an accident of geography, just happens to be connected to some Central American country.

The vast majority of Nicaragua's 450 kilometers of Atlantic coastline are unexplored, undeveloped, and unapproachable. Writer Edward Marriot called it "Nicaragua's jungle coast. Not the 'Caribbean'—despite cartographers' insistences—but, deliberately, the 'Atlantic.' . . . this was the Atlantic coast, with its mangrove swamps and alligators, hurricanes and stiff westers that washed up bales of high-grade cocaine, shrink-wrapped for export."

The Atlantic coast is languid and lazy, but it's got a rough edge too, bitter poverty and, thanks to the drug traffickers, increasing danger. It also has sultry mangrove estuaries, white, sandy beaches, and a relaxed lifestyle. The warm, humid breezes smelling of coconut palms and vegetation is a nice break from the dry, dusty highlands. Bluefields is a quintessential Caribbean port town, with enough fresh seafood to wear you out, an oppressive afternoon sun, and a no-hurry attitude. Corn Island and Little Corn Island are another scene altogether: the soft sand beaches and rustling palm fronds of your most primitive Caribbean

HIGHLIGHTS

☾ **Palo de Mayo Festival:** Sensual and rhythmic, Bluefield's joyous May Day cele-bration is one of the flashiest shows in the country (page 317).

☾ **Pearl Lagoon:** The quiet lanes of this waterside village beg to be explored. Follow them all the way out to the beach (page 329).

☾ **Wawachang and Khaka Creek Reserve:** Few foreigners have yet ven-tured up the Wawachang River to this guesthouse and forest reserve, one of Nicaragua's newest community-based eco-tourism ventures (page 331).

☾ **Picnic Center Beach:** This Corn Island classic is an uninterrupted crescent of white-sand hedonism; a wonderful beach and a bed await (page 335).

☾ **Diving:** Snorkel, swim, or scuba to visit the reefs and marine life just offshore of Little Corn Island (page 339).

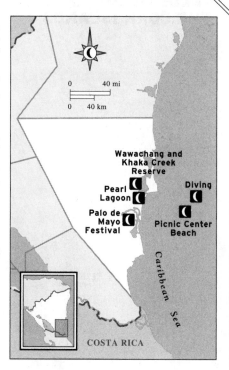

LOOK FOR ☾ TO FIND RECOMMENDED SIGHTS, ACTIVITIES, DINING, AND LODGING.

BLUEFIELDS

fantasy, plus an isolated feeling that's hard to find elsewhere.

PLANNING YOUR TIME

If you lay in a good stack of books, a bottle or two, and a jug of sunscreen, you could spend weeks on Nicaragua's right coast, exploring the islands, reefs, bays, and broad pine savannahs and villages along the coastline. Corn Island is worth a night or two unless you really crave remoteness, in which case you should beeline to Little Corn, the more rustic of the pair, where 2–4 days will provide ample opportu-nity to dive and explore the reefs. Remember

that everything except seafood is more ex-pensive here—expect to pay 2–3 times more than you would on the Pacific side for lodg-ing, beef, beer, and soft drinks. If you're trav-eling overland from Managua, schedule in one day for the trip and another to recover in Bluefields. Otherwise, take an afternoon flight to Bluefields and spend the rest of the day pok-ing around the city.

A night or two in both Bluefields and Pearl Lagoon is enough to get a basic taste of Creole culture, but if you have time, you can take a cooking class, sign up for Creole and Garifuna dance lessons, meet natural medicine

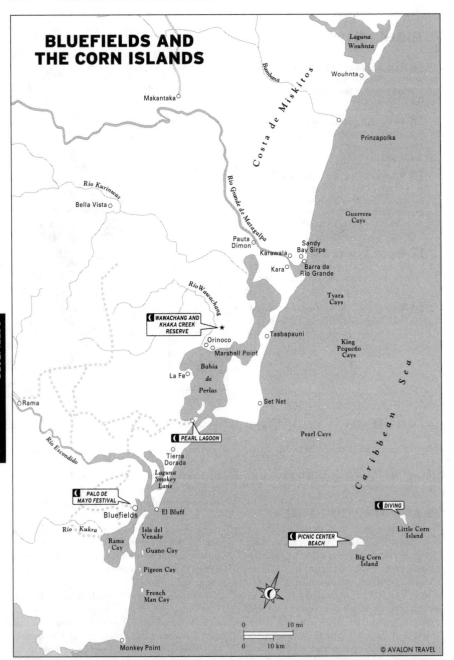

BLUEFIELDS AND THE CORN ISLANDS

BLUEFIELDS

Laguna
Wouhnta

Wouhnta

Makantaka

Costa de Miskitos

Bambana

Rio Grande de Matagalpa

Prinzapolka

Rio Kurinwas

Bella Vista

Guerrera
Cays

Pauta
Dimon

Karawala

Sandy
Bay Sirpe

Kara

Barra de
Rio Grande

Rio Wawashang

Tyara
Cays

☽ WAWACHANG AND
KHAKA CREEK
RESERVE

Orinoco

Marshall Point

Tasbapauni

King
Pequeño
Cays

La Fe

Bahía
de
Perlas

Set Net

Rama

Caribbean Sea

Rio Escondido

Pearl Cays

☽ PEARL LAGOON

Tierra
Dorada

Laguna
Smokey
Lane

☽ PALO DE
MAYO FESTIVAL

Bluefields

El Bluff

☽ DIVING

Little Corn
Island

Río Kukra

Isla del
Venado

☽ PICNIC CENTER
BEACH

Rama Cay

Guano Cay

Big Corn
Island

Pigeon Cay

French
Man Cay

0   10 mi

0   10 km

Monkey Point

© AVALON TRAVEL

doctors, poke around the two universities. Or head north on the early morning *panga* to Wawachang and the Khaka Creek Reserve. Spend a couple of days hiking, exploring the fauna and flora, and meeting local farmers. Then catch the twice-weekly *panga* back down the river to Orinoco, the Nicaraguan home of the Garifuna. Spend a day trying local foods and listening to village elders tell their unique history on a front-porch step. See if anyone wants to walk up to Marshall Point with you. A couple of days later, hop back on the (also twice weekly) *panga* and stop in Pearl Lagoon for as long as you desire.

When to Come

The Atlantic coast receives 3,000–6,000 millimeters of rain annually (with the higher levels falling in southern RAAS), making it among the wettest places on the planet. The rainy season is punctuated by hurricanes in September and October and can extend well into December, sometimes longer. The end of December is marked by cool, "Christmas" winds. Most visitors come during the period between late January and April when things are generally dry and sunny. The biggest crowds arrive for Christmas, Semana Santa (the Holy Week before Easter), and during various regional fiestas, when making reservations is a good idea.

Safety

Nicaragua's Atlantic coast is playing a growing role in drug trafficking, with important ramifications both for local communities and foreign travelers. South American drug runners make use of the unpoliced, unlit coastline and cays for pit stops, drug stashes, and worse. It's easy money for locals willing to participate, but now the locals are not only helping transport the drugs but getting into the local sales racket too, and with hard drugs—crack, in particular—come crime and violence.

You don't have to stay at home, but you do have to stay alert. To avoid robbery and sexual assault, we recommend the following guidelines: Do not walk alone or in pairs on any deserted beach, day or night. If you want to explore a deserted beach, do so with a large group and consult a trusted local before doing so. Under no circumstances should you agree to transport wrapped packages for strangers, much less make a purchase. Be aware of "fishermen" driving particularly luxurious boats ("catch any white lobster today, amigo?"). Foreigners caught with narcotics can anticipate a long and uncomfortable stay in Nicaragua's prisons.

HISTORY

The Atlantic coast of Nicaragua was originally populated primarily by the native Miskito, Mayangna (Sumu), and Rama people, who settled along the rivers and coastline and lived on fishing and small-scale agriculture. Columbus described the coast when he cruised by in 1502, but throughout the 16th century, its general inhospitality kept the coast relatively unvisited.

Spanish friars hoping to Christianize the Mayangna, Tawaka, and Miskito (Guanae) peoples were killed immediately, and Spain subsequently lost interest in the Caribbean coast. That made it attractive to English and Dutch pirates like Dutchman Abraham Blauveldt in the 1630s, whose name in English, Bluefields, came to represent the bay and later the coastal city.

In the 1700s, the English organized the Atlantic coast into a British protectorate, establishing "Miskito Kings" whom the British educated and maintained in power. England armed the Miskito and Sambo people, and encouraged them to raid nearby lands and incidentally, the Spanish territories of western Nicaragua, where the bellicose Miskitos reached as far as Nueva Segovia and Chontales. The sparring lasted until 1790.

German Moravian missionaries integrated with the communities beginning in the early 1800s; their legacy is a largely protestant population and beautiful, spartan churches. In 1860, the British departure was followed by the advent of American businesses, which established timber and banana company camps all along the Atlantic coast. Bluefields became a thriving commercial center with regular steamship connections to New Orleans, Baltimore, Philadelphia, and New York.

Such was the state of Bluefields and the Atlantic coast when President José Santos Zelaya ordered its military occupation in 1894. General Rigoberto Cabezas sailed down the Río Escondido in February, deposed the Miskito government, and officially united Nicaragua from Atlantic to Pacific for the first time. But once united to Spanish-speaking Nicaragua, Managua felt free to tax and ignore the Atlantic coast, and Zelaya and successors roundly abused indigenous rights for centuries. The foreign companies began to withdraw, and Sandino and his anti-imperialist troops brutally attacked those tempted to linger. In the aftermath and right up to the present, the Atlantic coast has decayed into a state of corruption, financial mismanagement, and ruin.

Costeños were decidedly apathetic about their supposed Sandinista "liberation" in 1979.

Since the war ended, Spanish-speaking Nicaraguans have arrived en masse, putting the black and indigenous populations in the minority for the first time ever. Considering their long-held isolation and resistance to the Managuan government, this is no small change. Tensions rise as the "Spaniards" (as Costeños have always referred to mestizos) seek housing and employment, and at the same time, attempt to import their language, music, food, and other cultural aspects to their new home.

Bluefields

Bluefields is a rich waterfront melting pot of nearly 50,000 souls, many of whom make a living in the fishing and timber industries, or working on cruise ships, where their bilingual skills are prized. The city has never been connected to western Nicaragua's highway system and can be reached only by water or air. Bluefields Bay remains an important Atlantic port, and the city itself is the capital of the RAAS and home to several universities. Despite all the activity, unemployment is acute and drugs and crime are on the increase. Bluefields's primary attraction is its Creole culture. Do not miss the Palo de Mayo celebrations, an exuberant and erotic calypso-inspired dance and music event, unique to the city and celebrated fervently throughout the month of May.

ORIENTATION AND GETTING AROUND

From the Bluefields airport take a taxi for the several-kilometer approach to town for the fixed price of $0.75. Overlanders traveling from El Rama will arrive by *panga* at the municipal wharf downtown. Parque Reyes is located three blocks west of the waterfront road. Bluefields is small enough that you should need a taxi only to go to the extremes of town—the URACCAN campus at the north and the airport at the south, or when you feel unsafe. Two nearly identical bus routes run 6 A.M.–7:30 P.M. Get on and off where you like for $0.25.

SIGHTS AND ATTRACTIONS

The red-roofed **Moravian church,** built in 1848 with English, French, and Caribbean influence was the first of its kind on the Central American coast. About a block and a half west, the whitewashed wood and stained glass **Catholic cathedral** is captivating, airy, and modern. Ms. Edna Cayasso (tel. 505/572-1877, nicachild_87@yahoo.com, $20 pp or $12 pp for a group of two) offers a fun Caribbean **cooking class,** from *rondon* to stewed beans and coconut delicacies. Call ahead and she will pick you up from your hotel. Mr. Selso (tel. 505/845-4137 or 505/572-2176) is a traditional and fascinating Miskito **"Bush Docta"** and

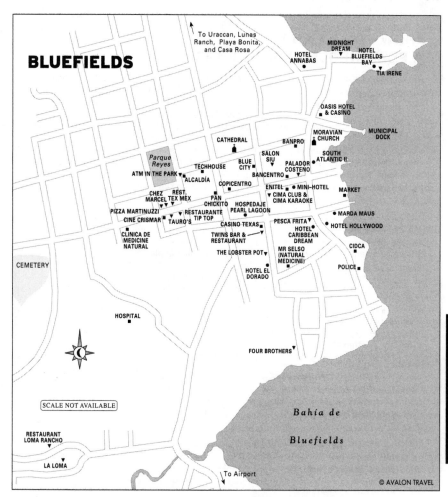

BLUEFIELDS

To Uraccan, Lunas Ranch, Playa Bonita, and Casa Rosa

MIDNIGHT DREAM
HOTEL ANNABAS
HOTEL BLUEFIELDS BAY
TIA IRENE

OASIS HOTEL & CASINO

MORAVIAN CHURCH
MUNICIPAL DOCK

CATHEDRAL
BANPRO
SALON SIU
SOUTH ATLANTIC II
Parque Reyes
TECHHOUSE
BLUE CITY
PALADOR COSTEÑO
ATM IN THE PARK
ALCALDÍA
BANCENTRO
COPICENTRO
ENITEL   MINI-HOTEL
MARKET
CHEZ MARCEL   REST. TEX MEX
PAN
CIMA CLUB & CIMA KARAOKE
CHICKITO
HOSPEDAJE PEARL LAGOON
PIZZA MARTINUZZI
MARDA MAUS
CINE CRISMAR
RESTAURANTE TIP TOP
TAURO'S
HOTEL HOLLYWOOD
CASINO TEXAS
PESCA FRITA
CLINICA DE MEDICINE NATURAL
TWINS BAR & RESTAURANT
HOTEL CARIBBEAN DREAM
THE LOBSTER POT
MR SELSO (NATURAL MEDICINE)
CIDCA
CEMETERY
HOTEL EL DORADO
POLICE

HOSPITAL

SCALE NOT AVAILABLE

FOUR BROTHERS

Bahía de

Bluefields

RESTAURANT LOMA RANCHO

LA LOMA

To Airport

© AVALON TRAVEL

BLUEFIELDS

Obeah practitioner who is highly sought after for spiritual, emotional, and medical issues that doctors trained in western medicine have been unable to resolve.

The small Clinica de Medicina Natural en Terapias Alternative (Barrio Teodoro Martinez, Avenida Cabeza, in front of Escondito bar, open 5:30–8 P.M.) is a **natural medicine** clinic offering bach flower therapy, healing massage, and medicinal plants.

Palo de Mayo Festival

Also known as the ¡Mayo Ya! festival, Bluefields's May Day celebration is unique in Central America. In North America, this pagan-rooted party is about springtime, fertility, and the re-awakening of the earth after a long winter. In Bluefields, May falls on the cusp of the rainy season, and the entire month is a bright burst of colors, parades, costumes, feasting, and, most importantly, dancing around the maypole.

"HOW YOU MEAN?"
A FEW CREOLE EXPRESSIONS

Put your Spanish dictionary away in Bluefields – you're in Creole country! Creole is a complete language system, currently being documented by the Institute of Linguistic Promotion, Investigation, and Rescue of the Culture (IPILC) at the University of the Autonomous Regions of the Atlantic coast of Nicaragua (URACCAN). Popular books are being written to teach Creole students to read and write in their first language. The campaign slogan is: *Kriol iz wi langwij, mek wi rait it!* (Creole is our language, let's write it). At times, the rhythms of the Costeño tongue are difficult to understand, but not so tough to speak. And, of course, coastal communication slides easily in and out of English and Spanish. For instance, *"Dem aprovecharing beca dem mama no de"* means "That person is taking advantage of the fact that his mother is not home." Listen for the following expressions – and try them out, if you're feeling up for it.

Creole	English
"She done reach Raitipura."	She arrived at Raitpura.
"How you mean?"	Explain that please.
"No feel, no way."	Don't worry, it's okay.
"I no vex."	I'm not angry.
"Dat nasty."	That's awesome!
"That ain't nothing."	Thank you.
"Check you then."	Goodbye.
"Make I get tree o dem."	Give me three of those.
"She feel fa eat some."	She's in the mood to eat.
"He own"	His.
"It molest we."	It bothers us.
"Nice."	"It's all good," or goodbye.
"Uno jus keep walking."	You all just keep walking.
Wabool	Cassava pounder, or penis
Coco	Coconut, or vagina

(Big-up to "Dr. G.," a.k.a. Georgie Cayasso, Bluefields native and distinguished Creole linguist.)

Every night is a party, and the festival comes to a rip-roaring peak at the end of the month. Look for it throughout the month of May.

Palo de Mayo isn't the only festival in town. Bluefields exuberantly honors its patron saint, **San Jerónimo,** on September 30. The party rolls right into the city's birthday celebrations which last throughout the month of October, culminating on October 30. This is the anniversary of the 1987 passage of the Autonomy Law; its commemoration features cuisine competitions between all the ethnic groups. This is a great time of year to sample the foods of the coast, learn about the autonomy process (and its history), and meet community leaders and politicians.

NIGHTLIFE AND ENTERTAINMENT

Bluefields likes its music loud. You'll hear the reggae bumping wherever you go, from dance hall, roots, *soka, punta,* and Palo de Mayo to reggae *romantica,* and of course, long sets of Bob Marley. Interestingly, the Atlantic coast's second favorite is American country music, which locals proudly call their "coastal music."

The Spirit Dancers are a professional music and dance group dedicated to celebrating, promoting, and educating locals and foreigners about the unique Garifuna history, culture, dance, and music. They are hard to catch, but if they are performing while you are in town, their show will astound you.

Discos

Four Brothers (six blocks south of the park, open 9 P.M.–2 A.M. Thurs.–Sun.) has been the heart of the Creole social scene since the 1990s. Expect a small, cramped juke joint with a wooden-plank dance floor and ice-cold beer. You'll need that beer before you can master the sensual Caribbean grind enjoyed by lovers and strangers alike—women, keep a stiff arm's distance between you and your dance partner if you'd rather not feel a stranger's *wabool.* You should strongly consider arriving around 10 P.M. and leaving by midnight, before the crowd gets drunk and rowdy.

Bluefields's famous Palo de Mayo parade

© SWENJA JANINE SCHLEGEL

BLUEFIELDS

Cima Club (half block up from Bancentro on the left, 2nd floor) features a Creole crowd, an intimate dance floor; and downstairs, to your right, **Cima Karaoke** offers louder music, a spacious dance floor, a longer bar, and a more diverse crowd (both are open seven days a week). **Midnight Dream** (Barrio Pointeen, two long blocks from the Moravian Church, open daily), popularly known as Baghdad, is owned by former mayor and town celebrity "Lala," a.k.a. Lawrence Omeir. This is a prominent drinking and dancing social center for the Creole community and features a dark, open-air bar and dance floor with a great view of the bay.

Radio and Cinema

Soak in the culture with programs like "Roots Rap Reggae" (9 A.M. on Radio Zinica, 95.9 FM), "Energía Volumen" (4–6 P.M. on Radio La Morenita, 102.1 FM), and "Caribbean Breeze" (1 P.M. on Radio Punto Tres, 90.7 FM). Radio La Costeñísima plays regular sets of Miskito music (101.1 FM). Hear the "Voice of America" daily at 6 A.M. on Radio Bluefields

BLUEFIELDS

AFRICAN-DERIVED SPIRITUAL PRACTICES OF THE ATLANTIC COAST

A distant cousin to the voudoun ("voodoo") of Haiti and Benin, **Obeah** refers to sorcery, folk magic, and other religious practices brought by Central- and West African slaves to the Americas. Using herbal teas and baths, charms, amulets and prayer, Obeah is best described as a method of communication with the supernatural world, and a means of calling on metaphysical powers through shamanistic rituals.

Obeah was frowned upon by Christian missionaries and slave masters, resulting in the awkward Christianization of modern Obeah: Many African deities now bear the names of Catholic saints. Obeah is most commonly used in the West Indies, but is widely practiced in Caribbean and Latin American nations whose African descendants have maintained a connection to this aspect of their ancestry, including the Creole, Garifuna and Miskito people on Nicaragua's Atlantic Coast.

Contrary to popular belief, Obeah is not always used for negative purposes. In fact, often times Costeños pay a practioner to heal a medical, emotional, or spiritual problem; to influence events in a person's favor; to achieve success in a particular endeavor; or to find out the answer to an important question (such as who is my husband sleeping with, who stole my cows, etc.).

However, amongst the Miskito and Afro-Caribbean peoples negative Obeah is not unheard of: Locals will even resort to Obeah revenge rather than the police department. Whether you personally believe in Obeah or not, on the Atlantic Coast you are entering a world where the practice and the belief of Obeah are a large part of the culture, and every Costeño believes just a little, in its power.

When visiting the Caribbean coast of Nicaragua, there is no need to fear Obeah (unless you take away another's lover)! Moreover, the way that most Costeños approach Obeah is indicative of their overall spiritual perspective on life. For example, in Creole culture, there is a strong nine-day ritual that follows a person's death: As soon as the person is pronounced dead, word begins to spread amongst the Creole community. The family's closest friends and family quickly arrive at the house to clean, cook, and receive the multitudes that will soon come to accompany the family during their grief. This set-up occurs 24 hours a day (though most people come at night) and appears to be like a party without the music – crowds of people eating, drinking rum, and talking. On the ninth night, the night before the person is finally buried, a very specific ritual occurs: The same close friends and family of the deceased go through the house and remove all bed linens, tablecloths, and curtains. At exactly midnight, all present begin to sing to the spirit of the deceased the following words to signal to the spirit that it is now time to descend to heaven: "TBA." It is widely believed that failure to perform this ritual will cause the spirit of the dead person to wander the earth as a miserable ghost, causing trouble, harm, and sometimes death to the living.

For more information check out the novels and memoirs of Jamaica Kincaid, or *Vampire The Masquerade, Unburnable,* and *Brown Girl in the Ring* by Nalo Hopkinson.

(Contributed by Phoebe Haupt-Cayasso, trip leader and experiential learning consultant with a decade of experience working with students in Bluefields and Atlantic coast communities.)

Estereo (96.5 FM), followed by a country music show. On 97.7 FM, Radio Riddim hosts Creole talk radio programs about local politics and autonomy, as well as good reggae and dance hall music.

Cine Crismar shows three movies ($1.50) once each night at 5:15 P.M., 7:15 P.M. and 8:45 P.M. There's also high-speed Internet, international phone calls, and a restaurant.

SHOPPING

Joyeria y Artesania Gutierrez (Barrio Central in front of the SOS Farmacia) sells Caribbean-inspired wood carvings, also on sale at the bigger hotels. **Julio Lopez,** a Garifuna originally from Orinoco (Barrio 19 de Julio, in front of INAFLOR) and Miskito **Leo Bolanos Padilla** (Barrio 19 de Julio, *"contiguo donde fue la cocotera,"* or "next to where the *cocotera* used to be," tel. 505/572-0070) are local artisans. **Mr. Rene Hodgson** (tel. 505/572-1658) is a talented, self-taught Creole painter and local Adventist pastor whose work is frequently displayed at the Bluefields Bay Hotel.

CHARTER FISHING

For professional catch-and-release river and deep sea fishing (and wildlife tours) contact Gerald Lewis and the **Casa Rosa Lodge** (tel. 780/970-3015, randyrosa97@hotmail.com, www.rumbleinthejungle.net). For $250 a day, you get a chance to land some huge fish and lots of fun. The price includes a large room, all meals, guide, boat, and gear. Bar drinks and tip not included.

ACCOMMODATIONS

Crack cocaine makes Bluefields more dangerous than most other Nicaraguan cities, and the city is grimy and less sanitary in general—just get an eyeful of all the dirty water and mangy mutts slithering down the roads. This is one place where "roughing it" in the cheapest flophouses is asking for trouble, so we strongly recommend you avoid the cheapest accommodations. If you do decide to go for one of the budget hotels, assess both its security measures and the kind of people hanging around. Insist

on either a window with screens and/or a mosquito net. Avoid the Pension Lopez, famous for drunk men and hourly room rentals.

Under $10

Hospedaje El Dorado (Barrio Punta Fría, across from the Cruz Lorena, tel. 505/572-1435, $6.50–10) is one of your best options if you are determined to stick to a strict budget. The hotel offers relatively clean, well-maintained rooms with private bath and cable TV. **Lobster Pot** (on the main drag in Barrio Central, no phone, $6.50–$8 pp) is owned by a Creole-speaking, Cayman Islander who runs a large establishment that rents many of its rooms to permanent guests. The clean rooms with a shared bath are better than some other run-down places but that's about it. **Hospedaje Laguna de Perla** (Barrio Central, across from the UNAC, tel. 505/572-2411, $5.50) offers very basic rooms with fan, "but we don't accept drunks or scandalous behavior, and you cannot come in past midnight."

$10-25

Bluefields Bay Hotel en Casa URACCAN (tel. 505/572-2143, kriol@ibw.com.ni, $25 and under) is right on the water, away from the hustle and bustle of the central barrio, yet still within walking distance of town. It's a uniquely Costeño establishment that helps fund university programs.

Hotel Caribbean Dream (Barrio Punta Fría, 30 meters south of the main market, tel. 505/572-0107, www.hotelcaribbean dream.com) offers spacious, well-appointed rooms with private bathroom, closets, cable TV, new air-conditioning units, hot water, wireless Internet (for $2 per day), an on-site restaurant, a bright atmosphere and an upstairs veranda.

◖ Mini-Hotel Central (Barrio Central, across from Bancentro, tel. 505/572-2362, $12 with fan, $25 with a/c) has been a mainstay of Bluefields since 1983 and is nearly always booked. It has a popular restaurant and outside veranda, and clean, well-maintained rooms with private bath and cable TV.

PALO DE MAYO

Celebrated every day in the month of May, the Palo de Mayo, or maypole dance, is the most well-known and colorful feature of Nicaragua's vibrant cultural Caribbean stew. In English and Nordic tradition of the 19th century, on the first of May young men and women would collect freshly cut flowers. This was known as "going-a-maying." A long, straight pole was set in the center of town and decorated with the fresh flowers and colored ribbons anchored to the top of the pole. The celebration ushered in the spring and expressed hopes for happiness and a good harvest.

How the Palo de Mayo got to Bluefields and the Atlantic coast of Nicaragua remains a mystery, though it very probably passed directly from England during the years the Atlantic coast was an English protectorate, or possibly by way of Jamaica, where it evolved into something more Caribbean and erotic. To date, the Palo de Mayo is celebrated, in such disparate locales as Austria, Spain, and amongst the Wenda and Galla people of Africa.

The Palo de Mayo refers to two things: a massive celebration and outpouring of joy held the first of May every year in Bluefields, Pearl Lagoon, and the Corn Islands, and also the name of a dance and style of music. The dance has gotten progressively more sensual in recent decades – sometimes appearing as simulated sex on the dance floor – and the more conservative Costeños have started a movement to return the dance to its more respectable origins.

Most cultural presentations on the Atlantic coast and elsewhere in Nicaragua include a version of the Palo de Mayo that you should make an effort to see, if possible. Set typically to the tropical rhythms of Dimensión Costeña, the popular Bluefields party band, dancers in brightly colored satin costumes go through a series of provocative routines of gyrating hips and shimmying chests.

$25-50

Hotel Anabas (Barrio Central, next to Radio Sí Nica, tel. 505/572-1144) is a step up from Mini-Hotel Central, plus hot water, ceiling fans, and better beds but no wireless Internet. Expect slightly higher prices for this smaller hotel and look for the bigger and better Gran Hotel Anabas sometime soon.

South Atlantic II (Barrio Central, next to the gas station Levy, tel. 505/572-1022, $28–50) is a friendly, centrally located, Creole establishment, popular with Nicaraguan business travelers. They offer a safe environment and well-maintained, spotless rooms with air-conditioning, cable TV, hot water, and an on-site restaurant and travel agency.

Over $50

Oasis Hotel (on the corner near the municipal wharf, tel. 505/572-2812, www.oasis hotelcasino.net, $65–120 pp includes breakfast) was opened in 2005 by a U.S. businessman who also owns the two casinos in town (one of which is on-site). This is the classiest act in town, with a warm, intimate environment, carpeted and hardwood floors, and lovely sparkling bathrooms, plus a presidential suite.

FOOD
Caribbean Baked Goods

Start at the Bluefields Bay Hotel, where you'll find **Ms. Emma Rose's** baked goods; for a delicious, filling afternoon snack, arrive around 3 P.M. to place an order for a loaf of her famous bun, the official sweet bread of the Atlantic coast, often with raisins, coconut milk, and hand-ground cinnamon and nutmeg. Pick it up between 4–5 P.M. Fridays she also makes a mean "patti"—a spicy beef empanada.

Soro (Barrio Central, across the street from Galileo) sells a variety of typical Nicaraguan and Costeño baked goods. Try the moist Coco Cake for a true coast snack: grated taro with coconut milk, cinnamon, nutmeg, and sugar. For savory small loafs of coconut bread, bun, soda cake (coconut bread with ginger and sugar), and *pico* (bread with sugar and cheese), go to

SEA TO SOUP: ATLANTIC COAST COOKIN'

Atlantic coast cuisine is marked by its simplicity and freshness. That lobster on your plate was probably picked off the ocean floor this morning; the fish were swimming hours ago. The only way you'll get fresher fish is by cooking it on the ship – or eating it raw: **ceviche** with lime juice, tomato, and onion. Seafood on the Nicaraguan Atlantic is cheap by international standards, delicious by anyone's standards, and well worth the wait (most Bluefields restaurants are slow, even by Nicaraguan standards). If your travel complaints don't evaporate in the garlicky steam of lobster under your nose, then you obviously are going to need to spend another couple of days.

Start off with **yellowfin, snapper,** or **sea bass,** grilled or fried. **Conch,** when tenderized correctly, is soft and delicate, less briny than other seafood but with a soft texture. Or enjoy a lobster *al vapor*, bulging with delicate, white meat you can pull from the shell with your fingers, drenched in butter and lime.

Mixed soup is served in a helmet-sized bowl choked with crab, lobster, conch, and fish. Not hearty enough? Then reach for **rondon,** or "rundown," a thick stew of fish (or endangered turtle), vegetables, and coconut milk thickened with starchy tubers and plantains. In August, don't miss the Corn Island **Crab Soup Festival,** when Costeños cook tons of soft crabmeat into a festival you won't forget. Atlantic coast crabmeat is particularly soft, with a delicate flavor unique to the tropics.

You don't have to stick to seafood to eat well on the Atlantic coast. Even the *gallo pinto* tastes better here: That's because it's

© KATHLEEN SILK

Creole cooking with Ms. Edna

cooked in sweet coconut oil. Between meals, fill up with **coco bread** – football-sized loaves of soft, rich wheat flour cooked up with coconut and served hot out of the oven. Another treat is kind of like cinnamon rolls but without the cinnamon: hot coconut **bun** is sweet and sticky.

See *Sights and Attractions* for information on Creole cooking classes with Ms. Edna Cayasso.

the woman who is in front of Pan Chickito (also known as Mercadito Mas y Menos) in Barrio Central.

Breakfast

One of the only establishments serving pancakes, sausage, and eggs is **Salon Siu** (across from Blue City Tech House, open daily at 7 A.M. for under $3). But **Bluefields Bay** **Hotel** features the best Costeño breakfast in town with coffee/tea, fruit, eggs, and fresh, warm coconut bread for $2.50.

Street Food and *Frito*

In Bluefields, Creole *fritanga* (usually just $1.50) features stewed chicken with a savory brown and salty sauce, served in a small, plastic bag with *tajadas* and Creole cabbage salad.

Try **Mr. William's** shop, Thursday–Sunday, located to the left of Four Brother's disco (which also sells good, Creole *frito* and soups Thurs.–Sun.).

The mestizo version of *frito* consists of fried or slow-roasted chicken plus all your favorites from Spanish-speaking Nicaragua. Try **Comedor Arlen** (Barrio Central, right across the street from the well-known Galileo store), or on the corner across from the Texas Casino. Enchiladas that cost $0.25 and cheap beef tacos are on the menu at **Pulpería El Guayabo.**

Inexpensive Restaurants

The following restaurants offer good value for decent portions. **(Bar Tauro's** (Barrio Central, next to the Tip-Top) is a tiny place well loved for loud music and a good menu, including *rondon* (or "rundown") soup for less than $4. It's known also by the name of the new owner, Bam Bam. **Mini-Hotel Central Café** offers a wide range of well-prepared Nicaraguan and Costeño dishes at reasonable prices. **Pizza Martinuzzi** (next to Parque Reyes) comes pretty close to the real thing, and next door, **Restaurante Tex Mex** sells a plate of beef fajitas for $5. **Dragon Chino** (Barrio Santa Rosa, Calle Alcalde) is almost but not quite what you expect, at about $6 per plate.

Upscale Restaurants

Twins Seafood and More (Barrio Central, next to Texas Casino) is the new, hip restaurant in town, specializing in seafood, vegetarian, and salads. After 4 P.M., the bar and dance floor upstairs are popular with the moneyed Creole crowd. But **Loma** (near the Bluefields Bay Hotel) is the most elegant restaurant in town. The view from your table and the variety in the menu make the steeper prices well worth it. Feel free to down the ice (they have a water purification system for ice and fresh drinks), a delicious piña colada, or a fresh fruit punch.

(Tía Irene Bar and Restaurant is located over the water below Bluefields Bay Hotel; its one-of-a-kind view of the bay and reliable quality have kept this restaurant a local favorite from the time it was known as Manglares. **Lunas Ranch** is a well-known restaurant in the newer part of town (Barrio Loma Fresca, almost across from URACCAN). Decorated with the traditional thatched-roof design, the restaurant offers great food, midrange prices, and a very professional staff. **Chez Marcel** is another longtime standby, especially if you're craving a steak, located near Pizza Martinuzzi.

Playa Bonita (jeanlouis.vigo@gmail.com) was opened in 2007 by a French-Bluefields couple and offers a varied menu in an open-air, waterfront setting in Barrio Loma Fresca. Given its remoteness, we do not recommend going alone, even in a taxi. **Casa Rosa Lodge** (www.rumbleinthejungle.net), a small, family-run restaurant specializing in seafood, is located next to Playa Bonita and also on the waterfront.

INFORMATION

The INTUR office (tel. 505/572-1111) can't hold a candle to CIDCA, the Research and Documentation center for the Atlantic coast (affiliated with the UCA, 50 meters north of the police station, open 8 A.M.–5:30 P.M. Mon.–Fri., with a break for lunch). CIDCA makes available to the public a wide selection of materials about Caribbean cultures and languages, including several Miskito-only publications. Meanwhile, www.bluefieldspulse.com keeps you current on the social scene.

SERVICES
Emergency

The fire department (tel. 505/572-2298) is just north of the Moravian church; the police (tel. 505/572-2448) are on the same side of the street, three blocks south; and the Red Cross (tel. 505/572-2582) can be found in Barrio Fatima. Hospital Ernesto Sequeira (tel. 505/572-2391 main switchboard or tel. 505/822-2621 emergency) is located about five, long blocks south and west of the park.

Phones and Mail

The ENITEL/CLARO phone office is located next to Mini-Hotel Central (open 8 A.M.–5 P.M.

© RANDALL WOOD

Nicaraguan puddle-jumpers fly daily between Managua and the Atlantic coast.

Mon.–Fri., 8 A.M.–noon Sat.). The post office is half a block west of the Texas Casino building, and the two Western Union offices are located one and two blocks east of the park.

Banks

Banpro (formerly Caley Dagnall) is the older of the two banks on the Atlantic coast and is located in front of the Moravian Church. Bancentro is located just around the corner on Calle Cabezas. Both are open 8 A.M.–5 P.M. Monday–Friday and 8 A.M.–noon Saturday. Money changers are on the corner between the two banks and are both safe and useful.

ATMs

Both banks now feature 24-hour ATM service, though the one at Banpro dispenses the money in much more reasonable denominations (100 *córdoba* vs. 500 *córdoba* bills, which can be hard to change in Bluefields). The town hall (or Palacio) also has a 24-hour ATM booth, located just east of the park, across the street.

Internet

Bluefields has faster Internet access than much of western Nicaragua. For the best chance of securing a decent computer without a long wait, check out the original Bluefields cybercafe, **Copicentro.** For higher quality computers, air-conditioning, and better service, go to **TechHouse** (one block east of the park, open 8 A.M.–9 P.M. Mon.–Fri, condensed schedule on weekends). **Blue City** is run by Mark Narcisso, who spent part of his childhood in the U.S.; it offers a nice atmosphere, many computers, air-conditioning, beverages, CD burning, printing, and a music studio (same basic hours as TechHouse). All offer Internet access for about $0.75 per hour and international phone calls to the U.S. for about $0.10 per minute.

Film

The Kodak store (open 8 A.M.–6 P.M. Mon.–Fri., 8 A.M.–noon Sat.) is located kitty-corner from Cima Club and now features a fairly high-tech, self-service photo-printing machine. Bluefields is so humid your negatives will seal

ATLANTIC COAST FLIGHT SCHEDULE

Two small, independent airlines connect Nicaragua's two coasts with regular flights. Please note: At the time of publication, this information was accurate and will most likely remain so for some time. However, schedules change, as do prices, so please check airline websites and phone their offices to double-check our data. Round-trip flights from Managua to Bluefields cost about $130; from Managua to Corn Island, you'll pay $165 round-trip.

AIRLINES

Atlantic Airlines
(www.atlanticairlinesint.com)
Managua: tel. 505/270-5355 or 505/233-2791, fax 505/270-5259
Bluefields: tel. 505/572-1299 or 505/572-0259
Puerto Cabezas: tel. 505/792-2586
Corn Island: tel. 505/575-5055 or 505/575-5151

La Costeña
(www.tacaregional.com/costena)
Managua: tel. 505/263-2143 or 505/263-2142, fax 505/263-1281
Bluefields: tel. 505/572-2500
Corn Island: tel. 505/575-5121

FLIGHT TIMES

Managua-Bluefields
La Costeña ....6:30 A.M., 10 A.M. (except Sun.), 3 P.M.
Atlantic......................6:45 A.M., 10:30 A.M., 2:10 P.M.

Bluefields-Managua
La Costeña ....7:30 A.M., 8:30 A.M., 11 A.M. (except Sun.), 4 P.M.
Atlantic......................9:10 A.M., 11:45 A.M., 4 P.M.

Managua-Corn Island
La Costeña ....6:30 A.M., 3 P.M.
Atlantic......................6:45 A.M., 10:30 A.M., 2:10 P.M.

Corn Island-Managua
La Costeña ....7:30 A.M., 3 P.M.
Atlantic......................8:35 A.M., 3 P.M.

Managua-Puerto Cabezas
La Costeña ....6:30 A.M., 10 A.M., 2 P.M.
Atlantic......................6:30 A.M., 10:30 A.M.

Bluefields-Puerto Cabezas
La Costeña ....12 P.M. (Mon., Wed., and Fri. only)

Puerto Cabezas-Bluefields
La Costeña ....11 A.M. (Mon., Wed., and Fri. only)

© RANDALL WOOD

El Rama's international port

themselves to each other the instant you carry them out of the shop unless you protect them in well-sealed plastic bags.

GETTING THERE AND AWAY
By Land

The overland route is no longer the heroic journey it was before they repaved the highway to El Rama in 2002–2003, but you'll still need some stamina. Leave Managua for El Rama at night, then board a predawn *panga* and soak up two hours of fresh air, sunrise, and a beautiful trip down the Río Escondido to Bluefields (bring a sweater for both parts of the trip). While this route is cheaper than flying, it also offers you a true appreciation for Nicaragua's girth and the Atlantic coast's geographical isolation. See the *El Rama* section in the *Chontales and the Nicaraguan Cattle Country* chapter for more detailed information on the companies that offer a bus-boat combination package.

By Air

Both La Costeña and Atlantic Airlines offer regular, daily flights between Bluefields,

Managua, and Big Corn Island. The trip from Managua to Bluefields takes about one hour and costs $83 for a one-way ticket ($127 round-trip). To fly directly from Managua to Corn Island will cost you $107 ($165 round-trip). The flight from Bluefields to Corn Island costs $65 ($99 round-trip). It is easy to buy a Managua–Corn Island round-trip ticket with a stopover in Bluefields on the way to Corn Island for $197. Buying an "open" ticket means no dates are fixed, so you can arrange your onward flight with either of the two airlines by calling or visiting the airport, or by dealing with one of their many ticket brokers around town—South Atlantic II hotel is a good one, or look for the Costeña and Atlantic signs elsewhere in town.

By Boat

Passenger-boat traffic to El Rama, Pearl Lagoon, Orinoco, and Pueblo Nuevo (up the Wawachang River) originates from the main municipal dock. Pay the $0.10 entrance fee at the first window (pays for their cable TV connection). Trips to El Bluff ($1.50 each way)

originate at a much smaller MINSA dock next to the municipal market (inquire at the market). Old cargo-passenger boats leave three times a week for Corn Island. If you choose this route instead of flying (as most travelers do), take lots of water, sun protection, and a sense of humor; the eastward voyage produces some major barf-bag swells.

Near Bluefields

EL BLUFF
Located on the spit of land separating Bluefields Bay from the Caribbean Ocean, El Bluff used to be connected to Bluefields by land—before Hurricane Joan breached the bar in 1988. The breach was bridged only in 2006 by a pedestrian walkway. El Bluff's principal attraction is a fabled stretch of classic Caribbean sand in front of a lovely patch of turquoise sea (when the sun's out anyway); the place is known only as "the beach by El Bluff," across the strip from Bluff's hulking industrial park and fish-packing facilities, all on the bay side. The harbor was built by Bulgarian engineers in the 1980s with hopes of creating a supertanker port. Wander around the docks and check out the enormous steel ships of Nicaragua's Atlantic fishing fleet before making your way to the beach.

You can usually hire the same *panga* that took you to Bluff to get to the beach if you ask your driver. It's only a five-minute ride and should cost no more than $1. To walk to the beach, look for Hotelito El Bluff, the only *hospedaje* in town, right next to the park. As you walk out the main entrance of the hotel, take your first left onto a paved path and follow it through a residential area until it ends (about 10–15 minutes). Keep going straight for about 200 meters at which point you will be able to see the beach. Make sure to go with a group of friends; going alone could be dangerous. On the weekends only, there is a disco on the beach that sells beverages.

Accommodations, Food, and Entertainment
Hotelito El Bluff (tel. 505/577-0059, $5 s or d) is located right next to the park and is the town's only lodging. The hotel offers basic rooms with cable TV and fan, and has a no-frills on-site restaurant. You can also eat at **La Casona Bar and Restaurant** (open nights Tues.–Sun.), located along the paved path towards the beach. There is also a basic food stand in the park. For dancing at night, check out the same La Casona or **Beach View Ranch** (along the paved path to the beach, about 50 feet from La Casona), which offers a view of the beach.

Getting There and Away
Pangas leave for El Bluff all day from the MINSA dock next to the municipal market in Bluefields for $1.50 (30-minute ride), embarking as soon as they fill up with 12 passengers. The last boat returns to Bluefields around 4 P.M.

RAMA CAY
Fifteen kilometers south of Bluefields is Rama Cay, ancestral home of the Rama people. About 800 souls live on this small island. According to historians, the Rama people are originally descended from the Chibchas and Aruac Rama from the Amazon basin; several oral histories explain how the Rama came to occupy this isolated island at the end of the 17th century. Rama culture is now disappearing: Only a small handful of elders still speak the language.

A tour of the island is available to visitors for $3 ($6 if you want lunch). When you arrive on the island, ask for Sonia Omeir who was the coordinator of the program at the time of this books' publishing. Getting to Rama Cay is an easy $6 *panga* ride from Bluefields; it takes about an hour to cross the bay.

RESERVA SILVESTRE GREENFIELDS

On the outskirts of Kukra Hill, Reserva Silvestre Greenfields (tel. 505/278-0589 or 505/434-4808, www.greenfields.com.ni) is a protected reserve, characterized by its scenic beauty, silence, and proximity to nature. Privately managed as an ecotourism business, you can hike more than 25 kilometers of trails, canoe through jungle watercourses, or rest and enjoy the silence surrounded by lush vegetation. Price includes lodging, meals, and guided tours. You can make this a day trip (no lodging, no meals) for $15 per person or $50 per group (up to six persons), and enjoy excursions with guides by foot or canoe, the botanical park, the bathing pier, and more. All trips must be previously arranged and reservations need to be received at least four days in advance.

KARAWALA AND SANDY BAY

Sandy Bay, located three hours north along the Caribbean coast, is one of the only Miskito communities accessible from Bluefields, and nearby Karawala is the last indigenous Ulwa site in the world (the Ulwa are related to the Mayangna but have distinct cultural characteristics and language). The boat ($14 one-way) to both places leaves the *muelle* (dock) in Bluefields on Mondays and Fridays at 10 A.M.—or whenever they fill up; it returns on Wednesdays and Fridays. There's not much to do in Sandy Bay for nonanthropologists, although the beach is nice. Karawala, however, is situated between pine forest and mangrove swamps and offers world-class tarpon fly-fishing. In town, you'll find basic accommodations and simple meals. Sand flies in both places can get pretty bad, so be prepared with long pants and baby oil.

◖ PEARL LAGOON

Tucked away one lagoon north of Bluefields, Pearl Lagoon (Laguna de Perlas) is a small community whose natural, green splendor is a welcome respite from Bluefields. Its sandy streets are easily explored on foot. This little village gives access to local Miskito communities and the enchanting Pearl Cays. The locals earn their living from the water—you'll see boats of the five companies that deal in fishing and fish processing tied up along the docks or moored in the lagoon. Denmark and Norway have been active in the economic development of the region, constructing municipal piers in Pearl Lagoon, Haulover, Tasbapauni, Kakabila, Brown Bank, and Marshall Point to assist local fishermen in getting their catch to market.

Sights and Entertainment

Of interest in town is the **"the great gun,"** as the locals lovingly call the iron cannon (mounted in front of the ENITEL building). Embossed with the seal of the British empire and the year 1803, it dates back to the protectorate. The clean architectural style of the most eye-catching building in town, the whitewashed **Moravian church,** was typical of the period. Attending an evening service there is memorable (dress appropriately).

Don't miss a night of reggae at one of Pearl Lagoon's several small ranches, or clubs, the most popular of which is **Cultural Vibrations** (known locally as Stiff Cock, no joke). Cultural Vibrations and **Consumé Club** are open all week.

Pearl Lagooners love baseball, and compete on teams with names like the Buffalos, Mariners, Young Stars, Hurricanes, Sweet Pearly, First Stop, Young Braves, and the Haulover Tigers—watch them battle it out at the stadium on Saturdays and Sundays September–January.

Accommodations

The best of the family-run guesthouses is ◖ **Green Lodge Guesthouse** (tel. 505/572-0507, $15), a pleasant place on the main drag. **Hospedaje Ingrid** (tel. 505/572-1777, $8) has a quiet veranda with hammocks and chairs. It's located towards the back of Pearl Lagoon, to the left of the stadium in Barrio 4th of May. All rooms have private bath and some have TV. Right on the

© RANDALL WOOD

the Moravian church in Pearl Lagoon

main drag in front of the dock, the **Sweet Pearly's** (tel. 505/572-0520, $10–13) is another standby with 11 small, clean rooms with fans, plus bar, restaurant, and ice-cream parlor downstairs.

Casa Blanca Hotelito y Restaurante (tel. 505/572-0508, $10–30) is clean, well liked, and run by a Danish-Creole couple intent on making your trip pleasurable.

Food

Miss Betty's Bread Shop is the place to go for pastries, juices, and sweets. The **Green Lodge** serves fresh, well-prepared food; their plate of the day costs $3–5, though breakfast is cheaper. **Hospedaje Ingrid** and **Cool Spot** also offer good cooking from $3. The basic **Pearl Paradise** is on the second story of the building adjacent to the municipal dock. The **Casa Blanca Hotelito y Restaurante** has the best menu in town, served in a pleasant ambience, though a few readers have told us it is not the friendliest place in town. Shrimp dishes start at $5 and lobster at $6.50.

Services

The ENITEL office and a police post are in the center of "town" by the wharf. The health clinic is a few blocks south, to the right of the Moravian church. Four pharmacies can take care of basic medical needs. For more serious medical emergencies, you will be strapped into a *panga* and rocketed off to Bluefields. With that in mind, stay safe.

Getting There and Away

The *panga* trip up the Río Escondido and then north through a complex network of waterways to Pearl Lagoon is a thrilling, beautiful ride that takes under an hour and costs $6 each way. On the way, you'll pass several shipwrecks, and the active dock at Kukra Hill, named after a long-assimilated cannibalistic tribe. Go to the municipal dock in Bluefields around 7 A.M. to sign up for the Pearl Lagoon *panga*. Boats leave as soon as they have 20 passengers, all day until 3 P.M. The last *panga* back from Pearl Lagoon leaves between noon and 3 P.M. but won't leave if the boat isn't full.

© RANDALL WOOD

the Pearl Cays

THE PEARL CAYS

Most of the 18 specks of land that make up the Pearl Cays archipelago remain untouched and relatively accessible, though a few cays are being built up by wealthy foreigners, and controversy over their ownership and development is building. The cays (pronounced KEYS) are six kilometers east of a small Miskito coastal village called Set Net. Hire a boat from Pearl Lagoon and enjoy the ride through the harbor, into the open Caribbean, then up the empty coastline to the cays.

For the most part, the Pearl Cays have zero tourist facilities, so bring water and your Gilligan's Island kit. Arrange a trip through La Casa Blanca or Hospedaje Ingrid in Pearl Lagoon. A round-trip *panga* ride to the Pearl Cays can cost $150, so the more people chipping in, the cheaper it'll be. If you find yourself sharing one of the islets with local fishermen, you may find them cutting down coconuts and telling fishing stories over a fire on the beach; strike up a deal for some fresh fish.

VILLAGES NEAR PEARL LAGOON
Awas

The town of Pearl Lagoon sits on the southeast side of a small prominence jutting out into the bay. Walk west from the town (to the left of the dock) to get to the broad, shallow lagoon-beach community of Awas. This half-hour walk down a flat, sandy road will cross a saltwater estuary and a small footbridge. When you get to the Miskito community of Raitipura (Miskito for "on top of the cemetery"), turn left and follow the road to Awas. Rent a small palm-thatch hut from one of the locals for $2–4, kick back, and relax. Take advantage of the new **Bar and Restaurant Tropical View,** built out over the water.

Tasbapauni

Farther up the coast, on the Caribbean side of the land, is the community of Tasbapauni (two hours from Pearl Lagoon, no lodging), set on a thin strip of land right between the Caribbean and the lagoon, close to the Man of War Cays. Beware of the sand flies when the breeze is not blowing (same with visiting Set Net). From Bluefields, you can go directly here via *panga* for $13 each way.

Pueblo Nuevo

To hear the Bluefielders tell it, Pueblo Nuevo, 45 minutes up the Wawachang River just to the west of Orinoco, is home to farming families that began slashing and burning back in the Pacific, and mowed their way east until they hit the Atlantic. FADCANIC is here teaching organic farming and forest management in order to save the only remaining tropical forest in the region. Catch the Pueblo Nuevo *panga,* departing Bluefields on Sundays and Wednesdays ($12 pp each way), and returning on Mondays and Thursdays. He passes Wawachang and the Khaka Creek Reserve on his way to Pueblo Nuevo. It's harder to catch *at* Pueblo Nuevo, when it might already be full. Either way, reserve your return seat in the boat on your way upstream.

◖ Wawachang and Khaka Creek Reserve

Located about a kilometer up the river from Wawachang, Khaka Creek Reserve is the epitome of the local, grass-roots ecotourism movement which is providing alternate means of subsistence in a delicate ecosystem. Run by FADCANIC, new, modern tourist facilities allow you to take advantage of this wilderness area, from hiking trails to eight cabins and trained guides knowledgeable in local flora and fauna.

An all-inclusive package (food, lodging in the guesthouse, and trail guide) costs $30 per night plus $24 for round-trip transportation to and from Bluefields. The center is ideal for ecological research and is equipped with solar energy, Internet access, screened windows, and purified water. The guesthouse offers seven rooms that can accommodate 25 people, one with a double bed and private bath. To pay for your services separately, it's $15 per night for lodging, $2.50 per meal, and $5 for the services of a local trail guide for half a day ($10 full day). Contact them via the Wawachang Center (tel. 505/572-2386, mruizg1964@hotmail.com). To arrange your trip from Bluefields, stop by the FADCANIC office, located just up from Mini-Hotel and speak with Reynaldo, Silver, or Marcos (or any of the Agro-Forestry or Wawachang staff).

The whole Wawachang region is serviced by the Foundation for the Autonomy and Development of the Atlantic Coast of Nicaragua (FADCANIC). Founded by a small group of passionate Creole leaders in the early 1990s, FADCANIC manages a number of successful development programs, financed largely by the Norwegian government and various NGOs. The **Wawachang Center for Sustainable Agro-Forestry Development** is FADCANIC's largest microcredit program. Stop by it to visit the Agro-Forestry high school and walk the fields, seedling nursery, and model farm.

ORINOCO AND MARSHALL POINT

Orinoco is the southernmost home of the Garifuna people, a distinct ethnic group with strong West African roots unique to Central America. On May 18, 2001, UNESCO proclaimed the Garifuna language, music, and dance a "Masterpiece of the Oral and Intangible Heritage of Humanity." Their dancing, drumming, and singing manifests strongly African roots. Try to visit on November 19, the Garifuna Arrival Day in Nicaragua and National Day for the Garifuna People, featuring talented Garifuna singers, drummers, and dancers from the coast, as well as from Belize, Honduras, and Guatemala.

Marshall Point is a typical, small Creole community. You can reach Marshall Point by going to Orinoco and then walking or hiring a *panga* to take you around the corner. Do not walk alone. Tip: Grease the edge of your shoes with a thick line of Vaseline as you arrive in Orinoco and Marshall Point, as grass lice can be abundant.

Try to sample some *fufu,* a cassava dish common throughout West Africa, or the Garifuna *ereba* or *bami,* flat bread also made from cassava. Invite community leaders Frank Lopez, Ramon Martinez, and Fermin Gonzalez to lunch to hear about the history and culture of the Garifuna and Orinoco. You may extraordinarily witness a *walagallo,* or *dugu,* ceremony, a healing ritual that has been known to bring people back from the brink of death. The spirit of an ancestor appears to someone in a dream, giving the specific recipe for that particular *walagallo.* Dancing, singing, and sacrificing of chickens then continues until the dying person gets up from the sickbed to start dancing, signifying to the crowd that he or she has been cured. The chickens don't do as well.

Accommodations and Food

The only lodging option in Orinoco is the **Hostal Garifuna** (www.hostalgarifuna.com, $8–16), a nice, new guesthouse with seven large rooms and a pleasant area for relaxing. Arrange to eat your meals at the hostel to experience authentic Garifuna cooking.

Getting There and Away

From the municipal dock in Bluefields, take a *panga* ride up into the Laguna de Perlas (the water body, not the town) to Orinoco and Marshall Point. The famous "hardway *panga*" ($11 one-way) leaves Bluefields on Mondays, Thursdays, and Saturdays, and returns to Bluefields on Mondays, Tuesdays, Thursdays, and Fridays. You can sometimes catch this boat from Pearl Lagoon, depending on whether or not they filled up with passengers in Bluefields. You can also try to catch the Pueblo Nuevo boat, but remember: This is the coast and no schedules are set so stay flexible.

Corn Island

Eighty-three kilometers due east of Bluefields Bay's brackish, brown water, the Corn Islands are a pair of Tertiary period volcanic basalt bumps in the Caribbean, politically Nicaraguan but Caribbean in spirit. Formerly home base for lobster fishermen and their families, the islanders are increasingly turning to tourism for their future. How well the fragile island ecosystem will support it will determine the fate of the islands.

Corn Island is 10 square kilometers of forested hills, mangrove swamps, and stretches of white coral beaches. The mangrove swamps and estuaries that line several stretches of coastline are crucial to the island's water supply, and the islanders have fiercely resisted attempts by foreign investors to drain or fill them. The highest points are Quinn Hill, Little Hill (55 and 57 meters above sea level, respectively), and Mount Pleasant (97 meters).

Three distinct layers of reef, composed of more than 40 species of coral, protect the north side of the island. Though the diving and snorkeling are still impressive (divers regularly see nurse sharks, eagle rays, and lots of colorful fish), the reefs closest to shore have deteriorated over the past decades, victims of overfishing, predatory algae (which grow as a result of increased nutrient levels in the water from sewage runoff), sedimentation, and global warming. Of the six sea turtle species swimming off Nicaragua's shores, four live in Caribbean waters. On land, Corn Island boasts three endemic species of reptiles and amphibians, all threatened by the continued swamp draining.

HISTORY

Pirates on their way to maraud the coast of Central America and Nicaragua's Río San Juan first visited here in the 16th century, sometimes by accident after the reefs tore the bottom of their ships open. But Corn Island was inhabited long before that by the Kukras, a subtribe of the Mayangnas whose penchant for consuming the bodies of their enemies (in a light coconut sauce, we're sure) inspired the first English visitors to call them the Skeleton Islands. The Kukra were eventually assimilated into the Miskitos. Nowadays, the native Creole population shares the island with an increasing number of menial laborers from the mainland, who have overtaken the Creoles in number and have increased the island's total population to nearly 9,000 people.

Native islanders are direct descendants from several of the more infamous European pirates, as well as English royalty and plantation owners—don't be surprised if you meet people with names like Kennington, Quinn, Dixon, or Downs.

ORIENTATION AND GETTING AROUND

From the new airport building, it's a five-minute taxi ride to almost anywhere on the island. A walk to Brig Bay, which is the "downtown" area, is around 2.5 kilometers. A paved road circumnavigates the island and bicycles can be hired at some hotels, including Morgan's Hotel. The municipal docks are in Brig Bay with *panga* service to Little Corn.

The nicest beaches on Big Corn are in the southern half: Both South West Bay and Long Bay are gorgeous but have almost no daytime services, including food. The north half of the island tends to be rocky with sharp coral formations but a few sandy stretches allow you to get into the water—in front of Dorsey Campbell's Yellowtail House, for example, for fantastic shore snorkeling.

Taxis cost under $0.75 to go anywhere on the island, prices double at night. Minibuses circumnavigate the island twice an hour and cost $0.35.

SIGHTS AND ENTERTAINMENT

The garish and incongruous **Golden Pyramid** on the top of Quinn Hill was built in 2006 by the Soul of the World society, a group whose

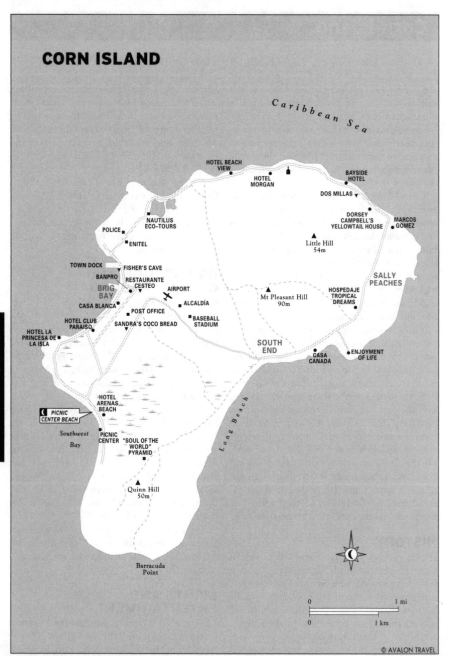

CORN ISLAND

Caribbean Sea

HOTEL BEACH VIEW

HOTEL MORGAN

BAYSIDE HOTEL

DOS MILLAS

DORSEY CAMPBELL'S YELLOWTAIL HOUSE

MARCOS GOMEZ

NAUTILUS ECO-TOURS

POLICE

ENITEL

Little Hill 54m

TOWN DOCK

FISHER'S CAVE

BANPRO

RESTAURANTE CESTEO

BRIG BAY

AIRPORT

SALLY PEACHES

ALCALDÍA

Mt Pleasant Hill 90m

HOSPEDAJE TROPICAL DREAMS

CASA BLANCA

POST OFFICE

BASEBALL STADIUM

HOTEL CLUB PARAISO

SANDRA'S COCO BREAD

HOTEL LA PRINCESA DE LA ISLA

SOUTH END

CASA CANADA

ENJOYMENT OF LIFE

HOTEL ARENAS BEACH

Long Beach

PICNIC CENTER BEACH

Southwest Bay

PICNIC CENTER

"SOUL OF THE WORLD" PYRAMID

Quinn Hill 50m

Barracuda Point

0   1 mi

0   1 km

© AVALON TRAVEL

members believe Quinn Hill is one of eight spots in the world where the vertices of a cube—with a diameter the same as the earth itself, and placed inside the Earth's orb—intercepts the land surface of the globe. Got that? The other vertices are found in the Cocos Islands (Indian Ocean), Hawaii, Santiago de Compostela (Spain), South Island (New Zealand), Buryat (Siberia), Tierra del Fuego (Argentina/Chile), and the Kalahari desert (Namibia).

◖ Picnic Center Beach

The most popular swimming beach, South West Bay is a long, golden crescent of soft sand and turquoise water, with a smattering of cheap restaurants and not-so-cheap hotels. Or go to **Long Beach,** just as pretty, but a bit rougher and with fewer services.

Other Sights and Events

For a good walking adventure, tackle the shore between Marcos Gomez's hotel and the South End Cemetary in Sally Peaches, or break a sweat on the hike up Mount Pleasant where the view from the top of the old lighthouse tower is well worth the effort. A path leads up to Mount Pleasant opposite the **Casa Canada** hotel. When you reach the local school, take the path that winds up behind the school to the left.

Weekends, the islanders dance to island rhythms at **Reggae Palace,** just south of the docks in Brig Bay, and at **Nico's** in the South End. Corn Islanders are serious about their **baseball:** A league of eight teams (including two from the Little Island) play in the quite-nice stadium east of the airport.

Be here at the end of August (27–28) for the age-old **Crab Soup Festival,** a commemoration of the islanders' emancipation from British slavery in 1841. The governor of this then-British protectorate, sitting miles away in Kingston, Jamaica, was authorized to pay slave owners compensation for the loss of their "assets," while the newly freed slaves scrambled to put together a meal out of what was most handy—crabs. Be sure to catch the crowning of Miss Corn Island, Miss Coconut, and Miss Photogenic.

DIVING

The island's only dive shop, **Dive Nautilus** (tel. 505/575-5077, www.divebigcorn.com) offers scuba gear and the dive-master services of "Chema" Ruiz, a jolly Guatemalan with a wall full of framed scuba diplomas and a full-service, modern dive shop: $75 for an introductory course, $60 for a two-tank dive, $250 for open-water certification, or $90 for two dives at Blowing Rock.

Corn Island's diving is well recommended. **Blowing Rock** is a rock formation with lots of color and dozens of varieties of tropical fish.

ACCOMMODATIONS

Traditionally more expensive than elsewhere in Nicaragua, stiff competition on Corn Island has kept prices more reasonable, though you'll still drop a few more bones than back west. There are now at least two dozen hotels and guesthouses on Big Corn island, and another 11 on Little Corn. Hotels with restaurant service will make your stay a lot more pleasant, as eateries elsewhere on the island are few and far between. There is a comprehensive hotel listing at www.bigcornisland.com.

Under $10

Prices have increased across the board over the past couple of years, and practically the only place on the island with a room for less than $10 now is **Hospedaje Angela** (tel. 505/575-5134). A shared room costs $5 per person, a single room $7. It's located behind the airport and somewhat distant from the water.

$10-25

For $10, you can stay with the impressive family of **Marcos and Jeanette Gomez** (tel. 505/575-5187, $10) who rent clean, safe rooms out of their house or additional outbuildings. Nearby **Dorsey Campbell's Yellowtail House** offers two self-catering private cabins ($10 per night) plus boat or accompanied dive trips from the shore out to the reefs ($10 per hour). Dorsey knows the reefs better than anybody. No meals, but Seva's Dos Millas is conveniently right around the corner.

C Hotel Morgan (tel. 505/575-5052) on the north side has individual cabins with simple rooms for about $15, $35 with air-conditioning, fridge, TV, and private bath. They serve three meals a day in the restaurant, or climb the stairs to the open-air balcony for drinks and a top-notch view.

Hotel Best View (tel. 505/575-5082, $30) is less fancy and cheaper, with a nice second-story balcony overlooking the water. **Anastasia's on the Sea** (tel. 505/575-5001) is under renovation and has a restaurant on stilts over the water which is a fun experience, but is likely to be in a different price category when back in operation.

$25-50

C Paraíso Beach Hotel (tel. 505/575-5111, www.paraisoclub.com), tucked away on its own grounds in Barrio Brig Bay, has 14 cabaña-style rooms with private baths, and fan or air-conditioning for $45–70, the latter a honeymoon suite. Laundry service and snorkel gear are also available. Under Dutch management since 2005, the hotel offers excellent service and the restaurant, though expensive, has the best menu on the island (breakfasts from $4 and $5 burgers, all the way up to the $17 surf and turf) and is open till 10 P.M. Snorkel rental and a half-block walk to the beach make snorkeling simple.

Locally owned **South End Sunrise Hotel** (tel. 505/828-7835) has double rooms for $45 with air-conditioning, TV, and hot shower.

Over $50

C Casa Canada (tel. 505/644-0925, Canada and U.S. tel. 514/448-8339, $75) has a superb location at South End overlooking a turquoise bay and reef. Owned by four partners from—guess where?—the whole place is classy, from sumptuous towels and hot showers to the minibar, cable TV, air-conditioning, fridge and coffee machine. Each cabin features queen-size beds and overstuffed sofa and chairs; dip in the infinity pool, or explore the beach and rocks. The restaurant serves

excellent seafood and at breakfast, copious, strong coffee.

The **Centro Turistico Picnic Center** (tel. 505/575-5204, $65) enjoys the best uninterrupted crescent of white sand on the island but under new management has unfortunately raised prices rather than the quality of the services. Rooms are equipped with air-conditioning, TV, queen-size beds, and private baths and superb hot showers. The restaurant is an enormous, palm-thatched open-air patio. **Arenas Beach** (tel. 505/575-5223 or 505/456-2220) has large, clean, and well-equipped bungalows with deck verandas, all finished in tropical timber, on the same South West Bay for $90 per night for three people, and $20 for each extra person up to seven people. Rooms in the main building are $75 per night. It has a bar on the beach, and next door you can rent golf carts to tour the island ($30, half day).

La Princesa de La Isla (tel. 505/854-2403, www.laprincesadelaisla.com) is a secluded and recently remodeled beachfront hotel at Waula Point, run by a very amiable Italian and his family, who of course offer excellent Italian cuisine. It is at the south end of Brig Bay and accessed by a beach road that passes by the shrimp processing plant. Cabins are $50 per night, bungalows $65.

FOOD

Outside the hotels, there are very few restaurants. One exception is **Fisher's Cave,** adjacent to the docks, with a breezy deck over the water of the bay and a small, open aquarium with sharks, turtles, and parrotfish. **C Seva's Dos Millas** (Two Miles) on the north side of the island has seen better times, but still serves reliably tasty seafood and ice-cold beer. A meal at **Anastasia's by the Sea** will convince you lobster tastes best by the water. Meals are served in a building on stilts directly over the water. A couple of hundred meters south of Brig Bay town, **Comedor La Rotonda** makes a mean *gallo pinto* with toasted coco bread for $2.

Fill up on **coconut bread,** which usually comes out around midday. Ms. Sandra, 50 meters south of the Banpro building (look for a small roadside sign) bakes the best coco bread on the island, as did her mother.

INFORMATION AND SERVICES

There is no post office. Cell phone services are available from the two main local carriers, Movilstar and ENITEL, and roaming services are available to be able to use your own cell phone, if you have brought it with you. Internet is available from most of the hotels on the island. ENITEL (the phone office) is north of the docks and around the corner. Banpro is the only bank on the island, occupying a new building in Brig Bay, at the corner where the road turns parallel to the runway. Dive shops and larger hotels take credit cards, but some only take Visa. There is a small and improving hospital with limited ability.

GETTING THERE AND AWAY
By Air

Both Atlantic Airlines and La Costeña airlines offer daily flights to Corn Island (see sidebar *Atlantic Coast Flight Schedule*).

By Sea

The *Captain D* leaves Bluefields (El Bluff, actually) bound for Corn Island on Wednesdays and returns Sundays. It's a 4–6-hour, sun-baked trip. Contact the Emusepci office just inside the gates of the municipal dock for current ship schedules (open 7 A.M.–5:30 P.M.), or call their office in El Rama (tel. 505/572-1467) if you have a lot of patience. The same ship can take you all the way upriver to El Rama. To travel in relative luxury, try the *San Nikolas* (tel. 505/277-0970, www.semarflu.com), a weekly RORO freighter between El Rama and Corn Island, which will actually arrange your entire overland journey from Granada. The ship leaves at midnight on Thursdays from El Rama and arrives at Corn Island at 4 P.M. on Friday. Cost is $17 each way.

Little Corn Island

A humble, wilder version of Big Corn, "La Islita" is a mere three square kilometers of sand and trees, laced with footpaths and encircled by nine kilometers of coral reef. Little Corn is a delicate destination, visited by an increasing number of travelers each year. There are clever accommodations for several budgets here to meet the demand, but rough boat transport from Big Corn—an experience one traveler likened to pursuing a *narco-panga* across 15 kilometers of open swell—will help hold the masses at bay. Bring a flashlight, your snorkel gear, and a good book.

Unfortunately, Little Corn Island is irregularly policed and has experienced a handful of violent attacks on tourists in recent years. The security situation is sometimes better, sometimes worse, so be sure to ask your hotel for the latest news—and advice on staying safe. Above all, don't walk alone at night.

ORIENTATION AND GETTING AROUND

Unless you make special arrangements with your *panga* driver to take you elsewhere, you will be let off at the southwestern-facing beach, where you'll find a cement sidewalk that runs the length of the village. This is called the "front side" by islanders and is the center of most social activity.

Walk north along that sidewalk to the school, baseball field, and phone office before the road deposits you in the unsavory barrios where miserable migrant workers camp out in huts of black plastic and corrugated steel. Turn right at the school for the walk up to the lighthouse and the north side

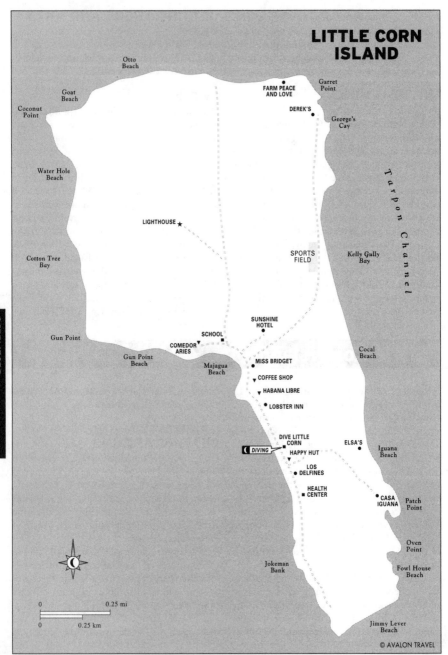

LITTLE CORN ISLAND

Otto Beach

Goat Beach

Coconut Point

Garret Point

FARM PEACE AND LOVE

DEREK'S

George's Cay

Water Hole Beach

Tarpon Channel

LIGHTHOUSE ★

Cotton Tree Bay

SPORTS FIELD

Kelly Gully Bay

Gun Point

SUNSHINE HOTEL

SCHOOL

COMEDOR ARIES

Gun Point Beach

Majagua Beach

Cocal Beach

MISS BRIDGET

COFFEE SHOP

HABANA LIBRE

LOBSTER INN

DIVE LITTLE CORN

🌙 *DIVING*

HAPPY HUT

ELSA'S

Iguana Beach

LOS DELFINES

HEALTH CENTER

CASA IGUANA

Patch Point

Oven Point

Jokeman Bank

Fowl House Beach

0   0.25 mi

0   0.25 km

Jimmy Lever Beach

© AVALON TRAVEL

© RANDALL WOOD

Little Corn Island: the view from Casa Iguana

of the island, or follow the red muddy track from Miss Bridget's place through forests and swamps to the north beach and Derek's place. Just south of the dive shop is another muddy track that leads across to the "breezy side" of the island and the Casa Iguana.

Circumnavigating the island on the beach is ill-advised, as the sandy shoreline is interrupted by long, rocky, impassible sections, both at Goat Beach and the southern tip of the island. Elsewhere, there are long sandy stretches of beach to enjoy and explore.

SPORTS AND RECREATION

Beach hikes, snorkel excursions, and lots of time reading and swinging in your hammock will fill your day. Casa Iguana offers fishing, snorkeling, and picnic trips, and most of the beachfront hotels have snorkel gear for rent. For a rewarding hike, walk to the school, turn right and follow the sidewalk to its end; then follow the foot path up and to the left to reach the **lighthouse** (about 20 minutes from the waterfront), perched on Little Corn's highest peak. You can climb up to get a view of the entire island.

◖ Diving

The island's bigger scuba shop, **Dive Little Corn** (www.divelittlecorn.com), operates out of a wooden building just south of the new pier on Pelican Beach. They offer morning and afternoon dives for novice through advanced divers, night dives by appointment, hourly and all-day snorkel trips, PADI certification, and kayak rentals. Hotel Delfines also has **Dolphin Dive.**

Most dives around the island are shallow (less than 60 feet), but a few deeper dives exist as well. Little Corn's delicate reef system is unique for its abundance of wildlife and coral formations—these include overhangs, swim-throughs, and the infamous shark cave.

Fishing

Within a couple kilometers of shore, you'll find schools of kingfish, dolphin, amber jack, red snapper, and barracuda. Fly fishers can catch tarpon and bonefish right from the beach, or Casa Iguana will take you out for $35 a person. Boat trips can also be arranged with a number of locals, or at Hotel Delfines—ask around on the front side for a good deal.

BLUEFIELDS

Fishing is the mainstay of the Atlantic coast economy.

© RANDALL WOOD

ENTERTAINMENT AND NIGHTLIFE

The best place on the island to sip a drink and enjoy the gorgeous waterfront view of the big island on the horizon is **Habana Libre,** owned by a Cuban transplant to the island ("I married an islander. Everyone here has the same story," laughs owner Ronaldo). They offer the best *mojito* on the Atlantic coast, with mint fresh from the garden. The bar is also homebase for the Island Braves baseball team. The **Happy Hut** is another option, a reggae-colored building on the front side, which is a grinding good time on weekends.

ACCOMMODATIONS

A variety of accommodations are available on Little Corn, from palm-thatch huts to cabins to conventional hotel rooms with color TVs. How close to nature do you want to be?

Casa Iguana (www.casaiguana.net, $35–75) is a cinch to recommend: Located on the cliffs of the southeast, breezy side of the island, the Casa Iguana consists of a dozen raised, wooden cabins clustered around a communal, hilltop lodge where guests gather to eat, drink, and listen to the waves. The 11 cabins are a clever compromise between rustic simplicity and comfort, and include soft mattresses, outdoor showers, private, breezy porches with hammocks, and shelves full of books. Join the other guests each morning for breakfast and each evening for happy hour and family-style dinner, frequently the day's catch. Casa Iguana provides a host of services, such as snorkel gear rental, picnic excursions to Goat Beach, fishing trips ($45 a person, $10 each additional person), and satellite email.

There are two conventional hotels that offer modern rooms with private baths and all the amenities. **Hotel Los Delfines** (tel. 505/892-0186 or 505/285-5239, hotellosdelfines@hotmail.com, $20–60) is larger, with individual, air-conditioned concrete and glass cabins. They'll be glad to arrange trips for you. Local-owned **Sunshine Hotel** (tel. 505/883-9870, $45) is rather quiet. A bit simpler but still breezy and clean, **Hotel Lobster Inn** ($20 pp) has basic rooms with no air-conditioning, but a full menu in the restaurant downstairs.

SPORTFISHING IN NICARAGUA

Sportfishing trips are available out of San Juan del Sur, the Corn Islands, an increasing number of Pacific beach towns, and along the Río San Juan. Saltwater sportfishing on the Pacific coast is focused primarily on *hurel* (jacks), *pargo* (snapper), and *pez gallo* (roosterfish) inshore and bonito, *pez vela* (sailfish), and *dorado* (mahimahi) offshore. All commonly reach sizes in excess of 50 pounds.

In addition to casting for kingfish, amber jack, red snapper, and barracuda off the Corn Islands, bonefishing in the flats around Little Corn Island is exciting, but you'll have to have some idea of what you are doing, as experienced guides are limited.

There are freshwater fish to be caught in Lake Apanás and El Dorado in Jinotega, and of course, in Lake Cocibolca and down the Río San Juan. The giant freshwater bull sharks and sawfish are all but gone, but mammoth *sábalos* (tarpon), bigger than your mother and carrying up to 50 pounds of meat, are still abundant, as are *robalos, guapote,* and the basin's newest resident, tilapia. The introduction of the tilapia has had a disastrous effect: One study shows that diseases introduced by tilapia have resulted in a 50 percent decline in Lake Cocibolca's total biomass and another reports that the foreign fish have eliminated all aquatic vegetation in the Laguna de Apoyo.

There are several cheap *hospedajes* offering not-so-special accommodations: Check out the **Guess House Sweet Dreams** ($15 pp), for example. Otherwise it's back to nature: **Derek's Place** ($4 pp camping, $14 thatch hut, $20 raised cabin) is a long hike to the north end of the island, and from his place to the west you'll find **Ensueños, Wichos,** and **Casa Sunrise** ($20 pp), all of which offer bare-bones accommodations in palm-thatch huts or similar. One of the better options is five minutes north up the beach from Casa Iguana, ◖ **Sweet Breeze** (from $10 pp), a locally run establishment and backpacker favorite with cabins made from traditional bamboo and palm thatch, and hammocks slung from the coconut trees just meters from the shoreline. It is run by several Miskito Indian families with surprising skill in the kitchen.

Derek's offers a single meal a day Monday–Friday, and Ensueños makes breakfast, but otherwise you'll have to hike back into town for a meal or carry your provisions with you. The easiest way to the north shore is to strike a deal with your *panga* driver to take you around the island. The next easiest is to follow the coast. Cut to the east side of the island as though you were heading to the Casa Iguana and then strike north along the beach. It's about a 45-minute walk: When you reach a rocky, difficult-to-pass point, you're about halfway. For the intrepid, try going overland: Follow the track from Miss Bridgett's east and northward, crossing a rugged, muddy ballfield, bearing left at the coconut swamp, and keeping the concrete fencepost line to your right. If you have a compass, follow that track for as long as you're headed north-northeast. Good walking shoes are a must.

Hard to find but worth the effort, **Farm Peace Love** (farmpeacelove@hotmail.com) has a guest room for $40 a couple including breakfast, and a fully-equipped (washer, dryer, full kitchen) guesthouse for four people ($65 per night, five-night minimum). Get your boat to drop you off to avoid the 45-minute overland trek.

FOOD

Nearly every accommodation offers meals. **Elsa's Great Food and Drinks** offers just that, but slowly, in a beachside barbecue setting on the east side of the island. On front side, **Bridgett's First Stop Comedor** is a good choice for home cooking. **Hotel Lobster Inn** is more formal and offers chicken and steak as well. Knock on the door at the blue house past the school to inquire about coconut bread.

Italian native Paola Carminiani will cook a

legitimate three-course Italian meal for $12 a person at her place, **Farm Peace Love.** Have the dive shop radio her at least one day in advance.

SERVICES

The ENITEL office (open 8 A.M.–5 P.M. Mon.–Fri.) is the yellow building with the satellite dish, across from the big blue *acopio*. You can find a wimpy health clinic just south of the Hotel Delfines. Anything more complicated requires a *panga* ride back to the big island, or even Bluefields.

GETTING THERE AND AWAY

Sometimes one, sometimes two *pangas* ply the route between Corn Island and Little Corn Island ($6 each way, 40 minutes) and are coordinated with the departure and arrival of the two rounds of daily flights. Boats depart from Big Corn Island (pay a $0.20 harbor tax) at about 9 A.M. and 4 P.M.; boats depart Little Corn Island at 7 A.M. and 2 P.M.

The trip to Little Corn is often choppy and rough, especially when the seas are up. During the windiest time of year (December–April), if it gets too rough, the port authority can stop shuttle service until conditions are safer. You can expect to get wet regardless the weather. Also, the *panga* drivers sometimes enjoy racing their friends, tipping a cold one before getting behind the wheel, and gunning it on waves to catch mad air. Seats in the front afford a more violent bashing; seats in the back are prone to more frequent splashes of spray. The *pulperías* across from the dock on Big Corn sell heavy, blue plastic bags that fit over a backpack for less than $1—an essential investment for keeping your gear dry. Alternatively, rent your own boat and driver, which runs $70–90 each way. Smooth-drivin' Charlie, on Little Corn, provides this service; he can be contacted through any of the hotels there.

A number of larger fishing boats travel between the islands, and these may agree to take on a paying passenger. See Miss Bridgett for the day's schedule. Also, coming soon: boat service for up to 50 passengers between Bluefields and the Corn Islands on Captain Emíldo's ship, *The Adventurer.* The best and cheapest way ($4 pp) is to take the *San Nikolas* freighter which makes a return journey between the two islands on Sundays, leaving at 8 A.M. from the dock in Big Corn Island and at 2 P.M. from the front beach on Little Corn Island.

PUERTO CABEZAS AND THE RÍO COCO

Isolated from all of Nicaragua and even Bluefields and the rest of the Atlantic coast, Puerto Cabezas and the Río Coco region is remote, wild, and unique. It is far and away the most indigenous region of Nicaragua, as well as the only area where learning Miskito is worth your time. At first glance, Puerto Cabezas and the Río Coco might have the air of a drowsy backwater unchanged through the centuries, but to the contrary, modernization and the advent of illicit narcotics trafficking are equally exerting tremendous pressure on mestizos and indigenous communities alike.

The Río Coco is Central America's longest river and the cultural and spiritual heart of the Miskito people, who live a rather traditional lifestyle on both banks of the waterway. The whole region burned white-hot during the revolutionary years, and the scars run deep, but these days the rhythm of the days revolves around fishing and farming, as it has for centuries. Hurricane Felix gave this area a wallop in 2006 that will take years to recover from, and many a house even in Puerto Cabezas is sporting a new tin roof in the storm's aftermath.

Inland, the mining triangle (the three pueblos of Siuna, Bonanza, and La Rosita) no longer produces the gold or guerilla warriors it once did, and is looking for a new identity more in keeping with the 21st century. And

© JAMES SAVAGE

HIGHLIGHTS

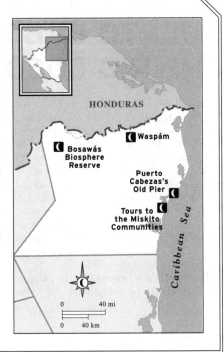

◖ Puerto Cabezas's Old Pier: Any farther east and you're in Barbados. This old dock is the heart of the town and a picturesque look at the 19th century (page 348).

◖ Tours to the Miskito Communities: Nicaragua's indigenous fishing communities are practically a country unto themselves and AMICA, an association of indigenous women, will take you there (page 354).

◖ Waspám: This is the spiritual home of the Miskito people and gateway to Central America's longest river, the Río Coco. It's about as rough and remote as you can get in Central America (page 356).

◖ Bosawás Biosphere Reserve: No corner of Central America is wilder or less explored than this unbroken stretch of cloud forest (page 360).

LOOK FOR ◖ TO FIND RECOMMENDED SIGHTS, ACTIVITIES, DINING, AND LODGING.

offshore, the photogenic Miskito Cays offer tremendous tourist—not to mention ecological—potential, unless the nocturnal narco-boats complete their takeover of the mangrove archipelago and convert it into a Caribbean battleground.

Spanish-speaking Nicaragua has always felt nationalistic about its right to alternately claim and ignore this far-off corner of the country. Managua has painstakingly incited neighboring Honduras over the subtleties of the national boundary, yet the only road to Puerto Cabezas degenerated into bumpy oblivion decades ago, making Puerto somewhat of an island in itself. Needless to say, tourism is undeveloped throughout this region, which for some travelers, makes it all the more enticing.

PLANNING YOUR TIME

It's safe to say Puerto Cabezas, the mining triangle, and the indigenous communities along the Río Coco don't figure prominently into the travel itineraries of many, so if you're looking northward it's because you already had a reason to go, be it anthropology, humanitarian assistance, or development projects. But the north is the jumping-off point for Nicaragua's most rugged adventure, the sprawling and untamed Bosawás Reserve, which intrepid backpackers can experience for as long as your supplies last. Though it's easy enough to hop a puddle jumper in Managua for an hour-long flight to Puerto, Siuna, or Waspám, you should always plan more time than you think you'll need when traveling in these areas.

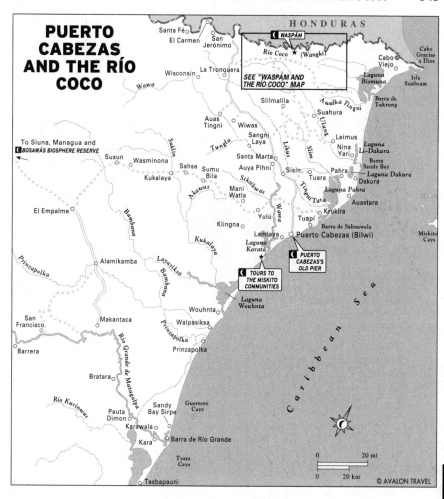

HISTORY

The Mayangna inhabitants that settled in Puerto Cabezas gave it the name Bilwi, in reference to the great quantity of *wi* (leaves) and the equally great number of snakes hidden in the foliage ("Bil"). Renamed after the general that President Zelaya sent out to the Atlantic coast to unify the nation, Puerto Cabezas—like much of Nicaragua's Atlantic coast—has seen more glorious days. Its zenith was probably at the start of the 20th century, when Puerto was the center for exportation of Atlantic coast lumber and mineral products, including gold from the mining triangle. Its airstrip was, in 1964, the longest in Central America. Testimony to the wealth of Puerto Cabezas during the lumber boom is the enormous wooden dock that juts into the Atlantic, built in the mid-1940s out of locally cut hardwoods.

Somoza was well liked in Puerto and the northeast because he largely left the area alone. Puerto locals fondly recall the times

the beach at Puerto Cabezas

© JAMES SAVAGE

Tacho would arrive on the Atlantic coast in his private plane, barbecuing with the locals and telling jokes. Their fondness for Somoza made the Sandinista years even more bitter for the Miskito people. Somoza had largely left the Atlantic coast to its own devices and Costeños generally viewed the goings-on in Managua as news from a foreign country. What followed was arguably one of the Sandinista regime's greatest misjudgments and internationally condemned disgraces.

The revolution collided with a growing sense of Native American autonomy worldwide. Miskito and Creole leaders up and down the coast formed a political group called MISURASATA, a concatenation of the words Miskito, Sumu, Rama, Sandinista, and the Miskito word for together. Originally intending to work with the Sandinistas, MISURASATA then turned away, and disputed Sandinista authority to rule the Atlantic coast. The Sandinistas retaliated by forcing the relocation of entire Miskito communities and razing the villages, ostensibly to deny

support to Contras. Ten thousand Miskito villagers resettled in refugee camps, while another 40,000 Miskito and Mayangna escaped over the Río Coco to Honduras, some of whom returned as Contras themselves. In 1985, Minister of the Interior Tomás Borge conciliated, and the Río Coco communities have slowly rebuilt their original villages in the delicate autonomy now granted to the two departments of the Atlantic coast.

Today, with the war behind them and the people back in their ancestral homes, Puerto Cabezas is largely a coastal backwater and commercial hub for the northeast. Its small economy is based on commerce—particularly of lobsters, wood, fish, and transport. The Nicaraguan military maintains a naval base here, from which it patrols the northern Atlantic coast and Miskito Cays. There are scattered jobs in the timber and fishing industries, and a lot of people looking for a legitimate way to earn a living. While a significant number of Puerteños work in government jobs—Puerto is not only the departmental

HEALTH AND SAFETY CONCERNS IN NORTHEAST NICARAGUA

Due to its lowland and wet geography, the Río Coco area is particularly prone to malaria and dengue fever outbreaks. All travelers here should ensure they're taking chloroquine to prevent malaria, as well as standard precautions to prevent being bitten by mosquitoes: Keep your skin covered, try to stay indoors around 5 P.M., and use repellent and a mosquito net. A major issue is the availability (or lack) of medical facilities and supplies in the region.

At the same time the Río Coco is venerated, it is also the public toilet for most of the communities that line its shores. Don't be surprised to see someone scooping a bucket of river water out for cooking just downstream of someone defecating. Although the water is usually treated with chlorine, you should pay extra attention to the food and beverages you ingest, and especially all water and water-based drinks. Treat all water with iodine pills or a portable water filter before drinking. That goes double any time you are downstream of Waspám. If you are not carrying bottled water from Managua, it is recommended that you use a good water filter. While it is possible to purchase bottled water in Waspám, the supply is not always guaranteed, so don't rely on it.

This health warning needs to be taken even more seriously since hurricane Felix devastated the northeast part of the country in August 2007. Flooded latrines have contaminated wells and various disease vectors have multiplied alarmingly.

In addition, the Río Coco was a heavily mined area in the 1980s. Though the land mines have largely been cleared away, known mined areas still exist and have been cordoned off with ribbon or wire. Ask the locals before you go wandering too far from the road or riverbank. Additionally, the locals took care of some land-mine clearing operations themselves, to speed the process of returning to their homes, by scooping up the mines and throwing them into the river. Some of them probably settled down into the mud, and others were carried downstream. Be wary at all times.

Finally, the entire Atlantic coast is experiencing the effect of drug trafficking from Colombia, and the Río Coco area provides particularly good hiding spots. The delta at Cabo Gracias a Dios is a known point of entry for small smugglers who take advantage of the almost total lack of police vigilance there. Watch your back.

capital, but also the center of the indigenous community's government—several thousand workers were laid off when the Chamorro government replaced the FSLN, and the city has never quite recovered.

Another mainstay is "red gold": lobster. Since 1990, a $50-million export industry has emerged and now comprises 10 percent of Nicaragua's foreign trade—but at an enormous cost. In the last couple of years, the international press began reporting that a horrific number of Miskito lobster divers were being crippled and killed as they dove deeper and deeper in search of lobster, usually with faulty equipment and a lack of safety training. Former Miskito divers in wheelchairs outnumber tourists on many white-sand beaches

and untold hundreds have died from the bends. One World Bank report stated that close to 100 percent of (Miskito) divers show symptoms of neurological damage—"presumably due to inadequate decompression."

Life struggles on in Puerto and the surrounding villages, with a wary eye on the future. Tankers from Venezuela and Curaçao periodically pull up at the dock to replenish the town's supply of petroleum, and a Louisiana-based engineering company continues to fuss with plans to build a modernized port complex complete with grain silos, a power plant, container storage, industrial cargo cranes, and facilities for deepwater tankers; but after years of talk, there is still only the decrepit old dock. In the meantime,

Puerto Cabezas continues to experience a two-headed wave of immigration: poor Miskito families from the Río Coco area in search of a better life, and wealthy families from Managua who are starting businesses and buying beachfront properties.

Puerto Cabezas (Bilwi)

Far away from everything, Puerto Cabezas (or just Puerto, or even Port, as it is affectionately known) is connected to Pacific Nicaragua only by semipassable, seasonal roads (the bus ride to Managua is 24 hours), and has no connection with the rest of the coast. Most travelers prefer to fly to this outpost city.

It is entirely possible that you'll be the only traveler in this town of 56,000 inhabitants, but enough foreign volunteers and missionaries have passed through that you won't draw too much attention. In Puerto, most streets are nothing more than streaks of bare red earth connecting neighborhoods of humble wooden homes set on stilts. It's a glimpse of many worlds, with Miskitos tying wooden canoes alongside steel fishing boats at the pier. Puerto is homely and accessible, and it's an easy walk from anywhere in town to the water's edge for a swim in the Caribbean.

This is one of the most important economic centers for the Miskito communities of the northern Atlantic coast and the Río Coco. Outside of Waspám and the communities of the Río Coco, it's one of very few places in Nicaragua where you're less likely to hear Spanish than Miskito—or even Mayangna—spoken on the street.

SIGHTS AND ATTRACTIONS
◖ Old Pier
The old wooden pier is the mainstay of the town and certainly worth a look. Built in the 1940s of precious woods culled from the nearby forest, the pier has been on its last legs for years due to extensive hurricane damage, saltwater, and old age. Tied up there are usually a motley crew of old fishing freighters, Miskito double-ended sailboats, and small fiberglass *pangas*.

The pier is beautiful during the day, but dangerous at night.

Other Sights
Near the center of town is an interesting house/museum/hotel, the **Casa Museo** (entrance $1), commemorating the life and work of Judith Kain Cunningham, a local painter who passed away in 2001. A prolific artist, her subject matter was the Río Coco and the Miskito communities of the Waspám. Also on display are works of macramé, sculpture, artifacts celebrating local indigenous movements, and more.

At the north end of town just past Kabu Payaska restaurant is **La Bocana,** a sandy Atlantic coast beach. Enjoy a swim or a splash in the surf, or walk north along the beach to explore the shipwreck of an old fishing boat that wandered in too close to shore.

In Barrio El Cocal, in the northern part of town, the **Moravian church** has services in Miskito every Sunday morning. Puerto has several other pretty churches: the Moravian church and school in the center of town, the **Catholic church** with its stained glass, and the remnants of the former Catholic church behind it.

The **URACCAN** campus is located a few kilometers down the road out of town. There's a good library there, as well as people with a wealth of information about the area.

ENTERTAINMENT AND EVENTS
The **Malecón** is Puerto's overall most happening nightlife venue, with inside and outside tables overlooking the beach and two dance floors that start throbbing on the weekends. **Disco Maria** (two block west of the park)

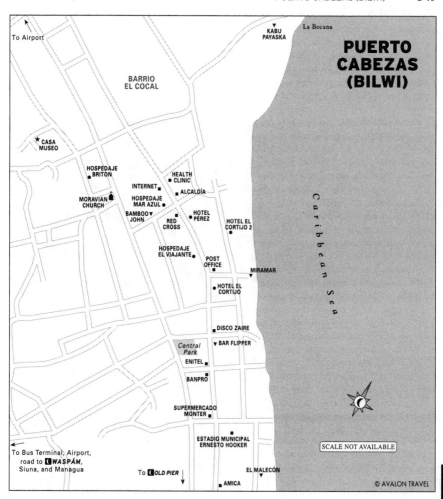

PUERTO CABEZAS (BILWI)

To Airport

KABU PAYASKA

La Bocana

BARRIO EL COCAL

★ CASA MUSEO

HOSPEDAJE BRITON

HEALTH CLINIC

INTERNET

ALCALDÍA

MORAVIAN CHURCH

HOSPEDAJE MAR AZUL

BAMBOO JOHN

HOTEL PÉREZ

RED CROSS

HOTEL EL CORTIJO 2

HOSPEDAJE EL VIAJANTE

POST OFFICE

MIRAMAR

Caribbean Sea

HOTEL EL CORTIJO

DISCO ZAIRE

BAR FLIPPER

Central Park

ENITEL

BANPRO

SUPERMERCADO MONTER

ESTADIO MUNICIPAL ERNESTO HOOKER

To Bus Terminal, Airport, road to WASPÁM, Siuna, and Managua

To OLD PIER

EL MALECÓN

SCALE NOT AVAILABLE

AMICA

© AVALON TRAVEL

PUERTO CABEZAS

rules the disco scene but there's *reggaetón* at **El Rincón** (north of town just past the Petronic gas station). On the east side of the park is **The Flipper Bar,** an old Caribbean classic with $0.50 beers in the pool hall out back. *Soka* and salsa beats throb at **Disco Zaire,** and a group of other discos that surround the park.

Semana Santa in Puerto Cabezas is an unforgettable event that many overseas Puerteños try to return home for. The town sets up dozens of thatch *ranchos* at La Bocana beach, and the 24/7 party lasts at least a week: food, drink, music, and nonstop Caribbean grinding.

ACCOMMODATIONS
Under $10

Hospedaje Mar Azul (half a block west of the Alcadia, tel. 505/792-2263) is cheap, safe, and central, with rooms from $7 for shared bath. Family-run **Hospedaje Britton** (tel.

© JAMES SAVAGE

Puerto's old wooden pier is the center of activity in town.

505/450-8504) has eight rooms for $5, with shared bath and fan; the American owner (an American dot-com bubble refugee) can arrange everything from day trips to swimming holes on the Río Tuapi to sailboat tours and lobster dives.

$10–25

El Cortijo (tel. 505/792-2340, $27) is on the main drag, a block south of the mayor's office with air-conditioning, private bath, and cable TV. **(El Cortijo 2** (tel. 505/282-2223, $25) is classier and more elegant, two blocks away and sitting atop a bluff over breaking surf. Guests here enjoy stained hardwood interiors, a wonderful ocean-facing deck, garden, and a semiprivate beach at the bottom of the stairs.

Hotel Pérez (tel. 505/792-2362, $11–22) has eight different rooms, some with air-conditioning, all set in an old wooden house on the main drag. All rooms have their own bathroom. Breakfast is available, or use the kitchen. **Hotel Casa Museo** (tel. 505/282-2225 or 505/792-2225, casamuseojudithkain@hotmail

.com, $12–27) was built in and around the Judith Kain Cunningham museum; a handful of accommodations on wooden stilts with bright, well-appointed rooms surrounds a central garden with sprawling comfy sofas, tables, benches, and other sitting areas. The on-site café serves breakfast and lunch as well as coffee and sodas throughout the day.

FOOD

Three excellent restaurants are evenly distributed through town, all offering essentially the same menu of shellfish, fresh fish, soups, beef, and chicken. At the north end of town, the best meal in the city is at **(Restaurante Kabu Payaska** (Sea Breeze), serving seafood on a beautiful grassy lawn overlooking the ocean; $6–8 for lobster, shrimp, or fresh fish. More toward the center of town, **Miramar** is a fraction cheaper and has a view just about as good. Dancing on weekends makes some people think of it only as a disco. At the south end of town near the dock is **El Malecón,** with very much the same type of environment and menu.

If for some reason you find yourself out, about, and hungry between the hours of 9 P.M.–3 A.M., stop by **Karen's Fried Chicken.** Karen, a Miskito woman, has been frying chicken at her street stand half a block up from the northeast corner of the park for ages, and whatever hour of the night, you'll wait in line behind a crowd of locals.

INFORMATION

For a taste of life in Puerto and Nicaragua's northeast, tune in to one of the local radio stations for news and commentary—even more interesting if you speak Miskito. Radio Miskut (104.1 FM) has lots of Miskito music and other programming. Radio Van (90.3 FM) presents itself as "The Voice of the North Atlantic," but throws in a cheesy *ranchera* song now and again just for good measure.

SERVICES

Supermercado Monter has a surprisingly full repertoire of canned and dry goods, fresh foods, and basic housewares. The post office (open 8 A.M.–noon and 1:30–5 P.M. Mon.–Fri., until noon Sat.) is located two blocks northeast of the park. ENITEL (open 7 A.M.–9:30 P.M. Mon.–Fri.) is located a block southeast of the park; BancPro (across from ENITEL, tel. 505/792-2211, open 8 A.M.–4:30 P.M. Mon.–Fri., till noon Sat.), with an ATM, is the only bank in town, so lines can be horrendous—you may easily have to wait an hour to change money. Your best bet is at noon, when everyone else in town goes home for lunch; otherwise, bring a book.

Internet cafés at CECOM (half a block south of El Cortijo) and at Bilwinet (behind the Pegatel). There's also a decent Internet place with air-conditioning right across from the mayor's office and next door to Casa Museo. The run-down municipal hospital is a block from the bus terminal.

GETTING THERE AND AWAY
By Air

Until Venezuela's President Hugo Chávez comes through with the road construction

project he has promised, a quick flight from Managua or Bluefields is the only practical way to get to Puerto Cabezas. From Managua, Atlantic Airlines has flights departing at 10:30 A.M. and 4:30 P.M., and La Costeña at 6:30 A.M., 10:30 A.M., and 2 P.M. (no 2 P.M. flight on Sunday).

From Puerto, Atlantic flies to Managua noon and 6 P.M. Monday–Saturday (at noon on Sunday). La Costeña has flights to Managua at 8:30 A.M., 12:30 P.M., and 4 P.M. Monday–Saturday and at 8 A.M. and noon on Sunday. The flight from Managua takes about 90 minutes.

One flight per day (every day except Sunday) leaves Bluefields at 12:10 P.M., arriving in Puerto at 1 P.M. From Puerto to Bluefields, La Costeña has one flight per day every day except Sunday leaving at 11 A.M. In Puerto Cabezas, the Atlantic Airlines phone numbers are tel. 505/282-2586, 505/282-2255, or 505/282-2523; La Costeña can be reached at tel. 505/282-2255 or 505/282-2586. Always confirm flights beforehand; reservations or advanced ticket purchases are recommended. If you need to make changes to flight reservations it is best to do this at the local office.

By Land

The difficulty of this trip can not be understated. Two daily buses (9 A.M. and 1 P.M.) make the arduous 24-hour journey through Nicaragua's muddy interior. The municipal bus terminal in Puerto Cabezas is located on the western edge of town. Puerto buses leave Managua's Mayoreo terminal, or you can piece the trip together from Jinotega's north terminal on a bus bound for Waslala; from there, you board a second bus to Siuna, and then another to Puerto Cabezas. There's an alternate road from Matagalpa to Siuna by way of Río Blanco and Mulukuku. Both roads are largely impassable during the wet season.

GETTING AROUND

Puerto Cabezas has no bus system, though the mayor's office is trying to put a couple of local city buses in place. In the meantime, Puerto has an astounding number of taxis. The price is

YATAMA AND THE STRUGGLE FOR INDIGENOUS SELF-DETERMINATION

Fraught with frequent reversals and setbacks, the struggle of Nicaragua's indigenous people for human rights, electoral privileges, and autonomy has never been easy. The Somoza government was popular in the Atlantic coast primarily because Anastasio and his sons largely ignored non-Spanish-speaking Nicaragua. The Miskito people of Puerto Cabezas fondly recall the days when Tacho would fly into the northeast for a visit, accompanied by tons of fresh meat he would distribute. To this day, Tacho is popularly associated with summer barbecues and relative isolation. The Sandinistas, however, paid quite a bit of attention to the Atlantic coast.

The FSLN came to power just when a sense of unity and independence was growing among the Miskito people. The new government gave the native peoples a unique opportunity to press for their own interests and historic demands. The Sandinistas moved quickly to attempt to incorporate the indigenous movement into their own organizational structure, but soon learned the Miskito people were not even remotely interested in being a part of any group led from Managua. The indigenous peoples of the Atlantic coast instead organized themselves into the political group MISURASATA and renewed their fight for self-determination.

The Sandinistas blundered badly in their early years on the Atlantic coast. Attempts to break up indigenous patterns of life and form state-sponsored cooperatives, mandates on which crops were to be planted and for how much they would be sold, and expropriations of foreign-owned companies alienated the indigenous peoples of the Atlantic coast from the start.

The Sandinistas met the growing resistance with violence and repression. Labor strikes and other organized disruptions led to a massive increase in government military presence, and, in 1981, more than 30 Miskito leaders were rounded up and arrested on the grounds that they were inciting the indigenous peoples to rise up against the Nicaraguan state. Whether the charges were true or not, the arrests cemented the Miskito's mistrust of the new government into hatred and many communities packed up and moved across the Río Coco to Honduras, where the Contras tried to win them over. The rancor was mutual: The Sandinista government broke ties with MISURASATA, forcefully relocated the remaining Miskito villages to refugee camps outside of Puerto Cabezas, and burned the old villages to make sure roving bands of Contras couldn't make use of them.

Against insurmountable odds, MISURASATA leaders, like the controversial Brooklyn Rivera, hoped to convert the entire Atlantic region into an autonomous, self-governing reserve for indigenous peoples. Sandinista minister of state Tomás Borge offered them instead a few concessions that, when accepted, eventually helped to restabilize the region: a limited form of autonomy and self-policing and the chance to return to their ancient homelands. In 1987, after just over two years of consulting with the Atlantic coast communities, the government went a step further in reaching out to the indigenous peoples of the coast: They signed into law an autonomy statute.

The statute reshaped the Atlantic coast like nothing else had since the days of the British. It guaranteed self-rule and first-class citizenship for all minority groups on the Atlantic coast without sacrificing their cultural roots or identities. The statute permitted them to use their own languages, common land, and have a say in the development of the Atlantic coast's natural resources. The statute called for two 45-member coastal governments to be formed, one each for the northern and southern regions, responsible for governing trade, the distribution of goods, and the administration of health and education. The statute's one weakness was its flexibility, which opened the door for internecine feuds and leadership rivalries among the Atlantic coast peoples.

The Miskitos, who eventually found their way into the ranks of the Contras during the 1980s, organized themselves into a group called Yatama (Yapti Tasba Masraka Nanih Aslatakanka, or Sons of the Mother Earth). With the advent of the Chamorro government, the Yatama Contras generally disbanded and turned in some of their weapons in exchange for land to farm. Yatama made the conversion from armed movement to political party. Chamorro's effort to stabilize the region, plus her government's respect for the newly created autonomous regions earned her the respect of the indigenous peoples.

In contrast, the government of Arnoldo Alemán apparently tried to set the indigenous movement back a hundred years, causing the entire political climate in Puerto Cabezas and the Atlantic to become more tense as a result. Not lost on the indigenous peoples of the Atlantic coast is the auspicious fact that Alemán was of the same political party as Zelaya, who integrated the Atlantic coast at gunpoint a century ago. The now infamous "Pact," in which the Sandinista and Liberal parties essentially divided the government between themselves, imposed election criteria that makes it nearly impossible for small or new parties to get a foothold in the elections.

During the departmental elections of 2000, violence erupted when Yatama was completely excluded from appearing on the ballot or taking part in the elections. Representatives of Yatama vowed that unless they were permitted to participate in the municipal elections, there would be no elections. The military was sent to Puerto Cabezas and bullets flew in armed confrontations with protesters. Several people were killed. During the elections, there was significant Miskito abstention, resulting in the election of a Sandinista mayor.

Yatama supporters accused Alemán of trying to politically eradicate the indigenous community, abandoning the Miskito, Mayangna, and Rama peoples to continued poverty and exploitation. The Bolaños government (2002-2007) largely ignored Yatama, whose leaders were subsequently wooed into an alliance with the Sandinistas for the 2006 Presidential and National Assembly elections. Brooklyn Rivera now serves as a deputy in the National Assembly for the FSLN, and Steadman Fagoth, another of the former Contra Miskito leaders, now heads the Fisheries Ministry in the Sandinista government. This political about-face is so complete, Sandinista cadres on the Atlantic Coast complain that Yatama has effectively displaced them in regional governments. How long it will be before the FSLN feels it has to retake control remains to be seen; the FSLN has never been comfortable for too long with independent-minded allies. This story is far from over.

© RANDALL WOOD

You can catch boats northbound from Puerto Cabezas.

fixed at about $0.35 per person to go anywhere in town, a bit more to go from the airport to the pier or bus terminal.

NEAR PUERTO CABEZAS

Tuapí, just 10 kilometers north of Puerto, has a popular swimming hole on the banks of the eponymous river. Buses leave for Tuapí several times a day from the terminal in Puerto. It's also possible to travel by boat north or south along the Atlantic coast to visit Miskito communities.

Getting Around

For points north, make arrangements with a boat owner at the old dock in Puerto Cabezas. You'll have better luck in the early mornings when the boats are setting out for a day's fishing. Someday, travelers will have interesting adventures in the gorgeous beachfront community of Sandy Bay (two hours from Puerto Cabezas) and the Miskito Cays (two hours across the open sea from Sandy Bay), but as of press time,

both locations are known rendezvous points for drug runners and other dangerous types.

For points south, take a bus or taxi ($3.50 per person) to the community of Lamlaya; or hop a bus or truck in front of Hotel El Cortijo for $0.50. From there, boats leave daily for Wawa and Karata between noon and 1 P.M., charging $3 one-way for a *panga,* and $2 for a "punkin" local boat (which takes twice as long). Or hire a boat to Prinzapolka, quite possibly the single hardest destination to reach in Nicaragua and the statistically poorest community in the nation. You should have a basic command of Miskito to visit these communities on your own, both to avoid suspicion and to be able to communicate.

◖ Tours to the Miskito Communities

Hurricane Felix pummeled many Miskito communities in 2007 and recovery will be slow. Truckloads of donated food arrive daily in Puerto, but take a long time to reach remote villages. Most people are incredibly friendly,

THE ATLANTIC COAST DRUG TRADE

Long the territory of pirates plying the waves in tall ships, the hidden and sparsely populated rivers, cays, and lagoons of Nicaragua's Atlantic coastline are a favorite haunt of drug merchants. As South Americans pass through with their cargo of refined cocaine bound for United States cities, Nicaragua finds itself a part of the shadowy, violent world of narco-trafficking that threatens to unravel the social fabric of the entire Atlantic coast.

During the 1980s, each Atlantic coast community had a Sandinista police force and a boat to patrol the coastal waters and estuaries. Succeeding governments had until recently done away with that police presence for lack of the resources to sustain it; in the vacuum of power, the Atlantic coast became a lawless and virtually unpatrolled haven. Drug runners would land onshore to refuel their boats and reconsolidate, divide, and distribute their merchandise. The Nicaraguan military's meager resources have been a poor match for the well-equipped drug boats sporting 250–500 horsepower engines with the latest in GPS, radar, and weaponry.

It's a well-known fact that many drug boats pass through the wilds of the Miskito Cays, an archipelago of islets, mangrove swamps, and trackless lagoons where the police have found stashes of gasoline. Other points of entry to Nicaragua include Cabo Gracias a Dios and the Río Coco, the city of El Rama and the Río Escondido, the northern half of the Pearl Lagoon, Corn Island, and the community of Sandy Bay. Some traffickers purchase gasoline from willing locals, paying with bales of high-grade, uncut product.

Other drugs come to shore when Colombian traffickers transiting Nicaraguan waters jettison their cargo into the sea when threatened

with boarding or capture, either abandoning it or circling back later, using their ample knowledge of the Atlantic currents to predict where the packages will turn up on the beach.

Whether recovered off the beach by locals or traded offshore by Nicaraguan traffickers, some of the Colombian cocaine inevitably makes it to the communities of the Atlantic coast, where its resale value is irresistible in a region so rampant with unemployment and a rapidly declining quality of life. No one knows for sure just how much coke is passing through Nicaragua's Atlantic coast, though the unofficial word on the street is that 10 kilos change hands every day in Puerto Cabezas alone.

In early 2001, three Colombians turned up dead in the coastal community of Sandy Bay, with no explanation; supposedly, they were assassinated by Yatama for trying to hook the locals on their product, which they were offering at ridiculously low prices. In 2004, hired gunmen burst into the police station at Bluefields, blowing away six officers in a carefully planned hit. But even just aiding in the trafficking of drugs has deteriorated the coastal societies, which find themselves suddenly caught in the kind of turf wars and gun battles that South Americans and the residents of inner cities of the United States know too well.

Since the new Nicaraguan police chief, Aminta Granera, a one-time trainee to become a nun, was appointed at the end of 2006, the war against the drug barons has turned serious. The police and military presence on the Atlantic coast has increased dramatically and major busts are becoming a weekly occurrence. Because of drug trafficking crackdowns, you can expect police to thoroughly inspect your bags at every dock and airport.

PUERTO CABEZAS

living in very rustic circumstances. The best way to visit and experience local indigenous communities is with **AMICA** (Asociación de Mujeres Indígenas de la Costa Atlántica, tel. 505/792-2219, asociacionamica@yahoo.es), an organization making an effort to promote the empowerment and development of women along the northern Atlantic coast. AMICA gives training in gender development, reproductive health, leadership, and AIDS, plus the laws that affect indigenous women. AMICA offers trips to the Miskito communities of Haulover, Wawa Bar, and Karata, with homestays, nature tours, and dance or cultural presentations. Accommodations aren't as rustic as you'd think—including box spring mattresses and towels. Prices depend on recent transport costs; renting a boat adds considerably to the cost (about $65 pp per night, meals around $2, all negotiable depending on number of people and number of nights). In all cases, it's crucial to call at least three days ahead. The office is located one block south of the baseball stadium.

Norton Perilla (tel. 505/450-8504, elvin kind@yahoo.com), an American expat, can arrange day trips to the mainland Miskito communities of Tuapí and Boom Serpi.

Waspám and the Río Coco

◖ WASPÁM

Waspám, in the far northern reaches of the Miskito pine savanna and at the edge of the mightiest river in Nicaragua, is the gateway, principal port, and economic heart of the Miskito communities that line the banks of the Río Coco. It is, in itself, a difficult place to get to, yet it is really the first step of the voyage to places even farther away still. The communities here would prefer to be left to their own ways, but this has not been the case, and the Miskito peoples of the Río Coco suffered more than most during the 1980s, including a massive relocation that is still cause for resentment.

Waspám is not expecting travelers: It's exactly why it's such an engaging place to visit. You will find no package tours here, no one hawking T-shirts, real estate, or their new bed-and-breakfast. Rather you will be immersed in a community that lives in a very traditional way, that retains a strong cultural identity despite growing mestizo influence, and that is prepared to show you exactly what it is, not what it expects you are expecting. If places like Granada and León seem over run with foreigners to you, Waspám might seduce you.

Once you have gotten a feel for town, a trip up the Río Coco is the natural way to glimpse the communities—usually just a couple of families living together—that make up the Miskito landscape. This endeavor is neither inexpensive nor easy, but you will find it rewarding, moreso if you can speak enough Miskito to speak with the locals. In fact, some basic Miskito is nearly obligatory throughout your exploration of this region.

Accommodations and travelers' facilities in the traditional sense of the word are practically nonexistent. The chance to visit this frontier—and it is truly frontier—to live and travel amongst the Miskito people, and to feel the spiritual power of the mighty Río Coco should not be missed. For a successful journey, travelers in this region absolutely must speak decent Spanish and make an effort to learn and use at least some rudimentary Miskito.

The Miskito people are reserved but friendly—once you've broken the ice, you'll find them helpful and inquisitive. They like to be left alone but they will certainly greet you with a smile if you approach them. They're also more conservative than other Nicaraguans, so leave the short shorts and bikini tops back home. The Miskito people speak Spanish as a second language and practically no English at all. Foreigners who speak languages other than Spanish or Miskito will inevitably be called

Miriki (American). Even Nicaraguans from the Pacific region are considered foreigners and are referred to as mestizos. The Miskito people live largely off the river, fishing for small freshwater species, and off their small, neatly tended fields of corn, beans, and even upland rice. Their version of the ubiquitous tortilla is a thick, wheat-flour cake, which is fried in coconut oil. Starch makes up the rest of the diet along the Río Coco, including tubers like *quiquisque* (taro) and yucca. *Rondon* is a fish stew (and along the Río Coco it will be made of fish, not turtle, like on the coast), and the *gallo pinto* is cooked in coconut milk. Wild game also finds its way onto the menu; don't be surprised to find boar, deer, and armadillo.

Remember the Río Coco area is particularly prone to malaria and dengue fever. Make sure your *hospedaje* provides you with a mosquito net, or use your own. You can't rely on a fan to keep the mosquitoes away, as the electricity often fails or is cut off during the night.

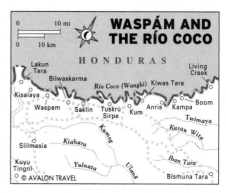

Accommodations

There are several very basic places to stay—expect bucket baths and pit latrines. Located right across from the airport is **Hospedaje Rose.** In the main house, all the rooms have private bathrooms and 24-hour electricity; three meals are available, as well as Internet and satellite TV. Rose also has a small movie theater. **Las Cabañas** offers bamboo huts for around $3.50. **El Piloto** is located on the main road, about two minutes from Wangki. They have air-conditioned single rooms with private bathrooms and a kitchen area with meals available ($25).

Food

There are several small eateries in town, most serving rice and beans accompanied by a hunk of meat, sometimes fish. You can ensure fish—or shrimp—for dinner by arranging beforehand with the restaurant where you intend to eat later that day. Vegetables are scarce and any salad usually consists of cabbage and some tomatoes in vinegar; eggs are usually available as well. Ask to try some *wabul*, a thick, warm,

green banana drink, which has many variations. Coconut bread can usually be found at the market during the evening, when it's still warm from the oven, or in the early morning. The **Restaurant Funes** is well recommended and has a splendid view of the river. They use lots of *chile cabro,* a spicy bonnet chili pepper grown here. **El Ranchito** feeds you for less than $3. For cheap late-night eats, pay a visit to the *frito* lady down by Bar Freddy.

Information and Services

The ENITEL phone office (open 8 A.M.–noon and 1–5 P.M. most weekdays, until noon Sat.) is located just west of the Rotonda Centroamerica. The post office—a private home with a Correos de Nicaragua sign posted out front—is along the airstrip.

There is a local, underequipped police station in town and a health clinic with very basic services. The Catholic church has a private clinic with slightly better service and more supplies; in case of an emergency go to the convent and tell the nuns. One of the attending doctors speaks good English.

Getting There and Away

La Costeña (tel. 505/263-2814) is the only airline that services the dusty little airstrip at Waspám. Upon approaching the runway, the pilot radios ahead to have someone shoo the cattle off the runway. Daily morning flights leave Managua most of the week; the flight is about 90 minutes long over some of the most

PUERTO CABEZAS

SPEAKING MISKITO

The Miskito language doesn't use the vowel sounds "e" (as in bread) or "o" (as in boat), which makes it a flowing, rhythmic language of "a," "i," and "u," as in the following sentence, which exhorts the locals not to let the Yellow Coconut Virus infect the coconut plantations: *Coco lalahni taki pruiba sikniska alki takaskayasa.*

Here are a couple of words you might come across during your travels in the northeast:

English	Miskito	English	Miskito
Hello	*Naksa*	Dirty	*Taski*
Goodbye	*Aisabi*	Clean	*Klin*
What is your name?	*Ninam dia?*	Meat	*Wina*
How are you?	*Nahki sma?*	Chicken	*Kalila*
Fine	*Pain*	Rice and beans	*Rais n bins*
Bad	*Saura*	Fish	*Inska*
Sick	*Siknis*	Small boat	*Duri*
Thank you	*Tingki pali*	Lagoon	*Kabu*
Food	*Plun*	River	*Awala*
Toilet	*Tailit*	Birds	*Natnawira nani*
Water	*Li*	Parrot	*Rahwaa*

exotic scenery in Nicaragua; $97 one-way ($149 round-trip).

Land transportation to Waspám can be arranged in Puerto Cabezas. The grueling bus trip takes 5 hours when the road is in good condition and it isn't raining; in the rainy season the trip can take as long as 12 hours. Two or three daily Waspám-bound buses leave Puerto at the crack of dawn; get there early for the 6 A.M. bus. The following day, the same buses leave Waspám at the crack of dawn bound for Puerto Cabezas. Because all the buses leave their respective starting points in the morning, day trips are impossible.

Additionally, there's a truck that leaves Puerto Cabezas every morning between 5 and 6 A.M.— a lumbering, diesel-belching IFA—and many

opt to travel with El Chino Kung Fu, a local character with a decent pickup truck who makes regular trips between Waspám and Puerto Cabezas. Ask around and try to form a group to share the costs. Bear in mind that hitchhiking runs the danger of being an unknowing accomplice to transporting narcotics.

RIVER TRIPS FROM WASPÁM

Waspám is your gateway to the Río Coco, and small boats—fiberglass *pangas* and dugout *batu* canoes—are your means of transport. One local volunteer recommends the *panga* trip to San Carlos, which has a simple *hospedaje*. In the upriver villages located between Waspám and Leimus, visitors are not common and facilities are somewhere between limited and

© RANDALL WOOD

traveling on the Río Coco

nonexistent. Don't plan on staying overnight or finding food for sale.

Nothing is easy or cheap, by the standards of travelers accustomed to the prices of the Pacific side. In general, expect to pay $35–100 per person per day for boat transportation along the Río Coco, which includes the boat, the gasoline, and the boatman. The dream adventure is a trip all the way up to Wiwilí, the upstream port town. El Bailarín makes the trip from time to time, but charges $1,000 round-trip per person for the extended 550-kilometer voyage one-way.

Two tributaries to the Río Coco, the Yahuk and the Waspuk, are both home to waterfalls the locals say are beautiful places to visit, but make for long trips. To visit the Yahuk, for example, you'd have to hire a boat for two days. The first day, you can motor up the Río Coco to the Yahuk and continue upstream to the falls, then spend the night in San Carlos, and return the following day. The Waspuk falls are reportedly a site of religious significance to the Miskito people. The trip is just upwards of 130 kilometers in each direction.

TRIPS BY LAND FROM WASPÁM

Travel is difficult, transportation infrequent, and food and lodging service nonexistent. If necessary, you can try arranging a meal with a local family, for which you'll pay. There are two local villages that are close to Waspám: Kisalaya (five kilometers) and Ulwas (three kilometers). Locals will point you in the right direction. There are two taxis in town, which might be able to take you to Ulwas, where you might be able to find a small store to buy cookies, crackers, and maybe a warm soda. Bilwaskarma (10 kilometers; approximately a 45-minute walk from Waspám) is a pleasant village with a small health center that was a world-famous nursing school before the conflict of the 1980s.

Siuna and the Mining Triangle

Heart of the nearly-derelict mining triangle, Siuna is now gaining fame as the point of entry for the Bosawás reserve and home to a growing number of Mayangna Indians who have gradually migrated from the Atlantic coast's tropical interior and the Río Coco.

HISTORY

In the early 20th century, Siuna was a bustling mining town that drew workers from as far away as Jamaica. But in 1968 the foreign companies running the mines decided to close up shop (Yamana Gold out of Toronto, Canada has recently taken a renewed interest). Distant and poorly patrolled, the whole triangle made an easy target for Contra operations during the 1980s, and indeed several serious skirmishes took place in the region. When the war ended, an uneasy peace ensued, for the entire area was peppered with land mines, now lost or abandoned, and many well armed but still unemployed men gave up guerilla warfare for a life of petty banditry.

Regaining a sense of civility took over a decade, despite groups like the FUAC (Frente Unido Andres Castro) terrorizing farmers, stealing cattle, kidnapping ranchers, and otherwise causing havoc. But demining operations concluded in 2001 and the bandits mostly gave up the lifestyle, notwithstanding a gun battle in 2001 between Nicaraguan police and some renegade FUAC commanders, one of whom was killed. There have been no attacks on foreigners with the 1999 exception of Manley Guarducci, a Canadian mining engineer who was kidnapped and held for ransom for five weeks before being released unharmed.

NIGHTLIFE AND ENTERTAINMENT

Not surprisingly, beer joints are everywhere. Locals prefer **El Secreto** (right on the landing strip in the center of town), a gritty disco that seems to be full all weekend; eat at the *fritanga* right outside. **El Machin** and **Las Praderas** are a distant second and double as restaurants.

ACCOMMODATIONS AND FOOD

Hotel Siu (Barrio Sol de Libertad, $6) and **Los Chinitos** are two of the nicer, cleaner places in town.

La Terraza serves basic meals, and also run an Internet café next door. **Las Praderas** (Barrio Campo Viejo, near URACCAN) is recommended for dining, or rub elbows with the cowboys over steaks at **El Machin. Doña Azucena** (across from Los Chinitos, Barrio Luis Delgadillo) serves an especially good breakfast featuring eggs any style, fresh bread, and coffee.

◖ BOSAWÁS BIOSPHERE RESERVE

Located 350 kilometers north of Managua, the 730,000 hectares of forest, mountains, and rivers collectively known as Bosawás are located within the municipalities of Waspám, Bonanza, Siuna, El Cuá–Bocay, Wiwilí, and Waslala. Although inhabited by some 40,000 widely dispersed people (more than half of whom are Mayangna and Miskito), most of Bosawás remains unexplored, unmapped, and untamed. Its name is derived from the region's three most salient features: the Río Bocay (BO), Cerro Saslaya (SA), and the Río Waspuk (WAS).

It's the largest uninterrupted tract of primary rainforest north of the Amazon, and besides unparalleled stretches of cloud forest, Bosawás contains tropical humid forest, rainforest, and a wealth of disparate ecosystems that vary in altitude from 30 meters above sea level at the mouth of the Waspuk River to the 1,650-meter peak of Cerro Saslaya. Bosawás is a Central American treasure, an immense genetic reserve of species that have vanished elsewhere in Mesoamerica, including jaguars, rare small mammals, 12 kinds of poisonous snakes, and many bird species, including the gorgeous scarlet macaw and 34 boreal migratory species.

Bosawás was designated a protected reserve

in 1997, but where there is no money, there is little enforcement and few rangers—there are many more desperately poor who continue to make a living from this ancient land. In many cases, this translates into slash-and-burn clearing of the forests and the continual push of the agricultural frontier, mostly for subsistence. The 1.8 million acres of protected area was declared a part of the Nature Conservancy's international Parks in Peril program in 2001.

Visiting the Reserve

To do anything in Bosawás, you *must* receive permission (at time of printing, free). Talk to the Bosawás Office (office at central park near the stadium not far from Los Chinitos, tel. 505/794-2036, www.tmx .com.ni) who will help arrange a guide. The MARENA office in Managua can also help (tel. 505/233-1594). Guides are both obligatory and absolutely necessary and cost about $7 per day plus food. You may be convinced to hire two guides for your trip, a recommended safety and comfort precaution.

Unless you have months to explore the reserve, you'll have to pick and choose from various possible destinations. Get off the bus at Casa Roja (1.5 hours from Siuna) to stage an ascent of Cerro Saslaya (4–5 days); or continue to Santa Rosita (2.5-hour bus ride) for a two-

hour hike to the river or trailhead to Cerro El Torro (4–5 days). Waslala is a 4–5 hour ride from Siuna and home to the original tomb of Carlos Fonseca (his remains were moved to Managua after the revolution's victory).

Be advised: Any trip in Bosawás is a serious backcountry undertaking and should not be attempted without proper supplies, some wilderness experience, a tolerance for dampness and discomfort, and a basic survival instinct. You should already have supplies like water bottles, a mosquito net, and some kind of pump or purifying tablets for water (start your hike with at least three liters in your bag; a fresh source is available in the park), a brimmed hat, sunscreen, sturdy shoes, and a medical kit. Additional supplies that can be purchased in Siuna include rubber boots (for snakes and knee-level mud), four yards of heavy black plastic for a roof in the jungle, a piece of plastic or waterproof cover for your backpack, a machete, a hammock, extra rope, and food.

Take a local bus to Rosa Grande, then walk or rent a horse ($5 per day) to Rancho Alegre. From there the journey is a challenging one-hour hike through the community of Rancho Alegre to a series of waterfalls at Salto Labu. Another hour hike up a steep path leads you to Mirador, a lookout and an incredible view of an absolutely stunning waterfall before you reach the primary forest on the path into Bosawás.

BACKGROUND

The Land

The largest and lowest Central American country, Nicaragua is a nation of geographical superlatives. Located at the elbow where the Central American isthmus bends and then plummets southward to Panamá, Nicaragua is almost dead center between North and South America. Part of a biological corridor that for millions of years has allowed plant and animal species from two continents to mingle, it boasts an extraordinary blend of flora and fauna.

In the 16th century, Nicaragua's geographical beauty enchanted the conquistadores, who reported, "The Nicaraguan plains are some of the most beautiful and pleasant lands that can be found in the Indies because they are very fertile with *mahicales* and vegetables, *fesoles* of diverse types, fruits of many kinds and much cacao."

Nicaragua is roughly triangular in shape and dominated by two large lakes in the southwest. The northern border with Honduras is 530 kilometers long, the longest transect across the Central American isthmus. To the south, the southern shore of the Río San Juan defines the better part of the Nicaraguan–Costa Rican border. Wholly within Nicaragua, the San Juan has been a continual source of conflict with Costa Rica, whose attempts to navigate and patrol the river have been met aggressively by the Nicaraguan government. To the east and west

© JOSHUA BERMAN

lie the Caribbean Sea and the Pacific Ocean, respectively. With 127,849 square kilometers of land area, Nicaragua is approximately the size of Greece or the state of New York. Nicaragua has lost some 50,000 square kilometers to her neighbors over the past several centuries. The eastern third of what is now Honduras, as well as the now–Costa Rican territories of Nicoya and Guanacaste were considered Nicaraguan during colonial times.

Administratively, the nation is divided into 15 units called *departamentos,* and two vast autonomous regions on the Atlantic coast known as the North and South Atlantic Autonomous Regions (RAAN and RAAS). The departments, in turn, are divided into a total of 145 municipalities. The two autonomous regions elect their own officials on a separate electoral calendar. Nicaragua's three largest cities are Managua, León, and Granada, followed by Estelí, Masaya, and finally the remaining department capitals.

GEOGRAPHY

Nicaragua's favorite nickname for itself—The Land of Lakes and Volcanoes—is indication enough of its geography, which is indeed dominated by two great lakes and a chain of striking volcanoes. Nicaragua's water and volcanic resources have had an enormous effect on its human history, from the day the first Nahuatl people concluded their migration south and settled on the forested shores of Lake Cocibolca (Lake Nicaragua) to the first Spanish settlements along the lakes to the many as yet unrealized plans to build a trans-isthmus canal (see sidebar *Canal Dreams Past and Present* in the *Solentiname and the Río San Juan* chapter).

Geologic History and Formation

The earth that comprises Nicaragua, like all of Central America, took shape 60 million years ago (MYA) when the isthmus formed. Geologically speaking, the land that makes up Nicaragua's northern third is the most ancient. In the area of Telpaneca and Quilalí, rocks dated at 200 million years old are thought to have once been part of a small Jurassic-Cretaceous continent that included the modern-day Yucatán

Peninsula in Mexico and the Antilles Islands. To the south, what are now Costa Rica's Talamanca Mountains formed an archipelago of isolated volcanoes. During the Tertiary period (65–1.7 MYA), intense volcanic activity and erosion produced large amounts of sediment and volcanic flows that accumulated underwater.

There were at least two periods of intense volcanic activity: one in the Eocenic-Oligocenic epoch (55–25 MYA) when the lesser features of Nicaragua's central highlands were formed, and a second in the Miocene (25–13 MYA) that produced the larger mountains in Matagalpa and Jinotega. Eleven million years later, the Pacific region formed when shifting tectonic plates in the Pacific and Caribbean lifted the seabed.

When the so-called Cocos plate slid under the Caribbean plate, the main volcanic mountain range that runs northwest–southeast across the Pacific plains blistered to the surface. Ocean water from the Atlantic rushed in along a broad sunken valley of the Pacific plate now known as the Nicaraguan Depression, and pooled, forming the lakes. Some geologists believe the Atlantic and Pacific actually connected at this point in time and were later cut off by volcanic sedimentation. Erosion began pulling material from the landmass outward to the sea, building up Nicaragua's Pacific region and gradually forming the Atlantic coast.

Plate tectonics theory, in spite of being widely accepted since the 1960s, is most frequently criticized for its failure to adequately explain the geology and geography of several regions of the world, including Central America. It is highly probable that our concept of the geological events that formed Central America will change as geologic science progresses. Regardless of the mechanism, however, the convergence of the plates ensures crustal instability, which manifests itself in frequent volcanic and earthquake activity in all of Central America, and especially Nicaragua.

Volcanoes and Mountain Ranges

Nicaragua has about forty volcanoes, a half dozen of which are usually active at any time,

HURRICANE MITCH

It was late October 1998, and the rainy season had been reduced to sporadic drizzle, just right for the red beans that were slowly gathering strength in the fields. The newspapers mentioned a hurricane forming in the Atlantic, but Nicaragua seemed spared when the storm, called Mitch shifted to the north instead of making landfall on the Caribbean coast.

Instead, on October 28, rain began to fall steadily from a leaden sky over most of Nicaragua. Mitch had come to a near complete stop off the north coast of Honduras, and thick gray arms of clouds swept in long spirals across the entire Central American isthmus, greedily gathering strength from both the Caribbean and Pacific Ocean, while winds around the eye of the hurricane reached 290 kilometers per hour. The rains fell day and night for seven days. The country roads of red earth turned muddy, then became dangerous rivers of coffee-colored water coursing through the center of towns, while cattle that had been left in the fields found high ground or were drowned and swept away. Swollen to 10 times their normal size, Nicaraguan rivers flared over their banks, tearing out trees, snatching away homes, and breaking apart (or just tearing around) every bridge in their path. On October 29, the electricity failed in most of the north as power lines fell and poles were swept away. In Sébaco, the Río Viejo and the Río Grande de Matagalpa, which normally pass within a kilometer of each other, rose and combined before tearing through Ciudad Darío.

The waters of Lake Xolotlán rose three meters over the course of three days. Overtopping the basin, the waters barreled through the old, dry channel of the once-intermittent Río Tipitapa, raising the level of Lake Cocibolca and the Río San Juan; the town of Tipitapa, built in the low saddle between the two lakes, was completely inundated. On the Pan-American Highway, the enormous bridge that crossed over the Tipitapa River was damaged, then destroyed, and finally carried away completely. By October 30, the entire northern half of the country was isolated: Major bridges had been demolished in Sébaco and Tipitapa, and

whether venting light, constant clouds of gas or actually erupting. Running parallel to the Pacific shore, Nicaragua's volcanoes are a part of the Ring of Fire that encompasses most of the western coast of the Americas, the Aleutian Islands of Alaska, Japan, and Indonesia. The Maribio (Nahuatl for the "giant men") and Dirian volcano ranges stretch nearly 300 kilometers from the Concepción and Maderas in the middle of Lake Nicaragua to Cosigüina, which juts into the Gulf of Fonseca.

The first volcanic event in recorded history was a major eruption of Volcán Masaya in the early 1500s. The lava formed the present-day lagoon at the base of the mountain. Another great lava flow occurred in 1772, leaving a black, barren path still visible today where the Carretera Masaya highway crosses it. In 1609, Spanish settlers abandoned the city of León when Momotombo erupted. And in January of 1835, Volcán Cosigüina violently blew its top, hurling ash as far away as Jamaica and Mexico, covering the area for 250 kilometers around the volcano in ash and burning pumice and forcing the entire peninsula into three days of darkness. All this volcanic activity is responsible for the exceptional fertility of Nicaragua's soils, most notably the agricultural plains around Chinandega and León.

Volcán Masaya is the most easily accessed of Nicaragua's volcanoes and boasts a paved road leading right to the lip of the crater. Volcán Masaya is actually formed of three craters, the largest of which, Santiago, is the only crater in the Americas that contains a visible pool of incandescent liquid lava in its center. The visibility of this lava fluctuates on a 30-year cycle and was best seen 1965–1979.

For some boot-packing travelers, climbing a few Nicaraguan giants is a central part of their trip to the country. San Cristóbal is every bridge without exception between León and Managua had been destroyed.

But Mitch was cruelest in Posoltega, Chinandega, where the equivalent of a full year's rainfall came down in under four days. The intense rains filled the crater of Volcán Casita with rainwater, and at 2 P.M. on October 30, the southwest edge of the crater lip tore away, unleashing a deadly avalanche of mud, water, and rock 1.5 kilometers wide and three meters high on the three small communities below. Thousands died immediately, as the mudflow poured southwest more than four kilometers to the highway, crossed it, and continued southwest into the town of Posoltega. In the aftermath, there was no hope of recovering or even identifying victims.

By the time the rains finally stopped, Hurricane Mitch had reduced Nicaragua's GDP by half and destroyed more than 70 percent of the country's physical infrastructure. Hundreds of health clinics and more than 20,000 homes were carried away, and arable farmland was reduced by 11,550 hectares. Overall, economic losses sustained by this already poor nation were around $1.5 billion. Mitch also opened up political and social scars less obvious than deforested hillsides. Under duress, political divisions reopened as relief money poured in and politicians – particularly President Alemán – struggled to divert it for their own interests.

Though the press called Mitch "the storm of the century," scientists estimate it was much more severe even than that and declared it the most deadly storm event in at least 200 years. However, the hundreds of millions of dollars of aid money that poured into Nicaragua in the aftermath have provided Nicaragua with a much-needed opportunity to strengthen and rebuild, and much effort has gone into ensuring that the Nicaraguan government and people are more capable of dealing with future disasters through training programs, flood-warning detection systems, computer models, and more. These are crucial to Nicaragua's future well-being, because Hurricane Mitch will surely not be the last storm to wreak havoc in Nicaragua.

---

the highest, at 1,745 meters. A smaller peak adjacent to San Cristóbal, Volcán Casita still bears the immense scar of the landslide that buried thousands in an avalanche of rock and mud during Hurricane Mitch—and trembled briefly again in January of 2002. Other popular treks are found on Isla de Ometepe, but always hire a guide, as several foreigners have gotten lost and perished.

In general, the most active volcanoes are Momotombo, San Cristóbal, and Telíca, all of which tremble and emit plumes of poisonous gases, smoke, and occasionally lava. La Isla de Ometepe's Volcán Concepción (1,610 meters) last blew its top in 2005 and 2007. The other half of Ometepe (Nahuatl for "two peaks") is Volcán Maderas (1,394 meters) which sleeps, its crater drowned in a deep lagoon that feeds a thriving jungle.

Volcán Telíca, just north of León, erupts approximately every five years. Gas vents at its base churn out boiling mud and sulfur. Neighboring Cerro Negro is one of the youngest volcanoes on the planet: It protruded through a farmer's field in the middle of the 1800s and has since grown in size, steadily and violently, to a height of 400 meters. Cerro Negro's last three eruptions have been increasingly powerful, culminating in 1992 when it belched up a cloud of burning gases and ash seven kilometers high, burying León under 15 centimeters of ash and dust. Eight thousand inhabitants were evacuated as the weight of the ash caused several homes to collapse. Volcán Momotombo's (Nahuatl for "great burning peak") perfect conical peak is visible from great distances across the Pacific plains, as far away as Matagalpa. Momotombo is responsible for approximately 10 percent of Nicaragua's electricity via a geothermal plant located at its base. It hasn't erupted since 1905, but Momotombo's menace has in no way diminished. Increased seismic activity and rumbling in April 2000 caused Managua residents great concern until the mountain eventually quieted back down.

A popular day trip from Granada is to visit the cloud forest park and coffee plantations of Volcán Mombacho (1,345 meters), a dormant volcano whose explosion and self-destruction is thought to have formed the archipelago of *isletas* in Lake Cocibolca. Mombacho took its modern shape in 1570 when a major avalanche on the south slope buried an indigenous village of 400 inhabitants and left the crater open and exposed.

The central and northern areas of Nicaragua are dominated by three lesser mountain ranges: the Cordilleras Isabelia, Huapi, and Chontaleña. These three ranges radiate northeast, east, and southeast, respectively, from the center of the country, gradually melting into the lowland jungle and swamps of the Atlantic coast. These mountains include a half-dozen prominent peaks and were the scene of intense fighting during several conflicts in Nicaraguan history. Nicaragua's highest point, Cerro Mogotón, at 2,107 meters, is located along the Honduran border in Nueva Segovia.

Laguna de Apoyo, near Masaya, is inviting on a hot day.

Lakes and Lagoons

Two lakes, Cocibolca (Lake Nicaragua) and Xolotlán (Lake Managua), dominate Nicaragua's geography, occupying together nearly 10 percent of the country's surface area.

Lake Xolotlán, although broad (1,025 square kilometers), is shallow with an average depth of only seven meters. It reaches its deepest—26 meters—near the island of Momotombito. Lake Managua is, for the most part, biologically dead, after a century of untreated human waste and extensive dumping of industrial wastes during the 1970s, including lead, cyanide, benzene, mercury, and arsenic. The tremendous opportunities for tourism, recreation, and potable water for human consumption that a clean lake would facilitate have led to an ambitious plan to detoxify Xolotlán. Backed by loans from Japan and the World Bank, the project entails collecting and treating Managua's

sewage and, gradually, cleansing the lake itself in water treatment plants to be built on the lakeshore.

Lake Cocibolca is the larger of Nicaragua's two lakes and is one of Nicaragua's greatest natural treasures. At 8,264 square kilometers and 160 kilometers long along its axis, Lake Cocibolca is nearly as big as the island of Puerto Rico and lies 31 meters above sea level. It's also deep—up to 60 meters in some places, and relatively clean. The prevailing winds, which blow from the east across the farmlands of Chontales, make the eastern part of Cocibolca calm and the western half choppy and rough. A massive pipe system is presently being designed which, if built, will carry drinking water from Cocibolca to the city of Managua to meet the needs of the capital's rapidly growing population and industrial sector.

Nearly a dozen stunning lagoons mark the maws of ancient volcanic craters. Around

Managua are the Nejapa, Tiscapa, and Asososca lagoons. West of Managua, the picturesque twin craters of Xiloá and Apoyeque form the Chiltepe peninsula. Near Masaya, the 200-meter-deep Laguna de Apoyo was formed sometime in the Quaternary period (1.6 MYA) by what is thought to be the most violent volcanic event in Nicaragua's prehistory. Not far away is Laguna de Masaya, at the base of the volcano of the same name. Other gorgeous lagoons flank Volcán Momotombo and occupy the craters of the volcanoes Maderas and Consigüina.

Rivers

To the original Spanish settlers in Granada, the Río San Juan was the elusive "drain" of Lake Cocibolca; since then, the possibility of traveling up the Río San Juan, across Lake Cocibolca, and then by land to the Pacific Ocean has made the San Juan the most historically important river in Nicaragua. In the years of the gold rush, thousands of prospectors navigated up the Río San Juan en route to California; some made the return trip laden with riches, others with nothing. These days, several sets of rapids and decades of sedimentation reduce its navigability, exacerbated by shifts in the riverbed from occasional earthquakes. Cattle ranches and small farms primarily producing basic grains line both shores (farmers on the southern shore identify more closely with Costa Rica and even use its currency).

Formed by the confluence of three major rivers—the Siquia, Mico, and Rama—the Río Escondido is the principal link in the transportation corridor from Managua to Bluefields and the Atlantic coast. Produce and merchandise (and busloads of travelers) reach El Rama and then proceed down the Escondido. The Escondido and its tributaries are important to the cattle industry in Chontales, but massive deforestation along its banks have unleashed dangerous floods that frequently put the river port of El Rama under water.

The 680-kilometer-long Río Coco is the longest river in Central America, fed by headwaters in both Nicaragua and Honduras. Also known as the Río Segovia or by its indigenous name Wanki, the Coco traverses varied terrains that include several minor canyons and vast stretches of virgin forest. Small communities of the indigenous Miskito people, for whom the river bears great spiritual significance, make their homes along its shores.

The Estero Real (Royal Estuary), at 137 kilometers in length, is the most consequential body of water on the Pacific coast and is one of Nicaragua's best places to spot waterfowl. It drains most of northwestern Nicaragua through extensive mangroves and wetlands to the Gulf of Fonseca and is the nucleus of extensive shrimp-farming operations.

Soils

In the Pacific region, soils are typically of volcanic origin—highly fertile and rich with minerals. The mountainous north and central regions of Nicaragua are less fertile basalt, andesite, and granite-based soils, and their steeper slopes are prone to erosion and soil degradation. The better soils are usually found alongside rivers where deforestation and fierce storms such as Hurricane Mitch haven't carried it away, stripped it of its nutrient value, or buried it under thick layers of sand. In the north and northeast of Nicaragua, the soils are quartz-based and mostly useless for farming, though they typically bear thin stands of white pine. The Sébaco Valley is thought to have once been the bed of an immense lake. The claylike black soils there retain moisture, which impedes the production of corn or beans but greatly facilitates wet rice farming. Nicaragua's rice industry centers around the city of Sébaco.

CLIMATE

Located between 11 and 15 degrees north latitude, Nicaragua has a tropical climate. Temperatures range 27–32°C (81–90°F) during the rainy season, and 30–35°C (86–95°F) in the dry season, but regionally vary remarkably: In the mountains of Matagalpa and Jinotega, the temperature can be 10°C cooler, while in León and Matagalpa, they can be 10°C warmer, making ordinary travelers feel like glazed chickens roasting over the coals. Nicaragua's *invierno* (winter, or rainy season) lasts approximately May–October, and *verano* (summer, or dry season) lasts November–April—rain during these months may mean just a quick shower each afternoon, or it may go on for days. As you travel east toward the Atlantic coast or down the Río San Juan, the rainy season grows longer and wetter until the dry season only lasts the month of April.

Flora and Fauna

Nicaragua's variety of ecosystems, and its position at the biological crossroads between North and South America and between the Atlantic and Pacific Oceans have blessed it with an astonishingly broad assortment of vegetation and wildlife.

FLORA

Of the world's known 250,000 species of flowering plants, an estimated 15,000–17,000 are found in Central America. It is estimated Nicaragua is home to some 9,000 species of vascular plants, many of which are thought to be of medicinal value. But while a few areas are relatively well protected, little effort has been made to protect the rest, where the majority of the land set aside by the government continues to experience intense pressure from the agricultural frontier and the scattered human settlements within the confines of the reserves.

Trees

The *madroño (Calycophyllum candidissimum)* is the national tree of Nicaragua. The hills south of Sébaco form the southern limit of the pine family found on the continent; south of Nicaragua, the pines are out-competed by other species. At the turn of the millennium, Nicaragua had a forest area of 5.5 million hectares, the majority of which is broadleaf forest, followed by pine forest *(Pinus caribea* and *P. oocarpa).* At altitudes greater than 1,200 meters, the forests also include the conifers *P. maximinoi* and *P. tecunumanii.* A full 2.5 million hectares of forest are considered commercial timber forest. Though often privately owned, the exploitation of forest products is under the control of the Nicaraguan government.

Principal Ecosystems

Nicaragua's varied topography and uneven rainfall distribution, not to mention the presence of tropical reefs, volcanoes, and volcanic crater lakes, result in a phenomenal diversity of terrain and ecosystems. This can be easily appreciated during any road trip through Nicaragua, as you watch prairie grasslands melt into rolling hills into near-desert into craggy mountain ranges whose peaks are draped in cloud forest. You can burn your feet on an active volcano's peak and cool your heels in ocean surf the same day. Nicaragua's higher peaks are isolated ecosystems in their own right and home to several endangered as well as endemic species, and the streams, rivers, and two very different coastlines furnish myriad other distinct ecosystems. In general, the land can be divided into the following ecological zones:

Pacific Dry Forest: The lowlands of the Pacific coast, specifically the broad, flat strip that borders the Pacific Ocean from sea level to approximately 800 meters in altitude, are a rain-stressed region dominated by thorny, rubbery species. The region typically receives less than 2,000 millimeters of rain per year. Both trees and non-cactuslike plants in this ecosystem shed their leaves in the middle of the dry season in preparation for the rain to come, and often burst into flower in April or May.

Upland Pine Forest: With the exception of the slopes of several Pacific mountains, namely San Cristóbal and Las Casitas in Chinandega and Güisisíl in Matagalpa, the majority of Nicaragua's pine forests are found in the north near Jalapa and Ocotal. Pines particularly thrive on poor, acidic soils, which erode easily if the area is logged.

Lower Mountainous Broadleaf Forest: Nicaragua's higher peaks are cloud covered for most of the year and home to a cool, moist biosphere, rich in flora and fauna. Most of these areas are the more remote peaks of Matagalpa and Jinotega, like Kilambé, Peñas Blancas, Saslaya, and Musún. It's easier to enjoy this ecosystem on the beautiful and easily visited peaks of Volcán Mombacho near Granada, and Volcán Maderas on Ometepe.

Caribbean Rainy Zone: The Atlantic coast receives rain throughout nearly 10 months of the year and the humidity hovers around 90 percent year-round. Most of the Atlantic coast is covered with tropical forest or even lowland rainforest, with trees that often reach 30 or 40 meters in height. In the north along the Río Coco are the remains of Nicaragua's last extensive pine forests *(Pinus caribaea),* presently subject to intensive logging by national and international concessions.

FAUNA

Nicaragua is home to a great deal of exotic wildlife, much of which—unfortunately—you'll only see for sale on the sides of the highways and at intersections in Managua, where barefoot merchants peddle toucans, reptiles, ocelots, parrots, and macaws. This is a considerable, largely unchecked problem, more so because, of the animals that are captured for sale or export in Nicaragua, 80 percent die before reaching their final destination. To view fauna in their natural habitat involves getting out there, being very, very quiet, and looking and listening. Most critters are shy and many are nocturnal, but they're out there. To date, 1,804 vertebrate species, including 21 species endemic to Nicaragua, and approximately 14,000 invertebrate species have been defined. However, Nicaragua remains the least-studied country in the region, and it is thought that excursions into the relatively unexplored reserves of the north and northeast will uncover previously undiscovered residents of the planet.

Mammals

There are 176 mammal species (including sea life) known to exist in Nicaragua, more than half of which are bats or small mammals, including rodents. Nicaragua has at least three endemic mammal species, two of which are associated with the Caribbean town of El Rama—the Rama squirrel *(Sciurus richmondi),* considered the tropical world's most endangered squirrel due to reduced habitat, and the Rama rice mouse *(Oryzomis dimidiatus).*

Nicaragua is also home to six big cat species, but there's no guarantee they'll be around for long. All six listed as endangered, most seriously of all the jaguar and puma. Both were once common, but require vast amounts of wildland on which to hunt. The Pacific region of Nicaragua, home to extensive agriculture for so many consecutive years now, is most likely devoid of big felines, with the possible exception of isolated communities on the higher slopes of some forested volcanoes like Mombacho. In the Atlantic region, small communities of cats eke out their survival in the dense forests of the southeast side of the Bosawás reserve. These species are unstudied and untracked, and are presumably preyed upon by local communities. Better off than the pumas and jaguars are smaller felines like ocelots and *tigrillos* trapped in the central forests, the latter of which are notorious chicken killers in rural farming communities.

There are three kinds of monkeys in Nicaragua: the mantled howler monkey *(Alouata palliata),* known popularly in Nicaragua as the *mono congo;* the Central American spider monkey *(Ateles geoffroyii);* and the white-faced capuchin *(Cebus capucinus).* Of the monkeys, the congo is the most common. One thousand individuals roam the slopes of Mombacho alone. You can also find them (or at least hear their throaty, haunting cries) on La Isla de Ometepe and the mountains of Matagalpa, particularly Selva Negra. Howler monkeys are able to project their voices an incredible distance; you can easily hear them several kilometers away. They eat fruits and leaves and spend most of their time in high tree branches. The white-faced capuchin is most frequently found in the forests in southeastern Nicaragua and parts of the Atlantic coast. It is a threatened species, but more so is the spider monkey, whose population has nearly been eliminated.

The Baird's tapir is present in very small numbers in eastern Nicaragua; it is estimated that several communities of this three-toed ungulate inhabit Bosawás. Nevertheless, this species is severely threatened with extinction.

The agouti paca (a large, forest-dwelling rodent known in Nicaragua as the painted rabbit), the white-tailed deer *(Odocoileus virginianus)*, and the collared peccary *(Tayassu tajacu)*, a stocky piglike creature with coarse, spiky fur, though abundant, are under much pressure from hunters throughout northeastern Nicaragua. You may still see an agouti or peccary in Jinotega and to the east, if you're lucky.

Aquatic Life

Nicaragua is home to a wide variety of both saltwater and freshwater species of fish, due to its two large lakes, two ocean coastlines, and numerous isolated crater lakes. Among Nicaragua's many saltwater species are flat needlefish *(Ablennes hians)*, wahoo *(Acanthocybium solandri)*, three kinds of sole, spotted eagle rays *(Aetobatus narinari)*, the Gill's sand lance *(Ammodytoides gilli)*, two kinds of moray *(Anarchias sp.)*, croakers *(Bairdiella sp.)*, triggerfish *(Balistes sp.)*, hogfish *(Bodianus sp.)*, eight kinds of perch *(Diplectrum sp.)*, sea bass *(Diplectrum sp.)*, and a dozen kinds of shark, including blacktip *(Carcharias limbatus)*, great white *(C. carcharias)*, silky *(C. falciformis)*, and spinner *(C. brevipinna)*.

Among the freshwater species are needlefish *(Strongylura sp.)*, grunts *(Pomadasys sp.)*, introduced tilapia *(Oreochromis aureus)*, catfish *(Hexanematichthys sp.)*, mojarra *(Eucinostomus sp.)*, and snook *(Centropomus sp.)*. Some species of cichlid *(Amphilophus sp.)* found nowhere else in the world swim in Nicaragua's varied crater lakes.

At least 58 different types of marine corals have been identified in the Atlantic, specifically in the Miskito Cays, Corn Island, and the Pearl Cays. Nicaragua's most common coral species

include *Acropora pamata, A. cervicornis,* and *Montastrea anularis.* Brain coral *(Colypophylia natans)* and black coral *(Antipathes pennacea)* are common. Studied for the first time in 1977 and 1978, the shallow reefs of the Pearl Cays contain the best coral formations in the nation, but are currently threatened by the enormous sediment load discharged by the Río Grande de Matagalpa.

The manatee *(Trichechus manatus)* is an important species currently protected by international statutes. In Nicaragua, it can occasionally be found in the Caribbean in the mouth of the Río San Juan and in the coastal lagoons, notably in Bluefields Bay. In 1993, the freshwater dolphin *(Sotalia fluviatilis)* was first spotted in Nicaragua and is most commonly sighted in Laguna de Wounta. The northern range for the freshwater dolphin was previously thought to be limited to Panamá.

Birds

As a result of its prime location along the Central American biosphere corridor, many thousands of species migrate through the area. To date, 676 species of birds in 56 families have been observed here, the more exotic of which you'll find in the mountains of the north and east, and along the Atlantic shore. Nicaragua has no endemic bird species of its own, but hosts 87 percent of all bird species known. The most exotic species known to reside in Nicaragua is also its most elusive, the quetzal *(Pharomacrus mocinno)*, known to inhabit highlands in Bosawás, Jinotega, and Matagalpa, especially along the slopes of Mt. Kilambé, and in Miraflor in Estelí.

Nicaragua's elegant and colorful national bird, the *guardabarranco (Momotus momota)*, is more easily found than you'd think. The Guardian of the Stream (as its Spanish name translates) can be found catching small insects in urban gardens in the capital. It is distinguished by its long, odd-shaped, iridescent tail, which it carefully preens to catch the eye of the opposite sex. The *urraca* is a bigger, meaner version of the North American blue jay, with a dangly black crest on the top of its head. It's one of the larger of the common birds in Nicaragua and can frequently be found in treetops scolding the humans below. Though the *urraca* are everywhere, a particularly sizeable population patrols the slopes of Ometepe's twin volcanoes and the Isletas by Granada. Also in the Isletas, look for the brightly colored oropendolas *(Psarocolius wagleri)* that hang their elaborate, suspended bagnests from the treetops around the lakeshore.

Reptiles

Of the 172 reptile species that make their homes in Nicaragua, nearly half are North American species, found in Nicaragua at the southern limit of their habitat, while 15 species are found only in Central America and another five are endemic to Nicaragua.

Nicaragua's several species of marine turtles are all in danger of extinction. The Paslama turtle *(Lepidochelys olivacea)* in the Pacific and the Carey turtle *(Eretmochelys imbricata)* and Green turtle *(Chelonia mydas)* in the Atlantic are protected, and much effort has gone into setting aside habitat for them, particularly nesting beaches. However, the struggle is fierce between those who aim to conserve the turtles and those who'd like to harvest their eggs, meat, and shells. There are approximately 20 beaches in the Pacific that present adequate conditions for the nesting of these turtle species, most of which play host to only occasional nesting events. Two beaches, Chacocente and La Flor on the Pacific coast, are the nesting grounds of the Paslama turtle. Massive annual egg-laying events between July and January (primarily during the first and third quarters of the moon) involve between 57,000 and 100,000 turtles, which crawl up on the moist sand at night to lay eggs. It's a safety-in-numbers approach to survival—only 1 out of 100 hatchlings makes it to adulthood. Armed guards on these beaches do their part to make sure the youngsters make it to the sea instead of the soup.

Frequently seen along the Río San Juan and some larger rivers of Jinotega are alligators, crocodiles *(Crocodilus acutus)*, caimans *(Caiman crocodilus)*, and the *Noca* turtle *(Trachemys scripta)*.

The *garrobo* is a bush lizard the size of a small house cat you're more likely to see suspended by its tail on the side of the road than in the wild. It is hunted by poor *campesino* children and then sold to passing motorists who take it home and make an aphrodisiac soup from the meat. Similarly, the *cusuco (Dasypus novemincinctus)* is a type of armadillo with plated sides and sharp-clawed feet, commonly found in drier areas of the countryside. (For information on snakes, see the *Health and Safety* section in the *Essentials* chapter.)

Amphibians

Nicaragua's humid forests and riversides are inhabited by 64 known species of amphibians, four of which are endemic, including the Mombacho salamander *(Bolitoglossa mombachoensis)*, the miadis frog, the Cerro Saslaya frog *(Plectrohyla sp.)*, and the Saslaya salamander *(Nolitron sp.)*.

Insects

Each of Nicaragua's different ecosystems has a distinct insect population. Estimates of the total number of species reach as high as 250,000, only 1 percent of which have been identified. Notable species to seek out are several gigantic species of beetles, including *Dynastes hercules* (found in cloud forests); several species of brilliant green and golden Plusiotis (found in Cerro Saslaya and Cerro Kilambé); the iridescent blue butterfly *Morpho peleides,* common all over the country, and its less common cousin, *M. amathonte,* found at altitudes of 300–700 meters, especially in the forests of Bosawás. Nocturnal moths like the Rothschildia, Eacles, and others are common. For more information about bug hunting in Nicaragua, you'll want to contact Belgian entomologist Jean-Michel Maes (jmmaes@ibw.com.ni), who, with nearly 20 years of research experience in Nicaragua, knows his stuff. He runs the entomological museum in León (normally closed to the public), and sells a CD-ROM entitled *Butterflies of Nicaragua* ($30). There is an increasing number of *mariposarios* (butterfly farms) in Nicaragua, notably in Los Guatuzos, Papaturro, El Castillo (Río San Juan), and San Ramón (Matagalpa).

National Parks and Reserves

Nicaragua's complex system of parks and reserves encompasses more than two million hectares. The Sistema Nacional de Areas Protegidas (SINAP) is made up of 76 parks, reserves, and refuges classified as "protected" by the Ministerio del Ambiente y los Recursos Naturales (Ministry of the Environment and Natural Resources, or MARENA). Of these, many are composed of privately owned land, making enforcement of their protected status difficult. That, combined with MARENA's paltry resource base and budget, has led to the decentralization of park management. Since 2001, MARENA has been experimenting with the "co-management" model in six natural reserves, handing natural-resource management responsibilities over to local NGOs who work with the communities within the areas to create sustainable alternatives to natural resource use and ecotourism infrastructure. Co-management is a novel, ongoing experiment, and while it has been surprisingly successful in some areas, the great majority of protected lands in Nicaragua remain unmanaged, unguarded, and completely undeveloped for tourism. They are sometimes referred to as "paper parks," existing only in legislation and studies, not in reality. The Río Estero Real, a wetlands preserve in the northwest corner of the country, is one of those, where half of the "protected" territory has been granted to private shrimp farmers who have eliminated most of the mangrove swamps and lagoons where shrimp once bred naturally, replacing them with artificial breeding pools.

Occasionally, being left alone results in untouched, virgin forests and wetlands protected by their own remoteness and natural tropical hostility. More commonly, however, it means that some of Nicaragua's richest treasures continue to be plundered by foreign and national cattle, logging, and mining interests, as well as destructively managed by *campesino* populations that are given little incentive or education to do otherwise. In the latter case, a typical example is the government's declaring "protected" an area where people have been living traditionally for generations, and who are suddenly expected to drastically alter their fishing, hunting, and planting patterns to protect a "park" that is and always has been their homeland. That has been the experience in the Bosawás Biosphere Reserve, where Mayangna and Miskito people were not consulted during the planning of the reserve and have consequently fought against the new regulations, which interfere with their traditional lifestyle.

Conversely, Fundación Cocibolca, in management of La Flor, has relied heavily on local residents, both for staffing the reserve and for ideas on how to run it. Tourism can go a long way toward bolstering local incentive to protect—rather than consume—the natural world.

The following is a selection of some of the more accessible (or just spectacular) of Nicaragua's protected areas.

NATIONAL PARKS
Volcán Masaya

Nicaragua's best-organized and most easily accessed park features a paved road leading to the crater, a museum, interpretive center, and paid guides to take you through more than 20 kilometers of nature trails. Declaring the 5,100 hectares that surround Volcán Masaya a national park was one of the last things President Anastasio García Somoza did before the revolution took him from power in 1979. The park's extensive lava fields are home to coyotes, *garrobo* lizards, white-tailed deer, and *cusucos*. A rare variety of sulfur-tolerant parakeets inhabits the inside of the crater's walls.

Zapatera Archipelago

Comprised of the Zapatera Volcano (629 meters) and the eight islets that surround it, the park is located in Lake Cocibolca between the Isla de Ometepe and the city of Granada, 34 kilometers to the north. Although owned by private landholders, the islands were given

© RANDALL WOOD

Volcán Masaya

national-park status in the 1980s in recognition of their immense natural, cultural, and historical value, and the government subsequently took control over much of the land. The islands still contain virgin forests and lovely shorelines, but are perhaps most famous for the pre-Columbian statuary that was found there. Many of the statues are observable today in the Convento San Francisco in Granada. Others were sold or plundered, to be spirited off to the far corners of the world. The park and adjacent mainland peninsula served as a massive burial ground for the indigenous people there.

BIOLOGICAL RESERVES
Miraflor

Draped with Spanish moss and carpeted with orchids and lush vegetation, the more than 5,600 hectares of the Reserva Natural Miraflor is a cloud forest, considered one of the most important natural reserves of its type in Nicaragua. The area is privately owned in its entirety, and is managed by several different groups of farmers and *campesino* cooperatives. This is one of the few places in Nicaragua to spot the exotic (and elusive) quetzal and up to a third of the total number of bird species observed in Nicaragua.

Río Indio-Maíz

The 3,618 square kilometers of jungle pressed between the Indio and Maíz Rivers, La Gran Reserva as it is known, abut two additional protected areas, the Punta Gorda Nature Reserve to the north, and the Río San Juan Wildlife Reserve to the south. Together, the reserves are part of the Biósfera del Sureste de Nicaragua, an immense chunk of southeastern Nicaragua dedicated to the preservation of animal and plant species along with their natural ecosystems in the Río San Juan watershed. The reserve is one of the few remaining areas in the Americas where you can experience virgin tropical humid forest as it was 200 years ago (and all the rain, insects, and heat that goes with it). The extent of the wildlife in the reserve has still not been completely determined, but it is, at the very least, one of the last refuges in Nicaragua for ocelots and other big cats.

Cayos Miskitos

Defined as all the cays and small islands found in a 40-kilometer radius from the center of Isla Grande in the Atlantic Ocean off Puerto Cabezas, plus a 20-kilometer swath of shoreline from Cabo Gracias a Dios to the south, the Reserva Biológica Cayos Miskitos has important economic and cultural significance to the Miskito people, who depend on it for fish and shellfish. The Cayos Miskitos are an ecological treasure whose impenetrable lagoons, reefs, mangrove forests, and swamps are home to marine turtles, manatees, dolphins, and several types of endangered coral species. The mangrove forests give shelter to bird species, such as *pancho galán, garza rosada,* and the brown pelican. Substantial petroleum deposits lie below the continental shelf in the Cayos Miskitos area, so the management of the region will warrant much caution and a careful balance. In the meantime, the cays' most immediate threat is drug traffickers, who use the area as a lair.

WILDLIFE RESERVES
Río Escalante-Chacocente

Named for the peculiar smell of *choco* (rotting turtle egg shells after a hatching), the Refugio de Vida Silvestre Río Escalante-Chacocente encompasses 4,800 hectares of dry tropical forest along the edge of the Pacific Ocean. The area was declared a reserve primarily because of its importance as the nesting ground of the endangered tora and Paslama turtles, incredible multitudes of which crawl up on the beach each year to lay eggs in the sand. Exotic orchids, like the *flor de niño* and *huele noche* fill the nocturnal air with a sweet, romantic fragrance. But Chacocente is also home to important forest species, mangrove systems, and the "salt tree." Check the treetops for howler and white-faced monkeys, and keep an eye peeled for the many reptiles, pelicans, white-tailed deer, and *guardabarrancos* that are watching you from the forest edges.

Don't try this at home: crocodile wrangling at Los Guatuzos Wildlife Refuge.

© ROMAN YAVICH

La Flor

This southern Pacific beach, a gorgeous white sandy crescent at the edge of an 800 hectare broad strip of tropical dry forest, is one of the most beautiful beaches in Nicaragua. Thousands of Paslama turtles beach themselves here annually to nest and lay eggs, one of just a handful of beaches in the world that witness such a spectacle. Many *garrobo negro,* iguana *verde, lagartijas,* monkeys, coyotes, raccoons, and skunks (some of which prey on the turtle eggs) also make their home in the reserve. The skies at La Flor are full of bird species that make their homes in the relatively intact dry forest: *urracas, gavilanes caracoleros, chocoyos, querques, garzas,* and *sonchiches.*

Los Guatuzos Wildlife Refuge

The 43,000 hectares of protected wetlands that separate the southern shore of Lake Cocibolca from the Costa Rican border are a remnant of a Sandinista-era wildlife reserve called Sí-a-Paz (a play on words meaning yes to peace). Los Guatuzos preserves both the spirit and the wildlife of the reserve and offers valuable habitat to hundreds of different species, plus several small border settlements of people.

NATURAL RESERVES
Volcán Cosigüina

In the farthest northwestern corner of Nicaragua, more than 12,000 hectares of the Cosigüina peninsula have been declared a natural reserve. The area has been quietly revegetating itself since the volcano's massive eruption in 1835, predominantly as dry tropical forests of *genícero, tempisque,* and *guanacaste* trees. Its nearly inaccessible crater has become the home to spider monkeys, coyotes, black iguanas, white-tailed deer, and coatis, but more obvious to the naked eye are the hundreds of bird species, notably the scarlet macaw. Climbing the volcano offers a phenomenal view of the crater lake (which began filling after the eruption 150 years ago), the Gulf of Fonseca, and beyond.

Isla Juan Venado

Much more than a sandy barrier beach island, Isla Juan Venado contains 4,600 hectares of estuary and coastline along the Pacific coast west of León. Its vegetation is successional, going from mangroves at the water's edge to inland dry tropical forest. Isla Juan Venado is rife with bird species due to the estuary system—its mangroves are home to the nests of thousands of parrots and herons—as well as crabs, mollusks, and more than 50 species of mammals and reptiles.

Volcán Mombacho

A scant 41 kilometers from the lowland heat of Managua is an otherworldly island of cloud forest atop an ancient and dormant volcano. Volcán Mombacho's lower slopes are dedicated to agriculture, cattle raising, and coffee production, but its upper third—above 800 meters—is a spectacular, misty wildlife and cloud-forest reserve. Mombacho is managed by the Fundación Cocibolca, which has done an admirable job of constructing trails and low-impact guest and research facilities. Mombacho is home both to several endemic species of butterflies and the endemic Mombacho salamander.

Chocoyero-El Brujo

The closest natural reserve to Managua, Chocoyero–El Brujo makes up for its small size with the sheer quantity of *chocoyos* (parakeets) that inhabit its cliff caves. There's no excuse for not exploring Chocoyero–El Brujo some lazy afternoon at sundown when the skies fill with the ruckus of thousands of squawking green *chocoyos*. Chocoyero is set in a semihumid forest of stately *pochote, tigüilote,* and cedar trees, and in addition to its famous birds, provides habitat for several types of owls, monkeys, and squirrels.

Estero Padre Ramos

In the northwest corner of the department of Chinandega, Estero Padre Ramos is a mangrove forest reserve with more than 150 bird species, and untouched, pristine beaches as far as the eye can see. The fingers of the estuary are a sea kayaker's dream, or you can try the local *botes.*

Other Reserves

There are many more nature reserves, typically small and designated as such in an attempt to protect a very specific resource. In addition to those mentioned previously, there are 11 reserves that protect volcanic or coastal lagoons, 16 that protect specific peaks, such as Kilambé and Pancasán, six that protect volcanic complexes, such as San Cristóbal or Pilas–El Hoyo, plus dozens of others.

BIOSPHERE RESERVES

Nicaragua's two biosphere reserves were indirectly based on a model proposed for protecting several vast areas in the southeast United States. The strategy is to create a central "nucleus zone," with wilderness status totally preventing human activity. The nucleus is then surrounded by various levels of buffer zones with increasing, but still regulated, resource exploitation permitted as the distance increases from the center. That's the intention, anyway. The virgin lands of Bosawás and the Río San Juan areas have long served as "safety valves" for Nicaragua's expanding population, accommodating *campesinos* as they look for new forestland to clear and farm. Several hundred *campesino* families currently inhabit the Bosawás reserve, and in the absence of regulation, more will surely follow.

Located in the remote north-central wilds of Nicaragua, Bosawás is the largest continuous expanse of virgin cloud forest in Central America. In the extreme southeast of Nicaragua, the Refugio de Vida Silvestre Río San Juan stretches from El Castillo southeast to the Atlantic Ocean along the north edge of the Río San Juan. In addition to the river itself, an important part of the reserve are the four interconnected lagoons at the river's mouth and their related pools, all of which are crucial habitat for manatees and several other mammals.

PRIVATE RESERVES

Another category of protected areas are called *Reservas Silvestres Privadas* (Private Wilderness Reserves). These are entirely private landholdings whose owners have applied to MARENA to become officially declared as part of SINAP. The landowners must meet a number of criteria as well as present a management plan to be classified as protected. At present, there are a handful of approved private reserves and more pending. The areas are usually near other parks or reserves, contain substantial vegetation and wildlife, and are often a part of some biological corridor. At this early point in the game, they are in varying stages of developing their tourism infrastructures. The original six private reserves are Montibelli near Chocoyero, Domitila outside Nandaime, La Maquina on the road to the coast from Diriamba, Toromixcal in San Juan del Sur, César Augusto in Jinotega, and Greenfields near Pearl Lagoon. Look for them in the appropriate regional chapters.

Environmental Issues

The problem with Nicaragua's environmental issues is that they are entangled in a rat's nest of bigger problems, including politics, land rights, population pressure, war, and natural disasters. The remedies are anything but simple.

Chief among Nicaragua's immediate problems is the rapid loss of its forests—at the rate of 150,000 hectares harvested per year. Some analyses indicate Nicaragua's timber reserves will be completely depleted by 2015. The extent of the problem is not entirely clear, as the calculations of remaining forest are based on figures collected in the 1970s.

The great majority of families in the countryside use *leña* (firewood) as their prime fuel source for cooking, which has put tremendous pressure on forest resources as Nicaragua's increasing population expands into previously unsettled lands. Population pressure and the swelling cattle industry have caused a progression of the agricultural frontier from both the Atlantic and Pacific sides of the country, reducing Nicaragua's forests by 4.6 million hectares from 1950 to 1995. On the Atlantic coast, much of the hardwood logging is happening at the hands of U.S., Canadian, and Asian companies that have negotiated fat timber concessions with Nicaragua's successive cash-strapped governments.

As if forest depletion due to humans hasn't been enough, the remaining pine forests in Nueva Segovia were further devastated by a massive outbreak of pine bark beetles that began in October 1999 in Teotecacinte, Nueva Segovia. By March 2001, an estimated 6,000 hectares were destroyed in the seven departments that make up northern Nicaragua, with the area around Jalapa being the worst hit. The beetle attacks both young and mature pines weakened by fires, resin harvesting, and poor management. The insects bore through into the tree to feed on the resin between the wood and the bark. At the start of each rainy season, young beetles disperse and fly longer distances. The infestation can spread up to 20 meters per day, spreading a full kilometer in just under two months.

Regardless of the mechanism of deforestation, the process leaves the fragile tropical soils exposed to rainfall; ensuing erosion leads to

© ALVARO MOLINA

Solid waste disposal is one of Nicaragua's biggest environmental problems.

the contamination and elimination of water sources, and outright microclimate changes. This is the case in much of Nicaragua, where within one human generation, rivers and streams that were once perennial now flow only sporadically, if at all and as any *viejito* will tell you, "it doesn't rain as much as it used to." On the Pacific coast, decades of chemical-intensive agriculture and wind erosion have caused the loss of once-rich volcanic soils as well. In general, the entire Pacific, central, and northern regions of the country are at immediate risk of sustained soil erosion.

Massive efforts are underway to attack the problem from all sides, from environmental education of the youngest children in order to change destructive habits, to active replanting of hillsides via tree-nursery projects, to the teaching and implementation of less-destructive agricultural techniques.

History

PRE-COLONIAL YEARS

Even older than the famous 6,000-year-old footprints baked into the mud in a quiet corner of Managua are the remnants of a Caribbean people known as *Los Concheros* (the shell collectors), who inhabited—or frequently visited—the Atlantic coast around 2,000 years earlier. Deposits of shells from their fishing and collecting forays have been discovered in several locations, but little else is known about Nicaragua's first inhabitants. Agriculture began around 5,000 years ago with the cultivation of corn. Pottery making followed 2,000 years later.

Sometime in the 13th century, the Chorotega and Nicarao people, under pressure from the aggressive Aztecs in Mexico, fled south through the Central American isthmus,

A BRIEF HISTORY OF U.S. INTERVENTION IN NICARAGUA

In President Teddy Roosevelt's addition to the Monroe Doctrine of regional dominance, he proclaimed that the United States, by virtue of its status as a "civilized nation," had the right to stop "chronic wrongdoing" throughout the Western Hemisphere. Subsequently, the so-called Roosevelt Corollary was used to justify troop deployment to Latin America 32 times between the end of the Spanish-American War and the years of the Great Depression. President William Howard Taft provided further rationalization for aggressively dominating Latin America with his Dollar Diplomacy, an unabashed strategy to advance and protect U.S. businesses in other countries. Nicaragua, which had been host to U.S. fruit, mining, and transportation interests since the 1850s, was a frequent recipient of such foreign policy.

U.S. Marines landed at least seven times during the aforementioned period, and spent a total of 21 years occupying Nicaragua. Official reasons for these visits included "pacification of Nicaragua," "prevention of rebellion," and, of course, "protection of U.S. interests and property." It would be unfair to call these visits uninvited, since nearly all were ostensibly serving the purpose of one or more Nicaraguan parties, usually the Conservatives.

The following is a more detailed list of gringo interventions.

1853: Washington sends U.S. Navy commander George H. Hollins to Greytown to extract an apology from local British officials for having insulted U.S. diplomat Solon Borland. Those responsible were nowhere to be found, so, reports a U.S. Marine Corps historical website, "Hollins' only alternative was to bombard the town, and this he tried to do in the most humane manner possible." Hollins allowed 24 hours for evacuation, then commenced firing. "At 0900 on 13 July, 177 shells plowed into Greytown. That afternoon a landing party of Marines and seamen completed the destruction of the town." Humanely, of course.

1853-1856: U.S. citizen William Walker usurps power and declares himself president of Nicaragua; he is briefly recognized by Washington before the other Central American nations briefly unite, drive him out, and eventually execute him by firing squad.

led by a vision of a land dominated by a great lake. The Chorotegas settled on the shores of Lake Cocibolca and around the volcanic craters of Masaya and Apoyo, and the Nicaraos farther south.

COLONIALISM (1519-1821)

Christopher Columbus, known in the Spanish world as Cristóbal Colón, first set eyes on Nicaragua in July of 1502, on his fourth and final trip to the Americas. Searching for a navigable passage through the land mass, Columbus skirted Nicaragua's Mosquito Coast, then continued on to South America without noticing the outlet of the San Juan. Seventeen years later, the conquistador Pedro Arias Dávila returned under orders from the Spanish crown to explore the land bridge of Nicaragua. During his brief foray, another Spanish explorer, González, encountered the caciques (tribal leaders) Nicarao and Diriangén, who engaged González's men in a brief battle. This gave the Spanish a hint of the warrior spirit of the original Nicaragüenses—a warning that went unheeded amongst the Europeans who would frequently face the same rebelliousness over the next few centuries.

Francisco Hernández de Córdoba arrived not long after González, entrusted with the duty of establishing Spain's first settlements in the new land. Córdoba settled Granada alongside the Chorotega communities on the banks of Lake Cocibolca, and, pushing farther inland and up the Tipitapa River, the settlement of León on

1894: The U.S. Marines under Lieutenant Franklin J. Moses have a monthlong occupation of Bluefields.

1896: From May 2-4, when fighting near Corinto "endangers American holdings," 15 Marines, under First Sergeant Frederick W. M. Poppe, and 19 seamen land in Corinto and stand guard in a "show of force."

1898: As President Zelaya extends his tenure for still another term, the local U.S. consular agent requests the U.S.S. *Alert,* at anchor in the harbor of Bluefields, to stand by in case of an attack on the city. On the morning of February 7, the U.S. flag on shore rises "union downward" over the consulate, signaling a force of 14 Marines and 19 seamen to land; they withdraw the following day.

1899: Another display of force lands, this time with a Colt automatic gun "to prevent both rebels and government troops from destroying American property."

1910: Marines and navy vessels concentrate in Nicaraguan waters and land in Bluefields and Corinto on May 19 "to guard American property."

1912: Nicaraguan president Adolfo Díaz requests the support of U.S. forces. The United States complies when the U.S.S. *Annapolis* arrives in Corinto, deploying a contingent of naval officers to Managua on August 4. Three companies of marine infantry also land and are transported to Managua by train.

1927-1933: President Coolidge sends Marines to find Sandino and "gun the bandit down." They fail.

1981-1990: The CIA runs a secret command operation directing and financing Contra forces in their attempt to topple the Sandinista government. U.S operatives carry out supply and intelligence activities, train commanders and soldiers, plant harbor mines, and sabotage Sandinista holdings.

(All citations from "Marine Corps Historical Reference Series, The United States Marines in Nicaragua," by Bernard C. Nalty, Historical Branch, G-3 Division, Headquarters, U.S. Marine Corps, Washington, D.C.)

the western shores of Lake Xolotlán. Nicaragua remained a part of Spain's overseas possessions for the next 300 years under the governance of the colonial capital in Guatemala.

INDEPENDENCE (1821)

Central America won its independence from Spain in 1821, and for a short time remained united as the five provinces of the Central American Federation. The belief that Europe would act militarily to return the former colonies to Spain forced the United States to issue the Monroe Doctrine in 1823, declaring the New World off limits to further European colonization and interference. It was the first step in two centuries of political domination in Latin America. The Central American

Federation was a short-lived pipe dream, however: When Nicaragua withdrew from the federation in 1838, the remaining states opted to become individual republics as well and the federation dissolved. Reunion of any form remains nearly impossible.

The Birth of a Rivalry

Newly independent, Nicaragua underwent several years of complete anarchy. The two primary cities, León and Granada, operated as independent city-states until a national government was finally agreed upon in 1845.

The conflict between León and Granada in the 1800s is noteworthy because it established political rivalries that endure to this day. In the early 19th century, Nicaragua's principal exports were cacao, indigo, and cattle, the sale of which allowed the landed and merchant classes to accumulate considerable wealth— on the backs of the Native Americans and landless farmers, of course, who worked the farms and ranches essentially as indentured servants. At the same time, the aspiring bourgeoisie, influenced by the Liberal teachings of the universities in León and by the American and French Revolutions, sought to liberate the poor working classes of their feudal labor obligations, thus making their labor available to all at market prices. The landed class, mostly based in Granada and loyal to the aristocratic system that favored them, resisted. The León Liberals–Granada Conservatives split was responsible for more than 100 years of civil war and continues into modern political-party rivalries.

The Canal, William Walker, and the U.S. Marines

Nicaragua's unique geography has resulted in an uninterrupted history of unrealized transcontinental-canal plans, some of which continue through the present. During the California gold rush (1849–1856), the Central American isthmus served as the route for many a prospector bound for California—and not a few impoverished ones headed back east. Steamship baron and businessman Cornelius Vanderbilt established a cross-isthmus transport company to challenge the Pacific Steamship Company then operating in Panamá. Travelers bound for California sailed up the Río San Juan and across Lake Nicaragua to the small port at San Jorge. There, they were taken by horse cart 18 kilometers across the narrow isthmus through Rivas to the bay of San Juan del Sur. Ships waiting in the harbor then carried the travelers north along the Pacific coastline to California. Vanderbilt dredged the channel of the Río San Juan and built roads, railroads, and docks on both coasts to accommodate the traffic. At about that time, the Leóneses, embroiled in a bitter battle with the Conservatives of Granada, enlisted the help of William Walker, an American filibuster who eventually installed

himself as president of Nicaragua, razed the city of Granada, and caused a whole lot of trouble (see the *Granada* chapter).

Though the relative peace of the Conservative period fostered many advances in infrastructure and technology—including the train from Granada to Corinto and the introduction of the telegraph—the famous "Thirty Years" were also a time of economic stagnation that kept Nicaragua several decades behind its neighbors in coffee exportation. Under the leadership of Liberal General José Santos Zelaya, the bourgeoisie rebelled, and Zelaya became president. He was a fierce nationalist who, among other things, marched troops to the Atlantic coast in order to refute Britain's territorial claims and officially incorporate the Atlantic region into the nation. (The two administrative units of the Atlantic coast bore Zelaya's name until the 1990s.) As a staunch nationalist, he promptly raised the ire of the United States, who arranged his ouster. Zelaya rejected Washington's proposals to build a cross-isthmus canal through Nicaraguan territory while at the same time courting Great Britain to finance the construction of a transcontinental railway.

The United States, which had been constructing the Panama canal since 1904, was threatened by the idea of a nationalist dictator encouraging a competing transport mechanism and in 1909, forced Zelaya out with pressure from the U.S. Marines. The U.S. intervention reestablished the Conservatives in power, but in 1912, the Liberal and nationalist Benjamin Zeledón led a rebellion that provoked the United States to step in again. This time, the invasion was on a much larger scale; 2,700 marines landed at Corinto and took immediate control of the railways, ports, and major cities.

Military aggression aside, the U.S. government was subtly gaining control over Nicaragua in other ways. Following the 1912 attack, U.S. financial institutions began to quietly acquire coffee-export businesses and railway and steamship companies, forcing Nicaragua into a credit noose. Under the watchful eye of the U.S.

Marines, governmental control was handed over to the Conservatives, whom Washington thought would more faithfully represent U.S. interests. But the Liberals resisted, staging 10 uprisings between 1913 and 1924, all of which the U.S. military quelled.

In 1924, Conservative President Bartolomé Martínez instituted a novel form of government—a power-sharing arrangement between the Liberals and the Conservatives at the local level. The United States withdrew Marines in 1925 but they were back within the year. No sooner had power sharing begun than ambitious Conservative Emilio Chamorro staged a coup d'état, seized power, and sparked the Constitutional War. The United States stepped in to prevent the imminent takeover by the Liberals, but because the Conservatives had discredited themselves, the United States was unable to simply hand the power back to them. The deal they worked out was known as the Espino Negro Pact (named after the town where it was signed; Spanish for Black Thorn). It was a crucial moment for the Liberals. One of their generals, Augusto C. Sandino, was opposed to the pact, and fled with his men to the northern mountains to start a guerrilla war in opposition of the continued presence of the United States in Nicaragua. The leader of the Constitutional Army was forced to declare, "All my men surrender except one."

The U.S. military tried unsuccessfully to flush Sandino from the mountains in spite of drastic measures, which included the aerial bombing of the city of Ocotal, so in 1933, Washington tried a new approach. Withdrawing U.S. troops from Nicaragua, the United States formed a new military unit called the National Guard, placed young Anastasio Somoza García at its head, and handed the power over to them and the new president, Juan Bautista Sacasa. Sandino enjoyed overwhelming support in Nicaragua's northern mountains and had achieved two of his goals—the removal of both U.S. armed forces and the Conservative oligarchy from power. Sandino represented a major threat to Somoza's political and military ambitions. So in February of 1934, Sandino went to Managua at Sacasa's invitation to negotiate, and when he left the presidential palace that night, several National Guard members ambushed and assassinated him on the streets of Managua. Sandino's assassination was quickly followed by a government-sponsored reign of terror in the northern countryside, destroying cooperatives, returning lands to their previous owners, and hunting down, exiling, imprisoning, or killing Sandino's supporters.

THE SOMOZA ERA (1937-1979)

The formation of the National Guard paved the way for its leader, General Anastasio Somoza García, to seize control of Nicaragua in 1937 and begin an enormously wealthy and powerful family dynasty that would permanently reorient and completely control Nicaraguan politics for the following 42 years. So formidable was the rule of the Somoza family that many Nicaraguans and foreigners alike refer to the nearly continuous succession of three Somoza presidents as one all-powerful "Somoza." The Somozas were wily politicians with a near-genius for using existing political conflicts to their personal advantage; they were also expert practitioners of a favorite trick of Latin American dictators, *continuismo*, in which a puppet leader would be elected but resign shortly afterward, handing the power back to the Somozas. Five such "presidents" were elected during the 42-year reign of the Somozas, not one of which lasted longer than three years. The Somozas maintained a strong foothold in the national economy as well (much to the dismay of merchants in Granada) by manipulating the government licensing mechanisms and importing contraband for local markets with the complicity of the National Guard. If there was money to be made anywhere in Nicaragua, the Somozas took notice and squeezed out the competition. They extracted personal income from public utilities and the financial sector, monopolized the cotton industry when it surged in the 1950s and, later, meat, shrimp, and lobster export in the 1960s and 1970s. They owned the nation's

AUGUSTO CÉSAR SANDINO (1893-1934)

The term Sandinista is easily associated with Nicaragua, but less well known is the story of the man, who, through his fight against imperialism, became a legend in Nicaragua and the world, and is recognized today by just the merest rendering of his famous broad-brimmed hat.

Augusto C. Sandino was born in Niquinohomo (Nahuatl for "valley of warriors"), the bastard son of a wealthy, landed judge and one of his servant women. But while the judge lived well in town, Sandino's family was so poor they often resorted to stealing crops to eat. Sandino grew disgusted at Nicaraguan society, which engendered such inequity, and questioned both civil society and the Catholic church, which he believed was guilty of propping up the aristocracy. At the age of 17, Sandino witnessed the U.S. Marines's invasion of Nicaragua to prop up Adolfo Díaz's failing Conservative presidency. When they crushed a rebellion led by General Benjamin Zeledón, their parading of Zeledón's dead body through the streets of Masaya affected Sandino deeply. Nine years later, Sandino fled to Mexico, where

he was inspired by Tampico laborers struggling to unionize in spite of resistance from the U.S.-owned oil companies. Sandino returned to Nicaragua with a new sense of purpose and a strong self-identity shaped by anarchy, socialism, and armed conflict.

He became a renegade general from the Liberals and set up his camp in the mountains outside San Rafael del Norte, Jinotega, where he became one of the first to practice guerrilla warfare, staging effective hit-and-run raids against U.S. Marine installations in Ocotal and the north. Sandino's men, who grew to number nearly 1,800 by 1933, attacked some mining and lumber companies with enough force to drive them away from the Atlantic coast.

Sandino and his troops were brutal – they sometimes killed prisoners of war or slit the throats of the dead and pulled the tongue out and down through the gash, like a necktie. The U.S. military struggled diligently but fruitlessly for seven years to flush Sandino out of the hills. In the words of one U.S. Army lieutenant, "Sandino poses as the George Washington of Nicaragua but he is only a cut-throat

---

prime food-processing industries; sugar refining; cement production; the cardboard, tobacco, and recording industries; and sea and air transport. In fact, it is said that by the late 1970s, the Somoza family owned everything in Nicaragua worth owning.

Anastasio Somoza García
(Presidencies: Jan. 1, 1937–May 1, 1947; May 6, 1950–Sept. 21, 1956)

Born in San Marcos, Carazo, and educated in Philadelphia, Somoza García's English language proficiency and business sense helped him ascend rapidly through the military. The Roosevelt administration overlooked his rapacious greed, questionable politics, and strong-handed military tactics in exchange for a Central American ally. World War II was an economic windfall for Nicaragua— and Somoza's industries, which exported raw

material, but just in case, Somoza declared war on Germany and Japan as a pretext for confiscating the valuable German-owned coffee land.

Somoza García's administration oversaw construction of the Chinandega–Puerto Morazán railway, Managua's city water system and International Airport (originally named Aeropuerto Las Mercedes) and perhaps most importantly, the Pan-American Highway, which began in 1942 (and which not coincidentally happened to connect several of his personal farms). Under increasing political pressure to step down from the presidency, Somoza García handed power over to a series of puppet governments and then stepped back into power in 1951, maintaining his presidency through a series of constitutional reforms that eliminated the need for elections. Popular frustration grew until 1956, when, at a celebratory and a bandit, preying upon foreigners and the law-abiding citizens of his country." But he was slippery: In Sandino's advantage was a profound knowledge of the land, vast popular support, the willingness to live poor, and an uncanny ability to vanish into thin air.

While Sandino's struggle was ostensibly to force the U.S. military and business interests out of Nicaragua, he represented much more than brute nationalism. In the Segovias, where Sandino enjoyed massive popular support, he formed agricultural cooperatives of landless peasants, imposing taxes on wealthy ranchers and businessmen to support them. He also fought in support of the exploited timber, banana plantation, and mine workers.

During the Great Depression, the Marines eventually left Nicaragua, and the new president of Nicaragua, Anastasio Somoza García, had Sandino assassinated in February 1934. Sandino's body was never found.

Thirty years after Sandino's death, a young idealistic student named Carlos Fonseca Amador resurrected Sandino's image and ideals as the basis of a new political and guerrilla movement, which he called the Frente Sandinista de Liberación Nacional (FSLN) – the Sandinista Front for National Liberation. The FSLN greatly exaggerated Sandino's reputation as a peasant who fought righteously against the imperialistic designs of the United States, because it suited their ideology. Contrary to FSLN doctrine, Sandino was no communist. Rather, Sandino's crusade was often against the bourgeois Nicaraguan Conservatives. His ideology was a mix of his own peculiar leftism with a curious indigenous mysticism; he changed his middle name from Calderón to César in honor of the Roman emperor, claimed he could give orders to his troops using silent mental communication, and predicted Nicaragua would be the site of Armageddon, where "armies of angels would do battle alongside more temporal troops."

Nevertheless, to this day, Sandino remains a hero to Nicaraguans and the world's leftist community. He spearheaded a movement that fought for drastic social and political change and sought to make up for centuries of class discontent that continues even today.

ball in the Social Club of León, he was assassinated by the poet, political idealist, and frustrated nationalist Rigoberto López Pérez.

Luís Somoza Debayle
(Presidency: Sept. 21, 1956-May 1, 1963)

Upon his father's assassination, Luís Somoza Debayle, a.k.a. Tacho, took the reins. An agronomist by training, he showed great political skill at keeping the nation stable despite political agitation that filled the years of his presidency. Some of the tension was due to his younger brother Anastasio Somoza Debayle's political aspirations, but there were several attempts on Tacho's life as well, including a 1959 (Cuban-inspired) aborted uprising that led to the surrender of all 100 insurgents after only two weeks. But Tacho built the hydropower plant and reservoir of Lake Apanás in Jinotega; the improved port facilities at Corinto; the highway from San Benito to El Rama, which helped unite the Atlantic and Pacific coasts; and the nation's first social security system (INSS). In 1963, Tacho lost in popular elections to the Liberal Renée Schick, and died of a heart attack four years later.

Anastasio Somoza Debayle
(Presidencies: May 1, 1967-May 1, 1972; Dec. 1, 1974-July 16, 1979)

As "Tachito," a 1964 graduate of the West Point Military Academy, rose to power, the nascent Sandinista (FSLN) movement was gaining attention in the north through attacks and kidnappings; over the next decade, they would prod Tachito into becoming the cruelest president the nation had ever seen.

The earthquake of December 1972 provided Tachito a unique opportunity: Appointing himself head of the Emergency Committee, he did little more to rebuild the country than funnel aid money into his own bank accounts. He was reelected in 1974, but Tachito's increasingly flagrant human rights violations including the assassination of journalist Pedro Joaquín Chamorro, and his increasingly violent responses to FSLN attacks earned him much international opprobrium. When the FSLN finally ousted him on July 16, 1979, he fled to Miami, and then to Paraguay, where on September 17, 1980, he was assassinated by an anti-tank rocket that pulverized his limousine.

THE SANDINISTA REVOLUTION (1979-1990)

Guerrilla groups opposed to the Somoza dynasty and inspired by Fidel Castro began training in clandestine camps in the northern mountains of Nicaragua in the early 1950s and coalesced a decade later when Carlos Fonseca Amador, Silvio Mayorga, and Tomás Borge formed the **Frente Sandinista de Liberación Nacional (FSLN).** Carlos Fonseca's ideas, an inspired combination of Marxism (which he'd experienced firsthand in a trip to Moscow) and the nationalist, anti-imperialist beliefs of Augusto Sandino formed their ideological framework: Sandinismo.

Early Sandinista insurrections in Ríos Coco and Bocay (1963) and Pancasán (1967) were crushed but the actions helped legitimize the FSLN. Growing opposition to Tachito fueled the dictator's increasing brutality. In January 1978, Pedro Joaquín Chamorro, the editor of *La Prensa,* was gunned down in Managua. A relentless critic of Somoza, his death fooled no one. One month later, the largely indigenous population of the Masaya neighborhood of Monimbó protested for five days. The National Guard responded by massacring hundreds. Trade unions, student organizations, and popular movements, both private and religious, all threw their weight behind the Sandinista insurgency. By May 1979, the guerrillas were ready for the final insurrection, which would last 52 days.

Combat erupted simultaneously around Chinandega, León, and Chichigalpa in the Pacific, and in the mining triangle in the northeast. At the same time, Sandinista troops began pressing north from the border with Costa Rica. They entered León, capturing the city after a two-day battle. The rest of the nation began a massive general labor strike.

On June 8, 1979, Sandinista soldiers and supporters began marching from Carazo, just south of Managua, into the capital itself. The National Guard responded by shelling Managua. Most of the fighting in Managua took place in the lower-middle-class neighborhoods of Bello Horizonte and El Dorado, where extensive networks of concrete drainage ditches made easy battle trenches. On the streets, the people tore up the concrete *adoquines* (paving stones) of the streets and erected barricades (Somoza's own factories produced the *adoquines,* a much-loved irony to this day). The world watched, appalled, as Somoza's aircraft indiscriminately strafed the capital.

Meanwhile, in the north, Matagalpa fell to the FSLN on July 2, 1979, and the strategic town of Sébaco fell the day after, leaving the entire north in the hands of the Sandinistas. The military barracks in Estelí—the last and most important barracks outside of the capital—fell on July 16; FSLN forces surrounded the capital. Trapped by the Sandinistas and abandoned by the United States, Somoza fled Nicaragua in the predawn hours of July 17. The Somoza era had ended.

The FSLN Government

The exuberance of military victory quickly faded as the new leaders struggled to convert revolutionary fervor into support for the new nation they wanted to build. They were starting from scratch: Somoza had run Nicaragua as his own personal farm, and overthrowing him had meant obliterating the entire institutional infrastructure of a nation. The sweeping economic, political, and social reforms of the Sandinista revolution therefore made Nicaragua a real-time social experiment, and the entire world looked on with fascination and fear.

The new Nicaraguan government was a

battleground of competing interests exacerbated by the dire need to reactivate the economy. The "Group of Nine" fatigue-clad FSLN *comandantes* nudged a supporting conservative alliance aside and revealed their legendary "Plan 80," which formulated Nicaragua's economy as a delicate balance between private ownership and steadily increasing state control. The nation's commercial sector and upper class wanted nothing of the sort, and evacuated for Miami, returning a decade or two later, after the Sandinistas were out of power; their exodus contributed to the economic failure of the FSLN.

Land reform proceeded immediately. Two million acres of Somoza's holdings were confiscated and distributed to the poor. This was a first in Central America, socially significant, but also environmentally negligent, as previously unexploited and delicate hillsides were soon cleared and planted, unleashing massive deforestation and erosion problems. Worse, the best pieces of land were distributed not to needy *campesinos* but to the Sandinista elite, which they retain to this day.

A massive and world-acclaimed literacy campaign to combat Nicaragua's abominably high illiteracy rate followed not long after. The year 1980 was proclaimed "The Year of Literacy" and thousands of volunteers—typically zealous university students—marched out to the rural corners of Nicaragua to teach reading, writing, and basic math skills. The literacy rate soared to nearly 90 percent, but its Cuban-inspired mix of education and revolutionary propaganda meant many a *campesino*'s first reading lessons taught revolutionary dogma, and the math exercises frequently involved counting items like rifles and tanks. Nonetheless, the literacy campaign encouraged young idealists to explore and take pride in their own country and culture, and has reinforced Nicaragua's nationalism and self-identity to the present.

The Contra War

In their zeal to "defend the revolution at all costs," Sandinista leaders ran into opposition from all sides—from the business community (represented by the business organization COSEP, led by future president Enrique Bolaños); from Somoza's former cronies who missed their days of wealth and privilege and were enraged by the policy of confiscation; from the former members of the National Guard, many of whom regrouped outside of Nicaragua and became the nucleus of the military *contra-revolucionarios* (Contras); and lastly, from the United States, who, under President Reagan, were deeply suspicious of the Sandinistan Communist tendencies. Reagan immediately launched a political, economic, and military program designed to strangle the Sandinistas out of power.

The Sandinistas were not only openly collaborating with Cuba and the Soviet Union but also exporting their revolution to El Salvador by supporting the FMLN. In the context of heightened Cold War tensions, the United States imposed an economic embargo in 1985. But the desire and the ambition to remove the Sandinistas was not North America's alone—many moderate Nicaraguans felt betrayed by the Sandinistas, who, they felt, had imposed a Marxist-Leninist regime on the nation without their approval and had simply replaced one political elite with another. The land confiscation didn't end with Somoza's land; the Sandinistas confiscated the land of any Nicaraguan that opposed them, and in many cases, kept the best properties for themselves.

Gross economic mismanagement by the Sandinistas, plus the embargo, caused the economy to collapse. By 1985, export earnings had plummeted to half their pre-revolution figures, and much of the confiscated agricultural land converted into cooperatives remained unproductive and was administered at great expense. The business class, in fear of further expropriations, refused to invest, and many of Nicaragua's skilled laborers fled the country in search of profitable employment elsewhere. In order to combat the Contras, the Sandinistas increased military spending and sent much of the country's productive labor force into battle. Austerity measures didn't earn the Sandinista government many friends either, as previously

OF BEANS AND BULLETS:
WHO WERE THE CONTRAS?

The Contras remain one of the most powerful, divisive, and enigmatic elements of Nicaragua's recent history. They owe their name to the Sandinista leaders who christened them *contra-revolucionarios*. The Contras preferred to call themselves La Resistencia, and others called them "freedom fighters," "bandits," "heroes," and "outlaws."

Not long after the Sandinistas took power in 1979 and long before the Contra movement even had a name, discontent was already swelling among some groups of *campesinos*, who sensed that the Sandinista revolution had gone wrong: Small farmers were being forced to join collectives or were jailed; political meetings were frequent; government propaganda smacked of atheism (or dubious support for the Catholic church); the government was full of Cuban advisors; price controls were making it hard to turn a profit in agriculture; and a lot of people were incarcerated, including many indigenous Miskito people, who had never wanted much more than to be left alone. The revolution was supposed to have made the lives of the poor farmers easier, not harder.

As the first *campesinos* picked up arms and slipped across the northern border into Honduras, they encountered another group eager to see the Sandinistas return to where they had come from: former members of Somoza's National Guard, professional military personnel who longed for their former positions of power and prestige and thirsted for one more battle.

Though they received some early training and organizational help from Argentine military advisers, the Contras weren't an organized force per se until late in the game. Even then, they were composed of numerous factions rife with internal divisions, petty grudges, and ambition among and within their units. Many were simple farm boys looking for fame and fortune at the end of a rifle; others were would-be warlords who used the armed maneuvers to settle old civil disputes or have some vengeance on former drinking buddies. The Contras survived on limited supplies, donations from sympathizers in Miami, and whatever they could take at gunpoint.

The only thing that united the various Contra groups was the feeling that the Sandinista revolution had been a step in the wrong direction. That group included U.S. President Ronald Reagan, who in March 1986, said, "I guess in a way they are counterrevolutionary, and God bless them for being that way. And I guess that makes them Contras, and so it makes me a Contra, too." At various points in the 1980s, the U.S. government played a critical part in the financing and arming of the Contras, in violation of its own laws and without the knowledge of the public.

Based out of camps along the Honduran border, the Fuerza Democrática Nicaragüense (FDN) staged raids in Jinotega, Matagalpa, and Chinandega, and was led primarily by ex-National Guard officers and groups of farmers who called themselves Milicia Popular Anti-Somoza (MILPA, a play on the Spanish word for corn patch). Fighting a completely separate battle along the Río San Juan from camps

common goods, like toothpaste and rice, were parsimoniously rationed and shoddy Eastern-bloc goods replaced imports of better quality.

And to fight the increasingly violent Contra attacks in Matagalpa, Jinotega, and much of the east, the Sandinistas instituted a roundly-hated obligatory draft, forcing Nicaraguans to defend a revolution in which they were rapidly losing faith. *Servicio militar patriotico* (patriotic military service), or SMP, was parodied by young men as *Seremos Muertos Prontos* (soon we will be dead).

In 1984 the Sandinistas easily won an election international observers declared fair and transparent, but Washington continued to fund the Contra "refugees."

By the close of the 1980s, both the Contras and the Sandinista government were physically over the Costa Rican border was the Alianza Revolucionaria Democrática (ARDE), led by the infamous Edén Pastora, a.k.a. Comandante Cero (Zero), former Sandinista militant turned Contra. ARDE was a military disaster from the start, so thoroughly riddled with Sandinista spies it never had any hope of victory. Pastora was a would-be *caudillo* who hated organization, refused to delegate authority, and kept his own men divided to prevent any claims to his throne. His macho posturing and reputation for womanizing made him an easy target for sexy female Sandinista spies, a half dozen of whom coaxed him to pillow-talk away just about every military secret he had. Pastora's own men feared he was really a Sandinista sympathizer sent to lead them into military devastation.

Though the Sandinista military committed its share of mistakes and atrocities, the Contras' propensity for brutality and terror is well documented and undeniable. Militarily, they were best at short, sharp raids and random ambushes of military and civilian vehicles. Complicated operations that required timing or planning nearly always went awry, and communication and coordination problems plagued them throughout the war. What they were best at was seeding terror in the hillsides. Their tactics were barbaric: Reagan's "Freedom Fighters" regularly disemboweled victims, chopped their limbs off, and tore bones out of bodies which they shook at the victims' family members. Columns of hungry Contra troops didn't think twice about taking at gunpoint anything they needed from local *campesinos*, from cattle to liquor to boots. On the way, many young women and girls were taken away to be raped and killed, sometimes by decapitation. Young boys and men were routinely castrated and mutilated before being killed.

The Contras commonly targeted suspected Sandinista sympathizers, including government workers in nonmilitary organizations. They brutalized and killed mayors, doctors, nurses, judges, schoolteachers, clergy, policemen, even the staff of utility offices and wealthy townspeople suspected of supporting the new government. Often, those victims who escaped death at the hands of the Contras were forced into the mountains at gunpoint to become soldiers. Intent on derailing the Sandinista economy by preventing the harvest, Contras frequently burned the installations of agricultural cooperatives and massacred anyone who stayed to defend them.

The Contras never had the satisfaction of a military victory. Rather, when the Sandinistas lost public elections and handed power over to the Chamorro government, the incentive to be a Contra vanished. Though some Contras rejected the peace accords and slipped back into the mountains to continue fighting, most disarmed and went back to farming their beans and corn. In the end, though foreign powers had helped the Nicaraguans to nearly destroy themselves over ideology and geopolitics, the Contras who returned to the land knew the struggle to defeat the Sandinista government was simple – the right to a piece of land, to be left alone to work it, and to sell their crops at a fair price.

and economically exhausted. The Sandinistas lost their primary source of funding when the Soviet Union collapsed, while the Contras had little hope of a military victory. The Iran-Contra scandal in the United States, in which arms were secretly and illegally sold in the Middle East to raise money for Contras, ended all further funding for Reagan's "Freedom Fighters." The moment was propitious for a peace initiative, and Costa Rican president Oscar Arías supplied it. In 1987, five Central American presidents attended talks at Esquipulas, Guatemala, and emerged with a radical peace accord. The Sandinistas organized elections in 1990 to show the world that their government was committed to democratic principles and to give Nicaraguans the chance to reaffirm their support for the FSLN.

To their surprise, the Nicaraguan people overwhelmingly voted them out of office. The revolution had ended. On their way out the door, the Sandinistas looted the state of everything it could—hundreds of millions of dollars of property. FSLN party heads privatized many state companies under anonymous cooperatives and passed a series of decrees ensuring they would retain some power—a disgrace now known as the *Piñata.*

THE NEW DEMOCRACY (1990-PRESENT)

Upon losing the elections, the Sandinistas handed power to **Violeta Barrios de Chamorro,** widow of the slain journalist Pedro Joaquín Chamorro and center of a ragtag coalition of Sandinista opposition groups called the Unión Nacional Opositora (UNO).

Doña Violeta's charismatic ability to reconcile and unite the nation as though it were a shattered family set a reassuring tone for an embattled populace. Her administration reestablished diplomatic and economic ties with the rest of the world, ended the draft, brought the army and the police under civil control, and slowly began disarming and reassimilating the Contras. As a peace offering, Doña Violeta offered them 1,600 square kilometers of land, including much of the Río San Juan area, to resettle and enter the agrarian labor force. Other Contra communities can be found in Jinotega and Matagalpa. Though Doña Violeta successfully enticed the international aid community back to Nicaragua to help with the reconstruction, Nicaragua's economy was anemic through much of the early 1990s. To her credit, she negotiated so that much of the accumulated international debt was pardoned.

The elections of 1996, run without the massive international funding that characterized previous elections, were rife with abnormalities, near-riots, and chronic disorder: Polling places opened hours late, bags of discarded ballots were found afterward in the houses of officials, and the communication network failed. Not surprisingly, in the aftermath, all sides had

reason to accuse the others of vote-rigging and fraud. Even so, Nicaraguans turned out in record numbers and elected Managua's slippery PLC (Partido Liberal Constitucionalista) mayor, Arnoldo Alemán over Daniel Ortega, by a margin of 49 to 38 percent.

Arnoldo Alemán was a political conservative and hard-core capitalist lawyer with a sworn aversion to all things Sandinista and a professed admiration for the Somozas, whose proclivity for political manipulation and capacity to accumulate personal fortune Alemán imitated. Alemán oversaw the continued growth of the economy, boosted the development of *zonas francas* (free trade zones) and the construction of *maquiladoras* (export clothing assembly plants). Politics returned to the back room, where endless scandals of kickbacks, insider deals, and frenzied pocket-filling embarrassed and infuriated the nation. He became a larger-than-life figure as the head of the PLC party, negotiated deals with the Sandinistas when it suited him to do so, as his personal fortune soared from $20,000 when he took office as mayor of Managua, to $250 million, when he was voted out in 2001. But as he came under increased political and popular pressure for corruption, he and Ortega engineered the infamous **El Pacto.** The agreement provided them both diplomatic immunity and a lifetime seat in the Assembly, and divided up the government's most important roles between the FSLN and PLC, including the Supreme Court and the Consejo Supremo Electoral (which runs the elections). Together, Nicaragua's top two *caudillos* (political strongmen) had eviscerated Nicaraguan democracy.

Midway through Alemán's presidency, on October 28, 1998, Hurricane Mitch, the worst storm in recorded history, struck Nicaragua, killing thousands and destroying the already decrepit road system. Alemán took time from planning his lavish wedding to berate the Sandinista mayor of Posoltega as a liar when she first reported the disaster. The Nicaraguan people were appalled, but rising popular opposition to his increasingly corrupt administration was unable to touch him.

Enrique Geyer Bolaños, Arnoldo Alemán's nondescript vice-president and former head of COSEP (the Nicaraguan private industry association), came to power in 2002 with the PLC party and an anticorruption platform. His pledge to clean up Nicaraguan government resonated with Nicaraguans fed up with the abuses Alemán had subjected them to, and they elected him over Daniel Ortega with a 56 percent majority. But despite good intentions, even Bolaños was unable to overcome the powerful party dynamics that have maintained the Nicaraguan political elite in power for centuries. The PLC, which had brought Bolaños to power, was bloated with corruption, and by attacking it Bolaños destroyed the political support he needed to be an effective leader.

Upon entering office, Bolaños moved quickly to bring indictments against high-ranking PLC officials, including Alemán himself. Alemán under other conditions might have been able to muster the support to resist the charges, but, as his allies slipped away, he was stripped of diplomatic immunity. In December 2003, a Nicaraguan judge found him guilty of corruption and money laundering, and sentenced him to 20 years in prison. This was the first time in recent Latin American history that a blatantly corrupt leader has been convicted and punished. But Alemán continued to wield considerable political influence even from house arrest, and the majority of the PLC turned against Bolaños in retribution for attacking one of their own. Consequently, Bolaños had considerable trouble enacting meaningful legislation, as very few members of the Congress, evenly divided between PLC and FSLN members, supported him, and the PLC mounted a vindictive effort to convict him of corruption himself, alleging his 2001 election campaign was financed by government funds. Ironically, Enrique Bolaños had better political support from the rest of the world and international institutions than he does from his own political party.

The Pact allowed Daniel Ortega to gain in

strength, and through the Sandinistas in the National Assembly he methodically weakened and divided the political opposition like a pro. Mayoral elections in 2004 went overwhelmingly to the Sandinista party, while Bolaños's new coalition, APRE, suffered significant defeats in most departments.

Ortega Returns

By 2006, Ortega had expelled most of the old guard from the FSLN. After three consecutive failed bids for the presidency since 1990, Daniel campaigned on a platform of unity and moderation. People began speaking of Sandinistas and Danielistas as though they were no longer one and the same. Meanwhile, with Arnoldo Alemán still under a very loose house arrest, the Liberal party was in disarray.

Nicaraguans turned out in record numbers to vote and were stunned to discover Daniel Ortega had won the presidency with only 38 percent of the vote. In his favor was a law passed by Sandinistas and Liberals together that had lowered the minimum percentage required to win the presidency without a runoff from 40 percent to 35 percent (simultaneously, Alemán was released from house arrest—coincidence?). But to win back power, Ortega also renounced everything he had ever believed in, embracing the Catholic church (his Sandinista supporters in the National Assembly passed a last-minute law forbidding abortion even when the mother's life is at risk, which won over the devout but appalled everyone else), apologized for some of the worst offenses of the war against the Contras, and spoke lovingly about investment and private property. Says Álvaro Vargas Llosa, "What this farcical saga tells us is that Daniel Ortega was much more interested in being president than in being principled."

During his first two years in power, Daniel's support for capitalism devolved into frequently incoherent ranting against America as he strengthened diplomatic ties with Libya's Mohammar Qhadaffi, Iran's Mahmoud Ahmadinejad, Venezuela's Hugo Chávez, and of course Cuba's Fidel Castro.

How revolutionary Ortega's return becomes depends on his ability to maintain the delicate balancing act of courting Chávez's new socialists and appeasing the investment and donor communities that help keep Nicaragua's economy afloat. Slipping polls indicate Nicaraguans on the whole are not overly eager to return to the 1980s. William Easterly quotes, "It took the Sandinistas twelve years to make a saint of Somoza; it took Violeta only five years to make saints of the Sandinistas; Alemán needed only two years to make a saint of Violeta." The cycle continues. . . .

Government and Politics

It's tempting to think Nicaraguan politicians' sole purpose for governing is to gerrymander the system to ensure their indefinite power and/or enrichment. And with the sole exception of perhaps Violeta Chamorro and Enrique Bolños, that's essentially true. But talk to any Nicaraguan and you will find Nicaraguan politics are infinitely subtle and the battlefield is constantly being redrawn.

ORGANIZATION

The Republic of Nicaragua is a constitutional democracy, which gained its independence from Spain in 1821. In addition to the national government, there is a parallel government responsible for the administration of the two autonomous regions of the Atlantic coast. The government of the autonomous regions elects its own leaders separately from the rest of the nation.

Branches of Government

Nicaragua's government is divided into four branches. The executive branch consists of the president and vice president. The judicial branch includes the Supreme Court, subordinate appeals courts, district courts, and local courts, plus separate labor and administrative tribunals. The Supreme Court oversees the entire judicial system and consists of 12 justices elected by the National Assembly for seven-year terms. Many consider the judicial system ineffective and plagued by party interests and manipulations by the rich, but it does have some points in its favor, including an approach that attempts to reduce crowding in jails by having the aggressor and the aggrieved meet to strike a deal. For minor offenses, this is an effective tactic. There is no capital punishment in Nicaragua, the maximum sentence being 30 years (though the abominable conditions of Nicaraguan prisons makes one wonder if the sentence isn't equally harsh).

The legislative branch consists of the Asamblea Nacional (National Assembly), a chamber in which 90 *diputados* (deputies) representing Nicaragua's different geographical regions vote on policy. The *diputados* are elected from party lists provided by the major political parties, though defeated presidential candidates that earn a minimum requirement of votes automatically become lifetime members, and by law, former presidents are also guaranteed a seat.

The fourth branch of Nicaraguan government is unique to Nicaragua: The Consejo Supremo Nacional is in charge of running democratic elections. Politicized since the Pact of 2000, the body is often accused of furthering the interests of Arnoldo Alemán and Daniel Ortega.

Prior to his election, Ortega attempted repeatedly to implement a parliamentary system that would weaken the executive and permit a sort of power sharing favorable to the Sandinistas, without success. Now that he is again president, he is pushing for a direct or participatory democracy through Chavez-esque **Consejos de Poder Ciudadanos,** which would ostensibly

THE PACT

Seldom have two bitter enemies been such good friends. In January 2000, outgoing president Arnoldo Alemán was struggling to find a way to avoid charges of embezzling over $100 million during his presidency, and sideliner Daniel Ortega was looking for a way to avoid facing charges of sexual abuse of his stepdaughter Zoilamerica Narvaez, the gentlemen's (may we use that word?) agreement now known as El Pacto suited them both politically.

The Pact is essentially a power-sharing agreement between the two men's respective political parties. It granted political impunity to ex-presidents (which, when later revoked, landed Alemán in jail), and guaranteed seats on the Assembly to outgoing presidents. It also ensured all government bodies were enlarged and filled with an equal number of PLC and FSLN party representatives.

To ensure no additional parties arise to challenge either party's power, the Pact enacted more stringent requirements for the formation of new parties as well as the requirements for individual candidates for mayor, which worked marvellously to its intended effect, the political abandonment of potential political menace Pedro Solorzano.

The Pact has single-handedly eviscerated the democratic apparatus of post-revolutionary Nicaragua and ensured the ongoing political shenanigans of both Ortega and Alemán are not only tolerated, but lead inevitably to their personal political benefit. As such it is universally criticized as the single most important factor in Nicaragua's future political and economic development. And an entire generation of Nicaraguans suddenly looks back on the Somoza years with a bit of nostalgia, wondering in a sense of horror if things were actually better back then.

provide more voice to the electorate but would moreover ensure easy manipulation of the public to strengthen the FSLN's political base.

Elections

The Nicaraguan people vote for their president and *diputados* every five years. The president cannot run for consecutive terms. The Consejo Supremo Electoral (Supreme Electoral Council, or CSE) consists of seven magistrates elected by the National Assembly for five-year terms. The CSE has the responsibility of organizing, running, and declaring the winners of elections, referendums, and plebiscites. Electoral reforms put in place in 2000 allowed the FSLN and the PLC the new ability to name political appointees to the Council, politicizing the CSE to the extreme. The international community decried the fact that the entire process of recognizing new political parties, declaring candidates, and managing the mechanics of holding elections could be so easily subverted to ensure the two strongest parties—the PLC and the FSLN—divide the spoils of government between themselves. These "reforms" have led to a perceived reduction in the transparency of the Nicaraguan government as a whole.

Note another trend as well: Nearly every Nicaraguan presidential candidate (with the exception of Doña Violeta), has been, at one time or another, jailed by a previous administration. Tachito jailed Ortega, and Ortega in turn jailed at one point or another both Arnoldo Alemán and Enrique Bolaños.

THE CONSTITUTION

The present constitution, written in 1987 by the FSLN administration, was amended in 1995 to balance the distribution of power more evenly between the legislative and executive branches. The National Assembly's ability to veto was bolstered and the president's ability to veto reduced. It was revised again in 2000 to increase the power of the Supreme Court and the comptroller-general's office.

Civil Liberties

Among Latin American societies, the people of Nicaragua enjoy unequaled freedom. Most notable is their nearly unparalleled freedom of speech, a right guaranteed by the constitution and exercised with great vigor by Nicaraguans of all persuasions. The repression, censorship, and brutality of Somoza's dictatorship ended within the recent memory of many Nicaraguans, and they do not take the freedom they enjoy in the 21st century for granted. There is no official state censorship of the media in Nicaragua, though there have been occasional governmental attempts to exert influence through subtler means, such as the embargo of government-sponsored ad revenue of newspapers that seem overly critical.

The constitution additionally guarantees freedom of religion, freedom of movement within the country, freedom of foreign travel, emigration, and repatriation, and the right to peacefully assemble and associate. Domestic and international human rights monitors are permitted to operate freely and interview whomever they wish.

The Nicaraguan constitution prohibits discrimination in all forms, including discrimination by birth, nationality, political belief, race, gender, language, religion, opinion, national origin, or economic or social condition. In practice, however, there are many social forms of discrimination, from former president Alemán's public derision of Managua Mayor Herty Lewites as el Judío (the Jew) to the day-to-day behavior of a *machista* society that, in addition to imposing a double standard on women, also associates lighter-skinned people with the aristocracy and darker-skinned people with the labor force, regardless of whether that's the case. As a popular graffito in Managua exhorts, *"No hay democracia posible en una sociedad de clases."* (Democracy is not possible in a society of classes.)

Nicaraguans are permitted to form labor unions. Nearly half of the workforce, including much of the agricultural labor, is unionized. The trade unions receive much international support from labor groups overseas, who often step in on behalf of Nicaraguan laborers in disputes in the free-trade zones, most recently in a failed campaign against union firings of the Taiwanese Chentex corporation. Alemán's administration earned some bad press by preventing one group of union officials from the United States from entering the country.

POLITICAL PARTIES

It's easy to believe that the concept of the political party in Nicaragua is more for organizational convenience than for conviction of principles. Nicaraguan politicians change from one political party to another as necessary to suit their own ambitions. At the same time, smaller parties continually coalesce into alliances that later fracture into new arrangements. Infighting and division have been an integral part of the Nicaraguan political scene for well over a century, starting with the split between the Conservatives and Liberals in the 1800s that defined political disputes for a century. No other major political party came onto the scene until the FSLN took power in the 1980s. By 1990, no fewer than 20 political parties had risen in opposition to the FSLN; Doña Violeta's UNO coalition was formed from 14 of them.

By 1996, the number of parties swelled to 35, all of which participated in the elections on their own or as one of five coalitions. In 2000, new legislation was enacted to prohibit such a free-for-all at the polls and to make entry more difficult for the smaller political parties. The requirements a political party had to meet to become eligible to run in elections were made prohibitively stringent, which prevented many political parties from participating in the national elections. Popular perception was that it was more of the same political maneuvering in an effort to exclude any newcomers from taking a piece of the government pie.

Three parties were represented in the presidential election of 2001: the FSLN; the PLC; the Partido Conservador Nicaragüense (PCN), the moderate-right representatives of the Conservative party; and the PLC-dominated

Alianza Liberal (Liberal Alliance), which ultimately won the election. At present, the Liberals and Conservatives have formed an alliance, and their respective strongmen, Eduardo Montealegre and Arnoldo Alemán are duking it out for its leadership. If the alliance holds, the balance of power may shift away from Ortega and the FSLN.

The Economy

Two successive governments have had to jumpstart the Nicaraguan economy from an essential standstill: the Sandinistas, who picked up the shattered remains upon ousting Tachito, and Doña Violeta, who had to recover from the war and a decade of socialism. Her administration made dramatic progress, reducing the foreign debt by more than half, slashing inflation from 13,500 percent to 12 percent, and privatizing several hundred state-run businesses. The new economy began to expand in 1994 and these days is growing at just over 4 percent, despite several major catastrophes, including Hurricane Mitch in 1998, which decimated agricultural production.

Nevertheless, Nicaragua remains the second poorest nation in the Western hemisphere with a per capital gross domestic product of $780 and its external debt ratio—nearly twice the gross national product—is a serious constraint to growth. Unemployment is a pervasive problem: More than half of the adult urban population scrapes by in the informal sector (selling water at the roadside, for example), and population growth is probably going to keep it that way. High demand for jobs means employers can essentially ignore the minimum-wage requirement, especially in the countryside, where agricultural laborers typically earn as little as $1 a day, insufficient for survival even by Nicaraguan standards. Nearly 600,000 people face severe malnutrition.

Nicaragua has an economy almost entirely based on agricultural export of primary material, though in recent years tourism and several nontraditional exports have gained in importance. Export earnings are $700 million and rising: Agricultural programs in 2000 and 2001 that helped increase Nicaragua's ability to export beef and milk give hope that exports will rise in the latter part of the decade. Traditional export products include coffee, beef, and sugar, followed by bananas, shellfish (especially lobster tails and shrimp), and tobacco. New nontraditional exports are on the rise as well, including sesame, onions, melons, and fruit.

The upward trajectory of Nicaragua's economy has slowed radically under President Ortega, and rolling blackouts left much of Nicaragua without energy in 2006 and 2007. This was the combined result of Hugo Chávez's failure to deliver the cheap petroleum he'd promised and ostracism by foreign energy suppliers. Ortega's long-term economic plans remain muddled.

DEBT, THE HIPC, AND FOREIGN AID

For years, Nicaragua has been one of the most highly indebted nations of the world. When Somoza fled the country, he took the capital reserves of the banks with him, leaving behind $1.6 billion of debt. The Sandinistas, through a combination of gross economic mismanagement, extensive borrowing (primarily from Eastern bloc nations), the U.S. economic embargo, and high defense expenditures augmented the national debt by a factor of 10, nearly half of which was in arrears. By 1994, Nicaragua had the highest ratio of debt to GDP in the world, a challenge every successive administration has had to deal with. Germany, Russia, and Mexico were the first nations to forgive Nicaraguan debt entirely.

Propitious to Nicaragua's future economic growth was its inclusion in the Highly Indebted Poor Countries (HIPC) debt relief initiative in 2000. Inclusion in the initiative means

Cattle ranching is an important part of the Nicaraguan economy.

Nicaragua will be exonerated from the majority of its international debt upon compliance with an International Monetary Fund (IMF) and World Bank program, but that program mandates several austerity measures, debt restructuring, and the opening of its economy to foreign markets. More hotly contested is the mandated privatization of public utilities, including the telephone system (privatized in 2002) and municipal water distribution. City water systems have not yet been privatized and the issue is extremely controversial with those who consider water a human right rather than a commodity. Central to the HIPC initiative is Nicaragua's continued effort toward macroeconomic adjustment and structural and social policy reforms, particularly basic health and education.

AGRICULTURE

Nicaragua is, above all, an agricultural nation—a third of its gross domestic product is agriculture-based, and agriculture represents the fastest growing economic sector, at 8 percent growth per year. However, much of the new land put into agricultural production is opened at the expense of the forests, the indiscriminate harvesting of which has a negative overall effect on the environment and water supply. Agriculture employs 45 percent of the workforce. Outside of the small, upscale producers who export to international markets, the majority of Nicaraguan agriculture is for domestic consumption, and much of that is subsistence farming. Drought years often require importing of basic grains.

Subsistence farmers typically grow yellow corn and red beans. The choice of red beans over black beans and yellow corn over white corn is cultural and presents additional challenges to farmers, as red beans are more susceptible to drought (and less nutritious) than black or soybeans.

The Sébaco Valley is an agriculturally productive area and the primary source of wet rice for local consumption; it's also widely planted with onions. Extensive irrigation of rice plantations caused the water table in the Sébaco Valley to drop more than three meters in the

1990s. Jinotega's cool climate is a major source of fruit and vegetable production, including cabbage, peppers, onions, melons, watermelons, squash, and tomatoes.

THE COFFEE ECONOMY

There's no underestimating the importance of coffee to the Nicaraguan economy. Coffee is produced on more than 100,000 hectares of Nicaraguan land, contributes an average of $140 million per year to the economy, includes more than 30,000 farms, and employs more than 200,000 people, about 10–20 percent of the agricultural workforce. Nicaragua exports its beans primarily to North America, Europe, and Japan—to the tune of 1 million 100-pound burlap sacks every year. These beans are roasted and ground (usually abroad) to produce 11 billion pounds of java.

Because most Nicaragua growers produce full-bodied Arabica beans under the shade of diverse trees at altitudes of 900 meters and higher, the quality of its crop is recognized the world over. The June 2004 issue of *Smithsonian* magazine reported Nicaragua as "the 'hot origin' for gourmet coffee, with its beans winning taste awards and its decent wages for many small farmers a hopeful beacon for a global coffee market under siege." It also declared Nicaragua a country where "the goals of a better cup of joe, social justice and a healthier environment are nowhere more tightly entwined." This is important as Nicaragua struggles to emerge from the worst crash in the global coffee economy in a century.

The Coffee Crisis

Producing and selling Nicaraguan coffee, challenging even in good times, was dealt a staggering blow in 1999, when low-quality Vietnamese and Brazilian Robusta beans drove world prices to their lowest rates in 30 years (discounting for inflation, they were the lowest prices in a century). This was compounded by corporate consolidation in the trading and roasting industries, which dealt coffee farmers a blow while well-off overseas consumers were spared the extra costs. With market prices well below the costs of production, the effect on rural Nicaraguan coffee workers has been devastating.

Conditions bottomed out when hacienda owners could no longer afford to even feed their workers, let alone pay them wages, and thousands of families (called *plantónes*) migrated to the cities, marched and camped along the highways, and demanded assistance from the government, including land, food, education, and temporary work. With the help of the cooperatives and some of the hacienda owners, the farmworkers union finally negotiated most of their demands and now more than 2,000 families are getting the title to their own land. The next step will be to see, if the crisis continues, whether they will be able to keep their small allotments in the face of neo-liberal national governmental policies.

The Future of Coffee

Discerning North American and European java swillers have created an enormous demand for a superior cup of coffee—and they are willing to pay extra for it, as we all well know. If the Nicaraguan coffee industry is to continue to gain ground, it must maintain its reputation for quality coffee. This requires a government-level effort to address environmental issues, like soil fertility and water contamination, the modernization of processing methods, and the resolution of severe microcredit and marketing issues. The industry will also need to pay higher prices for top-quality coffee, and even Fair Trade and organic coffee price premiums have failed to keep up with the costs of sustainable production. Addressing the coffee crisis may provide the framework for dealing with the social ills inherent in modern coffee production, such as the feudal system of ownership and labor that still exists at many of the larger hacienda-style plantations; on these farms, seasonal pickers and their families are paid the barest survival wages and are sucked into a never-ending debt cycle that keeps them desperate and working.

The future of sustainable coffee production, many agree, is in family-run cooperatives in

CAFTA: BOON OR BUGBEAR?

CAFTA, the Central American Free Trade Agreement, was ratified in 2005 and resembles the similar North American Free Trade Agreement. While the agreement generated much debate and more than a few anxious farmers, CAFTA's immediate economic provisions appear amenable to Nicaragua. The United States agreed to import a greater quantity of Nicaraguan goods — notably beef and sugar — while permitting Nicaragua to protect domestic farmers from most American foodstuffs. Quotas were raised for most Nicaraguan exports and they are scheduled to increase further over time, giving Nicaraguan farmers a better opportunity to export their crops. But Nicaragua's biggest win was for the textile industry, where Nicaragua negotiated the right to import cloth from Asia, assemble clothing, and sell it duty-free in the United States. Nicaragua was the only nation in Central America to receive this concession. Nicaraguan-produced clothing will be even more competitive after 2005, when China's right to do the same expires.

But you've got to give to receive, and not surprisingly, CAFTA comes with a sting. The United States earned the right to export yellow corn for chicken feed, as well as powdered milk. While Nicaraguan farmers produce white (not yellow) corn, they and the cattle ranchers are understandably anxious about the effect corn and milk imports will have on their livelihood.

Opponents of CAFTA bring up other concerns as well. For one, CAFTA promotes the Washington consensus export-economy model, where Nicaragua exports cash crops and imports basic foodstuffs. With little leverage in the marketplace, that increases Nicaragua's vulnerability to prices. The textile provisions will certainly promote job creation, but because the Nicaraguan government has taken few steps to protect its workers, women working in the Free Trade Zones are subject to abuse and are often not permitted to freely form unions. Finally, studies of CAFTA's predecessor, NAFTA, have failed to show a notable improvement in the lives of the Mexicans it claims to affect. Whether CAFTA will be any more beneficial to the Nicaraguans will largely depend on whether the big shots in Managua are willing to protect their people, and history has shown they are not.

---

which small-scale farmers, rather than a single, rich hacienda owner, possess the power to control their product. At present, nearly 20 percent of Nicaraguan coffee is grown by 8,000 small-scale *campesino* producers working as members of nine cooperatives in the country's northlands (that's an increase of 10 percent and 2,000 farms since our last edition). As much as 80 percent of their coffee can be marketed as specialty coffee for the specialty, Fair Trade, and organic markets, making these growers less vulnerable to the extreme price oscillations of conventional coffee.

Nicaragua has a number of other advantages over other similarly struggling coffee-producing nations in the region. First of all, nearly 95 percent of Nicaraguan coffee is grown under a forest canopy that provides shade for coffee bushes and, at the same time, habitat for migratory birds. This can earn a grower a "Bird Friendly" sticker, which, like organic certification (not using chemicals and properly disposing of waste products), gains a significantly higher market price.

Coffee families and their communities also benefit enormously from the Fair Trade certification program (www.transfairusa.org), in which participating companies must comply with strict economic, social, and environmental criteria, guaranteeing producers a fair price. The small-scale farmers who represent most of the certified-organic producers and those linked to Fair Trade markets recently organized to represent their interests at the national and international level by forming an association of small-scale coffee farming co-ops called Cafenica.

Finally, a number of coffee growers,

© JOSHUA BERMAN

Tourism to Nicaragua (especially Granada and San Juan del Sur) has taken off only in the last few years.

especially those who own their own land, have diversified their income with various non-coffee crops and activities, including several awesome ecotourism projects. For information on visiting one of the small-scale coffee cooperative families, please see the *Matagalpa and Jinotega Highlands* chapter.

INDUSTRY

Industrial production in Nicaragua reached its zenith in 1978 under Anastasio Somoza, who encouraged industrial expansion in Managua at the expense of the environment, especially Lake Xolotlán. Investment policies of the time exonerated industries from the need to worry about environmental protection. Industry—even agro-industry—has been underdeveloped in the years following the revolution. There is a small amount of production for domestic and regional markets, including cement processing, petroleum refining, and some production of plastic goods. Another aspect of Nicaragua's export industry is the steadily increasing number of Zonas Francas (free trade zones) near

Managua, Sebaco, Masaya, and Granada, where tens of thousands of Nicaraguans are employed in foreign-owned sweatshops.

TOURISM

The so-called "industry without smokestacks" is widely hoped to be a panacea to Nicaragua's economic ills. The govermnet agency in charge of tourism development and marketing is El Instituto Nicaragüense de Turismo, better known as **INTUR** (www.intur.gob.ni). At present, tourism represents the third largest source of foreign exchange. Public Law 306 provides a 10-year tax break to newly constructed tourist facilities that meet certain criteria. More beneficial still are travelers like you, who spend a little money and hopefully take home a good impression of Nicaragua. Since the mid-1990s, investment in tourism has skyrocketed, notably in Managua, Granada, and San Juan del Sur. The total number of visitors to Nicaragua has increased from under 600,000 visitors in 2001 to more than 800,000 in 2005, the majority arriving from Central and South

FREE TRADE AND THE *MAQUILAS*

Free trade zones *(zonas francas)* – areas that assemble manufactured goods (usually clothing) for duty-free export – have multiplied like rabbits since the Alemán administration and currently employ somewhere between 50,000 and 70,000 Nicaraguan workers, mostly women. Free trade zones don't generate any tax revenue for the government but provide jobs for a nation that desperately needs them. That desperation has not been overlooked by those who do business there.

Apparel magazine reports that Nicaragua's "disciplined and low-cost work force" make it the newest regional competitor in the free-trade factory frenzy, as evidenced by the Korean, Taiwanese, and North American garment companies raising scores of assembly warehouses in Tipitapa, Sébaco, Ciudad Sandino, and Masaya (the largest free trade zone, Las Mercedes, abuts the airport in Managua and is clearly visible from your plane). These firms scour the globe for the absolute cheapest production sites, and Nicaragua is a prime option. At last count, there were 60 such assembly plants in the aforementioned areas, producing goods for well-known brands like Target, J.C. Penney, Talbots, Polo Ralph Lauren, Levi Strauss & Co., Gap, Wal-Mart, Kohl's, Kmart, and Mervyns.

Proponents of this industry argue that in a nation with nearly 70 percent unemployment, *maquila* jobs are better than nothing, regardless of the pay or conditions. But labor activists, human rights monitors, and other critics counter that the mere creation of jobs is unjustifiable if it comes at the cost of conditions that deprive workers of dignity, respect, and basic human rights, like the right to assemble or organize. Someone is making lots of money in these free trade zones (exports grew from $2.9 million in 1992 to $400 million in 2003 at a rate only surpassed by Costa Rica) but it's not the workers: They are paid in continuously-devaluing *córdobas* at a fixed rate that makes their pay worth less every month, halving their monthly earnings over the aforementioned period of export growth.

Critics of free trade zones call it a global "race to the bottom," in which international companies flock to the nations where they can

---

America. Most foreign visitors come from North America and Europe. In 2007, nearly half a million people arrived by international flight to Nicaragua.

Ecotourism

The word ecotourism was created in the 1980s with the best of intentions. The idea is to prevent tourism from spoiling the environment, or to use it to provide an alternative to spoiling the environment. The success of the concept and its marketing value led to a worldwide boom in the usage of that prefix that we know so well, even when its actual practice has sometimes fallen short of original intentions. Indeed, the warm and fuzzy "eco" has been used, abused, prostituted, and bastardized all over the world, and Nicaragua is no exception. Alternative tourism goes by many other names as well: "sustainable," "responsible,"

"ethical," "rural," or "fair trade" tourism, to name a few.

The concept of protected areas and national parks is relatively new in Nicaragua and is, in some places, viewed with skepticism—especially by poor *campesinos* who live near (or sometimes within) these areas and have always used the forests to supplement their paltry incomes. They need wood for fuel, land for farmland, and game for protein. MARENA, the government ministry charged with protecting Nicaragua's vast system of parks and refuges, has scant resources to prevent such activities. If money comes from nature-loving visitors, an alternative use for the forest has been created. Foreigners come to see the local waterfall or coffee cooperative and need to eat breakfast, hire a guide, rent a horse, and witness how people in this particular corner of the continent live. We've both pay the least and encourage governments like Nicaragua's to overlook fundamental labor rights, i.e. paying a living wage and paying it on time, compensating for overtime, and allowing the workers to form unions. Every one of these abuses has occurred in the *zona francas;* some have been addressed, many have been ignored, and, on more than one occasion, the company has closed its doors and relocated to other nations even more desperate for foreign investment.

Nicaragua's sweatshops pay by the piece, not by the hour, and enforce minimum-piece counts before a worker earns her first *córdoba.* A favorite subterfuge is to raise the minimum whenever it seems the workers are attaining it. *Maquila* workers thus work long (usually 10-hour) shifts and endure frequent verbal, physical, and sexual abuse from factory supervisors who, among other things, strip-search them on the way out (to "prevent theft") and monitor bathroom breaks. Workplace injuries are ignored, and attempts to form unions are met with mass firings, trumped-up criminal charges, and use of riot police. The Nicara-

guan government has made no effort to protect workers and does not intervene in these cases, fearing mass unemployment would be worse than mistreated workers. Indeed, the Nicaraguan workforce was abused long before the days of foreign investment.

The alternative? One idea is the **Fair Trade Zone,** like that formed by a group of unemployed women in Ciudad Sandino called the **Nueva Vida Womens Sewing Cooperative** (tel. 505/269-7073, jhc@jhc-cdca.org, www .fairtradezone.jhc-cdca.org). As owners of their factory, workers at Nueva Vida decide what hours they work, what salaries they are paid, what their labor policies are, and how they share their business's profits amongst themselves. Contact them directly to place an order for your company or organization, or support them by shopping at Michigan-based **Maggie's Functional Organics** (U.S. tel. 800/609-8593, www.maggiesorganics.com). To learn more about the labor rights movement, check in with Campaign for Labor Rights (www.campaignforlaborrights.org) or Global Exchange (www.globalexchange.org).

pointed out community-sponsored tourism efforts wherever we found them, namely in Granada, Isla de Ometepe, Matagalpa, and the Miraflor region of Estelí. Here, existing cooperatives have arranged homestay opportunities that involve volunteer work, Spanish language class, alternative agriculture, and trips to local sites.

The People

POPULATION

Nicaragua's population is fast approaching six million, about a full third of whom live in Managua. Nicaragua is both the least populous Central American nation and the fastest growing, at just over 3 percent annually. At this rate, the country's strained resources will have to support between 9 and 12 million people by the year 2030. In addition, well over a million Nicaraguans live outside of the country, particularly in Costa Rica (679,000) and the United States (500,000), not to mention thousands more living in Mexico and other Central American nations.

ETHNIC GROUPS

While Nicaraguans can trace their ancestry back to many sources, most of the population is a blend of Spanish, Native American, and sometimes other European stock. Indigenous blood runs most strongly in the northeast, where the Spanish had less influence, and on the mid-Atlantic coast, where English and African influences were dominant.

In the Pacific region, the indigenous population thinned from 800,000 when the Spanish arrived to less than 60,000 after a couple centuries of conquistador policy (i.e., war, slavery, genocide, and diseases). The native peoples of the northeast, including Matagalpa and Jinotega, were less affected, and thus retain larger indigenous populations today.

Mestizos

The term *mestizo* refers to any mixture of Spanish and indigenous blood and describes the majority of Nicaraguan citizens, whose Spanish colonial ancestors began intermingling with the locals about as soon as they got off the boat. A second wave of *mestizaje* (mixing) occurred from the 1860s through the 1890s, during the wave of rubber and banana production along the Atlantic coast, and again in the 1950s as Pacific farmers moved eastward in search of new agricultural lands at the expense of the Sumu-Ulúa and Miskito peoples. Note: Mestizo Nicaraguans sometimes use the term "Indio" as a derogatory label for anyone with Native American features (high cheekbones, straight black hair, short eyelashes, and dark brown skin).

Creoles

After decimating the indigenous peoples of the New World, the Spanish realized they lacked laborers; so they imported African slaves to their colonies in the Americas. Beginning in 1562, English slave traders, and later Dutch, Spanish, and others, supplied the colonies with human cargo. Along the Atlantic coast of Nicaragua, African slaves intermingled with Miskitos, giving birth to the Zambo (or Sambo) people. They also bred with the Spanish and English, forming the Creoles, primarily found today in Bluefields and San Juan del Norte. Creoles speak a form of English that still bears traces of 19th-century Queen's English, as well as Caribbean and Spanish traits. Their culture includes distinct African

elements, including the belief in a form of African witchcraft called *obeah* or *sontín,* the latter a corruption of the English "something," or "something special."

Miskitos

Modern-day Miskitos are really a mixture of several races, and include traces of English and African blood. The Native American Bawihka people, whose territory extended from the Río Coco (Wangki) at Cabo Gracias a Dios south to Prinzapolka, mixed with the African-slave refugees of a Portuguese ship that wrecked on the Miskito Cays in 1642. They later mixed with the English during their long occupation of the Atlantic coast. Over the centuries, the word "Miskito" has been written many other ways, including "Mosquito," "Mosca," "Mískitu," and others. The name derives not from the insect but from the Spanish word *mosquete* (musket), a firearm the British provided to the locals to ensure a tactical advantage over their neighbors.

The Miskitos' warlike nature and superior firepower helped them subdue twenty other Native American tribes along the Atlantic coast of Central America. They were valuable allies to the English, who used them in raids against inland Spanish settlements, and crowned their "kings" in an Anglican church in Belize City. The Miskitos also absorbed the Prinsu tribe (located along the Bambana and Prinzapolka Rivers) and the Kukra tribe.

Today the Miskitos inhabit much of the Atlantic coast of Nicaragua, from Bluefields northward and all along the Río Coco, which they consider their spiritual home. There are additional Miskito settlements on both Corn Islands, but their two principal centers are Bilwi (Puerto Cabezas) and Waspám. Their language, Miskito, is the old indigenous Tawira language enriched with English and African vocabulary.

The Kukra

The Kukra people were assimilated by the Miskitos over the last two centuries and no longer exist as a tribe. Of unknown but reportedly

CORN CULTURE

The planting cycle of *maíz* (corn) has governed the life of Nicaraguans and their Mesoamerican descendants ever since the first yellow kernels were laid in the dark volcanic soil. *Maíz* is as central to the Nicaraguan diet as white rice is to the people of Southeast Asia. Beans are just as critical a staple (and a nutritionally critical complement), but in Nicaragua, corn is prepared with more variety, taste, and frequency.

Corn is prepared and consumed in more than a hundred different ways: hot, cold, cooked, ground, and liquefied, in both food and in beverages. Tortillas are, of course, flat cakes of corn dough softened with water and cooked on a slightly rounded clay pan known as a *comal*. The only place you'll find a flour tortilla is in a Mexican restaurant in Managua; Nica corn tortillas are thick, heavy, and (hopefully) hot off the woodstove and slightly toasted. When the same dough is fortified with sugar and lard, then rolled into small lumps and boiled while wrapped in yellow corn husks, the result is a *tamal*, steaming heavy bowls of which market women balance on their heads and loudly vend in the streets. *Nacatamales*, a Nicaraguan classic, are similar but with meat – often spiced pork – in the middle. *Atol* is corn pudding, and *güiríla* is a sweet tortilla of young

corn, always served with a hunk of *cuajada* (salty white cheese).

Elote is corn on the cob, especially tasty when roasted directly over open coals until the kernels are dry, hot, and a little chewy. When harvested young, the ears of corn are called *chilotes* and are served in soup or with fresh cream. Corn is also oven-baked into hard, molasses-sweetened cookie rings called *rosquillas*, flat cookies called *ojaldras*, and many other shapes. The same dough is also combined with cheese, lard, and spices to produce dozens more items, including *perrerreques*, *cosas de horno*, and *gofios*.

What do you wash it down with? More corn, of course. *Pinol*, drunk so frequently in Nicaragua Nicaraguans proudly call themselves *pinoleros*, is toasted and ground corn meal mixed with water. *Pinolillo* is *pinol* mixed with cacao, pepper, and cloves; *tiste* is similar. *Pozol* is a ground cornmeal drink prepared from a variety of corn with a pinkish hue. The ultrasweet, pink baggies of *chicha* are made from slightly fermented cornmeal (especially strong batches are called *chicha brava*). Then, of course, there is crystal clear, Nicaraguan corn tequila, or *la cususa*.

Corn: It's what's for breakfast, lunch, and dinner.

---

cannibalistic Caribbean origin, they once inhabited Bluefields, the Corn Islands, and the area around Pearl Lagoon. Today, the only trace of them is the name of the small Pearl Lagoon community of Kukra Hill.

The Garífuna

The Garífuna, as a distinct culture, are relative newcomers to the world. Their history began on the Lesser Antillean island of San Vicente (Saint Vincent), which in the 1700s had become a refuge for escaped slaves from the sugar plantations of the Caribbean, including Jamaica. These displaced Africans were accepted by the native Carib (Arawak) islanders, with whom they freely intermingled.

As the French and English settled the island, the Garífunas (as they had become known), established a worldwide reputation as expert canoe navigators and fierce warriors, resisting the newcomers. The English finally got the upper hand in the conflict after tricking and killing the Garífuna leader, and in 1797 they forcefully evacuated the Garífunas from San Vicente to the Honduran Bay Island of Roatán. From there, many of the Garífunas migrated to the mainland communities of Trujillo, Honduras and Dangriga, Belize. Today, they exist up and down most of the Central American Caribbean coast, with a small but distinct presence in Nicaragua, primarily around Pearl Lagoon. Orinoco (originally Urunugu) is the largest settlement of Garífunas in Nicaragua, established in 1912 by the Garífuna John Sambola. The communities of San Vicente and Justo Point are both Garífuna as well. During the 1980s, the Contra war forced many Garífunas out of their communities and into Bluefields, Puerto Limón (Costa Rica), and Honduras.

The Mayangna

"Sumu," is a derogatory word the Miskito used for all other peoples of Ulúa descent (it means stupid; conversely, the Mayangna name for the Miskito was *wayas,* which means "stinky"). The Mayangna, as they prefer to be called, are a combination of several Ulúa tribes, including the Twahka, Panamka, and Ulwa, who once settled the Kurinwas, Siquia, Mico, Rama, and Grande Rivers of the Atlantic coast. Mayangna tradition has it that in the 9th and 10th centuries they were the inhabitants of a territory that extended from the Atlantic coast and Río Coco to the Pacific, but they were forced off the Atlantic coastal lands by the more aggressive and warring Miskito and out of the Pacific by the Nahuatls, Maribios, and Chorotegas. The Mayangna are now centered around the mining triangle and the massive forest reserve of Bosawás.

The Rama

The Rama are the least numerous indigenous people in Nicaragua, numbering only several hundred. Their language is distinct from Miskito and Mayangna and is closely related to the ancient tribal languages of Native American tribes of Panamá and Colombia. Today, only several dozen people can still speak Rama and anthropologists are scrambling to document what they can of the language before it disappears entirely. The Rama people inhabit the pleasant bay island of Rama Cay in the Bay of Bluefields, where they fish and collect oysters. They also grow grains and traditional crops on small plots of land on the mainland of Bluefields Bay and along the Kukra River. The Rama people are reserved and keep mostly to their traditional ways, even using traditional tools and implements. They are excellent navigators and fishermen.

Culture, Conduct, and Customs

Nicaraguans are generally open, talkative, and hospitable. In most areas of the country, Nicaraguans are accustomed to seeing foreigners, but they are still curious—and not very discreet about it. Expect blunt questions right off the bat about your age, marital status, and your opinions about Nicaragua. The reaction is nearly always one of curiosity, hospitality, and friendliness.

Despite their directness, Nicaraguans are prone to circuitous, indirect behavior associated with the cultural concept of "saving face." When asked something they don't know, people often invent an answer so that neither party is embarrassed (this is especially true about directions and distances; as Allan Weisbecker observed, "no one, *no one,* south of the Mexican border has any idea how long it takes to go from anywhere to anywhere else"). Business contracts are rife with implied obligations neither party wants to discuss openly, even simple payment details and the work to be done.

Many Nicaraguan city dwellers are, in fact, recently immigrated *campesinos,* and they often bring their country ways—and livestock—with them to the city.

Anti-Americanism, in our experience, is rare, Nicaraguans being particularly adept at distinguishing between a nation's people and its government's policy. In addition, because most Nicaraguan families adore cable TV and have at least one relative sending money back from Miami, Houston, or Los Angeles, many are quite fond of the United States and maintain the dream of traveling there one day. The word "gringo" is used more often as a descriptive, casual term for anyone who comes from north of the Mexican border. In rare cases, it is meant as an insult (in which case, it will likely be preceeded by *"pinche"*). Likewise for *chele, chela,* and their diminutives, *chelito* and *chelita,* all of which simply mean pale or light-skinned, and are in no way disrespectful. In fact, many cries of, *"Oye, chele!"* ("Hey, whitey!") are used as much for light-skinned Nicaraguans as for foreigners.

FAMILY

The Nicaraguan family is the most basic and strongest support structure of society, and, like in most Developing World nations, it is usually large—rural women have an average of 4–6 children, and families of a dozen or more aren't uncommon. Urban couples, particularly in Managua, typically have no more than three or four children. In addition, extended families—cousins, in-laws, aunts, and uncles—are all kept in close contact and relied upon during hard times (which, for many, is their whole lives). Families live close together, often in small quarters, and the North American and European concepts of independence and solitude are not well understood.

Nicaraguans' traditional dependence on large family structures mandates that they take care of stragglers. If, for example, you were stranded in a strange country town in the pouring rain, it would not be strange or uncommon for someone to invite you into their home for coffee—or a bed.

CLOTHING AND NEATNESS

Nicaraguans place a great deal of importance on cleanliness. Even the poorest *campesino* with the threadbare and patched clothing takes great care to tuck his shirt in and keep his clothes clean and wrinkle-free. Managuans are just as conscientious about looking good and smelling clean. Nicaraguans only wear shorts for playing sports or lounging around the house. Nicaraguan women dress the spectrum from long, conservative dresses to bright, tight, and revealing outfits.

Unshaven *internationalistas* wearing stained shorts, ripped T-shirts, and natty dreads stand out like sore, malodorous thumbs, even without their trademark bulky backpacks. If you plan on being taken seriously in any kind of day-to-day business activities, a little effort into your wardrobe and hygiene will go a long way…and will help do away with the question, "Is it true that people in your country don't bathe because it's too cold?" If, however, you prefer to remain true to your filth, seek out the bohemian population of tattooed Managuans who take well to carefully unkempt foreigners with Che T-shirts and creative facial hair.

CONCEPT OF TIME

Hay más tiempo que vida. (There is more time than life.) So why hurry? The day-to-day approach to living life in Nicaragua may come from the necessity of survival, or it may just be an effect of the hot sun. Probably both. Nicaraguan life, in general, goes according to La Hora Nica (Nica Time), which means a meeting scheduled in Managua for 2:30 P.M.

© ROMAN YAVICH

Villagers in the greased-pole competition in a *fiesta patronales,* or Saint's Day party.

OLD WIVES' TALES: NICARAGUAN *CREENCIAS*

Like any society with a tradition of rural folk culture, Nicaraguans have hundreds of unique beliefs, or *creencias*, which explain mysteries, offer advice, and dictate practices that prevent or cure common health ailments. In general, most behaviors are associated with causing harm to oneself, and Nicaraguan mothers can be heard admonishing their children, *"¡Te va a hacer daño!"* ("It will cause you harm!").

Nicaraguans are sensitive to subtle differences in temperature, and many of the *creencias* involve avoiding hot things when you are cold, or vice versa. Conventional wisdom dictates that intense bodily harm can come from drinking a cold beverage after eating something hot, bathing in the evening after a hot day in the sun (or bathing with a fever), and ironing with wet hair. If you come in from the fields on a hot day and you're sweaty, drinking a cold glass of fruit juice or water can make you sick, especially your kidneys. Better is a cup of hot coffee. If you want to walk outside at night after drinking coffee, however, you should protect yourself by draping a cloth over the top of your head, being careful to cover the ears. Dietary rules tie into the same theme and other worries as well: no fish, eggs, or beans while menstruating, no citrus when sick, and no fish soup when *agitado* (worked up or sweaty).

The belief in the *mal de ojo* (evil eye) is not unique to Nicaragua, although the local version states that a drunkard who looks directly into an infant's eye can kill the child or make it evil. A person well versed in the art of applying the evil eye can cause birth defects in newborn babies, stroke, paralysis among the living, and other woes like the loss of a job or bad luck. You'll frequently see children wearing a red bracelet with two small gray beads – this is to protect the child from *mal de ojo*. Similarly, if a sweaty man looks at a baby, the only cure is to wrap the baby up in the man's sweaty clothes. To guard against the risk, many babies are kept well covered when out of the house. Allowing dew to fall on a baby's brow will stunt its growth (look for women holding umbrellas over their children on a clear night), and letting a baby look in a mirror will cause his or her eyes to cross permanently.

If you have trouble with bats, you can keep them away by hanging a red cloth from the rafters. To keep flies off your food, suspend a bag of water over the table. To avoid family fights, don't cook with a knife in the pan.

Some Nica *creencias* coincide with North American and European practices even if the reasoning is different. For example, Nicaraguans recommend you don't walk around barefoot, but not because you run the risk of contracting ringworm; rather, walking barefoot, they claim, is an unhealthy temperature combination (hot feet on cold floor). Foreigners tempted to make fun of the "crazy" Nicaraguan beliefs will do well to remember our own societies' *creencias*. Whether scientifically grounded or not, Nicaraguan beliefs are popular because they have been passed from generation to generation, and should be given proper regard.

might not start until 3 P.M., or an hour later in the countryside. Foreign travelers accustomed to La Hora Gringa, in which everything starts and stops exactly when planned, will spend their days in Nicaragua endlessly frustrated (and consistently early for meetings). Appointments and meetings are loose, and excuses are easy to come by and universally accepted. Gradually, as you experience Nicaragua, this concept of time will win you over; just be careful when you go home.

ALCOHOL
Rum

It goes largely undisputed that Nicaragua makes the best rum in all of Central America. Period. Flor de Caña is the highest caliber, of which the caramel-colored, seven-year-old Gran Reserva is only surpassed by the 12-year Centenario (which is twice as expensive). Flor de Caña produces a half-dozen varieties of rum, which increase in price and quality as they age. A *media* (half-liter) of seven-year, bucket of ice,

© JOSHUA BERMAN

Flor de Caña is Central America's best rum.

bottle of Coke, and plate of limes (called a *servicio completo*) will set you back only $5 or so. Rum on the rocks with a squirt of Coca-Cola and a spurt of lime is called a Nica Libre.

Reach for a clear plastic bottle of Caballito or Ron Plata, and take a giant step down in price, quality, and class. Enormously popular in the *campo*, "Rrrrron Plata!" is the proud sponsor of most baseball games—and not a few bar brawls. Bottles are $1 or less.

But wait—you can get drunk for even less! Most street corners and town parks are the backdrop for many a grimacing shot of Tayacán, or its homemade, corn-mash equivalent, often served in clear plastic baggies. West Virginians call this stuff "that good 'ole mountain dew"; Nicaraguans call it *la cususa, el guaro,* or *la lija,* brought down from the hills by the moonshine man on his mule. *La cususa* is gasoline-clear, potent in smell (including when you sweat it out the next day), and will bore a hole through your liver quicker than a 9-millimeter. It's sold by the gallon for about $4, often in a stained,

sloshing, plastic container that used to contain some automobile product, and then resold in baggie-size portions that look like they should have a goldfish swimming in them.

Beer

The national beers—Victoria and Toña—are both light-tasting pilsners and, well, you can't really say anything bad about an ice-cold beer in the tropics. Expect to pay anywhere from $0.80 to $2 a beer, depending on your environs. Recent additions to the beer selection are Premium, Bufalo, and Brahva, largely indistinguishable. Brahva is the only alcoholic beverage whose production or distribution isn't controlled by the Pellas family, which produces every other beverage mentioned in this book. Together, Victoria, Toña, and Flor de Caña are known affectionately as "Vickie, Toni, and Flo."

Alcoholism

Alcohol abuse is rampant in Nicaragua and increasingly acknowledged as a problem. Most towns have an Alcoholics Anonymous chapter, and many churches forbid their members to drink. Nevertheless, most otherwise religious holidays (including Sundays)—in addition to all nonreligious events—serve as excuses to get falling-down drunk. Just about all men drink and are firm believers in the expression *"una es ninguna"* ("one is none"). Their benders often start before breakfast and end when the liquor does. In small towns, women are socially discouraged from drinking, though they sometimes do so in the privacy of their own homes or with close friends. Bigger towns and cities, of course, are more modern in this regard.

Should you decide to partake in this part of the culture and find yourself drunk *(borracho, bolo, picado, hasta el culo)*, be sure you have a decent understanding of your environment and feel good about your company. Remember that most travelers' disaster stories begin with "Man, I was so wasted . . ." Always take it slow when drinking in a new place, and remember that your hydration level has an enormous impact on how drunk you get.

PAINTED ROOSTER:
A GUIDE TO NICARAGUAN DINING

Desayuno	**Breakfast**
Huevos	Eggs
Enteros, Revueltos, Volteados	Hardboiled, scrambled, over-easy

Almuerzo y Cena	**Lunch and Dinner**
Carne/res	Beef
Desmenuzada	Shredded and stewed
A la plancha	Served on a hot plate
Churrasco	Grilled steak
Filete jalapeño	Steak in a creamy pepper sauce
Puerco/cerdo	Pork
Chuleta	Porkchop
Pollo	Chicken
Empanizado	Breaded
Frito	Fried
Al vino	Wine sauce
Rostizado	Rotisserie
Valenciano	A chicken and rice dish
Mariscos	Seafood
Pescado entero	The whole fish
Langosta al ajillo	Lobster in garlic sauce
Camarones al vapor	Steamed shrimp
Sopa de conchas	Conch soup
Huevos de Paslama	Endangered turtle eggs

Platos Tradicionales	**Traditional Dishes**
Baho	Plantain and beef stew
Nacatamales	Meat-filled corn tamal, wrapped and boiled in banana leaves
Indio viejo	Beef, veggie, and cornmeal mush
Caballo bayo	A sampler's plate of traditional dishes
Gallo pinto	Red beans and rice, generously doused in oil and salt
Cuajada	White, farmer's cheese
Leche agria	A sour cream-yogurt combo
Vigorón	Pork rinds with yucca and coleslaw, served on a banana leaf

Bocadillas	**Appetizers**
Tostones	Thick, fried, green plantain chips
Tajadas	Crunchy, thin strips of green plantain
Maduro	Ripe, sweet plantains fried in their own sugar
Ensalada	Shredded cabbage, tomatoes, and a dash of lime
Tortilla	Heavy, floppy discs of toasted white corn

daily special: plantains, cheese, roast pork, boiled yucca, and *gallo pinto*

Bebidas y (Re)Frescos	Drinks and Fruit Juices
Tiste	Toasted cooked corn with cacao, pepper, and cloves
Pinol	Toasted, milled corn
Pinolillo	Pinol with pepper, cloves, and cacao
Horchata	Toasted and milled rice with spices
Chicha	Rough-milled corn with vanilla and banana flavors, sometimes fermented

Postres	Desserts
Flan	Flan
Sorbete	Sherbet
Helado	Ice cream

There are dozens of stately Catholic cathedrals throughout Pacific Nicaragua.

And oh, by the way, rum does *not* make you a better dancer, but it may improve your Spanish.

RELIGION

Officially, the Republic of Nicaragua endorses no religion. In practice, the overwhelming majority of Nicaraguans call themselves Catholic, with over a hundred evangelical Protestant sects comprising about 9–15 percent and increasing annually. Beginning in the early 1970s and continuing through the revolution, Nicaragua created its own version of liberation theology, a school of Christianity and bourgeois thought that equated Jesus's teachings with Marxism. The degree to which biblical parables were equated to the Marxist struggle varied, and the most radical versions placed Sandino as Jesus or Moses, Somoza as the Pharaoh, and the Nicaraguan masses as the Israelites searching for their promised land through revolutionary struggle.

A tiny percentage of Nicaraguans are descendents of one of the several Jewish families that found refuge here during World War II. Some of them still identify themselves as Jewish, but there is no real practicing community. The only synagogue was dismantled and sold in 1980. A Torah did not return to Nicaragua until 2008. Most Nicaraguans, especially in the countryside, have little concept of Judaism as a modern religion, relating the word *judío* only to the ancient race of *hebreos* they read about in the Old Testament.

LANGUAGE

Spanish is, according to the Nicaraguan constitution, the official language of the republic, though indigenous languages are respected and even used officially in certain areas of the Atlantic coast. Ninety-six percent of Nicaraguans speak Spanish as their first language, 3 percent speak indigenous languages (Miskito, Mayangna and Rama), and 1 percent speak languages of African origin (Criollo and Garífuna). To hear pure Miskito, travel north from Bluefields or visit Puerto Cabezas or any village along the Río Coco; in

A FEW *NICARAGUANISMOS*

The textbook Spanish you learned back home will be understood without trouble, but Nicaraguans take pride in the fact that their version of the old-country Castilian is decidedly unique. When you try to look up some of the new words you're hearing and realize they're not in the dictionary, you'll see what we mean.

Blame it on *campesino* creativity and the Nicas' propensity for inventing words they need; blame the centuries of educational starvation, during which language evolved on its own; blame the linguistic mishmash of pre-Columbian Central America and the words left behind. Or just get out your pencil and paper and try to write down some of the unique vocabulary and phrases you hear, because you won't hear it anywhere else. Nicaraguan Spanish uses some old, proper Spanish no longer used in the Old World, and has assimilated pre-Columbian words from Nahuatl and Chorotega tongues as well (especially local plant and animal names). Still other words are pure onomatopoeia. Those interested in pursuing the topic should seek out Joaquim Rabella and Chantal Pallais's *Vocabulario Popular Nicaragüense*, available in some bookstores in Managua. Here's an incomplete sampling (with the Castilian in parentheses when possible).

arrecho: extremely angry *(enfurecido)*
bochinche: a fistfight among several people
boludo: lazy, unmotivated *(haragán)*
bullaranga: loud noises, ruckus *(tumulto, alboroto)*
curutaca: diarrhea *(diarrea)*
cususa: country moonshine *(aguardiente)*

chapa: earring *(arete)*
chigüin: little kid *(bebé)*
chinela: sandal *(sandalia)*
chingaste: the granular residue of a drink like coffee *(poso, resíduo)*
chunche: any small, nameless object *(cosita)*
chusmón: mediocre
guaro: general term for booze or alcoholic beverages
hamaquear: to rock something rhythmically *(mecer rítmicamente)*
moclín: perverted old man
ñaña: excrement *(excremento)*
panzona: big bellied, implies pregnant *(embarazada)*
pinche: cheap *(tacaño)*
pipilacha: small airplane *(avioneta)*
salvaje: awesome; literally, "savage," fun response to *"¿Como estás?"*
timba: big belly *(barriga)*

EXCLAMATIONS

¡Chocho!: Holy cow! Dude!
¡A la puchica!: Wow!
¿Ideay? (eedee-EYE?): What was that all about? What do you mean?
Va pué: OK then; see you; I agree; or whatever (short for *va pués*)
Dalepué: OK, I agree, let's do that.
¡Qué barbaridad!: What a barbarity! How rude! What a shame!
¡Sí hombre!: Yeah man!
hijueputa: extremely common, from the vulgarity *hijo de puta* (son of a whore), pronounced hway-POO-tah and used liberally.
Tranquilo como Camilo: Chillin' like Dylan; fun response to *"¿Como estás?"*

---

some of these villages, Spanish is completely unknown.

Nicaraguan Spanish is probably unlike any Spanish you've ever come across. The chameleon-like ability of the Spanish language to adapt to new areas of the world is strong in Nicaragua, where it is spoken rapidly and liquidly, the words flowing smoothly together and eating each other's tails. Central

Americans enjoy making fun of how their Latin neighbors talk, and the Honduran nickname for Nicaraguans, *mucos* (bulls whose horns have been chopped off), is a reference to the Nicaraguans' habit of chopping the "s" off the ends of spoken words. Backcountry *campesino* Nicaraguan Spanish is inevitably less intelligible to the untrained ear than its urban counterpart, but it is also distinctly more melodic, with a cadence and rhythm distinct to the countryside and celebrated in many of Carlos Mejía Godoy's songs.

And then, of course, there are the vulgarities. Ernest Hemingway wrote, "There is no language so filthy as Spanish. There are words for all the vile words in English and there are other words and expressions that are used only in countries where blasphemy keeps pace with the austerity of religion."

In Nicaragua, even a simple fruit or vegetable name can cause a room to break out in wild laughter if said in the right tone and context (and if accompanied by the appropriate hand gesture). After you've learned a few dirty words, be careful—the degree to which most *vulgaridades* are considered offensive varies depending on the gender of your company, their age, your relationship with them, and a variety of other factors. Cussing can be a fun, complex, and subtle game if you have the patience to learn—*y los huevos. . . .*

Body Language

Limber up your wrist and stretch out those lips. You'll need 'em both if you want to communicate like a true native. Watch people interact on the buses, in the markets, and on the streets, and see if you can spot any of the following gestures in action—then try some out yourself.

Probably the single most practical gesture is a rapid side to side wagging of the index finger. It means "no," and increases in strength as you increase the intensity of the wagging and the amount of hand and arm you use in the motion. In some cases, a verbal "no" in the absence of the **Finger Wag** is disregarded as not serious enough. Use this one liberally with pushy vendors, beggars, and would-be Romeos.

To pull off the **Nicaraguan Wrist Snap,** simply join the tips of your thumb and middle finger and let your index finger dangle loosely. Then with a series of rapid wrist flicks, repeatedly let your index finger slap against the middle one, exactly as you would do with a round tin of tobacco dip. The resulting snapping noise

serves to either emphasize whatever it is you're saying, refer to how hard you've been working, or, when combined with a nod and a smile, infer something like, "Damn, that's good!"

You can ask, "What?" (or "What do you want?") with a quick **Cheek Scrunch,** occasionally performed with a subtle upward chin tilt. Use the **Lip Point** rather than your finger to indicate something by puckering up as if for a kiss and aiming where you want. Or, if you are listening to a friend's dumb story, point to the speaker with your lips while looking at everyone else to imply, "This guy's crazy or drunk."

The gesture North Americans would normally use to shoo something away—the outstretched, waving, down-turned hand—means just the opposite in Nicaragua, where the **Downward Wave** (occasionally combined with the whole arm for emphasis) means "Come here." This one is a favorite with drunks in the park who love to talk at foreigners for as long as they are tolerated. The North American "come here," i.e., the upturned and beckoning index finger, is a vulgar, possibly offensive gesture. Speaking of vulgar, a closed fist atop a rigid forearm indicates the male sex organ, and an upturned, slightly cupped hand with the fingertips pressed together into a point is its female counterpart. Here's one more for the road: Make a fist, lock your elbow into the side of your body, and move your hand up and down; combined with a dramatic grimace, the **Plunger Pump** tells the whole world you have diarrhea.

ETIQUETTE AND TERMS OF ADDRESS

Latin America is not homogenous across state borders when it comes to addressing each other: While Costa Ricans tend to gravitate toward the formal *usted* form of address among themselves, Nicaraguans prefer the friendly *vos* (second person) form with each other, although *tú* is widely understood. For travelers, it's best to use *Usted* until you've really gotten to know someone (or mastered the tricky *vos* form), particularly after a night out

typical Nicaraguan meal: *tostones, gallo pinto, cuajada,* and *frijoles*

or a long drinking session (you'll be surprised how quickly alcohol lubricates friendships at this latitude).

The term *don* for men and *doña* for women is a colonial term of respect usually related to aristocracy or landownership, but in Nicaragua it's far more commonly used than elsewhere in Latin America, and indicates a higher level of respect or affection, particularly for the elderly, the important, or the wealthy. Practitioners of certain careers sometimes drop their names entirely and go by their profession. That is, it's not uncommon to be presented to someone everyone calls simply *"la doctora," "el ingeniero,"* or *"la abogada."* Just go with it and smile.

It's customary to kiss women on the cheek when greeting, but women will provide the signal whether that's appropriate or not by turning their cheek toward you. Men will offer you their hands for a stiff handshake. When someone new enters the room, rise from your seat to greet them, and when you're ready to end a conversation or leave the room,

a friendly *"con permiso"* will pave the way to the door.

TABLE MANNERS

Dig in! Grab that fried chicken between two hands and gnaw at it, shovel down *vigorón* from its banana-leaf wrapper as best as you can without letting all the shaved cabbage and *chile* spill down your shirt. Chase it with long swigs of a cold drink. Nicaraguans enjoy good food and good times, and if you're too dainty, the signal is all too clear you're not pleased with the meal. There are limits, of course, so keep an eye on your dining companions for what's appropriate and what's not, but while you're picking away at your fried cheese and sweet plantains, the guy next to you has finished his meal, pulled his shirt up with one hand and is happily rubbing his belly with the other. Don't be afraid to enjoy what's on your plate. If you'd like to get a laugh out of your Nicaraguan hosts or waiters, after you've finished your plate, tell them, *"Barriga llena, corazón contenta"* (Belly full, happy heart).

The Arts

Nicaraguans are by nature a creative people, and the many countries and cultures that have taken part in their country's history have each left an unmistakable mark on dance, sculpture, painting, writing, and music. There are many opportunities to experience traditional dance and song, but equally vibrant are the artisans, writers, and performers who are creating in the present, helping to form an artistic environment that's very much Nicaragua's own.

LITERATURE

"Nicaragua," wrote the poet Pablo Neruda, "where the highest song of the tongue is raised." José Miguel Oviedo called the writing of Nicaragua, "the richest and most tragic national literary tradition on the continent." Most start the story of Nicaraguan literature with the groundbreaking words of Rubén Darío. It continues with the vanguardists of the 1950s and 1960s, the subsequent generation of revolutionary poets and novelists, and the current wave of soul-searchers.

Though poverty has placed books out of the economic reach of most Nicaraguans, the Casa de los Tres Mundos art gallery in Managua doubles as ground zero for the Society of Nicaraguan Writers, and is a good place to start if you have questions about readings, book releases, or other events. There are a few bookstores in Managua that carry Nicaraguan and Latin American selections, as well as Spanish translations of foreign works; Estelí and León also boast interesting bookstores to explore.

Poet and author Gioconda Belli was called one of the 100 most important poets of the 20th century. Her work deals with the themes of feminism, mystical realism, and history, all mixed with a breath of sensuality. Her books *Wiwilí, Sofía de los Presagios,* and *El País Bajo Mi Piel* (The Country Under My Skin) are widely acclaimed.

The writing of Ricardo Pasos Marciacq reflects not only his appreciation for the long and tumultuous history of Nicaragua but for the richness of its society. His books *Maria Manuela Piel de Luna* and *El Burdel de las Pedrarias* are modern classics; the former evokes the years when British-armed Miskitos were wreaking havoc on the Spanish settlements of the Pacific.

Rubén Darío is loved throughout the world of Latin American literature and is considered the father of modernism in Spanish literature. A few of the many other books by Nicaraguan writers worth reading if you have the time and the facility of the language include *El Nicaragüense* by Pablo Antonio Cuadra, *Nicaragua, Teatro de lo Grandioso* by Carlos A. Bravo, and *El Estrecho Dudoso* by Ernesto Cardenal.

DANCE AND THEATER

Nicaragua's traditional folk dances are often mixed with a form of theater, like a play in a parade. There are several dance institutions in Managua that teach folk classics alongside modern dance and ballet, and sponsor frequent performances. The presence of dance schools outside the capital is on the rise, which means fortunate travelers have a good chance of seeing a presentation outside of Managua, especially in Masaya, Diriamba, Matagalpa, León, and Granada. "El Güegüense," for example, is a 19th-century dance of costumed dancers in wooden masks that satirically represents the impression Nicaragua's indigenous people first had of the Spanish and their horses. This dance and others are often featured at *fiestas patronales* (patron saint celebrations), notably in the Masaya and Carazo regions. "El Viejo y La Vieja" ("The Old Man and Woman") pokes ribald fun at old age and sexuality. One dancer, dressed up as an old gentleman with cane and top hat, and the other, dressed up as a buxom old woman, perform a dance that usually involves the old man trying to dance with young female members of the audience while his wife chases him, beating him with her cane. "Aquella Indita" is a celebration of

THE POET IS THE HIGH PRIEST

In *Risking a Somersault in the Air*, Margaret Randall wrote, "Throughout Nicaraguan culture, the poet is the high priest. The prophet. The maker of visions. The singer of songs. The one who knows and can say it for others the way others feel it but cannot say it for themselves." Salman Rushdie was equally impressed when, during his tour of Nicaragua and the Sandinista government in the mid-1980s, he found himself surrounded by young warrior-poets at all levels of society.

Indeed, an inordinate number of the revolution's leaders were published writers – including Minister of the Interior and Head of State Security Tomás Borge, and President Daniel Ortega, both of whom published poems from Somoza's prisons in the 1970s (Somoza's forces found and destroyed the only manuscript of the book Ortega wrote during the same time period). Ortega once told Rushdie, "In Nicaragua, everybody is considered to be a poet until he proves to the contrary."

Literature (and painting, pottery, theater, music, and crafts) was strongly supported by the Sandinista government, whose Ministry of Culture, Father Ernesto Cardenal, stayed busy instituting poetry workshops and publishing magazines and books. Cardenal's poetry is internationally acclaimed and widely translated. Another revolutionary, Gioconda Belli, whose work evokes the sensuality of her country's land and people, was named one of the 100 most important poets of the 20th century. But Nicaraguan poetry, no matter how entwined with the revolution, goes way back, before the life of Sandino.

Invariably, one must turn to Nicaragua's literary giant, Rubén Darío, who 100 years ago set the stage for his nation's love affair with poetry by producing a style unprecedented in Spanish literature. Darío is called the father of the modernist movement in Spanish poetry, a literary style that shed long, grammatically intricate Spanish phrases for simplicity and directness. His experimentation with verse and rhythm made him one of the most acclaimed Latin American writers of all time. Darío's legacy stands firm, and stories about his drinking bouts and international exploits still abound. Poet, journalist, diplomat, and favorite son of Nicaragua, Rubén Darío has become the icon for all that is artistic or cultural in Nicaragua. Today, his portrait graces the front of the 100 *córdoba* bill, his name is on most of the nation's libraries and bookstores, and his sculpted likeness presides throughout the land. His legacy is incredible, and Randall asks if today's poets owe everything to him or to the fact that they, like their hero, glean their inspiration "from that violent expanse of volcanic strength called Nicaragua."

A hundred years later, the Sandinistas pointed to Darío's anti-imperialist references, including a passage written at the time of the Spanish-American War in which he denounces the North Americans as "buffaloes with silver teeth."

The muse still reigns in today's generation. *Rubén's Orphans* is an anthology of contemporary Nicaraguan poets, with English translations by Marco Morelli, published in 2001 by Painted Rooster Press. Also, seek out Steven F. White's book, *Poets of Nicaragua, a Bilingual Anthology*, which covers the poets following Darío up to the revolution (1983, Unicorn Press).

WOLVES, DOGS, AND THE BEST PIECE OF CHICKEN: POPULAR NICARAGUAN SAYINGS

Nicaraguans in general, and *campesinos* in particular, love to speak using *refranes* (sayings or refrains). They're an easy way to make a point, and both the way they are phrased and the points they make say much about the country folks' way of thinking. If you learn a refrain or two and throw one out once in a while in casual conversation, you will be sure to earn broad smiles.

Hay más tiempo que vida. – There is more time than life. (There's no need to rush things.)

Él que a buen árbol se arrima, buena sombra le cobija. – He who gets close to a good tree will be covered by good shade. (He who seeks protection will find it.)

Perro que ladra no muerde. – Dogs who bark don't bite.

No hay peor sordo que él que no quiere escuchar. – There's no deaf person worse than he who doesn't want to hear.

A cada chancho le llega su sábado. – Every pig gets his Saturday. (Everyone eventually gets what he deserves.)

Indio comido, puesto al camino. – An Indian who has eaten, gets up immediately from the table. (A way of pointing out someone ready to leave as soon as he/she gets what he/she wants.)

Quien da pan a un perro ajeno, pierde el pan y pierde el perro. – If you give bread to someone else's dog, you'll lose the bread and lose the dog.

Él que madruga come pechuga, él que tarda, come albarda. – He who gets up early eats the best piece of chicken, he who gets up late eats the saddle.

Él que no llora no mama. – He who does not cry does not suckle. (If you don't complain, you'll never get any attention.)

Él que anda con lobos, aullar aprende. – He who walks with wolves, learns to howl. (A warning about the company you keep.)

Barriga llena, corazón contento. – Full belly, happy heart. (Lean back and use this one after a big meal.)

Él que tiene más galillo, traga más pinol. – He who has a bigger throat, drinks more *pinol*. (Being aggressive will get you farther.)

---

the Nicaraguan woman and her reputation for being graceful and hardworking. "El Solar de Monimbó" ("Monimbó's Backyard") is a traditional dance from the indigenous neighborhood of Masaya, which captures the spirit of community and celebration.

Besides the traditional folk pieces, Nicaraguans love to dance. Period. And there is no occasion (except maybe a funeral) at which it is inappropriate to pump up the music and take to your feet. The ultrasuave, loose-hipped movements associated with merengue, salsa, *cumbia,* and reggae are most commonly seen at discos, street parties, or in living rooms around the nation. The Palo de Mayo is a popular, modern Caribbean dance form featuring flamboyant costumes, vibrating chests, and not-so-subtle sexual simulations. When you see mothers rocking their babies to loud Latin rhythms, and two-year-old girls receiving hip-gyrating lessons, you'll understand why Nicaraguans are able to move so much more fluidly on the dance floor than you are.

VISUAL ARTS

There are a number of Nicaraguan sculptors and painters whose work is displayed at galleries in Managua, Granada, León, and other

© JOSHUA BERMAN

Musicians often participate in country processions as part of local *fiestas patronales* and other religious events.

places. Though the primitivist painters of Solentiname have gotten the lion's share of the press, there is much more in Nicaragua to be seen. In Managua, there are frequent expos of art, often accompanied by buffets or musical performances. More detail is provided in the Managua chapter.

MUSIC

Music, in an infinite variety of forms, is incredibly important in Nicaraguan society. Expect to find loud, blaring radios in most restaurants, bars, vehicles, and homes. It may seem strange at first to find yourself listening to fast, pulsing merengue beats at six in the morning on a rural chicken bus (or in your hotel lobby at midnight for that matter) when the only people listening are sitting calmly in their seats or rocking chairs. Realize, however, that this behavior is seen as a way to inject *alegría* (happiness) into the environment, or alternately, to get rid of

the sadness that some Nicaraguans associate with silence.

Radio mixes are eclectic, featuring the latest Dominican merengues, Mexican and Miami pop, cheesy *romanticas,* plus a bizarre U.S. mélange of Backstreet Boys ("Los Back," for those in the know), Air Supply, and Guns N' Roses. Another wildly popular genre is the *ranchera,* which comes in the form of either polka beats or slow, drippy, lost-love, mariachi tearjerkers, performed by one of a handful of super-celebrity Mexican crooners. Old, rootsy, U.S. country music is extremely popular on the Atlantic coast, and in northern Nicaragua, Kenny Rogers (pronounced "Royers") is recognized as the undisputed king of "La Musica Country."

Managua is host to a small, exciting scene of young local bands and solo musicians, most of whom are direct descendants—children, nephews, cousins—of the generation of musicians

NICARAGUAN BASEBALL FEVER

A hundred years of North American and Cuban influence has engendered a nation of baseball fanatics unrivalled in Latin America. Soccer (fútbol) has a few fans in Nicaragua – especially in the Carazo region – but it's *el béisbol* that gets most Nicas' blood boiling.

Throughout Nicaragua, very few pueblos lack a ball field of some sort, even if the kids put together games with homemade bats and balls of wound twine and tape. The casual traveler is more often than not welcome to join. A plethora of municipal leagues, town leagues, little leagues, competitions between universities, and even between government ministries, make up the bulk of the national sport. Nicaragua's pro league seems to be constantly in flux, often to due to funding problems. At last check, only four teams were competing in the top division – Managua (El Boer), Masaya (San Fernando), the León Lions, and Chinandega Tigers. These teams play with professional ringers from the U.S. who come to Nicaragua to stay in shape during their off-season. The other division consists of ballclubs from Estelí, Granada (Los Tiburones – the Sharks), Matagalpa, and Rivas. **The Federación Nicaragüense de Beisból Asociado** (tel. 505/222-2021) has an office in the national stadium in Managua.

There are several concurrent seasons, with the pros playing November–February, and the minors starting around January. Playoff games and a seven-game championship series are played in the spring. The games are serious – as are the fans – but the series' charm is its humility: Unlike elsewhere, baseball is a sport and a pastime, not a mega-marketed seven-figure-salary circus. Not that Nicaraguan players don't dream of one day making it big in "The Show" like their colleagues, Vicente Padilla and Marvin Bernard. Padilla is a star pitcher who, at the age of 26, signed a $2.6-million contract with the Philadelphia Phillies in 2004. Bernard took $4.2 million from the San Francisco Giants in 2003. Being the only two Nicas playing in the big leagues, they are followed passionately in the Nicaraguan sports pages.

Going back a few years, one of Nicaragua's most admired national heroes is **Dennis "El Presidente" Martínez,** the kid from Granada who left home in 1976 to make it to the big leagues, where he pitched more winning games than any other Latino. In 1991, he pitched the 13th perfect game in major league history against the first-place Dodgers. Nicaraguans followed every detail of his career with avid determination, as he pitched for the Baltimore Orioles (1976-1986), Montreal Expos (1986-1993), Cleveland Indians (1994-1996), Seattle Mariners (1997), and finally the Atlanta Braves (1998). Martínez was a breath of fresh air and a source of much-needed relief throughout the 1980s, when his pitching and hitting stats were the only good news associated with this war-torn nation; talking baseball was a popular respite from the tragedy and destruction. Martínez retired in 1998 and today, his name graces the stadium in Managua, as well as several chari-

---

that brought Nicaraguan folk music to the world. Their acts range from quiet acoustic solo sets to the head-banging throaty screams of a couple of angry, politically minded metal bands. Common venues to catch live music are Bar Chango, Bar La Cavanga, and Guantanamera.

Live music is also found at most *fiestas patronales,* performed by one of several Nicaraguan commercial party bands whose sets imitate the radio mixes of the day. Among the most popular bands is Los Mokuanes (named after the enchanted mountain and its resident witch in La Trinidad, Estelí), who have been around in one form or another for more than three decades. During the war, they were conscripted by the government to don fatigues and perform at army bases throughout the country. Other favorite bands are Macolla and, representing the Palo de Mayo side of things, Sir Anthony and his Dimensión Costeño.

The Masaya baseball team is known as "San Fernando."

table foundations, like the **Dennis Martínez Foundation** (www.dennismartinezfound ation.org).

Also respected is Puerto Rican-born Pittsburgh Pirate, **Roberto Clemente.** Clemente was so moved by the distress in Nicaragua's capital after the 1972 earthquake that he rounded up a planeload of clothes, blankets, and food, and flew to Managua to personally distribute it. He never arrived. Immediately after taking off from San Juan, Puerto Rico, his DL-7 plane faltered and plunged into the Caribbean. Investigators suggested the unrestrained cargo shifted during flight and threw the plane off balance; five additional people perished trying to rescue him.

ESSENTIALS

Getting There and Away

BY AIR

American Airlines has daily flights to Nicaragua via Miami, and Continental Airlines via Houston. Latin American airlines TACA, LACSA, and Sansa have service between Miami and Nicaragua, as well as to other Central American destinations. Iberia has one flight per day to Miami with connections to European destinations. In 2007, Spirit Airlines began offering discount service between Fort Lauderdale and Managua. Be aware of the $30 cash-only exit fee when flying out of Nicaragua; it's often included in your ticket price, but be sure.

BY LAND

The three legal northern border posts are (from west to east): Guasale (in Chinandega), El Espino (near Somoto), and Las Manos (near Somoto). While entering Nicaragua from eastern Honduras north of Puerto Cabezas, is technically possible, it is a guaranteed lengthy series of risky and expensive challenges. On the southern border, the legal crossings are

© JOSHUA BERMAN

Peñas Blancas on the Pan-American Highway, and Los Chiles, reached via an hour-long boat ride from San Carlos. The feasibility of crossing into Costa Rica via the Río Colorado to Tortuguero is undetermined, but would most likely involve convincing the migration officer in San Juan del Norte that you are not trafficking drugs or jaguar pelts.

Crossings by foot, boat, or bus are pretty standard at both the Honduran and Costa Rican borders. Sometimes, you breeze right through; sometimes there are multiple bag and document checks. Remember that you *always* need an exit and an entrance stamp—at some borders, when leaving Nicaragua, it is possible to walk into the neighboring country with your Nicaraguan exit stamp, and then miss the line for the other country's customs; you'll have a lot of explaining to do at your next passport check.

Driving Across the Border

If you are driving your own vehicle, the process to enter Nicaragua is lengthy, but usually not difficult. You must present the vehicle's title, as well as your own driver's license and passport. You will be given a temporary (30-day) permit to drive in Nicaragua, which will cost $10—should you lose the permit, you will be fined $100.

By International Bus

All bus lines between Managua and other Central American capitals are based out of Barrio Martha Quezada, and have competing schedules and prices (see sidebar *International Bus Departures*). Several have affiliate offices in other Nicaraguan cities, like Rivas and León.

TicaBus (two blocks east of the Antiguo Cine Dorado, tel. 505/222-6094 or 505/222-3031, ticabus@ticabus.com, www.ticabus.com) is the oldest and best-established Central American international bus company, servicing all of Central America with connections all the way to Mexico. Across the street, **King Quality/Cruceros del Golfo** (tel. 505/228-1454) is a more comfortable ride and offers both breakfast and a drink cart, for a

INTERNATIONAL BUS DEPARTURES

TO SAN JOSÉ, COSTA RICA (CONTINUING TO PANAMA CITY, PANAMÁ)

TicaBus	6 A.M., 7 A.M., 12 P.M. ($10)
King Quality	1:30 P.M. ($15)
Central Line	5 A.M.
TransNica	5:30 A.M., 7 A.M., 10 A.M. ($10)
TransNica luxury bus	12 P.M. ($20)

TO TEGUCIGALPA, HONDURAS

TicaBus	4:45 A.M. ($20)
King Quality	4 A.M., 11 A.M. ($23)

TO GUATEMALA CITY, GUATEMALA

King Quality	4 A.M., 11 A.M. ($49)

TO SAN SALVADOR, EL SALVADOR

TicaBus	6 A.M. ($10)
King Quality	4 A.M., 11 A.M. ($26)
TransNica	5 A.M. via Choluteca, Honduras

The 11 A.M. King Quality bus to Guatemala spends the night in San Salvador and arrives the next morning.

The TicaBus to Panama City, Panamá, stops first in San José, Costa Rica, then continues through the night, arriving in Panama City the following morning.

slightly higher price. Right next door to King Quality, **Central Line** (tel. 505/254-5431) offers service only to San José, Costa Rica. **TransNica** (Rotonda Metrocentro 300 meters north, 25 meters east, across from DGI, tel. 505/277-2104 or 505/882-7600) services El Salvador and Costa Rica. Their noon bus to Costa Rica costs double but is the most pleasant trip on the market, with meals and drinks included.

Getting Around

BY AIR

Nicaragua's two local carriers, La Costeña and Atlantic Airlines, are both based at the International Airport in Managua (tel. 505/233-1624, www.eaai.com.ni) and, between them, offer daily flights to Puerto Cabezas, Waspám, and Siuna in the northeast, Bluefields and Corn Island in the east, and San Carlos in the south. Flights are in single- and double-prop planes and may be a little bouncy at times. Don't be surprised if your pilots (who you'll practically be sitting next to) kick back and take a nap or read the morning paper after they gain altitude and throw on the cruise control (we're not kidding). Flights within the country generally cost $50–70 each way.

BY BUS

Nicaragua has a massive fleet of old yellow school buses, retired from the First World and customized to transport Nicaraguans to and from the farthest reaches of their country. Each major population center has one or two bus hubs, with regular and express service to nearby cities and to Managua, plus rural routes to the surrounding communities. Generally speaking, Nicaragua's bus system is safe, cheap, and sure to be one of the most memorable parts of your travels. Enjoy being a part of the chatting, smiling, sweating crowd, even when you are packed so tightly into the mass of real-life Nicaragua that you confuse your limbs with someone else's.

In theory, *expresos* are buses that do not stop to pick up extra passengers en route to their destination. This is occasionally true and we recommend paying the 25 percent more for an *expreso* ticket, which sometimes gets you a reserved seat and can save you an hour's travel or more. To points west and south from Managua, there is an especially large number of express microbuses (minivans or *interlocales*) that leave every 20 minutes—or whenever they fill up.

Local buses are called *ordinarios* or *ruteados* and take their sweet time, stopping for every Tom, Dick, and Pedro who waves his hand—hell, they'll stop for a chicken if he flaps his wing too close to the highway. *Microbuses,* sometimes called *interlocales,* are small, express minivans that depart when full.

In some bus terminals, you'll purchase your ticket before boarding, but usually, you'll board the bus, find a seat, and then wait for the *ayudante* (driver's helper) to come around and collect your *pasaje* (fare). Asking the Nica sitting next to you how much the ride should cost will help you avoid being ripped off (very rare). In some cases, if the *ayudante* doesn't have change, he'll write the amount owed to you on your ticket, returning later in the trip to pay you. This is normal. Most buses have overhead racks inside where you can stow your bags. Less desirable, but common, is for the *ayudante* to insist you put your backpack on the roof or in some cargo space in the back of the bus. It is obviously safer to keep your stuff on your lap or at least within sight, but sometimes you don't have much choice but to trust your chauffeurs.

Urbanos

We advise against using the Managua bus system unless you are with a Nicaraguan or another traveler who has experience with it. The routes are long and confusing and you and your fancy backpack are obvious targets for thieves. *Urbanos* are, of course, much cheaper

© RANDALL WOOD

hailing a taxi on the Río Coco

than taxis, but it only comes down to a couple dollars—or less. You can decide how much it's worth to not feel a knifepoint in your side. Actually, urban buses probably aren't too dangerous during the day, but during rush hour and nighttime, the risk shoots up. Most other major cities have a basic *urbano* bus loop and are much safer than the ones in Managua.

BOATS

In several regions of Nicaragua—notably Solentiname, Río San Juan, Río Coco, and the entire Atlantic coast—boat travel is the only viable means of transportation. Because gas prices are as high as $3–4 a gallon in these areas, locals get around in public water taxis called *colectivos* that help cut costs. For recreation, there are a handful of sailboats that can take you out in San Juan del Sur, and some boat-based tour companies out of Granada.

TAXIS

There are new Japanese models slowly joining Nicaragua's taxi fleet, but the vast majority remain the same tin-can Russian Ladas that were imported during the 1980s and, miraculously, are still chugging along. Granted, many windows don't open, windshields are shattered, and the seats are shot—but who cares when the engine works and there's a sound system more powerful than the one you had in your freshman dorm. In every city except Managua, urban taxis operate on a fixed zone rate, usually no more than $0.35 within the central city area. In the capital, however, it's a different story, and you should never get into a cab before settling on a price. Strangely, most old Nicaraguan taxis have no handle with which to roll the windows down. If you can't stand the heat, ask the driver for the *manigueta de la ventanilla;* he's probably got it stashed up front.

DRIVING
Vehicular Safety

The most dangerous thing you will do in Nicaragua, without a doubt, is travel on its highways. Outside the cities, roads are poorly

© JOSHUA BERMAN

Traveling on Nicaragua's highways is the most dangerous part of your trip.

lit, narrow, lacking shoulders, and are often full of axle-breaking potholes, unannounced speed bumps, fallen rocks, and countless other obstacles. Even in Managua, you can expect to find ox carts, abandoned vehicles, and grazing horses wandering the streets. Because there are no shoulders for taxis to use when boarding passengers, they stop in the right lane and let traffic swerve around them. Also expect macho, testosterone-crazed bus drivers trying to pass everything they can on blind, uphill curves. The fact that beer and rum are sold at most gas stations should give you an idea of how many drivers are intoxicated, especially late at night.

When possible, avoid traveling during peak rush hours in the cities, and after dark anywhere. New highway projects since 2000 have improved the situation in many parts of the country, but road and vehicle conditions are still hazardous and many drivers even more so, occasionally taking advantage of the newly repaved straightaways to speed like bats out of hell. Everywhere you drive, keep an eye out

for dogs crossing the road. Experienced drivers suspect the canines are specially trained and then released on the roads to test driver reactions.

Renting a Car

Car rental services (including Avis, Budget, Hertz, Econo, and Hyundai) are easily found in Managua at the airport, the fancier hotels, and a number of agency offices and lots. In terms of price, renting a car here is comparable to the United States or Canada, so by Nicaraguan standards, it is a huge chunk of your travel budget. However, if you have a group of five people or so, it can be a reasonable way to make a road trip to see the turtles, or to go anywhere else with limited public transportation.

Getting Pulled Over

So how's that Spanish coming along? This is where your language skills will really pay off—literally. Police in Nicaragua are well known to be fairer and less corrupt than elsewhere in Central America, but with their dismal salaries, they are still often on the lookout for a little baksheesh. Commonly called *la pesca* (a reference to fishing), Nicaragua's finest are often seen in groups at intersections and traffic circles, surrounded by construction cones, flourishing bright orange gloves, and pulling over everything in sight—especially gringo drivers without diplomatic plates. Drivers complain that the cops' definition of *mala maniobra* (moving violation, literally bad driving) is just about any movement of your vehicle within their sight. Have your papers ready when the officer approaches your window, and know that calling him *"compañero"* is likely to double the bribe. The latest method used by police is to confiscate your license and threaten to hold it hostage until you come in the following week to pay the fine—unless, of course, you'd rather take care of the issue right then. Speaking of bribes, slick talk and some quick cash will get you out of some situations; however, honest Nicaraguan cops, who not only won't accept your 500 *córdobas* but will ticket you for the attempt, are known to exist. Also, paying off the police only serves to encourage and perpetuate corruption.

In Case of a Traffic Accident
Do not move your vehicle from the scene of the crime until authorized by a police officer, even if it is blocking traffic. For lack of high-tech crime-scene equipment, the Nicaraguan police force will try to understand how the accident occurred based on what they see at the site. Drivers who move their vehicle at the scene of the accident are held legally liable for the incident—even if you just move your vehicle to the side of the road. Any driver in Nicaragua who is party to an accident where injuries are sustained will be taken into custody, even if the driver has insurance and does not seem to be at fault. This custody will be maintained until a judicial decision is reached (sometimes weeks later) or until the injured party signs a waiver releasing the driver of liability. In many cases, to avoid a lengthy court proceeding and horrifying jail stay, it may be worth your while to plead guilty and pay a fine (which will probably not exceed $1,000, even in the case of a death).

TWO WHEELS
If you intend to ride a motorcycle or bicycle in Nicaragua, be sure to bring your own helmet, an item largely ignored by Nicaraguans—even when baby, junior, and grandma are all crammed onto the motorcycle or bike, with dad driving (or peddling).

Interested in donating a bike? **Bikes Not Bombs** (www.bikesnotbombs.org) is a Boston-based nonprofit that supports community bicycle projects in Nicaragua and El Salvador. Another organization that can ship your used bike to Nicaragua and other places in need of cheap transport is **Pedals for Progress** (www.p4p.org).

Visas and Officialdom

PASSPORT AND VISA REQUIREMENTS
Every traveler to Nicaragua must have a passport valid for at least six months following the date of entry. A visa is required only for citizens of the following countries: Afghanistan, Albania, Bosnia-Herzegovina, Colombia, Cuba, Haiti, India, Iran, Iraq, Jordan, Lebanon, Libya, Nepal, Pakistan, People's Republic of China, People's Republic of Korea, Somalia, Sri Lanka, Vietnam, and Yugoslavia. Everyone else is automatically given a tourist pass good for three months which can be extended by going to the Office of Immigration (Dirección General de Migración y Extranjería, 1.5 blocks north of the *semáforos* Tenderí, tel. 505/244-0741, 505/244-1320, or 505/244-3960, open 8:30 A.M.–noon and

NICARAGUAN CONSULATES AND EMBASSIES ABROAD

Nicaragua does not maintain a consulate in Canada. For additional consulates in Europe and Latin America, visit www.intur.gob.ni.

IN THE UNITED STATES

Washington, DC (Embassy and Consulate)
1627 New Hampshire Ave. NW
Washington, DC 20009
U.S. tel. 202/939-6531 or 202/939-6532
fax 202/939-6574

Houston, TX
8989 Westheimer Rd., Suite 103
Houston, TX 77063
U.S. tel. 713/789-2762 or 276/789-2781

Los Angeles, CA
3550 Wilshire Blvd., Ste. 200
Los Angeles, CA 90010
U.S. tel. 213/252-1171 or 213/252-1174
fax 213/252-1177

Miami, FL
8532 SW 8th St., Suite 270
Miami, FL 33144
U.S. tel. 305/265-1415
fax 305/265-1780

New York, NY
820 2nd Ave., 8th Floor, Suite 802
New York, NY 10017
U.S. tel. 212/986-6562
fax 212/983-2646

San Francisco, CA
870 Market, Suite 1050
San Francisco, CA 94102
U.S. tel. 415/765-6821, 415/765-6823, or
415/765-6825
fax 415/765-6826

IN CENTRAL AMERICA

Costa Rica
Avenida Central No. 2440, Barrio
La California
San José, Costa Rica
tel. 506/222-2373
fax 506/221-5481

El Salvador
71 Avenida Norte y Primera Calle Poniente
No. 164
Colonia Escalon, San Salvador
tel. 503/298-6549
fax 506/223-7201

Guatemala
10 Avenida, 14-72, Zona 10
Guatemala
tel. 502/268-0785
fax 502/337-4264

Honduras
Colonia Tepeyac, Bloque M-1, No. 1130
Tegucigalpa, Honduras
tel. 504/232-7224
fax 504/239-5225

Panamá
Intersección de Avenida Federico Boyd
y calle 50
Apartado 772, Zona 1
Corregimiento Bella Vista
Ciudad de Panamá, Panamá
tel. 507/223-0981
fax 507/211-2080

© JOSHUA BERMAN

Be sure your passport is in order before your trip to Nicaragua; most visitors do not need a visa.

2–4:30 P.M. Mon.–Fri.); show up at least four days before it expires with your passport, current visa, and $25. There's no guarantee you'll be given an extension. If the gods smile on you, the extensions will be for one month at a time. Remember to look presentable. If you're traveling on a simple tourist visa, it may be less cumbersome to simply cross into Costa Rica or Honduras and return the same day. Additional requirements exist for those who intend to work, study, reside for an extended period, or engage in nontourist activities. Contact your nearest Nicaraguan embassy for details about the requirements.

CUSTOMS AND IMMIGRATION

Upon entering Nicaragua, tourists are required to pay a $5 entrance fee. You also must be in possession of a valid passport, an onward/return ticket, and have evidence of sufficient funds (though the latter two are almost never checked). As you exit baggage claim, a red light indicates your luggage will be searched, a green light means keep walking. Should they go through your luggage, you can expect to be taxed for carrying items you obviously don't intend to use yourself, including electronics, jewelry, and perfume. If your iPod, camera, or laptop computer isn't in its original box or accompanied by several more of the same, you will pass through customs in a flash. When leaving Nicaragua by plane, an airport tax of $30 in U.S. dollars only (no credit cards) may or may not be included in your ticket price.

FOREIGN EMBASSIES AND CONSULATES IN NICARAGUA

All diplomatic missions in Nicaragua are located in Managua, mostly along Carretera Masaya and Carretera Sur. The city of Chinandega hosts consulates from El Salvador, Honduras, and Costa Rica, and the city of Rivas has a consulate from Costa Rica.

GUIDE TO NICARAGUA'S FIESTAS

Each community's annual *fiestas patronales* revolve around the local saint's birthday, but the actual party may extend days or even weeks before and after. This guide should help you catch (or avoid) *fiestas patronales* as you travel; the events are associated with special masses, processions, alcohol, dancing, carnivals, show horses, contests, and more alcohol.

Year-round weekly events include the following: Thursdays in Masaya are Jueves de Verbena, Fridays in Granada are Noches de Serenata, and Sundays in León are Tertulias Leonesas. Semana Santa (Easter Week) is a particularly big deal – everyone parties like rock stars at the beach and prices skyrocket across the board.

JANUARY
1: New Year's Day
18: Fiestas Patronales, El Sauce
Third Sunday: Señor de Esquipulas, El Sauce (León)
Third weekend: Viva León Festival, León
Third weekend: San Sebastían, Acoyapa (Chontales), Diriamba, Carazo (San Sebastián)
Last weekend: La Virgen de Candelaria, La Trinidad (Estelí)

FEBRUARY
Second weekend: Music and Youth Festival, Managua

MARCH
Third weekend: Folklore, Gastronomy, and Handicraft Festival, Granada

APRIL
Semana Santa
First week: Religious Ash Paintings in León
19-21: Fiestas Patronales, San Jorge (Rivas)

MAY
1: Labor Day
1: Fiestas Patronales, Jinotega
15: San Isidro Labrador, Condega (Estelí)
30: Mother's Day
Third weekend: Palo de Mayo Festival, Bluefields

JUNE
16: Virgen del Carmen, San Juan del Sur (Rivas)
24: St. John the Baptist, San Juan de Oriente (Carazo), San Juan del Sur (Rivas), San Juan de Jinotega (Jinotega)
29: St. Peter the Apostle, Diriá (Masaya)
Last Friday: El Repliegue Sandinista (Managua)

United States and Canada

Americans living or traveling in Nicaragua can register with the **U.S. Embassy** at the international travel page of the U.S. State Department website (travel.state.gov). This is not a legal requirement, but the embassy encourages you to do so that they can send you updated travel and security advisories regarding Nicaragua. These advisories—and the warden messages on the embassy website—are invariably very conservative, as far as risk assessment. The new U.S. Embassy (they moved in November 2007) is located at Kilometer 5.5, Carretera Sur. The main phone is 505/252-7100, the Information Resource Center is 505/252-7237, and you can contact American Citizens Services by email at ACS.Managua@state.gov.

The **Canadian Embassy** in Managua is actually an outpost of their main embassy in San José, Costa Rica. The address in the Bolonia neighborhood is "costado oriental de la Casa Nasareth, una cuadra arriba, Calle El Nogal," tel. 505/268-0433 or 505/268-3323, fax 505/268-0437, mngua@international.gc.ca. For urgencies involving Canadian citizens, call the emergency consular service in Ottawa collect at 613/996-6885.

JULY
Second Saturday: Carnaval, Somoto
15-25: Fiestas Patronales, Somoto
19: National Liberation Day
25: Santiago, Boaco, Jinotepe (Carazo)
26: St. Ana, Nandaime (Granada), Chinandega, Ometepe

AUGUST
1-10: Santo Domingo (Noches Agostinas), Managua
10: St. Lorenzo, Somotillo (Chinandega)
14: Gritería Chiquita, León
15: The Assumption, Granada
14-15: Fiestas Patronales, Ocotal
15: The Assumption and Fiesta del Hijo Ausente, Juigalpa
Third weekend: Mariachis and Mazurcas Festival, Estelí

SEPTEMBER
10: San Nicolás de Tolentino, La Paz Centro (León)
14: The Battle of San Jacinto
15: Independence Day
14 and 15: Fishing Fair, San Carlos (Río San Juan)
15: Patron Saint Festival of Villa Nueva, Chinandega
20: San Jerónimo, Masaya
24: La Merced, León, and Matagalpa

Fourth weekend: Polkas, Mazurcas, and Jamaquellos, Matagalpa; Festival of Corn, Jalapa

OCTOBER
12: San Diego (Estelí)
Second weekend: Norteño Music Festival in Jinotega
24: San Rafael Arcángel, Pueblo Nuevo
Penultimate Sunday: Fiesta de los Agüisotes, Masaya
Last Sunday: Toro Venado, Masaya

NOVEMBER
2: All Souls' Day
3-5: Equestrian Rally in Ometepe
4: San Carlos Borromeo, San Carlos (Río San Juan)
12-18: San Diego de Alcalá, Altagracia (Ometepe)
Fourth Sunday: Folkloric Festival, Masaya

DECEMBER
First Sunday: Procesión de San Jerónimo, Masaya
6: Lavado de La Plata, Virgen del Trono, El Viejo (Chinandega)
7: Purísimas (Immaculate Conception Celebrations) in Managua, Granada, Masaya, and León

Central America

Costa Rica: half a block east of Estatua Montoya along Calle 27 de Mayo, tel. 505/268-7460. There is also a consulate in Rivas and Chinandega.

Cuba: Carretera Masaya from the third entrance to Las Colinas, two blocks east, 75 meters to the south, tel. 505/276-2285.

El Salvador: Las Colinas, Ave. El Campo Pasaje Los Cerros no. 142, tel. 505/276-0160.

Guatemala: Carretera Masaya Km 11, tel. 505/279-9834.

Honduras: Carretera Masaya Km 12, 100 meters toward Cainsa, tel. 505/279-8231.

Panamá: third entrance to Las Colinas, then two blocks east and 75 meters south, tel. 505/276-0212.

Europe and Asia

Austria: from the Rotonda El Güegüense, one block north, tel. 505/266-0171 or 505/268-3756.

Belgium: Consulado de Bélica, Reparto El Carmen across from the Esso station, Calle 27 de Mayo, tel. 505/228-2068.

Denmark: Plaza España one block west, two blocks north, half a block west, tel. 505/268-0253.

Finland: Bolonia, one block north, 1.5 blocks west of the Hospital Militar, tel. 505/266-3415.

France: Reparto El Carmen, 1.5 blocks west of the church, tel. 505/222-6210.

Germany: 1.5 blocks north of the Rotonda El Güegüense, tel. 505/266-3917.

Great Britain: Los Robles, from the old Sandy's on Carretera Masaya, one block south, a half-block west, tel. 505/278-0014 or 278-0887.

Italy: one block north and half a block west of the Rotonda El Güegüense, tel. 505/266-6486.

The Netherlands (Holland): Bolonia canal 2, half a block north, one block west, tel. 505/266-4392.

Norway: one block west of Plaza España, tel. 505/266-4199.

Russia: Las Colinas, Calle Vista Alegre No. 214, tel. 505/276-0131.

Spain: Las Colinas Avenida Central No. 13, tel. 505/276-0968.

Sweden: one block west, two blocks north, and half a block west of the Rotonda Plaza España, tel. 505/266-8097.

Switzerland: Consulado de Suiza, one block west of the Las Palmas Clinic, tel. 505/266-5719.

China: Planes de Altamira, from the Copa office 200 meters south across from the tennis courts, tel. 505/267-4024.

Japan: Bolonia, from the Rotonda El Güegüense one block west, one block north, tel. 505/266-1773.

OFFICIAL HOLIDAYS

Expect all public offices to be closed on the following days. Also remember that Nicaraguan holidays are subject to decree, shutting the banks down without warning to suit some politician's inclination.

- January 1: New Year's Day
- Late March/early April: Semana Santa, including Holy Thursday, Good Friday, and Easter
- May 1: Labor Day
- May 30: Mother's Day
- July 19: National Liberation Day
- August 1: Fiesta Day
- September 14: Battle of San Jacinto
- September 15: Independence Day
- November 2: Día de los Muertes (All Souls' Day)
- December 8: La Purísima (Immaculate Conception)
- December 25: Christmas Day

Like the rest of Latin America, each town and city has its own patron saint whom the residents honor each year with a prolonged party that lasts from one to three weeks. These **fiestas patronales** combine holy religious fervor with a fierce celebration of sin that features alcohol consumption of biblical proportions. Highlights of the celebration include Virgin and Saint parades, special masses, fireworks, cockfighting, rodeos, concerts, gambling, and show-horse parades. Many towns have additional celebrations of specific events in their history.

Semana Santa (or Holy Week) is the biggest celebration of the year, occurring during the week leading up to Easter Sunday. The weeklong vacation sends most city folk to the beach for sun and debauchery (and usually a couple of drownings, too) while shops close their doors and everyone takes a breather. Expect lots of trouble traveling during this time period, as many buses stop running and many hotels hike their rates exponentially.

Tips for Travelers

TRAVEL WITH CHILDREN

There's no reason you can't travel with your children and there are no set rules about how young is too young. The family unit is strong in Nicaragua and children everywhere are cherished and adored, not seen as a burden. You may find that traveling with your children helps form a new connection between you and Nicaraguans you meet. That said, be aware that your children will have to endure the same lack of creature comforts, change in diet, and long bumpy bus rides you do.

Nicaraguan children generally grow up with cloth diapers, which are painstakingly washed out and hung to dry in the sun. Disposable diapers are available in supermarkets, but they're imported from elsewhere, so they're not cheap. Other necessities available in Nicaragua include powdered milk for formula, pacifiers (*pacificadores* or *chupetas),* and bottles (*pachas).*

WOMEN TRAVELERS

In Nicaragua, as in all of Latin America, women are both adored and harassed to their wits' end by "gentlemen" hoping for attention. Catcalls and whistles are everywhere, often accompanied with an *"Adios, amorrrr,"* or a sleazy, *"Tss-tss!"* More often than not, the perpetrators are harmless, immature young men with struggling moustaches. It will either comfort or disgust you to know that Nicaraguan women are forced to endure the same treatment every day and you should note how they react—most ignore the comments and blown kisses entirely, and some are flattered and smile confidently as they walk by. Acknowledging the comment further is probably ill-advised, as it will only feed the fire. Be prepared for this part of the culture, and decide ahead of time how you plan to react.

Physical harassment, assault, and rape are much less common in Nicaragua than elsewhere in Central America, but certainly not unheard of, especially when alcohol is involved. Take the same precautions you would anywhere

else to avoid dangerous situations. For more, download a copy of "Her Own Way: Advice for the Woman Traveller" at the Canadian Consular Affairs website (www.voyage.gc.ca); also find good advice and tips at www.journeywoman.com.

As for feminine hygiene products, tampons can be difficult to find, as almost all Nicaraguan women use pads (*toallas sanitarias).* Most pharmacies and *pulperías* carry pads, usually referred to by the brand name Kotex, regardless of the actual brand. Nicaraguan women favor pads over tampons due to custom as well as social stigma, as tampons are sometimes associated with sexually active or aggressive women.

GAY AND LESBIAN TRAVELERS

As of March 2008, consensual gay sex is no longer a criminal act in Nicaragua, though the Catholic church still forbids it. Nica society is generally tolerant of homosexuality. The gay or lesbian traveler should feel neither threatened nor endangered in Nicaragua provided they maintain a modicum of discretion and choose their situations wisely. Managua and Granada have a few openly gay clubs and gay-friendly hotels. Elsewhere same-sex couples may find local gay communities that will help orient them to tolerant clubs and bars. For more track down the 25-minute 1993 film *Sex and the Sandinistas* for a look at homosexuality in revolutionary *machista* society.

TRAVELERS WITH DISABILITIES

Travelers with disabilities should contact **AccessibleNicaragua** (accessiblenicaragua @gmail.com, www.accessiblenicaragua.com), the only tour company in Nicaragua that eases the way for people with disabilities—as much as possible, anyway. Founder Craig Grimes, a disabled traveler himself, is offering one- and

SINFUL SOUVENIRS

Looking for a gift that keeps on giving? Nicaragua offers a selection of ephemeral pleasures, including fine **cigars** and **rum.**

Nicaragua's hand-rolled cigars start with Cuban seed and the good earth around Estelí. Find them for sale in the Huembes market in Managua, El Mercado Viejo in Masaya, or the cigar shops around Granada's central plaza (or at the source at cigar factories in Estelí). Gringos: Just because you can buy Cuban Cohibas in Nicaragua (which may or may not be genuine), U.S. customs may still enforce their anti-Cuban embargo – whether your cigars are real or counterfeit! Remove the labels to be sure.

The cheapest place to pick up souvenir bottles of **Flor de Caña,** widely accepted as one of the smoothest rums in all Latin America, is in a supermarket or corner *pulpería;* hotel gift shops and airport kiosks often charge double what you should be paying. Nicaragua customs limits you to six liter-sized bottles of rum at the airport and if you're catching a connecting flight in the U.S., you'll have to transfer your liquids to your checked luggage, so plan ahead and make sure you have space to do so.

two-week trips that he says are "not for the faint-hearted by any stretch of the imagination; some people may find it really tough going, but it will be a great experience for those that decide to come."

Nicaragua's *descapacitados* (disabled) get around with much difficulty because of ruined sidewalks, dirt roads, aggressive crowds, and open manholes. While Nicaraguans agree people with disabilities have equal rights, no attempt is made to accommodate them, and the foreign traveler with limited mobility will certainly struggle, but will no doubt find ways to get by.

The Los Pipitos organization, based in Managua with 24 chapters around the country, is devoted to providing support, materials, and physical therapy to Nicaraguan children with disabilities and their families. Los Pipitos is always looking for volunteers and support. The Managua office is located half a block east of the Bolonia Agfa (tel. 505/266-8033).

WORKING AND VOLUNTEERING

In light of Nicaragua's exceeding poverty and sky-high unemployment rate, you'll have a tough time finding paying work. Additionally, immigration laws force you to prove your job couldn't have otherwise gone to a Nicaraguan. Still, there are plenty of foreigners who've pulled it off. Start your job search with your embassy and the many NGOs that work in Nicaragua, including CARE, Save the Children, ADRA, Project Concern International, and Catholic Relief Services. If you are a licensed English teacher you might also try the universities in Managua, though your salary will be the same as a Nicaraguan's (i.e., you'll be able to sustain yourself from day to day but you'll wish you had a cousin in Miami sending you checks). Universidad Centroamericana (UCA), Universidad Nacional Autónoma (UNAN), and Universidad Americana (UAM) all have English departments that may be looking for staff. For more ideas, check out the book, *Work Abroad,* edited by Clay Hubbs, available at www.transitionsabroad.com.

However, because of its history of poverty and social experimentation, Nicaragua has always attracted altruistic groups and individual volunteer-oriented tourists. Shortly after 1979, hordes of *internacionalistas* poured in from all over the world to participate in the Sandinista revolution—they picked coffee, taught in schools, wrote poetry and editorials of solidarity, put themselves in the line of fire, and protested in front of the U.S. Embassy (the less ardent, Birkenstock-clad of these were called Sandalistas). Today anyone with an independent head on their shoulders and a couple

U.S. SISTER CITIES WITH NICARAGUA

Some of the following pairings were formed during the 1980s to express solidarity with the Nicaraguan people. They have continued to exist as small-scale development organizations that often organize brigades to their sister towns. For more on sister cities or to find ideas of how you can become involved in your local program, contact your city council, or go to www.sister-cities.org.

Amherst, MA	La Paz Centro	Hudson Valley, NY	Larreynaga
Ann Arbor, MI	Juigalpa	Lansing, SC	Tipitapa
Bainbridge Island, WA	Ometepe	Madison, WI	Managua
Baltimore, MD	San Juan de Limay	Merced, CA	Somoto
Beckley, WV	Mina El Limon	Milwaukee, WI	Ticuantepe
Bend, OR	Condega	Montclair, NJ	Pearl Lagoon
Bennington, VT	Somotillo	Moscow, ID	Villa Carlos Fonseca
Berkeley, CA	León	Newark, DE	San Francisco Libre
Bloomington, IN	Posoltega	New Haven, CT	León
Boulder, CO	Jalapa	Newton, MA	San Juan del Sur
Brookline, MA	Quezalguaque	New York, NY	Tipitapa
Burlington, VT	Puerto Cabezas	North Plainfield, NJ	Masaya
Concord, MA	San Marcos (RAAN)	Norwalk, CT	Nagarote
Fresno, CA	Telpaneca	Pittsfield, MA	Malpaisillo
Gainesville, FL	Matagalpa	Pittsburgh, PA	San Isidro
Gettysburg, PA	León	Platteville, WI	Mateare
Hartford, CT	Ocotal	Portland, OR	Corinto
Holyoke, CO	Las Mangas	Racine, WI	Bluefields
		Richland Center, WI	Santa Teresa
		Rochester, NY	El Sauce
		Sacramento, CA	San Juan de Oriente
		Santa Cruz, CA	Jinotepe
		Stevens Point, WI	Estelí
		South Haven, MI	Quilalí
		Tampa, FL	Granada
		Tucson, AZ	Santo Domingo
		Waukesha, WI	Granada
		Yellow Springs, OH	Jicaro

hundred dollars a month for living expenses can still come to Nicaragua and find some way to help. They come in organized tours, government programs, through academia, and by themselves—grants and awards abound for such individuals. Just be aware that sustainable solutions to poverty take time. A long time. Expect things to happen differently than you expect and learn some Spanish.

Throughout *Moon Nicaragua,* we've included sidebars listing regional opportunities to volunteer. Organizations (both faith-based and secular) work throughout the country to assist with construction, education, translation, agriculture, and general solidarity. Check www.volunteerabroad.com for the most

updated listing of available assignments or inquire about opportunities with the following organizations:

Habitat for Humanity (www.habitat.org) is active building homes throughout Nicaragua. **American Jewish World Service** (www.ajws.com) has a program called the Jewish Volunteer Corps, which provides support for professionals looking to volunteer in Nicaragua and other countries—to practice the Hebrew commandment "to heal the world."

If your organization wants to travel with a group to Nicaragua, **Bridges to Community** (U.S. tel. 914/923-2200, www.bridgestocommunity.org) will help plan a trip, find a project, and facilitate logistics. They can get you

TOUR OPERATORS

For a current list of active tour operators in Nicaragua, go to www.intur.gob.ni. Nicaragua's independent tour companies offer a huge variety of trips, from afternoon city tours to weeklong pirate cruises in the farthest reaches of the country, the logistics of which would be nearly impossible for the solo traveler. These adventures cost money, and of course, as part of a group, you lose some independence – then again, you are provided with security and freedom from making plans. In general, an all-inclusive nine-day tour costs about $1,000, but each company varies.

Tours Nicaragua (www.toursnicaragua.com) focuses on ecotourism, adventure, and special interest packages.

Nicaragua Adventures (tel. 505/883-7161, www.nica-adventures.com) focuses on high-energy hiking, biking, and volcano packages.

Explore Nicaragua Tours (tel. 800/800-1132, www.explorenicaragua.com) has 17 years of experience in the business.

Solentiname Tours (tel. 505/265-2716, www.solentinametours.com, zerger@ibw.com.ni) offers several best-of tours of up to two weeks, and a personal touch, having lived in Nicaragua since long before it was a popular tourist destination.

Careli Tours (tel. 505/278-2572, www.careli tours.com), owned by the Chamorro family, errs on the side of luxury.

Soltours Nicaragua (tel. 505/266-7164, www.soltoursnicaragua.com) has 15 years of experience and can help arrange tours that connect you to other Central American countries as well.

ALTERNATIVE TOURS

Global Exchange (www.globalexchange.org) offers a Reality Tours in Nicaragua. These educational trips explore various social justice issues, including the fair-trade coffee economy, monitoring elections, and learning about labor rights in free trade zones.

Witness for Peace (www.witnessforpeace.org) is a grassroots organization "committed to nonviolence and led by faith and conscience." Based in Managua, Witness for Peace has maintained a permanent presence in this Central American country since 1983; they offer trips that "combine international travel and education with the struggle for peace, economic justice, and sustainable development."

Wonder-Full Tours to Nicaragua (www.wonder-full-tours.com) specializes in service and learning trips including yoga retreats, Granada and San Juan del Sur, and special-topic trips to explore environmental conservation and sustainable development.

to small Nicaraguan communities to work on construction, health, and environmental projects.

Peace Corps Nicaragua

El Cuerpo de Paz, as the organization is known in Spanish, is a U.S. government–funded program created by John F. Kennedy in 1961. More than 45 years later, 200,000 Americans have served as Peace Corps volunteers (PCVs) in over 130 countries; there are currently about 7,000 volunteers serving in more than 90 countries around the world. Participants sign up to receive an intensive three-month training in their host country's language and culture, as well as in technical aspects of their assignment, followed by a two-year tour during which they receive a bare-bones living allowance. The first Peace Corps volunteers arrived in Nicaragua in 1969, then took a hiatus during Sandinista control and were invited back in 1991. About 150 volunteers currently serve in some of the most remote corners of Nicaragua, and in many major towns and pueblos—except Managua and the Atlantic Coast. PCVs work in one of five sectors: Environment, Agriculture, Small Business Development, Youth at Risk, and Community Health. To learn more, visit www.peacecorps.gov.

Study Abroad

There are many possibilities for spending a summer, semester, or extended internship in Nicaragua. Programs range from biological fieldwork at remote research stations to language training and social justice programs. You'll find additional listings at **www .studyabroad.com.**

School for International Training has been running a semester program in Managua for years, entitled "Revolution, Transformation, and Civil Society" (U.S. tel. 888/272-7881, www.sit.edu). **World Leadership School** (www.worldleadershipschool.org), based in Denver, Colorado, has extensive experience with international travel, leadership training, and managing student groups overseas; their Nicaragua program is on La Isla de Ometepe. Also on Ometepe, near the village of San Ramón is **Estación Biológica de Ometepe** (lasuerte.org), a biological field station frequented by student groups and researchers from all over the world. At the **Mariposa Eco-Hotel and Spanish School** (www.spanishschoolnica .com), the owner Paulette Goudge, PhD, offers a three-month course in the "Politics of Development."

SPANISH SCHOOLS IN NICARAGUA

Nicaragua has a strong network of independent Spanish schools, and an increasing number of visitors to the country choose to combine their travels with a few days, weeks, or even months of language study. Most schools follow the same basic structure, mixing language instruction with cultural immersion: 2–4 hours of class in the morning, community service activities or field trips in the afternoon, and optional homestays with Nicaraguan families.

To a certain extent, choosing a school is as much a question of geographical preference as anything else. If possible, it's a good idea to come down and personally look into a few

options before making a long-term commitment. Get a feel for the teachers (ask about their experience and credentials), the professionalism of the business, and the lesson plan. Do not trust everything you see on the websites.

Also, please note that keeping up with prices is difficult in the competitive world of Spanish schools, so always confirm what we've listed here and, in general, expect to pay around $150–250 per week, depending on the quality of services offered. This usually includes room, board, instruction, and sometime tours. Schools in the northern regions are generally cheaper. You can create your own language tour by studying at several of the schools below for a week or two in each place, using your class schedule and family homestays as a way to travel throughout Nicaragua.

Once in the classroom, remember that gaining a language takes time—you must learn one word at a time until they start flowing together in sentences. Be patient, do your homework, and be ready to laugh at yourself (along with everyone else) as you make mistakes. ¡*Suerte!*

Managua

Viva Spanish School (tel. 505/877-7179 or 270-2339, www.vivaspanishschool.com) offers intensive classes (20 hours per week), catering to students of all ages and backgrounds—one week of instruction, including all materials is $155 (or $210 per couple). There are less intensive classes as well in-home study and classes for kids. Modules of study are available for missionaries, medical students, and businesspeople, covering specialized vocabulary in each area; also advanced courses, tourist Spanish, a Literature Class, and a specially developed Childrens Program which includes games, art, and other activities. Private lessons, tutoring, and guide services are offered by **Raúl Gavarrette** (tel. 505/233-1298, cell 505/776-5702, aige@tmx.com.ni).

Granada

Granada's status as ground zero for the Nicaragua tourism scene (from backpackers to upscale) makes it a natural choice for many students who love the city's aesthetic as much as its bar scene. Roger Ramírez's **One-on-One Spanish Tutoring Academy** (on the Calle Calzada, four blocks west of the central park, tel. 505/552-6771, www.1on1tutoring.net) receives a constant stream of students. A week of 25 hours of instruction costs $95, plus $65 for room and board with a family. Custom, group, and cultural activities can also be arranged, as can shorter lessons, or classes by the hour.

Casa Xalteva (across from the church by the same name, tel. 505/552-2436, www.casa xalt eva.com) offers a similar package, $150/week, with a stress on volunteer activities; it's highly recommended by former students, has a quiet location, and is part of a small group home for boys, which is supported by your tuition.

Skilled teachers give classes in the patio of **Maverick's Reading Lounge** (see the *Granada* chapter), and there are classes offered in the beautiful **Palacio de Cultura** (tel. 505/552-7114), in a grand building on the west side of Granada's main plaza.

Los Pueblos Blancos

Tucked into the forest off the road to the village of San Juan de la Concepción (also known as La Concha, 12 kilometers west of Ticuantepe, under an hour from Managua), **Mariposa Eco-Hotel and Spanish School** (tel. 505/418-4638, www.spanishschoolnica.com) offers language classes in a rural setting under an hour from Managua or Granada; there are views of Volcán Masaya, a small pool, riding horses, hiking trails, and a library. A great retreat for families. All-inclusive Spanish school packages for $250 a week (please see Mariposa's listing in the *Masaya* chapter for more).

Laguna de Apoyo

If you prefer to avoid the bustle and nightlife of the city, **Proyecto Ecologico Spanish School and Hostel** (tel. 505/882-3992, www.gaianicaragua.org) is the only Spanish school in Nicaragua in a purely natural setting—the lakeside lodge is in the crater of an ancient volcano. The spot is incredible, only an hour from Managua, less to Granada, yet still tucked away in its own green world. Lodging and food are excellent (homestays are possible too), and the organization is not-for-profit. One week costs $190 and includes classes, activities, and room and board in their lodge.

San Juan del Sur

One of the best deals in the country is **Doña Rosa Silva's Spanish School** (located two blocks south of Hotel Villa Isabella, tel. 505/621-8905, www.spanishsilva.com), offering four hours of daily instruction, up to six days a week; $180 a week includes three meals a day.

Latin American Spanish School (tel. 505/820-2252, www.latinamericanspanishschool.com) is a good option, run by a half dozen entrepreneurial and professional Nicaraguan Spanish instructors with significant experience teaching foreigners. They offer a basic 20-hour instruction and activity package for $120, plus $90/week for lodging with private bath and three meals a day, plus homestay and volunteer activities.

Down the block across from the bank (right on the beach!) is the **San Juan del Sur Spanish School** (tel. 505/568-2432, www.sjdsspanish.com) with all-inclusive packages for $195 per week; the teachers are very experienced.

León

Va Pues Tours (tel. 505/606-2276, www.vapues.com) recently began offering an intensive, full-immersion Spanish course: $195 for 20 hours of one-on-one class (over five days), includes room and board. Check the **Casa de Cultura** class schedule, or the bulletin board at the **Vía Vía Hospedaje** for private tutors and lessons.

Estelí

You'll find a cool climate and a number of natural excursions available at one of the three schools here, all of which have been around since the early '90s. **Escuela Horizonte Nica** (located two blocks east and half a block north of INISER, tel. 505/713-4117, www.ibw.com.ni/~horizont) has one of the longest track records in town and proffers the lofty vision of "promoting peace and social justice for those living in poverty, those struggling against class, race, and gender prejudices, and those fighting for political freedom." It donates part of its profits to local organizations and has an afternoon activity program that includes visits to local cooperatives and community-development programs. One week of class, with 20 hours of intensive study, afternoon activities, and homestay with a family costs $165, discounts for groups.

The **CENAC Spanish School** (Centro Nicaragüense de Aprendizaje Cultural, tel. 505/713-5437, cenac@ibw.com.ni, www.ibw.com.ni/~cenac) has been around since 1990. Room and board plus 20 hours of class cost $140 a week. It's located on the west side of the Pan-American Highway, 150 meters north of the Shell Esquipulas (or half a block south of Bodegas de Enebas).

Spanish School Güegüense (250 meters east of the Shell Esquipulas, tel. 505/713-7172) offers afternoon activities, including trips to Jinotega, Quilalí, San Juan del Río Coco, and local Estelí attractions. Class and homestay cost $120 per week.

Matagalpa

This is a great, slightly off-the-beaten-path city in which to spend a few weeks, and it's got a single top-rate Spanish school to set it all up: **Spanish School Matagalpa** (matagalpatours.com) offers "a holistic vision of cultural immersion, enabling students to build friendships in the local community." As a part of Matagalpa Tours, you'll have immediate access to a range of day trips and backcountry hiking expeditions in the surrounding mountains. The school is also right next door to one of the country's chillest cafés, the Artesano.

Health and Safety

BEFORE YOU GO
Resources
Dirk G. Schroeder's *Staying Healthy in Asia, Africa, and Latin America* is an excellent and concise guide to preventative medicine in the Developing World and is small enough to fit in your pocket. Consult the "Mexico and Central America" page of the U.S. Centers for Disease Control (CDC) website for up-to-date health recommendations and advice (www.cdc.gov) or call their International Travelers Hotline (U.S. tel. 404/332-4559 or 877/394-8747). You can also contact the Nicaraguan embassy in your country.

Vaccinations
Required: A certificate of vaccination against yellow fever is required for all travelers over one year of age and arriving from affected areas.
Recommended: Before traveling to Nicaragua, be sure your tetanus, diphtheria, measles, mumps, rubella, and polio vaccines are up-to-date. Protection against hepatitis A and typhoid fever is also recommended for all travelers.

MEDICAL ATTENTION
Medical care is in short supply outside of Managua, and even in the capital city, doctors in public hospitals are underpaid (earning about $200 a month) and brutally overworked. Though there are many qualified medical professionals in Nicaragua, who studied abroad in Mexico, Cuba, or the United States, there are also many practicing doctors and medical staff who have less-than-adequate credentials. Use your best judgment. Hospitals and medical facilities typically expect immediate payment for services rendered, but their rates are ridiculously cheaper than they are back home. Larger facilities accept credit cards and everyone else demands cash.

Government-run health clinics, called

When eating *fritanga* street food, be sure the meat is hot and well cooked.

Centros de Salud, exist in most towns throughout the country, usually near the central plaza. They are free—even to you—but often poorly supplied and inadequately staffed.

We've pointed out the main hospital or private clinic in most regional chapters, but we should also mention here that the newest and most modern hospital in the country is **Hospital Vivian Pellas,** a $23-million private institution seven kilometers south of Managua on the Carretera Masaya. For **dental emergencies,** or even just a check-up, seek out the bilingual, well-trained services of Dr. Esteban Bendaña McEwan (300 meters south of the Enitel Villa Fontana tel. 505/270-5021 or 505/850-8981, estebanbm@hotmail.com); Dr. Bendaña is accustomed to dealing with foreign patients and his prices are reasonable.

As for natural medicine, many *campesinos* have excellent practical knowledge of herbal remedies that involve teas, tree barks, herbs, and fruits. The first medicines came from the earth, and the Nicaraguans haven't lost that connection. Try crushed and boiled papaya seeds, oil of *apazote* (a small shrub whose seed is crushed for medicinal use), or coconut water to fend off intestinal parasites, *manzanilla* (chamomile) for stress or menstrual discomfort, or *tamarindo* or papaya for constipation. A popular cold remedy involves hot tea mixed with two squeezed limes, *miel de jicote* (honey from the *jicote* bee), and a large shot of cheap rum, drunk right before you go to bed so you sweat out the fever as you sleep.

Medications and Prescriptions

Many modern medicines, produced in Mexico or El Salvador, are sold in Nicaragua. Because of a struggling economy and plenty of competition, some pharmacies may sell you medicine without a prescription. For simple travelers' ailments, like stomach upsets, diarrhea, or analgesics, it's worth going to the local pharmacy and asking what they recommend. Even relatively strong medications like codeine can be purchased over the counter (in Alka-Seltzer tablet form).

Birth Control: Condoms are cheap and easy to find. Any corner pharmacy will have them, even in small towns of just a few thousand people; a three-pack of prophylactics costs less than $2. Female travelers taking contraceptives should know the chemical name for what they use. *Pastillas anticonceptivas* (birth control pills) are easily obtained without prescription in pharmacies in Managua and in larger cities like León, Granada, and Estelí. Other forms of birth control and sexual protection devices, such as IUDs, dental dams, and diaphragms, are neither used nor sold.

STAYING HEALTHY

Ultimately, your health is dependent on the choices you make, and chief among these is what you decide to put in your mouth. One longtime resident says staying healthy in the tropics is more than just possible—it is an "art form." Nevertheless, as you master the art, expect your digestive system to take some time getting accustomed to the new food and microorganisms in the Nicaraguan diet. During this time (and after), use common sense: Wash or sanitize your hands often. Eat food that is well cooked and still hot when served. Avoid dairy products if you're not sure whether they are pasteurized. Be wary of uncooked foods, including ceviche and salads. Use the finger wag to turn down food from street vendors and be aware that pork carries the extra danger of trichinosis, not to mention the disgusting diet of garbage (and worse) on which most country pigs are raised.

Most importantly, be aware of flies as transmitters of food-borne illness. Prevent flies from landing on your food, glass, or table setting. You'll notice Nicaraguans are meticulous about this, and you should be too. If you have to leave the table, cover your food with a napkin or have someone else wave their hand over it slowly. You can fold your drinking straw over and put the mouth end into the neck of the bottle to prevent flies from landing on it, and put napkins on top of the bottle neck and your glass, too. Have the waiter clear the table when you've finished with a dish—and beware the

waiter who, in response to your complaints about the flies, comes back and douses you and your dinner in an aerosol cloud of pesticide that's been banned in the United States for decades.

Sun Exposure

Nicaragua is located a scant 12 degrees of latitude north of the equator, so the sun's rays strike the Earth's surface at a more direct angle

---

GETTING IN HOT WATER

In the cooler parts of the country, namely Matagalpa and Jinotega, some hotels and *hospedajes* offer hot water by means of electric water-heating canisters attached to the end of the shower head. Cold water passing through the coils is warmed before falling through the spout. The seemingly obvious drawback to the system is the presence of electric wires in and around a wet (i.e., conductive) environment. While not necessarily the electric deathtraps they appear to be, they should be approached with caution. Before you step into the shower, check for frayed or exposed wires (or the burned carcasses of former hotel occupants on the shower floor). Set the control knob to II and, very carefully, turn the water on. Once you're wet and water is flowing through the apparatus, it's in your best interest not to mess with the heater again.

To save you many cold showers trying to figure out how the darned thing works, we'll let you in on the secret: If the water pressure is too low, the heater isn't triggered on, and the water will not be heated, but if the water pressure is too high, it will be forced through the nozzle before it's had sufficient contact with the coils, and the water will not be heated. Open the faucet to a moderate setting, and rub-a-dub-dub, you're taking a hot shower. When you've finished, turn the water off first and dry off, then turn the little knob back to Off.

¿DONDE ESTÁ EL BAÑO? A GUIDE TO NICARAGUA'S TOILETS

Nicaragua boasts an enormous diversity of bathrooms, from various forms of the *inodoro* (modern toilet) to the full range of dark, infested *letrinas* (outhouses). Despite so many options, there is a general shortage of actual toilet seats, so having to squat over a bare bowl is common. Also important is mastering the manual flush, useful when the normal pump mechanism breaks down or when the city water pressure fails. Use the bucket that should be sitting beside the toilet to dump water into the bowl all at once, forcefully and from high up to ensure maximum turd swirlage.

Additionally, with most flush toilets, always assume that used toilet paper is to be put in the basket next to the toilet, not in the bowl, so as not to clog up the weak plumbing. You'll get used to it. The most commonly encountered toilet paper is pink and made of recycled paper in a plant in Granada. It's not so soft – you'll get used to that, too. If not, pick up some luxury rolls to travel with, available in most supermarkets. Smart travelers carry their own *papel higiénico*, protected in a plastic bag and easily accessible. Otherwise, try the following phrase with your host when their can runs out of paper: *"Fijase que no hay papel en el baño."*

any muscles as you kick yourself for being so stupid. Treat sunburns with aloe gel, or better yet—find a fresh *sábila* (aloe) plant to break open and rub over your skin.

Drinking the Water

While most Nicaraguan municipal water systems are well treated and probably safe, there is not much reason to take the chance, especially when purified, bottled water is so widely available. But rather than contribute to the growing solid waste problem in Nicaragua, why not bring a single reusable plastic water bottle and refill it in your hotel lobby's five-gallon purified water dispensers? If you are diligent about refilling, it is entirely possible to spend a week or more in Nicaragua drinking purified water without using a single plastic throwaway bottle.

If you'll be spending time in rural Nicaragua, consider a small water filter or, alternately, use six drops of liquid iodine (or three of bleach) in a liter of water; this will kill every organism that needs to be killed, good if you're in a pinch, but not something you'll find yourself practicing on a daily basis. Bringing water to a boil is also an effective means of purification.

Standard precautions include avoiding ice cubes unless you're confident they were made with boiled or purified water. Canned and bottled drinks without ice, including beer, are safe, but should never be used as a substitute for water when trying to stay hydrated.

Oral Rehydration Salts

Probably the single most effective item you can carry in our medical kit are these packets of powdered salt and sugar known in Spanish as *suero oral*. One packet of *suero* mixed with a liter of water, drunk in small sips, is the best immediate treatment for all of the following: diarrhea, sun exposure, fever, infection, or hangovers. Rehydration salts are essential to your recovery as they replace the salts and minerals your body loses from sweating, vomiting, or urinating, thus aiding your body's most basic cellular transfer functions. Whether or

than in northern countries. The result is that you will burn faster and sweat up to twice as much as you are used to. Did we mention that you should drink lots of water?

Ideally, do like the majority of the locals do, and stay out of the sun between 10 A.M. and 2 P.M. It's a great time to take a nap anyway. Use sunscreen of at least SPF 30, and wear a hat and pants. Should you overdo it in the sun, make sure to drink lots of fluids—that means water, not beer—and try not to strain not you like the taste (odds are you won't), consuming enough *suero* and water is very often the difference between being just a little sick and feeling really, really awful.

Sport drinks like Gatorade are super-concentrated *suero* mixtures and should be diluted at a ratio of three to one with water to make the most of the active ingredients. If you don't, you'll urinate out the majority of the electrolytes. Gatorade is common in most gas stations and supermarkets but *suero* packets are more widely available and much cheaper, available at any drugstore or health clinic for about $0.50 a packet. It can be improvised even more cheaply, according to the following recipe: Mix one-half teaspoon of salt, one-half teaspoon baking soda, and four tablespoons of sugar in one quart of boiled or carbonated water. Drink a full glass of the stuff after each time you use the bathroom. Add a few drops of lemon to make it more palatable.

DISEASE AND COMMON AILMENTS
Diarrhea and Dysentery
Everyone's body reacts differently to the changes in diet, schedule, and stress that go along with traveling, and many visitors to Nicaragua stay entirely regular throughout their trip. Some don't. Diarrhea is one symptom of amoebic (parasitic) and bacillic (bacterial) dysentery, both caused by some form of fecal-oral contamination. Often accompanied by nausea, vomiting, and a mild fever, dysentery is easily confused with other diseases, so don't try to self-diagnose. *Examenes de heces* (stool-sample examinations) can be performed at most clinics and hospitals and are your first step to getting better (cost is $2–8). Bacillic dysentery is treatable with antibiotics; amoebic is treated with one of a variety of drugs that kill off all the flora in your intestinal tract. Of these, Flagyl is the best known, but other non–FDA approved treatments like Tinedazol are commonly available, cheap, and effective. Do not drink alcohol with these drugs, but do eat something like yogurt or acidophilus pills to refoliate your tummy.

Generally, simple cases of diarrhea in the absence of other symptoms are nothing more serious than "traveler's diarrhea." If you do get a case of Diriangén's Revenge, your best bet is to let it pass naturally. Diarrhea is your body's way of flushing out the bad stuff, so constipating medicines like Imodium-AD are not recommended, as they keep the bacteria (or whatever is causing your intestinal distress) within your system. Save the Imodium (or any other liquid glue) for emergency situations like long bus rides or a date with Miss Nicaragua. Most importantly, drink water! Not replacing the fluids and electrolytes you are losing will make you feel much worse than you need to. If the diarrhea persists for more than 48 hours, is bloody, or is accompanied by a fever, see a health professional immediately.

Malaria
Malaria is present in Nicaragua, and to date, the newer chloroquine-resistant strains of the disease have not been detected. Though the risk is higher in rural areas, especially those alongside rivers or marshes, malaria-infected mosquitoes breed anywhere stagnant pools of water (of any size, even in an empty bottle cap) are found, including urban settings.

Malaria works by setting up shop in your liver and then blasting you with attacks of fever, headaches, chills, and fatigue. The onslaughts occur on a 24-hour-sick, 24-hour-feeling-better cycle. If you observe this cycle, seek medical attention. They'll most likely take a blood test and if positive, prescribe you a huge dose of chloroquine that will kill the bug. Allow time to recover your strength. Weekly prophylaxis of chloroquine or an equivalent is recommended, and the CDC specifically recommends travelers to Nicaragua use Aralen-brand pills (500 mg for adults). Begin taking the pills two weeks before you arrive and continue taking them four weeks after leaving the country. A small percentage of people have negative reactions to chloroquine, including nightmares, rashes, or hair loss. Alternative treatments are available, but the best method of all is to not get bit (see the *Mosquitoes* section in this chapter).

Dengue Fever

Dengue, or "bone-breaking," fever will put a stop to your fun in Central America like a baseball bat to the head. The symptoms may include any or all of the following: sudden high fever, severe headache (think nails in the back of your eyes), muscle and back pain, nausea or vomiting, and a full-bodied skin rash, which may appear 3–4 days after the onset of the fever. Although the initial pain and fever may only last a few days, you may be out of commission for up to several weeks, possibly bedridden, depressed, and too weak to move. There is no vaccine, but dengue's effects can be successfully minimized with plenty of rest, Tylenol (for the fever and aches), and as much water and *suero* as you can manage. Dengue itself is undetectable in a blood test, but a low platelet *(plaquetas)* count indicates its presence. If you believe you have dengue, you should get a blood test as soon as possible to make sure it's not the rare hemorrhagic variety, which can be fatal if untreated.

AIDS

Although large numbers of HIV infections have not yet appeared in Nicaragua, especially compared to other Central American countries, health organizations claim that geography, as well as cultural, political, and social factors will soon contribute to an AIDS explosion in Nicaragua. Currently, there are about 1,500 HIV-positive cases registered with MINSA (the Government Health Ministry), but one World Bank official estimated actual cases at 8,000. Exacerbating the spread of AIDS (La SIDA) is the promiscuous behavior of many married males, an active sex-worker trade, less than ideal condom-using habits, and growing drug trouble. AIDS is most prevalent in urban populations, mainly Managua and Chinandega, and is primarily transmitted sexually, not through needles or contaminated blood.

That said, blood transfusions are not recommended. Travelers should avoid sexual contact with persons whose HIV status is unknown. If you intend to be sexually active, use a fresh latex condom for every sexual act and every orifice. Condoms are inexpensive and readily available in just about any local pharmacy; in Spanish, a condom is called *condón* or *preservativo.*

Other Diseases

Cholera is present in Nicaragua, with occasional outbreaks, especially in rural areas with contaminated water supplies. Vaccines are not required because they offer incomplete protection. You are better off watching what you put in your mouth. In case you contract cholera (the symptoms are profuse diarrhea the color of rice water accompanied by sharp intestinal cramps, vomiting, and body weakness), see a doctor immediately and drink your *suero.* Cholera kills—by dehydrating you.

Leptospirosis is caused by a bacteria found in water contaminated with the urine of infected animals, especially rodents. Symptoms include high fever and headache, chills, muscle aches, vomiting, and possibly jaundice. Humans become infected through contact with infected food, water, or soil. It is not known to spread from person to person and can be treated with antibiotics in its early stages.

Hepatitis B also lurks in Nicaragua. Avoid contact with bodily fluids or bodily waste. Get vaccinated if you anticipate close contact with the local population or plan to reside in Nicaragua for an extended period of time.

Most towns in Nicaragua, even rural ones, conduct a yearly **rabies**-vaccination campaign for dogs, but you should still be careful. Get a rabies vaccination if you intend to spend a long time in Nicaragua. Should you be bitten, immediately cleanse the wound with lots of soap, and get prompt medical attention.

Tuberculosis is spread by sneezing or coughing, and the infected person may not know he or she is a carrier. If you are planning to spend more than four weeks in Nicaragua (or plan on spending time in a Nicaraguan jail), consider having a tuberculin skin test performed before and after visiting. Tuberculosis is a serious and possibly fatal disease but can be treated with several medications.

BITES AND STINGS
Mosquitoes

Mosquitoes are most active during the rainy season (June–Nov.) and in areas near stagnant water, like marshes, puddles, or rice fields. They are much more common in the lower, flatter regions of Nicaragua than they are in mountains, though even in the highlands, old tires, cans, and roadside puddles can provide the habitat necessary to produce swarms of *zancudos* (mosquitoes). The mosquito that carries malaria bites during the night and evening hours, and the dengue fever courier is active during the day, from dawn to dusk. They are both relatively simple to combat, and ensuring you don't get bitten is the best prophylaxis for preventing disease.

First and foremost, limit the amount of skin you expose—long sleeves, pants, and socks will do more to prevent bites than the strongest chemical repellent. Choose lodging accommodations with good screens and if this is not possible, use a fan to blow airborne insects away from your body as you sleep. Avoid being outside or unprotected in the hour before sunset, when mosquito activity is heaviest, and use a *mosquitero* (mosquito net) tucked underneath your mattress when you sleep. Hanging-type mosquito nets are available in Nicaragua, or you can purchase *tela de mosquitero* anywhere they sell fabric and have a mosquito net made by a seamstress. Also, many *pulperías* sell *espirales* (mosquito coils), which burn slowly, releasing a mosquito-repelling smoke; they're cheap and convenient, but full of chemicals, so don't breathe in too much smoke.

Spiders, Scorpions, and Snakes

Arachnophobes, beware! The spiders of Nicaragua are dark, hairy, and occasionally capable of devouring small birds. Of note is the *picacaballo,* a kind of tarantula whose name (meaning horse-biter) refers to the power of its flesh-rotting venom to destroy a horse's hoof. Don't worry, though; spiders do not aggressively seek out people, and do way more good than harm by eating things like Chagas bugs. If you'd rather the spiders didn't share your personal space, shake out your bedclothes before going to sleep and check your shoes before putting your feet in them.

Scorpions, or *alacránes,* are common in Nicaragua, especially in dark corners, beaches, and piles of wood. Nicaraguan scorpions look nasty—black and big—but their sting is no more harmful than that of a bee and is described by some as what a cigarette burn feels like. Your lips and tongue may feel a little numb, but the venom is nothing compared to their smaller, translucent cousins in Mexico. For people who are prone to anaphylactic shock, it can be a more serious or life-threatening experience. Be aware, in Nicaragua the Spanish word *escorpión* usually refers not to scorpions but to the harmless little geckos (also called *perros zompopos*) that scurry around walls eating small insects. And in spite of what your *campesino* friends might insist, those little geckos are neither malevolent nor deadly and would never, as you will often hear, intentionally try to kill you by urinating on you.

There are 15 species of poisonous snakes in Nicaragua, but your chance of seeing one is extremely rare, unless you're going deep into the bush. In that case, walk softly and carry a big machete. Keep an eye out for 1 of 11 pit viper species (family *Viperidae*), especially the infamous fer-de-lance *(Bothrops asper),* or *Barba amarilla;* the most aggressive and dangerous snake in Central America, the fer-de-lance is mostly confined to the humid central highlands and the Caribbean coast. Less common pit vipers, but occasionally seen in western parts of the country, are the Ponzigua *(Porthidium ophryomegas);* the Central American rattlesnake *(Crotalus durissus),* known in Spanish as *cascabel;* and a relative of the copperhead, the Cantil, or Castellana, *(Agkistrodon bilineatus).* In addition, there are four rarely seen species of the *Elapidae* family (three coral snakes and the pelagic sea snake). Remember, there are many coral mimics out there with various versions of the famous colored markings; the true coral (only one species of which is found on the west side of the country) has ring markings in only this order: red, yellow, black, yellow.

Chagas' Disease

The Chagas bug (*Trypanosoma cruzi*) is a large, recognizable insect, also called the kissing bug, assassin bug, and cone-nose. In Spanish it's known as *chinche*, but this word is also used for many other types of beetlelike creatures. The Chagas bug bites its victim (usually on the face, close to the lips), sucks its fill of blood, and, for the coup de grâce, defecates on the newly created wound. Chagas bugs are present in Nicaragua, found mostly in poor *campesino* structures of crumbling adobe. Besides the downright insult of being bitten, sucked, and pooped on, the Chagas bug's biggest menace is the disease it carries of the same name, which manifests itself in 2 percent of its victims. The first symptoms include swollen glands and a fever that appear 1–2 weeks after the bite. The disease then goes into a 5–30-year remission phase. If and when it reappears, Chagas' disease causes the lining of the heart to swell, sometimes resulting in death. There is no cure.

CRIME

Believe it or not, Nicaragua is, for the moment, still considered one of the safest countries in all of Latin America. If you're traveling south from Honduras, El Salvador, or Guatemala, you should feel your anxiety level drop noticeably—Nicaragua has been more successful at preventing the gang violence that has plagued its northern neighbors. You're more likely to be harassed than attacked in Nicaragua, and most physical assaults involve alcohol. Avoid traveling alone at night or while intoxicated, and pay the extra dollar or two for a cab. Women should not take cabs when the driver has a friend riding up front.

Pick-pocketing (or hat/watch/bag snatching) occurs occasionally in crowded places or buses, but again, this is a situation that can usually be avoided by reducing your desirability as a target and paying attention. Try to avoid urban buses in Managua and, whenever possible but especially when visiting the markets, avoid wearing flashy jewelry, watches, or sunglasses. Keep your cash divided up and hidden in a money belt, sock, bra, or underwear.

If you are the victim of a crime, report it to the local police department immediately (dial 118). Remember, if you've insured any of your possessions, you won't be reimbursed without a copy of the official police report. Nicaraguan police have good intentions but few resources, lacking even gasoline for the few patrol cars or motorcycles they have—don't be surprised if you are asked to help fill up a vehicle with gas. This is not uncommon, and remember that a full tank of gas should cost no more than $30. Travelers are often shocked to find that the police occasionally do recover stolen merchandise. While police corruption does exist—Nicaraguan police earn a pitiful $55–60 per month—the Nicaraguan police force is notably more honest and helpful than in some Central American nations.

Bigger cities, like Estelí and Chinandega, have their shady neighborhoods to avoid, and, because of its size and sprawl, Managua is the most dangerous of Nicaraguan cities. Still, it's a pretty simple task to stay out of the unsafe barrios. Although still nowhere near the urban violence being experienced in nearby Honduras and El Salvador, worsening poverty and unemployment have led to a surge in gang membership in the Nicaragua's poorer neighborhoods, and drug use—including crack—is also reportedly on the rise. Still, by not entering unknown areas, not walking at night, and sticking with other people, you can reduce the chances of anything bad happening.

In general, the countryside of Nicaragua is peaceful and safe. Until a few years ago, the one exception was El Triangulo Minero, a mountainous northeastern region around the mining towns of La Rosita, Bonanza, and Siuna. The area was home to a loose band of armed ex-soldiers infatuated with the bandit lifestyle and calling themselves FUAC (Frente Unido Andrés Castro). Today, however, most of their members and leaders have been hunted down and picked off by the army and police, notably in a few gun battles in 2001.

Always check the latest crime and U.S. State Department reports.

LAND MINES IN NICARAGUA

Nicaragua has the ignominious honor of having had more land mines – more than 135,000 in place and another 136,000 stockpiled in the wilds of the northeast – than any other country in the Western Hemisphere. This is one of the most brutal and pernicious legacies of the conflicts of the 1980s, and the focus of a major de-mining cleanup effort by the Nicaraguan Army and the Organization of American States (OAS). In fact, no other country in the world is making a greater effort than Nicaragua to clear the land of mines.

The de-mining process, though ongoing, can largely be considered a success: Since the beginning of operations, 75 percent of installed antipersonnel mines have been located and destroyed, and more than 3.8 million square meters of minefield have returned to productive use. The de-mining effort takes place in six-month modules that concentrate on known trouble spots, during which specially trained troops and dogs trained to sniff out explosives comb the territory. After every square meter has been checked for explosives, the region is certified mine-free. The weapons, when uncovered in the field, are detonated on-site. Stockpiles are transferred to and destroyed at one of two special detonating zones: the Escuela de Sargentos Andres Castro outside Managua and the ENABI army base a few kilometers south of Condega, Estelí.

There are currently four areas where OAS troops are actively searching for and destroying land mines: outside of Matagalpa and Jinotega, outside of Murra (Nueva Segovia), and the lands around Jalapa (Nueva Segovia). Both Sandinista and Contra troops mined Nueva Segovia heavily during their repeated confrontations, and, in 1998, flooding and mudslides caused by Hurricane Mitch washed many known minefields downstream, burying other sites under a layer of earth. Since 2002, OAS troops have been combing the Honduran border from Las Sabanas (Madriz, just south of Somoto) through Jalapa to Wamblán, Jinotega, a distance of nearly 150 kilometers. The department of Chinandega and the border with Costa Rica were declared free of mines in late 2001, and the Río San Juan in 2002.

Antipersonnel explosives have crippled nearly a thousand Nicaraguans and injured countless more (to this day, about 20 people per year). More frequent still are losses of cattle, which go unreported but are the subject of many a *campesino* story. For this reason, an intensive education campaign aimed at the *campesinos* in the affected areas employs comic books with a story line discussing the danger of land mines and what to do if you suspect you've found one.

What does the presence of land mines mean to the traveler? That you should ask a lot of questions if you leave the beaten trail, particularly in the north: Nueva Segovia, Jinotega, Matagalpa, and Jalapa, as well as eastern parts of Boaco. Loose mines don't lie scattered randomly in the hillsides; they were placed at strategic locations, like radio towers, bridges, air strips, and known Contra border crossings. The locals are your best sources of information. They'll be able to tell you if there were battles or heavy Contra presence in the area, if there are known minefields, and if the OAS teams have already passed through. In towns like El Cuá and Bocay, you'll find parcels of land in chest-high weeds even though the land on both sides is intensely farmed. Ask around, and look for the yellow "Area Minada" signs, then move on.

Numerous international organizations work both to clear minefields around the world, such as the UN-sponsored Adopt-a-Minefield program (www.landmines.org), and to ban the devices (www.icbl.org).

Illegal Drugs

Nicaragua is part of the underground high-way that transports cocaine and heroin from South America to North America and, as such, is under a lot of pressure from the United States to crack down on drug traffickers passing through in vehicles or in boats off the Atlantic coast. Drug-related crime is rapidly increasing on the Atlantic coast, particularly in Bluefields and Puerto Cabezas. All travelers in Nicaragua are subject to local drug-possession and use laws, which include stiff fines and prison sentences of up to 30 years.

Marijuana, an herb that grows naturally and quite well in the soils and climate of Nicaragua, is known locally as *la mota, el monte,* or, in one remote Matagalpa valley, *pim-pirim-pím.* Marijuana prohibition is alive and well in Nicaragua, despite regular use of the plant throughout the population. This controversial antiganja policy (critics call it a waste of public funds) allows harsh penalties for possession of even tiny quantities of *cannabis sativa,* for both nationals and tourists alike. Canine and bag searches at airports, docks along the Atlantic coast, and at the Honduran and Costa Rican border crossings are the norm, not the exception.

As a foreign, hip-looking tourist, you may be offered pot at some point during your trip, especially on the Atlantic coast and in San Juan del Sur. The proposal may be a harmless invitation to get high on the beach, or it may be from a hustler or stool pigeon who is about to rip you off and/or get you arrested. Use the same common sense you would anywhere in the world, with the added knowledge that Nicaraguan jails are a major bummer.

Prostitution

The world's oldest business is one facet of Nicaragua's economy that has more than tripled in recent years, especially in Managua, Granada, Corinto, and border/trucking towns like Somotillo. Though illegal, *puterías* (whore-houses), thinly disguised as "beauty salons" or "massage parlors," operate with virtual impunity, and every strip club in Managua has a bank of rooms behind the stage, some with an actual cashier stationed at the door. Then there are the commercial sex workers on Carretera Masaya, and the nation's numerous auto-hotels, which rent rooms by the hour. The situation is nowhere near as developed as the sex tourism industries of places like Thailand and Costa Rica, but it is undeniable that foreigners have contributed in no small way to Nicaragua's sex economy. Travelers considering indulging should think seriously about the social impacts that result from perpetuating this institution, and should start by reading the section on AIDS in this chapter.

BEGGING

In general, it is assumed that foreigners with the leisure time to travel to Nicaragua have lots and lots of money. Expect poor children and adults to occasionally ask you for spare change wherever you travel, usually by either a single outstretched index finger or a cupped, empty hand, both accompanied with an insistent, *"Chele, deme un peso"* ("Whitey, give me a coin"). It's low-key, nothing like the aggressive beggars in countries like India, so don't be worried or afraid. Another poignant sight, encountered at sidewalk restaurants and market eateries, are wide-eyed, hungry children watching as eagerly as the skeletal dogs standing behind them as you finish your meal. Your leftovers will not go to waste here as they would at home—a small concession. In many cities, including Granada, many children and adolescents asking for money are *huele-pegas* (glue sniffers) and your money will only go to buy them more of H. B. Fuller's finest. *Huele-pegas* are identified by glazed eyes, unkempt appearances, and sometimes a jar of glue tucked under a dirty shirt. Do not give them money, but feel free to give them some time, attention, and maybe a little food. In general, giving money to beggars, especially in tourist centers, is a bad idea which perpetuates dependency, bad habits, and children skipping school (sometimes at their parents' request) to ply tourists for coins and dollars. There are many other ways to direct your good intentions.

Information and Services

MONEY
Currency
Since 1912, Nicaragua's currency has been the *córdoba,* named after Francisco Hernández de Córdoba, the Spanish founder of the colony of Nicaragua. It is divided into 100 *centavos* or 10 *reales.* In common usage, the *córdoba* is also referred to as a *peso.* The U.S. dollar is also an official currency in Nicaragua and the only foreign currency you can hope to exchange (although many communities along the Río San Juan also use Costa Rican *colones*). Travelers from nations other than the United States should bring their money to Nicaragua in U.S. dollars. The currencies of neighboring Central American nations can only be exchanged on the borders. Even in Managua, trying to exchange Central American currency is nearly impossible. As of January 2001, only Bancentro exchanges Euros, but the rate is not favorable.

The runaway inflation of the Sandinista years (as much as 30,000 percent) is now a mere memory, and the currency these days is relatively stable. However, to offset inflation, the *córdoba* has been steadily devalued since its inception at the rate of approximately US$0.37 every six months and has led to the introduction in 2003 of a fancy new C$500 bill for larger purchases. You can do the arithmetic yourself before arriving in Nicaragua, or find the latest rates at the Central Bank of Nicaragua's website, www.bcn.gob.ni.

Costs
Nicaragua is still a budget traveler's paradise, as prices for lodging and food are lower than other Central American nations, notably Costa Rica. You can comfortably exist in Nicaragua on $50 per day, less if you're not traveling and have simple needs. Because there's more to do in Managua than other cities, and taxi costs add up, budget a little more while in the capital. Needless to say, you can travel for less by eating the way the locals do and forgoing the jalapeño steak and beer. Budget travelers interested in stretching their money to the maximum should eat at *fritangas* and market stalls, take the slow bus, and avoid prolonged stays in the major cities.

Bank Machines
Known in Spanish as *cajeras automáticas,* ATMs are no longer a novelty to Nicaragua—since 1999, they've appeared in dozens of gas stations all over Managua. Any bank card affiliated with the Cirrus logo will work. You will receive your cash in *córdobas,* and you won't get a good exchange rate.

Wiring Money
There's a branch of Western Union in just about every midsize and large city in Nicaragua. Western Union is the most convenient way for someone to wire you cash, but the transaction fee is steep at 25 percent.

Bank Hours
Unless noted otherwise in this book, all bank hours are 8:30 A.M.–4 P.M. Monday–Friday and 8:30–noon Saturday. Nicaraguans receive their pay on the 15th and 30th or 31st of every month. Should you need to go to a bank on those days, you can expect the lines to be extra long. Bide your time by watching businesspeople carry away large sums of cash in brown paper lunch bags.

Travelers Checks
U.S. dollar *cheques viajeros* are growing increasingly obsolete in this world of ATMs and online banking. They are accepted in some banks, notably Bancentro, one of the only places which will cash a non–American Express check. Travelers checks for currencies other than U.S. dollars will not be cashed. You will need to show your passport to cash travelers checks, and be sure that your signature matches your previous one or you'll convert your precious dollars into a worthless piece of

Money changers on the streets of major cities are often sanctioned by the banks and offer fair exchange rates.

paper. Some banks actually demand to see your original receipts—the ones you are supposed to keep physically separate from the checks!

Credit Cards

Many hotels and restaurants accept credit cards (Visa, MasterCard, American Express, or Diners Club), but still mostly just in Managua, San Juan del Sur, and Granada. Always check ahead, though, because credit cards are still not ubiquitous and steep charges may apply.

Sales Tax

Nicaragua's sales tax (IGV or Impuesto General de Valor) is a whopping 15 percent—the highest in Central America. You'll find it automatically applied to the bill at nicer restaurants, fancy hotels, and upscale shops in major cities. Elsewhere, sales tax is casually dismissed. Should you decide to splurge on a fancy dinner (places where you'd expect to spend more than $6–10 a meal), expect to pay 25 percent of your bill for tax and tip. Prices in this book usually do not include the IGV; hotels who do not charge it are breaking the law and making you complicit.

Tipping

In better restaurants, a 10–15 percent *propina* (tip) will be graciously added on to your bill, even if the food was undercooked, the beer flat, and the service atrocious. You are under no obligation to pay it if it is unmerited. You might want to give a little something after getting your hair cut: 10 percent is appropriate. Skycaps at the International Airport in Managua will jostle to carry your luggage out to a waiting taxi. Tip what you'd like (a few dollars is appropriate) and never accept the services of someone not wearing an official airport identity badge. Taxi drivers and bartenders are rarely tipped and don't expect to be unless they are exceptionally friendly or go out of their way for you. If you accept the offer of children trying to carry your bags, find you a hotel, or anything else, you have entered into an unspoken agreement to give them a few *córdobas*.

BUYING REAL ESTATE IN NICARAGUA: CAVEAT EMPTOR

For better or worse, Nicaragua is the latest tropical country chosen by international speculators with hopes of carefree retirement and lucrative appreciation on their new plot of Central American soil. A steady stream of aging baby boomers, aspiring financial managers, and alcoholic ne'er-do-wells on the run from ex-spouses and the tax man continue to find their way to southwestern Nicaragua. Healthy foreign investment? Or the new face of Yankee imperialism? You decide.

Potential real estate moguls typically wind up in Granada (and its nearby *isletas*), Rivas, and San Juan del Sur, all of which buzz with both independent and corporate real estate agents of mostly U.S. and Canadian origin. Before signing that check, however, take a breath, open your eyes, and ask a lot of questions. Start by visiting your embassy. The U.S. Embassy (www.usembassy.state.gov) has made land reform a priority for its relations with the Nicaraguan government; experienced buyers also seek out Pro-Nicaragua (www.pronicaragua.org), an "Investment Promotion Agency" that can help with information and contacts. We also recommend the companion volume to this book, by the same authors: *Moon Living Abroad in Nicaragua*.

Good deals are still found, but not without some risk. Much of the valued property that is up for grabs has two distinct and viable chains of title ownership: one that dates back to the Somoza period, and one that dates to the Sandinista government's failed agrarian reforms in which they confiscated land, Robin Hood-style, and redistributed it to the masses. Some of this land is still owned by cooperatives and *campesino* families, and some was given to powerful supporters (and leaders) of the Sandinistas. In the aftermath of the revolution, many of these seizures have been contested, many still stand, and very frequently two or three people present legitimate claims to the same lot. Make sure you – and your lawyer – know the history of the property back to 1978, and buy title insurance just in case. More than one new land owner has been surprised to have a stranger confront him with an obviously falsified property title. The Nicaraguan court system may or may not back you up. Title insurance is valuable because the companies that offer it not only research and defend your title, they also know their way around the Nicaraguan court system, no small thing. In the case of contested property, your policy may cover fraud and forgery. Florida-based First American Title Insurance Company is at present the only option (U.S. tel. 877/641-6767).

Don't completely entrust the job to others – do your own research on the region, the lot, community relations, year-round road conditions, etc. Was an environmental-impact statement done, as is required by law? If so, what did it conclude? Does your new piece of paradise have a freshwater supply? Lastly, watch out for the word beachfront. Under Nicaraguan law, land 30–80 meters from the high tide line (depending on who you ask) cannot be bought or sold, but only leased from either the national government or the local municipality as a "concession." Newly elected municipal governments (i.e., small-town mayors with grudges) often change policies on concessions, frustrating many a would-be gringo beach bum.

You can start your research at www.GoTo Nicaragua.com, a site run by the authors of this book.

Bargaining

Looking for a good deal is a sport in Nicaragua—half social, half business, and is expected with most outdoor market vendors and taxi drivers. But be warned: Bargaining is *al suave!* Aggressive, prolonged haggling is not cool, won't affect the price, and may leave ill feelings. To start off the process, after you are given the initial price, act surprised and use one of the following phrases: *"¿Cuánto es lo menos?"* ("What is your lowest price?") or *"¿Nada menos?"* ("Nothing less?").

Remember these guidelines when bargaining:

- Bargaining is social and friendly, or at least courteous. Keep your temper under wraps and always smile.

- Go back and forth a maximum of two or three times, and then either agree or walk away. Remember that some Nicaraguans, to save face, may lose a profit.

- Once you make a deal, it's done. If you think you've been ripped off, remember the $5 you got overcharged is still less than you'd pay for a double-tall mocha latte back home. Keep it in perspective and be a good sport.

- When bargaining with taxi drivers in Managua, bargain hard, but agree on a price *before* you enter the cab—once the vehicle is moving, your leverage has vanished in a puff of acrid, black exhaust.

MAPS

The overall champion map of Nicaragua is published by **International Travel Map** (ITM, www.itmb.com), scaled at 1:750,000, colored to show relief, and with good road and river detail. They also offer an excellent Central America regional map. It's found in many bookstores and travel shops, but not in Nicaragua.

A new favorite is the Nicaraguan map by German cartographers **Mapas NaTurismo** (www.mapas-naturismo.com) whose 1:500,000 country map is water resistant and features detailed tourist attractions and natural reserves better than any other; it also has a few handy inserts, including Isla de Ometepe at 1:200,000; samples available on their site.

The **Nelles Central America** map (1:1,750,000) offers a quality overview of the region (plus more detail on Costa Rica) and is good if you are traveling the whole area and don't intend to venture too far off the beaten track.

INETER, the Nicaraguan Institute of Territorial Studies, produces the only complete series of 1:50,000 maps (or "topo quads") of Nicaragua. Produced in the 1960s and photo-revised in the 1980s with Soviet help, these are the most detailed topographical maps of Nicaragua that exist. They can be purchased from the INETER office in Managua (and occasionally at regional offices) for $3 each. The Managua office is located across from Policlinica Oriental and Immigration, tel. 505/249-2768; open 8 A.M.–4:30 P.M. Monday–Friday.

Tactical Pilotage Charts (TPC K-25B and TPC K-25C) cover northern and southern Nicaragua, respectively, with some coverage of Costa Rica, Panamá, and Honduras at 1:500,000 scale. Designed for pilots, these maps have good representation of topography and are useful if you do any adventuring in the eastern parts of the country (far easier than carrying a stack of topo maps). Many smaller towns are shown, but only major roads.

TOURISM INFORMATION

Begin with the website of the authors of this book: www.GoToNicaragua.com, where you can ask us—and your fellow travelers—about specific concerns regarding Nicaragua travel.

The Instituto Nicaragüense de Turismo (INTUR, one block west and one north of the Crowne Plaza Hotel, tel. 505/222-3333, www.intur.gob.ni), an institution of the national government, is based in Managua, with a number of regional offices around the country. They staff a kiosk in the airport as well, which you'll pass after immigration. How useful INTUR is to you depends on your agenda in Nicaragua; most offices can give you a list of the year's upcoming festivals, a fistful of hotel brochures, and in some places, can help arrange tours with local operators. INTUR's regional offices are small and underbudgeted. INTUR Managua produces and sells maps as well as local guides and listings, and has a visitor's desk for tourists (8:30 A.M.–2 P.M. Mon.–Fri.).

Nicaragua Living (www.nicaragualiving .info) is the self-described "intelligent life-style magazine" of Nicaragua. *Between the Waves* is a free English-language magazine, available in the airport, bookstores, and hotels. A myriad other tourist-targeted, real-estate–funded glossy publications are always on hand in hotel lobbies across the country. Granada-based *Anda Ya!* (andayanicaragua .com) is particularly packed with helpful contacts and listings.

One underrated resource is the *Guía Telefónica* (national phone book), with basic tourism information and updated hotel listings; pick up a free copy at the Publicar office next to the Plaza España Colonia supermarket.

FILM AND PHOTOGRAPHY
Film Processing and Supplies

Really? You still use film? Don't worry, quality film and basic camera supplies are widely available in Nicaragua, and there are modern camera shops in most cities. Film processing is considerably more expensive (up to $20 a roll with no doubles) and often lower quality than back home. The biggest company is Kodak Express with a presence in nearly every major city (see *Information and Services* in the *Managua* chapter for info on their largest store). Black-and-white film and slide film are rarely available and processed at great expense.

For digital, always come equipped with a large memory card or your own laptop to store and edit your photos; otherwise, find a reliable cyber café, where most provide the service of burning your shots onto a CD at minimal cost.

Photo Tips and Etiquette

Cameras are by no means foreign objects in Nicaragua, but in many towns and neighborhoods, they are owned only by a few local entrepreneurs who take pictures at weddings, baptisms, graduations, etc. and then sell the print to the subject. Because of this, some rural Nicaraguans may expect that the photo you are taking is for them, and that you will either charge them for the photo or that you are going to send them a free copy. In general, people love getting their pictures taken, but often insist on dressing up, stiffening their bodies, and wiping all traces of emotion from their faces. The only way to avoid this (apart from making monkey noises to get them to laugh) is to take candid, unsolicited photos, something adults may perceive as bizarre and possibly rude. A solution is to ask first, concede to a few serious poses, and then snap away later when they are more unsuspecting but accustomed to your happy trigger finger. If you promise to send someone a copy, take down their address and actually do it.

COMMUNICATIONS AND MEDIA
Mail

The national postal system is called **Correos de Nicaragua**, and is surprisingly effective and reliable. Every city has at least one post office, often near the central plaza and adjacent to the telephone service (but not always). Legal-size letters and postcards cost about $0.70 to the United States, and a little more to Europe. Post offices in many cities have a gorgeous selection of stamps. Correos are open standard business hours (with some variations), almost always close during lunch, and are open until noon on Saturday.

To receive packages, have the sender use a padded envelope instead of a box, even if the shipment must be split into several pieces; keep the package as unassuming as possible, and try writing Dios Te Ama (God Loves You) on the envelope for a little help from above. In general, mail service to Nicaragua is reliable, even to remote areas. Boxes, on the other hand, of whatever size, are routed through the *aduana* (customs). This means traipsing to their office at the airport in Managua and enduring a horrific and uncaring bureaucracy intent on *not* giving you your goods. Most major international courier services have offices all over Nicaragua, including DHL and Federal Express, but they too are subject to the *aduana*.

Telephone and Fax

The national phone company, completely privatized in 2003, is **ENITEL** (Empresa Nicaragüense de Telecomunicaciónes, tel. 505/278-3131, fax 505/278-4012, www.enitel .com.ni), but it is just as commonly referred to by its old name, TELCOR. Every major city has an ENITEL, as do most small towns. In many villages without an ENITEL office, you'll find a local family renting out their private phone or contracted through ENITEL.

When you enter the ENITEL building, go to the front desk and tell the operator where you'd like to call. The operator will place the call for you, and if it goes through, will then send you to one of several private booths to receive it. When you complete the call, go back up to the front desk to pay. Alternately, look around for ENITEL and Publitel payphones, each requiring a different kind of prepaid card; there are also many Bell South coin-operated phones in corner stores, but these are usually more expensive.

Remember, when making calls within Nicaragua, you must prefix your number with a "0" when dialing out of your municipality or to any cell phone. Cell numbers begin with "88," "86," and "77," and cost extra to call. Satellite phones are wickedly expensive to call, begin with "892," and do not require a "0" beforehand.

Most ENITEL offices have fax machines. A two-page international fax may cost you $4–5; a local fax will cost about $1. Also check in copy shops, Internet providers, and post offices.

Important Numbers

- Information: 113

- Long-distance and collect-call operators: 110 and 116

- Police: 118

- Firefighters: 115 and 120

- Red Cross: 128

A 24-hour ENITEL customer service operator is available by dialing 121, and their main office in Managua is located 300 meters west of the Rotonda Centroamérica, second floor.

International Calls

Its ease and incredibly low cost have made Internet-based calling all the rage, especially in tourist sites with fast connections, like Granada, where competition drives rates to as low as $6 per hour to call the United States, Canada, or Europe. This phenomenon is sure to expand, the prices sure to fluctuate; always ask at the most modern Internet place in town about *llamadas internacionales*.

Mobile phone rates to the U.S. and other countries are usually reasonable. To make old-fashioned direct calls overseas, step up to the nearest ENITEL desk and give them the number. You'll need to know your country code: Canada and the United States are 1, Germany is 49, Spain 34, France 33, and Great Britain and Ireland 44. A complete listing of the country codes you'll need is in the phone book.

You can also use your calling card account from back home; tell the operator to connect you with the international bilingual operator for your company, or dial directly: AT&T tel. 1/800-0164, MCI 1/800-0166, Sprint 1/800-0171. Once you connect with the international operator, tell them your card's 800 number, then enter your card number and place your call as you would back home. In many larger cities, the ENITEL offices will have specially marked booths with direct hookups to international companies like MCI or AT&T, circumventing the need to use an operator.

Cell Phones

A number of companies provide expanding coverage throughout most of Nicaragua's populated areas. The more popular are Movistar and Claro (run by ENITEL, better coverage but more expensive). Some North American

© JOSHUA BERMAN

Internet access is easily found in Nicaragua, especially in Granada.

cell phones come equipped with a replaceable SIM chip to lock you into the various local networks available in Nicaragua. Ask your provider if this is possible. Otherwise, it's just as easy to purchase a mobile phone (they cost as low as $15) once you arrive in Nicaragua, then proceed to buy scratch-off cards to add minutes to your phone. To sign up with either company, just walk into a brightly painted cell phone booth, kiosk, or office (there are thousands throughout the country) where you can buy a phone and minutes as easily as picking up some carne asada from the corner *fritanga*.

Internet

The information superhighway came to Nicaragua as early as 1993 but wasn't widely accessible until 1999, when makeshift Internet cafés began appearing in Managua. Today, there are Internet cafés in just about every city in the nation, and even small villages, where the web squeaks by on horrible dial-up lines or hit-and-miss satellite connections.

If you are staying a significant time in Nicaragua and have your own computer, there are several options for opening your own account, which you can access by dial-up anywhere in the country. IBW Communications (tel. 505/278-6328, www.ibw.com.ni) has reasonable monthly rates, including options with or without Internet access ($10 a month for an email account). For your own ibw.com.ni address, visit IBW's Managua office (200 meters north of the Semáforos ENITEL Villa Fontana), or one of its regional offices around the country. They will install the necessary software and configure your computer, as well as provide reliable tech support as long as you are a customer. Other options are ENITEL or Cablenet (tel. 505/255-7280, www.cablenet.com.ni).

Free WiFi connections are spreading like the plague across Nicaraguan restaurants, hotels, and cafés—especially in Granada and San Juan del Sur. In a few years, you can probably expect near-global coverage in some of these places.

Macintosh

Most of Nicaragua is PC, but for Mac devotees and those who enjoy surfing with the best hardware on earth, the **iMac Center** (in Managua one block east and half-block south of the Semáforo UCA, tel. 505/270-5918) is a certified dealer and service provider, with all kinds of Macintosh-related services, repairs, and products (including iPods), plus cheap Internet service.

Newspapers and Magazines

Street vendors are out before 6 A.M. every day hawking the various daily papers, but you can often pick one up in most corner stores. *La Prensa* offers fairly conservative coverage and the front page contains a list of events for the week. *La Prensa* was so anti-Somoza in the 1970s, the dictator allegedly had the editor, Pedro Joaquín Chamorro, bumped off. Needless to say, it didn't help his press. Not long after the revolution, *La Prensa* turned anti-Sandinista and has remained so to this day. During election campaigns, *La Prensa* typically runs a regular series of "flashback" articles recalling the atrocities of the Contra war in the 1980s and dredging up every unresolved Sandinista scandal available. *El Nuevo Diario* is more blue-collar and sensationalist—its coverage of popular scandals is often hilarious.

International papers and magazines are sold in Managua at the Casa de Café, a kiosk on the first floor of the MetroCentro mall, and in the lobbies of the major hotels.

WEIGHTS AND MEASURES
Time

Nicaragua is in standard time zone GMT-6, i.e., six hours earlier than London. Daylight saving time is not observed, which means that during standard time, Nicaragua is in Chicago's time zone, and during daylight saving time, it is one hour behind Chicago. Don't forget, no matter what your watch says, you're always on "Nica time"—everything starts late, and your whining can't change it.

Electricity

Nicaragua uses the same electrical standards as the United States and Canada: 110V, 60 Hz. The shape of the electrical socket is the same as well. Travelers from Europe and Asia should consider bringing a power adapter if they want to make extensive use of electrical appliances brought from home. Laptop users should bring a portable surge protector with them, as the electrical current in Nicaragua is highly variable. Spikes, brownouts, and outages are commonplace.

Measurements

Distances are almost exclusively in kilometers, although for smaller lengths, you'll occasionally hear feet, inches, yards, and the colonial Spanish *vara* (about a meter). The most commonly used land-area term is the *manzana*, another old measure, equal to 1.74 acres. Weights and volumes are a mix of metric and non-metric: Buy your gasoline in gallons, your chicken in pounds, and so on.

RESOURCES

Glossary

alcaldía mayor's office

arroyo stream or gully

artesanía crafts

ayudante "helper" – the guy on the bus who collects your fee after you find a seat

barrio neighborhood

beneficio coffee mill

bombero firefighter

bravo rough, strong, wild

cabo cape

cafetín light-food eatery

calle street

cama matrimonial "marriage bed" – motels and hotels use this term to refer to a double, queen, or king-sized bed; a bed meant for two people.

camión truck

campesino country folk

campo countryside

carretera highway, road

cayo cay

centro de salud public MINSA-run health clinic; thereís one in most towns

centro recreativo public recreation center

cerro hill or mountain

cerveza, cervecita beer

chele, chela gringo, whitey

chinelas rubber flip-flops

ciudad city

colectivo a shared taxi or passenger boat

colonía neighborhood

comedor cheap lunch counter

comida corriente plate of the day

complejo complex (of buildings)

cooperitiva cooperative

cordillera mountain range

córdoba Nicaraguan currency

corriente standard, base

coyote illegal-immigrant smuggler; or profit-cutting middleman

cuajada white, homemade, salty cheese

departamentos subsection of Nicaragua, akin to states or counties

empalme intersection of two roads

entrada entrance

estero estuary or marsh

expreso express bus

farmacia pharmacy, drugstore

fiestas patronales Saint's Day parties held annually in every town and city

fresco natural fruit drink

fritanga street-side barbecue and fry-fest

gallo pinto national mix of rice íní beans

gancho gap in a fence

gaseosa carbonated beverage

gringo North American, or any foreigner

guaro booze

guitarra guitar

guitarrón mariachi bass guitar

hospedaje hostel, budget hotel

iglesia church

isla island

laguna lake

lancha small passenger boat

lanchero lancha driver

malecón waterfront

manzana besides an apple, this is also a measure of land equal to 100 square *varas*, or 1.74 acres

mar sea or ocean

mariachi Mexican country/polka music
mercado market
mesa/meseta geographical plateau
mosquitero mosquito net
muelle dock, wharf
museo museum
ordinario local bus (also *ruteado*)
panga small passenger boat
panguero *panga* driver
pinche stingy, cheap
playa beach
pueblo small town or village
pulpería corner store
puro cigar
quintal 100-pound sack
rancheras Mexican drinking songs
rancho thatch-roofed restaurant or hut
rato a short period of time
reserva reserve or preserve
río river
sala living room
salida exit, road out of town
salon large living room, gallery
salto waterfall
sierra mountain range
suave soft, easy, quiet
tope a dead-end, or T intersection
tranquilo mellow
urbano public urban bus
vara colonial unit of distance equal to roughly
  one meter
volcán volcano

ABBREVIATIONS

ENEL Empresa Nicaragüense de Electricidad
  (electric company)
ENITEL Empresa Nicaragüense de Telecomu-
  nicaciónes (telephone company)
FSLN Frente Sandinista de Liberación Nacional
  (Sandinista party)
IFA (EEH-fa) East German troop transport, used
  commonly in Nicaraguan public transportation
  system; it probably stands for something in
  German, but in Nicaragua, it means *imposible
  frenar a tiempo* (impossible to brake on time).
INETER Instituto Nicaragüense de Estudios
  Territoriales (government geography/geol-
  ogy institute)
MARENA Ministerio del Ambiente y los Recur-
  sos Naturales (Ministry of Natural Resources
  and the Environment), administers Nicaragua's
  protected areas
MYA Million Years Ago
NGO Nongovernmental Organization
PCV Peace Corps Volunteer
PLC Partido Liberal Constitucionalista, the
  conservative anti-Sandinista party
SINAP Sistema Nacional de Areas Protegidas
  (National System of Protected Areas)
UCA Universidad de Centroamerica
UN United Nations
UNAN Universidad Nacional Autónoma de Ni-
  caragua
USAID United States Agency for International
  Development, channels congressionally ap-
  proved foreign aid

Spanish Phrasebook

For particularities of Nicaraguan Spanish and a dictionary of regional phrases, see the sidebar *A Few Nicaraguanismos* in the *Background* chapter.

PRONUNCIATION GUIDE

Spanish pronunciation is much more regular than that of English, but there are still occasional variations.

Consonants

c as "c" in "cat," before "a," "o," or "u"; like "s" before "e" or "i"

d as "d" in "dog," except between vowels, then like "th" in "that"

g before "e" or "i," like the "ch" in Scottish "loch"; elsewhere like "g" in "get"

h always silent

j like the English "h" in "hotel," but stronger

ll like the "y" in "yellow"

ñ like the "ni" in "onion"

r always pronounced as strong "r"

rr trilled "r"

v similar to the "b" in "boy" (not as English "v")

y similar to English, but with a slight "j" sound. When standing alone, it's pronounced like the "e" in "me."

z like "s" in "same"

b, f, k, l, m, n, p, q, s, t, w, x as in English

Vowels

a as in "father," but shorter

e as in "hen"

i as in "machine"

o as in "phone"

u usually as in "rule"; when it follows a "q," the "u" is silent; when it follows an "h" or "g," it's pronounced like "w," except when it comes between "g" and "e" or "i," when it's also silent (unless it has an umlaut, when it is again pronounced as English "w")

Stress

Native English speakers frequently make errors of pronunciation by ignoring stress. All Spanish vowels – a, e, i, o, and u – carry accents that determine which syllable of a word gets emphasis. Often, stress seems unnatural to nonnative speakers – the surname Chávez, for instance, is stressed on the first syllable – but failure to observe this rule may mean that native speakers may not understand you.

USEFUL WORDS AND PHRASES

Nicaraguans and other Spanish-speaking people consider formalities important. Whenever approaching anyone for information or some other reason, do not forget the appropriate salutation – good morning, good evening, etc. Standing alone, the greeting *hola* (hello) can sound brusque.

Hello. *Hola.*

Good morning. *Buenos días.*

Good afternoon. *Buenas tardes.*

Good evening. *Buenas noches.*

How are you? *¿Cómo está?*

Fine. *Muy bien.*

And you? *¿Y usted?*

Awesome! *De acachimba!*

So-so. *Más o menos.*

Thank you. *Gracias.*

Thank you very much. *Muchas gracias.*

You're very kind. *Muy amable.*

You're welcome. *De nada* ("It's nothing").

yes *sí*

no *no*

I don't know. *No sé.*

It's fine; okay *Está bien.*

Good; okay *Bueno.*

please *por favor*

Pleased to meet you. *Mucho gusto.*

Excuse me (physical) *Perdóneme.*

Excuse me (speech) *Discúlpeme.*

I'm sorry. *Lo siento.*

Goodbye. *Adiós.*

See you later. *Hasta luego* ("Until later").

more *más*

less *menos*

better *mejor*
much, a lot *mucho*
drunk *hasta el culo*
a little *un poco*
large *grande*
small *pequeño, chico*
quick, fast *rápido*
slowly *despacio*
bad *malo*
difficult *difícil*
easy *fácil*
He/She/It is gone; as in "She left" or "he's gone." *Ya se fue.*
I don't speak Spanish well. *No hablo bien el español.*
I don't understand. *No entiendo ni papas.*
How do you say... in Spanish? *¿Cómo se dice... en español?*
Do you understand English? *¿Entiende el inglés?*
Is English spoken here? (Does anyone here speak English?) *¿Se habla inglés aquí?*

TERMS OF ADDRESS

When in doubt, use the formal *usted* (you) as a form of address. If you wish to dispense with formality and feel that the desire is mutual, you can say, *"Me puedes tutear"* ("You can call me 'tu'").

I *yo*
you (formal) *usted*
you (familiar) *vos*
you (familiar) *tú*
he/him *él*
she/her *ella*
we/us *nosotros*
you (plural) *ustedes*
they/them (all males or mixed gender) *ellos*
they/them (all females) *ellas*
Mr., sir *Señor*
Mrs., madam *Señora*
Miss, young lady *Señorita*
wife *esposa*
husband *marido or esposo*
friend *amigo* (male), *amiga* (female)
sweetheart *novio* (male), *novia* (female)

son, daughter *hijo, hija*
brother, sister *hermano, hermana*
father, mother *padre, madre*
grandfather, grandmother *abuelo, abuela*

GETTING AROUND

Where is... ? *¿Dónde está... ?*
How far is it to... ? *¿A cuanto está... ?*
from... to... *de... a...*
highway *la carretera*
road *el camino*
street *la calle*
block *la cuadra*
kilometer *kilómetro*
north *norte*
south *sur*
west *oeste; poniente*
east *este; oriente*
straight ahead *al derecho; adelante*
to the right *a la derecha*
to the left *a la izquierda*

ACCOMMODATIONS

Is there a room? *¿Hay cuarto?*
May I (we) see it? *¿Puedo (podemos) verlo?*
What is the rate? *¿Cuál es el precio?*
Is that your best rate? *¿Es su mejor precio?*
Is there something cheaper? *¿Hay algo más económico?*
single room *un sencillo*
double room *un doble*
room for a couple *matrimonial*
key *llave*
with private bath *con baño*
with shared bath *con baño general; con baño compartido*
hot water *agua caliente*
cold water *agua fría*
shower *ducha*
electric shower *ducha eléctrica*
towel *toalla*
soap *jabón*
toilet paper *papel higiénico*
air-conditioning *aire acondicionado*
fan *abanico; ventilador*
blanket *frazada; manta*
sheets *sábanas*

PUBLIC TRANSPORT

bus stop *la parada*
bus terminal *terminal de buses*
airport *el aeropuerto*
launch *lancha; tiburonera*
dock *muelle*
I want a ticket to... *Quiero un pasaje a...*
I want to get off at... *Quiero bajar en...*
Here, please. *Aquí, por favor.*
Where is this bus going? *¿Adónde va este autobús?*
round-trip *ida y vuelta*
What do I owe? *¿Cuánto le debo?*

FOOD

menu *la carta, el menú* ·
glass *taza*
fork *tenedor*
knife *cuchillo*
spoon *cuchara*
napkin *servilleta*
soft drink *agua fresca*
coffee *café*
cream *crema*
tea *té*
sugar *azúcar*
drinking water *agua pura, agua potable*
bottled carbonated water *agua mineral con gas*
bottled uncarbonated water *agua sin gas*
beer *cerveza*
wine *vino*
milk *leche*
juice *jugo*
eggs *huevos*
bread *pan*
watermelon *sandía*
banana *banano*
plantain *plátano*
apple *manzana*
orange *naranja*
meat (without) *carne (sin)*
beef *carne de res*
chicken *pollo; gallina*
fish *pescado*
shellfish *mariscos*
shrimp *camarones*

fried *frito*
roasted *asado*
barbecued *a la parrilla*
breakfast *desayuno*
lunch *almuerzo*
dinner (often eaten in late afternoon) *comida*
dinner, or a late-night snack *cena*
the check, or bill *la cuenta*

MAKING PURCHASES

I need ... *Necesito...*
I want ... *Deseo...* or *Quiero...*
I would like ... (more polite) *Quisiera...*
How much does it cost? *¿Cuánto cuesta?*
What's the exchange rate? *¿Cuál es el tipo de cambio?*
May I see ...? *¿Puedo ver...?*
This one *ésta/ésto*
expensive *caro*
cheap *barato*
cheaper *más barato*
too much *demasiado*

HEALTH

Help me please. *Ayúdeme por favor.*
I am ill. *Estoy enfermo.*
pain *dolor*
fever *fiebre*
stomachache *dolor de estómago*
vomiting *vomitar*
diarrhea *diarrea*
drugstore *farmacia*
medicine *medicina*
pill, tablet *pastilla*
birth-control pills *pastillas anticonceptivas*
condom *condón; preservativo*

NUMBERS

0 *cero*
1 *uno* (masculine)
1 *una* (feminine)
2 *dos*
3 *tres*
4 *cuatro*
5 *cinco*
6 *seis*

7 *siete*
8 *ocho*
9 *nueve*
10 *diez*
11 *once*
12 *doce*
13 *trece*
14 *catorce*
15 *quince*
16 *dieciseis*
17 *diecisiete*
18 *dieciocho*
19 *diecinueve*
20 *veinte*
21 *veintiuno*
30 *treinta*
40 *cuarenta*
50 *cincuenta*
60 *sesenta*
70 *setenta*
80 *ochenta*
90 *noventa*
100 *cien*
101 *ciento y uno*
200 *doscientos*
1,000 *mil*
10,000 *diez mil*
1,000,000 *un millón*

TIME

While Nicaraguans mostly use the 12-hour clock, in some instances, usually associated with plane or bus schedules, they may use the 24-hour military clock. Under the 24-hour clock, for example, *las nueve de la noche* (9 P.M.) would be *las 21 horas* (2100 hours).

What time is it? *¿Qué hora es?*
It's one o'clock *Es la una.*
It's two o'clock *Son las dos.*
At two o'clock *A las dos.*
It's ten to three *Son las tres menos diez.*
It's ten past three *Son las tres y diez.*
It's three fifteen *Son las tres y cuarto.*
It's two forty-five *Son las tres menos cuarto.*
It's two thirty *Son las dos y media.*
It's six A.M. *Son las seis de la mañana.*
It's six P.M. *Son las seis de la tarde.*
It's ten P.M. *Son las diez de la noche.*
today *hoy*
tomorrow *mañana*
morning *la mañana*
tomorrow morning *mañana por la mañana*
yesterday *ayer*
week *la semana*
month *mes*
year *año*
last night *anoche*
the next day *el día siguiente*

DAYS OF THE WEEK

Sunday *domingo*
Monday *lunes*
Tuesday *martes*
Wednesday *miércoles*
Thursday *jueves*
Friday *viernes*
Saturday *sábado*

Further Study

SUGGESTED READING

A prodigious amount of literature emerged from the Sandinista years, when Nicaragua was the setting of the hemisphere's most celebrated—and criticized—socialist experiment of the century. You'll find more titles on Nicaragua in the used-book section than you will on the new releases shelf. Following is an extremely eclectic (and incomplete) list of your options.

Fiction

Sirias, Silvio. *Bernardo and the Virgin*. Chicago: Northwestern University Press, 2005. *Bernardo* stands head and shoulders above other books about Nicaragua for sheer originality, real-life texture, and ingenious use of voices and characters. This historical novel tells the true story of the Virgin Mary's appearances to a *campesino* in Cuapa, while portraying a thick slice of Nicaragua's past and present. If you only have time to read one book before your trip, this may be the one.

History and Current Events

Babb, Florence. *After Revolution: Mapping Gender and Cultural Politics in Neoliberal Nicaragua*. Austin, Texas: University of Texas Press, 2001. Professor of Anthropology and Women's Studies at the University of Iowa, Babb has also published scores of academic papers on Nicaragua, mainly on issues of gender and sexuality.

Barrios de Chamorro, Violeta. *Dreams of the Heart*. New York: Simon & Schuster, 1996. A very human history of Nicaragua from the Somoza years through Doña Violeta's electoral triumph in 1990 (she served as Nicaragua's president in the early 1990s).

Belli, Gioconda. *The Country Under My Skin: A Memoir of Love and War*. New York: Anchor Books, 2003. Stephen Kinzer writes, "Belli's memoir shows us a side of the Sandinista revolution we have not seen. It also introduces us to an astute veteran of two eternal wars, one between the sexes and one that pits the world's poor against its rich."

Cabezas, Omar. *Fire from the Mountain (La Montaña es Algo Más que una Grán Estapa Verde)*. Phoenix, AZ: Crown, 1985. A ribald, vernacular account of what it's like to be a guerrilla soldier in the mountains of Nicaragua; one of the few books about the early stages of the revolution.

Cardenal, Ernesto; Walsh, Donald D. (translator). *The Gospel in Solentiname*. Maryknoll, NY: Orbis Books, 1979. Transcripts of the masses given by Cardenal on Solentiname that helped spawn the *Misa Campesina* and liberation theology movements.

Chomsky, Noam. *Turning the Tide: U.S. Intervention in Central America and the Struggle for Peace*. Cambridge, MA: South End Press, 1985. Succinctly and powerfully shows how U.S. Central American policies implement broader U.S. economic, military, and social aims, with Nicaragua and El Salvador as examples.

Davis, Peter. *Where is Nicaragua?* New York: Simon & Schuster, 1987. Davis breaks down the revolution and Contra war, and ties them into the country's greater history; he articulates the complexity of the situation in a graspable manner.

Dickey, Christopher. *With the Contras*. New York: Simon & Schuster, 1985. Dickey was the *Washington Post* correspondent in Honduras and gives an exciting account of his experience with the secret Contra army.

Kinzer, Stephen. *Blood of Brothers: Life and War in Nicaragua*. New York: G. P. Putnam's Sons, 1991. Kinzer, the *New York Times*

Managua bureau chief during the war, sensed that Nicaragua was "a country with more to tell the world than it had been able to articulate, a country with a message both political and spiritual."

Lancaster, Roger N. *Life Is Hard: Machismo, Danger, and the Intimacy of Power in Nicaragua*. Berkeley: University of California Press, 1992. Lancaster is an anthropologist and this is an ethnography studying not current events, but their effect on the Nicaraguan individual and family. It is intimate and offers details about Nicaraguan life that one can only get living with the people in their very homes. Lancaster pays attention to issues often passed over, like homosexuality, domestic violence, broken families, and the roots of machismo.

Mejía, Camilo. *Road from Ar Ramadi: The Private Rebellion of Staff Sergeant Mejía*. New York: The New Press, 2007. In 2004 Mejía, who grew up in Managua and Costa Rica before emigrating to Miami with his mother, became the first U.S. National Guardsman who refused to return to fight in Iraq. He applied for a discharge as a conscientious objector after serving eight months in a combat zone in Iraq and was promptly court-martialed for desertion. His memoir comes after serving nine months in a military jail and provides a rare first-hand glimpse of life in wartime Iraq form the unique perspective of a Sandinista-bred son of Nicaragua's most famous musician, Carlos Mejía Godoy. Mejía is now a leading member of Iraq Veterans Against the War.

Pastor, Robert. *Not Condemned To Repetition: The United States And Nicaragua*. Boulder, CO: Westview Press, 2002. Robert Pastor was a U.S. policymaker in the period leading up to and following the Sandinista revolution of 1979. A decade later, he organized the International Mission led by Jimmy Carter that mediated the first free election in Nicaragua's history. This updated edition covers the events of the democratic transition of the 1990s and extracts lessons to be learned from the past.

Randall, Margaret. *Sandino's Daughters: Testimonies of Nicaraguan Women in Struggle*. Point Roberts, WA: New Star Books, 1981. Explores the role of feminism in the Sandinista revolution, via a series of interviews with participants.

Rushdie, Salman. *The Jaguar Smile*. New York: Viking, 1987. Representing the pro-Sandinista Nicaragua Solidarity Campaign in London, Rushdie takes readers on a poetic, passionate jaunt through Nicaragua as part of a government cultural campaign; he offers a careful (if short) examination of their policies.

Squier, Ephraim George. *Nicaragua: Its People, Scenery, Monuments, and the Proposed Interoceanic Canal*. New York: D. Appleton, 1852. Squier remains one of Nicaragua's most prolific writers; this massive, multivolume tome is available for hundreds of dollars in rare bookstores. The discussion is divided into five parts in which he describes geography and topography; the events during the author's residence, including accounts of his explorations; observations on the proposed canal; notes on the indigenous of the country, including information regarding geographical distribution, languages, institutions, religions, and customs; and the political history of the country since its independence from Spain.

Zimmerman, Matilde. *Sandinista: Carlos Fonseca and the Nicaraguan Revolution*. Durham, NC: Duke University Press, 2001. This is the first English-language biography of the legendary leader of the FSLN and arguably the most important and influential figure of the post-1959 revolutionary generation in Latin America.

Art Books

Belli, Alejandro et al. *The Nicaraguans.* Managua, 2006. One of the best photography book about Nicaragua. Period. Go to www.thenicaraguans.com to learn more about this stunning collection of images celebrating the people of the country. In the foreword, Sergio Ramírez Mercado writes, "these photographs, taken by Nicaraguans observing other Nicaraguans who are simply getting through the day, reveal the multifaceted face of peace, which today also embodies our identity."

Gentile, William Frank. *Nicaragua: Photographs by William Frank Gentile* New York: W. W. Norton & Company, 1989. These are some of the deepest, most powerful photos you'll ever see, with fantastic juxtapositions of Contra and FSLN soldiers.

Kunzle, David. *The Murals of Revolutionary Nicaragua 1979–1992.* Berkeley: University of California Press, 1995. Many murals were strictly political, but most intertwined the revolutionary process with cultural, historical, and literary themes. All are celebrated in Kunzle's book; 83-page introduction and 100 color plates.

Poetry, Language, and Literature

Morelli, Marco, editor. *Rubén's Orphans.* New Hyde Park, NY: Painted Rooster Press, 2001. An anthology of contemporary Nicaraguan poets, with English translations.

Rabella, Joaquim and Pallais, Chantal. *Vocabulario Popular Nicaragüense.* This big, red linguistic bible is a wonderful, dictionary celebrating Nicaraguan Spanish, complete with regional usages, sayings, and plenty of profanities; available in the UCA bookstores in Managua.

Randall, Margaret. *Risking a Somersault in the Air: Conversations with Nicaraguan Writers.* San Francisco: Solidarity Publications, 1984.

Just as much about literature as it is about the revolution, this is a fascinating series of interviews with Nicaraguan authors and poets, most of whom were part of the FSLN revolution and government.

White, Steven, translator. *Poets of Nicaragua: A Bilingual Anthology 1918–1970.* London: Unicorn Press, 1983.

Miscellaneous

Hulme, Krekel, and O'Reilly. *Not Just Another Nicaragua Travel Guide.* Redwood, CA: Mango Publications, 1990. An ebullient and fascinating guidebook for traveling Sandinista Nicaragua in the 1980s. Get it if you can find it; only 1,000 copies were printed.

Marriot, Edward. *Savage Shore: Life and Death with Nicaragua's Last Shark Hunters.* New York: Owl Books, 2001. A curious and descriptive journey up the Río San Juan and beyond.

SUGGESTED VIEWING

The World Stopped Watching, a 2003 Canadian film by Peter Raymont and Harold Crooks, was shot in 56 mm. Nicaragua dropped from the spotlight after the end of the Contra war. This documentary, shot in late 2002 and early 2003, picks up the pieces of what happened next. Essentially, this is a sequel to *The World is Watching,* a critically acclaimed documentary from the 1980s, involving many of the same characters.

Walker, a 1987 anachronistic biography of the infamous soldier-of-fortune from Tennessee, stars Ed Harris. Filmmaker Alex Cox (of *Sid & Nancy* fame), wanted to show that "nothing had changed in the 140-odd years between William Walker's genocidal campaign and that of Oliver North and his goons." One reviewer wrote, "What is so amazing about *Walker* is that it got made at all. It's a film condemning capitalism funded by a capitalist studio. Since it was filmed on location, its production money went straight into a country that the United States was currently at war with." Critics mostly panned the film as "sophomoric black comedy," but confirmed Nicaphiles will surely get a kick out of it.

Carla's Song, a 1996 drama by Ken Loach, stars Robert Carlyle and Oyanka Cabezas. Set in 1987, Scottish bus driver George Lennox meets Carla, a Nicaraguan exile living a precarious, profoundly sad life in Glasgow. George takes her back to her village in northern Nicaragua to find out what has happened to her family, boyfriend, and country. Notable for its real and gritty location shots, in both Scotland and Nicaragua, *Carla's Song* is enjoyable and touching and, notes its writer, Paul Laverty, "is just one of thousands of statistics, hopefully reminding the viewer that everyone in this war had a story." *Carla's Song* was awarded a gold medal at the Italian Film Festival in Venice.

Internet Resources

THE AUTHORS' SITES

www.GoToNicaragua.com

The authors' homebase, where you can chat with fellow Nicaphile travelers and expats, ask questions directly to Josh and Randy, plan routes, post travelogues, read the latest Nicaragua headlines, and check for updates to this edition.

www.therandymon.com

Randy Wood's personal site.

www.joshuaberman.net

Joshua Berman's personal site and blog.

NICARAGUA PORTALS

www.xolo.com.ni

Xolo is a Nica-run portal with lots of info on music, books, and theater, plus links to many of the hotels and restaurants mentioned here.

www.ibw.com.ni

IBW Internet Gateway is a Spanish language portal that is a good introduction to the nation's print and visual media, plus links to Nicaraguan government and NGO websites.

http://news.bbc.co.uk/2/hi /americas/country_profiles

The BBC's Nicaragua portal is an excellent overview of current news and themes; a great way to get a flavor of what the hot topics are during your trip.

http://lanic.utexas.edu/la/ca /nicaragua

The Latin American Network Information Center boasts a ton of Nica-sites, including many academic links.

OFFICIAL

www.intur.gob.ni
www.visitanicaragua.com

Visit the Nicaraguan government tourism agency's sites for a current list of active tour operators in Nicaragua.

http://nicaragua.usembassy.gov

The official U.S. embassy page for Nicaragua.

http://travel.state.gov/travel

U.S. State Department's fact sheet for travelers in Nicaragua, including security overview.

www.voyage.gc.ca

Ditto, from the Canadians. The Canadian government has never really been politically involved in Nicaragua, so its travel warnings provide a good reality check for what you read at the U.S. State Department's site.

https://www.cia.gov/library /publications/the-world-factbook

CIA World Factbook provides current statistics on Nicaraguan geography, people, government, economy, etc., courtesy of the folks who brought you the Contra war.

www.marena.gob.ni

For more information on specific parks and reserves, this is the Nicaraguan Natural Resources Ministry home page.

POLITICAL/SOLIDARITY

www.nicanet.org

For more than 20 years, The Nicaragua Network, a coalition of U.S.-based non-profits (many of them regional sister city organizations), has been committed to social and economic justice for the people of Nicaragua.

www.witnessforpeace.org

Witness for Peace is a politically independent, grassroots organization whose mission is to support peace, justice, and sustainable economies in the Americas by changing U.S. policies and corporate practices that contribute to poverty and oppression in Latin America and the Caribbean. Join a delegation or work brigade in Nicaragua and beyond.

www.globalexchange.org
Global Exchange is a human rights organization dedicated to promoting environmental, political, and social justice around the world. It has long had a focus on Nicaraguan issues and sends delegations there.

www.amigosdenicaragua.org
Amigos de Nicaragua is the official site for Returned Peace Corps Volunteers of Nicaragua.

www.buildingnewhope.com
Building New Hope supports a number of worthy projects, mostly in the Granada area.

COFFEE AND FAIR TRADE

www.transfairusa.org
Transfair USA is the place to start your fair trade research and offers Nicaragua-specific information.

www.nicaraguancoffees.com
Specialty Coffee Association of Nicaragua offers the latest international "Cup of Excellence" winners.

www.thanksgivingcoffee.com
CEO Paul Katzeff has done more for small-scale Nicaraguan coffee farmers than we have room to describe; read about California-based Thanskgiving Coffee Company's latest exchange with Nicaraguan farmers here, then buy a few pounds of beans.

www.maggiesorganics.com
Fair trade organic clothing products made by women's cooperatives in Nicaragua.

www.pachamamaworld.com
Go shopping: Pachamama features international Fair Trade cooperatives and tours

to show firsthand how people are building sustainable futures for themselves in Nicaragua.

TRAVELING AND TOURISM

www.vianica.com
Vianica provides a well-designed, informative overview of travel destinations throughout Nicaragua and can help you plan your trip.

www.planeta.com
Planeta provides a lively public space devoted to "the development of conscientious tourism that benefits travelers and locals alike" with a full section on Nicaragua.

www.sanjuandelsur.org.ni
An extensive network of local businesses in the southwestern corner of Nicaragua.

www.transitionsabroad.com
Listings of work, volunteer, and study opportunities in Nicaragua and beyond.

www.nicaliving.com
A vibrant online community of opinionated expats and travelers.

PHOTOGRAPHERS

http://agstar.blogspot.com
Tomás Stargardter is a Nicaragua-based photojournalist whose website features a wide range of Nicaraguan images, from the natural to the extreme to the political.

www.christoph-grandt.com /nicaragua.html
Christoph's photos capture the human vibe; photos he sells provide for donations to needy families.

www.nicaraguaphoto.com
Richard Leonardi, a U.S.-born photographer based in Managua, offers a number of interesting galleries and books.

Index

Map Index

Acknowledgments

For our daughters, Valentina Joelle Wood and Shanti Ayla Berman—may they come to enjoy Nicaragua as much as we have.

We receive and respond to many hundreds of reader letters each year. Rereading your suggestions and corrections is the first of many tasks that go into each update of *Moon Nicaragua*. We offer our sincerest *agradacimientos* to each and every traveler who took the time to write to us. Please stay in touch by joining us on the reader forum at www.GoToNicaragua.com.

This new edition was made possible by our crack team of writer-researchers who painstakingly helped us comb the Nicaraguan countryside: Tim Coone, Roman Yavich, James "El Salvaje" Savage, and Phoebe Haupt: *gracias.* Thank you to our Berkeley editing squad: Kathryn Ettinger, Domini Dragoone, Albert Angulo, and the rest of the team at Avalon.

Thanks to Donna Tabor, Olin Cohan, Paul Phelan, Stephanie Garnica, Pat Sweikowski, Marie Mendel, Erin Dunlap, Shaya Honarvar, Alvaro Molina, Miranda Jennings, Kenia Ramirez, Jenny Epstein, Jarryd Widhalm, Rebecca Johnson, Leora Mallach, Swenja Janine Schlegel, Kevin Cohen, Erik Winkler, Jon Brill, Steve "OurManinGranada" Jackson, and Dr. G. There are many other names that belong on this list, that got lost somewhere in the thousands of emails; forgive us and thank you.

Big-up to Nica Quinze.

Hugs of gratitude go to the Escoto family in La Trinidad (Darwin, Karla, Darling, and Karling) for their neverending affection and *gallo pinto;* and to the *familía* Jiménez in Ticuantepe (Mama Mercedes, Julio Negro, Lastenia, Mardis, Neyda, and Edén, *mi hermano, que descansa en paz).*

Finally, the hundreds of hours it takes to crunch out a decent guidebook update used to be less complicated a task before we both started reproducing. Our indebedtedness to our wives for putting up with the process is beyond words. Sutay and Ericka—at various stages of pregnancy and birth—simultaneously created life *and* endured our late-night, hours-long exchanges about chapter titles, captions, maps, and a million minutiae. *Las queremos mucho.*

www.moon.com

DESTINATIONS | ACTIVITIES | BLOGS | MAPS | BOOKS

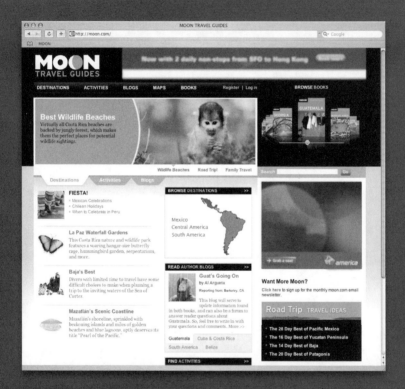

MOON.COM is all new, and ready to help plan your next trip! Filled with fresh trip ideas and strategies, author interviews, informative blogs, a detailed map library, and descriptions of all the Moon guidebooks, Moon.com is all you need to get out and explore the world—or even places in your own backyard. As always, when you travel with Moon, expect an experience that is uncommon and truly unique.